The Dundas Despotism

As the cartoonist, James Gillray, saw him: Dun-Shaw, Dundas the Bashaw, combining the figure of kilted Scot and turbaned oriental despot, with one foot in the city of London, the other in Bengal, and power to command the sun and moon. (Reproduced by kind permission of the Trustees of the British Museum.)

The Dundas Despotism

MICHAEL FRY

EDINBURGH UNIVERSITY PRESS

© Michael Fry, 1992
Edinburgh University Press
22 George Square, Edinburgh

Typeset in Linotron Goudy
by Koinonia Limited, Bury, and
printed in Great Britain by
the University Press, Cambridge

A CIP record for this book is available from the
British Library.

ISBN 0 7486 0352 2

The publisher acknowledges subsidy from
the Scottish Arts Council towards
the publication of this volume.

Contents

THE DUNDAS

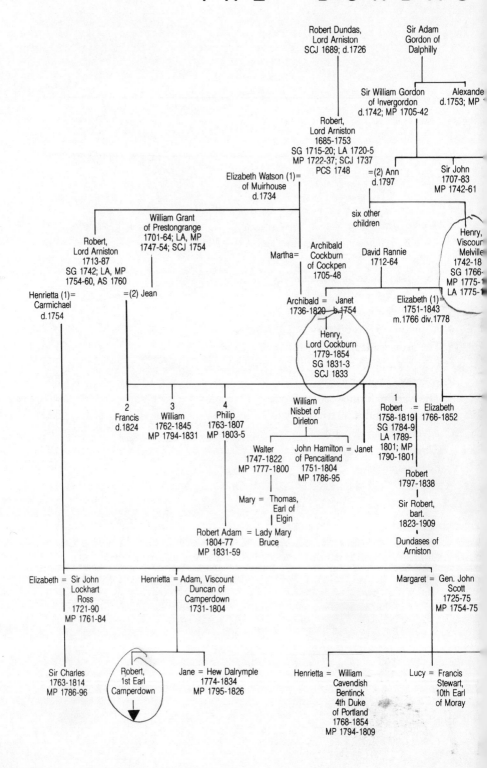

Robert Dundas,
Lord Arniston
SCJ 1689; d.1726

Sir Adam
Gordon of
Dalphilly

Sir William Gordon
of Invergordon
d.1742; MP 1705-42

Alexande
d.1753; MP

Robert,
Lord Arniston
1685-1753
SG 1715-20; LA 1720-5
MP 1722-37; SCJ 1737
PCS 1748

=(2) Ann
d.1797

Sir John
1707-83
MP 1742-61

Elizabeth Watson (1)=
of Muirhouse
d.1734

six other
children

Henry,
Viscour
Melville
1742-18
SG 1766-
MP 1775-1
LA 1775-1

William Grant
of Prestongrange
1701-64; LA, MP
1747-54; SCJ 1754

Robert,
Lord Arniston
1713-87
SG 1742; LA, MP
1754-60, AS 1760

Martha=

Archibald
Cockburn
of Cockpen
1705-48

David Rannie
1712-64

Henrietta (1)=
Carmichael
d.1754

=(2) Jean

Archibald =
1736-1820
Janet
b.1754

Elizabeth (1)=
1751-1843
m.1766 div.1778

Henry,
Lord Cockburn
1779-1854
SG 1831-3
SCJ 1833

2
Francis
d.1824

3
William
1762-1845
MP 1794-1831

4
Philip
1763-1807
MP 1803-5

William
Nisbet of
Dirleton

1
Robert = Elizabeth
1758-1819 1766-1852
SG 1784-9
LA 1789-
1801; MP
1790-1801

Walter
1747-1822
MP 1777-1800

John Hamilton = Janet
of Pencaitland
1751-1804
MP 1786-95

Robert
1797-1838

Sir Robert,
bart.
1823-1909

Mary = Thomas,
Earl of
Elgin

Dundases of
Arniston

Robert Adam = Lady Mary
1804-77 Bruce
MP 1831-59

Elizabeth = Sir John
Lockhart
Ross
1721-90
MP 1761-84

Henrietta = Adam, Viscount
Duncan of
Camperdown
1731-1804

Margaret = Gen. John
Scott
1725-75
MP 1754-75

Sir Charles
1763-1814
MP 1786-96

Robert,
1st Earl
Camperdown

Jane = Hew Dalrymple
1774-1834
MP 1795-1826

Henrietta = William
Cavendish
Bentinck
4th Duke
of Portland
1768-1854
MP 1794-1809

Lucy = Francis
Stewart,
10th Earl
of Moray

CONNECTION

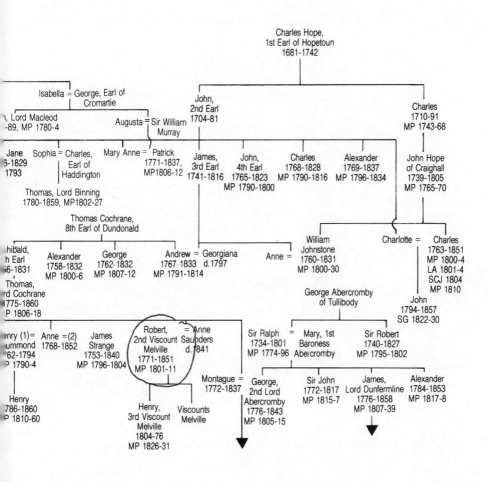

Charles Hope,
1st Earl of Hopetoun
1681-1742

Isabella = George, Earl of Cromartie

..., Lord Macleod
-89, MP 1780-4

Augusta = Sir William Murray

John, 2nd Earl 1704-81

Charles 1710-91 MP 1743-68

Jane 3-1829 1793

Sophia = Charles, Earl of Haddington

Mary Anne = Patrick 1771-1837, MP1806-12

James, 3rd Earl 1741-1816 MP 1790-1800

John, 4th Earl 1765-1823

Charles 1768-1828 MP 1790-1816

Alexander 1769-1837 MP 1796-1834

John Hope of Craighall 1739-1805 MP 1765-70

Thomas, Lord Binning 1780-1859, MP1802-27

Thomas Cochrane, 8th Earl of Dundonald

William Johnstone 1760-1831 MP 1800-30

Charlotte = Charles 1763-1851 MP 1800-4 LA 1801-4 SCJ 1804 MP 1810

.hibald, h Earl 6-1831

Alexander 1758-1832 MP 1800-6

George 1762-1832 MP 1807-12

Andrew = Georgiana 1767-1833 d.1797 MP 1791-1814

Anne =

George Abercromby of Tullibody

John 1794-1857 SG 1822-30

Thomas, rd Cochrane 775-1860 P 1806-18

enry (1)= Anne =(2) James ummond 1768-1852 Strange 62-1794 1753-1840 1790-4 MP 1796-1804

Robert, 2nd Viscount Melville 1771-1851 MP 1801-11 = Anne Saunders d.1841

Sir Ralph 1734-1801 MP 1774-96 = Mary, 1st Baroness Abercromby 1760-1831

Sir Robert 1740-1827 MP 1795-1802

Henry 786-1860 1810-60

Henry, 3rd Viscount Melville 1804-76 MP 1826-31

Viscounts Melville

Montague = 1772-1837

George, 2nd Lord Abercromby 1776-1843 MP 1805-15

Sir John 1772-1817 MP 1815-7

James, Lord Dunfermline 1776-1858 MP 1807-39

Alexander 1784-1853 MP 1817-8

Jean, scountess Canning = George Canning 1760-1837 MP 1793-1827

KEY: only Scottish offices are noted—

SG   Solicitor General
LA   Lord Advocate
SCJ   Senator of the College of Justice
PCS   Lord President of the Court of Session

For MPs, only dates of first election and
final retiral are noted.

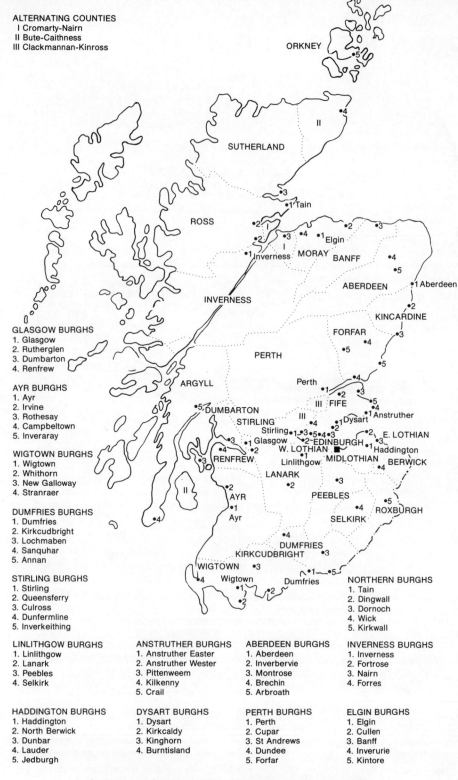

ALTERNATING COUNTIES
I Cromarty-Nairn
II Bute-Caithness
III Clackmannan-Kinross

GLASGOW BURGHS
1. Glasgow
2. Rutherglen
3. Dumbarton
4. Renfrew

AYR BURGHS
1. Ayr
2. Irvine
3. Rothesay
4. Campbeltown
5. Inveraray

WIGTOWN BURGHS
1. Wigtown
2. Whithorn
3. New Galloway
4. Stranraer

DUMFRIES BURGHS
1. Dumfries
2. Kirkcudbright
3. Lochmaben
4. Sanquhar
5. Annan

STIRLING BURGHS
1. Stirling
2. Queensferry
3. Culross
4. Dunfermline
5. Inverkeithing

LINLITHGOW BURGHS
1. Linlithgow
2. Lanark
3. Peebles
4. Selkirk

HADDINGTON BURGHS
1. Haddington
2. North Berwick
3. Dunbar
4. Lauder
5. Jedburgh

ANSTRUTHER BURGHS
1. Anstruther Easter
2. Anstruther Wester
3. Pittenweem
4. Kilkenny
5. Crail

DYSART BURGHS
1. Dysart
2. Kirkcaldy
3. Kinghorn
4. Burntisland

ABERDEEN BURGHS
1. Aberdeen
2. Inverbervie
3. Montrose
4. Brechin
5. Arbroath

PERTH BURGHS
1. Perth
2. Cupar
3. St Andrews
4. Dundee
5. Forfar

NORTHERN BURGHS
1. Tain
2. Dingwall
3. Dornoch
4. Wick
5. Kirkwall

INVERNESS BURGHS
1. Inverness
2. Fortrose
3. Nairn
4. Forres

ELGIN BURGHS
1. Elgin
2. Cullen
3. Banff
4. Inverurie
5. Kintore

SCOTTISH PARLIAMENTARY CONSTITUENCIES 1707-1832

27 counties returned one member · 6 counties had alternating representation
Edinburgh returned one member · 65 other burghs were arranged in districts, each returning one member

Preface

The Dundas despotism is the name, derived from Henry Cockburn, given to the half-century of Scottish government straddling 1800. It was dominated by two cadets, father and son, of the family of Dundas of Arniston, later elevated to the peerage as Viscounts Melville. The system over which they presided, though perfectly satisfactory to Scots of the time, has in ours attracted a peculiar degree of academic opprobrium; about the least damning judgment of it, by Christopher Smout, was that it grew 'so moribund as to be scarcely relevant any longer to a general history of Scottish society'. One of my main aims in the story told below is to prove him and others wrong: to show not only that Scotland's political experience during the period was significant, but also that it can be convincingly linked to those contemporary experiences which have won scholarly interest and approval, and which go collectively under the name of the Scottish Enlightenment. With this established, it will be natural to assert that the political experience was worthy of note in a wider context too. Here I shall offer a contribution to the recent efforts, made mostly outside Scotland, to rewrite British history as something more than the activities of a few hundred people in London. Further, since this was an era when, largely through the Dundases' agency, their countrymen played a part out of all proportion to numbers in the Empire and in war, I hope to demonstrate that Scottish influences were also channelled into imperial policy and generally into Britain's conception of her place in the world. Altogether, I should like to assist in rescuing the modern history of Scotland from the parochialism often imputed to it by non-Scots, in which it just as often confines itself.

The influences did not, of course, flow only in the one direction. The Dundases, the first home-based Scots since 1707 to rise to and stay at the summit of politics in the United Kingdom, completed the Union in a certain sense, by more equitable distribution of its benefits and by finding a definition of their nation's role in it acceptable on both sides of the border. Scotland regretted what of herself she had to sacrifice. The Dundases compensated by helping to establish new identities for her and for Britain, identities so durable that they have come into question only with the loss of Empire. The father, Henry Dundas, was thus by any standards a key figure in Scottish history and a major one in British history. Yet there has been no full-length study of him since a pair of biographies in the 1930s, each anyway limited in scope. Given the advances meanwhile in the historiography of the eighteenth century, a fresh look at him is long overdue.

The son, Robert Dundas, was only a minor figure in British history but still an important one in Scottish history. He has found no biographer at all.

One cannot quite say that they have been neglected, because in Scotland at least their reputation has meanwhile passed through several stages of increasingly bizarre mutant growth. Correction of that, and reassessment in the light of later knowledge, has been hindered by dispersal of their papers. These, which by my reckoning must originally have comprised about 80,000 pieces, formed till the 1920s one of the greatest extant archives from the late eighteenth and early nineteenth centuries, a record of two men's service to the state spanning more than sixty years. But then their family, like others among the British aristocracy, fell on hard times. The papers were sold, though this could not stop the lands then the castle of Melville at last coming under the hammer too. The loss of such a vast collection would have been irreparable, had not the National Library of Scotland managed to acquire the most important of the specifically Scottish material. In recent years, this has been supplemented through the generosity of the senior line of the family, which still resides at Arniston, in making available at the Scottish Record Office photocopies of the manuscripts remaining in its possession. Even so, a good third of the total has wandered, much of it overseas. A true appreciation of the Dundases requires reading it in its entirety, which is what I have undertaken during the last five years.

Transforming it into narrative has made great editorial demands. The bulk of Henry Dundas's papers concentrates on India and the French Wars. The problem is not only to bring this mass within manageable compass, but also to stop the result becoming unacceptably lopsided. Since neither of those subjects lacks excellent specialist historians, I decided to be firm in keeping them in due pro-portion to the rest of what I had to say. For India it will be clear that I have relied heavily on the interpretations of previous authors. For the wars I sought to detach from the bottomless operational detail the main lines of Dundas's thinking and strategy, subjects which have been neglected; the actual course of the fighting is therefore taken rather as a backdrop. For the rest, he was so omnipresent in public affairs that a determinedly exhaustive biography would have to be several times longer, and little less than a political history of the entire age. To limit myself to the matters on which he set some personal stamp has been formidable enough a task.

Nor are the manuscripts easy to work with. Dundas's handwriting was awful, his style prolix, faults that grew worse with age. Many major documents are uncannily resistant to the telling quote, and have had to be more or less resolutely pruned. In quotations, I have neither pedantically preserved contemporary spelling and punctuation nor relentlessly modernised: my concern has been for clarity of presentation to the reader and, if possible, for pace or colour in the narrative. To give a different example, parliamentary reports in the eighteenth century were usually written up in indirect speech; I have had no compunction in turning them back into direct speech. Again, I have always preserved Scots usage as in the manuscripts. In one important case, the remarkable collection at the National Library of Scotland listed as Accession 9140, I have given lengthy excerpts verbatim, on the grounds that none of these letters has ever been published and that they contain all the conceivable dirt on Dundas.

The best guide to the material hitherto has been the typescript introduction to the first volume of the inventory of Melville Papers held at the Scottish Record Office. It is still not complete or accurate. It mentions one apocryphal collection, supposed to be at the Archive départementale de la Vienne, Poitiers (which may, though, contain letters of French émigrés that passed through Dundas's hands). It mentions a second at Keltie Castle to which I have not been able to gain access, and which must be regarded as closed to the public. It does not mention the holdings at Yale, or at the Bank of Scotland. In the latter case this may be all to the good since those manuscripts, used by Sidney Checkland as recently as 1975, appear meanwhile to have been lost. There must also still be Melville Papers in private hands, for they occasionally come on to the market (from which the National Library of Scotland has a laudable policy of acquiring them). I should be grateful to hear from readers of any others. Meanwhile, my own list of the extant collections appears at the head of the bibliography, with the abbreviations by which reference is severally made to them.

I have examined such further papers of contemporaries as have come to my attention; these are specified by name in the notes. For alas, the Melville Papers proper by no means exhaust the available material, as will appear from the second list in the bibliography. The best sources on Robert Dundas are actually in London, among the correspondence of his ministerial colleagues. Men at the centre of affairs were anyway bound to scatter their letters liberally. Helped in their limitless business by no more than a couple of clerks, they usually managed to keep the incoming ones, but it was a matter of chance whether they copied or even recorded the outgoing ones. At the National Library of Scotland and at the British Library, many can be traced by excellent systems of cross-reference (that at the Scottish Record Office is less full). I am sure there must be more collections containing letters from or to the Dundases which I have had no means of detecting: again, I should be grateful to hear of them.

I am, of course, immensely indebted to those many scholars whose publications have illumined the dauntingly wide range of matters to which the Dundases applied themselves. In the general bibliography, I have not observed a distinction between primary and secondary sources, but placed all printed works, as well as doctoral theses, in one consolidated list. This is for ease of reference from the notes where, for each chapter, author and date are given only at the first mention, and author alone at subsequent mentions, unless it is necessary to distinguish more than one work by the same author.

Arduous endeavours like this could not have been finished without direct help and encouragement from numerous quarters. My most profound debt is to the Wingate Foundation, and especially to its administrator, Jane Reid, for the generous grant that enabled me to survey the relevant American archives. I have been sustained, too, by fellow labourers in the Scottish vineyard. My thanks go to Alexander Murdoch and Richard Sher for first planting the idea of the biography in my mind. I am grateful to Stewart J. Brown, Roger Emerson, Michel Faure, Irma Lustig, Vincenzo Morelle and Donald Withrington for several particular references. Then I owe an immeasurable debt to the legions of librarians who proved so unstinting in their services to me. I cannot possibly mention them all, but equally

I cannot omit to express my appreciation of the special trouble taken by Albert Bardovics, Robert Cox, Mark Dilworth, William Erwin, Irene Innes, Alice Loranth, Christina Robertson and R. N. Smart to guide me through the collections in their care. The Earl and Countess of Glasgow, Major Crichton-Maitland of Houston, James Hunter-Blair of Blairquhan and Oliver Russell of Ballindalloch kindly allowed me to examine their families' papers in their homes. I am grateful to the Duke of Buccleuch, the Earl of Dalhousie, the Earl of Harewood and Viscount Thurso for permission to quote from manuscripts owned by them but held in public repositories. Thanks are also due to Willis Pickard, editor of *The Times Scottish Education Supplement*, and Grant Baird, editor of *The Royal Bank Review*, for permission to reproduce material originally published in their journals.

I have incurred more personal debts as well. Althea Dundas-Bekker received me for an unforgettable visit to Arniston, and filled out a number of interesting but obscure points from her knowledge of her family's history. Stewart Lamont, Ross Leckie and David and Mary Ross accommodated me when I had to undertake research in distant corners of Scotland. My sister and brother-in-law, Denise and John Reynolds, and Michael and Hilary Shipman performed the same service in London, as did Eamonn and Maire Lawlor in Dublin. While I was in the United States, John and Bunty Wilkinson, Robert and Barbara Cain, Donald and Marie Livingston, Jacqueline Murphy and Joseph Vogelson offered me hospitality surpassing even the legendary American standards.

Finally, I have to express my gratitude to Vivian Bone and the staff of the Edinburgh University Press for seeing this volume through. It is my deepest regret that I cannot do so to its late Secretary, who was besides a delightful companion and a good friend. I had looked forward during my transatlantic journey to a reunion with him in New York, which he was to visit on business. It was only when, in late November 1990, I telephoned home to fix some rendezvous that I learned of his death after an operation. My thanks to him must go for ever unsaid, but at least I can state publicly that no publisher could ever have been kinder to an author and that without his aid and support my work might have overwhelmed me. And so I set down in sorrow, but in affectionate and admiring remembrance too, the name of Martin Spencer, and dedicate my book to him.

MRGF
Edinburgh

1

'The great house of Arniston'

On hearing about the death of Robert Dundas, second Viscount Melville, in July 1851, Henry Cockburn wrote: 'Is the great house of Arniston to end with him? It has been the greatest house in Scotland in the greatness which depends neither on rank nor on fortune, but on talent and public situation, for the last two centuries.'[1]

Cockburn was right in thinking that this gifted and ambitious clan, whose blood ran in his own veins, had fallen from the peak of its achievement. He had known and, despite their differences, admired Henry Dundas, first Viscount Melville, one of the most powerful men in the British Empire. The grandson and namesake now succeeding to the peerage had been among the many scions of an *ancien régime* who saw their political prospects blighted by parliamentary reform. He was introduced early to the House of Commons as member for Rochester, a seat in the gift of his father, then First Lord of the Admiralty. But he went out in 1831 and did not return. He followed instead a military career, vigorously suppressing the Canadian rebellion of 1837 and repelling a band of Yankee brigands at Prescott, Ontario. For this he became aide-de-camp to Queen Victoria. He did not like her much and, one evening after dinner at his club, was imprudent enough to say so. Prince Albert, getting wind of it, had him dismissed from all his appointments. Yet the services of such a gallant soldier were not easily dispensed with. He left for the old family fief of India, where he so distinguished himself in the Sikh War that he won royal forgiveness and a knighthood. Coming into the title he was made Commander-in-chief, Scotland, then governor of Edinburgh Castle.[2] Later descendants were, like him, faithful but never outstanding members of the imperial proconsular class: soldiers, sailors, diplomats, colonial administrators. Except in cleaving to the Toryism of the Melvilles, they took little part in politics.

The senior but not noble line, Dundas of Arniston proper, went much the same way. Robert, its head at the time of the Reform Act of 1832, might thus far have hoped to rise easily to high judicial office, which had been his family's for the asking. He had taken a first step at the age of 25, when he became an advocate-depute, the most junior of the Crown's law officers in Scotland. After 1832, though, and the electoral triumph of the Whigs, preferment was reserved to them. Robert retired to his estate. Plagued by inherited ill-health, he died in 1838, aged only 41.[3] There had been talk of putting him forward as parliamentary candidate for Midlothian, which Dundases had represented, on and off, since the seventeenth century. It came to nothing. This was true also of his son, another Robert, plain laird and pillar of the county, the local government of which he ran for thirty years. In acknowledgement, he received a baronetcy in 1898. More conspicuous was his sister Anne, one of a group of formidable, and usually unmarried, ladies of Edinburgh who constituted what might be termed Scotland's first feminist movement. They demanded in particular the admission of women to the universities, an object attained, after twenty-five years' campaigning, in 1892.

The family made money, something it had never really managed before, from lucky inheritances and from coal found on its land. The miners' village of Gorebridge was built a safe mile or two from Arniston. It still 'presents a picture of solid Victorian prosperity; stone houses, rather sooty, stepping downhill on a slight curve'. A church, hall, library and school testified to the Dundases' munificence. With their money they also repaired again to Edinburgh, eleven miles distant. This time it was not the quirky quaintness of the Old Town that drew them, and the picturesque foibles of the Parliament House within it, but the New Town constructed – under the Dundas despotism – on high classical principles of reason and proportion. Amid these memorials to the nation's wealth and enterprise in a new age, banks and investment houses were already finding productive use for the proceeds of Scottish thrift anywhere from the American frontier to Hong Kong. After this financial community's wont, Sir Robert appointed friends and relations to the boards of his companies while they appointed him to theirs. In the North British & Mercantile Insurance, in the Scottish Widows, in the Bank of Scotland and so on, Dundases sat till the 1930s.[4]

The belated prosperity came in time to preserve Arniston House itself, in the family and in its original state:

> O Arniston! seen lovely 'mid its woods,
> From the distasteful neighbourhood of towns
> And villages most happily removed;
> Free, grand and open, as befits thy soul,
> As planned thy genius, as thy taste improves.

Designed by William Adam, it was built in two stages, around 1730 and around 1760 – this because of the perennial troubles with money, which for years forced the Dundases to shift as they could in an unfinished home. Even a century later it was 'without any water laid on above the basement, no means of lighting or heating, no bells and only about four or five servants'. But, according to one authority, it 'approximates more closely to Palladian concepts than any other country house of its period in Scotland'. Perhaps it did so at the Dundases' own behest, for they had an edition of Palladio. It was among the first examples of a seat designed for a Scot below noble rank, artfully garbing his need to work for a living in graceful classical elegance. For such customers, Adam 'evolved a style which reflected their wealth but avoided pretence and unnecessary extravagance'. The exterior does show a certain Scottish severity. A stuccoed hall, on the other hand, 'is one of Adam's most ambitious essays in his grandiloquent Vanbrughian manner'. Again, a playfully ornate rococo dining room, with a frieze of pheasants lurking among fronds of antique foliage, speaks only of *la douceur de la vie*.[5]

One owner, whom we shall come to know as the Chief Baron, not only enlarged and embellished the estate but was a lover of Edinburgh and keen antiquarian long before Cockburn made of the city's past a popular passion. When buildings were being demolished, this Dundas would rescue bits of them to work into his schemes of improvement at Arniston. The royal arms which had once surmounted the façade of the old Scots Parliament, dating from the 1630s and destroyed in 1808, adorn the pediment with which he relieved one previously plain front. Elsewhere, gates and bridges are wholly constructed of stones from the same hallowed halls. At an entrance to the policies, the pillars are surmounted by frolicsome lions which 'stood in front of Mr Mitchelson's, afterwards Dr Bennet's house in Nicolson Street, and were purchased by me for 20 guineas. They were erected when I was a boy at the High School about 1766 or 1767, and it was one of the first houses in that street.'[6]

The Dundases acquired Arniston in 1571. The line from which they sprang had settled in the twelfth century at a castle overlooking the main passage of the Forth, above Queensferry on the Lothian shore. The district was still Gaelic-speaking and they named themselves after their home, Dùndeas, the southern fortress. There they could safely multiply, and did it so prolifically that their branches in the end spread from Shetland to Berkshire. It was an indigent younger son who set up at Arniston, with a gift from his mother. While today this stretch of the South Esk is sheltered and leafy, almost lush after a fashion rare in Scotland, that has only come with two centuries of improvement. Rising to high, windswept moors, it would have been bleak before. In the 1790s the minister of Temple, the parish where most of the estate lay, wrote in the *Old Statistical Account* that 'from the situation the air is cold; the frost sets in early in the season, and continues late in the spring. At other times the air is damp, occasioned by the hills attracting the showers and the moss retaining the moisture.' In the upland parts nothing but bere, an inferior barley, could be grown. Little more than subsistence was possible, especially as there were no roads. The natives found it easier to move themselves than their crops. The population had fallen to 593, compared with 905 in 1755. Enclosure doubtless prompted the drop, for

> the proprietors have also been at considerable pains and expense to second the natural tendency of the soil to pasturage, and have, with this view, laid out much of their best land in grass-fields, cultivated in a superior style, and which now make great returns. But till of late the farmers have shown no spirit for improvement. Six years ago, none of them but one raised turnip, and ten years ago none of them but one raised clover and rye-grass.

The Revd James Goldie went on to note that 'the people are in general quiet and no disturbers of the public peace' – quite sensibly, one would have thought, when the law officers of Scotland were their landlords. He cannot always have been content in this chilly and remote charge, with its doltish peasants: he complained that his church was freezing in winter because it had no ceiling and the doors would not shut properly. But he was the sort of clergyman who could easily divert himself with the coursing and shooting, and survived to write his piece for the *New Statistical Account* forty years later.[7]

Here, without their extraordinary gifts, the Dundases of Arniston would probably have remained just like hundreds of other Scottish lairds, poor but proud, fierce but pious, violent but insecure, by turns obsequious to authority and almost insanely defiant of it. In important respects they were closer to the rest of the people, who tilled the land for themselves, than to the nobles by or through whom it was ruled. The Lothians provide an illustration.

A line drawn southwards from Edinburgh to pass Arniston would bound a broad, fertile coastal plain to the east, much of it occupied by great estates. Here were the seats of the Earls of Haddington and Lauderdale, of Seton and of Winton (these attainted after 1715), of the Marquises of Lothian and of Tweeddale, above all of the Duke of Buccleuch, the grandest magnate of the Lowlands: he could, it was said, ride from sea to sea without leaving his domains. This was a feudal aristocracy, a *noblesse de l'epée*. Rank and fortune, to use Cockburn's terms, guaranteed its scions' greatness. They had done very nicely out of Union and if, unlike their Irish counterparts, they were still rooted in their country and proud of it, they nevertheless no longer looked for greatness in Scotland, but in London.

To the west was a hilly landscape of inferior soils where lesser landowners lived as a matter of course on their own estates, or as near as made no difference if they happened to have a town-house in Edinburgh. The Union, which had opened opportunities for the highest rank, closed many for this second one, in particular by drastically reducing the political places available. Yet national affairs were of no great interest or importance to the lairds. What mattered was their own localities. And while not so rich or potent as the nobles, they nevertheless firmly held the levers of power there. As heritors, they supervised the revenue and ran what welfare the state afforded, in education, relief of the poor and patronage of the Church. As justices, they set wages and otherwise adjudicated between masters and servants, built roads, maintained bridges and ferries. As barons, they sat in judgment in the barony courts till these were abolished in 1747.

But they were always under an economic compulsion. Scotland was owned at the end of the century, as at the beginning, by a mere 8000 people. Among them, only 400 had land with an annual rental above £2000, and only another 1000 had land worth more than £500. It was a self-consciously static society, yet not entirely immobile. Its Jacobite families genteelly withered. Its younger sons were obliged in any event to make their own way in a trade or profession. Meanwhile, wealthy merchants, lawyers, manufacturers or nabobs could pay the entrance fee with the purchase of an estate. If only for the sake of higher rents, all this made the lairds into great agricultural improvers. Every one of the most famous, Cockburn of Ormiston, Grant of Monymusk and Barclay of Urie was below the rank of peer. It also roused their eagerness for the remaining salaried public positions, of which the main source was the law. In the seventeenth century, lawyers had enjoyed a low social status. But after the Union, in the absence of a feudal aristocracy, something of a *noblesse de robe* came into existence. And of this the Dundases of Arniston stood at the very peak.[8]

The first to attain judicial office was James (1620–79). He sat in Parliament for Midlothian in 1648. After the Restoration of 1660, he was appointed a judge in the Court of Session. But he stepped down within months when required by the royalist Government to renounce the Covenant, which he had subscribed in his youth.[9]

These were awkward times for rigorous Presbyterians, even for those dwelling quietly on their lands. His son Robert went abroad, if possibly for the innocent purpose of studying law. In any case, he returned with William of Orange and in 1689 was appointed straight to the Bench. He also represented Midlothian in Parliament till 1707, the two functions not then being incompatible. Though a retired and bookish man, he was one of the thirty-one commissioners for the Union. The Earl of Stair wrote to the Earl of Mar in January 1706: 'My lord Arniston is very current for the treaty and that we should take the best terms we can get.' He died in 1726, just as he began to build his new seat. He was the only man to have held public office continuously since the Glorious Revolution.[10]

His eldest son, James, turned out the black sheep in a family of stern Whigs. He was a Jacobite. Worse, he insisted on advertising it, for he was also a pamphleteer. One effort, in 1710, urged the country not to fear a Tory landslide in the impending General Election: 'Unanimity is the greatest blessing can attend a society.' If his sentiments were there still veiled by ambiguity, the next year he let himself go with an effusion of unmistakable intent. The law officers got wind of it, stopped the printing and sent a copy south. Not only was it pored over in Cabinet but, according to Sir John Clerk of Penicuik, 'the Queen called it a villainous pamphlet'. A subsequent letter from somebody in Windsor Castle noted that

> one Mr Dundas, who was described by the Lord Advocate as a light, pragmatical, headstrong young man, had printed a pamphlet which under pretence of defending the loyalty of that society [the Faculty of Advocates] was the most violent libel against the Revolution, the settlement of the Crown, the past and present reign, the Union and the whole English nation.

The writer suggested it might have been done as an exercise in satire after the manner of Daniel Defoe.[11]

If that was truly young Dundas's aim, he was remarkably foolish to go on and urge the Faculty to accept into its collections a medal bearing the likeness of the pretended James VIII, offered to boot by the Duchess of Gordon, whose husband had in 1689 held Edinburgh Castle against the Dutch William. He carried his colleagues with him and was deputed by them to convey to her their thanks, at which he hoped for 'the restoration of the King and Royal Family, and the finishing of rebellion, usurpation, tyranny and Whiggery'. This proved too much: James was charged with sedition and disinherited by his father. What happened afterwards is not known for certain. One tradition had it that James was kept locked up at Arniston for the rest of his days. Another said he fled to France, where his perversity overtook him. Badly served at a fashionable restaurant, he later reserved there a table for three. He arrived with two dogs which he seated on either side of him and addressed as Monsieur le Comte and Monsieur le Chevalier. A real comte or chevalier happening to be present objected, challenged him to a duel and killed him.[12]

Both the ability of his father and the contrariness of his brother came out in the next heir, Robert. A pious man who hated bishops and intellectuals, he warned his own son against 'throwing too much money away on books: when that turns disease 'tis as bad as pictures.' Of Lord Kames he averred: 'His fault is a fondness for concerts, by which he neglects and confounds [his] solid principles.' Alexander

Carlyle, the literary minister of Inveresk, called him 'ill-looking, with a large nose and small ferret eyes, round shoulders, a harsh croaking voice, and altogether unprepossessing; yet by the time he had uttered three sentences, he raised attention and went on with a torrent of good sense and clear reasoning that made one entirely forget the first impression.' He was indeed 'one of the ablest lawyers this country ever produced, and a man of high independent spirit.' John Ramsay of Ochtertyre esteemed him more, as the greatest Scots lawyer of the century: 'besides being a profound feudalist and civilian, he was confessedly one of the closest and clearest reasoners of his time … Notwithstanding the heat and impetuosity of his temper, which could ill brook contradiction in conversation, his lordship was a most patient and dispassionate hearer of counsel.'[13]

Juries owed to him their option of returning a verdict of not guilty. Till 1728, when he secured a change in the procedure, they could only declare the facts of a case proven or not proven and had to leave the judges to decide whether the guilt of the accused was then to be inferred. Dundas boldly took his inititative during a trial of high political delicacy, though it arose from a mere drunken brawl at Forfar. He led for a defendant who had killed Lord Strathmore, ancestor on the maternal side of her present Majesty, but a Jacobite who had cursed the man for a Hanoverian lickspittle and thrown him in a brimming ditch. By the success of his manoeuvres, Dundas got him off.

After the law, his passion was drink, in such volume as still to be talked of a century later. Walter Scott told in the notes to *Guy Mannering* how Dundas, after finishing work one Saturday noon, was booted and saddled for the return to Arniston. But a colleague, seeking advice on some ticklish legal point, inveigled him into taking just a glass or two while they discussed it. Impromptu drinking bouts were even then a hazard of the capital's life, and they emerged at nine that night. Dundas still sat down and wrote an opinion till the small hours. We are assured that not five words of it had afterwards to be corrected. His habits were indeed 'considered rather as a proof of a vigorous brain than treated as an outrage on decorum.' Sometimes vigour and decorum could be combined: 'There was a tremendous silver vessel at Arniston Castle, not reserved for any one person, but brought into the dining room after dinner, when the ladies had left the table and the serious drinking had got under way, for the general comfort of all the men.'[14]

In a wider sense, the national spirit coursed through Dundas's veins. Ramsay recalled him as

> one of the last of that illustrious group of Scots lawyers who adhered really to the dialect, manners and customs of their ancestors. At his outset, and even on going into Parliament, he did not think it incumbent on him to study the niceties of the structure and articulation of the English language like a schoolboy. This was no doubt an insuperable bar to his being well heard in the House of Commons; but he was satisfied with displaying his unpolished manly eloquence at the Scottish bar, where he was sure of finding admirers. Trusting to the extent of his intellectual powers, and to skill in his own profession, he held the graces of style by pronunciation perhaps too cheap. Be that as it may, he left it to younger men to bow to the Dagon of English taste. Though Scotland had lost its rank among the nations, he could say, as

the Trojan did of his city after the fall, Fuimus Troes, fuit Ilium et ingens gloria Teucrorum.[15]

He was the first Dundas to go seriously into politics, if with no great zeal. His individualism anyway meant he would not get far. He attached himself to the Squadrone Volante. It had won its name by opportunism but, being largely composed of nobles out of favour in London, was in fact fairly consistent in its resistance to executive immoderation. To that extent, it had more principles than the Court party, with its habitual support for anyone in power, to which, in the erratic politics of the age, the Squadrone was sometimes allied and sometimes opposed. After 1715 when the Jacobites, the third faction, put themselves beyond the pale, it took office under the Duke of Roxburghe as Secretary of State. Dundas, Solicitor General in 1717 at the age of 32, found his position sensitive. His superior, the Lord Advocate, Sir David Dalrymple, scarcely hid a sympathy for the rebels whose lands were threatened with confiscation. When he was eased out in 1720, Dundas succeeded. His election to Parliament for Midlothian followed in 1722, though he found in his turn that he could not do without the Jacobite vote. A previous member for the seat, George Lockhart of Carnwath, the Pretender's principal agent in Scotland, agreed not to stand against him on condition that he 'would preserve some honest men's estates from being forfeited'.

The pact was needed at that year's General Election. For in the preceding Whig Schism, the Squadrone had chosen the wrong side and come out against Sir Robert Walpole. He was thus looking for someone new to run Scotland and picked the second Duke of Argyll, whose followers, dubbed Argathelians, triumphed at the polls. From Scotland's forty-five representatives in the Commons the Tories were virtually eliminated, while the Squadrone was reduced to a dozen, three afterwards unseated by Walpole's ample majority at Westminster. Its leaders stayed in office, but could not last long. In 1725, the Prime Minister decided once more to impose a malt tax on the Scots. The peers had actually moved for dissolving the Union at the previous such attempt in 1713, so high did feelings run. This time it brought in Glasgow riots and in Edinburgh a calamity: the brewers went on strike. The Scots Ministers refused to toe London's line, the Lord Advocate indeed concerting popular opposition to it – what Lockhart called 'a right Scots part'. All were sacked amid much acrimony. Roxburghe deplored that Dundas 'was the first Advocate for Scotland that had been dismissed the service without any gratification or compensation'. It left him with large debts which twenty years later he was still trying to get repaid.[16]

To him, however, there was a deeper, constitutional issue, for it was by the terms of the Treaty of Union that the Scots claimed their exemption from the tax. Dundas wrote: 'It is not in the power neither of the representatives of South Britain nor of North Britain, nor of them both together, to alter any part of what was contracted and agreed to by the articles of the Union.' He conceded, however, that 'I have no hope of persuading either the Parliament or any other person that the representatives for Scotland have a negative upon the representatives of England in all questions touching the unalterable articles of the Union.' Still, when it was proposed in the Commons the next year that the malt tax might be made more acceptable by an explanatory Act to justify it under the Treaty, he 'thought explaining ane article of the Union by ane Act of Parliament was a dangerous thing and could not help telling my sentiment that it was more than perhaps Parliament could do, that I should never be for explaining because I was afraid that if we came to that the articles would soon be explained away.' He thus stated what was to become a standard Scottish argument for the sanctity of the contract of 1707 against English claims for the absolute, unlimited sovereignty of Parliament.[17]

It looked meanwhile like the end of Dundas's political career, at least so long as the Scottish roost was ruled by Argyll, who called him a madman and a knave. Not a large proprietor in his county, he still dug himself in – 'though by no means opulent, he was no lover of money, few lawyers having ever refused so many fees or working harder without them. He made it a rule never to take money from a freeholder of Midlothian or a clergyman.' He yet prospered at the Bar, and kept a public position as Dean of the Faculty of Advocates. Nor was he politically negligible. He continued to lead a tiny Squadrone in the Commons, supported from home by those magnates who would not pander to Argyll. In 1734, Dundas whipped up resistance, albeit unsuccessful, to the 'King's list' – the system under which the sixteen representative peers elected to each Parliament were named in advance by the Government. In February he resignedly told his son Robert, a student at Utrecht:

> There is no such thing as writing to you anything that passes here, all our letters being opened; there are a far greater number of opposers in the House of Commons than hath been seen at any time before; and to be sure, the generality of the whole nation is quite dissatisfied both with our Minister and his measures, but, as they have a majority in the house, corruption and oppression in elections will probably increase it, and so we will be left to struggle for the sinking liberty of our country till God in his providence interpose to save us; and if he hath destined us for destruction, to be sure we must fall into it. For the other house, nothing can be expected from them; such a sixteen as we have. God pity them![18]

The Calvinist mood was deepened by affliction. In the previous winter his wife and three of his children had been carried off by smallpox.

This was his nadir. But he was resilient enough to pick himself up within months. A second marriage, to Ann Gordon, gave him a new lease of life. He combined the penning of letters to her almost incoherent in their passion with still more diligent work at the Bar. And suddenly his political position improved too. In its wrath following the Porteous Riot of 1737, the Government tried to humiliate Scotland, and her capital in particular. The normally self-serving Argyll could not stomach that. He spoke out in the House of Lords against the pains and penalties proposed. It was the start of his estrangement from Walpole. In these new circumstances, he cast about for allies. One immediate beneficiary was Dundas. As his talents without doubt warranted, he was raised to the Bench. Lord Arniston, however, refused to be disarmed by this. In 1740 mutual friends discreetly arranged a meeting between the Duke and him with the aim of formal reconciliation. But he failed, as they intended, to invite his Grace home. When Arniston arrived there his lady, in on the plot, asked where Argyll might be, for dinner was nearly ready.

Porteous
Riot
1737

He said: 'My dear, rather than let him within my door I would burn the house. But come, let this great dinner be served up in form. I asked a friend or two to dine with the Duke, and they shall certainly not be disappointed.'[19]

He stood still better before long. In 1742 Walpole was put out of office. Argyll stayed in opposition, followed now by only a dozen members in the Commons, and anyway died the next year. The leader of the Squadrone, the Marquis of Tweeddale, became Secretary of State for Scotland with Robert Dundas younger, aged 29 and but five years back from Holland, as Solicitor General. Arniston too was active for the Ministry, ever ready with suggestions and advice: 'I do think the Crown's church favours are in wretched, worthless hands'; it would be a 'good thing if a way could be fallen upon to get hold of the town of Edinburgh' of which the Lord Provost might in certain circumstances 'be brought to model the town of Edinburgh our way and himself to be with us.'

Tweeddale, weak and idle, exasperated him. Never a man to mince his words, Arniston once wrote: 'I looked again and again to find how many of your Lordship's recommendations had been taken the least notice of, I think I find none.' Another time, after only just successfully managing a by-election, he groused: 'Instead of having any assistance from those who have been continued in the King's service we had all their weight against us, which indeed is no more than I had always told your Lordship would happen.' In fact this interlude was only a temporary setback for the Argathelians. No purge of them took place and Lord Milton, their man of business, carried on in his offices. The Dundases lost few chances to pick a fight with him.[20]

It fell to this querulous crew to face the second Jacobite rising. Arniston, a martyr to gout, was lucky that he had to spend the latter half of 1745 taking the waters in various southern spas, for the Scottish establishment showed itself utterly incompetent in the face of Prince Charles's threat; not that the English one was much better. Tweeddale preferred to dither in London, nursing his own gouty feet. The Lord Advocate, Robert Craigie, was busy to no purpose. Sir John Cope, the local commander, went with a mere 2000 troops on a futile march round the North, before shipping them back by sea towards the capital: only towards, because the Prince had just taken it unopposed. There survives a distracted letter from Mrs Dundas, telling her husband how she was caught there by the Highlanders' occupation but managed to talk her way out and escape to Arniston driving her own carriage. Robert Dundas and the other officers of the Government were already away, first to Haddington, then to Dunbar. When the Prince beat Cope at Prestonpans in late September, they fled into England. Dundas cautiously returned to Berwick in October, and to Edinburgh only in November. Two months later all the Scottish Ministers resigned or were dismissed. The Government vented its spite by abolishing the Secretaryship altogether.[21]

The way ought to have been clear for an Argathelian restoration in the person of the new, the third Duke, better known by his previous title, Earl of Ilay. But neither King George II nor the Pelham Ministry would give him a free hand. They thought him, with his vast Highland connection and attachment to ancient privileges, soft on Jacobitism: the Duke of Cumberland's approach was much preferred. The one possible counterpoise to Argyll lay in the shattered remnant of the Squadrone, but it was plainly inadequate for the purpose. Some successes were scored. The Heritable Jurisdictions Act was passed on the Squadrone's votes. Argyll had little say in the appointment of sheriffs, who in the consequent legal reform were named by the Crown to administer justice in each county. Above all, Arniston was promoted Lord President of the Court of Session in 1748, over the head of Milton – he exulted to see 'that puppy' thrust aside. Yet right down the line concessions had to be made to Argyll too. He got the highest payment in compensation for loss of the old jurisdictions. The sheriffs' terms were limited to seven years, so that he would before long have a second chance to fill these posts with his clients. And Milton was consoled with another judicial office. It had become obvious that Argyll was just too mighty to be toppled. All that the Government could hope for was a balance of power in Scotland.[22]

The Earl of Albemarle, succeeding Cumberland as commander there, found Arniston 'a violent patriot'. But the Dundases were left as adjuncts to a faction in London which demanded yet more loyal unionism than the Argathelians had shown. There was nothing to be done. At least the best man had the Lord Presidency. 'Even his abrupt manner, which degenerated at last into absolute crabbishness, contributed to accelerate business; for nobody cared to say more than enough to a man so fiery and peremptory, who understood business perfectly and meant excellently well.' His mind was as strong and sour as ever. A foe of all episcopacy, he dragooned the court into sitting over Christmas. He did not mind if that discomfited his brother judges, for he thought little of them. Blaming years of corrupt Argathelian patronage, he saw himself as sitting 'betwixt persons not unsuspected [of Jacobitism] and a set of whimsicals disposed to thwart everything wherein the Government may seem to have a concern'. The law officers did not impress him either: 'How they came to be employed is not fit for me to explain, because it would disoblige a great man [Argyll], if he knew it, whom it would be insolent in me to offend.' He called the Duke of Newcastle, actually his best political ally at Westminster, 'that brute'. His abuse was at any rate even-handed, and ought not to obscure the fact that judicial patronage did at his urging become less partisan. But age and illness soon sapped him. For two or three years before his death in 1754 he could do his job only with difficulty. At the end he was said to be 'very doited'.[23]

His son, Robert, had just entered Parliament for Midlothian, after a more convincing truce with Argyll. The Duke wrote to the Prime Minister, Henry Pelham:

> Mr Dundas of Arniston and I are in all human appearance on a very good footing; he was so good as to say … that he would not stand unless I approved it. He came to see me at Edinburgh and I returned the compliment by begging him to stand … He seems to be a sensible pretty kind of man; but some of his own friends say he is as hot as his father.

They shared a keen, if crabbed intelligence, for the son was 'in no period of his life distinguished for laborious application to study', indeed, 'never known to read a book'. Rarely assenting to follow the herd, he was held more in respect than in affection. His nickname, Bumbo, can have been no endearment when it so often prefaced abusive letters to him.[24]

Almost at once the incumbent Lord Advocate, William Grant of Prestongrange, went on to the Bench. Dundas's succession was eased by the fact that, having lost his first wife, he was about to marry Grant's daughter. Certainly Newcastle pushed him forward in order to forestall any Argathelian rival. Back from him came the usual lowering reaction of a Dundas: 'This step in life is no doubt great but would in many things carry a gloomy aspect.' He was soon well regarded at Westminster, though, and named by Horace Walpole as one of only about thirty members who could truly be termed orators. His sole speech of which record has survived was in favour of press-gangs. But an era of good feeling followed in Scottish politics. Both old parties were represented in the Ministry, co-operating on measures for the Highlands and legal reform. Their conflict was damped, at least on the surface.

Yet manoeuvring for advantage continued behind the scenes. When a minor appointment came up in the capital, Dundas wrote to Newcastle: 'I ingenuously own that I am the more desirous of obtaining this favour that the town of Edinburgh and many in it may see that your Grace does me the honour to listen to my recommendations, which in such a trifle as the present being given to be known to be under my influence increases, I must be forgiven to say, your Grace's interest and weight in this place.' His Grace sent his regrets saying that Argyll 'will suppose that the meaning of any recommendation, not his own, to that employment is with a view to lessen his credit and influence in the city of Edinburgh, that it would be breaking with him to give it to any recommendation but his own. You know how much I always desire to oblige your lordship when it is in my power, and I am sure you will excuse me when it is not.'[25]

It was apparently considered safer all round for politics to be reduced to personalities, but the Lord Advocate fought spirited running battles with his special bugbears. One was Lord Provost George Drummond, who has won immortality by his enlightened projection of a New Town for the capital. Dundas, however, had the satisfaction of ensuring that Drummond himself never saw a single house rise on the further side of the Nor' Loch by thwarting his every attempt during his lifetime to extend the burgh's boundaries, without which work could not start. Dundas also opposed the appointment of the popular David Hume as keeper of the Advocates' Library in 1752. According to the philosopher, it was a political manoeuvre. He wrote that the Dundases, father and son,

> who used to rule absolutely in this body of advocates, formed an aversion to the project, because it had not come from them; and they secretly engaged the whole party called Squadrone against me. The bigots joined them, and both together set up a gentleman of character, and an advocate, and who had got favour on both these accounts. The violent cry of deism, atheism and scepticism was raised against me; and 'twas represented that my election would be giving the sanction of the greatest and most learned body of men in this country to my profane and irreligious principles.

Hume was all the same elected. Even then, Dundas harried him and demanded removal from the library of purportedly dirty books ordered by 'le bon David' from France. One was, to be sure, the Comte de Bussy-Rabutin's *Vie amoureuse des Gaules*, but another was La Fontaine's *Contes*. The affronted Hume wrote to Dundas:

There is a particular kind of insolence which is more provoking as it is meaner than any other, 'tis the insolence of office ... By the by, Bussy-Rabutin contains no bawdy at all, though if it did, I see not that it would be a whit the worse. For I know not a more agreeable subject for books and conversation, if executed with decency and ingenuity. I can presume, without intending the least offence, that as the glass circulates at your lordship's table, this topic of conversation will sometimes steal in, provided always there be no ministers present. And even some of these reverend gentlemen I have seen not to dislike the subject.[26]

The remark was pointed. Keep though he might to the straight and narrow, on two wives Dundas sired ten children. They were of great value in extending connections: one girl, for instance, married a rich old general in Fife and bore three daughters, who became respectively Duchess of Portland, Countess of Moray and Mrs George Canning. Nor was Dundas at all inhibited in other social activities. His household got through sixteen hogsheads of claret a year, equivalent to fourteen modern bottles a day. His boon companion was indeed a reverend gentleman, Dr Alexander Webster, former Moderator of the General Assembly, minister of the Tolbooth kirk, leader of the High-flyers, the popular or evangelical party in the Church of Scotland. Their moral programme might be summed up as opposition to all indecencies save alcoholic ones. Married to a lady worth £4000 a year, Dr Webster became 'a five-bottle man, he could lay them all under the table.' He was given the affectionate cognomen of Magnum Bonum, for 'a love of claret not being reckoned in those days a sin in Scotland, all his excesses were pardoned'. Yet he efficiently fulfilled the commission from Dundas to carry out a Scottish census – which computed the population in 1755 at 1,265,380.

What his fellow High-flyers thought of it all was unclear. Webster himself commented that 'I drink with gentlemen and vote with fools'.[27] He certainly in himself refuted the view that the popular party, if redeemed in the light of its history by its democratic sentiments, was at heart a collection of crude, plebeian bigots. But that view anyway rested on the writings of their opponents, who took for themselves the winsome name of Moderates. They preened themselves on being polite, tolerant and firmly attached to an aristocratic social order. The Dundases stood by their family's tradition with the popular party, but neither in the Kirk nor anywhere else were they ever party hacks. The underlying tensions in all this – religious, political, social, cultural – emerged in the curious controversy over *The Tragedy of Douglas* in 1756–7.

Its author was the Revd John Home, the young minister of Athelstaneford in East Lothian. He composed an exceptionally tedious farrago of declamatory rhetoric. Its significance lay in its supposedly giving Scotland, which had produced no works worth reading for a century and more, a literary monument on a par with those of the Greeks, of the Romans, not to speak of the English. Hence the cry, on the tumultuous first night in Edinburgh, 'Whaur's yer Wullie Shakespeare noo?' As Carlyle recorded, 'there were a few opposers, however, among those who pretended to taste and literature'. At the head of these in retrospect discriminating men was the Lord Advocate. He joined with others at the General Assembly in passing a resolution that ministers should shun the theatre. But he had a motive of his own. Home was patronised by Argyll and more especially by Milton, whom Dundas had evidently forgiven nothing. The tragedian was also about to resign his charge and become private secretary to the Earl of Bute, waiting eagerly on the accession to the throne of his pupil, the future George III. The Prince and Princess of Wales actually went to see the wretched play in London, where it was put on at Covent Garden through the good offices of no less a personage than William Pitt the elder.

Carlyle, whose demeanour earned him the apt nickname of Jupiter, loftily commented that 'this conduct of Dundas might in part be imputed to his want of taste and discernment in what related to the belles lettres, and to a certain violence of temper, which could endure no-one that did not bend to him'. We might be inclined to put things the other way round and commend him for his inability to resist goading his adversaries, especially if they were also in authority. The latest Commander-in-chief, General Humphrey Bland, wrote: 'Neither the favours nor frowns of the great men in this city can bias him from telling the truth … He is free from the underhand low cunning peculiar to his countrymen, an enemy to the jobbing so much practised to the destruction of justice and the ruin of this kingdom.' Certainly he was short with those who crossed him. And, as a good Presbyterian, he could only be expected to show a certain degree of hypocrisy.[28]

In himself he represented something wider: a class which was acquiring the confidence and willingness to enter public affairs alongside the old aristocrats, even to establish a social authority independent of theirs. The Dundases were among the first to rise above rude rusticity and prim Presbyterianism, to attain thus a life of greater comfort, elegance and prestige, or what they dubbed politeness. Not that their imitation of metropolitan manners was always convincing. They habitually spoke Scots. James Boswell, one of the most touchy in a nation soon afflicted by acute linguistic sensitivity, was dismayed when standing in Parliament House one day to receive a thunderous clap on the back and to hear, bellowed in his ear, 'Hoo's yer faither the day, Jamie?' This was Robert Dundas, by then Lord President of the Court of Session. He, even amid the splendours of Arniston House, liked to dine off cock-a-leekie, cockle hags and sheep's heid.

Such was his reputation as a lawyer, however, that nothing could harm his prospects. He had not, as it happened, prospered much at the Bar. Hating the written pleadings which were the staple diet at Parliament House, he often declined briefs and had an income of only £280 per year. But as a judge his professional despatch was in every way exemplary. He kept an hourglass on the bench and silenced advocates who were not done when it ran out. If they became vague or tiresome, he would pick it up and wave it at them. Boswell likened pleading before him to an encounter with a fierce dog: 'He is chained and does not bite you. But he barks wowf, wowf and makes you start; your nerves are hurt by him.'

On his appointment as Lord President in 1760, the Court of Session was still wading through the causes of 1755. He dealt with the whole backlog, besides disposing of current business, in thirty months. And never again, during the quarter-century he remained in charge of it, did the court fall into arrears.

Rigorously impartial and intellectually formidable, it enjoyed under his presidency a golden era. He was concerned that the law should be not only efficient but also accessible. To this end he penned with his own hand in 1777 a layman's guide to *The Nature and Constitution of Rights, heritable, movable and personal* – the only time he went into print. On another occasion, he committed to paper 'the principles which ensured what success in life I have enjoyed: first, studying mankind to learn their tempers; second, accommodating myself to various tempers; third, preserving inflexible integrity'.[29]

We have been tracing the history of a leading legal family and its acquisition of interest and influence outside Parliament House. If the Dundases were pre-eminent in this, they were by no means unique. Lawyers figured among those who gained most from a Union at first deeply unpopular and not a little shaky, but now turning out beneficial. Years passed, however, before Scotland assimilated the constitutionalism ennobling English public life. It had been wanting in her own past. The Scottish state during its last decades was a constant prey to noble feuding, disruptive of such regular government as might have been possible and held in check only by bribes from London. Moreover, the Revolution of 1688 ended attempts in Britain to emulate the unifying absolutism which in this era was the vehicle of progress elsewhere in Europe. The diverse social forces previously subjected to the monarchy were preserved distinct and robust. Here, England lost less of the colourful medieval heritage than any continental country.

When Scotland entered the Union, then, bringing her laws and institutions with her, they could be easily fitted in. Indeed, they were probably thus protected. There was no telling what other end there might have been to the worsening relations between the two countries which prompted Queen Anne's démarche of 1706, with the appointment of commissioners on each side to treat for a Union. The result rendered Scotland's own national and religious interests relatively unimportant. And there followed during the first decades of Union a phase of economic, political and cultural disorientation. But afterwards material and intellectual advance renewed and quickened, preparing the country for spectacular progress into the agricultural and industrial revolutions. By a miracle the Union was working, something its authors had hoped but dared not expect.

Yet it would be idle to maintain, given the episodes already recounted, that relations proved uniformly harmonious. Blatant breaches of the Treaty of Union occurred. One was the Patronage Act of 1712. It ended the guarantee, won with the Presbyterian settlement of the Church in 1690, that congregations could elect their ministers. That was indefensible. A second came with the abolition of heritable jurisdictions in 1747. But that was negotiated and paid for, an augury of greater English tolerance and sensitivity. The earlier examples were in truth a bad guide to how matters would eventually turn out. For Scots in these times were more fortunate than other small European peoples drawn into the orbit of larger neighbours. Effectively they could pick and choose for themselves which elements of their nationhood to retain and which to discard. Yet the English legal theorist, William Blackstone, was already asking whether the guarantees in the Treaty were not illusory, whether it could in reality be abrogated by Parliament's breaching its terms. He took a view which has since prevailed: that by the Union a new body politic had been created, which nothing could prevent from exercising sovereign power. That power was vested in a united Parliament. It could thus override the Treaty, done though that might be by outvoting the Scots.[30]

Still, however much the Scots claimed to be North Britons – a claim anyway rejected by many Englishmen besides John Wilkes – they were still unready for full integration. That ensured the survival of Scottish modes of thought and action. Scottishness was not extinguished. It could be preserved, indeed aroused. In fact, for nearly three centuries after the Reformation, social development formed a continuum. There was no sudden break at the Union and no need for Scots to adopt a defensive nationalism against loss of statehood. Their Parliament had never been the same revered wellspring and focus of national life as England's. It had been one among a range of such focuses – the nobility, the law, the schools and universities, the royal burghs, above all the Kirk. These others were maintained by the Treaty. The major institutions shaping the lives of the people remained native, and through them Scotland held on to a semi-independence. If their vices were at times more prominent than their virtues, they gave her some benefits of full statehood without tiresome responsibility. In latter days, a separate Scottish administration has made analogous arrangements possible. But for a long time after 1707, most things were run by lawyers.

By now, Scots law was a mature system. It had been virtually created by Lord Stair at the end of the previous century. It was at any rate set, by his *Institutions of the Law of Scotland*, on a firm rational foundation. Lord Cooper of Culross described them as 'an original amalgam of Roman law, feudal law and the native customary law, systematised by resort to the law of nature and illuminated by many flashes of ideal metaphysic'. Now, 'development proceeded at a steadily increasing pace with reliance upon the law of Rome and with a revival of interest in feudal law in consequence of the forfeitures and redistribution of lands following upon the Jacobite rebellions'.[31]

The system remained fertile not only because lawyers continued to build up an edifice of new rules to meet new circumstances, but also because they were precisely fitted into the existing framework by further institutional writers. Through this pertinacious and impressive intellectual effort, Scots law retained its coherence. Had a state been present, one would have said that it was codified. If the impulse was owed ultimately to Roman law, in fact this influence declined. Absolute and eternal though Justinians's principles might be, and not inappropriate to the Scotland of the eighteenth century, their spirit was authoritarian. The procedure reinforced it. There were, for example, no juries in civil causes, a bugbear to those who thought Scotland should by now have won the blessings of English forms of liberty. The rigour of this jurisprudence could not but be soothed by the sweeter reason of the Enlightenment. Stair's natural law yielded to the insights of historical sociology. This was a sea-change in a system priding itself on adherence to principle. Now the law, like everything else, was found to be conditioned by the state of society: which meant it could be amended.

Scots law has always had its arcana, what with hamesucken and horning, sasine and servitudes, teinds and tailzie, mysteries to any but the initiate. But perhaps

they helped the judiciary to retain its prerogatives intact. Under the Treaty there
was in criminal cases no appeal from the highest Scottish instance, which fact
would be crucially confirmed by Lord Chancellor Mansfield, a Scot trained in
England. The Lords' appellate jurisdiction for civil causes had, however, been
established as early as 1711, to Scotland's surprise and disgust. It was done by one
of those wicked manoeuvres in the early years of the Union in order to let off an
obnoxious Episcopalian clergyman who broke Scots law by using the English
liturgy. Their later lordships must have rued it. It brought them a rising burden of
Scots appeals, most on the fiendish intricacies of feudalism. Lord Chancellor
Erskine, despite a curriculum vitae similar to Mansfield's, confessed: 'I know
something of the law, but of Scotch law I am as ignorant as a native of Mexico.' It
span out an already labyrinthine procedure. Nor did it expedite for the future the
questions submitted to Westminster. The Court of Session, always disliking case
law, by no means regarded judgments pronounced there as binding in similar
matters.[32]

    The fact remained that the law, exposed to a foreign influence, was hard to
reform systematically without a resident legislature. Besides, strong prejudice
existed against changing statutes without irrefutable reason, a feeling explicitly
embodied in the Treaty of Union's securities for national institutions and private
law. Attempts to meddle with them could be ignorant, heavy-handed and unpopular, yet Scottish affairs were in general not thought weighty enough to take up
much of Westminster's time. Governments came to prefer sending the drafts of
important measures to be mulled over at Parliament House in consultation with
the parties concerned, and if all agreed on their final form there was little trouble
in getting them through. Legislation as such was not usually a major official
preoccupation, however, most of it being proposed and passed by private members.
Scotland's undersized delegation at Westminster offered only a meagre basis for
such initiatives, which thus had to rely on reluctant ministerial backing. In
practice it was usually left to lawyers to codify, interpret, indeed reform the law.

    Perhaps Lord Cooper's statement above only rationalised the fact that all along
Scots law had had to abandon some statutes on grounds of desuetude, enlarge
others as occasion demanded, create novel topics almost from nothing and, for the
criminal side, declare new offences on that basis: this with the straight-faced
pretence of stating the law as it had ever been. 'Native vigour' was what they called
it. It gave the Scots judiciary something like the function which the Supreme
Court of the United States enjoys today. Within it could be observed the same
tension between a conservative jurisprudence, handing down verdicts on a strict
construction of existing law, and a progressive one, shaping the law by its decisions
to answer changing needs. The system was creative and fecund, on the whole
keeping English influences at bay. Thus, as a great academic lawyer of modern
times declared, 'Scotland's supreme courts have sat on in Parliament House in
Edinburgh, symbolising, as it were, the nation's survival in her laws'. Not for
nothing had they taken over the old place in 1707.[33]

    Together with the character of the jurisprudence, that of the judiciary also
changed. Till well on into the eighteenth century, the feudal aristocracy could still
state and enforce the law. It happened, first, because of heritable jurisdictions.

They were a peculiar Scottish institution which, in territories owned or dominated by certain noblemen, reserved the judicial function to them. Guaranteed by
the Treaty, the arrangement was yet revealed as dangerously obsolete by the
Jacobite risings. In its most exalted form, the regality, the hereditary judge had to
all intents and purpose the status of a king, from whose verdict there was no
appeal. It excluded one-third of the country from the authority of the central
courts, as from the local policing entrusted after the Union to justices of the peace,
an office originally imported from England.

As if this was not enough, there sat extraordinary lords in the Court of Session.
They were noblemen named by the Crown as supernumeraries to the regular
judges, for their political weight rather than for any legal expertise. Their presence
tended to keep the judicial system under the thumb of the high aristocracy, or at
least amounted to a confession that verdicts could not be universally enforced
without its good grace. No new ones were named after 1723, though the last,
Secretary of State Tweeddale, did not die till 1762; by then the heritable jurisdictions had also been gone fifteen years. Now, the law was administered locally
through sheriffs, officials of the state fulfilling a function which the English
entrusted to the gentry of the shires in quarter sessions. At the same time, a more
efficient central administration generally extended the rule of law, so that it was,
if anything, rather more rational and systematic than in the South.

None of this ended political appointments to the judiciary. In Scotland, unlike
England, they have always been accepted as normal, and to them the Dundases
among others owed their standing. But partisan machination differed from feudal
vendetta. The reason for the crumbling of feudal institutions was the transformation of society beneath them. The conduct of those taking part in public life had
once been governed by kinship and regulated by feud. In defending his interests, a
man relied first on his own family; if wronged, and if able to seek redress for
himself, he went out with them and killed. It was, after all, hardly worth turning to
courts which had yet to define due process and which had few means of enforcing
their verdicts.

Yet even before the Union, in a Scotland where the medieval past was hardly
shaken off, her people at least started to go to court to settle differences. The
process was furthered by its economic consequences. At first, it caused depression.
Depression caused bankruptcy. Bankruptcy caused the sale of land or problems
with succession. There was an upsurge in litigation out of which lawyers profited
so handsomely that their profession, once something for the grubby bourgeois,
became fit, indeed desirable, for gentlemen. These began to send their sons into it.
The more that went, the more that had to follow. If Scots would no longer kill for
a kinsman, they would certainly take his side in a law-suit. The litigious classes
thus needed a foothold in the right places. And the places were legion. In
Edinburgh hundreds of lawyers, members of the Faculty of Advocates or Writers to
the Signet, thronged the central courts to service the needs of the landed class
with which their interests were inextricably linked. Together they constituted 'an
estate of lawyer-lairds not unlike the scholar gentry of medieval China'.[34]

Out of it all they became richer and more aware of their status. Apart from
private practice in the courts and outside, they had ladders of advancement open

to them in all important areas of public life: in the whole range of the judiciary, in local administration through the sheriffdoms, in political management, in agencies of the state. Professionally they embodied – except for the clergy, whose role was diminished since the Union – the country's one large concentration of trained minds. And with an absent high nobility, it was no surprise that the lawyer-lairds came to see themselves as custodians of the nation or, on occasion, as defenders of its imperilled liberties. J. G. Lockhart, Walter Scott's son in-law and biographer, wrote: 'It is not to be denied that the Scottish lawyers have done more than any other class to keep alive the sorely threatened spirit of national independence in the thoughts and feelings of their countrymen.'[35]

In the absence of a Parliament, equally, the courts became something of a substitute, just as did the General Assembly of the Church of Scotland and the Convention of Royal Burghs in their different ways. Political conflicts had to come out somewhere. They hardly did so at Westminster, because after 1745 the rivalry of the surviving Scottish factions all but ceased. This was in part for adventitious reasons, in part also because the Scots realised they would be better governed and get more out of the English if they did not openly squabble; a lesson taken perhaps too much to heart for the future.

The truce was reflected in judicial appointments. Though partisan interests were fiercely involved in them, some recognition obtained that a rough division of the spoils was preferable to proscribing the side which happened for the moment to be out: political life had lately become too unstable for that. Even so, there was in the courts no lack of opportunity for flyting. As Scott observed, 'a court of 15 men, trained to polemical habits from their youth, is more fitted for the dexterities of a popular debate than for the gravity and decorum of judicial deliberation'.[36] Such debate often clothed in legal language the real political questions of the time. One example was in the tension between the absentee magnates, interested in Scotland mainly as a territorial base for their pretensions in London, and the gentry, who had not forsaken their country for the fleshpots of the South and who felt it was now for them to state what its interests were and how they should be served.

These tensions could surface in struggles between the Argathelians and the Squadrone, though each was bound together primarily by personalities and they often swapped positions on matters of substance. With political concepts so fuzzy, it would be vain to expect consistency from born individualists like the Dundases. But it was surely no accident that the second Lord President Arniston exerted himself to suppress the electoral manipulation which allowed the great nobles of Scotland a tighter grip on the parliamentary representation than their English counterparts had. He was constantly thwarted by his compatriot Mansfield in the Lords: not that it affected their warm friendship.

Lest any jump to conclusions about the progressive nature of these lesser landowners, let us also recall how conservative they could be. From what they retained of their fathers' martial values and of classical rudiments learned at school, they tended to believe the modern age degenerate, and they set limits to the social change they might countenance. Though eager to get rich, they did not subscribe without qualification to a merely material code. If they had been to

London, they would have returned, as Scots still do, half-bewitched and half-appalled, in any case with their prejudices confirmed. 'The question is whether', David Hume wrote, 'it be for the public interest that so many privileges should be conferred on London, which has already arrived at such an enormous size, and still seems increasing.'[37]

Through that and other deplorable influences they thought society threatened with dominance by men they called 'mushrooms', who could spring up overnight out of any old midden. One held to typify them was the overbearing and ambitious Sir Lawrence Dundas of Kerse. A distant kinsman of the Dundases of Arniston, he was quite as much of family as they, even if his own branch had fallen on hard times. Himself the son of a draper, he had started his career selling stockings in the Luckenbooths of Edinburgh. He afterwards made a fortune, first as commissary to Cumberland in his march against the Jacobites, then to the British army during the Seven Years' War. Now he had bought the whole of Orkney and Shetland, and seemed to be doing the same with Stirlingshire. If upstarts like him could acquire such huge estates, then the number and power of the smaller proprietors would be inexorably reduced, and never restored. Just when the feudal nobility was being tamed, a parvenu caste would spring up to subvert the rights of honest old-time lairds. They thus wanted laws to protect them.[38]

Such questions perplexed a Scotland so poor and so aware of it. They had animated, in fields far from home, the precocious economics of William Paterson, the retired pirate from Dumfriesshire who founded the Bank of England, and of John Law, gambler, murderer, Duke of Arkansas, financial genius too fast for the French. All agreed that Scotland's first necessity was to become a trading nation. Without it there could be no growth and no progress. The immediate answer was to open the nearest, the English market. In this, one of the main aims in 1707, the unionists could be credited with pricking the fondest notions of economic science, such as it then was. They made a decisive choice, later articulated by Adam Smith, against mercantilism; not that Scotland could anyway have followed its injunction to cultivate a trading surplus at other countries' expense.

Yet, reciprocally opened to the market, she faced economic, political, indeed moral demands potentially conflicting with her social order. The Patriot, Andrew Fletcher of Saltoun, warned that it would crumble unless historic institutions held it together, whatever the Union's benefits. Thus he turned against the Treaty, though in fact it secured much of what he wanted. To this the Enlightenment offered the answer that a free market, with exchanges among people remote in time and space, could still sustain the cohesion of society if their ethics instilled in them a mutual sympathy. The prosperity offered by economic freedom did not on this interpretation threaten social order, and could thus prove congenial to the Scots ruling class.[39]

Here we might see, however, how central to the whole process was the law, where ethical and economic demands might be reconciled. Given the right legal framework, Scotland would be sure of the tranquillity needed for the flourishing of arts and sciences that kept growth going. At the University of Glasgow, Francis Hutcheson, professor of moral philosophy 1729–46, and his pupil Adam Smith, neither a lawyer by profession, yet studied and taught law as part of their social inquiry. It was a sign of how in contemporary Scotland legal concerns, otherwise in European tradition so notoriously narrow, could become fundamental to the development of the country as a whole.

One channel through which lawyers applied their thoughts to general questions was in the intellectual clubs of enlightened Edinburgh. It would certainly be unsafe to assume that nothing enlightened could take place outside such circles, yet their importance for the production and exchange of ideas was undeniable. The most renowned of the clubs was the Select Society, founded in 1745. Under the potent direction of a failed lawyer, David Hume, of a successful one, Henry Home, later Lord Kames, and of the wigmaker-poet Allan Ramsay, it sought 'the most effectual method of promoting the good of society'. By 1759 it had 133 members, of whom at least forty-eight were lawyers, the rest mostly professors and clergymen. They constituted almost the entire personnel of the Enlightenment in Edinburgh. The link of land, law and letters here found its apotheosis.[40]

This was the world where Henry Dundas first saw light on April 28, 1742. His father, Arniston, was away at Rossdhu on Loch Lomond, drinking goat's whey for his gout. Through his mother he had a heredity not just independent-minded but positively swashbuckling. She was a daughter of Sir William Gordon of Invergordon, who died six weeks later, a fine early example of a Scotsman on the make. Of ancient lineage, he was himself a moneylender's son and followed a shady financial career. Into the Mississippi scheme of his crony Law he was said to have put in £500 and to have realised £9000 before it crashed. In England, he arranged to acquire stock of the South Sea Company without payment but with an option to sell back once a profit was made. He did not lack, even so, a certain public spirit. He was active against the Jacobites in 1715 and, a member of the Squadrone, sat in five Parliaments for Sutherland. He rose regularly from his death-bed to vote for the Ministry, looking like 'Lazarus at his resuscitation'.[41]

Ann Dundas, now 36, bore seven children, including five sons, of whom Henry was the fourth. Hale indeed, she reached the age of 92; George III regretted the passing of a 'most respectable woman'. She was by all accounts a splendid character, strong-willed and bursting with vitality. She had no qualms about holding forth on matters then thought quite beyond the ken of a gentlewoman. When the Revd James Beattie, the Aberdonian professor and drinking companion of Henry, published his first attack on Hume, she wrote:

> I do not believe there is a single person of candour who will not allow the truth of Mr Beattie's reasoning, nor a single person whose judgment is equal to the task of inquiry and weighing arguments who in their heart will not allow the strength of his arguments, nay more, that he has fully confuted Mr Hume's sceptical system.

This robustness she not only kept till her end but passed on to her son. He, having lost his father when just 12, was deeply attached to her. During a busy career, he never failed to stay in touch. And for the rest of his life he was more attracted by dames and crones, by termagants and even amazons than by the demurer ladies whom conventional taste extolled. In later years, when his time for Edinburgh was limited, he always took an afternoon off and 'might be seen going about and climbing up to the most aerial habitacula of ancient maidens and widows.'[42] If he had a father-figure, it was his half-brother, the second Lord President Arniston, thirty years his elder.

His birthplace lay off the High Street of Edinburgh, in a house called Bishop's Land just to the east of what is now the North Bridge. It was so named because it had been the residence of John Spottiswoode, the primate on James VI's restored bench of bishops; behind it stood Old St Paul's, the main chapel of the Episcopalians, still suspected of Jacobitism. The house burned down in 1814, to be replaced by an ugly tenement. But Robert Chambers's description of it survives: 'The ground floor of the mansion … was formed of a deeply arched piazza, the arches of which sprang from massive stone piers. From the first floor there projected a fine brass balcony.' Like other houses in Edinburgh at the time, it had a mixed population. One neighbour was Lady Jane Douglas, sister of the childless Duke of Douglas. Remarkably, she produced twin sons at the age of 50, heirs to the vast lands of that ancient line. Or did she? Arniston would have to judge the cause. Another denizen, Sir Stuart Threipland of Fingask, must surely have been the last of the Jacobites. He was out in 1745, but did not die till 1805. At the top dwelt a tailor. 'All the various tenants, including the tailor, were on friendly terms with each other – a pleasant thing to tell of this bit of the old world, which has left nothing of the same kind behind it in these days, when we all live at a greater distance, physical and moral, from each other.'[43]

Little is known of Henry's youth. But his mother, a widow with so many children, could not have found life easy. Because of a strict entail on Arniston, it was impossible to pay the portions destined for them by the Lord President's will. The Government agreed, in recognition of his services, to set up a trust of £5000 in their favour in 1756. It was still not enough, and pensions of £200 a year each were granted them in 1759. For his education, Henry was first sent to the grammar school at Dalkeith, to be taught by James Barclay, who had a high reputation for imparting the classics. Indeed a student friend, George Buchan-Hepburn, recalled that 'we of course spoke to each other in Latin when conversing on the law'. As late as 1795, Henry composed a letter in that language to Chan Ta Zhin, governor of Canton and Kwansi, intended for translation by the catholic fathers at Macao. He asked protection for British merchants and signed himself gracefully off: 'Nihil mihi gratius accidere poterit, quam ut de valetudine tua secunda et salute integerrima audiam.'

In other respects, his education seems to have been wanting. Henry was on sundry occasions in later life reproached for his spelling, his grammar, his geography, his French and his handwriting – for the last by the King, no less, who called it 'the worst and most ungentlemanlike he had ever met with'. He was anyway noted for his 'vigour and rough jocularity rather than learning', though at the age of eight he caught smallpox, then a common disease of childhood. It left him unmarked and unharmed otherwise. He grew up tall and robust, with genial, open features, the most prominent a big Dundas nose.[44]

He went on to the High School of Edinburgh which, in the Scots' democratic system, was quite normally attended both by the sons of local gentlemen and the boys from the burgh. No record of him remains there. Following still the habitual

Advocate
1763

path, he proceeded to the city's university, and was admitted an advocate in 1763, just before coming of age. His *Disputatio Juridica* concerned the legal status of acts by guardians. He also found time to bloom socially. In Buchan-Hepburn's recollection, 'we generally indulged ourselves once a month with half a crown's worth of punch' – modest indeed by their later standards. On another occasion, Henry was reported to be especially fond of oysters and porter followed by brandy.[45]

An intimate of these early years, as of many later ones, was his cousin Archibald Cockburn of Cockpen, likewise a scion of Midlothian's gentry, and father of Henry Cockburn. Soon the bonds were made still faster. The two blades espied the most eligible co-heiresses, Elizabeth and Janet, of David Rannie, who had died in 1764 after acquiring the rank certainly of captain and possibly of knight in the course of a life spent as an East Indian merchant and afterwards as a shipbuilder. If his career was obscure, little needed to be known of him except that he had left his daughters large fortunes. They were promptly caught by our intrepid cradle-snatchers. Henry married his Elizabeth in 1765 and Archibald his Janet in 1768, each girl being a mere 15 years old at the time. Henry got besides Rannie's residence at Melville Castle, just outside Dalkeith, with an estate of 600 acres valued at over £1500 a year. It had once been the home of David Rizzio, the murdered Italian secretary of Mary Queen of Scots.[46]

In attaining this respectable station, Henry learned more than good living. Jupiter Carlyle wrote:

> Although his brother and guardian, the Lord President, had been much alienated from the most distinguished literati, [he] no sooner approached to man's estate than he overcame all his family prejudices, and even conquered his brother's aversion, and, courting their society, soon became the favourite and friend of all the men who were eminent for learning or fine talents.

He was certainly open to intellectual stimulation. Among the books at Melville which may have been personally bought by him, about one quarter were Scottish, from the works of James VI to those of the Enlightenment. The rest was about equally divided between English publications, most literary but many of a serious political or historical nature, and others in foreign, including the classical, languages. Offered the range of intellectual clubs, he went for the Speculative and the Belles Lettres – the latter, patronised also by the older literati, being regarded as a junior Select Society. He first spoke there on religious liberty, afterwards on whether law or divinity was the preferable career and whether in the theatre love should be mixed with tragedy: all very raffish for a Dundas. The Revd Thomas Somerville recalled that he

> excelled in readiness and fluency of elocution, but he reasoned feebly, and often digressed from the question. In discussions of a political nature, he always professed an enthusiastic attachment to Whig principles. The eminence which Mr Dundas afterwards attained as a statesman and able debater surpassed the expectations I had formed from his appearance in the Belles Lettres Society.

His family were freemasons, and he probably joined them about now.[47]

Naturally Henry looked to the Bar for his career. When called, he possessed a mere £60; one story reduces this to a golden sovereign, which he used to buy a gown. He found humble chambers off a turnpike stair at the head of Fleshmarket Close, a little way up the High Street from his birthplace. He took a year or so to start prospering. His first recorded case reached a verdict in July 1764. He supplemented his income as an assessor to the town council and enhanced his reputation by pleading as a lay elder in the General Assembly of the Church of Scotland. His name certainly helped. It was a treasured belief in the profession that judges were more likely to lend a favourable ear if their sons or other kin appeared before them. Boswell was always amused at how his work increased when his father was on the Bench, though their relations could hardly have been worse. Solicitors took care to ply such people with briefs. Yet Dundas certainly had talents of his own. Carlyle said that he entered 'so warmly into the interest of his client as totally to forget himself, and to adopt all the feelings, sentiments and interests of his employer.'[48]

Indeed, within quite a short time he was taking in his stride some of the biggest cases. One was his defence of Katherine Nairn, in a trial for a fine Scots murder spiced with adulterous incest.[49] Katherine was of family, daughter of Sir Thomas Nairn of Dunsinnan, but wilful enough to marry beneath her station. Her choice was Thomas Ogilvy of Eastmiln, a dreary fellow, the sort who wore a nightcap in the daytime, too old at 40, valetudinarian and with good reason. The union was greeted with scarcely less horror among her relations than among his.

For Ogilvy had two brothers, Patrick, invalided home from India, and Alexander, a rake. Living with the latter's widower father-in-law, 'a common porter', was also a cousin, Anne Clark. These were eager that the head of their clan should do what he was always saying he would do, that is, die. They were more eager still that he should do so without issue. Patrick not being expected to last long, Alexander would in due course succeed to the estate, where his *ménage à trois* could live happily ever after. Depressed by the wedding, they perked up when Katherine tired of her tedious spouse and took Patrick as her lover. Anne Clark revealed this to the husband, who not surprisingly ordered his brother out of the house. His wife then killed Ogilvy with poison procured from her paramour, though not before the unlucky man had brought their conduct to the notice of the local justices. Katherine and Patrick were therefore jailed at Forfar. Yet appearances may have been deceptive. Certainly Anne and Alexander urged matters on, and the latter had with indecent haste sold the whole stock of the family's farm, applying the proceeds to settlement of his gambling debts. So there was enough doubt about the character and motives of this pair for Dundas to work on.

The trial had other notable aspects. It was the first occasion in Scotland on which a judge, here Kames, charged the jury with the points to be weighed in the verdict, a procedure which became standard. And it was during an attempt to take the case to the Lords that Mansfield definitively declined on their behalf an appellate jurisdiction in Scottish criminal causes. For Patrick Ogilvy had been found guilty and sentenced to death. While efforts were made at Westminster to save him, he passed his time in the Tolbooth playing the violin. He may have derived some satisfaction from the furious wrath aroused on the Scottish Bench by his appeal. When the editor of a newspaper in Edinburgh made so bold as to seek the opinion on it of an English barrister, he was hauled up and rebuked for submitting the College of Justice to a 'high indignity'. Patrick was led out to his death in November 1765.

Dundas had likewise failed to exculpate Katherine. Found pregnant after conviction, she secured a deferral of the sentence. Having given birth, she was ordered to appear early in March 1766 to hear her doom. Protesting herself still not well enough, she got another stay. Now the Scottish enthusiasm for celebrating the turn of the year came to her rescue. One of the several excuses for it fell on March 15, a festival dating from the times before New Year was shifted forward to January 1, thus known as Old New Year. While the jailers of the Tolbooth were keeping this feast, Katherine slipped out dressed as a midwife. It was rumoured that she hid with her uncle, the advocate William Nairn, a friend of Dundas. She escaped abroad, by various accounts to Holland or America, and had a large family. A quite different tale sent her to a nunnery in France, whence she fled to England during the Revolution. In any event her love-child died, her remaining brother-in-law Alexander fell out of a window in Edinburgh and the house of Eastmiln came to a sorry end.

Despite these excitements Dundas could not be fully satisfied with a career in the courts. It involved an immense amount of paperwork. While the judgments were oral, the pleadings were usually written – quite the reverse of modern practice. According to Boswell,

> one half of the business before the Court of Session is carried on by writing. In the first instance a cause is pleaded before the Lord Ordinary, that is to say by one of the 15 judges who sits in his turn for a week in the Outer House. But no sooner does he give judgment that we give him in replies and answers and replies and duplies and triplies, and he will sometimes order memorials to give him a full view of the cause. For it is only in causes of great consequence that the Court order a hearing in presence. This method of procedure is admirable, for it gives the judges a complete state of every question, and by binding up the session papers a man may lay up a treasure of law reasoning and a collection of extraordinary facts.

Dundas took no such sanguine view. He later complained that his profession had tired and bored him.[50]

For experience in public speaking, an advocate had to turn elsewhere, for instance to the intellectual clubs. Moreover, as Carlyle recalled, 'it was about this time that the General Assembly became a theatre for young lawyers to display their eloquence and exercise their talents'. Here too, social change was beginning to make rivalries sharper and more political. Being by law established, the Church's place in society was apparently safe. It found visible expression at the General Assembly every May. Two-thirds of the commissioners were clergymen, but the others were lay elders, usually of high social standing. Somerville explained that 'many Lords of Session, advocates and county gentlemen of rank and opulence sat as ruling elders on the benches of the General Assembly, and, both by their presence and the part they took in business, contributed to the dignity of the court.'[51]

This was presbyterianism in practice. Yet the definitive victory it thought to have won in 1690 had been undermined by the 1712 Patronage Act. The second

Duke of Argyll, in particular, was notorious for his cavalier exploitation of this law. To him clerics were the merest pawns of patronage, to be preferred or not according as how they would truckle to secular authority. Since the Crown presented to a quarter of the livings in Scotland, he was able to build up in the General Assembly a corpus of votes subservient to his will. It could mean at the same time ignoring the wishes of the faithful in the parishes concerned. To many, this was outrageous. Certainly it offended a fundamental presbyterian principle, that pastors, if not elected, should at least submit themselves to the approval – in the parlance, to the call – of their flocks. The fact that that did not happen gave perennial proof of the Church's subordination to the state, and negated the equality for it claimed by Scottish doctrines.

Against the abominable Patronage Act the Kirk entered an annual protest, but with the passage of time had had no choice except acquiescence. The people, however, were less submissive. Unwanted ministers could sometimes only get into their churches with the aid of troops. Since the civil power would always back up its clerical creatures in this way, those scandalised could only secede altogether. In 1733 Ebenezer Erskine, minister of Stirling, was deposed by the General Assembly (contrary to the Dundases' advice) for preaching against lay patronage. He and three others responded by setting up independent congregations, in what became the Original Secession Church.

The Squadrone, with its closer links to the popular party, made a difference when it came back into office in 1742. The next year it gained the upper hand in the General Assembly, which elected as Moderator the Revd Robert Wallace. Arniston recommended him to Tweeddale as 'a right ministerial honest man, knowing far above most of them, prudent and judicious and who would be most acceptable to the clergy'. The aim was to start building an anti-Argathelian interest in the Kirk. But this also had implications for patronage. A laird like Arniston was not against it on principle: he himself had rights of presentation at Temple and Borthwick. He did object, however, to the 'very bad use that hath been made of the Crown's patronage, presentations given sometimes as rewards of corruption to a bailie or councillor's brothers, etc., sometimes to anybody named by a voter as a great man without the least regard either to heritors of a parish or people'. He even wished that 'care would be taken to dispose of royal presentations so as might best suit the inclinations of the parishes'. His son, as Lord Advocate, continued trying to forestall clashes over patronage. When the Crown wanted to assert a doubtful right of presentation to a charge at Leith, he wrote that 'the most effectual method of getting this accomplished will be by presenting the person most agreeable to the inhabitants who will probably concur and acquiesce in the royal presentation as they are the only persons who can create any disturbance'.[52]

Meanwhile the Argathelian system in the Church, as in the state, was being restored by its clerical agent, the Revd Patrick Cuming, Moderator in 1749 and 1752. His influence survived for a decade and even beyond his retiral in 1761. Quite undismayed by the third Duke of Argyll's passing in the same year, Milton, his man of business, actually tried to extend secular control. Following the municipal election of 1762 in Edinburgh, which strengthened his position and brought back the evergreen George Drummond as Lord Provost, they made so bold as to revive the practice of presentation to the city's charges, in abeyance since the Revolution.[53]

A reaction also set in. A new generation of ministers, led by the Revd William Robertson and the Revd John Home, had been prepared to act with the Argathelians on lay patronage. They did so to decisive effect in disputes with local presbyteries which were resisting objectionable presentees at Torphichen in 1751 and Inverkeithing in 1752. Yet they were never happy with Cuming. Indeed, their aims were different from his. They wanted to restore a Kirk equal, not subordinate, to the state.

Unlike the Church of England, the Church of Scotland could offer no fat bishoprics or other privileged emoluments. That had created a situation which Carlyle, in oleaginous mood, may be permitted to describe:

> Till this period the clergy of Scotland, from the Revolution onwards, had in general been little thought of, and seldom admitted into liberal society, one cause of which was, that in these days a clergyman was thought profane who affected the manners of gentlemen, or was much seen in their company.

Doubtless he had in mind the objections to his own presentation to Inveresk by the Duke of Buccleuch, namely that he was 'too young and full of levity, and too much addicted to the company of superiors', he 'danced frequently in a manner prohibited by the laws of the Church', he wore his hat 'agee' and 'had been seen galloping through the links one day between one and two o'clock'.[54]

Not everyone went to the same lengths to get into the right circles. But Carlyle and his cronies thought patronage the means by which the standing of ministers, hitherto considered ill-bred and fanatical, might be more generally raised. With such patronage at its disposal, the gentry would be inclined to select for the parishes ministers of its own kidney. The clergy, by the same token, would have to cultivate its mind and manners. Learning and morality would blossom. The tone of society as a whole would improve. The gap between the enlightened upper class and the bigoted multitude could be closed, and the social order more firmly secured.

On exactly the same grounds, this rising generation wished to modify the high Calvinist view that held the fallen world in holy horror. They wanted a Church in and of it, embracing all strands of national life, hallowing the secular from inside, not just preaching at it from outside, perhaps in vain. Only in that way, at any rate, was it likely to have a real effect in the magic circles ruling Scotland, to make them treat it on equal terms rather than as an object of patronage. To the Evangelicals this merely represented the danger of the Kirk being secularised in the new age. Yet one ought to remember that these younger ministers never abandoned, nor tried to abandon, the Calvinist standards. Standing between the two extremes they encountered, it was not unfitting that they should call themselves Moderates.[55]

They, too, were strongly represented in the personnel of the Scottish Enlightenment. As it proceeded, they rose to dominate the Church. That could not have happened, however, without astute management. It was found under Robertson. From 1744 to 1758 he held the obscure charge of Gladsmuir in East Lothian, only a hamlet even today, and then among the bleaker and emptier spots of an otherwise fertile county. But ministers with academic pretensions often settled in a backwater. For Robertson, employing the time and leisure to work on his best-selling history of Scotland, published in 1759, it paid off handsomely. He was at length translated to the fashionable parish of Old Greyfriars in Edinburgh, in its turn a springboard to his becoming a royal chaplain in 1761, principal of the university in 1762 and Moderator in 1763. At his outset he was promoted by Milton. But after the fading of the Argathelians he could dispense with a patron. Relying on little more than his own natural authority, he was to lead the Kirk for two decades in a fashion clever and devious but conciliatory, strong-willed and far-sighted. Moreover, as a truly learned man, he made his university the finest in Europe. With all these qualities, he established the Moderate regime.

Though his aim was harmony rather than conflict, he also knew it needed firmness in the face of threats from below. He repeatedly showed himself ready to act on that knowledge: the Church of Scotland had to demonstrate itself at least as efficient and disciplined, and as respectful of the law, as the agents of the state with which it was proposing to treat on equal terms. Robertson insisted that the General Assembly should be able to enforce its judgments on the inferior courts of the Kirk and, in any crisis, found means to ensure that they were obeyed.

Against him, however, the High-flyers also rallied. Sound though the Moderates' policy might appear to right-thinking people, it gnawed at the presbyterian conscience. Robertson and his followers were never quite convincing enough in depicting their opponents as merely old-fashioned and illiberal. It was to be said, a century later, by Principal Robert Rainy, leader of the Free Church of Scotland, that 'a hard disregard of the feelings of conscientious men, and a pleasure in breaking them to the yoke, if possible, characterised the party throughout.'[56] Moreover, the Moderates were not certain of a majority in the presbyteries – the further away from the capital, the weaker they tended to be. To maintain their ascendancy, they had to rely on the General Assembly's lay members.

A considerable political effort was therefore required to outmanoeuvre the popular party yet to keep it in the Kirk. By the 1760s, the Original Secession Church had grown to about 100 congregations. In that decade also, the Relief Church was formed. Still, secession remained for the Evangelicals a deeply distasteful prospect. The principle of a national Kirk was dear to almost all Scots, including seceders, who usually saw themselves as only temporarily out of it. They made few changes in doctrine or liturgy and never ceased to declare themselves ready to return to the bosom of mother Church once she had righted her relations with the state.

On such ground, the High-flyers could mobilise support from both clergy and people. But their stumbling-block was the General Assembly where, accordingly, their efforts had to be concentrated. In the early 1760s this otherwise sedate gathering was repeatedly rent by bitter disputes over patronage. In Carlyle's words,

> for a few years at this period there was a great struggle in the General Assembly against the measures supported and carried through by Robertson and his friends, and we had to combat the last exertions of the party who had supported popular calls; and it must be confessed that their efforts were vigorous. They contrived to bring in overtures from year to year, in which

they proposed to consult the country, in the belief that the result would be such a general opinion over the kingdom as would oblige the General Assembly to renew their application for the abolition of patronage.[57]

What he referred to above all was the 'schism overture' of 1766. An overture was the preliminary stage of the Kirk's legislative process. This one would have set up an inquiry into why so many were leaving it. The inevitable answer, in the Evangelicals' view, would be because of patronage. The move had therefore to be nipped in the bud. Dundas, known socially to the Moderates, was called in to argue their case. If not an ostentatiously religious young man, he was at least a regular churchgoer. More to the point, he proved, according to Carlyle 'the most strenuous advocate for the law of the land respecting presentations, and the ablest and steadiest friend to Dr Robertson and his party that ever appeared in my time'. Over the next two decades, he sat eighteen times in the General Assembly and played a valuable part in consolidating the Moderate regime. For the moment, he succeeded in suppressing the schism overture against the High-flyers' advocate, Henry Erskine. It was 'the last blow that was aimed at patronage, for whatever attempts were made afterwards were feeble and ineffective'.[58] The question was not to be raised again in any form that could seriously worry the authorities till the prelude to the Disruption seventy years later.

Dundas had just become, at 24, Solicitor General. In February 1766 he went to London to be put through his paces in appeals to the Lords. The impression he made was favourable and, for his future, decisive. Sir Alexander Gilmour, member for Midlothian, wrote to the Lord President congratulating him 'on the appearance Henry made at the bar. His pleading was sensible, in good language, moderate and concise, and indeed in a word it gave universal satisfaction to all your lordship's friends within and without the bar.' For others, however, his advancement was a surprise, and not always welcome. Boswell, who had been with him at university, fairly goggled. He wrote to a third friend, William Temple: 'Do you remember what you and I used to think of Dundas? He has been making £700 a year as an advocate, has married a very genteel girl with £10,000 fortune and is now appointed His Majesty's Solicitor General for Scotland.' Temple agreed that 'we used to think little' of Dundas. They were wrong. He had cut a figure, made himself useful to a powerful party, combined the ability of his clan with a degree of independence from it, all at once. A more general opinion was that of George Dempster, independent member of Parliament for the Perth Burghs: 'Henry Dundas is a great acquisition … He appears to have an exceeding good capacity and a very good heart.' A young man could hardly hope for a better start.[59]

Notes

1. Cockburn (1874a), 265.
2. Peel Papers, BL Add MSS 40511, ff. 165–70; 40515, f. 113; Lee & Stephen (1908), vi, 191.
3. Haldane Papers, NLS MS 6043, ff. 47 et seqq; Brash (1968), xxxi.
4. McWilliam (1978), 220–1; Hughes & Scott (1980), 49.
5. Haldane Papers, NLS MS 6043, f. 32; McWilliam, 79–82; Tait (1969), 132; Cosh (1984), 214 et seqq; Macaulay (1987), 70.
6. *Book of the Old Edinburgh Club*, xix, appendix, 17.

7. *Old Statistical Account*, x, 497 et seqq.
8. Saunders (1950), 14; Smout (1964), 218; Kettler (1965), 20 et seqq; Hobsbawm (1980), 7.
9. Omond (1888), 14.
10. Lee & Stephen, vi, 193; HMC Mar and Kellie MSS (1906), 214; Graham of Fintry MSS (1909), 273.
11. Dundas (1710); NLS Adv MSS 19.3.28; Clerk of Penicuik Papers SRO GD 18/5274/55; HMC Drummond Moray MSS (1885), 145.
12. Murray Papers, NLS Adv MSS 29.1.1, iii, f. 82; Arnot (1777), 2; Lee & Stephen, vi, 40; Craik (1901), 96.
13. Hardwicke Papers BL Add MSS 35447, f. 129; Carlyle (1860), 249–50; Ramsay (1888), 67.
14. Craik, loc. cit.; Johnson (1970), 387.
15. Ramsay, 75.
16. NLS Adv MSS 19.1.35, ff. 31–2; Bricke (1972), 109; Hayton & Szechi (1987), 253 et seqq; Szechi (1989), 179, 270.
17. Clerk of Penicuik Papers, SRO GD 18/3194/4 & 10.
18. Mar and Kellie Papers, SRO GD 124/15/1223/3; Ramsay, 70; Omond, 81.
19. Ramsay. loc. cit.; Bricke, 38.
20. Yester papers, NLS MS 7046, f. 47; 7049, f. 83; 7058, f. 146; 7060, f. 125.
21. NLS MS 3036, ff. 42, 155; Omond, 20.
22. Bricke, 157 et seqq.
23. Hardwicke Papers, BL Add MSS ff. 112, 310; Carlyle, 230; Ramsay, 69; Fleming, 256; Terry (1902), i, 366; Yorke (1931), 622; Phillipson (1967), 13; Jewell (1975), 38.
24. Ferguson (1761), passim; Tytler (1789), 5; Chambers (1875), 511; Brooke & Namier (1964), ii, 362.
25. Newcastle papers, BL Add MSS 32856, f. 173; 32857, f. 67; Paul Papers, NLS MS 5156, f. 137; Elliot (1897), 338; Bricke, 87, 131.
26. Greig (1932), i, 165, 210; Mossner (1980), 253; Murdoch (1991), 163.
27. Carlyle, 239.
28. ibid., 312; Brooke & Namier, loc. cit.
29. Arniston (1777); Brunton & Haig (1836), 536; De la Torre (1953), 200; Forman (1953), 26; Timperley (1977), 227 et seqq; Phillipson, 14.
30. Cobban (1969), 154–9.
31. Cooper (1957), 44.
32. Smith (1961), 68.
33. ibid., 61.
34. Miller (1975), 4.
35. Lockhart (1819), ii, 67.
36. Scott (1808), 350.
37. Rotwein (1955), 95.
38. Dwyer & Murdoch (1981), 226.
39. Phillipson (1976), 97 et seqq; (1981), 22, 28.
40. *Scots Magazine*, xvii, 1755; Clive & Bailyn (1954), 206.
41. Sedgwick, ii, 69.
42. WLP I, Dec. 22, 1798; NLS MS 547, 23; Ord and Macdonald Papers, MS 14841, f. 8; Lockhart, ii, 35.
43. Grant (1883), i, 205.
44. NLS MS 547, 26; MS 1069, f. 116; SRO GD 235/8/3/3; Newcastle Papers, BL Add MSS 33055, f. 135; 32890, f. 405; Hutton (1885), 88.
45. Melville (1763); NLS MS 547, loc. cit.; Saltoun Papers, NLS MS 16700, f. 27.

46. SRO GD 51/11/1/1; Cockburn & Cockburn (1913), 211–12; Pottle & Reid (1977), 266; Timperley, 233.
47. SRO GD 51/10/56; Somerville (1861), 41; Cockburn, H. A. (1910), 173; Carlyle, 242; Grant, iii, 283; Craik, 103.
48. Carlyle, 245.
49. Roughead (1913), 106 et seqq.
50. De la Torre, 186.
51. Carlyle, 248; Somerville, 97.
52. Yester Papers, NLS MS 7046, f. 62; MS 7055, ff. 47, 64; Newcastle Papers, BL Add MSS 32737, f. 352.
53. Cater (1970), 70 et seqq; Dalzel (1793), xxii–xxv.
54. Carlyle, 216.
55. Sefton (1977), 203 et seqq; Sher (1985), passim.
56. Rainy (1883), 103.
57. Carlyle, 446–9; Mathieson (1916), 103.
58. Carlyle, 474–5.
59. Matheson (1933), 24; Fergusson (1934), 221.

2

'Goth against Goth'

The Government into which Henry Dundas had been called was headed by the Marquis of Rockingham, one of the brief administrations that filled the gap between the fall in 1763 of George III's first favourite, the Earl of Bute, and the rise a decade later of his supposed strongman, Lord North. The Marquis's, formed in 1765, was the most Whiggish of the sequence. He even managed to bring back into the Cabinet the Duke of Newcastle, grandest of the grandees so discomfited by the refusal of their new monarch to truckle to them. Amid the King's efforts to restore the royal prerogatives, Rockingham's greatest service lay in keeping Whiggism alive, and linking its past with its future. He himself was so attached to Revolution principles that he had, as a boy, run away from school to join the Duke of Cumberland's army in pursuit of Prince Charles. After he stepped down, his faction remained coherent: thus the chance was preserved of an alternation of parties.

Not that it made much difference in Scotland, where politics had a rhythm of its own. Her Ministers came and went with little regard for what was happening at Westminster. Usually they felt no obligation to resign with their principals. This time, however, there was a reshuffle. The incumbent Solicitor General, the immensely rich but modest Sir James Montgomery of Stanhope, member of Parliament for Peeblesshire, had won his place in 1760 on the recommendation of Lord President Arniston. He was now able to repay the debt, moving upstairs to be Lord Advocate and thus making room for young Dundas. This pair then serenely held their offices through the several changes of Government in London right till 1775.

Yet the Scottish political system was undergoing a crisis too: as it turned out, a long one. The third Duke of Argyll, who had managed it for so many years, died in 1761. An effort to take over was made by the Earl of Marchmont, noted for 'brilliancy of genius', once a friend of Viscount Bolingbroke, the Earl of Chesterfield, Alexander Pope and the Duchess of Marlborough – in fact one of the old Tories who, welcoming the monarchist revival, now moved into support even of a Hanoverian Crown. Not, however, a self-seeking or partisan man, he could be outflanked by the Earl of Mansfield. The Lord Chief Justice, while eschewing a special role in Scotland for himself, had the means, through his membership of the Cabinet and his standing in the upper House, to queer the pitch for anyone else.

A shadow of the former regime lingered on for a while under the Dundases' *bête noire*, Lord Milton. He continued to perform most day-to-day business in Edinburgh when the dominant influence passed to the Earl of Bute, who was also the dead Argyll's nephew. The two houses had been closely related, by marriage and politics, for many years. They quarrelled in 1758. But a new King in London and a new Duke at Inveraray called for a patching up. Bute himself had not lived in Scotland since 1745 and, whatever his countrymen's hopes, did not intend to deal personally with her affairs: he was far too busy being a bad Prime Minister. If Milton's skills and knowledge were indispensable, for advice – as opposed to proficiency – the Earl relied on two younger men, William Mure of Caldwell, made a Baron of Exchequer, and John Home, the tragedian, who between them knew all the rising stars in the Church and universities. At Westminster, business was first entrusted to another of Bute's acolytes, Gilbert Elliot, member for Selkirkshire. He wrote to Milton: 'I protest I do my part in it from a mere sense of duty, for this detail is to me no amusement, and hardly comes within the pale of what is called ambition.' Soon, therefore, the Earl summoned his brother, James Stuart Mackenzie, back from a budding diplomatic career, made him member for Ross and set him to work on all that Scots drudgery. Amid these shifts, however, much patronage was let slip to English Ministers over whom the new manager exercised no influence.[1]

He had in any event hardly time to get to work before Bute was hounded from office. The new Prime Minister, George Grenville, extracted from the King a promise that his predecessor 'should never directly or indirectly ... have anything to do with his business, nor give advice on anything whatsoever'. Retribution was not long in being visited on the caustic, cocky but careless Stuart Mackenzie. In 1764 he was dismissed as Lord Privy Seal for Scotland, banished from Court and cut off from all patronage.

This left the Scots with a great problem: who was now to manage them? The fourth Duke of Argyll, besides being too close to Bute, was too aged and uninterested, while another kinsman, the Earl of Breadalbane, was too old-fashioned a Whig. Grenville wanted to turn the tasks over to the Duke's sons, but the King refused. On the formation of Rockingham's Ministry, Newcastle asked the Lord President to act in Scotland for it. Arniston declined because he thought that incompatible with his judicial duties; a significant decision since it established thenceforth the political impartiality of the Scots Bench, if not of the Bar. In any case, Rockingham did not want a special Scottish Minister. The Duke of Grafton, who followed him as First Lord of the Treasury in 1768–9, apparently relied again on Stuart Mackenzie to carry out some of his former functions. James Boswell called Sir Alexander Gilmour the real power in Scotland: hardly a serious idea when he owed his seat to the Dundases. George III consulted the Duke of Queensberry from time to time, but he was far too eccentric for regular political business. Lord Stormont, Mansfield's nephew and heir, absented himself as ambassador in Vienna. The Dukes of Buccleuch, Gordon and Hamilton were minors, the Dukes of Atholl and Montrose, as well as the Marquis of Tweeddale, in their dotage.[2]

There had never since 1707 been quite such a vacuum in the management of Scotland, though it had been erratic at the best of times and often purely informal.

This was the result of having dismantled one system of government without taking care about an adequate substitute. Ministries always intended, of course, to control the country, but not let its concerns occupy more than a peripheral place in British politics. They hardly ever came up in Cabinet, for example. Further down the administrative chain in London, nobody knew anything of them. Yet they had to be shepherded through the bureaucracy by someone, else sink without trace.

When a Secretary of State was in office, he had of course supervised matters. It was done primarily through distribution of patronage: appointments to the public service (with its many sinecures), to the armed forces, to the Church and universities, sometimes to jobs in England or abroad, more seldom through beneficial expenditure and rarely through sheer bribery. One might say that almost every object of ambition among Scots came through this mechanism; equally, the recalcitrant could be excluded. The Argathelians in particular always ran it on narrowly partisan lines. But it meant that a Secretary of State for Scotland had, compared to his colleagues of similar rank, a minor post with trivial duties. London certainly wanted to prevent a mystique building up round any particular Scottish institution and endowing it with a power of its own. Mere persons on the other hand, could always be disposed of. So for long intervals the office was vacant, and in the end nonchalantly abolished. If the Argylls were meanwhile treated as viceroys at home, the second Duke was able to exercise all necessary authority over Scotland as Lord Steward of the Household, Master General of Ordnance and Governor of Portsmouth. Nor did the third Duke ever take office as Secretary of State, but arranged everything through his agent Milton.[3]

With the dismissal of Stuart Mackenzie, however, these oddities came home to roost. The chain of command was now thoroughly obscure. The Scots did not know to whom they should turn in London and had nobody there to speak for them who was not himself prey to the conflict of faction. All they could do if they wanted something was to approach a great man and hope for the best. London for its part neither knew nor cared who were likely to prove its more able or faithful servants in Scotland.

The plain fact was that for a decade or so nobody took charge of Scottish affairs, hardly even of the most routine patronage. At the heart of the system there had opened a void: 'the government here seems running into anarchy and confusion,' wrote Atholl. In June 1764, the Lord President suddenly found he had no quorum for his court, because several judges were ill and the commissions to fill two vacancies on the Bench had not arrived from London. They were hurriedly sent for, and with them came a note from the Secretary of State, the Earl of Sandwich, saying that 'to prevent any accidents of a like nature for the future, some proper person should be appointed in London to take out and regularly transmit all instruments relating to Scotland.' The fact that such an elementary matter was not normally attended to spoke for itself. Legislation naturally languished as well, and the General Election of 1768 was chaotic, probably the most corrupt of the century. But all this left the English absolutely cold. John Wilkes said while the House of Commons was considering a Scottish electoral petition: 'I'll have nothing to do with it! I care not which prevails! It is only Goth against Goth!'[4]

Yet perhaps the interregnum was a necessary transition from one power structure to another. That which crumbled had rested on the feudal nobility. That which rose in its place was grounded among the lesser landed families who, in the law and administration, had actually been running the country since 1707.[5] Dundas emerged as their most promising scion – though not yet. It was meanwhile possible to imagine that for the future Scottish public affairs would consist in little else than the law. Parties were moribund, and political debates showed scant shape or unity. The national institutions, above all the judiciary, might supervise the country sufficiently without any local surrogate for central power. There would be no Scottish Minister because none would be required.

Some basic tasks had nevertheless to be performed. The Government found it needed a decisive say in Edinburgh, notably with those national institutions. The apparatus of state being so rudimentary, means had also to be found of dealing with local pressures and claims, if not for the Ministry itself then to persuade particular interests in the counties and burghs to act in a congenial manner. Thus in practice the influence extended down a long way. Governments usually tried, for example, to make safe the capital's town council. They would want it to elect an acceptable member of Parliament. They would want to exploit its weight in the Convention of Royal Burghs, especially for the expeditious collection of tax (much of which came through the Convention and was paid by Edinburgh). They would want to ensure the right appointments to those posts of which the council disposed in Kirk and university, as well as protect vested interests there from popular or evangelical attack. They would want to enforce compliance with their purposes in the banks and public boards.

So it turned out that a manager was after all indispensable. Only amid the decay of the Argathelian hegemony, however, did such power as remained in Scotland pass in a rather casual way to the law officers. The standard history of the Lord Advocates exaggerates the extent to which this happened shortly after the Union, with its consequent severe paring of the old apparatus of state. The system did not depend on offices but on personalities, above all on their relationship with the house of Argyll. Thus all sorts of *ad hoc* arrangements could be countenanced. For example, effective authority was during quite long periods exercised by the Lord Justice Clerk, head of the criminal judiciary, even though he was excluded from Parliament. Almost everyone in the residual system of Scottish government had to be a jack-of-all-trades, a fact no less true of the law officers than of the others.[6]

The original main duty of the Lord Advocate, obligatorily a member of the Faculty, was as chief prosecutor for the Crown, which appointed and removed him at pleasure.[7] At first, his only responsibility beyond that was to make recommendations for the Bench. But other business devolved on him. He was the obvious person to issue proclamations and deal with the practical maintenance of public order, which lately had meant sniffing out treason, censoring the mails, taking an interest in military dispositions. He conducted the official correspondence between Edinburgh and the Secretary of State (when there was one) in London. The very fact that Scotland was turning *faute de mieux* to the law officers also caused a certain amount of patronage to flow through them. The Lord Advocate in particular thus came to run what political business needed to be run from home.

His stature grew not only there but in the South. He was usually a member of Parliament. Improved communications allowed him to move between the two capitals with greater ease, linking more effectively the administrations in them. At Westminster, he had started by giving advice to the Ministry on Scots law, which led to his having at least a little influence on general policy. He would act in the Commons as spokesman for the manager (during the first fifty years of the Union invariably a member of the Lords), and would whip his followers. He would frame Scottish legislation, receive Scottish petitions, act from the other end also as a channel between Ministers and Scottish interests. Yet there was nothing systematic about this: different Lord Advocates could concentrate on what appealed to them and neglect the rest. It was really only in the last third of the century that they emerged as the most important representatives of the state, and largely by accident. Other posts having fallen into the wrong hands, the essential work came willy-nilly to rest with the law officers. The Solicitor General, by the way, could take on any of the duties of a Lord Advocate who might be absent or too busy. But in practice he did not often escape the routine of the courts.

The courts could, however, occasionally offer something sensational. Of late years, Scottish noblemen had grown used to dying in their beds, but one who did not was the tenth Earl of Eglinton, a charming rake yet also a public-spirited representative peer. He was less pleasant to social inferiors, and would personally thrash trespassers on his land. On a fine morn in 1769 while riding over the sands at Saltcoats, which he owned, he came across a local customs officer, Mungo Campbell, carrying a gun. He had once before caught this man red-handed at poaching. Now he dismounted and advanced menacingly, demanding the weapon. Campbell backed away, but tripped over a rock. His gun went off, and Eglinton fell dying. Dundas prosecuted for murder. Though it was a tricky case, motives being so hard to read, Campbell was at length found guilty and sentenced to hang. He escaped this fate by killing himself in his cell. 'The body was then privately buried under the Salisbury Crags. But the Edinburgh rabble discovered the grave, took out the body, and tossed it about till they were tired. To prevent farther indecency and outrage, Campbell's friends caused the body to be sunk in the sea.' This was Dundas's major criminal trial during his term as Solicitor General.[8]

He also became embroiled in the greatest civil lawsuit of the century, the Douglas Cause. [9] For Scots, on the whole indifferent to the politics of Westminster, the courts were infinitely more exciting as a theatre of human, even national, destiny. And this case, in Boswell's words, 'shook the sacred security of birthright to its foundations'.[10] As we have seen, Scotland was an insecure nation, obsessed with status and safeguards for it. The Douglas Cause struck right through the inarticulacy of her political life to the heart of that obsession.

It had indeed all started as an affair of the heart, with Lady Jane Douglas, whom we met as neighbour of the Dundases in the High Street of Edinburgh. Few women have been so endowed with beauty and fortune for a life of sorrows. She was born in 1698, sister of Archibald, first and only Duke of Douglas, whose patrimony was as ancient as it was vast. Wild and vindictive, he never married. It thus fell to her to continue the line. This ought not to have proved difficult. Her youth's bloom was exquisite, her simple charm touched all. At the age of 22, she was betrothed to Francis, Earl of Dalkeith, heir of Buccleuch. It would have been a brilliant match, but the engagement was broken. One reason lay in Douglas's insane jealousy – he murdered a subsequent suitor, who also happened to be his natural cousin. Prudently, Lady Jane stayed in seclusion with her mother at Merchiston Castle, her loveliness paling if not fading. Nothing disturbed this long, drear spinsterhood but the mother's death, whereupon Lady Jane set up her own establishment at Drumsheugh, just to the west of Edinburgh.

Into her life there then swept a second time (for his suit had once before been politely rebuffed) Colonel Sir John Stewart, a tall, suave wastrel, a Jacobite who had been out in 1715. He fled to Sweden, whence he returned after years of soldiering, penniless as ever. He hung around Edinburgh in the autumn of 1745, seeing what he could pick up. Lonely Lady Jane fell for him. He took her to Holyrood to meet the Prince. With the Whigs back once the Highland army had marched on, he got her at some risk to hide Jacobite stragglers about Drumsheugh. In August 1746 they married in secret, and immediately left for Holland. It was no time for men like him to tarry, while she still had her brother to fear.

They were heard of only through the occasional letter home. In the spring of 1748, Lady Jane wrote one to the Duke confessing that she was wed. And that July, in Paris, she bore twin sons, Archibald and Sholto. In November they all went to London, where Stewart was promptly imprisoned for debt. With that affair settled, Lady Jane came back to Scotland, anxious to have her sons acknowledged heirs of Douglas, so that their careworn existence of destitute wandering could at last be brought to an end. But her brother had hardened his heart. He refused to see her, even though she lingered for three days with the boys before the gates of Douglas Castle. She was prostrated by grief when Sholto died in April 1753. She followed a few months later after a painful final illness, affirming to the end that Archibald was the true heir whether the Duke cared to recognise him or not.

He, on the other hand, went out of his way to show that their estrangement stretched beyond the grave. Quickly drawing up his will, he named as heir a cousin, the Duke of Hamilton. Seven years passed, till Douglas himself lay dying. Now, for reasons we cannot fathom, he suddenly relented, bequeathing all to his sister's son. The 13-year-old Archibald Stewart (henceforth calling himself Douglas) was served heir to his uncle's estates. The Hamiltons were not unnaturally aggrieved. In fact they would move heaven and earth to get the disposition overturned. Their man of business, Andrew Stuart, was an elegant, brilliant lawyer in Edinburgh, not yet 40, but solemn and cautious enough. Strangely, he had also worked for Douglas before the Duke's abrupt change of mind. In the course of these duties he convinced himself that Lady Jane, from whatever tragic reasons, was guilty of an imposture. In a preliminary probe, he tried to prevent Archibald's succession on a technicality of the land laws. It failed. At the end of 1762, he raised a new action calling on the Court of Session to declare that the young man was not the heir of Douglas, nor indeed Lady Jane's son at all.

The evidence, though circumstantial, proved difficult to ignore. It was odd that Lady Jane should have been a 50-year-old *prima gravida* in the first place, if not, of course, out of the question. Stranger still was that there seemed to be no witness of the births, except for an evasive servant. Four letters supposed to have been written by the French surgeon in attendance were patently botched up later by someone whose native language was English, probably by Colonel Stewart. He himself protested that the confinement had come to an end so fast that he had not had time even to finish dining and arrive at the bedside before his wife was delivered. He made a disastrous impression when cross-examined on his written interrogatories, randomly throwing out contradictory statements, smiling fool-ishly, shrugging fecklessly when pressed on them, all under Arniston's baleful eye. It came as no surprise, therefore, when the court decided in July 1763 that there was a case to answer: though Stewart, who died the next year, did not in the event have to answer it himself. The battle could begin in earnest.

Andrew Stuart extended his inquiries through agents in France, including Adam Smith who happened to be there as tutor to Buccleuch on a Grand Tour. A second action was raised in the parlement de Paris, accusing the Stewarts of 'supposition of children', a practice common enough to have been declared a crime, indeed a capital one, under French law. In fact it was a formal device to flush out more evidence, requiring anybody in the archdiocese of Paris to pass it to a curé. The coincidence was uncovered that, at the relevant date, the newborn son of a poor glazier had been sold to a distinguished foreign couple. Stuart's zeal got him into trouble at home, though. The terms of the edict he secured from the parlement, presupposing commission of a crime, offended a Court of Session jealous of its prerogatives. He was ordered to wind up his action in Paris. This proved time-consuming and cost the Hamiltons much sympathy meanwhile. Given the convoluted procedures of Scots law, it was June 1766 before they were ready to present their case in Edinburgh.

There the matter had become political. As the Revd Thomas Somerville wrote, 'it was a constant subject of conversation in companies of every description. Families of all ranks ranged themselves on different sides of the contest.' Public opinion split along lines not unfamiliar to us. Nearly all the literati were for Hamilton, whose case was held to conform more closely to enlightened principles. In David Hume's words, it had the 'force of Reason' on its side, while the argument for Douglas represented 'the most violent torrent of prejudice that ever was heard in a private cause.' There were also less exalted motives for this bias, for the guardians of the 11-year-old Duke of Hamilton included his mother, the dowager Duchess, who was shortly to marry the fourth Duke of Argyll, and Mure of Caldwell, the confidant of Bute and his Maecenas. It was altogether quite an Argathelian ramp.[11]

Douglas's interest, on the other hand, might be regarded as a popular party in court. That it should espouse the cause of Scotland's largest landowner-in-waiting was perhaps curious. But the people were genuinely moved by Lady Jane's sufferings, angered by the Hamiltons' rapacity and appalled at a callous determina-tion to rob young Archie of his inheritance. Not least, they could take revenge on the great noble house which for years had so haughtily manipulated their govern-ment and church. It would be going a little far to dub this sentiment, as one historian has, proto-radical. But he was surely right to point out that submerged social and political tensions can often find an outlet in highly personalised form.[12]

Dundas was one of the counsel engaged for Douglas, in a formidable team headed by the Lord Advocate himself. It included also James Burnet, who would within a year be elevated to the Bench as Lord Monboddo, and Robert Macqueen, whose dark brows, lowering looks, thick accent and growling voice already marked him out: when he became Lord Braxfield, they would terrify everybody. The other side was not quite so star-studded, and something of a political mixture. It included both Alexander Lockhart, Dean of the Faculty of Advocates, of the Jacobite family, and Sir Adam Fergusson, called by Dr Johnson 'a vile Whig' and by Boswell 'a prodigious dull fellow'. The pleadings began in July 1766 and lasted twenty-one days, the longest ever known in the Court of Session. Dundas spoke for several hours on July 9 and 10. At the end of it all, the judges, whose heads must have been reeling from the weight and complexity of the evidence, ordered it to be summarised for them in memorials. This was normal in very difficult cases. But it meant the proceedings, already four years old, would be dragged out still further. The court eventually had before it 173 documents printed in four volumes of nearly 4000 pages.

It was thus July 1767 before the Douglas Cause came to judgment. Half of Edinburgh seemed to throng Parliament House. All eyes were on Archie Douglas, 19 years old, who certainly looked like a common Frenchman, with a swarthy complexion and low brow, though he was much refined by his education at Rugby and Westminster. But many eyes doubtless wandered to the dowager Duchess of Hamilton, a strikingly handsome woman, representing her son, who stayed away for fear of the crush. The procedure was this: the judges would give their verdicts in order of seniority. If there was a majority among the fourteen Lords ordinary, that would determine the cause. If not, the Lord President had a casting vote.

A betting man (and wagers of £100, 000 were placed on the outcome) would surely have put his money on Arniston's declaring for Douglas. All his previous political and personal connections spoke for it; and, of course, he had his brother pleading on that side. But he was never a man to gratify expectations. He led off in his blunt way:

> The simple fact before us resolves into this question – is the defendant the son of Lady Jane Douglas or not? And I am sorry to say it, that my opinion in this great cause, after the utmost pains and attentions I could bestow, is clearly against the defendant; and that by the evidence brought, that he is not the son of Lady Jane Douglas ... Let us only consider the conduct of Lady Jane and Sir John, and see whether this will quadrate with the notion of a real birth, or a design of imposture. It is clear to me that their conduct is, upon the supposition of a real birth, improbable to the last degree.[13]

He spoke on a Tuesday, the delivery of other verdicts taking the whole of the rest of the week. By Friday, the votes stood at six for Douglas and six for Hamilton. When the court resumed on the following Tuesday, another was added to each side. Arniston thus had the casting vote, and few could doubt what he would do with it. He said tersely: 'As this is a cause of civil property, I think myself bound to give judgment according to my own opinion.'

In the Court of Session, therefore, Hamilton had won. But on so fine a balance an appeal was inevitable to the House of Lords – which did indeed reverse the verdict. With the necessary delays, the cause was not heard there till January 1769, nearly seven years after it had started. In London, passions ran as high as in Edinburgh. Stuart fought a duel with Edward Thurlow, one of Douglas's counsel, and a future Lord Chancellor of England. At this trial, the decisive voice was Mansfield's. A betting man would surely have wagered on his supporting the Hamiltons – again, all his previous connections spoke for it. But again a betting man would have been wrong. The Lord Chief Justice's peroration was magnificent:

> I never saw in any cause so much anger, so much disingenuity, so cruel a stand, so much dexterity and so much art to break truth, to wrest and distort evidence, to colour facts, to throw dust in the eyes, to foul the head, to mislead the heart and judgment. I never saw such a scene of rank and gross perjury.

But

> Lady Jane's reputation is unsullied and great. How is it possible to credit the witnesses, some of them of a sacred character, when they spoke of Lady Jane's virtues, provided we can believe her to have been a woman of such abandoned principles as to make a mock of religion, a jest of the sacrament, a scoff of the most sacred oaths, and rush with a lie in her mouth, and perjury in her right hand, into the presence of the judge of all, who at once sees the whole nature of man, and from whose all-discerning eye no secrecy can screen, before whom neither craft nor artifice can prevail, nor yet ingenuity and wit of lawyers can lessen or exculpate – on all of which accounts I am for finding the appellant to be the son of Lady Jane Douglas!'[14]

That was on February 27. At twilight on March 2, a lone, weary horseman rode up the High Street of Edinburgh to the Cross. It was Ilay Campbell, one of the delegation of advocates who had gone to Westminster. He was a small, usually impassive man with a dry, somewhat ineffective manner and a low, dull voice. But this time he raised it, with the cry 'Douglas for ever!' The town went wild. Three days of revels followed. The whole populace was exhorted to put on a celebratory illumination. The younger bloods needed not much heating before they conceived the jolly notion of stoning windows without candles in them. The first to be shattered were Arniston's in Adam Square, at what is today the corner of South Bridge and Chambers Street. The mob, it was quipped, were now giving their casting votes. When done with the judges who had voted for Hamilton, they turned to those who had voted against. Thus Lord Auchinleck, disdaining to illuminate, lost his windows too. At the front of the yelling, gesticulating crowd capered his son, Boswell.

Nor did a night's rest serve to cool tempers. The next day, Lord Hailes recalled,

> I was peaceably hearing a cause, when the alarm came, 'They are attempting to pull the President out of his chair'. In a moment everybody but a few lawyers and clerks left the Outer House; I had no idea at the time of any chair but the chair in court. I went to Lord Pitfour who was near me and said, 'They are pulling the President out of his chair. We must go and share fates with him!'. He followed me into the Inner House. There there was nothing but bare walls. This confirmed me in the opinion that Civil Justice was

annihilated. I called for a macer that I too might go out in form; I found immediately that the court had not been assembled, and that the confusion had been about the President's chair in the street.

Boswell, meanwhile, was hauled before the sheriff and questioned on his part in the last evening's events. He replied in his sauciest manner:

> After I had communicated the glorious news to my father, who received it very coolly, I went to the Cross to see what was going on. There I overheard a group of fellows forming their plan of operation. One of them asked what sort of man the sheriff was, and whether he was not to be dreaded. No, no, answered another, he is only a puppy of the President's making.

At this, the interview came to an abrupt end.[15]

It may be pleasant to relate that later, all passion spent, both Stuart and Douglas were among the phalanx of faithful Scots whom Dundas marshalled in the Commons. Stuart aged into a gentle genealogist, cherished at Westminster. His studies led him to conclude that he was the rightful senior representative of Scotland's ancient royal line. It was thus generous of him to urge Dundas in 1799 to grant a pension to Henry, Cardinal of York, younger brother of Prince Charles, rendered destitute by the French conquest of the Papal States. Douglas remained a rich dullard. Though he sired twelve children, he left no heir male. A daughter carried the inheritance to the Earls of Home, who also assumed the name. We may finally note that this was another occasion in which Dundas surmounted Scotland's spiteful hereditary enmities. Having elsewhere cast in his lot with the moderate, enlightened, aristocratic party, he here defended a popular cause. It was a useful stage of his education in the art of reconciling the country's divisions.

A society obsessed with birthright, with the land and with the status and privileges attaching to it, often went to court. It also grew interested in reforms. Since the Union, the most important had come on Westminster's initiative, paying little heed to local opinion. In the last third of the century, however, as social and economic change quickened, a different attitude could be perceived from those holding responsibility in the state, an effort to respond to pressures from within Scotland. For major measures Montgomery, the Lord Advocate, revived the practice, followed for the Heritable Jurisdictions Act, of wide consultation with judges, legal societies and freeholders in the counties before legislating – a process to which Dundas, when himself Lord Advocate, later resorted regularly.

In land law, reform seemed urgent. The original fabric of feudalism had been embellished in 1685 by a superstructure designed to preserve the social edifice as it then stood. The Entail Act of that year, promoted by Sir George Mackenzie of Rosehaugh, 'Bluidy Mackenzie', has since been judged an archaism even in its own time. But in the context of the violent seventeenth century it may have been understandable. Faced by the Crown's exercise of arbitrary power or by the lawless rapacity of their neighbours, landed families wanted some sure protection. By executing a deed under the Act and registering it in Edinburgh, a proprietor could keep specified lands in the ownership of his kin inalienably, and determine in perpetuity the lines of inheritance to them. Archaic or not, the measure had evidently answered a need. By 1765, the register listed 500 deeds for the estates of

300 proprietors, mainly large ones, representing about one-fifth of the country's total valuation and perhaps one-third of its area.[16]

It had now become clear, however, that the law exacted a price. The agricultural revolution was well under way, but improvement was always expensive and often slow to yield its benefits. Heirs of entail found themselves left behind, and they were at a special disadvantage because they could never, if matters went awry, sell. They thus could charge no part of the costs to successors who would reap the gains. They could not grant leases beyond the term of their own lives, which no sensible tenant would accept. They could not offer their land for security if they wanted to borrow for improvement or raise a mortgage, nor make any other provision to disencumber themselves of debt. This encouraged absentee landlordism from unprofitable estates, where neglect could continue. Heirs saddled with some such, through no fault of their own, had an incentive to take out as much as possible and put as little back. Thus the whole agricultural economy suffered. At its worst, entail was also inimical to humanity and justice. Should an estate be destined to pass from its owner's immediate family (for example, if he had only daughters and the deed specified succession to heirs male) then he could do nothing for his loved ones, nor in any way bind the distant kinsman who might inherit.

In any event, entail had not made the landed oligarchy impregnable to parvenus. On the contrary, upstarts with wealth from commerce could exploit the law for themselves. Sir Lawrence Dundas, that bugbear to conservatives, entailed his own acquisitions and set a seal on his displacement of the old lairds. Nor was he alone. Venerable families could only keep out these people by maintaining their prosperity. But entail was a serious obstacle to the requisite improvement, removing from the economic process a large share of one factor of production which Scotland possessed in some abundance.

Not surprisingly, then, the Entail Act found severe critics. Smith wrote in *The Wealth of Nations* that 'in the present state of Europe, where small as well as great estates derive their security from the laws of their country, nothing could be more completely absurd.' Lord Kames was the great enemy of entail and conducted a long campaign against it. He remarked in 1759: 'Entails are a perpetual source of discontent by subverting the liberty and independence to which all men aspire with respect to their possessions as well as their persons' and 'if the legislature interpose not, the period is not distant when all the land in Scotland will be locked up in entails'. These arguments struck home. In 1764, the Faculty of Advocates voted for repeal of the Act, the first time it had ever acted as other than a professional body. This was a good example of how, in a rapidly changing Scotland bereft of a legislature, a reforming impulse arose in other institutions. The advocates called for perpetuities to be abolished in respect of new heirs, and for entails to be limited to the lifetimes of their present holders. A Bill drawn up on these lines for deliberation at Westminster got nowhere, however.[17]

But in 1770, Montgomery, himself a keen improver, responded to the pressure. The preamble of his Act made pointed reference to the existing law of Scotland, 'whereby the cultivation of land in that part of the kingdom is greatly obstructed'. The Lord Advocate was more cautious, though, than the Faculty. Entails were not abolished; in fact their number increased for another half-century. Montgomery did make a difference in liberalising leases, enabling long ones, a precondition for the emergence of an improving tenantry, to be granted by proprietors of entailed lands. He also allowed three-quarters of any money laid out in development to be charged to their heirs. Again, where an estate's finances were straitened, property could be sold off to the extent necessary for settling its debts.[18] These details need not obscure the deeper significance. Scotland was precocious in freeing herself from the mercantilist notions of the past; the Union itself had been an example of it. Here the very people with most at stake in the existing social structure were to the fore in opening agriculture further to the forces of the market, so that these could have the same beneficial effect as in commerce.

Another example came in the reform of serfdom, that notorious relic of the old Scotland. Workers in the unpleasant occupations of coal-mining and salt-panning were hereditarily bound to them; newspapers sometimes carried notices of rewards for catching runaway serfs. One biography makes Dundas author of the Act of 1775 which emancipated them, but this must be wrong.[19] Though it first came into force when he was Lord Advocate, it had been framed and passed by Montgomery. Still, one may reasonably assume that his Solicitor General, by then prospective parliamentary candidate for a mining constituency, had a hand in it.

The Act's preamble said it 'would remove the reproach of allowing such a state of servitude to exist in a free country'. But this came only after a recitation of the expected economic benefits. Serfdom had been instituted primarily by coalmasters who thought it the only way to make sure they had a workforce at all for an industry where few survived long. But, as so often, regulation defeated its own purposes. Serfs were unlikely to suffer competition for their jobs. In fact the masters had to grant generous terms and conditions to keep the men they had, or else exemptions to attract new ones. Adam Smith, native of a coalfield himself, supported his contention that free was cheaper than servile labour with the striking difference in wages between miners in Scotland and northern England, the former being three times higher. John Cockburn of Ormiston noted in vexation how his colliers had plenty of time for 'sauntering through the toun, chatting in the smiddy, tippling in the alehouses and kissing the girls'. Perhaps that was all to the good, because the only way to increase the supply of labour was through their fertility.[20]

The 1775 Act provided that nobody should in future be reduced to servitude. Existing serfs were to be gradually emancipated, according to their age and years of working. This was felt vital to stability in a growing industry, though it had the effect, because of the miners' ignorance and inertia, of prolonging individual cases of serfdom for decades. The last of these wretches did not die till 1844.[21] It took a second Act in 1799, also passed with Dundas's encouragement, to give them the same conditions of employment as others.

That of 1775 was even so another stage in dismantling economic interference by the state, though some did continue. For example, the Board of Manufactures, formed out of fears for the consequences of the Union, tried to foster new industries such as spinning and weaving: Arniston had been a member since 1761. The Commissioners for the Forfeited Estates carried on improvement in the

Highlands, as well as equipping them with churches, manses and schools, if to little effect on the region's prosperity. Intervention of that kind, though, was soon dwarfed by the initiatives of the private sector. Landowners lucky enough to have coal on their land, like the Duke of Hamilton and the Earl of Wemyss, could from now on, with the greater mobility of labour, become mining entrepreneurs. Local industry was still too puny to absorb their output, so that their need to export broke down the trading monopolies of the royal burghs, supposedly guaranteed by the Treaty of Union. The lairds simply built their own ports, at Alloa, Ardrossan, Bo'ness, Grangemouth, Granton, Port Seton, Prestonpans, Saltcoats, Troon. Accumulating capital, they could then expand into other fields.

There was thus the curious spectacle of the Scottish economy taking off under the impetus of the gentry. Smith remarked that 'a merchant is accustomed to employ his money chiefly in profitable projects, whereas a mere country gentleman is accustomed to employ it chiefly in expense.' Here he was less than usually acute. True, many private schemes came to grief. But others did work: the New Town of Edinburgh was started; the Clyde was made navigable up as far as Glasgow; a canal was planned between there and the Forth.[22]

The latent tension between capitalism and landowning was resolved because at this stage in Scotland most capitalists were themselves landowners. Only these had the resources for long-term investment. Ideologues of improvement, they were never a deadweight to progress as in other countries. With the benevolent despotism of their social leadership unquestioned, they could get all classes working together for growth. Scotland was thus satisfied that there need be no contradiction between the established and the emergent social order, still controlled from the top. Initially, greater external trade, better internal communications and a higher standard of living for the ruling class were the tangible results. Industrialisation proper was just beginning, and not till towards the close of the Dundas despotism did it really get under way. Only then were the earlier assumptions being in any degree questioned. In the meantime a long period of expansion engendered a universal mood of confidence.

It also created a great demand for borrowing. Till the end of the Seven Years' War in 1763 this had been satisfied. War, as always, brought both growth and inflation. Afterwards, though, the flood of paper money had to be dammed, a matter of special concern in Scotland, where specie was little known. In case the Scots tarried, Parliament passed in 1766 its first measure for controlling their banks, so far unfettered by legislation. It forbade notes worth less than £1, as well as the 'optional clause', under which issuers could relieve themselves of an immediate obligation to redeem their notes. The chartered institutions, the Bank of Scotland, the Royal Bank of Scotland and the British Linen Bank, were anyway contracting their credit. The score or more of private and country banks which had blossomed in the absence of regulation could only follow. Soon the borrowing classes began to squeal.

Queensberry now intervened. Otherwise no politician, he yet knew a simple expedient when he saw one. If the borrowing classes lacked a bank to cater for their needs, why then, they should set up one which would. Into his scheme he drew young Buccleuch, just back from a childhood spent in England and his Grand

Tour with Smith. Perhaps it was during their sojourn in France that the Duke's interest in the fancier sort of economics awoke. For the project in which he now joined was in essence the bank based on real estate once proposed to that country, and previously indeed to Scotland, by John Law. This time, too, its business was to be secured not on gold or other assets which, inconveniently, it happened not to have, but on its stockholders' lands. The flaw in such inspired reasoning lay in the idea that a banknote and a Scottish mountain partook of a similar degree of liquidity, so that they could be used for settling liabilities in much the same way. But the flaw was as yet unnoticed. Among those flocking to enrol with the ducal duo were Dundas and his cousin Cockburn. Both had fortunes from their wives. Here was a chance to do something with them.

The firm of Douglas, Heron & Co., commonly known as the Ayr Bank, was formed in November 1769, with the backing of numerous Lowland gentry. It traded vigorously, mounting take-overs, opening branches, liberally extending credit, prodigiously printing banknotes. Before long, two-thirds of Scotland's circulation originated in Ayr. As Douglas, Heron & Co. expanded its business, so the chartered banks prudently took the chance of further contracting theirs. It would anyway not have been worth their while to concert an attack on a house so strongly supported by the great and good. Instead they left it to pick up all the bad business the country could offer – and waited.

The crash came in less than three years.[23] On June 8, 1772, Alexander Fordyce, a banker in London, absconded with debts of £243,000, fruit of his speculations on the Stock Exchange. It was a calamity for fellow Scots in the City, most not only creditors of his but clients of Douglas, Heron & Co. 'I think 25 capital Scotch houses have stopped here,' one wrote. The English were the ones who thought they had been robbed. A cartoon of the time showed a limp Britannia complaining that 'this Scotch paper diet has brought me to a consumption.' Above her a figure in tam o'shanter flew away on a broomstick loaded with bags of coin, scattering worthless bills behind him and cackling, 'The deil away wi' ye all, ye English pudding bags, ken ye nae that paper is lighter of digestion than gold.' Others of his countrymen pushed off in a rowing boat with the same cargo, to the chorus, 'We'll over the water to Charlie.'[24]

On June 12, a lone horseman again rode up the High Street of Edinburgh. The news he brought from London sent the city into panic. People with bundles of notes in hand clamoured at the banks' doors, pitiably begging gold and silver. They merely put up their shutters, and thirteen never took them down. Douglas, Heron & Co. tried to brazen things out, and proposed a rescue to the chartered institutions. Dundas, appointed an extraordinary director, anxiously peddled the idea. He wrote to a prospective trustee:

> I should have thought the heritable bonds proposed to be given, joined to the corroborative obligation of many respectable persons, the very best security I ever saw, both for punctual payment of interest and the certain recovery of the principal when demanded. It is truly a matter of national concern that the affairs of the company should be rounded up in such a manner as to enable them to give ease to their debtors in collecting their funds, for otherways the country must be brought under the deepest distress.

Only much later could he bring himself to admit that there had been 'an artificial circulation prevalent in the country founded on no solid basis'. Still the big banks would have none of it. They could not be blamed. The offender's liabilities amounted to more than £1 million, against nominal capital of £150,000. Liquidation took place in August 1773. The Bank of England sued Queensberry and Buccleuch for £300,000.[25]

Then, however, the authorities sensibly moved in to clear up the mess. The chartered institutions extended credit to the soundest private bankers, though only three survived. In 1774 Montgomery carried the Bank of Ayr Act. It created financial instruments by which the two dukes could at once meet their debts, and back them up properly later. In fact claims on the pair remained open for sixty years. Smaller fry could expect no such help. Less than half the 226 proprietors of Douglas, Heron & Co. remained solvent. Estates worth £750, 000 changed hands. Dundas and Cockburn just escaped the worst. Henry, his mother reckoned, lost no more than he staked; in any event, he could borrow on the security of Melville Castle. But Archibald was hard up for years, had eventually to sell Cockpen and rely for subsistence on a sinecure granted by his cousin. Dundas never learned care with money. Having squandered his wife's dowry, he would always have to work for a living. Yet in the long run the result was salutary. The lessons learned produced that remarkable Scottish achievement, an efficient monetary and banking system free of interference or control by a central bank, with an automatic stabilising mechanism in the note exchange at Edinburgh – Walter Scott's 'argus-eyed tribunal'. And for Smith it provided a useful passage in *The Wealth of Nations*.[26]

It was by the way lucky that Scotland had just been given a more rational law of bankruptcy. Till now, the first to lay an arrestment on a debtor's effects secured them all to the extent of his claims. This led to the abuse that the impending bankrupt could show preference to a particular creditor by informing him privately of his state of affairs. The Court of Session attempted a remedy in 1754, giving equal force to every claim lodged within thirty days of the initial arrestment. But that provision was only for seven years, and the court did not renew it. After the customary consultations, Montgomery and Dundas in 1772 drew up a Bill similarly securing the rights of all creditors. Enacted, it at once proved its worth in the banking crisis.[27]

The value of land was perhaps more easily realisable in a political than in an economic sense. In the right circumstances land, regardless of its productivity, brought with it a vote, and thus a certain political weight. Scottish mythology paints the electors of the time as venal dupes. But that is scarcely consistent with another picture we shall see unfold in these pages, of men enjoying high social status and acutely conscious of their constitutional position, together with the duties it imposed. Such virtue was not immune to corruption from inside or outside the constituencies. Nor, however, were the seductions of vice irresistible or irreversible. Still, we shall start with an example of how wrong the system could go.

The Dundases had ample experience of that, for Henry's maternal uncle, Sir John Gordon of Invergordon, had come off worse in a fierce struggle over the representation of Cromartyshire. It was an insignificant county, made up of detached stretches of land inside the larger Ross, with which it was to be united a century later. Its voters were numbered in single figures. What was more, under an odd arrangement in the Treaty of Union for the smallest counties, it sent a member only to every other Parliament, alternating for that purpose with Nairnshire. Yet in vain quest of such a meagre prize, Gordon blew the amazing sum of £20, 000 at the General Election of 1768. His foe was Sir William Johnston, a laird from Dumfriesshire who took the name of Pulteney on landing as a bride the heiress of the Earl of Bath, with her immense fortune. He spent a little of it swanning round Edinburgh's literary circles, and a great deal more on this contest. It reflected some of the social divisions we have observed, between new money and old (sometimes only slightly older) money, between large landowners and small, between cosmopolitan elitists and couthy provincials.

On these matters the Dundases usually knew where they stood. Arniston passed judgment against Pulteney when Gordon took him to the Court of Session in 1770, only to see the verdict overturned by Mansfield in the Lords. Yet Henry, employed as counsel, all along advised his uncle to settle out of court, to abandon the claim to the seat against compensation. He was certainly averse from using the case as a means to more general reform. While his opinion was tied to the circumstances, it showed how early his later, cautious views were being shaped:

> I differ from you in thinking this a proper time for any reformation in the political law of this country. It is clear that our political system requires many alterations, but I doubt much if sound and impartial alterations can be expected at a period where almost every person either from interest or prejudice is warped and blinded in his sentiments upon these matters. I rather think the time for procuring salutary regulations is after all political controversies are over and all disputed elections determined so that nobody has an interest to withstand reason and justice.[28]

The case arose from the manipulation of voting rights as they had been fixed before the Union, and of the decidedly mean representation Scotland had since enjoyed at Westminster. There she was given 45 seats (against 518 for England), 30 for the counties and 15 for the burghs. To quality for the franchise and for election, a man had in general to hold directly of the Crown (the system of tenure being feudal) land valued at 40 shillings of 'old extent', equivalent to £400 Scots or £35 sterling.[29] The suffrage was thus in effect restricted to large proprietors, keeping out the lesser gentry and small farmers who often possessed it in England. The total electorate in the counties never rose much above 2500.

Yet many who got the vote had no genuine interest in a county. Feudal superiority, rather than mere ownership, was the essential qualification. And the superiority could be sold separately from the land. A magnate might without real loss to himself split his into a number of smaller ones sufficient to qualify for the franchise, renting them out to friends and supporters for their lifetimes; or else they might be bought by social climbers or by lawyers who traded and speculated in them. These proceedings brought endless, complex, costly legal suits. But that did not prevent blocs of votes being built which were employed in impenetrably obscure and cunning battles for control of the constituency. The usual result was to strengthen still more the influence of the most powerful, inevitable when too many potential politicians were seeking too few seats. So an electorate's composition might be quite arbitrary. The true landed interest could be submerged by fictitious or 'faggot' votes, cast at the beck and call of one or two noblemen or of outsiders, especially the Government.[30]

In Scotland, there were thus nine pocket counties, something impossible in England: Argyll, Bute and Sutherland under the eponymous noble houses, Dumfriesshire and Peeblesshire under Queensberry, Selkirkshire under Buccleuch, Nairnshire under the Earl of Cawdor, Banffshire under the Earl of Fife, Caithness under the Sinclairs of Ulbster. All except the last two were controlled by men unable themselves to vote or sit in the Commons. Elections in the counties did not invariably require a fortune, but there was no point in fighting them unless the contestant could stand the cost of defending his votes if they were impugned. Wiser heads, such as Arniston, recognised that the system was scandalous, twisting the law and wasting the time of courts with better things to do.

This was what brought on the crisis in Cromartyshire, though it only carried to a baroque height excesses already alarming. The basic statute governing the franchise was an Act of 1681. Meant to keep the circle of voters narrow, it did so without undue distortion or manipulation before the Union and for a few years afterwards. But the splitting of votes soon set in. As early as 1716, a new law was passed requiring of electors an oath that their qualifications were genuine. An aspirant faggot voter was hardly likely to balk at thus perjuring himself. So in 1743 a further Act allowed at least a minimum of judicial inquiry into doubtful claims. It, too, remained a dead letter. On the contrary, the manufacture of votes began to spread. It was soon used not only to protect great interests, but to attack what gentlemen regarded as their natural rights in their own counties. Cromartyshire was just the worst example, with an insane expenditure of time and money to create new or extinguish old franchises.

Firmer control seemed imperative. Arniston was in a position to try exercising it. Even then, his motive could be suspect, as to one observer: 'The secret of the case is this, Lord Abercorn has taken it into his head to split votes, which threatens some day or other the independency of our darling county of Midlothian, where justice reigns, and therefore we must be tender that the infection doesn't spread otherwise our happy constitution may be blasted.' Arniston attempted to breathe life into the Act of 1743 by authorising minute questions to be put to dubious electors. This procedure was declared *ultra vires* by the Lords in 1770. John Ramsay of Ochtertyre commented: 'The Lord President and a majority of the judges were decidedly hostile to these votes, which they regarded as palpable evasions of a plain and well-drawn statute. Had not their repeated decisions been constantly reversed by the House of Lords, the evil would soon have been nipped in the bud.' As for Mansfield, 'it was evidently his purpose in those decisions to extend the right of suffrage to persons who derived their titles from peers or great commoners.' Arniston then gave up resistance as a bad job and set about manufacturing votes himself. He even urged his friend Auchinleck, who had been just as severe on the practice, to do the same, much to Boswell's disgust. The way now stood open for any rational electoral system to be destroyed, as it quickly was in certain counties. But Midlothian, with about 100 voters, remained on the whole free of abuse under the generally acceptable tutelage of the Dundases. They were anxious to keep it so because Robert had, of course, given up the seat on becoming Lord President. The time was coming when Henry, next in line, would be qualified to represent it in Parliament.[31]

His start in public life promised much, and these must have been exhilarating years for him. True, his wife's fortune had led him not into financial security but only into a mess. He never let it worry him. He was, according to one close friend, 'the worst manager of money matters I ever knew. He never knew anything of his own money concerns.' In another respect, his personal life began to turn a little tangled. He always had a roving eye, and about this time it was caught by Nancy Ord, daughter of a senior English civil servant posted to Scotland. In a surviving letter, he wrote: 'In spite of the constant gaiety in which I have been engaged since I had the pleasure of seeing you I have not forgot the inclination I feel to see you at Melville ... I think it a principal part of devotion to indulge social and friendly attachments.' There was nothing terribly shocking about that, but before long Dundas adopted a tone which went well beyond the usual limits of propriety in an age when conduct among close relations, let alone friends, was highly formal:

> John Mcgowan and I, over a bowl of punch of his making, are warmly engaged in a dispute which of all the beauties of nature have the most irresistible force upon the mind of man. He says a flowering shrub, I say a beautiful face with a live imagination and a glib tongue to tell what the imagination conceives – I hope ... you will give me the advantage of silencing Mr Mcgowans's flowering shrub.

Nevertheless, Dundas's marriage seemed at this stage successful enough, if one may judge by the fact that his wife presented him with four children: Elizabeth, born in May 1766; Ann, born in September 1768; Robert, born in March 1771; and a third daughter, Montague, her father's favourite, born in April 1772.[32]

Besides their seat at Melville, the family had a house in Edinburgh at 5, George Square. This was the capital's most salubrious and fashionable quarter before construction of the New Town, which was only started in 1767. The young, rising advocate took a public-spirited role in the neighbourhood's affairs. It lay beyond the burgh's bounds and so had lacked any administration. By an Act of Parliament in 1771, the citizens of this built-up stretch to the south were empowered to elect eight commissioners to supervise cleaning, lighting and security, for which they could levy a rate. Dundas, representative of George Square, was chosen chairman. The first meeting had just one item on the agenda:

> As it has been and still is the practice in several streets and other passages for boys to meet and play at football, to bicker and cast squibs to the great inconveniency and often danger and damage of the lives of the inhabitants, the meeting consider this a nuisance and recommend to the commissioners of the proper districts to take proper steps for preventing the above occurrences for the future.

A bicker was, by the way, worse than it sounds. It was the Scots word for a fight with stones or even weapons. Walter Scott, who himself grew up in George

Square, recorded that battles often took place between its young blades and the scruffs from Crosscauseway and Potterrow, with some warriors ending in the Infirmary.[33]

In his spare time, Dundas was devoted to the country pursuits of riding, hunting and shooting. When in town, he liked a game of bowls. As a convivial coming man, he was invited to all its fashionable tables. He might also be found in the coffee-houses and drinking-shops clustered round its courts, noted for their serious, incisive, witty talk. He was so clubbable that a club formed round him, the Feast of Tabernacles, 'composed of lawyers and literary men, whose bond of union was their friendship for Mr Dundas, and who met at Purves's tavern in Parliament Square'. Other members were his cousin Cockburn; Sir David Dalrymple, Lord Hailes, called by Boswell 'one of the best philologists in Great Britain', historian too, indeed 'father of national history' according to Scott; James Beattie, waspish Aberdonian clergyman, compiler of the notorious list of avoidable Scotticisms, pioneer of Common Sense philosophy; Henry Mackenzie, the 'Man of Feeling', novelist, literary arbiter; Alexander Abercromby, political boss of Clackmannanshire, campaigner for lower duties on spirits; William MacLeod Bannatyne, Gael, male chauvinist, lover of parenthesis; Robert Blair, future Lord President, of whom an advocate said, 'God Almighty spared nae pains, when he made your brains'; William Craig, favourite pupil of Adam Smith; Robert Cullen, 'courteous Cullen', political liberal, mimic and expert on sleepwalking; Cosmo Gordon of Cluny, rector of Marischal College and famous improver; George Hume of Wedderburn, the Clerk of Session who because of deafness at length yielded his job, though not the salary, to Scott; Baron David Hume, nephew of the philosopher, later an eminent, if reactionary, jurist; John Logan, another clerical playwright, whom his intolerant flock sent off to eke out a living as a hack in London; John Maclaurin, author of a spoof on the *Tragedy of Douglas* and systematiser of the law of Moses; William Richardson, professor of humanity at Glasgow, authority on Shakespeare; Alexander Fraser Tytler, afterwards professor of universal history (no less), foe of philosophical farming, translator of the German Sturm und Drang. It was a mixed bunch indeed, but most remained lifelong cronies.

Keeping the company he did, Henry was not slow in acquiring his ancestors' social habits. We catch a glimpse of him through Boswell's eyes on the morning of July 29, 1774:

> I went to the Parliament House a little after nine. I found the Solicitor, who had been with us last night and drank heartily, standing in the outer hall looking very ill. He told me he was not able to stay, so he went home. He had struggled to attend to his business, but it would not do. Peter Murray told me he had seen him this morning come out of a dram shop in the Back Stairs, in all his formalities of large wig and cravat. He had been trying to settle his stomach. In some countries such an officer of the Crown as Solicitor General being seen in such a state would be thought shocking. Such are our manners in Scotland that it is nothing at all.[34]

Yet Dundas was respected at the Bar. He handled the biggest cases with consummate skill. His reputation spread: the burgh of Glasgow was now paying him an annual retainer of £9 7s 6d to look after its legal business. He would help colleagues in a fix. Boswell went into one of his blind panics when an indiscreet letter to a client accused of forgery was seized along with other effects. If read by the Crown, it would have caused a great deal of trouble. Dundas retrieved it from a bank in Glasgow, after making sure that he would not be found out: 'My reason is that it should not be entrusted in too many hands that you are in such a scrape, because when many are in the knowledge, it unavoidably gets air, which is the very thing we are so anxious to escape.' This was doubtless irregular, not least in a law officer, but it harmed nobody. Dundas never had qualms about cutting corners. It was the sort of thing which wins a man loyalty (though that hardly held true in Boswell's case). Approbation came, however, from more potent people. Dundas went to London in March 1772, after which Mansfield wrote to the Lord President: 'Your brother will certainly go as far as his career can carry him.' The next year Kames was uncannily accurate in his prophecy: 'Henry Dundas possesses all the qualities of an able statesman – quickness of apprehension, a comprehensive understanding, fluency of language with public spirit: and will in a short time do honour to his country, by making as brilliant a figure as any of our Scotch representatives have done from the union of the two kingdoms.'[35]

But it said a good deal about the decay of Scotland's relations with London that when Dundas wanted to make contact with Lord North, now head of the Ministry in which he was serving, he felt obliged to write first and explain who he was. Having set out his qualifications, he went on:

> Your lordship can without any difficulty be fully informed as to these particulars by any person from Scotland acquainted with the state of this country and the inclinations of gentlemen with regard to their representation in Parliament ... Before the expiry of the present Parliament, I shall have been nine years in His Majesty's service and shall be glad, if, by being in Parliament, I can be more extensively useful in the service of my country. I flatter myself that none who are acquainted with the principles I hold with regard to government ... will entertain any doubt what will be the line I shall pursue.[36]

North had to be squared because the incumbent in Midlothian was also a supporter of his. An old soldier, Sir Alexander Gilmour had been brought in at a by-election in 1761 and, despite a previous association with Bute, faithfully followed the Dundases' directions to vote against the Earl. He adhered by turns to the Ministries of Rockingham, Grafton and North. He did in short everything that might reasonably be required of him.

One fault was to have fallen into debt, though that could hardly be held up to stricture at Arniston or Melville. The real objection to him was that he stood in the way of the Dundases' political ambitions, now again manifest. Henry smoothed his own path by striking up a friendship with Buccleuch, four years his junior. This promised within Scotland a vast interest and range of connections, among others with Argyll, to which house the Duke's mother belonged. It also opened access to the pinnacles of English society. Buccleuch's father had died young, leaving him the title at the age of five. The dowager Duchess married Charles Townshend, member of several Cabinets till his death in 1767. Only then could the Duke return to his Scottish lands and wed, his wife being Lady Elizabeth Montague (after whom Dundas's daughter was named), heiress of the Duke of Manchester. Her kinship included the families of Grenville, Halifax, Marlborough, Suffolk, Sussex, Temple and Torrington. Buccleuch soon made his mark at home, joining the independents to oppose the government's nominees at elections of the representative peers.[37]

In September 1770 Dundas let it be known that he meant to enter the next Parliament; the sitting one would be dissolved at the latest by 1775. He wished no quarrel, writing that 'my desire not to divide the county … and my regard for him [Gilmour] would incline me to leave the representation of the county with him, rather than that he should be put in a situation (I mean out of Parliament) which I knew, as his affairs were circumstanced, would be highly inconvenient for him.' The best thing, it was agreed, would be if one or the other could make a deal with a second constituency. But Dundas's attitude soon stiffened: 'If two seats should cast up, I still must insist upon his yielding up this county and betake himself to the other, except it could be supposed that an event should happen of any set of electors being determined not to accept of him but willing to accept of me.' He did not look very hard. Poor Gilmour, scarce an attractive catch elsewhere, somewhat fatuously decided to stay and fight in Midlothian. That gave Dundas his first taste of electioneering, which he relished.

The circumstances, related by his sister Christy, show a young man of independence and spirit, even amid the courtesies of gentlemen. Dining at Arniston in October 1771,

> Sir Alexander Gilmour told the President he was going to pay a round of visits in the county. He then called Harry aside and told him the same, who replied, he certainly meant something … Sir Alexander said Yes, he was to solicit for the next election, upon which Harry answered it was early but since that was the case he likewise would begin and accordingly sallied out at five next morning and being on horseback made his round in ten days.

After three of them he announced to Sir Gilbert Elliot that 'my success has exceeded even my expectation … I tell you as a friend and without boasting that I cannot find out the ground on which Sir Alexander proposes to stand.' To Buccleuch he was still more positive: 'I now have the satisfaction to inform your Grace that a majority of freeholders upon the roll have declared explicitly in my favour, even allowing every undeclared person to go with Sir Alexander Gilmour.'[38]

One may note also how soon Dundas spread his wings. In 1773 he advised an acquaintance in Dumfriesshire:

> Unless you have just and solid grounds to expect success by an opposition to the Duke of Queensberry, we ought not to enter into association with other interest which may have the effect of separating or weakening the present established interest of the county, an interest which you and I wish to see come entire into the hands of our friend.[39]

The friend was Buccleuch, whose electoral business Dundas was clearly set on doing even in places with which he had no personal links – including, besides, the Linlithgow Burghs, where he sought to extend the alliance to a second duke,

Hamilton. Conspicuous also was the long-term view: Buccleuch was Queensberry's eventual heir, though the dukedoms were not united till 1810.

Midlothian was, however, enough to be getting on with. The fight proved
good-natured; the two candidates 'behaved like friends and gentlemen to one
another, though they dined in different houses.' In the General Election of 1774,
which took place here on October 20, Dundas won by 57 votes to 21. It was the
only poll he ever had to contest. He lost little time in impressing himself on
Westminster. He delivered his maiden speech on February 20, 1775. In May,
Montgomery took the lucrative post of Chief Baron of Exchequer, the first Scot to
hold it since the Union. Dundas was at once made Lord Advocate in his stead.
Boswell would hardly have been surprised, but was again green with envy. 'Harry
Dundas is going to be made King's Advocate – Lord Advocate at 33!' he howled to
William Temple. 'I cannot help being angry and somewhat fretful at this. He has,
to be sure, strong parts. But he is a coarse, unlettered, unfanciful dog. Why is he so
lucky?'[40]

Notes

1. Emerson (1988), 151; Murdoch (1988), 117–40.
2. Newcastle Papers, BL Add MSS 32970, f. 375; Murdoch, 133; Mure
   (1854), i, 134; Omond (1888), 177–9; Ramsay (1888), i, 346; Brady
   (1965), 9.
3. Sunter (1986), 2–22; Chitnis (1986), 475 et seqq.
4. Redington (1878), June 28, July 3, 1764; Murdoch, 134–6.
5. Phillipson (1973), 199.
6. Omond, passim; Jewell (1975), 263.
7. Bricke (1972), 47–87.
8. Fraser (1859), 127; Braxfield (1777); Maclaurin (1777).
9. Steuart (1909), de la Torre (1953), utroque passim.
10. Boswell (1924), v, 28.
11. Somerville (1861), 112; Klibansky & Mossner (1954), 175.
12. Ross (1972), 113 et seqq; Lenman (1981), 157, 178.
13. Steuart, 41 et seqq.
14. de la Torre, 202.
15. ibid., 209.
16 Phillipson (1967), 5.
17. Kames (1774), ii, 413, 453; Lehmann (1971), 328; Phillipson (1976),
    113; Campbell (1977), 205.
18. 10 George III, cap. 51; *Edinburgh Review*, xliii, 1826, 44–61; Burgess
    (1976), 97.
19. Matheson (1933), 38.
20. 15 George III, cap. 28; Smout (1964), 230; Campbell & Dow (1968), 141;
    Duckham (1968), 115.
21. Boswell, iii, 202.
22. Smout, 218 et seqq.
23. Smith (1976), iii, 181.
24. Munro (1928), 133 et seqq; Hamilton (1955–6), passim; Checkland
    (1975), 127 et seqq.
25. SRO GD 51/5/167; Chatham Papers, Public Record Office 30/8/157/2/
    208; Brady (1973).
26. Gordon of Invergordon Papers, SRO GD 235/8/4/12; Scott (1826), 33; H.

& Sir R. H. Cockburn (1913), 211–12.
27. SRO RH 4/15/11, 36; Forbes (1860), 43.
28. Gordon of Invergordon Papers, SRO GD 235/8/6/21; Ferguson (1957), 202–88; (1984), 283 et seqq.
29. Thomson (1946), passim.
30. Ferguson (1957), 38–9.
31. Ramsay, 340; Pottle & Wimsatt (1960), 269; Murdoch (1981), 154; Lieberman (1989), 159–60.
32. Ord & Macdonald Papers, NLS MS 14841, ff. 56–7; Thompson (1927), 144.
33. Catford (1975), 73.
34. Pottle & Wimsatt, 240.
35. Somerville, 41; Renwick (1912), vii, 225; Matheson (1933), 28; Pottle (1966), 293.
36. NLS MS 16, f. 20.
37. Ferguson (1960), 84 et seqq; Murdoch, 118 et seqq.
38. SRO GD 51/17/117, 3; 235/8/4/14; Minto Papers, NLS MS 11019.
39. Fergusson of Craigdarroch Papers, SRO GD 77/224/6; Buccleuch Papers, GD 224/30/2/2.
40. Tinker (1924), i, 225; Pottle & Ryskamp (1963), 160; Brooke & Namier (1964), 478.

3

'The age is liberal'

The year 1775 was not an ideal time for a bright young man from Scotland to arrive in London. At the end of the previous decade, the city's Scotophobia had reached its height during the riots provoked by John Wilkes. Though the atmosphere had since cooled, the popular attitude towards Scots was perhaps not so different from that, in the early twentieth century, towards Jews. They remained foreign. They were sneered at yet sneakingly admired for their industry and intelligence. Their physiognomy and accent were mocked. Clannish anyway by nature, they clung defensively all the closer together. They would gather to get drunk in Scottish-owned taverns, trying to pretend they were still at home, talking of what they were missing there, thinking up ways to help each other along.

The English had already noted how the appearance of a Scot in any one place was automatically followed by the appearance of several more. The Whig politician, Henry Fox, though a favourite of the Earl of Bute, could write: 'Every man has at some time or other found a Scotchman in his way, and everybody has therefore damned the Scotch; and this hatred their excessive nationality has continually inflamed.' The Duke of Newcastle had once taken exception to the proposed appointment of General James St Clair as Commander-in-chief because he was 'certainly no great general, certainly a Scotchman who would fill the army with all Scotch, a low Scotchman.' What St Clair had actually done was to tide over his kinsman David Hume with a clerical job while he completed the *Inquiry concerning Human Understanding*, but perhaps his Grace could not have been expected to appreciate that. As late as 1777, the directors of the East India Company turned down General Alexander Mackay for its highest command on similar grounds.[1]

Naturally one would not wish to impute all of this to base prejudice. The English commonly complained that the Scots were hirelings of government. The charge arose from one of the deepest misunderstandings between the two peoples. The Union had yet to imbue the northern one with the stock southern attitudes to the constitution. The Scots' own old Parliament having been unimportant, they did not share the mystical reverence of the English for everything, including the mumbo-jumbo, that went on at Westminster. Anyway, ruling Scotland was not something in practice done there. Her administration was left to the landed gentry, to the ministers of the Kirk or to an embryonic bureaucracy. The courts resolved disputes, and made or interpreted rules in the light of existing law. The scope for governing was otherwise small. Parliament merely embellished, at times to no great advantage, the structure of semi-independence. The major Scottish legislation passed since the Union might justly be regarded as hostile in intent, and only of late had benevolent reforms been attempted.

It was unsurprising that the forty-five Scots in the House of Commons, acting together if possible, went south above all for the sake of the spoils they could bear home.[2] What they thus really wanted by way of political blessings from the Union was a clear-cut and efficient arrangement for distributing the bounty it offered. And that, for too long now, was just what they had not got. James Boswell saw this partly as a matter of national self-reproach, partly of accident (he could find no fault on the other side): 'The Scotch are so cold and selfish and cunning that I fear generous exertion would be lost on them; and political interest is, since the death of Archibald, Duke of Argyll, so divided among different families hungry for advantages that I doubt if an extensive influence can again be established in one family'.[3] His political judgment was, as usual, well wide of the mark.

The decay of the Scottish political interest in London might indeed be seen as a result of the decay of political interests inside Scotland. They certainly existed, though the lack of shape and unity in contemporary politics has often blurred or obscured them, with the exception of the Jacobites. But at the risk of simplification it is possible to descry in the great Whig tide two currents: the one, Argathelian, aristocratic, very unionist, benevolently despotic, erastian, enlightened, improving; the other, often represented by the Squadrone Volante, composed of lesser men, setting store by personal independence, more prepared to stick up for Scotland, presbyterian, anti-intellectual, suspicious, conservative. Both sides believed, however, that they held 'Revolution principles'.

The era of the highest Whiggery had really passed with the third Duke of Argyll, or at the latest with his nephew the Earl of Bute. The fourth Duke, indifferent to politics, had now been followed by a fifth. He was a member of the so-called Bloomsbury gang which survived with diminishing influence the death in 1771 of its leader, the Duke of Bedford. Argyll seems to have been content to carry on returning a Campbell as member for his own county and occasionally in one or two other seats, but to do nothing else about restoring a once potent faction.

Bute still lived, though he had decided some years ago to retire from the world 'before it retires from me'. He cared for his eleven children, cultivated a few friends and lived in splendour at Luton Hoo, designed for him by Robert Adam, collecting books, scientific instruments, Flemish paintings and botanic specimens. He resigned gratefully to his heir, Lord Mountstuart, his remaining political interest. This was not inconsiderable. He disposed of the county of Bute and of the Ayr Burghs. Ross was still held by his uncle, James Stuart Mackenzie, the long deposed manager. There were allies in Ayrshire, Dumfriesshire and West Lothian. Two or three seats in England and Wales could be counted on. Here was a group of half a dozen or so members, not a major interest but the potential nucleus of one. The clan was, however, dogged by the Earl's calamitous reputation, which Mountstuart, proud, indolent and remiss, could not efface. Hating Henry Dundas, he might have drawn together with Sir Lawrence Dundas, moved by the same sentiment, member for Edinburgh, patron of Stirlingshire and of Orkney, wire-puller in several other counties and burghs. But Mountstuart took a peerage in 1776 on accepting the embassy at Turin. With that, the Argathelian connection which had ruled Scotland for most of the time since 1707 can be said to have come to a definitive end.[4]

Everywhere else, political control was extremely fragmented. A great family could command the odd seat, perhaps two. But most were to be won only by inconstant and shifting coalitions of lesser interests among the landed gentry. Occasionally, in a few counties such as Ayrshire or Renfrewshire which happened to contain a large number of independent proprietors, there would even be something we might distantly recognise as a free election.

This emergence of the gentry as an important political class, if at first lacking organisation and leadership, had parallels in England, where it might better be described as a re-emergence. There, it is often regarded as a foretoken of the Toryism which dominated politics for the next half-century, defining itself in opposition to the Whigs' previous monopoly of power even while respecting established authority and customs. The same vapid pieties hid a somewhat different scene in Scotland. Her highest nobles had since 1707 usually been absentees, no longer ruling in person their several domains. As long as the lairds continued to accord the aristocracy a distant deference, they could move more easily into the local seats of power. Since they also often had a legal and admin-istrative background lacking in the superior ranks, a national governing interest, largely free of party, could be more easily formed – especially with the waning of conflict between the two in any case never rigidly separate sets of Revolution principles schematically set out above. It remained then for this interest to be bound together in connection with London. That was Henry Dundas's part.

He did it the more easily because he drew something from both sides. If his family had formed an awkward-squad in Scottish politics, he himself was an urbane child of the Enlightenment. Not a profound or original thinker, he nevertheless showed himself intelligent and receptive. He has been accused of lacking all interest in ideas. If that had been true, it was strange that the favourite pastime of his youth, which he could easily have spent just boozing and whoring, should have been to move in Edinburgh's literary circles, where ideas were ceaselessly discussed; strange, too, that he should have sought, won and kept the friendship and respect of the intellectual leaders of his age. Even Boswell, who usually pooh-poohed Dundas's mental equipment, could be impressed. He wrote at Christmas, 1775: 'Harry Dundas ... was with us, and he gave so many parliamen-tary speeches, and talked so seriously on the decline of learning in Scotland, that I saw what I had never seen before: a company of advocates free from drunken-ness'.[5]

The Scottish Enlightenment was indeed just about to pass its first peak. After Adam Ferguson's *Essay on the History of Civil Society* (1767), John Millar's *Observations concerning Distinctions of Ranks in Society* (1771) and Adam Smith's *Wealth of Nations* (1776), Scotland was not again, in what she called philosophy, to produce works of such range and depth. But the impetus would run on in leaders pursuing practical social improvement.[6] That was what Principal Robertson and the Moderate clergy did in the Church and universities. Lords Kames and Dalrymple were reshaping jurisprudence to the same ends. It remained for the effect to be reproduced in Scottish government, which by comparison clearly lacked direction and purpose.

Relevant questions were broached by Dundas's intellectual friends. The club formed of his circle, the Feast of Tabernacles, had survived when others were wound up; though with him engaged elsewhere, it was actually run by Henry Mackenzie. In 1779 Mackenzie began to bring out a magazine, *The Mirror*, the debut of which can be described in its own words:

> The idea of publishing a periodical paper in Edinburgh took its rise in a company of gentlemen whom particular circumstance of connection brought frequently together. Their discourse often turned upon subjects of manners, taste and of literature. By one of those accidental resolutions, of which the origin cannot be easily traced, it was determined to put their thoughts into writing, and to read them for the entertainment of each other. Their essays assumed the form and, soon after, someone gave them the name of a periodical publication.

In his mirror, Mackenzie declared, 'I mean to show the world what it is and will sometimes endeavour to point out what it should be.'[7]

It was thus moral journalism, praising virtue, damning vice, but with some effort to tackle real problems rather than preach in the abstract. It adopted what it deemed the ideal attitude of landed gentlemen, middling in rank, to economic and social change such as Scotland was undergoing. It found fault with aristocrats for too often succumbing to material temptations, especially if led astray by metropolitan luxury from performance of their proper duties in the social hierarchy. Those who had made a way in life through talent were in turn warned against being corrupted by material reward. Commerce, not deplorable in principle, could become so if it caused traditional virtues to be lost. Perhaps not everyone wanted to hear all this in a Scotland rapidly enriching herself. The *Mirror's* circulation never exceeded 600, and it folded after eighteen months. A further effort on the same lines, *The Lounger*, appeared for a little longer in 1785–7, and had the distinction of publishing the earliest review of Burns's poems. He remained grateful, recording: 'I had often read and admired the Spectator, Adventurer, Rambler and World, but still with a certain regret that they were so thoroughly and entirely English … I have just met with the Mirror and Lounger for the first time, and I am quite in raptures with them.'

Slightly extravagant claims have been advanced about how much light these ventures throw on Dundas's personal opinions. Not being given to literary graces, he is unlikely to have contributed any of their anonymous or pseudonymous articles. Nor is there direct evidence that he even read them. We must thus be cautious about making too much of his literary associations, such as they were. It may be worth pointing out that he had dedicated to him a magazine of a rather different, of a 'coarse and indelicate' character, namely the *Scots Spy*, published by Peter Williamson, who ran a favourite howff for lawyers and literati next to Parliament House. Still, the authors of the *Mirror* were close friends of Dundas, later the objects of his patronage. Perhaps it did offer a glimpse of how their discussions turned on the concerns of the people he represented in politics, a landed class left leaderless by absentee magnates, wishing to assert its direction of Scottish affairs.[8]

Those claims have been advanced in aid of a fashionable interpretation of the Scottish Enlightenment, which sees it as part of the civic humanist tradition resting on a concept of political virtù formulated in classical antiquity and rendered redundant only by industrial society. So fashionable has it become that some of these interpreters seem to regard it as the key to unlock all intellectual problems about the Scotland of the eighteenth century. As an elucidation of development in political theory it has its uses. But the enlightened were not disembodied minds engaged in contemplation of eternal verities; they spent rather less time worrying about their relationship with Aristotle than about the practical realities they faced. A political historian must therefore record some reservations.

The counterpart in everyday politics of civic humanism has been identified as the 'country' ideology. It enunciated the preconditions for men of independence to maintain their virtù: the jealous guarding of individual, local or parliamentary rights and privileges, with the limitation of executive power in order to keep government responsible. It found, however, little consistent expression, being espoused at different times by Whigs and Tories, and by people both in and out of office. A sensible conclusion might be that, given the lack of a true party system, or even of any real acceptance that opposition to established government was legitimate, country ideology amounted to little more than a ready quiver of arguments for expressing dissent. In any event, vigorous enough in England, it was in Scotland much weaker – not surprisingly, in view of a different history.

Its nearest representative was the Squadrone Volante: the parliamentary speeches of Dundas's father could be taken as typical expressions of country sentiment in a Scottish context. Perhaps Dundas himself inherited it. His career certainly bears witness to a belief that those should govern who govern best, the landed gentlemen who were natural rulers of the nation. But this belief offered only a partial response to the condition of Scotland when he embarked on his career. Landed gentlemen could deal with their localities. They could not by themselves deal with the national requirements for patronage and legislation, which only some efficient mechanism at Westminster could satisfy.

Scotland might go on to do one of two things. She might either turn herself, rapidly and irrevocably, into an English province (which was in practice unthinkable). Or else, she might somehow acquire a special category of governors deriving power from office rather than property (though they need not be themselves unpropertied). Dundas was a landowner, but only a smallish one, and had besides to work for a living. It was, to recall Henry Cockburn's formulation at the outset, talent and public situation rather than rank and fortune that made him what he would become; a difference unmistakable in comparison with the Dukes of Argyll. Scotland would still barter patronage from above for loyalty from below, but the transaction was to be conducted by an enlightened professional ruler.

Dundas would thus act in precisely the opposite way to what might be expected from one imbued with a country ideology grounded in the concepts of civic humanism. For that ideology saw in the emergence of a governing class as a distinct interest above civil society something inevitably harmful and corrupting to the polity, a fundamental obstacle to good government. It might, of course, be assumed that Dundas was merely abandoning his youthful principles. But it would have been improbable for all his intellectual friends to do the same; and throughout his career he could, as a matter of fact, rely on their willing help. In truth, however rich and relevant they may have found the concepts of civic humanism, and however eager they may have been to apply those concepts to public life, such effort was vain, for the concepts were effete.[9]

At any rate Dundas, a practical man, well realised that before anything else he had to prove himself an efficient Lord Advocate. Though he soon established a reputation in the Commons, he still devoted most of his energies to pleading in Edinburgh's courts or to Scottish appeals in the House of Lords (he needed the money too). Nor did he go down every session to London. He remained more than a year at home, for example, in 1776 and 1777, and for much of 1779. Among the cases he handled was that of Joseph Knight, a negro slave brought back to Perthshire by a gentleman who had made his fortune in the West Indies. Knight was intelligent, learned to read, and married. He then found his pocket money, sixpence a week, inadequate. A request for regular wages being refused, he gave his master notice that he would leave to look for a job. The cause went before the county justices, who decided against him. The sheriff, on the other hand, found for him. On appeal to the Court of Session, where Dundas led for Knight, his emancipation was upheld (contrary to the opinion, it may be added, of the Lord President). Boswell wrote: 'I cannot too highly praise the speech which Mr Dundas generously contributed to the cause of the sooty stranger.' This established that slavery was illegal in Scotland.

The Lord Advocate also nominated the Scots judges. He was anxious to promote his friend, Robert Macqueen, who had distinguished himself at the Bar and now, aged 50, wished 'to retire to the Bench', as Dundas put it in an application to Lord Mansfield. The latter was not pleased, for he had in mind an arrangement of his own, and declined to use his influence in Macqueen's favour. Dundas persisted. The standard biography of him put an ill construction on this conduct, implying it was the first example of a deplorable penchant for inordinate favours to his personal clique. In fact, Macqueen stood unrivalled among advocates for his understanding and acuity in the law, as later historians have acknowledged. Dundas was actually intent on rewarding merit.

Mansfield still held out instead for Alexander Lockhart, Dean of the Faculty. In this the Lord Advocate at length acquiesced, for the appointment would possess a political symbolism of its own. Lockhart was a son of the Jacobite agent whom we met in 1722 carving up Midlothian with Dundas's father. He had shown moral courage in defending prisoners from Prince Charles's army before English courts after the rebellion. The professional esteem he enjoyed was reflected in his election to the deanship, but fecklessness marred his ability. He was always needy, and notorious for his tattered appearance. In any event, he had in his seventy years found no other preferment. Now he became a judge, as Lord Covington. His colleagues' appreciation of this magnanimous gesture to an ill-used man may be gauged from the fact that Dundas was at once chosen Dean in his stead. He had finally buried the hatchet with the Jacobites. And as it turned out, he was soon able to appoint Macqueen also, with the title of Lord Braxfield.

For other duties, Dundas had at his right hand the Solicitor General, Alexander Murray of Henderland, an advocate of large practice, sardonic humour and forthright opinion, not a specially close friend but a loyal colleague. One day be met a star-crossed citizen of Edinburgh on his way to drown himself in the Nor' Loch, eagerly followed by an expectant crowd. The law officers did not stand on ceremony in those days. Murray flapped into the midst of the ghouls, rebuking their heartlessness in loud, broad Scots and warning the man that he would shortly face the devil. Taken aback, they dispersed while he turned round and went home.[10]

Perhaps Dundas was too committed to his profession, for in the summer of 1778 his wife, in the middle of an affair with a Captain Fawkener, left him. She complained of neglect; doubtless not the first Parliament House widow, she was assuredly not the last. Though people found her amiable and charming, Dundas won all the sympathy. The law of the age was merciless to such a woman. She forfeited the entire property she had brought into the family, and never saw her children again. Decades later, her son would discover by chance that she was still alive in Cornwall, where she died at the age of 98 in 1847. Dundas was cast into 'gloom and melancholy', but they did not ruin his life. The demands of work, relieved by casual dalliance, kept him wifeless for another fifteen years.[11]

Even with these private and professional burdens, Dundas also set out to make of the Lord Advocate's political duties a matter of the first importance. It was he who would establish that the chief law officer should, for want of anyone better, take the initiative as Minister for Scotland. This ensured that the concept of such a Minister would not vanish, as it might have done. Dundas's informal enhancement of the job did encounter problems, and was not to stand the test of centralism in later times. But his leadership from the 1770s signalled the start of that development which led to the resurrection of the Scottish Secretaryship and creation of the Scottish Office more than a century afterwards.[12] He was a self-conscious public servant. In his writings and speeches, he often reflected on what, in given circumstances, ought to be done by a hypothetical figure termed 'the wise statesman' (or something of the sort). This was a long way from the knee-jerking reactionary authoritarianism usually imputed to him. In fact reform stood high on his agenda.

At its head were the electoral laws. Since the Lords had set at nought his brother's efforts to suppress faggot votes, the creation of them had gone on at an alarming rate. Broadly speaking, till the mid-1770s most electors were men of standing in their own counties, even if they held nominal franchises in others. After that, the rolls began to fill up with lawyers from Edinburgh, merchants from Glasgow, residents of London and so forth. A solicitor was found in 1788 to have nine suffrages in places where he owned no real property. Eventually in Banffshire, for example, only about one in seven votes was genuine. A pamphlet of these years pointed out that 'a man may be a freeholder without being proprietor of a single acre; while, on the other hand, a man may be proprietor of lands worth £10,000 a year, and yet may not be qualified to be a freeholder.'[13]

The system was without doubt pernicious, and steadily becoming more so. At least, however, faggot votes had as their usual purpose the defence or expansion of existing local interests, so that they seldom brought in carpet-baggers. The successful candidates who emerged, even out of shady dealings, were almost invariably from old families, at one with and attentive to the fellows they represented. While some constituencies did become politically moribund, in others the member had to work hard, to an extent unnecessary in English seats, at courting, sweetening or cajoling the electors. These did not hesitate to instruct him on how to cast his vote in the Commons, something thought outrageous in the South. He could, after all, lose the next poll by the disaffection of just a few when electorates ranged in size from not many more than 200 in the most populous counties down to a handful in the smallest.[14] It was only following her deliverance at Liberal hands in the next century that Scotland came to know the aloof public figure who deigned to honour the constituency with his presence for a couple of days a year.

The system was thus not beyond saving. The hope that it might yet be saved was strong in many electorates, including Dundas's own in Midlothian. It contained big estates, notably the Duke of Buccleuch's, but most of the freeholders were public-spirited lawyers of wealth, culture and independence. They objected to the corruption and degradation of the franchise. If nothing else, it was prudent for Dundas to humour them, as he did at one public meeting: 'The abuse which has crept in of late years, of allowing gentlemen of large estates as many proxies in the election of a member of Parliament as they have qualifications on their estates, is a most shameful practice, utterly repugnant to the spirit and intention of the election laws, and totally subversive of the constitution.' Instead, the responsible nobleman should 'seek to gain influence not by a preponderating number of votes, but by the way he does his duty to his neighbours, and thus deserves popularity'.[15]

He was speaking in support of a Bill to define more strictly the qualifications of freeholders which he and Montgomery had together introduced early in 1775 and which, as Lord Advocate, he continued to sponsor. It would have repealed the Act of the Scots Parliament under which the feudal superiority of land, and the vote with it, could be separated from the ownership. Even if the superiority was transferred, the vote would henceforth have remained with the original fiar. That would have rendered impossible the creation of further nominal franchises. The Bill then dealt with existing ones, by stipulating that for purposes of qualification a superiority had to be genuine, not in temporary conveyance or subject to conditions. Finally, Dundas wanted to enact what the Lord President had tried to enforce by judicial decree, an oath on each freeholder that he truly fulfilled the terms of all the relevant legislation. Had the Bill passed, the magnates, with their faggot votes under challenge, could no longer have manipulated the polls from a distance. To retain their influence, they would have had rather to co-operate with the smaller resident landowners, in whose favour the elections would have been weighted. The reform was therefore of great potential importance. It aroused a public interest so lively that Dundas agreed to debate it openly in Edinburgh with its main opponent, the Earl of Fife. Such conduct of national politics *coram populo* was unheard of in Scotland.

In his speech, the Lord Advocate again took up the theme that the very rich 'ought to make themselves respectable by their hospitality, their benevolence and promoting the good of the country.' Fife argued that political power should correspond to property, and that a purified system giving one single vote even to the greatest landowner was on that account defective. He was, though a noted agricultural improver, fanatically conservative. Despite the name, his interests lay in a swathe of counties and burghs across the North-east. Despite the name also, his peerage was an Irish one, permitting him to sit in the House of Commons – at the time he represented Banffshire. Odd antecedents did not stop him hitting the nail on the head in speaking for the Scots aristocracy. It perforce resorted to the ingenuity complained of because its true political power had, by the terms of the Union, been inadequately reflected in its representation. But he was also defying the change in social conditions which certainly warranted Dundas's Bill. The debate was therefore between the traditional dominant forces in the Scottish political nation and new ones seeking their proper share of influence.

Dundas seems to have won the argument. When the Bill went the rounds of the electorates in the counties for comment, it was approved by eighteen of them – more than half the total, and an overwhelming majority of those expressing an opinion, for only two were against it and one was undecided. Yet Fife found support too.

A pamphlet, noting that Dundas was also engaged in attempts to prise open the oligarchy of Edinburgh's town council, accused him of riding 'upon the extremity of Whiggery' and demanded: 'May not this passion for democracy spread into the counties?'[16] Fife was indeed to win where it mattered, for Dundas's numerical majority among the genuine electors did not necessarily outweigh the opposing vested interests, the magnates and their faggot voters. It was a fact of political life that he could not, for the general purposes of management, afford to offend them. In those days the chances for Scottish legislation were slim unless it was backed by both an overwhelming consensus at home and by the Government in London. Neither condition obtained here. The Bill was lost in the maze of parliamentary procedure, and the Lord Advocate abandoned it.

The issue remained live enough, however, in the constituencies. Several combined to petition Parliament for redress in 1778. In 1782 the effort was intensified, with delegates from twenty-three counties convening in Edinburgh to deliberate on a new Bill. With relish, they proposed one identical to Dundas's, a challenge to him to repudiate his own past opinions. But they also attempted to draw up a second, more comprehensive measure to redefine the suffrage, because the abolition of faggot votes would leave the Scottish electorate far too small. Over that they descended into discord, giving Dundas the perfect excuse for inaction. By then he had accepted the logic of his position and declared against reform of the franchise anyway. In future he sought, where necessary, to win over the great landed interests rather than to limit them. This assuaging of Scottish conflicts had a value of its own.[17]

Dundas remained open-minded on other policies, notably on economic ones. A mark of these years was the start of the always steady and at times spectacular economic expansion which continued with only rare intermissions till the end of the Napoleonic Wars. So far Scotland had probably benefited most from the disappearance, for trading purposes, of her border. Now she took off on her own, with the yet more thorough restructuring of agriculture, the emergence of manufactures (at first mainly of textiles), the accumulation of capital and growth of financial institutions, the extension of communications, the development of remote regions and the embellishment of cities and country seats. At last her advance seemed to be matching England's, a token to her of equality and harbinger of a yet closer Union. If the state continued to intervene on a minor scale, the main burden of improvement still fell on individual landowners, who quite often ruined themselves. Even so, the conviction steadily gained ground that the country was best going to prosper through private enterprise in open markets.[18]

Dundas entered into correspondence with Adam Smith in 1775, at first mainly over the representation of Fife. The acquaintance deepened. In 1777, Dundas got Smith the well-paid job as commissioner of customs which allowed him to spend the remaining years of his life in comfort, usually at Panmure House in Edinburgh, where he was available for discussion and advice. Meanwhile *The Wealth of Nations* had been published. Dundas was certainly among the first to read, mark and inwardly digest it. Later he introduced Smith to William Pitt the younger and other parliamentarians. If the work of the father of political economy was by then well known, it would be fair to say that Dundas played some part in advancing the personal contacts and influence through which his views were disseminated in governing circles. He came largely to share Smith's general position, in favour of lowering unnecessary or unprofitable barriers while eschewing a fanatical pursuit of free trade.

We saw in his support for emancipation of colliers that Dundas was anyway disposed to liberalise. He could go to some lengths, as when he sought official permission for cultivation of tobacco in Scotland.[19] Contact with Smith allowed him to work out his ideas more systematically. An example came on the question of dismantling tariffs between Great Britain and Ireland. Dundas's frame of thinking was generous, as little metropolitan as parochial. The history of his own country since the Union showed him that, while an effort to make of the British Isles a common market could bring its difficulties, the benefits to the whole would eventually be greater. They might be dramatic for remote regions previously deprived of access to the richer markets. Here he knew that Ireland ran a large, constant trade deficit even with Scotland. In October 1779 he was to be found exhibiting a confident grasp of what is nowadays called the theory of comparative advantage, with a facility in applying it to the case in hand, due account taken of the political realities involved.

Dundas wrote to Smith:

> I doubt much if a free trade to Ireland is so very much to be dreaded. There is trade enough in the world for the industry of both Britain and Ireland, and if two or three places either in south or north Britain should suffer some damage, which by the by will be very gradual, from the loss of their monopoly, that is a very small consideration in the general scale and policy of the country. The only thing to be guarded against is the people in Ireland

being able to undersell us in foreign markets from the want of taxes and the cheapness of labour. But a wise statesman will be able to regulate that by proper distribution of taxes upon the materials and commodities of the respective countries. I believe an union would be the best if it can be accomplished, if not the Irish Parliament must be managed by the proper distribution of the loaves and fishes, so that the legislators of the two countries may act in union together ... It has often shocked me in the House of Commons for these two years past, when anything was hinted in favour of Ireland by its friends, of even giving them only the benefit of making the most of what their soil or climate afforded them, to hear it received as a sufficient answer that a town in England or Scotland would be hurt by such an indulgence.

Smith wrote back agreeing that natural conditions did, and ought to, influence the pattern of international specialisation: 'to crush the industry of so great and fine a province of the empire, in order to favour the monopoly of some particular towns in Scotland or England is equally unjust and impolitic'.[20]

Dundas also set out his views to the Commons: 'Ireland is known to be in imminent distress and should in my opinion become an object of immediate and effectual relief. That relief, too, must be liberal in its nature. The age is liberal, and a liberality, an unrestrained or at least unclogged system of commerce, is of its very essence.' Dundas retained his sympathetic attitude to Irish misfortunes all through his career, and a comment to the House some days later gave one reason why: 'I have ever been a declared and real enemy to local distinctions. I am of opinion that every part of the two kingdoms is entitled to equal and indiscriminate favour.' His and others' exertions in favour of Ireland brought partial removal of the barriers in 1780. This marked the first step in British official policy towards free trade. For Scotland in particular, it brought a vast expansion of Irish traffic, which largely offset disruption of American commerce.[21]

While in that case Dundas was ready to attack unfair privilege, he never allowed himself to be entirely seduced by tidy economic theory: he lived in a world of political interests, as well as of market forces. The keystone of protectionism in an agricultural economy was the Corn Laws. But prices to farmers had long been rising, so that exports of grain had petered out and imports had become normal. The laws, intended to produce the opposite effect, were suspended annually all through the 1760s, before being adjusted in 1773 to the new conditions. This progress in a liberal direction, being conditioned by the markets, was inevitably erratic, however. In 1777 a new Corn Bill included a proposal for raising by one-fifth the price at which oats, staple of Scotland's diet, could be sold there, threatening a steep increase in the cost of living. Merchants and manufacturers in Glasgow protested because they would then be forced to pay higher wages. The Bill was supported by landowners, though, on the grounds that without effective Corn Laws they faced impoverishment. The debate took a more piquant turn for following so soon on publication of *The Wealth of Nations*. It showed that, as Smith surmised, a country where many vested interests held sway would be wary of swallowing political economy whole. Even the Glaswegians had no quarrel with the principle of domestic protectionism, only with its detailed application. Dundas spent these months at home, so did not personally pilot the Bill through. But interestingly it reflected one view expounded in his intellectual circle, that the landowning pillars of society had to be shielded from adverse effects of free commerce.[22]

Dundas more generally showed sense in never forcing the pace of economic reform and was at times content to acquiesce in the old muddles. One example came with the independent system for the Scottish revenue, the failings of which greatly vexed the Treasury in London. The customs and excise, for instance, were hard to collect when smuggling was basic to the economy of many ports in the East; and it remained so till, in later years, the lowering or removal of duties made it less lucrative.[23]

At the top of the fiscal structure stood the Court of Exchequer, where five Barons exercised jurisdiction. Three of them, usually including the Chief Baron, were by convention English. The arrangement, dating from 1707, was designed to help the Scots learn standard taxation practice. But the Scots also held to a rooted conviction, which Dundas did not greatly care to shake, that they should never be taxed more than they had been then. And they proved all the less amenable now that they were really beginning to thrive: 'for the most part … the Court pursued a course of glorious inefficiency'.

For the main direct tax, on land, Scotland was assessed at only £48,000 a year, less than many English counties. Yet by 1780 payments were thirty months in arrears, and falling still further behind. The Receiver-general, John Fordyce, owed £100,000 to the Treasury. Not unnaturally it regarded him as careless and incompetent, and tried to get rid of him. Dundas at first inclined to an equally severe view. But the frantically worried Fordyce managed to persuade him that he was, if not quite as pure as the driven snow, at least largely a victim of the system, though it certainly helped that he was related by marriage to the Duke of Gordon, whom Dundas wished to woo on other grounds. The Lord Advocate conceded in November 1782 that 'the public revenues of Scotland are ill-collected, ill-managed and … of those collected a sufficient proportion does not reach the Treasury in England.' He proposed that a special commission should be appointed to investigate. There remained the problem of Fordyce. He, rather than boringly leave the untransmitted revenues on deposit, had laid them out in investments of his own: something shockingly irregular to us, but then common among public officials. Sadly, his speculations were not paying off. Instead of bankrupting him, which would have solved nothing, Dundas allowed him to settle up gradually, on an optimistic assumption that his financial judgment would improve. His public accounts still remained to be discharged at the time of his death in 1809. Meanwhile, he had managed to impress Dundas, William Pitt and even Charles James Fox with his assiduity and despatch. He made an unexpectedly successful career as liquidator of the royal family's debts, for which he must have been well qualified.[24]

In the early years of Dundas's administration, only one policy stood out as plainly illiberal, his effort to suppress emigration from the Highlands. Even this, however, was tempered by wider considerations. The conservative proprietors of the eighteenth century actually favoured – in contrast to their utilitarian successors – keeping and increasing the population on the land, as a social and economic good for the nation. In this particular, their hierarchical view of society was as yet untouched by liberalising ideas. It was also offended by the flood of emigration to America, beyond anything seen before, since the Seven Years' War. Thomas Miller of Glenlee, Lord Justice Clerk, warned there was a real danger of emptying the country. As a first measure of control, he proposed registering the emigrants. It was then found that nearly 4000 left Scotland between 1773 and 1776, the majority from Argyll, Inverness-shire, Perthshire and Renfrewshire. Recent research has put the total for the period 1760–75 at 40,000, about three per cent of the population and one-third of the whole British emigration to America.

Some special factors must therefore have been at work in Scotland. These seemed plain: the move to commercial agriculture, with enclosures and higher rents, made by the landowners themselves. Nor did they stop there. Sir James Montgomery, while Lord Advocate, had in the deepest secrecy tried – but failed – to turn the emigration itself to his profit by establishing settlements in Nova Scotia. How was the Scottish ruling class to resolve the dilemmas which its own actions revealed?

Dundas has now been given credit for analysing them more acutely than any contemporary. In a long memorandum written in September 1775, he gave due weight to the conventional explanation: 'The severity of some great proprietors by a precipitate and injudicious rise of rents was the immediate cause of emigration in some part of the country.' But this was by no means the whole story. Dundas went on to note that the traditional Highland chiefs had wanted as many men as possible on their lands to manifest their power. Stripped of it by the repression after 1745, they had little choice but to regard themselves as landlords, their dependants as mere tenants. There had, of course, always been emigration from the over-populated North, attested by the many Highlanders in the Lowlands: 'more than half of our day labourers, of our menial servants, our chairmen, porters, of our workmen of every kind.' But it was by the collapse of a social system that they were 'induced to look for protection on the other side of the Atlantic, or, to speak more properly, are induced to wander there for want of that cherishment and protection that their fathers had felt in their old habitation.'

The answer, then, would be to find some substitute for the traditional order. Striking was Dundas's conclusion that the state ought to see to this, though it followed from his view that legislation had helped cause the problem. He dismissed any objection that the state could not be expected to pamper an inherently rebellious race: 'It is to talk like children to talk of any danger from disaffection in the North. There is no such thing and it ought to be the object of every wise ruler in this country to cherish and make proper use of the Highlands of Scotland.' Moreover he doubted the value, not to say legality, of banning emigration: 'in a small country, and where there are daily opportunities of getting away, such an idea is impracticable.' Policy should instead be concentrated on inducements for people to stay. As a first step, for example, the estates forfeited by Jacobite families could be handed back to them, to symbolise a new policy of consciously repairing the social fabric.[25]

Unfortunately, the outbreak of war across the Atlantic demanded some more immediate expedient, since every able-bodied emigrant could add to America's strength and reduce Britain's. Highland proprietors, led by Sir James Grant, clamoured for Dundas to do something. In response he forbade the Scottish Board of Customs to clear from its ports, while hostilities lasted, any more ships carrying emigrants, and sheriffs instructed ministers to pass the news on to their flocks. But he insisted that this could not be, once normal conditions returned, a permanent solution: 'If there were no such pretence as that of rebellion in America, it would be wild to think of keeping your subjects at home by force.' He had seen clearly the true reason for the rising tide of emigration, the social and economic revolution which had overtaken the Highlands since 1745. He was the first politician to put his finger on that, and to draw the consequences: that there would have to be much more systematic thought about the region's problems and concentrated effort to solve them.[26]

In the only action open to him for the time being, however, Dundas's prime interest was military, an interest he never lost. Sabre-rattling sentiments were common among Scots, partly out of pride in their old prowess, partly out of a guilty perception that it had been sometimes misapplied since the Union, or at least out of a fear that the English would think it had. The matter was of special concern among the enlightened, with their care for the survival of the nation's strengths in a new age. They had been furious when, during the Seven Years' War, the Government raised a militia for home defence in England, but not in Scotland. The Dundases often supported such national causes, yet on that occasion Robert, the Lord Advocate, would have none of it. He had been one of only two Scottish members to vote with the Government against a motion for a militia in 1760. He despised the literati promoting it. More important, he owed much to Newcastle, who opposed it for a variety of reasons, from the fact that Scots had indeed not endeared themselves to him when they were last in arms, to the possibility that someone else would gain credit if it went through. Public opinion had condemned Dundas for his truckling, and seen its worst suspicions confirmed when he was soon afterwards appointed Lord President.[27]

Two decades later, this was another question on which, in public at least, Henry Dundas straddled previous divisions in his country. He joined the Poker Club founded, according to Adam Ferguson, to 'stir up' the question of a militia again during the American War. There seemed better reason for it now, especially with the renegade John Paul Jones raiding his native shores. London was less suspicious too. With home defence becoming necessary as the colonial struggle developed into a general European conflict, the hope there was that a militia might offer a pool of trained men for the regular army. It thus remained all the same a secondary issue for the Government, which professed itself happy so long as a good number of Scots regiments were directly raised to fight in America. While Dundas could see to that, he had little incentive to move on a militia.

If one was to be established, somebody else had to take the initiative. Into the breach stepped Mountstuart, then still aspiring to manage Scotland. He admitted to his friend Boswell that he wanted to use this cause to restore the Butes' moribund influence. The fate of his Bill in the session of 1775–6 showed how difficult that would be. Lord North, it turned out, would consider helping solely on condition that the militia might be used as a source of regular recruits. To the enthusiasts, for whom it was a national virility symbol, this seemed a niggardly attitude. Dundas sympathised, but declined to commit himself, saying he would wait to hear the country's reaction to the Bill once printed.

What eventually came before the Commons was a misbegotten compromise, with acceptance of North's stipulation but apparently without any guarantee of his support in return. Dundas soon complained:

> I am come to a full persuasion that a Militia Bill with a power to recruit out of it as our Bill now stands would be ruin to the country ... They would fish up our militiamen as fast as they were embodied. The clause therefore is a bad one in itself, at least undoubtedly so while a contrary provision takes place in England. Besides, it is a scandalous distinction between the two countries.

If the clause was deleted, however, the Government would turn openly hostile. Bogged down between these unacceptable alternatives, impeded by persistent English misgivings, the Bill was doomed.[28]

In fact, if Scots wanted to play at soldiers they were perfectly entitled to do so under an Act of their own Parliament, still in force, permitting fencible regiments. These could, however, only be raised for the duration of any war, and might neither leave Scotland nor be used for regular recruitment. In 1778, when American privateers got as far as Leith, attacking Stornoway, Aberdeen and Arbroath for good measure, bodies of the rattled citizenry began arming and training themselves. Dundas wrote deploring this unauthorised action to the Secretary of State, Lord Stormont, who replied by spelling out conditions on which it might be done.[29]

That kept the question on the boil. In 1782 the Marquis of Graham made another effort to persuade the Commons of the need for a Scottish militia. He too may have done it to bolster the influence of his house, Montrose. Once more Dundas gave verbal support, and joined him on the platform at a meeting he summoned in London of all Scots in both houses of Parliament together with any other notables he could find. An uninvited guest was the crazed Lord George Gordon, fresh from his acquittal for treason following the anti-Catholic riots named after him. Everyone's heart must have sunk when, as the meeting opened, he rose to speak. Somehow he was allowed to rant on, protesting first that he had not been summoned with others of his quality, then that Graham was of too low a rank to take the chair, and not a good enough presbyterian besides, having failed to subscribe to every one of the decrees, confessions and covenants issued by the Kirk in Reformation, Civil War and Revolution – all of which he rehearsed. The proceedings broke up in confusion and the hapless Graham's efforts in Parliament came to nothing. Again Dundas, without taking action on a plan of dubious prospects, was at least left with the credit of having adopted a favourable public stance. At this stage any other course would have been foolish, for in a year the war was over and the whole question otiose.[30]

If moved by political before idealistic motives, Dundas otherwise identified with the enlightened, and in particular sustained their institutional regime. He took a special interest in the Church, carefully disposing of benefices in the Crown's gift.[31] Principal Robertson's aim, to make out of presbyterianism an orderly and trustworthy national ecclesiastical polity, had been achieved during the interregnum between Bute and Dundas. The Moderates' control now looked solid, though they paid a price for their enforcement of lay patronage by driving many into dissent; the compensating benefit was independence in the internal government of the Kirk. Dundas's arrival on the scene disturbed none of this. But the principal may have been anxious lest his own disciples should appear too assiduous in currying favour with the new manager as well. Such ingratiation might not be rewarded in the expected measure, for Dundas seemed ready to seek sound, efficient, loyal men wherever he found them, and not exclusively among the Moderates.

The Moderates were, however, entrenched in the Church's hierarchy, in positions often entitling them to *ex officio* membership of the General Assembly. Since its composition changed every year, that was important for keeping a grip. How firm it was can be gauged from two elections in 1778 managed by Dundas and Robertson. The latter's son, William junior, defeated Henry Erskine for the post of procurator. His cousin, the Revd John Drysdale, was chosen for principal clerk, as a man 'so well acquainted with the state of the two parties in the Church that he used to calculate, with surprising exactness, what the issue of the votes would be in almost all the great questions that came before the Assembly. He would often, with that great good humour which marked all his conversation, tell his acquaintances of the opposite party, by how many votes they would lose the question.' If Moderates could make one wince, they still offered the best career prospects, for Drysdale 'also took the greatest pleasure in protecting, encouraging and bringing forward younger men who seemed to him to be possessed of talents, which promised to be useful ... either in church or state.'[32]

At Edinburgh University, Robertson had no need of a political prop, so firm was his leadership and authority in a system offering any of the Enlightenment's leading figures an academic billet if wanted. There was the odd case where the Moderates failed to appoint their man, for example, once when the town council insisted on a relation of the Lord Provost; Dundas could not help here because, as we shall see, he was still far from controlling it. Yet if patronage in general, and nepotism in particular, have been banes of modern Scotland, Robertson was remarkable not in disdaining resort to them, but in contriving to use them to enlightened ends. His protégés brought with them names and connections, yet also academic distinction and in many cases a permanent contribution to their studies. The prime function of his supremely well-run university was still to turn out a learned and diligent ministry. More important in retrospect, though, was how its lay graduates pushed back the frontiers of social and political thought. The ideology and culture of what had once just been the 'tounis college' came to stand at the forefront of Western civilisation.[33]

But events showed that, for the ideology and culture to be more widely disseminated, it was insufficient to fill the highest places in the land with the enlightened. This did not of itself ensure the triumph of reason and progress. The regime of Dundas and Robertson was about to be shaken to the roots by a sudden and wholly unexpected visitation of darker forces from Scotland's past.

The occasion was Dundas's Bill for relief of Scots Roman Catholics, which he intended to introduce in the session of 1778–9. It met, however, with such ferocious popular opposition, culminating in riots, burning and looting in Edinburgh and Glasgow, that an astonished and appalled Government had to drop it. Disabilities had been laid on papists since the Reformation, and intensified after the Revolution. Various laws forbade, under draconian penalties, the saying of mass and any form of Romish instruction or proselytising, as well as the inheritance of land by a papist if the nearest protestant heir objected. They had resulted not in any real persecution – at least not during recent times – but in a gradual shrinking of the catholic population. It included now only one resident noble family, Traquair, and no more than a handful of other landowners. The rest were poor, illiterate peasants, most in Highland fastnesses, numbering 30,000 at the outside, and perhaps only half that figure.[34] This minority being all but invisible, the penal laws had, even in a strongly protestant nation, fallen into disuse.

Why, then, did Dundas bother? The tapping of new sources of manpower for military service in America is the reason usually given. He is said to have sought Highlanders in particular because, apart from being warlike, they would not in their ignorance quibble over terms and conditions as more awkward Lowland recruits often did. Under the existing law, papists among them were deterred from joining up by having to take an oath in abjuration of their faith. Some took it regardless but were, of course, denied priestly ministrations and forbidden to attend mass once under arms. It was not for nothing that the Continental Congress – though with Ireland uppermost in its mind – had called on all British Catholics to emigrate to America, where they would enjoy the toleration withheld from them at home.

The idea of a Scottish Relief Bill probably originated with a friend and neighbour of the Dundases, Sir John Dalrymple.[35] He was full of schemes for shortening the war, one being to offer George Washington a dukedom. Experience during a campaign for recruitment in Ireland had made him aware of catholic conscientious objections to joining up. He afterwards ascertained that the same problem affected Scots. His informant was George Hay, Vicar Apostolic (with episcopal rank) for the Lowlands. This sometime Jacobite averred that 'repeal of the penal laws would attach Catholics wholly to His Majesty's person and government for ever.'[36]

A convincing case needed, however, first-hand evidence. Alexander Gordon, principal of the Scots College in Paris, who happened to be home for a visit, was sent on a winter's journey through the Highlands to inquire of Catholics whether they were ready for recruitment; and if not, why not? It was duly found, according to Hay, that their treatment under the penal laws presented an 'insurmountable difficulty'. Gordon added that, with repeal, 'from two to three thousand men might have been got willing to serve in any part of Great Britain or America, without asking bounty money, rank or half-pay, if disbanded after the war': music to official ears.[37]

Gordon's errand bespoke haste – 'he had to travel over hills covered with ice and snow, sometimes at the peril of his life.' For after the Catholics had been granted toleration in Canada in 1774, and some relief in Ireland in 1778, a Bill was in preparation for England also. The Scots papists being so powerless, their best chance of greater religious liberty lay in attaching themselves to its coat-tails. The haste was also nervous, for nobody could say how the idea might be received. Even Hay admitted that 'as a total repeal is not to be thought of, in the present state of affairs, and perhaps not even to be wished for, in my humble opinion, the removal of three impediments would suffice', namely, on the saying of mass, on inheritance by papists and on their admission to the forces without the offensive oaths. In March 1778, Dalrymple went to London to discuss these requests with the Government and with a committee of English Catholics. In Hay's narrative, 'being desirous of going hand in hand with the English in every step we proposed that both repeals should go on together in the same Bill; but this the committee absolutely refused ... and they resolved to carry on their own Bill alone and left us to shift for ourselves.'[38] No reason for this curmudgeonly attitude was given. One may guess that they did not care to open what they imagined to be a can of Jacobite worms.

Dundas had so far taken a friendly interest without being more closely involved. He was drawn in by an appeal to resolve the impasse from Lord Linton, heir to Traquair, and 'most cheerfully and readily undertook to carry through our Bill, looking upon it as a national cause.' His motives here, then, were not exclusively military: one could hardly contend that recruitment would have been affected by a change in the laws of inheritance. We have already seen him calling for equal treatment of every part of the Empire. Scotland ought therefore not to tarry if Canada, Ireland and now England were relieving their Catholics. A tract from his camp in 1780 explicitly argued that 'interested for the honour and national character of Scotland, he wished she should not be behind hand in manifesting a spirit as humane, as liberal, as her neighbours.' And in publicly announcing his intentions, Dundas himself said that 'the object is only to repeal a penal law, which from the beginning has been considered so cruel as to have been seldom executed.' His motives may have been calculating, but they were not solely that: there is evidence enough of a genuine desire for toleration. Let us recall that the first speech he ever made had been in favour of religious liberty.[39]

So Dundas committed himself to introducing a separate Scottish Bill, using the excuse that the relevant legislation dated from before the Union. While the English measure had sailed through unopposed, it was regrettably too late in the session of 1777–8 for him to do anything. He tersely declared that he would proceed during the autumn, eschewing detail so as not to stir things up at the General Assembly, about to meet in Edinburgh. But he also thus put himself at a political disadvantage. This Assembly was more than usually dominated by Moderates, and might well have been persuaded to approve firm proposals rather than vague intentions. Hastening back, Dundas personally addressed it, stressing the limited nature of the action so far taken. On the very next day, however, the first rumble of discontent was heard. A Glaswegian minister of the popular party called for a committee to monitor the effects of the English Relief Act. Robertson had the motion easily defeated. Though the principal took no great part in promoting the reform, it was clear enough where his sympathies lay.[40]

There matters rested over the summer. As late as September, Dundas was writing to Linton that 'the Bill in favour of the Roman Catholics in Scotland must certainly be moved next session of Parliament, and the nature of it seems to be very simple. The object will be to put the Roman Catholics in Scotland upon the same footing as the Bill of last session put those in England.'[41] Their leaders showed every sign of confidence, and met in Edinburgh to plan the way ahead. In fact a storm was about to break.

Three groups used the interval unwisely left them by Dundas to make their own preparations against him.[42] The Episcopalians were another small minority suffering disabilities on account of their former Jacobitism. They would certainly have had a grievance, though not one beyond the wit of man to answer, if the penal laws against them had stayed in force while those against the papists were lifted. A dog in the manger among them, William Drummond, wrote a pamphlet denouncing catholic relief which he managed to get respectably published by the Society for the Promotion of Christian Knowledge, and which appears to have played some part in arousing wider public disquiet.

More formidable, despite defeat in May, were the Evangelicals in the Kirk. Their leader, the Revd John Erskine, who shared Robertson's charge at Greyfriars, had won notoriety by preaching peace with America. It may seem odd that he could reconcile support for that progressive cause with the apparently reactionary opposition to catholic relief he now espoused, though historians have begun to caution us against assuming that the popular party was a liberal one. Erskine's opinions on popery were fierce: 'a sect which thinks it lawful, by fraud or violence, to deprive every other sect of ... natural and civil rights, and to tolerate no religion save their own, is a common enemy, against whose encroachments every other sect should guard, and solicit, if necessary, the public protection.' The link with his views on America lay in his aversion from despotism, an old Scots song often struck up by the High-flyers against what they claimed to be the Moderates' backsliding. His biographer wrote that he saw in Catholicism 'an implacable enemy to the general liberties of mankind, as well as to the free and happy constitution of Great Britain'.[43] Relief was thus represented as another plot in high places to subvert presbyterian freedom, an aping of Romish practice by which corruption (as in the abandonment of scriptural standards) always went in the guise of innovation.

The popular party's strength lay in the provincial synods. During the autumn a succession of them, in Glasgow and Ayr, Perth and Stirling, Angus and Mearns, in Galloway and in Ross, passed resolutions condemning Dundas's plans. Even in Lothian, the Moderates' stronghold, compromise wording had to be found to stop a hostile motion going through. A yet more ominous event was a riot in October in Glasgow, the most presbyterian city, where the mob broke up a mass in a private house. The celebrant escaped by throwing off his vestments and crying 'Where is the priest?'[44]

This was the first sign of what turned out to be the most startling and pregnant reaction to Dundas's policy. For it also aroused violent protest from the people, a force with next to no role in Scottish politics ever since its sentiments had been so conspicuously ignored in 1707. The third hostile group now to be organised, in Edinburgh in November, was the Committee for the Protestant Interest. Its members were a solicitor, a solicitor's apprentice, a schoolmaster, three clerks, a goldsmith, a merchant, a grocer, a hosier, an ironmonger, a dyer, and 'an intaker for several bleachfields': a cross-section, therefore, of an otherwise silent, or at least unheard, urban mass. They won wide support. When they eventually took to the streets, they raised the blue blanket, age-old symbol of a mob bent not on mindless destruction but on serious business with the state. The anarchic tradition of popular riot stretching back to the middle ages thus visibly connected with the first political movement in modern Scotland organised from below. It would be pleasant to record that they were the sturdy, freedom-loving radicals of our national mythology. And so some of them may have been: but they were bigots too.

Hay, the Vicar Apostolic, never ceased to stress that they belonged 'to the lower and ignorant class'. Others were, despite themselves, not quite so dismissive. Jupiter Carlyle later remarked:

> When the operations of the famous committee extended themselves to my parish, I was weak enough (never suspecting the consequences which followed) to be somewhat proud of the spirit shown by the people. I was much pleased with the Whipmen of Fisherrow, who declared that they would endure all that could be inflicted by scorpions and whips, rather than renounce the Protestant faith. I was truly delighted with the Butchers of Musselburgh, who like their worthy forefathers, would resist unto blood, rather than embrace the Romish superstition. I was charmed with the Journeymen Tailors of Newbigging, whose venerable ancestors had saved a remnant from the shears of popish persecution.[45]

Thus far, it seemed, the leaders of Scotland could or would not take the opposition seriously. In any event, Hay appeared for further talks in London, where Dundas refused to present to Parliament the petitions against his measure sent from Scotland. By the New Year, 356 had arrived: more than 160 from various ecclesiastical bodies, 120 from incorporations of trades and other private societies, over 60 from burghs, towns and villages, though only two from county freeholders. In Edinburgh, a number of the incorporations requested support from the town council (nominally composed, for the most part, of their representatives). Though it was controlled by Sir Lawrence Dundas, thus by a party inimical to the Lord Advocate, here too the popular pressure met only blank rejection.[46]

That really was no answer to the strength of it. The tension burst forth on January 30, 1779, when a crowd gathered at the absent Hay's house in Blackfriars Wynd, off the High Street of Edinburgh. They first contented themselves with breaking his windows and molesting his servants. But on the following afternoons people making their way home from work returned in a great rabble, and on February 2 they got out of hand. They stormed, pillaged and set fire to the house and to a chapel newly erected beside it – just in time for Hay himself to arrive, summoned back by alarming reports he had received in London.

> With his saddlebags on his arm … he went towards his house and was surprised to meet with such crowds of people as he approached towards it. At last seeing that they always increased the nearer he was to it he enquired of an old woman what was going on. 'Oh sir!' said she, 'we are burning the popish chapel, and wish we had their bishop to help the bonfire'.[47]

Hay could turn and flee, but there was no such luck for many of the other 300 papists living in the city, on whom the mob next rounded, smashing their homes and shops. The Scottish Catholic Archive is full of pathetic testimonies of small lives shattered by its fury. Angelo Tremamondo, master of the stables at Holyrood, did not stop running till he got to France, whence he wrote that he was 'réduit au bout de 16 ans être obligé de fuire comme un criminel et laisser tout le produit de mes travaux à la merci d'une populace enragée' – though he was to return and live happily in Edinburgh for 20 more years.[48]

Henry Dundas was also home from Westminster and now came up to the city. But there was little he could accomplish alone if the magistrates made no move to suppress the tumult. This they had omitted to do, perhaps hoping it would peter out, perhaps even sympathising with it; perhaps again, as creatures of Sir Lawrence, they were not sorry to see the other Dundas stew in his own juice. Indeed, when Buccleuch brought down soldiers from the castle, the Lord Provost, Walter Hamilton, forbade him to interfere in case he provoked the rioters further. That night, Dundas met Hamilton at Fortune's tavern in Princes Street. Stronger action was indispensable, he urged, but the Lord Provost blandly stonewalled: was it not rather for the Lord Advocate, who some thought the cause of the trouble, to bring it to an end? As far as one may tell from inconsistent accounts, Dundas then sold the pass. At any rate, Hamilton claimed later to have received 'a private intimation that the popish Bill would be dropped'.[49]

Before it could be broadcast, the riots started again. When a mob made towards Robertson's house at the university, Dundas insisted on deployment of troops. Dragoons were called up from Dalkeith and Musselburgh. Hamilton gave notice that they would open fire if the violence continued. Nineteen people were arrested and taken to the castle, though the Lord Advocate at once ordered their release. He still could not secure the magistrates' full co-operation. Not for another three days did Hamilton announce that the Bill was 'laid aside … to remove the fears and apprehensions which had distressed the minds of many well-meaning people in this metropolis, with regard to the repeal of the penal statutes against papists' – a view of the disturbances indulgent to the point of impudence.[50]

Nor were they over. It is unclear whether the situation in Glasgow was affected by a notice posted in the streets: 'Any person willing to encourage an original genius may have an opportunity of hearing an oratorical declaration against popery, this evening at six o'clock in the Weighhouse Hall. Admittance 2d each. N.B. If any gentlemen or ladies think the performance worthwhile, their further contributions will be gratefully received by the persons appointed to keep the door.' In any event a rabble went on the rampage here just as order was being restored in the capital. Unable to find any native Glaswegian on whom to vent its spite, it ransacked the house of an English papist. At Perth, a crowd planned to march against Stobhall, a tiny catholic enclave outside the town, but gave up at finding it would be defended. Further disturbances were forestalled by a statement from the Government in London on February 12, making clear beyond doubt that the Scottish Relief Bill was abandoned. 'Nothing', Dalrymple wrote to Lord Linton a few days later, 'can be so pitiful, timorous and cowardly as the … Advocate's conduct has been.'[51]

Was there any excuse for Dundas? He could be given credit for good intentions, but they were scarcely enough in a business which he otherwise thoroughly mishandled. He ignored warnings and, though hamstrung by the town council's bad faith, capitulated at the critical moment. His good intentions were then evidently diluted by a different calculation. Dalrymple, now a very hostile witness, surmised that 'there is party in this case ... and thus to gain a burgh, the affections of 25,000 of the most zealous subjects will be lost to the King'. In other words, Henry Dundas was prepared to go only so far in alienating Edinburgh, where he was already struggling to wrest control from Sir Lawrence, nominally to give it to Buccleuch, but actually to himself.

Even in his ignominy, he did not lose sight of that. A secondary political problem posed now was that ruined Catholics claimed compensation from the city. Sir Lawrence wanted them paid, to avert trouble from a Government which, on the precedent of the Porteous Riot, might fine, depose and disqualify the whole town council. But Buccleuch and Henry Dundas urged it to stand up for itself, vindicate its magistracy, and so concede none of the claims. It was noted that this, while hardly keeping faith with the poor papists whose cause they had so recently espoused, would not serve the councillors' best interests either. In fact, it was a transparent ruse to get them all thrown out, thus destroying Sir Lawrence's careful packing of the council and clearing the way for his rivals to take over. He let it be known he would rather pay the damages out of his own pocket. In hard-bitten haggling with his heir, Thomas Dundas of Castlecary, member of Parliament for Stirlingshire, Henry settled the total compensation at £1650 – half of what Hay demanded.[52]

Thwarted in Scotland, Henry was humiliated when he returned to London to face the Commons in March. John Wilkes, of all people, rose and accused him of surrender to the mob. Dundas lamely replied:

I have found such tumults and insurrections in Scotland, and so violent an opposition to the measure, that in the counties where I am interested I have done everything in my power to reconcile the people to it; but finding it in vain, I have consulted the principal Roman Catholics, who have given it as their opinion that it would be much better to decline all attempts to procure an Act in their favour, till time and cool persuasion shall remove the unhappy prejudices of the Protestants of that country against them.[53]

But the main victim on a personal level, apart from the Catholics, was Robertson. At the following General Assembly, he rendered an account of his part in the fiasco which even from the printed page bespeaks his pain. He stressed that he had always tried to act as a calming influence, having appealed, in turn and in vain, to his colleague Erskine and to Dundas himself for efforts at a compromise to defuse the protests:

Though I have observed with pleasure the rapid progress of liberal senti-ments in this enlightened age; though I knew that science and philosophy had diffused the principles of toleration through almost every part of Europe; yet I was so well acquainted with the deep-rooted aversion of Britons from the practice and spirit of popery, that I suspected this motion, for giving relief to papists, to be premature ... Even the prejudices of the people are, in my opinion, respectable, and an indulgent legislature ought not unnecessarily to run counter to them.[54]

Despite the excuses, it was still a mortifying experience. Yet many were surprised when Robertson stepped down the next year from management of the Kirk. Though in indifferent health, he was still only 59. One observer thought some of his brethren were pressing him to make the Moderate regime yet stricter and that he retired rather than resist. It has also been suggested that he found Dundas's demands increasingly irksome. That some estrangement had happened or was happening seemed clear from the later comment by Carlyle that Robertson 'deserted' Dundas – 'a cloud that was never dispelled'. But he alluded to events in 1782, when the Whigs were said to have won the principal over by offering his son control of ecclesiastical patronage. The matter remained obscure because he was always too crafty to reveal his political motives. It may well be that the blunder with the Relief Bill, and other difficulties shortly to be recounted, persuaded him that the Lord Advocate had no staying power. Even in 1784, when Dundas really was establishing himself, Robertson remained unimpressed. How much more advisable it must have appeared to him in 1780 to leave a sinking ship.

Since his judgment here proved wrong, he resigned himself for his remaining thirteen years to study and to works of religion; a few surviving letters to Dundas were in fact perfectly cordial in tone. Only once did he break his public silence, for motives again hard to fathom. It was on the centenary of the Glorious Revolution, in 1788. He preached a sermon with a reference to 'the events now passing on the Continent, which will produce an event which our neighbours will ere long have to celebrate like to that which has called us together'. Few were so prescient about France, or so sanguine about 'the deliverance of so many millions of so great a nation from the follies of arbitrary government'. Dundas would not in later times have recalled these sentiments with approval.[55]

The failure of catholic relief in Scotland was a trauma for the enlightened generally. All the political weight they could muster had been thrown on the side of a self-evidently liberal reform. That had not, however, impressed the people. Hay rubbed it in: 'Poor Scotland! Unhappy, fanatical Scotland! While all the other nations in Europe are adorned with the most humane and liberal sentiments and adopting every measure worthy of civilisation, to you alone is reserved the infamous character of being sunk in your ancient barbarity, and of nourishing in your heart the most ungenerous sentiments of intolerant bigotry!' From a man shortly to betake himself to Spain, this was a bit rich. Yet the so far irresistible force of the Scottish Enlightenment had indeed here come up against an immovable object. That force had to an extent lain in the attack by a forward-looking, increasingly confident elite on a backward, increasingly impotent figure: the ordinary Scotsman with his grim Calvinism and conservative prejudices. A point was now found beyond which he could not be pushed. In science, in literature, in economics and in politics the Enlightenment continued. But the encounter of reason with religion had really been the fountainhead of it all; and with this defeat for reason the impetus of enlightened religion was lost.[56]

All that, however, Dundas himself would surmount. His debacle might well have been blamed for helping to create the atmosphere in which the Gordon Riots broke out the next year in London. Though Scotland then remained quiet, we know that her protestant extremists had meanwhile been urging like-minded Englishmen to get their own Relief Act repealed, and that a delegation of them joined the mob's march on Westminster. The Lord Advocate escaped further censure, but remained chastened. In future, while he did not desist from reform, he was less interested in the bright ideas likely to rally a political constituency at home. To build it up, he concentrated rather on the mechanics of politics, as well as taking great care of his reputation in the South. He may there have followed the advice of well-wishers, most of whom still retained confidence in him. At the very time of the Gordon Riots, Adam Ferguson, professor of moral philosophy at the university of Edinburgh, wrote that

> he has many qualities fitting him to be a considerable man, temper, perse-
> verance, resolution, and what is of most consequence is felt by his friends as
> a man who will not desert them nor trifle with his connection. He has
> likewise shown a disposition to carry the opinion of respectable people along
> with him and as matters now stand if he does not appear to run too fast may
> securely outstrip his competitors. This town has long been thought of
> consequence, my opinion is that the way to gain it is not to make direct
> applications here but to show the possession of power and consideration at
> London.[57]

Dundas continued, however, to woo Edinburgh too. It was, after all, not only his home-town but a political centre of some importance. The man who controlled it disposed of a good deal of legal, civil and ecclesiastical patronage, besides having access to the precocious financial institutions – material to the indigent Dundas. To say that it was the key to Scotland would be a gross exaggeration. But it was without doubt a valuable prize.

It possessed along with other royal burghs distinct political arrangements. They had been represented in the Scots Parliament, and so were all granted a place at Westminster. But as they numbered sixty-six, some tiny, they were divided into districts of four or five, the capital alone keeping a member to itself. That gave them together fifteen seats. These constituencies were for the most part incon-siderable, indeed often subject to magnates in the countryside surrounding them, by whom they could be manipulated in less complex but more demeaning ways than a county would have tolerated. So far from there being any popular franchise, not even the richest and most respected citizens necessarily had the vote. The member was chosen by the town councils which, as variously defined in the sett (or constitution), were composed of certain interests, usually the old merchants' or craftsmen's guilds. Moreover, each council elected its successor, and was naturally inclined to elect itself. A minute fraction of the urban population thus enjoyed the franchise. Edinburgh had no more than thirty-three councillors, while the total sank as low as nine in the smallest burghs, some of them absentees. Irresponsibility, secrecy, lack of real social standing induced in the councils a crass venality, which the Government and other political interests were ever ready to satisfy. At the same time the grouping of scattered burghs (a typical district contained Lanark, Linlithgow, Peebles and Selkirk) made them hard to manage. Each might be suborned by a different local interest, or by someone more distant. That left a degree of independence at least to the larger. The capital in particular was always minded for the sake of its dignity to exercise in its parliamentary representation a free choice, and had to be tactfully coaxed towards a safe one.

There was no uniformity about the setts, so that elections in the burghs caused just as many legal complications as in the counties. In Edinburgh the subtleties were especially fiendish. Ordinarily, the city was governed by a council of twenty-five. It consisted, besides the magistrates, of councillors representing the Merchant Company (members of which enjoyed a monopoly of the chartered trading privileges) and of councillors representing the fourteen incorporated trades: surgeon-barbers, hammermen, goldsmith, baxters, fleshers and so on. The first group were mainly rich importers of wine or exporters of grain. The second might have brought in a more popular element, but seldom did so. To enter an incorporation, a man had to have a residence within the still narrowly drawn bounds of the burgh, and then pay higher taxes. So modest artisans preferred to live outside, beyond the West Port or down the Canongate. In reality, membership of the trades was open to bribes or jobbery just like everything else.

The sett seemed nevertheless grounded in the view that the incorporations were a potential source of popular influence, and sought to contain it. On the ordinary council, they had eight representatives. Two were hand-picked by the magistrates and merchant councillors. The other six had to be elected out of a body of fourteen, one from each trade, proposed for this purpose and known as deacons. Nor was an incorporation even free in its choice of deacon. It had first to draw up a leet of six candidates, of whom the magistrates and merchants struck out three. The deacon could then be selected from the remainder. This obstacle-course was designed to keep the cosy ruling clique free from troublemakers, and only a really determined incorporation could negotiate it. A little solace lay in the fact that the eight deacons not chosen for the ordinary council were entitled to sit on the extraordinary council, which was convened solely in order to elect the member of Parliament. These details may seem trifling, but their significance will become clear.[58]

Internal squabbles still occurred, with the trades intermittently protesting at the shortening of their leets and claiming some reciprocal right to choose the merchant members. The tensions could also represent wider conflicts, as when in 1762 a new majority on the council had re-asserted its right of presentation to the city's churches. The trades had responded by disputing the validity of the poll, in what was clearly an effort to protect the popular party in the Kirk. But on this occasion, as on others, they had been frustrated.

Local politics was then still dominated by the Argathelians under Lord Milton, with a municipal front-man in George Drummond. But inside a year or two they passed from the scene, leaving their ramshackle machine to still lesser men, notably to Gilbert Laurie, a failed lawyer turned apothecary. He ran the council till the mid-1770s, allegedly through introducing a lower class of person into it. Yet the Enlightenment touched him too. In these years, James Craig's design for the New Town was approved, Robert Adam's exquisite Register House was started and plans for the noble thoroughfare of Leith Walk were drawn up. While his fellow-citizens seemed to appreciate his efforts on their behalf, they would not overlook his self-seeking. He too had the sense to see that he could not fully control the council without the backing of a patron more powerful than himself.

Where, during a period of political confusion, was one to be found? Muscling his way in came the Nabob of the North (though also local lad made good), Sir Lawrence Dundas, then sitting in Parliament for an English seat. In 1764 he got himself appointed governor of the Royal Bank of Scotland. In 1767 he piloted through the Commons the Edinburgh Improvement Act, under which the New Town was constructed. And in 1768 he was elected member for the city, after donating lavishly to the Merchant Company and its charities. The merchants observed with notable disingenuity that 'it is more agreeable to our happy consitution that a member be chosen by the free voice of the electors than in consequence of solicitations or other more unwarrantable means.'[59]

Boswell called Sir Lawrence a 'comely, jovial, Scotch gentleman of good address but not bright parts.' He soon turned out a far from ideal choice, with no qualms about using his immense fortune to gratify himself. This did make him, at his best, a benefactor. He raised the money for the Forth-Clyde Canal and at its terminus founded the town of Grangemouth. But like many self-made men he was arrogant and imperious. For example, he appropriated in secret a site at one end of the first New Town, where he built a house, now headquarters of the Royal Bank. It was an elegant house, to be sure, but made a squat and undistinguished finish to what would otherwise have been a noble prospect eastwards along George Street. St Andrew's, originally designated for the spot to match a church at the western end, was instead set awkwardly to one side.[60]

Through a council led by Laurie, Sir Lawrence could be as insolent as he liked. The city soon felt itself a mere prop for his broader ambitions. Dozens of poisonous pamphlets appeared against 'the stout Earl of the German plains', mocking his antecedents, flashiness and yen for a peerage.[61] He was so past bearing that even the municipal worms began to turn. The trades, irate at his snubbing their claims for more say in the council, withdrew support for him at the General Election of 1774. The Lord Provost, James Stoddart, unexpectedly went along with them and contested it himself. Sir Lawrence smothered that attempt by bribery. Though exerting himself to eliminate dissidents, he could not seal the council off. He opened up the city's affairs somewhat by involving in them his heir, together with Thomas's social circle of richer, better connected men, such as the bankers James Hunter (later Hunter Blair) and John Dalrymple, brother of Lord Hailes, who in 1777 became Lord Provost.[62]

The rejuvenation of his interest was also needed to face the challenge soon thrown down by Henry Dundas, well-placed on becoming chief officer of government in Scotland to exploit the divisions for himself. He at once set about seizing patronage in Edinburgh, for example by trying to award Adam Smith a commissionership of customs: but the first time it went to Sir Lawrence's candidate and they were obliged to wait another two years. After the keenly contested municipal elections of 1776,

> clamours were heard over the city, that the trades were an injured and oppressed body; that the shortening of leets was an intolerable grievance;

that they laboured under many other hardships; which, in other words, meant that they had in view many other claims which they intended to assert, as opportunity should occur; but in the mean time, they restricted the object of their complaint to the shortening of leets, being advised by their lawyers that it would be better not to seek too much at once.

Henry was the lawyer who gave that advice. With his backing, the trades appealed in February 1777 to the Convention of Royal Burghs for a corresponding reform of the sett. A majority of the ordinary council, led by Dalrymple, asked the Court of Session to interdict the move. Despite the eloquence of Henry's pleading, it not only did so but, for good measure, made the interdict perpetual. Dalrymple's motives appear to have been not so much to protect Sir Lawrence as to preserve oligarchy. He was in fact playing a double game, as we are about to see.[63]

A cornerstone of Sir Lawrence's power structure was his governorship of the Royal Bank, through which he could organise his local wheeling and dealing. The largest shareholder, he owned £7700 out of a total stock of £110,000. But he was not the city's only tycoon. Edinburgh housed, besides the three public chartered banks, several private ones. Prominent in this sector was William Ramsay of Barnton, chairman of Mansfield & Ramsay, which had recently embarked on a rapid expansion of its holding in the Royal Bank. The market in the shares was not normally active: between 1763 and 1775 dealings averaged only ten a year. Suddenly, in 1776, there were forty-eight. The bulk of the increase came through systematic buying by Mansfield & Ramsay, or agents clearly acting for them. By November the purchases totalled £13,000 of the nominal stock, which would have cost about £25,000.

Some care was taken to restrict the circle of those in the know about these transactions. The document for each transfer had to be countersigned by one of the nine ordinary directors. Five never signed any of the direct transfers to Mansfield & Ramsay. These were evidently the hard core of Sir Lawrence's faction inside the bank, for four of them, including Laurie, were to depart with him. Others signed two or three each, but one signature comes up again and again – Dalrymple's. There must be a strong presumption that he was colluding in Mansfield & Ramsay's purchases, and concealing them from other directors.

Either through him or through Ramsay's partner, Patrick Miller, brother of the Lord Justice Clerk, Henry got wind of all this and saw how it could enable him to overthrow Sir Lawrence at the Royal Bank. He approached Ramsay, who at first was reluctant to help but, urged on by Miller, eventually agreed.[64] So, suddenly in December 1776, Mansfield & Ramsay started to sell – and sell, and sell. Within two months, they got rid of nearly all the shares bought during the previous year. To whom? Why, to Henry Dundas (£600 worth), to the Duke of Buccleuch, to half the senators of the College of Justice and to a whole list of the Lord Advocate's cronies at the Bar and elsewhere. Insider dealing was evidently not something about which Scots law then inclined to worry.

Just as the ground for a coup was thus prepared, Sir Lawrence came all innocently to its aid. He, too, sold some shares: £2000 to his son, much of the rest to solicitors, the stockbrokers of the time, who promptly resold to the opposing camp. He could not, of course, have known how deep the conspiracy ran in the legal establishment. Yet it is altogether unclear why he acted in this way. Perhaps he needed to go liquid for some reason, and the shares were the easiest means of realising cash. Be that as it may, it certainly argues his complete ignorance of the earlier transactions. With only £2000 of stock left in his own name, he soon found himself at Henry's mercy.[65]

In November 1777 a shareholders' meeting was held. Tantalisingly, the record is lost, and only a bare summary survives. There were complaints about the running of the bank, and efforts to limit the directors' terms of office. Sir Lawrence was anyway voted out. A month later another meeting took place 'for the election of a governor in place of the Rt Hon Sir Lawrence Dundas, he having disqualified himself by transferring his stock' – no fulsome explanation, but the silence on details was eloquent enough. Buccleuch became governor, and the rest of the board was filled with Henry's associates. The stock rose steadily in the coming years. Mansfield & Ramsay lamented the losses they thus made by selling at the bottom, yet at least in future they got all the business the Lord Advocate could put in their way. Ramsay later said: 'I most steadily and uniformly used my best endeavours to serve him and his friends.' Henry had won a famous victory not just for himself but for the system he was constructing.[66]

Sir Lawrence still fought back. He had allies among other moneyed men displeased with the outcome, because excluded from Edinburgh's grand new financial confederacy. In the council, his majority held against the assaults, and he at length replaced Dalrymple by his own lackey, Hamilton. In 1778 he curried favour with the Government by prompting the corporation to raise a regiment for service in America. All the leading citizens and public bodies were approached for money. The Faculty of Advocates alone refused, airily declaring that it was a national rather than a merely civic institution, and that in any case its funds could be applied only to its own purposes. One could well see the hand here of Henry, its Dean, who would have been loth to let someone else steal the patriotic mantle, whatever that did for the Faculty's martial reputation. Meanwhile, the Lord Provost made hay of Dundas's problems with catholic relief, while astutely avoiding penalties on the city of the kind which had followed the Porteous Riot.[67]

But time was not on Sir Lawrence's side. Aged 70, gout-ridden, he seemed as far as ever from the peerage he craved. He could obviously expect little of a Ministry which allowed its Lord Advocate to attack him so blatantly. In April 1780 he broke away and voted for Dunning's famous Commons resolution that the influence of the Crown had increased, was increasing and ought to be diminished (against which Henry attempted an inadequate defence). The Whigs' leader, Lord Rockingham, wrote to congratulate Sir Lawrence, or at least, 'I shall not condole with you that you are become an object of the malice and intrigues of the time-serving court party in Scotland.'[68] Edinburgh, which now found itself with an opposition member, was on the other hand not pleased at all: even the Merchant Company protested.

That gave Sir Lawrence's enemies an opportunity when, in September, Parliament was dissolved. Henry put up as rival candidate another scion of clan Miller, William, son of the Lord Justice Clerk. They reckoned that 18 of the 33 on the existing extraordinary council would vote for him. But a municipal election fell due at Michaelmas, September 29. Sir Lawrence calculated that if he could delay the parliamentary poll till afterwards, he could whittle away the hostile majority and secure his own return once again. The writ for the General Election was delivered to Lord Provost Hamilton on September 11. Being conveniently ill, he did not attend the next meeting of the council, on September 13, but merely sent word that the writ had come; to callers he said through a servant that he was in bed and had no other answer to give. At the meeting, the convener of the trades moved that a day for the parliamentary election should immediately be appointed. Others objected, on no good legal grounds, that this could only be done if the Lord Provost was present in person. Ten of the ordinary council and all eight deacons of the extraordinary council voted for the motion. The remaining 14 members of the ordinary council voted against. But which was competent here, the ordinary or the extraordinary council? In Hamilton's absence, the first bailie occupied the chair. He solved the problem by first, in his capacity as preses of the extraordinary council, ordering its members to assemble at six o'clock that evening; and then, as preses of the ordinary council, ordering them not to.

The session in the evening was attended by the 18 but not the 14. They set the parliamentary poll for three days later, when they chose Miller. Sir Lawrence's supporters ignored this, serenely awaiting the municipal election, which restored them to 17 seats, a majority of one, on the new extraordinary council. By that margin, they voted for a polling day early in October, and for Sir Lawrence when it came. His foes spoiled their case by turning up, thus implicitly admitting the procedure was valid. When they petitioned Parliament against the return, arguing that the Lord Provost 'had been for a considerable time deprived of his reason', they lost. According to reformers of later years, these high-jinks caused even Henry to declare it was time to clean out the burghs.[69]

The struggle only ended with Sir Lawrence's death in September 1781. A compromise candidate, Hunter Blair, succeeded as member for the city. Henry was at once resolute, rhapsodic and reflective:

> The party left by Sir Lawrence must be broke, and the town of Edinburgh brought under some respectable patron on which Government can rely, for they must not be permitted to govern the town by a knot of themselves without the imposition of some such patron, for, if they do, the first good opportunity offers some able individual among them who leads the rest will sell them to any rich person like Sir Lawrence whom vanity or desire of being in Parliament might prompt to make the purchase.

If that patron was Buccleuch (which in effect meant himself),

> the whole council of Edinburgh will be completely and permanently placed, as they used to be, in the hands of government. So much for Edinburgh politics, which I shall conclude with one reflection upon the vanity of all human ambition. When Sir Lawrence Dundas laid out £20,000 to build a house in Edinburgh and submitted for these 15 years to every species of disagreeable meanness to establish an interest in the town of Edinburgh, did he ever imagine that he would not only die without a coronet, but that within a few months of his breath being out there should not remain in any of his family the vestige of that interest which cost him so much?[70]

Dundas confided that 'hunting foxes, shooting partridges and laughing with my friends is a much pleasanter business than burgh electioneering.' This was fair comment on his experience so far of Scottish electoral politics, for it had not proved easy to fill the vacuum caused by decay of the old interests. At first, Dundas lacked the wherewithal, full control of patronage. He was thus obsessed with winning the office which would give it to him, that of Keeper of the Signet, who countersigned all royal warrants and commissions in Scotland. In 1777 his wish was granted, at least in part. On the death of the previous keeper he succeeded jointly with Andrew Stuart, veteran of the Douglas Cause and another new Scots member. They were to hold it, however, not – as was usual – for life, but only during His Majesty's pleasure.[71]

That rankled. In March 1779, Dundas wrote to his brother, the Lord President:
> I have decided myself not to be a beggar at the Treasury. I really see no reason why I should. I make more money by following my profession, and why should I court anybody, to receive from them what I can do for myself? When I say all this I have no doubt of accepting the whole signet if offered to me. It would adhere to me through life, and is no doubt an exceeding good office; but to speak plain language, I feel the administration is much more obliged to me than I can ever be to them. I cannot think of going to the Minister to ask him what he ought to beg of me to accept. You may think me very wild, but I cannot help it.[72]

When before long Stuart was found something else, the whole signet could be offered to Dundas, yet still only on pleasure. He was so angry that at first he refused, writing to North that 'in duty to my family I could not agree to accept of an alteration of my present situation on so precarious a tenure'; afterwards he changed his mind. The next year he heard of a minor Scottish sinecure being granted to someone for life, and was quite beside himself over the
> contempt – I will not say disingenuity – with which Lord North has treated me … He has uniformly stated to me with apparent regret that the only reason why I did not get my office for life was a rule His Majesty had adopted of not giving offices for life. It seems however that mine is the only Scotch office – or rather I am the only Scotch person – to which this rule is to be applied … I don't wonder this secret was kept from me with so much care.[73]

Even without the signet for life, however, Dundas had been able to start assembling a political coterie. At the General Election of 1774, while he was capably serving his own apprenticeship in Midlothian, the Dundases united an interest they held through marriage in Lanarkshire with the Duke of Hamilton's interest there to return his man of business, Stuart. The member for Fife, General John Scott, was husband to one of Henry's half-sisters. He also exerted some influence over the members for Selkirkshire and Roxburghshire through Buccleuch. The pair of them backed another crony, Sir Adam Fergusson, spearhead of a coup by the independent gentlemen of Ayrshire against the prevailing magnates' interests.

One biographer has it that, in the subsequent Parliament, Dundas led a faction of twelve, but he cannot be right. Indeed he is demonstrably wrong in respect of

certain members he names: the one in Berwickshire possessed for patron Lord
Marchmont, a foe; Sir Ralph Abercromby in Clackmannanshire was to become a
dear friend of Henry's, but at this stage felt obliged to follow, most unhappily, Sir
Lawrence, to whom he owed the seat; and the member for Dunbarton was put
there by Argyll. Rather, the beginnings of Dundas's interest were much more
modest. For the moment, not more than half a dozen members were reliably acting
in concert with him.[74]

Nor at first did be easily hold what he had. General Scott soon died, after a
riotous life that had brought him wins of £500,000 at the gaming tables. Dundas
was named guardian of his three young daughters. With a personal interest in Fife
thus established, it became important for him to maintain the political interest
too. Yet in this first foray on to debatable land he failed. His candidate, John
Henderson of Fordell, sprang from ancient local stock. But other men of substance
in the constituency, led by the family of Wemyss, decided on a contest, not from
any special animus towards Dundas but from a feeling that Fife was for the Fifers.
Their standard-bearer, James Oswald of Dunnikier, won by 61 votes to 60. On
appeal to the Court of Session, Lord Auchinleck confirmed the result; a judgment
about which Dundas, leading counsel for his own side, was so scathing that
Boswell nearly called him out to a duel. Then, in 1779, Oswald took an official
post. At the subsequent by-election Henderson was again soundly beaten. It was a
far from convincing start to an election manager's career.

With the investment in Edinburgh required of Dundas at the General Election
of 1780, his performance elsewhere was unimpressive. He did bring the venal and
insignificant Dysart Burghs under his control. A stalemate among contending
factions in Ross enabled him to suggest a compromise candidate of his own; it was
a convenient step back into favour, after long exile in Sweden, for his attainted
Jacobite cousin, Lord Macleod. Solicitor General Murray came in for Peeblesshire,
but owed it more to his connections with Queensberry than to any influence
Dundas could exert. And he failed to prevent the return of Sir Lawrence's son,
Charles, for Orkney and Shetland. All except a handful of the Scots members
continued to support the Government. But as most would have done so anyway,
this was no proof of a growth in Henry's personal influence. On the contrary, it
looked still rather meagre, and Scotland remained electorally fragmented.[75]

But he did stand out among the Scots members, most of whom never uttered a
word. If they spoke, they confined themselves to local concerns. Scottish legislation having been rare, they had scant opportunity to address themselves to national
questions anyway. Those who plunged into the affairs of the Union usually forgot
Scotland altogether. Dundas had made up his mind from the outset that he was
going to be in equal measure a Scottish and a British politician. He was the first of
a very few who have successfully played the double role; and his disappointments
in the first were more than compensated by his success in the second.

The memorialist, Nathaniel Wraxall, found Dundas could even turn his accent
to account, for like his father he never affected an English one: 'These very defects
of elocution or of diction, by the ludicrous effects that they produced, became
often converted into advantages, as they unavoidably operated to force a smile
from his bitterest opponents, and chequered with momentary good humour the

personalities of debate.' The impression conveyed was kept under careful control and never let slip, not at least while he was on duty. Yet in March 1778 Horace Walpole related 'a very remarkable incident' when Dundas, in his cups among cronies at one o'clock in the morning, 'broke out into an invective against the English. He said he would move for a repeal of the Union, that any ten Scots could beat any ten English: and if there were any competition, he was, and would avow himself, a Scot.' That, however, did little but add to his reputation as a character in the House.

It married with sterling qualities. According to Wraxall, 'far from shunning the post of danger, he always seemed to court it; and was never deterred from stepping forward to the assistance of Ministers by the violence of opposition, by the unpopularity of the measure to be defended or by the difficulty of the attempt. His speeches, able, animated and argumentative, were delivered without hesitation and unembarrassed by timidity.'[76]

Those qualities were evident even in his maiden speech, on February 16, 1775, when he boldly admonished a Ministry in which he was still the mere Solicitor General for Scotland. The subject he chose was America, now openly preparing for rebellion. North had put forward his so-called olive branch resolutions to forestall it. Dundas declared: 'I can never accede to any concessions whatever ... until the Americans do, in direct terms, acknowledge the absolute supremacy of this country; much less can I consent to such concessions, while they are in arms against it.' A fortnight afterwards, on a Bill to impose trading sanctions against New England, he waxed still fiercer, calling it just and merciful in comparison to what retribution the Americans' disobedience merited: 'When it is said that no alternative is left to the New Englanders but to starve or rebel, this is not the fact, for there is another way, to submit.' The speech won instant notoriety for Dundas's coining of the word starvation, which the English language owes to him. It was fastidiously omitted from the record, but he certainly uttered it, to be drowned by roars of laughter from a House of Latinists. He did not live it down for years, during which he was often referred to as Starvation Dundas. But, never abashed by rough parliamentary treatment, he continued to bang out the theme of no surrender. Indeed he did not often speak on anything other than America.[77]

Claims have been made that the war helped stimulate a liberal political awakening in Scotland. They are not tenable. One independent politician, George Dempster, opposed coercion, as did some prominent seceding or evangelical clerics. Otherwise Scots were notable for flag-waving support of the rights of Crown and Parliament. They had nothing to gain by seeming to countenance disloyalty. Even their genuine approval of the war was turned against them by an extreme antagonist like Horace Walpole: 'If the conquest of America should be achieved, the moment of the victorious army's return would be the destruction of our liberty. That army had been sent to fight for prerogative, was disciplined by Jacobite Scots and was to combat men that fought for freedom.' Nor was he alone in such egregious sentiments. Newspapers in London ranted about the 'ruinous Scotch contest with the Anglo-Americans' or the 'Scotch quarrel with English liberty'.[78]

The most vocal Scots opinion, represented by Dundas and friends, did indeed urge the hardest possible line in America. They acted in the Commons with others such as Alexander Wedderburn, Solicitor General for England (though also alumnus of the grammar school at Dalkeith) and Lord George Germain, whose pugnacity sat strangely with his own cowardly military record, including the persecution of helpless Highlanders after 1745. Germain it was, however, who took the reward after his group had proved itself right about the failure of the Government's initial bid for a compromise. At the end of 1775 he was appointed Secretary of State for the Colonies. The warmongers enjoyed an ascendancy till the first major British defeat at Saratoga in 1777.

This, followed by France's joining in on the rebels' side, gave everyone pause, not least Dundas. On the Ministry's again proposing conciliation in January 1778, he issued a veiled challenge to North to say if the war could still be won, though he was taken at the time as imputing bad faith. George III waxed furious:

> The more I think on the conduct of the Advocate of Scotland the more I am incensed against him; more favours have been heaped on the shoulders of that man than were ever bestowed on any Scotch lawyer, and he seems studiously to embrace any opportunity to create difficulties; but men of talents when not accompanied by integrity are pests instead of blessings to society and true wisdom ought to crush them rather than nourish them.

It was thus, contrary to what has been written elsewhere, his insubordination rather than sycophancy that offended.[79]

His views certainly grew more supple. In March he said he had been for taxing America while he thought it practicable, but had now seen it was not: 'No miraculous illumination can ever persuade me that government should attempt impracticable things.' So, he deduced, conciliation had to be tried. He even toyed with the idea of offering some form of federal union, rather than losing America altogether or letting her fall into the hands of France. Later, when the war reached stalemate, and later still, when fortune attended British arms in the southern colonies, he once more seemed to turn aggressive: 'A vigorous continuation of operations against [France] and against America will make both the one and the other wish for a dissolution of their treaty. America at present owes more than she can pay. Her debt is enormous. The present Ministry are almost sure of success if they pursue the American war with vigour.' As late as the summer of 1781, he called for Britain 'to exert all her powers and strength in order to reduce her subjects ... to acknowledge the sovereignty of the British legislature in as full and ample a manner as it had heretofore exercised and enjoyed it.' But this was the last time he spoke in such a way. By then he was dissembling.[80]

It has been suggested that Dundas performed these twists and turns solely to ingratiate himself with North.[81] That was, however, belied by what might nowadays be called his semi-detached attitude to the Ministry, which the King was not the only one to notice. If in those times no doctrine of collective responsibility really existed, he went further out of his way than most to stress that his support had to be earned. As the war dragged indecisively on and on, and parliamentary approbation of it wavered, it was rather North who had to pander to him. Being one of the few on the Treasury bench who could command the Commons' respect, Dundas was becoming indispensable, and he knew it.

Wisely avoiding absolute commitment to any point of view, he allowed himself to be guided by his realism. He was bellicose when victory seemed possible, much more cautious in periods of adversity. From his private correspondence it is clear that by the end of 1780 he had decided the war could not be won. This assessment came in a letter to Edward Thurlow, now Lord Chancellor of England, in October: 'Although my expectations were almost at an end, respecting America, previous to the success at Charleston, after that event I was full of hopes the business might still be done. I am now completely satisfied that the attempt is impracticable and consequently the pursuit of it wicked.' But he was biding his time to make this judgment public.

A year later, things went obviously and terribly wrong, with the siege and surrender of Yorktown. Britain had irrevocably lost the struggle, though she continued to fight, in ever-growing weariness, for another two years. Dundas, at Melville when the news arrived, immediately saw to the bottom of the situation. He wasted no time in setting off for London, where Parliament was about to reassemble. Yet the King's speech opening the session ignored what had happened. The realist in Dundas was appalled. It prompted his most significant intervention in the Commons to date, with one of those rare performances that actually swayed events.

When he rose on November 28 he started out, after a survey of the position, by restating his former view – for old times' sake, as it were – that victory would only come through yet more 'vigorous exertion' (which he and almost everyone else knew to be impossible). The alternative lay in accepting that victory would elude Britain, a message delivered not bluntly but through telling verbal gestures. Germain, he said, had acted a very manly part by sticking openly to his hard line – if he continued with it, he would have an opportunity of acting a still more manly part. In other words, he should recognise his policy as bankrupt and resign. Striking also was this passage: 'That minister who, to preserve his situation, can submit to concur in measures he condemns must be one of the meanest of mortals; he betrays his trust and deserves the execration of his country … The minister who sacrifices his opinion to preserve his situation is unfit for society.' And, the unspoken implication ran, that minister – North – ought to resign unless he could change the measures.[82]

Nobody who heard him doubted that what he had to say was important, but some could not quite see how. Walpole wrote: 'With all this air of frankness, few knew what he meant, nor whom he meant to blame, and the more he was pressed the more obscure and shuffling he grew.'[83] Fox tried to pin him down, but Dundas wriggled out of a direct reply. The performance rested on a degree of mystification, yet to those with ears to hear the message came over. Dundas, so far a hawk in public, was breaking the Government's facade of unity and revealing within it men like himself who now differed little from the opposition's view that the fighting had somehow to be ended. Fox latched on to that, a few days later approaching him privately to ask if the Cabinet was really about to change its mind. He replied, 'I believe not, but do press them.'[84]

The great obstacle was the King, refusing to renounce the sovereignty over America which he was incapable of exercising. What his bluster and obduracy could bring instead, as Dundas descried, was more military disasters and, quite likely, ruin to the careers of all those who continued to serve loyally in his Government. The prospects in that direction were grim indeed. Short of disaster, the only chance of a change in course lay through emboldening, as the speech was also designed to do, those who acknowledged with Dundas that an impasse had been reached. It was a remarkably daring and astute stance to be taken up by a still minor politician, with as much to lose as to gain from saying the unsayable, articulating the flaws in an untenable policy. Dundas performed a service for British politics, indeed for British history, and the event vindicated him.

That Dundas himself knew what he was about showed clearly in a letter he wrote next day to his brother:

> Matters here are in a very extraordinary state. It is said that His Majesty, notwithstanding the experience we have of the impracticability of con-tinual war, still adheres to the plan ... It is my belief that if a new army is moved in Parliament to be sent to America ... Government will be beat upon the question. I for one shall certainly oppose it, if the consequence should be a forfeiture of all the favour I have hitherto enjoyed, and of all the views of ambition I may have looked to in the future ... I have communi-cated these sentiments in private, and I spoke in a manner last night in the House of Commons which must soon compel administration to take their ground one way or another. I believe they felt it as the severest bomb ever thrown among them. I was happy they did, as I meant they should.[85]

Having taken the initiative, he pressed forward. The logical next step was to get sacked from the Cabinet the two Ministers urging a struggle to the bitter end, Germain and the Earl of Sandwich, First Lord of the Admiralty. Over Christmas and New Year, Dundas returned to Scotland, whence he wrote to North demand-ing dismissal of Germain in particular. No sentiment was wasted on a once close ally: 'While he remains everybody must believe it to be the resolution of His Majesty's servants that this country never was to have peace except upon terms which never could nor would be obtained.'

Yet the Prime Minister, finding it hard enough to scrape along on shrinking majorities, could see no purpose in losing Germain's services in the Commons while the King remained stubbornly against peace anyway. So by the time Parliament resumed towards the end of January 1782, nothing had happened. Dundas's place was empty. He came ostentatiously late the next day, but promptly left again, saying he would not return while Germain stayed in office. North was being forced to choose. He being, as others noted, 'strongly impressed with a fear of displeasing the Lord Advocate', there could be little doubt of the outcome. For if Dundas was the one to go, the Government's Scottish votes would doubtless go with him, and it would collapse at once. The axe therefore fell on Germain. He consented to depart in return for a peerage; at the final interview with his monarch, he managed to get the offer of a baron's rank raised to a viscount's. The offensive against Sandwich ended with an inquiry into his conduct. While refusing to utter a word in his defence, Dundas was at least persuaded to come down and sit on the front bench during the debate. 'The Lord Advocate will be satisfied with one human sacrifice,' North's secretary wrote.[86]

Rather, Dundas blithely took the chance of demanding once more the signet for life. The Prime Minister, needing to make fast his present support, though also genuinely wishing to reward him with some insurance for the future, gamely took this up again with the King:

> He has really, Sir, been the principal and almost the only support of Your Majesty's business in the House of Commons during these two or three years past: I could not have gone on without him, and in these last and most troublesome times he has stood so boldly and so openly against the opposition that he will probably be proposed as one of the first sacrifices. It seems good policy to protect in such a situation those who have, in a distinguished manner, stood forth in defence of the Government.

North tried repeatedly, right till his last days in office, but to no avail.[87]

Dundas was still not making things easy for his chief. He wanted the Ministry to survive if possible, but would brook no false prospectus, as his next speech to the Commons showed:

> The very reason that induces me to stand and confess the wish for peace in America is the very reason that made [Germain's] retreat necessary, that is to say, the very important and essential change in the affairs of the country. I was extremely happy to find, when the noble lord's retreat became necessary, that the Crown had been advised to render it honourable and dignified. It is right to show to the nation at large that the noble lord's conduct in office was approved, and that it was not from any sense of incapacity, neglect or error in any part of it that his services were dispensed with, but merely because, such was the unfortunate situation of our affairs that the noble lord's principles were no longer practicable.[88]

If peace was surely on the way, Dundas admitted to himself that time was in any event running out for the Ministry. To his brother, on March 9, the morning after another narrow vote, he stated that 'it is impossible the present administration can go on'. He told how North had recently called him in for a confidential talk and asked what to do. 'I answered without reserve and hesitation, because I thought so, that it was his duty to intimate to the King that with so strong an opposition he could not carry on the Government of the country longer, but I thought it was his duty all the same not to leave the country in immediate distress.' Though the King was trying to find extra support, Dundas forecast he would fail. 'If he had followed the advice which even so insignificant an individual as I gave him repeatedly in the early part of the winter he would now have a strong and connected government. By the delays and consequences of them, I think he will now be obliged to throw himself into the hands of the opposition.'[89]

In public, though, Dundas pushed the less drastic solution. When the Government's enemies made another attempt to break the camel's back on March 15, he accepted that 'a coalition of parties seems to be the general desire of the House.' He shared it, but still advised against voting down the present Ministry because that 'puts the Government into the hands of the opposition alone ... A coalition can only be formed by the substantial union and connection of all parties, and not by driving out half of those who ought to compose it.' So if a coalition was desired, the administration should stay on meanwhile. This time its majority was only nine, even with the twenty-nine Scots votes which were thus truly keeping North in office. For him, however, enough was enough. Faced with yet another motion of censure on March 20, he did not wait to confront it, but resigned.[90]

That unleashed one of the longest and deepest crises in British political history. During its course, great changes took place. The first Empire was given up. The experiment in government by royal prerogative came to an end. A new ministerial constellation was formed. Amid the upheavals, some men's careers were ruined, others' were made. Dundas's was one of the latter.

For the rest, George III might be pilloried as a tyrant by Whig oligarchs struggling to regain power, but he was dourly intent, if with no great intelligence, on maintaining what he saw as the national interest against political intrigue. He had tried so far to do it through North, who was likable, droll, resourceful, sensitive and a master of the House of Commons, yet also timid and lazy, thus disinclined to defy his master and vacillating in crises. The parliamentary opposition now given its chance consisted of two main groups. One had followed the late William Pitt the elder, and had since followed Lord Shelburne. He, if also genuinely committed to reform, was a thinker rather than a doer, his aloof, devious manner vitiating any leadership qualities he possessed – though his party had gained much strength by the entry into the Commons in 1780 of the younger Pitt, from the outset universally admired. The other group were the adherents of Rockingham, a faction which had survived the vicissitudes of twenty years. Its most formidable member was Fox, the learned rake, the sincere but injudicious champion of liberty.

The King reluctantly took Rockingham as his Prime Minister, who came in on detailed conditions: end of the war, no royal veto, public economy, a ministerial purge. Dundas, upset about the signet, wanted to go out with North. He was dissuaded by Thurlow, himself transferring to the new Government, who said

> that I was throwing away the greatest game that any man ever possessed – that administration was formed out of inveterate factions jealous of each other, and united only by the desire of getting into office – that the jarrings were already begun – that I had nothing to do but coolly and temperately to lay by; and that within a month I would be courted by both parties.

So it proved.

By the roundabout route of Adam Smith and Edmund Burke, Dundas let Rockingham know he was ready to move over too. He thus got himself kept on as Lord Advocate. Again, though, he made clear his support could not be taken for granted: 'I will not pledge myself to support Ministers in any particular motion, but I will attend day by day and give them every support in my power to measures I think for the public good.' In private, he warned his new colleagues that 'unless they change their ideas of government, and personal behaviour to the King, I do not believe they will remain three months.' Dundas shrewdly saw that the monarch, though battered by defeat, was yet unbowed. If he could not sustain his own unpopular Ministry, he might still make life impossible for a successor. He mistrusted his Prime Minister; of the Secretaries of State, he detested Fox, though he could tolerate Shelburne. Advertising these preferences, he found it all too easy to provoke dissension among them. Within the time forecast by Dundas, the Whigs were reduced to chaos. Then, in July, Rockingham died.[91]

The sovereign turned to Shelburne, who formed a Cabinet from his own faction, with Pitt as Chancellor of the Exchequer. Rockingham's followers, now led by Fox, joined North in opposition. The new administration was thus still shakier than the old, relying for survival on its foes' divisions. Scottish votes were needed more than ever, and Dundas could serve on as Lord Advocate in his third Government. He made the signet for life his price. Stuart was sent to plead the case to Shelburne with all an advocate's pathos. His report back to Dundas on the exchanges told how he had harped away on

> the apparent distrust of you, in not giving you the office during life ... it was not only your own opinion but that of your friends that you ought by no means to quit your profession and embark on the ocean of politics, attended with some great uncertainties, without having at least something secured that was permanent and beyond the reach of accidents.

Shelburne agreed, but still George managed to procrastinate for a few more months – at the end of which, however, the boon was at last granted. 'I feel myself much upon velvet,' an ecstatic Dundas said.

To keep him quiet meanwhile, he was made Treasurer of the Navy. By convention, he had then to go to the trouble of fighting a by-election in his own seat. So vital were his services that Shelburne could not even let him out of Parliament for as long as it took. He arranged for Dundas to represent in the intervening weeks the rotten borough of Newtown, Isle of Wight, available at once to the Government for a consideration to its patron.

Shelburne's main business was to make peace. During the negotiations, he squandered an anyway meagre stock of political goodwill. Tactlessly failing to take even the Cabinet, let alone Parliament, into his confidence, he then over-whelmed both with technical detail when he saw fit to reveal his exhaustive plans. He appreciated himself that he could not last, and vouchsafed the fact to Dundas in February 1783: 'I find that it will now be necessary for me to quit the Government, and as you are beloved by all parties, I wished you to have early notice of it, that you might be prepared for what must happen.'[92]

The solicitude was generous, for to Dundas, a man with little social or financial security, the political dangers now grew acute. The King's own preferred Prime Minister had fallen. So had, in succession, the leaders of the two great Whig connections. Who could possibly follow? Keeping cool, Dundas was clear-sighted enough to analyse matters at length in a letter to his brother.[93] 'Lord Shelburne hates Fox and vice versa,' he began, which was true. After their service together in Rockingham's Cabinet, Fox had cast Shelburne as a dissembling royal catspaw; their alliance was impossible. But Shelburne, the letter continued, 'of course has all along wished a coalition with Lord North to which his lordship was not averse.' It would besides be the most congenial to Dundas himself. Moreover, North was anxious to regain office because, in opposition, he felt vulnerable to impeachment for his conduct of the war. The stumbling block here was Pitt, who like his father thought North a villainous buffoon. No administration could hold them both, and Shelburne could not dispense with Pitt.

The latter's filial piety might dictate a quite different course. 'On the other hand,' as the letter further reasoned, 'Mr Pitt and the rest of the Ministers preferred and urged a coalition with Mr Fox and the Rockinghams.' For Dundas, though, that coalition would be utterly disastrous, spelling probably the end of his political career: he could not serve in it and it would be too strong to overthrow. To such a pass he was, however, not yet come, for 'while they are disputing about this some material friends of Mr Fox and Lord North had been successful in getting them together, and they will this day concur in some amendment to the Address and I shall think it odd indeed if they do not beat us.' The problem with this permutation was that Fox, more than anyone else, had brought North down, and that, on the vital questions of royal power and constitutional reform, they were diametrically opposed. Yet if North sought immunity, it almost had to be in alliance with Fox, for nobody else could assure him of it.

Dundas amused himself at a prospect which, from the divers points of view of everyone involved, was just the lesser of two evils, so perhaps the most likely to come about. Speaking on the amendment, he mocked its caution: 'The more I consider it, the more I am surprised. Could not the two noble lords [sic – he meant Fox and North], in the honeymoon of their loves, have begotten a more vigorous offspring? Is such a sickly child the first-born of such able parents, and are they obliged to usher it into life in a condition so rickety and impotent?'[94]

His wit could not prevent the amendment being carried against the Government, which crumbled a week later. Dundas reported in detail back to Arniston on the manoeuvres of the hectic final days of February, but he was no less baffled than everybody else as to where it would all end. Urgent business, not least conclusion of the peace, remained undone while Westminster presented a distracted scene of nerve-racked commotion and duplicity. Dundas was engaged daily in consultations so complex that at first he hardly took notice when, in a casual aside, Shelburne ventured that they might all end up serving under Pitt. But somehow the words lodged themselves in his mind, and they later came back to him in a flash of inspiration. He sat down and penned an excited note to Shelburne, urging that they should indeed line up behind Pitt. 'There is scarce another political character of consideration in the country to whom so many people from habits, from connections, from former professions, from rivalships and from antipathies will not have objections. But he is perfectly new ground.'[95]

Here at last was an imaginative solution to the crisis, which would at the same time avert the dangers to himself; though clearly the idea was not his, as he later claimed. Like others he had admired Pitt's debut in public life, taking the occasion of his maiden speech in June 1781 to praise his 'first-rate abilities, high integrity, a bold and honest independency of conduct and the most persuasive eloquence.' Initially, however, they had nothing much to offer one another. When Pitt began to stake his claims for political recognition with a motion for parliamentary reform in May 1782, Dundas voted against. A year later, to much ribaldry from his fellow members, he was to support a repeat of it. He had not been converted to the idea but, since he knew the motion would fall anyway, might safely pay this compliment to a man potentially useful to him.[96]

Stating indeed that 'if ever I engage in politics again it will only be at the instigation of Mr Pitt,' he now moved fast. A delegation of Dundas, Shelburne and Thurlow went to the King and advised him to call for Pitt. Their monarch was not less pleased with the ploy than they. Only the young man himself took pause. He asked for time to reflect, during which he was constantly visited by Dundas, who went over the state of the Commons trying to demonstrate that there was a majority there for the asking. He bubbled in anticipation of success: 'Not a human being has a suspicion of the plan, except those in the immediate confidence of it. It will create all universal consternation in the allied camp the moment it is known.'[97] But after two days he wrote to his brother describing how he had met Pitt at eight that morning and left him at eleven apparently resolved to accept the King's commission. Now it was two in the afternoon and he had just received a letter shattering his hopes. Pitt after all declined. He judged that the time was not ripe, chiefly because he could not be certain how North would react: 'I see that the main and almost only·ground of reliance would be this, that Lord North and his friends would not continue in a combination to oppose. In point of prudence, after all that has passed and considering all that is to come, such a reliance is too precarious to act on.' Dundas, who had reassured him on this very question, was mortified: 'I don't think I shall give myself any more trouble in the matter.'

Yet on reflection he was impressed by such coolness. He kept in touch and constantly urged to others his view that a Ministry under Pitt would be the cleanest end to the country's troubles. A little later, the young man undertook to accept a renewed offer if Fox and North failed to get their coalition together and no alternative was available. This set Dundas off again. On March 24, he informed his brother: 'I have seen him this morning and although I shall not be sanguine upon anything till it is actually fixed, I flatter myself that Mr Pitt will kiss hands as First Lord of the Treasury on Wednesday next.' The following day, the Tuesday, it was all over: 'I have altered my mind: and it is now my opinion that Mr Pitt will not accept of the Government. How all this anarchy is to end God only knows.'[98]

How it ended for the time being was indeed in the junction of Fox and North as Secretaries of State under the nominal leadership of the Duke of Portland – 'yon mixtie-maxtie queer hotch-potch, the coalition', in Burns's words. Incredibly, Dundas, who during six weeks' interregnum had done more than almost anybody else to prevent it, stayed on as Lord Advocate, though not as Treasurer of the Navy. He even managed to bring in as Solicitor General, after Murray's elevation to the Bench, his crony Ilay Campbell.

To him Dundas explained his position as the chief officer of government in Scotland in a letter which gives a striking insight into the political confusion and difficulty of the period. With the coalition,

> I certainly mean to have no connection, nor indeed with any administration of which Mr Pitt is not an effective part. Neither he nor I mean to go into opposition nor to be parts of any faction, but to act a fair, candid and honourable public part. Whether therefore I shall give any support to the new administration must depend entirely upon the measures they bring forward. As for the Advocate's gown I certainly do not mean to resign it, nor do I even suspect the new administration will wish me to do so, as it would be the badge of immediate direct hostility to their Government. If I cease therefore to be King's Advocate it must be by their turning me out which I believe they will not be rash in doing.

His still quite good relations with North were the basis of this confidence. He was reckoning, however, without the enmity of Fox, into whose hands he cavalierly played by boasting that 'no man in Scotland will venture to take my place.' Such insolence could not be long tolerated, and a terse letter of dismissal arrived in August.

There followed an attempt by a disparate band of Whigs to seize the local reins of power, through an alliance between Sir Thomas Dundas of Castlecary and the Foxites' chief election agent, William Adam, member for the Wigtown Burghs. The post of Lord Advocate went to Henry Erskine, and that of Solicitor General to Andrew Wight who, perhaps ominously, was an expert on the electoral system. But neither law officer sat in Parliament and neither had time to get there, so that their reformers' credentials went untested.[99]

Erskine was courteously congratulated: 'You will not expect from me to say that I approve the change, but you may believe me to be very cordial and sincere in wishing you all health and happiness to enjoy it.' A meeting in Parliament House proved tenser, allowing the new Lord Advocate to score with a couple of his ghastly puns, unaccountably much admired by contemporaries. After some conversation he broke off, saying he must go and order the silk gown of his office. Dundas interjected: 'It is hardly worthwhile for the time you will want it. You had better borrow mine.' Erskine returned: 'I have no doubt that the gown is a gown made to fit any party: but however short my time in office may be, it shall never be said of Henry Erskine that he adopted the abandoned habits of his predecessor.'[100]

Dundas was not downcast by this or his general position. On the contrary, his problems had been solved for him. He had to commit himself to Pitt, whose renunciations made clear he was nobody's pawn and would not take power save on his own terms. Dundas, never a royal favourite himself, was still objective enough to see that the Whigs' renascence, arising more from others' failures than from their own successes, could not crush the monarchy and decisively tip the constitutional balance their way. But means had to be found, now that George III was discredited, of restoring the moral authority of the state. A Government under Pitt might offer the means. Even then, someone had to take the young man in hand for the manoeuvres leading to this goal. Dundas, who knew the Commons like the back of his hand and could ceaselessly calculate the effects of shifts within it, was perfectly suited to the task. He and the King were called by Lord Rosebery 'the most acute political tacticians of their time.' In more homely terms, Burns admired 'a chap that's damned auldfarran, Dundas his name.'

Dundas thus became a partisan, if in a party hardly formed. But it ended a time during which, according to Boswell, he was 'a Swiss to every Ministry'. He has been much abused for it. But what else could be do? He was not a great lord. He had no money. His future depended on practical success in his chosen profession of politics, and he had to work with the situation as given. A realistic readiness to tack about was, amid such turbulence, the only sensible course for a man like him. With so many changing sides, it could scarcely count to his discredit if he did so with the best of them; and in fact right till his dismissal he was as loyal to North as circumstances permitted.[101]

Shrewd judgment and timely action in London compensated for what had eluded him at home. He said as much to his favourite nephew, Robert:

They must be blind indeed who can suppose that my power in Scotland arose from my being King's Advocate. In my hands it was a very good concomitant, but in itself independent of talents and consequence in the House of Commons, I hold it as nothing. What consequence in Scotland, although most respectable as Crown lawyers, did either Miller or Montgomery derive from that situation? I doubt much if any of them ever named a tide-waiter [nominated a customs officer].[102]

He had at least set out in pursuit of the right goal, to represent and promote the Scottish landed interest. He had thus done something new in his country's politics by devising an ideology, not of a party (for Scots were indifferent to parties) yet certainly of a class, the only one able to fill the vacuum in national leadership. If no idealist, he was an intelligent man with a certain idea of how Scotland could be well governed. In that, he showed himself more confident and assertive than anyone else since the Union. He was progressive too, though cautiously so, elaborately building consensus well in advance of his moves. Unfortunately this meant that little actually got done: his one effort at moving ahead of opinion proved a grave mistake. But Scotland was not geared to active and efficient government, nor to the political processes normal elsewhere. The mechanisms had to be constructed almost from scratch, and in the face of many vested interests. It was no surprise that inexperience, in him and in the system, produced setbacks.

During Dundas's temporary eclipse at Westminster, George III set about the destruction of Fox and North. Their coalition was a failure, solving no problems and scandalising much of the political nation, especially with its East India Bill, seen as a conspiracy for seizing enough patronage to place it in permanent power. Exposing that, Dundas (as well as everything else already an Indian expert) made himself extremely useful in opposition. But the King would not have the Bill anyway. He induced the Lords to throw it out on December 18. Pitt and Dundas, who had met continually since this final crisis began, were ready with a new Government. The next day, Dundas sought his seat on the opposition front bench. North, who the night before had sent his seals to the palace without going there, came and sat beside him. Then Fox entered, seized Dundas by the arm and cried: 'What business have you here? Go over to the Treasury bench!' He obeyed, taking the place he was not to leave for more than seventeen years.[103]

Notes

1. Murdoch (1988), 138; Brooke & Namier (1964), ii, 168 et seq.
2. Notestein (1946), 244–5.
3. Pottle & Ryskamp (1963), 268.
4. Brady (1965), 74; Brooke & Namier, ii, 357; Kay (1877), ii, 404; Christie (1958), 213.
5. Pottle & Ryskamp, 204.
6. Phillipson (1981), 38.
7. *The Mirror* (1781), iii, 339.
8. Sinclair (1905), 140–3; Couper (1908), 138; Cockburn, H.A. (1910), 142; Craig (1931), 28–9; Phillipson, 26; Dwyer, Mason & Murdoch (1982), 5, 222–3; Dwyer (1987), 24–41.

9. Dwyer & Murdoch (1982); Chitnis (1986); Riley (1984), 10; Brewer (1988), 155 et seqq.
10. Brooke & Namier, iii, 183; Malcolm (1942), 134; Furber (1931), 5–6; Matheson (1933), 51; WLC, July 22, 28, Dec. 31, 1776.
11. Arnot (1777), 16; Boswell (1924), iii, 213; Ross (1972), 146.
12. Campbell (1964), 18; Campbell & Dow (1968), 114–15.
13. Fergusson (1947), 119–22; Thorne (1986), 70 et seqq.; Anon. (1782d), 12.
14. Brooke & Namier, 478.
15. *Scots Magazine*, xxxvii, (1775), 569; Craik (1901) ii, 60; Kelly (1984), 178–9.
16. Meikle (1912), 27; Dwyer & Murdoch, 238–9; Ferguson (1957) 38–9, 93; Arnot, 2; Anon. (1782d), 19; SRO GD 51/1/196.
17. Meikle, 11–13; Thorne, loc. cit.; Fry (1987), 8.
18. Lenman (1977), 99–100.
19. Minto Papers, NLS MS 11140, f.1; MS 60, passim.
20. Auckland Papers BL Add MSS 34416, ff. 470, 472; SRO GD 51/1/355; Browning (1886), 308; Mossner & Ross (1977), 240; Skinner & Wilson (1975), 458.
21. *Parl. Hist.*, xx, cols. 1130, 1215.
22. Lenman, 136; Teichgraeber (1987), 351 et seqq.
23. Ward (1954–5), 289–306.
24. Brewer (1988), 23, 132; NLS MS 9370, f. 3; SRO GD 51/5/363; WLC, Nov. 2, 1782.
25. Auckland Papers, BL Add MSS 34412, ff. 352 et seqq; Campbell & Dow, 2; Fay (1956), 11 et seqq; Bumsted (1978), 78; (1982), 23; Bailyn (1986), 9, 26, 41–54, 57–70, 92, 394–9.
26. Seafield Muniments SRO GD 248/52/1/23; Bumsted, loc. cit.; Matheson, 38.
27. Robertson (1985), 112–14.
28. Seafield Muniments SRO GD 248/52/1/109; Buccleuch Papers, SRO GD 224/30/10/2.
29. Robertson, 129–32; Murdoch (1988), 135.
30. Robertson, 136–41, 169.
31. NLS MS 547, 29.
32. Dalzel (1793), xxxvi.
33. Sher (1985), 136ff; Phillipson (1975), 426.
34. Darragh (1953), 50; Macdonald (1964), 140 et seqq.
35. Donovan (1984), 188 et seqq.
36. Cooney (1983), 13.
37. Scottish Catholic Archive [thereinafter SCA], Scottish Mission Papers, 4/15/1, 5/19/10.
38. Cooney, loc.cit.; SCA, Thomson-Macpherson Papers, History of the Scottish Mission, sect. 13, 1778, 5.
39. ibid.
40. *Parl. Hist.*, xix, col. 1142; Sher, 280; Gordon (1867), 148.
41. SCA, Blairs Letters, 3/307/2.
42. Sher, loc.cit.
43. Donovan (1990), 82, 88, 90; Moncreiff Wellwood (1818), 278.
44. Donovan (1979), 62 et seqq.; Forbes Leith (1909), 371.
45. SCA, Scottish Mission Papers, 4/16/3, 4/17/2. 4/40/6; Anon., (1780a), 32 et seq.
46. SCA, Scottish Mission Papers, 4/17/2; Anon., (1780c), 301.

47. ibid., Thomson-Macpherson Papers, sect. 13, 1779 (5).

48. ibid., Scottish Mission Papers, 4/17/10; HO SRO RH 2/4/87/85.

49. ibid., Scottish Mission Papers, 4/40/9, 7.

50. ibid., 4/40/8; Anon., (1779a), passim.

51. Black (1963), 146; Sher, loc.cit.; SCA , Blairs Letters, 3/309/11.

52. Black, loc.cit.; SCA, Scottish Mission Papers, 4/19/1–2.

53. *Parl. Hist.*, xx, col. 280.

54. SCA, Scottish Mission Papers, 4/40/6; Anon., (1780a), 49–55.

55. Note by Sir Henry Moncreiff Wellwood in Stewart (1802), 297; Stanley (1879), 128; Clark I. D. L. (1963), 95, 406–7.

56. SCA, Scottish Mission Papers, 4/17/6.

57. Donovan, loc.cit.; SCA, Thomson-Macpherson Papers, sect. 13, 1780 (3); Writings and Notes of Sir Walter Scott, NLS MS 1583, f. 108.

58. Murdoch (1983), 1 et seqq; Colston (1891), xlvi et seq.

59. Arnot (1779), 517; Murdoch, loc.cit; Wood (1932), 73.

60. Pottle & Ryskamp, 5; Catford (1975), 114; Youngson (1966), 83–4.

61. Dwyer & Murdoch, 241.

62. Grant (1883), ii. 282; Brooke & Namier, 502; Arnot, 517; Wood, 77.

63. Arnot, loc.cit; Warner (1988), 77; Innes of Stow Papers, SRO GD 113/283/9.

64. Royal Bank of Scotland Archives, dividend book, dividend no. 96, midsummer 1775; transfer book, 1763–1778, nos. 721–50; Checkland (1975), 158–9.

65. Royal Bank of Scotland Archives, transfer book nos. 751–99; Innes of Stow Papers, loc.cit.

66. Royal Bank of Scotland Archives, notes from the minutes of the General Court of Proprietors, November 25, 1777; minutes of the Court of Directors, xii, 218; Checkland, loc.cit.

67. Murdoch (1981), 158.

68. Brooke & Namier, 360.

69. Heron (1903), 107; Bell (1812), 499 et seqq; Wight (1784), 378–99; Cunninghame Graham Muniments, SRO GD 22/1/315/45.

70. Furber (1931), 196.

71. Walpole (1845), ii, 94; Matheson, 45; Bricke (1972), 25.

72. Matheson, 54.

73. Ibid., 56–7, 66.

74. Matheson, 66; Brooke & Namier, 470–510, passim.

74. Brooke & Namier, i, 354.

76. Wheatley (1884), i, 426; Steuart (1910), 153–4.

77. *Parl. Hist.*, xviii, cols 332, 387.

78. Meikle (1912); Fagerstrom (1954), 254 et seqq; Colley (1989), 177.

79. *Parl. Hist.*, xix, col. 803; Fortescue (1928), iv, 41.

80. *Parl. Hist.*, xix, col. 951, xx, col. 338; HMC, lxxii, Laing MSS, ii, 503.

81. Lenman (1981), 71.

82. *Parl. Hist.*, xxii, cols. 493, 735–40; SRO GD 51/1/3.

83. Walpole, ii, 478.

84. Russell (1853–7), i, 270.

85. SRO GD 51/17/117, 81.

86. Fortescue, v, 332, 359, 361; Christie, 283 et seqq; Brooke & Namier, i, 354; Matheson, 75.

87. Fortescue (1927), 105, 117; Brooke & Namier, loc.cit.

88. Christie, 324–5.

89. Durdans Books, NLS MS 10225, f.1; SRO GD 51/17/117, 100.

90. ibid., Christie, 339, 355.
91. Durdans Books, NLS MS 10225, 6, 11; SRO GD 51/117/17/115; Burke (1963), iv, 448.
92. Cannon (1969), 26; Fortescue, vi, 81; Brooke & Namier, loc.cit.; Fitzmaurice (1876), iii, 343.
93. Cannon, 44–9; Matheson, 85; Durdans Books, NLS MS 10225, 28; SRO GD 51/117/17, 156.
94. *Parl. Hist.*, xxiii, col. 469.
95. Stanhope (1879), i, 83; SRO GD 51/17/117, 160; Durdans Books, NLS MS 10225, 33, 35; Rose (1911), 125.
96. *Parl. Hist.*, xxii, col. 493; Matheson, 91; Durdans Books, NLS MS 10225, 31.
97. Stanhope, loc.cit; Durdans Books, NLS MS 10225, 30.
98. Burns, ed. Kinsley (1968), 153.
99. Durdans Books, NLS MS 10225, 41, 44; Burns, ibid., i, 88–9; SRO GD 51/17/117, 187; Campbell of Succoth Papers, TD 219/6/69.
100. Fergusson (1882), 241.
101. NLS MS 63b, passim.
102. Matheson, 86; SRO GD 51/17/117, 140.
103. Omond (1883), 118.

4

'A saviour to this country'

We know from hindsight that a new political era started when William Pitt the younger came to power. But, as the year 1784 opened, that was not at all clear. The latest Government might understandably have been regarded as just another odd, even unprincipled alliance, hastily cobbled together and unlikely to last. It included men of the most disparate antecedents. Half the Cabinet had wanted to crush the Americans, half to conciliate them. Some key figures, not least Henry Dundas, might but for the grace of God have still been with the coalition when it crashed. In matters of the moment, he was as much a foe to parliamentary reform as his young Prime Minister was a friend: on both sides of the House that remained an open question. If Pitt himself offered perfectly new ground, the terrain around him stood scarred and exhausted. Yet the nation, and the King in particular, had little choice but to set him tilling it as best he could.

For four months Pitt faced a bitterly hostile House of Commons, refusing either to resign or dissolve. His enemies won by fifty-four votes on the first division they forced, and beat him a further sixteen times. Dundas fought for him like a lion. Day after day, night after night, often indeed till the morning, he was on his feet braving ceaseless attacks on the Ministry's motives and character. By a skill in debate second only to his chief's, he frustrated and wore down the opposition. On January 16 he was to be found appealing to the independent members to support George III's choice of counsellors, since it would be wrong of Parliament to usurp this executive function. 'The assumption of power and privileges which do not belong to it has once proved the overthrow of this constitution. We are verging towards the same precipice again.' If prerogative was not persuasive enough, he could mix it with a little democracy, as on February 2: 'No man can lay his hand on his heart and say that the present Ministers have not the confidence of the people … The ministry, now the objects of removal, are confided in, loved and caressed by the people.' Nor did he neglect to warn members what they might miss if they spurned his advice: 'I must again return to the obscurity of a dull and laborious profession.'[1]

Arduous though the business was, it exhilarated Dundas. He wrote home to his children:

> I am in great health and perfect spirits. The times are very troublesome, and exertions from all quarters are necessary. These are the circumstances which make me feel the present moment to be exceedingly pleasant. My attach-

ment to Mr Pitt personally grows more and more unbounded every day, and of course to fight by his side when he is annoyed from so many enemies gives me more heartfelt pleasure than I ever enjoyed since I was in Parliament. I feel him to be sent down from heaven as a saviour to this country and cannot without indignation look upon the perversions of those who refuse to receive so precious a gift … I believe from the letters I have received from Scotland, the people there believe Mr Pitt came into office for no other reason but to grant pensions. How can they be so silly?

The audacity succeeded in its purposes: to break the Whigs' morale and give the Government's managers time to organise for a General Election. At a division on March 8 it lost by a single vote. 'The effect is that they do not choose to fight us again … My opinion is that we should dissolve as soon as possible', Dundas wrote the next morning. Indeed Pitt went straight to the country.[2]

For this contest, unlike most others during the eighteenth century, there was no trouble in discerning the result. In a House of 558 members, the Ministry secured the return of at least 300. Those committed to opposition were reduced to rather less than 200, after the loss of 70 to 80 of 'Fox's martyrs', the remainder being independent, unreliable or absent. Dundas naturally took charge of the campaign in Scotland. He had, while engaged in his plots the previous winter, at first reckoned on winning over for Pitt 27 of the 45 Scots in the old House, with 14 against. Closer investigation, presumably by personal lobbying, caused him to reduce his forecast of support to 20, with 10 classed as hopeful or doubtful. It is against this background that one must judge his performance on his native heath, often thought curiously unimpressive.

In doing so, one must draw more closely a distinction already made between those members who were afterwards merely in the habit of voting with the Government, and those whose election and subsequent conduct were in some sense controlled by Dundas. The first were following the normal practice of Scots at Westminster. For example, General James Murray had sat for Perthshire in the Duke of Atholl's interest since 1773. He now supported Pitt, but because the Duke told him to, not Dundas. The latter's pull in Perthshire, or lack of it, was just the same as before. Of course, he extended his power wherever he could. But there was no quick or easy way to pick up and fit together again the fragments into which the Scottish political system had broken during the last quarter-century.

Dundas's personal strength lay in Edinburgh and the south-eastern counties. It was anyway still far from unquestioned, and he felt relieved at not having to face a challenge in Midlothian.[3] Two other seats, Selkirkshire and the Dysart Burghs, remained safely in the Ministry's hands. Elsewhere, some fellow travellers were replaced by trustier men. In the capital, James Hunter Blair, leader of the merchant faction which had helped overthrow Sir Lawrence Dundas, stood down in favour of Henry's bosom friend, Sir Adam Fergusson. The Duke of Buccleuch had as patron of Roxburghshire long indulged the erratic Sir Gilbert Elliot, whose adherence to the coaliton gave, however, an excuse to get rid of him in favour of the safe Sir George Douglas. Berwickshire, for decades under the thumb of the Humes of Marchmont, had been thrown open by their folly, at a by-election in

1779, of putting in a gambler and cheat. The outraged voters rebelled and chose a different scion of the family in 1780. So weakened was it by the quarrel that Dundas could now successfully promote a candidate from a different connection altogether, Patrick Home of Home. In the remaining constituencies, independent interests held sway. Some were fairly friendly, such as those in the Linlithgow Burghs and Peeblesshire, some in fierce opposition, such as a remnant of Sir Lawrence's faction in Stirlingshire, held by his son, Sir Thomas Dundas of Castlecary, and in Clackmannanshire. Henry went to a contest against various local combinations in Fife, West Lothian and the Anstruther Burghs, but failed in all. Of the region's sixteen members, therefore, he commanded six. Two others would normally vote with the Government, and three more were won over as, in the course of the Parliament, it proved durable.

In the West, some ex-coalitionists presented Dundas with easy targets. One was a friend, Andrew Stuart, whom he had nominated jointly with the Duke of Hamilton for Lanarkshire in 1780. Urged, indeed inclined, to reconcile himself, Stuart was yet too honourable to turn his coat so brazenly. He chose instead to retire in favour of Sir James Steuart, a nervous soldier sure never to cause trouble. In the Glasgow Burghs the merchants, with whom Dundas cultivated excellent relations, obliged him by turning out the sitting member and bringing in his Lord Advocate, Ilay Campbell. In Dunbarton, the incumbent, George Keith Elphinstone, struck a deal with his patron, the Duke of Montrose, who had opted for Pitt: he would stay on for now, but not fight again.

This alternation of interests was to become a standard feature of Dundas's electoral bargains. He also employed it in Ayrshire, which was safe for him but still in contention between rival sets of ministerialists. He neatly solved the problem by translating the sitting member, Fergusson, to Edinburgh and giving a turn to the other faction, represented by Hugh Montgomerie, heir to the Earl of Eglinton. Thus he controlled three of the eleven western seats, with the certainty of a fourth the next time. Apart from Renfewshire, where the contest was purely local, the rest was carved up among magnates, the Dukes of Argyll and Queensberry and the Earl of Galloway. If not ill-disposed to the Government, they were never absolutely reliable. But two or three of their members were regularly voting with it by the end of the Parliament.

Where Dundas conspicuously lacked influence was in the whole of the North. Ross, the sole constituency there successfully courted by him in 1780, fell into other hands, Lord Macleod having proved unsuitable. He did secure Forfarshire, where the incumbent Archibald Douglas joined his camp: the Douglas Cause paid off once more. The members for Perthshire and Aberdeenshire, General Murray and Alexander Garden of Troup, gave steady support, without being in any sense beholden to Dundas. The rest remained beyond his grasp. The Highlands were, if anything, Whig country; quite a change from 1745. William Adam still sat for the Elgin Burghs, as did Charles, a nephew of Sir Lawrence Dundas, for Orkney and Shetland. Fox himself occupied the Tain Burghs in the Sutherlands' interest while awaiting the outcome of his disputed poll in the city of Westminster.[4]

If Robert Burns was anything to go by, Scots were rather pleased at the downfall of the coalition, and at their part in it. A poem of his acknowledged that:

> slee Dundas aroused the class,
> Benorth the Roman wa', man.

It should be noted that the Scots 'slee' is of wider reference than the English 'sly'. It means skilled, clever, expert or wise, rather than merely crafty or cunning. In the final stanza, recounting what Scotland had done for Willie (Pitt), Burns fairly swaggered:

> But, word an' blow, North, Fox and Co.,
> Gowffed Willie like a ba', man,
> Till Southron raise, an' coost their claise
> Behind him in a raw, man:
> An' Caledon threw by the drone,
> An' did her whittle draw, man;
> An' swoor fu' rude, thro' dirt and blood,
> To mak it guid in law, man.

Dundas now headed the most important Scottish connection but he was, with just ten seats under his personal control, a long way from hegemony. About the same number of members again would of their own volition usually vote with the Government, or consented to be won over as it established itself. Others were added through Dundas's astute management of by-elections. Previous accounts have found his performance in 1784 wanting, but that is because they exaggerated his earlier influence. The Ministry came out of the elections in Scotland in about the same position as it went into them, though with this difference, that the core of constituencies owed directly to Dundas grew. It was no brilliant success for him, perhaps a relative failure, yet all the same a useful expansion of his individual interest. He expressed himself moderately satisfied, considering that he had not started with a *tabula rasa*: 'If too many of our best friends had not been bound up by compromises and engagements on occasion of former elections our present election would have been a triumphant one indeed.'[5]

For the first time he also paid heed to the representation of the peers. Their small numbers lent themselves to his management. The Union roll, which established their voting qualification, contained 156 titles, of which twenty-five were attainted and a few others extinct. Six had a permanent place in the House of Lords by right of a British patent granted before 1711: Argyll, for example, officially sat as Lord Sundridge of Coombe Bank, in the county of Kent. But the House passed a standing order in that year, excluding from its membership future beneficiaries of such creations. From the remaining pool of rather more than 100 eligible as representatives, potential trouble-makers could be easily weeded out. It was done by means of ministerial nomination through the King's list. In this cosy arrangement the Scots peers, with their canny fidelity to the powers-that-be and their (by southern standards) often meagre means, had been wonderfully content to acquiesce.

But their reputation suffered in return. They were held to constitute in the Lords, along with English bishops and officers of the royal household, a 'party of the Crown', a non-hereditary element on that account open to undue influence from the Government of the day. Or, to employ the language of the cruder smears, by prostituting themselves for patronage they compromised the independence of one half of the legislature. It has, however, been demonstrated that till 1774 the Scots were inactive in the House. During the Parliament then dissolved, some had never turned up at all and only four had attended regularly. So perhaps the representative status could be regarded as honorific and apolitical, much like membership of the Order of the Thistle or the Royal Company of Archers. In that case, the King's list would not have been quite as demeaning as it seemed.

All this was in any event now changing. The peers, increasingly proud of and enriched by their country's progress, were less willing to put up with second-class status. At the election of 1768, a protest against the King's list had been entered by the Earl of Buchan, though he was a bit of a crank. Yet he presaged the feeling among a new generation, Buccleuch in its forefront, which could not be so easily written off. With a sense of leadership born of their rank these noblemen began in effect to ask, just as the law officers were doing in the Commons, for the state occasionally to assume responsibilities towards Scotland going beyond an otherwise non-committal barter of loyalty for patronage. The quality of her representation then became a much thornier question.[6]

At a by-election in 1770, Buccleuch had (to Dundas's alarm) supported a champion of free election, the Earl of Breadalbane, who, without winning, attracted a sizeable vote. The Government wisely appeased him. Breadalbane himself got on to the King's list in 1774, as did another dissident, Eglinton, at a by-election in 1776. This more tactful management proved also more successful. At the General Election of 1780, in which there is no evidence of intervention by Dundas, the King's list was returned unopposed.[7]

The nobility of Scotland was still not entirely mollified, in particular not over the exclusion from the Lords of most in its ranks who had been elevated to the peerage of Great Britain. That irked when the promotion could only follow from some accretion in their fortune or conspicuous service to their country. Hamilton's patrimony, for example, was on a par with any English aristocrat's. He had at his own expense raised a regiment which distinguished itself in America. Yet he was unable to sit at Westminster because his great-grandfather had acquired a British title, Duke of Brandon: this was the case that had brought about the offensive standing order of 1711. In 1782 he resolved to test matters anew by petitioning the House for a summons to it. Given his patriotic exertions, he could not be refused, and the standing order was cancelled. A sort of poetic justice was thus rendered to his family. At the same time, a precedent was set for the rest of the peerage.[8]

Dundas only looked on but it was he, as much as anyone, who benefited. So far he had had nothing more than the Order of the Thistle and a few sinecures as baits for the Scots peers. Now he was free to recommend to the King's grace all – and they were not few – who wanted a British title. He urged Pitt to exploit the ambitions revealed: 'Consider then what their feelings now are when by the acquisition of immense independent fortunes, enabling them to hold complete intercourse in society with the peerage of this part of the kingdom, still in point of parliamentary situation the highest in rank, in Scotland, feel themselves inferior to the lowest of the rank of peerage in England.' Dundas took care, though, not to cheapen his new resource, and during the next two decades sponsored only thirteen promotions. It was enough to whet appetites, yet not enough to open himself to accusations of rank jobbery. There would be problems in finding sixteen suitable representatives from the remainder. But that lay in the future, and for now the Scots aristocracy's good behaviour was reinforced. Of the delegation elected in 1784, twelve supported the Government. More significant was the part Dundas thus came to play in a painless transformation of the parliamentary peerage, from being overwhelmingly English to representing all parts of the United Kingdom (for in due course the Irish would be drawn in as well). By 1832, British peerages had been granted to twenty-three Scots. In effect the native magnates were commingled in an order of nobility embracing the great aristocracies of three kingdoms, not only equal in rank but also, through the education and social relations they tended to have in common too, sharing political and economic interests.[9]

An otherwise excellent Scottish historian has called Dundas 'the complete eighteenth-century politician, out of season and run to seed.'[10] In fact his methods were neither behind nor ahead of their time. He just used the existing machinery better than most. If he is to be faulted, it is for his inability to foresee that modern academics would condemn him for sharing the political assumptions of his own era rather than of theirs. It is surely altogether more profitable to consider what Dundas achieved within a system which he did not by himself create and which he could not by himself change.

The constitutional theorists, A. V. Dicey and R. Rait, dated the 'moral unity' of the United Kingdom from 1784. Whether one accepts this will depend, of course, on definition of the terms. It would be as easy to set the critical juncture at 1815, or even 1832. But their choice has some justification. The history of the Union so far was not especially happy. In the 1760s it had turned abruptly unhappier and Scots, disheartened with a political system apparently washing its hands of them, channelled their energies instead into literature and economic improvement. Even so, during the struggle in America they gave ample proof of their loyalty to Britain and the Empire, as they had tried and failed to do during the Seven Years' War: accusations of Jacobitism were now merely preposterous. In the midst of this, Dundas arrived. 'Besides that his temper was to everyone generous and kindly, his heart warmed to a fellow countryman as such,' said Pitt's Victorian biographer, the Earl of Stanhope. It made all the difference to have a typically clannish Scot at the centre of affairs. Through shrewdly sticking to Pitt, author of a coming national revival, he stayed there, without losing his affection for, interest in and connections with his countrymen. For them he was thus able to push ever higher the ladders of British and imperial advancement. Since the Union, nobody but Dundas had been able to do that; and since Dundas, nobody else has done it with the same success.[11]

It would, all the same, have been extremely difficult for any Scot to reach such a position by his own efforts, and the relationship with Pitt proved crucial. He was not an easy man to know. Though, by all accounts, delightful in private, he could in outward demeanour be aloof to the point of chilling. It was the shared adversity of 1784 that forged his link with Dundas, a bond that grew ever stronger as the two worked in unison for the rest of the decade on extremely complex administrative problems and in the following one fought a war together. Amid the vagaries of political life, it loosened somewhat afterwards, but never broke. Right at the end of Pitt's days, in 1805 and 1806, it was restored to being as close as it had ever been.

Nathaniel Wraxall described the initial stage:

> If Pitt attained the first place in the state, Dundas may with truth be said to have gained the second; for though he was not a Cabinet Minister, yet in essential functions of official authority and influence, he far outweighed either of the Secretaries of State, or even the Chancellor [who were all in the Lords]. Dundas, by his presence on the Treasury bench, came into daily contact with Pitt during many months of the year.

Wraxall, an English member, was a ludicrous pest, but his judgments could be shrewd. Here he saw to the bottom of a situation which escaped many observers. They regarded Dundas as a politician decidedly of the second rank, diligent and useful to be sure, but probably having reached his limits – this may have been Pitt's opinion too. He himself made the difference by overshadowing his Cabinet and reducing it to a nullity. The way was then clear for Dundas, a man from outside the magic ruling circle and by no stretch of the imagination a rival, to reach an unusually powerful informal position. Informality was of its essence. His surviving correspondence with Pitt is small, and they rarely even had official meetings. They would discuss and settle everything when they went for a ride or walk at the beginning and end of the day, in summer often staying out till ten or eleven o'clock.[12]

The intimacy still seemed belied by the difference, indeed stark contrast, between the bluff, practical, knowing Scot and his boyish, reserved, high-minded leader. Many held that Dundas corrupted the best in Pitt, by coarsening with cynicism his finer nature, and brought out the worst, above all by urging him to drink. Dundas certainly could be coarse in manner and language, and at times exploited for his own and his countrymen's amusement the fact that behaviour quite untoward among them might shock the English. But he was not vicious. The comments that have come down to us show rather an acute awareness of how sensitive and vulnerable Pitt could be, caught up by public duty when scarcely out of a boyhood already cramped by hieratic training for it. With all this, in fact, drinking helped him come to terms; just as generally Dundas's warm earthiness rounded out, made more capable of realisation, the ideals, discerning but fastidious, of a cool English aristocrat. Wraxall perhaps got it right again, remarking that compared to Pitt, 'Dundas manifested more amenity of manners, more placability of temper, more facility of access, a more yielding, accommodating and forgiving nature. If Pitt subdued, Dundas conciliated adversaries.'[13]

The coincidence of their views was not always realised either. Lady Hester Stanhope, the only woman to whom Pitt ever opened his heart, maintained that 'because Mr Dundas was a man of sense, and Mr Pitt approved of his ideas on many subjects, it does not follow, therefore, that he was influenced by him.' When they first came together in government it was indeed their disagreements (for example, on parliamentary reform) that people chose, usually for polemical purposes, to stress.

In their practical tasks, however, they complemented each other perfectly. Pitt provided insight and inspiration, while Dundas saw to the hard labour and the dirty work, necessary in any administration but little to the taste of the Prime Minister. As their mutual respect and liking then grew, they could bring into play their basic agreement over broad fields of policy, on more open markets, on more efficient government, on orderly social progress within the constitution. Each claimed, and got, unstinted support from the other, because each learned to appreciate the other's role. At the same time, neither doubted their relative stations. Pitt, till his friend was ennobled, always wrote to 'dear Dundas'; he always replied, 'my dear Sir'.[14]

Dundas, now over 40, was a mature character. His mind would expand, but was on the whole set in its ways. As a politician he was tempered by adversity successfully overcome. Without being a great orator, he could compel the respect of the Commons where Wraxall saw him standing 'his countenance open, cheerful and pleasingly expressive, though tinged with convivial purple.' John Wilkes, who knew something of these matters, said of him: 'There is much sound sense, and no rubbish in his speeches.'[15]

While ready to find time for intellectuals, and glad of their advice in wrestling with problems, Dundas himself was a man of action, ambitious and decisive. An excellent judge of people and of events, he could tell as if by instinct who would win and what would work. Sir John Sinclair remarked:

> I never met with any individual who could go through more business in a shorter time, or on whose judgment more confidence might be placed in any critical emergency. He also had a stretch of thought, which enabled him to adopt measures, the completion of which could not be looked for, until a considerable period had elapsed.

Loyal and level-headed too, he was satisfied in proficient discharge of his duties without pursuing extravagances, always equable, always assiduous, always effective. Yet he was still recognisably human, worldly enough to use the foibles and aspirations of others, warm enough to exercise his growing power with sympathy and care. While indeed a master of expediency, he also knew the meaning of a fair deal.

His great vice remained drink and it was a wonder, with his consumption, that he got through the work he did. To the guzzling of claret and fortified wines favoured in Edinburgh's legal circles, he added a liking for English beer unusual in a Scot. He told the Commons that 'when I go every year to my own country, I find no beer that I can drink, it is such weak, disagreeable and poor stuff. Here it is so fine, so pleasant, so swelling a liquor, that I care little if I taste no other beverage all the while I stay here.' His hospitality was famous, though what ought to have been a lubricant of good times with friends or family could and did turn too easily into that common fault of his countrymen, a mindless, systematic drunkenness.

Even an age far from abstemious found some of his exploits remarkable. One night he and Lord Thurlow 'got most egregiously drunk. With that heroism which Bacchus always gives the Chancellor mounted his mare (though he had the piles at the time) and rode home after midnight … His soliloquy the next morning was most devout and edifying: "That damned fellow Dundas was born upon a rock and can drink up the ocean and what a damned fool I am to keep company with such a fellow".' Another story went the rounds, though the source is obscure, of how the same pair and Pitt, having dined well with Charles Jenkinson at Addiscombe, were riding home across a star-lit Surrey. They came to a toll-gate and, finding they had no money on them, decided to rush through without paying. The indignant keeper, taking them for highwaymen, fired his blunderbuss as they galloped guffawing away into the night. With a better aim, he might have changed the history of these isles.[16]

Yet there was rarely any flagging of Dundas's energy or industry. His daughter Montague described a working day:

> Papa is very much hurried. Indeed just now he is always out riding by seven o'clock in the morning. He sometimes breakfasts at Putney with Mr Pitt and sometimes at his own office in the City. From thence he goes to the India Board, where he stays until two or three o'clock. Then he sometimes comes home to dress, but he oftener dresses at the office and goes down to the House of Commons, or else he comes to Leicester Square and takes a family dinner before going down to the House. If there is nothing particular there, he goes to the India Board again at seven o'clock and stays until eleven, when he comes home to supper. I never see him the whole day unless he dines at home.

It was when something particular did come on in the House that matters tended to get out of hand. Having sat, according to Lady Hester Stanhope, till the small hours Dundas, Pitt and others would sup (presumably a euphemism) 'and then go to bed to get three or four hours' sleep, and to renew the same thing the next day, and the next and the next.'[17]

Taxing though Dundas's way of life was, it did at last offer some material security. His income had risen and credit was on the whole easier to come by; though he could write ruefully that Drummond's Bank in London, with which he was closely connected, 'are not fond of Scotch families'. He needed a residence grander than his habitual lodging in Leicester Square, and in 1786 he bought a mansion with spacious grounds on the western side of Wimbledon Common. Called Cannizaro after an Italian duke who had lived there, it proved perfect as a social venue for politicians, with 'burgundy and blasphemy' always on offer. Pitt, whose own country house at Holwood was too distant to visit simply for fresh air, often came to stay overnight. So did many others. In March 1787, Dundas wrote to Adam Smith: 'I am glad you have got vacation. Mr Pitt, Mr Grenville and your humble servant are clearly of opinion that you cannot spend it so well as here. The weather is fine, my villa at Wimbledon a most comfortable healthy place. You shall have a comfortable room and as the business is much relaxed we shall have time to discuss all your books with you every evening.' His arrival was the occasion when the company, on Pitt's insistence, stood till Smith was seated, because they were all his pupils. One would be hard-put to find a modern Scots politician on easy terms with the great thinkers of the age. It rather refutes the charge that his mind lacked 'anything that resembles an idea, let alone an ideal.'[18]

In Scotland he had in 1782 acquired a portion, twenty acres in extent, of a forfeited estate at Dunira, beside the Earn near Comrie, Perthshire. He built a modest house which became his favourite residence, his 'Paradise of the North', to which he eagerly invited anyone who could be bothered to make the journey. A lover of country pursuits, he hunted and fished there, planted trees, went for long, solitary walks or stayed indoors and played whist. He also set to work on Melville, which was rebuilt between 1786 and 1798 to designs of 'manifold ingenuity' by James Playfair. They recalled, perhaps not without reason, Argyll's great seat at Inveraray. The castle was thus turned into a 'three-storey toy fort with round, Gothic-windowed corner turrets and two-storey wings', and an 'astonishing stair-case' within. Across its policies, doubled in size with the inclusion of five tenant farms, it looked to the river North Esk. 'Who knows not Melville's beechy grove?' wrote Walter Scott in the *Minstrelsy of the Scottish Border* – not a pertinent query since the trees were Wellingtonias.[19]

When in Edinburgh, Dundas stayed in George Square with his mother, by whom his children were largely brought up. But he tried not to regard career and family as incompatibles: 'I confess myself clannish enough to wish to be able to show everybody that the most substantial interest of the country is that which I hold up as the interest of the family of Dundas. I have made every exertion to collect it together and make it as formidable as possible. It ought to be held together and act together.'[20] That was doubtless why he showed a worried eagerness to see his son and heir, Robert, do well, scolding him for 'love of his pillow'. He did not approve of English education and rebuked his brother for sending a son to Westminster School. While conceding that acquisition of a southern accent might offer a slight advantage, it could not, he thought, compensate for losing touch with Scotland. So Robert went, like the rest of the family, to the High School of Edinburgh.

Thence he was dispatched, still aged only 15, on a continental tour. He arrived in Paris in July 1786 complete with letter of recommendation from Smith to the Abbé Morellet, a liberal of the French Enlightenment who had cultivated links with Britain. It read:

> I now venture to introduce to your acquaintance my particular friend, Mr John Bruce, professor of logic in the University of Edinburgh. He accompanies on his travels Mr Dundas, a young gentleman of great modesty and propriety of manner and of great application to his studies and to all his other duties, the son of the gentleman who may be considered as our present Minister for Scotland.

For a lad of such admirable character, Robert was mercilessly badgered by Bruce, who granted that 'I have too anxious a temper' – not least with regard to the superior academic post at home which he hoped to wheedle out of Dundas senior. So the pupil was hauled off to a dancing master from eight to nine, to a fencing master from ten to eleven 'and from that time, till dinner, he resumes his far more important labour of the study of the history of science with myself.'[21]

From the abbé, 'Dr Smith's letter procured us a kind reception. I consider this as a most valuable connection, as it will introduce Mr Dundas to the first literary company of this place. Everything, you may be assured, shall be done, that is in my power, to promote your great object, his improvement.' By September, Robert had 'given all the time, which at present is necessary, for drawing of architecture, and is reading the books proper for illustrating the principles of these arts. In a day or two, he begins the German language ... Mr Dundas keeps the accounts for this quarter, and will transmit them to you when it is ended. I only act the parts of cashier and comptroller.' The pupil developed, in reaction to this force-feeding, a carapace of amiable complaisance which he never quite lost. He seems to have exacted revenge by spending far too much, despite the comptrolling. Later when they proceeded to Hanover, he was alarmed to be threatened with arrest for a debt of £8000 left unpaid by Sir Lawrence Dundas a quarter-century before. Finally he enrolled in the university of Göttingen, in what he called 'a state of absolute banishment, perfectly out the reach of any civilised people.' But the professors 'spoke of him as the most promising young man that ever came from Britain.'

Dundas senior remained, all the same, more impressed with his nephew, another Robert, the Lord President's heir. He was supposed to be 'not endowed with those brilliant talents which were conspicuous in many of his family.' Even so, Henry made him Solicitor General in 1784 at the age of 26, and Lord Advocate in 1789. To him he also married, in April 1787, his eldest daughter Elizabeth. The second one, Anne, had been wed the year before to Henry Drummond, of the London-Scottish banking family.[22]

They formed a big, sociable clan. Henry Cockburn recalled an outing which must have taken place during these years.

> It was a bright, beautiful August day. We returned to the inn at Middleton, on our way home, about seven in the evening; and there we saw another scene. People sometimes say there is no probability in Scott's making the party in Waverley retire from the castle to the howff; but these people were not with me in the inn at Middleton, about 40 years ago. The Duke of Buccleuch was living at Dalkeith; Henry Dundas at Melville; Robert Dundas, the Lord Advocate, at Arniston; Hepburn of Clerkington at Middleton; and several of the rest of the aristocracy of Midlothian within a few miles; all with their families, and luxurious houses; yet had they, to the number of 12 or 16, congregated in this wretched ale-house for a day of freedom and jollity. We found them roaring and singing, and laughing, in a low-roofed room scarcely large enough to hold them, with wooden chairs and a sanded floor. When their own lackeys, who were carrying on high life in the kitchen, did not choose to attend, the masters were served by two women. There was plenty of wine, particularly claret, in rapid circulation on the table; but my eye was chiefly attracted by a huge bowl of hot whisky punch, the steam of which was almost dropping from the roof, while the odour was enough to perfume the whole parish. We were called in and made to partake, and very kindly used, particularly by my uncle, Henry Dundas. How they did joke and laugh! with songs, and toasts, and disputations, and no want of practical fun. I don't remember anything they said, and probably did not understand it. But the noise, and the heat, and the uproarious mirth – I think I hear and feel them yet.[23]

We get a picture here of a Merrie Old Scotland hard to reconcile with what is otherwise remembered of our grim, Calvinist past. But in his tableau of a *fête champêtre*, or at any rate *hôtelière*, Cockburn was perhaps almost consciously evoking comparison with another *ancien régime*, just as sweet, just as carefree, destined to pass just as completely away – only much sooner.

Dundas's normal life, however, was one of unremitting toil. He no longer wanted to be Lord Advocate, but even so felt unable (wrongly as it befell) to do without some legal work. Pitt therefore re-appointed him Treasurer of the Navy, which would be 'not incompatible with my profession.' It was neither a great office of state, nor yet quite a sinecure. Before we go on to deal with his more important tasks, it would be as well to describe his services at this post which, though limited in scope, proved of great benefit to those affected by them.

The navy's finances were in a mess, making it all the harder to get sailors paid and ships equipped. At bottom this was because modern concepts of the continuity of government and of the independence of the civil service simply had not yet evolved. Bizarre as it may seem to us, the Treasurer conducted his transactions not through any official channel but through a private account, fed as necessary from drafts on the Bank of England. He and, with permission, his officials were thus free to employ unused balances for their personal purposes, a matter of no concern to the state so long as the money was eventually applied to the proper ones. Inevitably, however, confusion and delay resulted. It was therefore the practice for the Treasurer to keep his account open after his retiral till he (or, if he died, his heir) found himself in a position to close it. Over time, the system had degenerated into utter chaos. Some of the outstanding claims dated back to the previous century. Dundas came from a new generation of public servants to whom this antique nonchalance caused offence. Almost the first thing he did was to draft legislation, passed in 1785, which converted the Treasurer's account into a public one, so that official and personal transactions should no longer be mixed together. Yet his subordinates went blithely on in the same old haphazard way, a new rigour being evidently too bothersome. It was fatal negligence on his part that he failed to enforce his own law, for on those grounds he was one day to be disgraced.

Beyond that, Dundas did what he could for the welfare of men serving in the navy and of their families. An Act of 1786 required an officer as witness to any will or other instrument executed by a rating, so as to thwart the moneylenders who commonly preyed on drunken sailors and persuaded them to sign away their future pay. An Act of 1792 similarly protected dependants in the case of a seaman's death, by directing that every claim on his estate should be handled by a clergyman or officer of the revenue. An Act of 1795 allowed provision to be made for them while their breadwinner was at sea, since it was the practice to pay him in a lump-sum on his return. Extended to non-commissioned officers and to residents of Ireland, the measure eventually saved from destitution the families of about 30,000 seamen absent in their country's service. 'Mr Dundas held this distinguished office during a much longer period than any of his predecessors and his attention to the sailor's interest appears to have continued to the last.' Indeed, 'he was the sailor's friend and might justly glory in the name'.[24]

For a man of Dundas's energies, however, this did not add up to much. Besides being an ever present help to Pitt in the daily political round, he directed his exertions above all to the government of India, and built an empire there too. It was a commonplace of the time that 'Scotland and India Dundas ruled and fed the one with the other.' The Revd Sydney Smith wrote that 'as long as he is in office the Scotch may beget younger sons with the most perfect impunity. He sends them by loads to the East Indies and all over the world.' Or, in one of Rosebery's striking phrases, 'he Scotticised India, and Orientalised Scotland.'[25]

British activity in the East had been undergoing profound changes. It was no longer just a matter of pillage, though people still went there to make a fortune and most of those who survived did so. But if an alien and exotic world depraved some, others it fascinated – many an exile would now, his day done, return to his bungalow, don a dhoti, eat a curry, light a hookah, then enjoy a nautch by the girls from the zenana. It was a pity that these easy relations between the two races later became the subject of so much stricture. Meanwhile, however, they awakened interest in Indian culture, and produced the first orientalists.

They also brought concern for order and good government in India. Nominal sovereignty over the whole resided still in the Moghul Emperor at Delhi. But the talents of his line had spent themselves, so that he was in reality little more than a princeling. The central regions of the sub-continent came for the most part under the sway of the Marathas, headed after a fashion by the Peshwa at Poona. Their confederacy originated in the great Hindu uprising against Moslem oppression led by Shivaji in the previous century. It retained a swashbuckling character, and only in its heartland of Maharashtra had it a regular administration. Beyond, the Marathas still marauded, and represented a force for instability. To their south lay the dominions of the Nizam of Hyderabad, once an imperial official, who had been able to seize independence from the Moghuls. To the south again was Mysore, essentially a Hindu state where, however, a coup had recently given power to a resourceful and aggressive Moslem Minister, Hyder Ali. He was one of the few Indian rulers ever to show geopolitical sense, and through seeking French aid constantly unnerved the British.

The East India Company, still in outward form a commercial undertaking, had direct responsibility for three so-called presidencies. Bombay remained small and unimportant, cut off from a hinterland by the lofty Western Ghats. Madras, oldest of the stations, was now outshone by Calcutta, metropolis of Bengal, emporium of its trade in textiles, sugar and saltpetre. The Company's control already extended up the Ganges as far as Benares, so willy-nilly it had become a territorial and political as well as a commercial power. In, for example, efforts to supplant European rivals, it was obliged to deal as such with the native states. Amid the chaos of Indian politics, however, the Company had grown used to enforcing its will through war. War proved not just highly expensive, eating up the proceeds from trade, but also ruinous to native society. Bengal ought to have had in its agricultural and commercial structure everything necessary to flourish; in fact it could barely feed itself. That did not go unnoticed at home, where the Company was now engaged in a long and losing battle to fend off corrective action by the Government. Things could not in fact go on without help from that quarter, but it was bound to require in return a cleansing of the mess and doubtless some retribution to those who had made it. The fact that the Company was a mere creature of statute did not make the task easier. The fabulous wealth earned by its servants from their depredations allowed many, on their return home, to acquire property and seats in Parliament. Some appreciated the need for changes in India, but they were still in a position to obstruct any they did not like.

A good number of these nabobs were Scots, attracted to the Orient, as to every quarter of the globe where commerce flourished, by their education and enterprise. As early as 1750 they took more than one-third of the Company's appointments to Bengal. Under Warren Hastings in the 1770s, this proportion rose to about half. Later, when Dundas gained access to the patronage, it actually sank again, for his acute political antennae told him that he had to be wary of stirring up English Scotophobia. But at 30 to 40 per cent of the posts available, it still greatly exceeded Scotland's share of the British population.

Also disproportionate was the nabobs' impact at home. Because of the nature of Scottish patronage they were often, if by no means always, well-born and influential. When they returned with their wealth, they visibly enriched their native land. Major electoral interests, such as the Johnstones in the South-west or the Brodies and the Grants in the North-east, were built on Indian money, like many a country seat and improved estate. India contributed as well to the Enlightenment, offering its historicist methodology a living example of civilised society in a quite different state of development. Smith noted that 'the improvements in agriculture and manufactures seem … to have been of very great antiquity in the provinces of Bengal.' He ascribed their decline to 'the mercantile company which oppresses and domineers in the East Indies'.[27]

Dundas must have known these passages, but what has justly been called his intellectual passion for India probably had personal origins. His family had never quite made it as nabobs, though not for want of trying. Like many a needy Scots clan, they sent sons to the East. Three of Henry's brothers went, and two died there. One fathered a half-caste daughter, Maria. Doubtless a century later this would have been a matter for shame, and people like the Dundases would have left her to her fate. But in these times a touch of the tarbrush was of no consequence to them – they accepted absolutely their obligations to one of their own blood. As soon as the waif could travel, at the age of five, they brought her all the way home. She then lived with the rest of them at Arniston, to grow up a lively, intelligent and beautiful girl. There could scarcely be better proof of the absence of contemporary racial prejudice. Perhaps at length she might even have been married off elsewhere in the Scots landed gentry, but she died in her twenties. She was all that the family had thus far to show for its Indian connection. The financial return had been nil, unless we except the inheritance from Henry's father-in-law, also long lost.

In any event, as early as 1773, well before his parliamentary debut, he was corresponding on India with Allan Ramsay who, showing the usual versatility of Scots intellectuals, added an informed knowledge of imperial affairs to his prowess as a painter. Dundas's side of the exchange has not survived, but from the replies it seems clear that some ideas on which he later acted were already in his mind.[28]

At Westminster he gained the reputation of an expert just by intervening in Indian debates. Affairs as important and complex as these ought, one would have thought, to have opened up a sufficient field of interest for statesmen. Yet they bored Parliament, except for the nabobs. The latest definitive Indian legislation was the Regulating Act (1773). It established a politically responsible institution for the British territories, the office of Governor-general, which Hastings first held. But his was responsibility without power, for he could neither override the often hostile council in Bengal, nor expect help from a Company in a chaotic internal state. The directors sitting in London, chosen for life in ferociously competitive elections, were far too remote to impose any discipline over what went on in the East. Even if so minded, they could be, and often were, outvoted by the shareholders. In the general court of proprietors where these regularly met, a majority was enjoyed by the 'shipping interest', which in the most blinkered fashion resisted tooth-and-nail every dilution of the monopoly which the Company held on all trade between Britain and any point east of the Cape of Good Hope. Its opponents, the more disparate 'Indian interest', had been out and seen for themselves that some reform must come.

A crisis was visibly approaching by 1779, when renewal of the Company's charter had to be postponed because of a wrangle with the Treasury over how much revenue it owed. That prompted a debate on Indian government destined to last a decade. Dundas's crucial role in it started with his appointment in 1781 as chairman of a parliamentary inquiry, the so-called Secret Committee. Its remit was to probe the reasons for hostilities with Hyder Ali who, provoked by the folly of the government of Madras, had invaded the Carnatic, the coastal region round that city, effortlessly defeated the British forces and overrun it. This was followed by the arrival of a French fleet which for a time swept British ships from the southern Indian seas – an alarming turn of events when the American War was also going badly. Though Hastings kept his head and mastered the crisis, the resulting outburst of parliamentary anger staggered the already groggy Lord North. Dundas's organisation of the committee's proceedings so as not to embarrass a failing Government was a godsend. He manoeuvred them beyond awkward details by giving a chance to every malcontent inside and outside the Company to vent his opinions. Though not unduly swayed by any, Dundas could gather a stock of his knowledge and contacts from which to formulate ideas of his own.[29]

Another investigation into an earlier conflict, the Rohilla War, was at the same time being conducted by Edmund Burke's Select Committee, composed largely of North's foes. The respective prominence of the two inquiries waxed and waned with the Ministry's fortunes. Neither by itself achieved anything decisive, but in combination they drew attention to India at a critical point. With the British political system also in turmoil, the potent oriental interests were bound to be thrown into the balance as a new equilibrium was sought. Burke's eloquence persuaded Parliament that the state of affairs in the East had grown intolerable. Dundas's pragmatism set out the essential lines of action.

The nub of the problems as he saw them was expounded in his speech of April 1782, winding up a year of the Secret Committee's work in forty-five resolutions. The Company, he said, had been too eager to wage war, contrary to its instructions. It had corruptly interfered in disputes of the native powers. It had breached treaties. It had indulged in peculation and oppression. The directors at home had done nothing to prevent these abuses except when they felt their profits threatened. He called on Parliament to intervene, to refer his resolutions to a committee of the whole House, then to send out to India commissioners with the authority to put things right. 'I wish every servant of the Company,' he declared, 'to consider that it is and ought to be the first aim of his life to prove himself a faithful steward of the Company, and that he has no right to fancy he is an Alexander or an Aurangzeb and prefer frantic military exploits to the trade and commerce of the country.'

Dundas's impulse at this stage was simply to get British India cleaned out from bottom to top. A month later, he persuaded the Commons to pass another resolution which blamed Hastings for having condoned incompetence at Madras, and generally for having 'acted in a manner repugnant to the honour and policy of this nation and thereby brought great calamity on India'. In other words, the misrule exposed by the inquiries was ultimately the Governor-general's. His authoritarianism could not be denied. The real question at his eventual impeachment was whether it represented the cause of misrule or the only conceivable cure. It was a question too complex to be answered on impulse, however, or by parliamentary resolution. Nothing more was for the present done against Hastings (whom the House indeed soon voted to re-appoint for a further term), nor even against the similarly censured and manifestly culpable Governor of Madras, Sir Thomas Rumbold.[30]

These affairs were meanwhile overtaken by the wider crisis at Westminster. Not till Dundas was serving in Lord Shelburne's Government had he the chance to resume his Indian endeavours publicly. This he did in an emphatic manner, introducing in April 1783 a comprehensive bill which has been described as a 'landmark in the history of Indian legislation'. It showed the fruits of the contacts he had cultivated, but also of his own work on the information they provided. While it gathered together all the points previously made by reformers in a moderate, sensible, workmanlike manner, its purpose was not anaemic compromise. Rather, it introduced a clear new principle into Indian government, of effective sovereignty vested in central authorities. It impressed the Commons and, but for the Ministry's fall, would have had a good chance of passing.

Dundas set out to the House four aims. First, the administration at home was to be put on a fresh footing. The Government would be enabled to bypass the Company's resistance in essential matters, such as recall of senior officials. The shareholders' right to override the directors on political issues would be ended. Direction of this new apparatus was the role Dundas foresaw for himself (in his own mind perhaps as Secretary of State for India). Secondly, in the sub-continent the office of Governor-general would be given the power to match its responsibility, through control of the council in Bengal, as of the governors and councils in the lesser presidencies. To disarm objections, it was essential to choose the right man for the job, one who could be counted on as an improvement over Hastings and the rapacious nabobs. Dundas believed he would find the proper degree of *noblesse oblige* in Lord Cornwallis. He, despite his inglorious surrender at Yorktown in the American War, retained through good nature, honesty and ability the respect of his political masters. Dundas laid the praise on thick: 'Here there is no broken fortune to be mended! Here is no avarice to be gratified! Here is no beggarly, mushroom kindred to be provided for! No crew of hungry followers, gaping to be gorged!'

The wayward Company was thus to be subjected to a double constraint: by the Government in London and by the Governor-general in India. This might seem at odds with what we have observed of Dundas's principles, which tended otherwise to set limits to the powers of the state. But rigid adherence to them would, in respect of the first constraint, hardly have been sensible when he was dealing with misrule. And in respect of the second, his proposals conveyed something important about his political outlook. With here a free hand, he showed that while he may have wanted a limited, he did not want an impotent state, but on the contrary one within its limits strong, even strengthened. He knew what he was doing, and that it had to be justified. He could argue that, with a clear chain of command, the Company would not be dragged casually into wars, for the Governor-general was to be instructed to avoid, save in emergencies, interference with native powers. He could argue also that despotism was what orientals understood: 'As unfortunately the government of our Indian possessions is necessarily despotic, it surely the more behoves the House to the particular care that the government of India is conducted as well as possible.'[31] His scheme, with firm authority delegated from London to a man on the spot, proved to be of great utility and was for the future imposed generally on imperial possessions not colonised by the British themselves.

The Bill also tackled two major problems of misrule. Under one provision an effort was to be made to settle the debts of the Nawab of Arcot, a vexed matter which will detain us below. Dundas said they 'ought to be minutely inquired into, because though I doubt not that some of them may be just debts, still I am of opinion that the greatest part are debts of corruption.' Another provision set out to establish a regular system of land tenure in Bengal, for the sake of both order and revenue. The Company had never respected native property, but taxed and confiscated without restraint. Dundas – and, he surmised, the gentlemen he addressed at Westminster – was ready to perceive beneath the impoverishment of the country a lack of leadership from a class analogous to themselves. Some debate went on at large about the nature of property in Asia, whether it rested on real rights which could be enforced against the sovereign, or was held merely at his pleasure. Those who anyway saw a prosperous gentry as the foundation of an ordered society were eager to discover such rights. And Dundas's diligent researches had proved to his own satisfaction that they resided, though in degenerate form, in a class called the zemindars. In his day they had come to occupy a station midway between the landowners and the tax-farmers, a recipe for corruption among themselves and oppression of the peasants. Dundas therefore meant to restore the rights to property he supposed them to have enjoyed under the beneficence of the Great Moghul. It may not have mattered particularly whether he was right or wrong, since the origins of Indian social institutions were lost in the mists of time. But it is interesting how an enlightened Scot could both universalise his own conceptions and apply them sympathetically to such alien conditions.[32]

Contemporaries applauded Dundas's reforming intentions yet still found it hard to take the concentrations of power he had in mind. Modern assessments have been positive, one judging the Bill 'far ahead of its time'. Another has indeed seen in it an application of the principles of the Scottish Enlightenment, 'a legislative reflection of the spirit of optimism, rational tolerance for alien cultures, yet easy, philosophically abstract unconcern for regional details which was latent in the Scottish conjectural historians.' If it marked the highest point of their influence, 'by the same token it marks their practical failure in the legislative sphere at Westminster.'[33]

For though the measure did set an agenda in the continuing debate, Dundas abandoned it before it could be fully scrutinised. He had little choice, for he was by then serving only on sufferance in a coalition with definite Indian ideas of its own, as he was soon made to feel. His superiors gave no encouragement at all to his inquiries, commanded by the House, into Rumbold's conduct. Dispirited at the considerable waste of his time, he eventually recommended that the prosecution should be dropped. The Foxites then had the cheek to accuse him of corrupt motives. But without their co-operation, or enough independent support, it was pointless to persist.

When Fox revealed his plans, inspired by Burke, they made Dundas's version of despotism look feeble indeed, for they amounted to a sweeping attack on the Company's independence. Introduced in the Commons in November they provided for seven commissioners sitting in London to exercise all effective power in India, with even the Governor-general as their puppet. They were to be political appointees, named in the legislation and more or less irremovable for four years, with their successors to be chosen by the Crown. Even commercial affairs were to be for a time taken out of the shareholders' hands, and directed instead by nine assistant commissioners, also political appointees in the first instance, though after five years to be elected by the general court of proprietors.

This subjection of British India to parliamentary rule, its recurrent instability mediated only by labyrinthine legislation, has been criticised as 'a retrograde Whiggish notion'. One motive was clear enough, and not all bad: there would be a drastic effort to check misgovernment in the East. But to do this by putting a straightjacket on the local administration, when letters from London to Calcutta took six months, was self-defeating.[34] Moreover, other motives were suspect. A Ministry free for several years to remodel the Company's personnel to its liking might indeed impose efficiency, but might equally be tempted into corruption. It boded ill that the seven commissioners need know nothing of India. They would probably have included, for example, Fox and North, who thus might have held on to a vast resource of patronage long after their own Government had fallen. And what new one could have tolerated an Indian administration of a different political colour to itself?

The scheme was, in short, not only dangerous but impracticable, and a shared determination to thwart it brought Pitt and Dundas still closer together at this crucial time.[35] The latter, a connoisseur of Parliament, early anticipated the coalition's defeat on the issue. He aired his own views in a debate on December 1. The Bill was 'big with the most alarming consequences to the constitution. It creates an imperium in imperio. So far from increasing the influence of the Crown, it does, what is much worse, create a new, inordinate and unexampled influence which it places in the hands of the Minister of the present day and his party, for five years together.' The House still passed it, but before it came under considera-tion in the Lords an equally horrified George III intervened personally and brought Pitt to power amid the circumstances described at the end of the last chapter.[36]

Indian legislation was now Pitt's priority. Not only did he accept that condi-tions in the East and in London demanded it. He also wished through a better scheme to draw a sharp contrast with the coalition's. That would help establish his cleaner credentials and rally, perhaps increase, his own following. In January 1784 he brought in a new measure, which Fox, still hoping for a quick return to office, did not hesitate to have at once thrown out. The General Election then super-vened, giving Pitt all the scope he could want for early action in the new Parliament.

Without fixed ideas himself, he was content to take over some basic principles from Dundas's Bill of 1783. Still, they had to be drastically modified, if only in response to the outcry against tyranny and absolutism unleashed by Fox. Pitt therefore stopped trying to do too much, and stuck to the question of relations between the Government and the Company. His measure, in comparison to the previous ones, took less power for the first and left greater independence for the second. Under it, the Government was not actually to rule India; contrary to Dundas' persistent hopes, she would have no Secretary of State sitting in the Cabinet. The keystone of the new structure was instead to be what we should nowadays call a quango, the Board of Control. It would consist of six unpaid privy councillors 'to superintend, direct and control all acts, opinions and concerns which in anywise relate to the civil or military government or the revenues of the British territorial possessions in the East Indies'. Specifically, it would scrutinise every dispatch to and from India, with power to modify or reject the outgoing ones. If it passed them, the orders from the directors they contained could not afterwards be overruled by the proprietors, who were thus finished as a political force. Moreover, the directors themselves could be bypassed through a Secret Commit-tee of the Board, empowered to issue instructions without reference to them.

The danger of excessive interference was acknowledged, however. The Com-pany's constitution and status were not altered, apart from interposition of the Board. The Bill simply omitted to answer the obvious question of where formal sovereignty over our Indian territories lay. It renounced military adventures, cut the Indian forces and forbade declarations of war without reference to London: 'to pursue schemes of conquest and extensions of dominion in India are measures repugnant to the wish, honour and policy of this nation.' But it did not otherwise regulate the conduct of the Company's servants. Over patronage, the matter of greatest contemporary importance, power was diffused; the Ministry would name the Governor-general and the other most senior officials, but the rest of the appointments remained with the directors. Dundas stressed the checks and balances in speaking for the measure on July 16: 'it shows every degree of tenderness to the chartered rights and privileges of the Company. It is, in fine, one which I doubt not will produce that happy and desirable mixed government which every friend to the immunities of a wealthy people will cheerfully welcome and maintain.'[37]

Having comfortably passed both Houses of Parliament, the India Act came into force in the autumn. The first members of the Board were all senior political figures, including Pitt and Dundas. But the latter took practical charge from the start. With his chief's indulgence, he neutralised rivals and soon dominated the proceedings, not least through his indefatigable industry. He wrote in July 1787: 'When the last ship of this season leaves, which it will in a few days, I shall not leave an unanswered letter on the table of India House, which I found many years in arrears, and in future every ship that sails will carry out as regularly as the post the answer to the dispatches of the former ship.' Whigs complained that Indian government became unaccountable through Dundas's effective monopoly of the Board's business. But to his mind its function was indeed to control, not to rule – that being best done by the people out in India. The essential at this end was to have a political authority which the directors were obliged to respect.[38]

Dundas was supremely suited to a job demanding not only minute attention to matters, but also sage management of men. Yet even with his skill in compromise behind the scenes, he could not avoid further overt political action. Despite the greater powers conferred on the office of Governor-general, Cornwallis still declined to take it. An embarrassing interregnum followed. Lord Macartney, Governor of Madras, was given next refusal, but set such impossible conditions that Pitt retracted the offer. *Faute de mieux* a member of the council in Calcutta, Sir John Macpherson, was appointed acting Governor-general. This son of the manse from Sleat on Skye ran 'a system of the dirtiest jobbing', according to Cornwallis, a man not given to verbal extravagance.

So just two years after the primary legislation, an Amending Act had to be brought in. As an extra, and clinching, inducement to Cornwallis it enhanced the Governor-general's powers yet further in various particulars. Dundas was perfectly happy, for in effect this tidied up a piece of his unfinished business from 1783. He had now endowed the supreme office in India with much the same authority as his Bill then would have done. To one scholar he was thus exhibiting both his consistency, because in struggling through the tangle of recent Indian affairs he had not lost sight of an ultimate goal, and his administrative good sense, because he remained deaf to Whig cries of despotism. The Governor-generalship as established to his satisfaction was his most durable achievement. In essentials, it lasted till the end of the Raj.[39]

A second attempt also proved necessary to get relations quite right with the Company in London. Dundas genially but doggedly deprived the directors of political initiative and management. Yet he was still circumscribed by their remaining powers and privileges, preserved in the course of previous compromise and all the more jealously guarded now. A major revolt took place in 1788 when he proposed to reduce the size of the Company's army, send out more regular troops and generally consolidate the Crown's control over European forces in the East. The directors rejected this on the grounds of what they assumed to be his political motive, in robbing them of one more sphere of influence and patronage.

They thought he added insult to injury by making them pay for the reinforcements. And for once they outdid him in work behind the scenes, for they got the
court of proprietors to back them up, albeit by a single casting vote. Dundas
remained absolutely unyielding. He claimed that 'the Act of 1784 gives the Board
the power to apply the whole of the revenues of India to the defence of India, if
necessary, without leaving the Company a sixpence for their investments.' With
such resistance, however, he and Pitt had to bring in a Declaratory Act compelling
the Company to give way.

This, passed by majorities considerably smaller than they were used to, also had
its price. It demonstrated that Parliament was still not inclined to accept meekly
any Indian measure thrust on it. Guarantees were extracted against the growth of
ministerial patronage, guarantees so binding as to rule out for good the idea, still in
the back of Dundas's mind, that he might become Secretary of State for India. He
philosophically paid the price, explaining afterwards to his friend Sir Archibald
Campbell, Governor of Madras: 'By the system of Indian government under which
we act, the spirit of the times renders it necessary to leave the exercise of patronage
without control in the Company. If therefore they are obstinate on any question
of appointments either at home or abroad, we must acquiesce and so things must
remain until matters are otherwise arranged.' At least he was now sure of all the
rest: 'I trust the pains we have taken of late to secure an unbounded influence in
the court of proprietors, and of course in the court of directors, will relieve us in
future from any altercations whatever on any topics.'[40]

Still, he must have been disappointed. He got his way, but was shown that a
smoothly running administration in London would not emerge of its own accord
from minimal statutory regulation, with all else left to the informal methods at
which he was so adept. They had at any rate not averted a crisis which could be
solved only by formal extension of the state's powers. That rendered explicit what
Pitt and Dundas had implicitly conceded in 1784 when, because of Fox's previous
blunders, they left the Company more independence than was otherwise desirable. Unable to get rid of it, they now had to use it as best they could. Reform in
India was without doubt impeded. It did come, but not by a quick, radical break
with the bad old ways. Too many hardened in them still throve in the East; too
many even of those returned ready to champion change had made their pile by
means that would not bear much examination.[41]

Nothing illustrated it better than the problem of the debts of the Nawab of
Arcot, the leading native ruler in the Carnatic. Standing now at £3 million, they
arose partly out of the wars fought on his territory, partly out of his own misgovernment. For years he had kept himself afloat by borrowing large sums at enormous
rates of interest from servants of the Company, confident that the British authorities would one day bail him out. Sharing this confidence, the creditors gleefully
flocked round. Their capital was in effect guaranteed by their own Government,
while their earnings on it could be chosen by themselves. It was, even by the
standards of the Orient, an easy way to get rich. It was also an utter scandal, which
surely had to be cleared up if reform in India meant anything at all.

All this was, as usual, tangled with the Company's internal politics. Most of
those serving in Madras had profited, and on returning home they found it

advisable for mutual protection to band together in the so-called Arcot Squad. Its leader, Paul Benfield, 'Count Rupee', had his wife riding round London in a sky-blue chariot. For all the vulgar ostentation, it was a powerful interest group well represented in Parliament. Its money had supported the coalition till Fox's Bill ordered an investigation of the debts. It was then the first to desert to Dundas and Pitt, offering them a badly needed nucleus for a faction of their own inside the Company. Along with the rest of the Indian interest, the Squad voted for a slate of Pittite directors in the spring of 1784, then gave vital financial help at the General Election. The Ministry had thus itself incurred debts, of more than gratitude. But it did not follow, as the Whigs howled, that Pitt and Dundas were in the Squad's pocket. Once possessed of a comfortable parliamentary majority, they were (as all their other actions show) determined to assert their political authority. They refused, for example, to support Lawrence Sulivan, the Indian interest's candidate for chairman of the Company, on the grounds of his being too friendly by half with Hastings, then still ruling in Calcutta.

In any event, the India Act also ordered inquiry into the Nawab's debts, with settlement of the valid ones, as opposed, presumably, to those in some sense fraudulently contracted. But a strange thing happened when in the autumn of 1784 the directors drew up a dispatch to the authorities in Madras, instructing them to embark on such an inquiry. This they submitted, as required by law, to the Board. To their astonishment, it was returned amended in the opposite sense, in effect instructing the debts to be accepted in full, and allocating a large sum out of the revenues of the Carnatic for their repayment.[42]

The Whigs were up in arms, but a cooler view was possible. Cornwallis, without exactly approving, still did not condemn the decision. He wrote to Dundas: 'I can have no doubt that we must think alike about them [the creditors], and that you only consented that their fraudulent and infamous claims should be put into any course of payment, because you could not help it.' To this Dundas agreed: 'My prejudices were once as strong against the claims of the ... private creditors as any that you can entertain, and the feelings of all my colleagues at the Board were the same; against many of them the prejudice still remains, but from the time we examined the whole subject to the bottom, which we did in the most laborious manner, we became perfectly satisfied that every consideration of wisdom and policy suggested the propriety of the arrangement of December 9, 1784.'[43]

It was, of course, a rotten deal for the public. Though the old debt was paid off by 1804, it was found that through the liquidation scheme a new debt of £30 million had been contracted. Joseph Hume, radical scourge of the Dundas despotism, remarked:

> The actual loss by these proceedings of the Board of Control is not limited to the large sum which has been paid: for the knowledge of the fact that Mr Dundas had in that manner admitted, without any kind of inquiry, the whole claims ... served as a strong inducement to others to get ... obligations or bonds of any description, in hopes that some future good-natured President of the Board of Control would do the same.[44]

The episode was certainly not creditable, and the comments of Cornwallis and Dundas were cryptic. But the choice lay only between evils. Rigorous examination of the debts would have aroused furious resistance and probably systematic obstruction. Much time, effort and money might have been spent without any assurance of ever fully uncovering the facts, it being perhaps impossible to distinguish between genuine and fraudulent debts, and futile to try. Nobody could have been proud simply to pull down the curtain on such a sorry scene. It was a doubtless cynical decision by Dundas, but in practical terms also an understandable one.

That was not the only example of how hard it would prove for him, in a situation not of his making, to finish with the Indian past. Dundas and Pitt also wanted rid of Hastings, despite the devotion to him of many among their natural allies, the reformers in the Company. The Governor-general did not relish living with the India Act and, rather than await an inevitable recall under its terms, left anyway. As soon as he arrived home in the early autumn of 1785, his enemies in the Commons, led by Burke, moved for his impeachment.

In the chorus of recrimination, Hastings was always depicted as the evil genius of the old regime. And, in one way, the proceedings against him represented the eighteenth century at its progressive and civilised best, probing the conduct of colonial administration under a clear assumption that Indian states and subjects had the same rights as European ones: in other words, on principles of international justice and racial equality. Yet it is equally clear in retrospect that many matters were mischievously laid to Hastings's charge. For without doubt the new regime in India owed much to him, too. His iron hand had not only conquered and subjugated, but also built administrative, financial and judicial mechanisms without which later reforms could hardly have started. If his rule was no model of virtue, that was largely because of the parcel of rogues he had to rule with. To curb their corruption at all, he could only be hard, and this hardness often extended to the Indians conniving with them. The alternative, however, would have been a yet more culpable laxity.

Still, there was no open-and-shut case against Hastings, and since the initiative for the impeachment came from the opposition, the Government's attitude would be crucial. On the record of the House there already stood a condemnatory motion of Dundas's. But when he had next voiced an opinion, in July 1784, he said he was 'neither a harsh censor of that gentleman, or too enthusiastic a eulogist. My opinion of Mr Hastings at this moment is exactly what it has ever been.' In the debates which went on through the spring of 1786, his sentiment seemed to have become more favourable still:

> I do not think that the procedure of Mr Hastings amounts to criminality. I have examined his conduct minutely; and I always found that when there was any improper conduct observable in Mr Hastings, every possibility of annexing a criminal intention to it eluded my grasp, and there was always some letter of the court of directors or some strong reason to justify Mr Hastings at the bottom.[45]

Burke was not one to let pass a lurking ambiguity and craftily brought his main charge against Hastings's conduct during the Rohilla War, which Dundas had also voted to condemn in 1782. He could surely not demur this time without exposing himself as a double-dealer. But he sidestepped:

I moved for his recall avowedly on grounds of expediency, because he appeared to me to have lost the confidence of the native princes of India and because there was thence reason to imagine that Mr Hastings could not continue to hold the government of India with any advantage to the Company or any credit to Great Britain ... The Rohilla War was an unjustifiable measure, but it is not more so now than it was nine years ago. Since the period that it occurred, an Act of Parliament has been passed reappointing Mr Hastings Governor-general of Bengal. The statute, there-fore, may be considered as a parliamentary pardon.[46]

Dundas accordingly voted against the first charge – as did Pitt, amid much sneering that his usual high standards were being abased by his crony's influence. Without the Government's support, the motion was defeated.

The Whigs could then have expected to do no better with a second charge brought by Fox. It concerned Chait Singh, deposed as rajah of Benares for evading payment of an exorbitant £500,000 demanded in contributions to the military expenses of the Company. To the amazement of Burke, indeed of everybody, Pitt and Dundas this time switched sides and voted against Hastings, thus ensuring a majority for the charge. Far from being gratified, the Whigs immediately cried corruption.

Several of Dundas's own confidants wondered exactly what was going on, and wrote to ask him. To Cornwallis he replied that the impeachment was

not pleasant to many of our friends, and of course from that and many other circumstances not pleasing to us [Dundas and Pitt], but the truth is, when we examined the various articles of charges against him, with his defences, they were so strong, and the defences so perfectly unsupported, it was impossible not to concur.

His response to Buccleuch laid still greater stress on his reluctance:

Mr Pitt and I studied the case with the utmost care and perhaps a culpable anxiety to find grounds to bring him off, but every defence slipped from under our feet, and the force of evidence compelled us to take a decided part against him ... I really feel it with infinite regret, but if he should for want of legal evidence be acquitted in the House of Lords, I suspect that when the whole of his conduct is examined to the bottom, he will cease to appear that great man which the world have been accustomed to consider him.

In asserting that the charges had to be treated on their merits rather than as an expression of moral horror, Pitt and Dundas were clearly no witch-hunters. But their reticence went deeper than their posture of studious objectivity suggested. Even on the charge to which they saw some substance they would not commit themselves officially beyond their vote in the House. Dundas told Burke so: 'From many reasons we cannot agree to take upon us any share in the management of the prosecution, but we have given and shall continue to give that support to it which appears to us consistent with national justice, and the credit of the House of Commons.'

Thus in the trial before the Lords it would still be for the Whigs alone to sustain the accusations. This may seem elaborately Machiavellian and, not least, callous towards a man who Dundas correctly predicted would at length be cleared. The impression is reinforced by his comment, recorded in Fox's correspondence, that: 'I don't care what is done with [Hastings], for you and your friends in opposition have done our business, by keeping him out of the Board of Control.' But if Dundas really felt a deep antipathy publicly dissembled, one may ask why he did not also vote for the first charge, consistently with his position in 1782. Nor does the idea that Hastings threatened him in the Board stand up for a moment. That such a controversial figure could have been put on it was almost inconceivable anyway, and it was not conceivable at all that he could somehow have been forced on in the teeth of objections from the Government's Indian specialist. The only other explanation is that Dundas feared Hastings's appointment if a different Ministry came in. Yet one may be sure that Hastings would have been appointed to nothing if that Ministry had been drawn from an opposition led by Fox and Burke. We are left all the same with Dundas's actual words. What do they mean? Perhaps he was expressing himself loosely, as he too often did, intending to convey no more than relief at the end of Hastings's influence on Indian policy. But the detail remains puzzling.

What seems at any rate obvious is that Pitt and Dundas saw in the affair a minefield to be approached with extreme caution. If they had taken a stand against impeachment, they might have sent the wrong signals to India and all connected with her, signals that a blind eye could be turned to misconduct. If they had supported impeachment without qualification, they might have lent credence to the less laudable of the Whigs' undoubtedly mixed motives. For the high moral tone of Burke's public declarations masked among his colleagues a guilty aware- ness that their recent disasters were owed to their Indian policy and a vindictive desperation to retrieve that ground.

Of course, the motives of Pitt and Dundas were mixed too, and it would not have escaped their scrutiny that the accusations were framed with less than judicial rigour. As Conor Cruse O'Brien has observed in a recent comment, once the Commons had voted for the impeachment, 'the essentially rhetorical format of the articles of charge became an embarrassment'. And why were they so framed? Perhaps because the Whigs did not expect to carry the motions for impeachment, were instead engaged in scoring political points. The instant allegations of duplicity when Pitt and Dundas actually voted with them were of a piece with that. It was the sort of opposition that any Ministers would have been happy to leave stewing in its own juice. The line adopted by Pitt and Dundas had two other merits. It would allow justice to take its course if Hastings was culpable after all. And it would not impede efforts to extend their own influence in the Company, which had necessarily to be done in large part through his friends. To be deemed in some quarters inconsistent with their votes in the Commons was by comparison no great matter.[47]

It was in any event not inconsistent with the higher goal of consolidating a regime under which the crimes imputed to Hastings could not recur – in which case, the controversies he represented were dead. The great advantage of an impeachment carried out by the opposition lay in its obviating any need by the Ministry to defend the mistakes of the past. It meant that Dundas, as the man in charge of India, could separate the reform of defects in the system from the

124 The Dundas Despotism

punishment of delinquencies by individuals. Not being personally spiteful, he preferred it that way: 'He thought more as advocate, legislator and Minister than as judge.' For though punishment should be condign, punctilio could be a vice, especially if it undermined the rest of what he sought to achieve. That was first and foremost to make a fresh start, to introduce a new philosophy in Indian government that would turn it irrevocably from mercantilist pillage to responsible imperial administration. With the wars over, this was possible, but only if the other old problems were expeditiously settled.[48]

What we should therefore rather mark is the change which now took place not only in that government's personnel and instruments, but also in its purposes and attitudes. In India itself, the change is credited primarily to Cornwallis. Having yielded at last to official pleas, he arrived there in 1786. To Campbell in Madras, appointed at the same time and on the similar grounds of his probity, Dundas wrote: 'Lord Cornwallis and you have gone to India, not like former Governors for the purpose of enriching yourselves, or providing for needy connections, but you have undertaken the much nobler task of redeeming a lost empire, and upon that foundation establishing a monument to your fame in the gratitude and affection of your country.'

Cornwallis lost no time in enforcing the higher standards of conduct desired by London. The first Governor-general with no obligations to the Company, he was determined to root out corruption in it. He divided its servants strictly into those engaged in trade and those in administration, which they were not allowed to mix. He cut down patronage from home, instead encouraging promotions on merit from within the presidency where a vacancy occurred. Thinking the Indians still more dishonest than the British, he reversed Hastings's policy of running things with their help and, except for one judge, dismissed all from high positions. Otherwise, however, his despotism was benevolent towards them. Land and tax reforms eased the peasant's lot while raising agricultural productivity. A more humane criminal code was introduced. After a period of large but haphazard territorial expansion, war and indeed all superfluous entanglements with the native states were avoided, though Cornwallis acted vigorously when he had to. Altogether he established the British tradition of strong, incorruptible, paternalist government in India.[49]

For Dundas, political reforms in India had a further purpose as the prelude to economic ones. To draw attention to this aspect, he started presenting an annual Indian budget, an innovation of importance, even in a wider constitutional sense, for there was as yet no regular British budget. But the Commons yawned: rather than deliver his speeches, he sometimes merely handed them over to be entered in the record. Since the Company was to stay in business with its monopoly for the time being intact, he wanted its performance to improve. Its finances, like everything else about it, had previously descended into chaotic disorder. Its debts stood in 1785 at £8 million, and were set for a rapid rise of another £6 million by 1790. With peace in the East, there did at first appear to be some improvement. In the decade to 1793, the Company earned profits of £13 million. But this was deceptive.

Dundas had read in *The Wealth of Nations* how a monopoly could only be justified during the early stages of a trade, after which it should be fully opened. That was borne out by Indian experience. While the Company continued to supply the British market with valuable commodities, its efforts to balance them with exports proved useless. Often its ships on the outward voyages were laden with nothing but bullion: which, quite apart from being no matter of rejoicing to free traders, was by definition a disaster according to mercantilist orthodoxy. Even to the more vigorous commerce which now began to develop the Indian monopoly contributed little, the difference being made by trade with China, above all in tea.

Yet it obviously was possible for profits to be generated in the sub-continent itself. That happened on the unregulated fringe of the monopoly, the 'country trade': trade not originating in or destined for Britain, thus coastwise trade in India or trade between India and third countries. This indeed was where the Company's servants, conducting their own businesses on the side, amassed their inflated earnings. It did not escape Dundas that this traffic was also growing – and to the benefit of people who, when working for their Company, could barely cover its costs. This ought in itself to have been a decisive argument for free trade, but they of course took it the other way and preferred to believe that general liberalisation would ruin their rackets.

Unfortunately, though contemporary economic theory might explain what was happening, it could offer little by way of a remedy. Dundas was left to tackle largely by himself these convoluted yet critical problems and, through no real fault of his own, his ideas remained too narrow and unsound to solve them.[50] But in seeking a solution, he incidentally prompted a remarkable development of trade, the benefits of which far outweighed his financial failure. They allowed India's no longer merely pillaged resources to be applied to strengthening Britain's general economic position in the world.

Dundas was too canny to mount a direct attack on the monopoly, but he could unobtrusively subvert it. This was how he broached the idea to William Grenville, a member of the Board of Control, in September 1786:

> Do not be jealous of me when I mention the chance of the dissolution of the monopoly of the East India Company. But you will agree with me that there are events which may led to such a dissolution, and I cannot help considering it as an important point to try as early as a favourable opportunity offers what chance there is by transactions with foreign nations to ensure a certainty of remitting our Indian revenues (which prudence will admit to be remitted) but which we may perhaps not be able to remit through the commerce of our own subjects, whose capitals and navigation may be otherwise employed at the time we require such remittances, which as you know can only be done through the medium of commerce.[51]

The monopoly would thus be eroded by stimulating more diversified trade through new channels. Dundas intended the British to retain the largest share. But it was historically exceptional for one country to stop trying to shut out all others from intercontinental commerce. He believed that if he could deal fairly with foreigners in India and obviate grievances arising from British political dominance there, they would not conspire to sabotage it. Most anyway posed no such threat.

Portugal merely clung lethargically to her old factories (though Goa was one that Dundas would have liked to snap up). Spain readily entered into an agreement in 1788. Britain needed to keep no more than an eye on the Emperor's subjects at Ostend, in the Austrian Netherlands, who ran an illicit oriental trade. France had also faded from the Indian scene, and Dundas for now discounted the chance of her returning in strength. But with naval stations commanding long stretches of the eastward route, she could still alarm and annoy the British. The best thing was to consider on their merits, as he did, the claims of the Compagnie des Indes. A limited trade was accommodated for it, under British protection, in the French commercial treaty of 1786.

Britain's real competitor was Holland. She had East Indian possessions, in the archipelago now known as Indonesia, much greater in extent and linked more securely to the homeland by the best strategic bases in the Cape and Ceylon. The Dutch took umbrage when, in 1786, Dundas secured from a local sultan the cession of Penang (renamed Prince of Wales Island), on the Strait of Molucca, inside their sphere of influence. His aim was not to acquire territory at their expense, however, but to make sure Britain got a cut of the commerce in the Far East by laying down a chain of trading stations. He also appreciated that he had to tread delicately with Holland. She, too, had seen her greatest days, and was throughout the eighteenth century steadily debilitated by a complex of constitutional and commercial disputes. In their most recent stage during the American War, the Stadholder, William V of Orange, a nephew of George III, had wanted to support Britain. His opponents in the remnant of the old republican oligarchy were by contrast anxious for their trade with France. They insisted on their country taking that side – with disastrous results, including great damage to its fleet and expulsion from India. The Dutch were simply no longer strong enough for an independent foreign policy. It remained only to see whether they would become clients of the British or the French.

For the present France held the advantage, after entering into a treaty with Holland in 1785. If Britain was to undermine it, she had to be in good odour with that merchant elite, which Dundas could thus not allow the Company to antagonise. But in his view this did not mean banning it from the Far East. On the contrary, he thought these varied interests reconcilable. While Britain was building, with whatever security was needed, a wide oriental network of trade, the Dutch were only worried about their lucrative monopolies of spices. In September 1787 he wrote to Grenville, who was doubtful of his analysis, 'I do not see how there is any inconsistency between their having the exclusive spice trade and yet our having Trincomalee,' the great harbour in Ceylon, together with 'a free navigation in the Eastern seas for the purposes of our China trade, and likewise for the purpose of opening new markets both for our Indian and European manufactures.'[52]

At that time, Dundas was engaged in drawing up a package of proposals to put to the Dutch for division of the spoils. In the final version, he stressed that it was in the Company's interest to eschew expansionism, that it had no desire for navigation or settlement in their sphere of influence while relations between the two countries did not deteriorate. As a token of its goodwill, it would indeed restore to Holland the port of Negapatam, near Madras, seized in 1781, which could then resume its former brisk trade through the Strait of Molucca. In return, the British would gain free use of all Dutch harbours. The Government in The Hague was interested enough to negotiate, but with extreme caution. Even after four years, when the talks were overtaken by other events, Dundas had not allayed its suspicion there that he was merely plotting to seize the most strategic bits of Holland's empire.[53]

If Dundas made only inchmeal progress with this centrepiece of his commercial diplomacy, he could push ahead with something that proved in the long run far more beneficial, the opening of China. His fertile mind soon sprang to one exciting opportunity – 'if China could be supplied by the sale of British and Indian manufactures either directly or indirectly finding their way to China, it would render the benefit of our Indian Empire complete.' This would be the answer to the biggest problem in Britain's balance of payments, which arose from the growing deficit against imports of Chinese tea. Assuming Britain could send a greater volume of manufactures, displacing specie, to India, then a trading triangle might be constructed, though not without difficulty. Development of commerce from India to China, between which there was also a regular drain of bullion, really depended on new products, sources of which Dundas became increasingly anxious to acquire: textiles, pepper, sandalwood – the eventual answer was to be opium. But in the process Britain would turn itself into the pivot of a quickening trade between East and West.[54]

Dundas sent out several embassies to China, the first to Canton in 1786–7 with the aim of improving local commercial conditions, a second under Charles Cathcart, who for the purpose gave up his parliamentary seat of Clackmannanshire, but died on the way to Peking in 1788. The efforts were then interrupted by objections from some shareholders in the Company who had arrangements of their own with the mandarins at Canton. In 1789 Dundas, planning a new expedition, told Cornwallis: 'I feel so much the importance of establishing a commercial connection with the great emperor of China, that I am not disposed to be discouraged from the plan by any trivial obstructions.'[55] He asked the Governor-general to dispatch a trustworthy agent for him from India, well out of sight of the pests in London. Finally, a successful official mission departed under Lord Macartney in 1791–2.

That was one illustration of how, by the end of the long process of reform starting in the 1770s, the Crown had won the essential of what it wanted in the East: control of the broad lines of British policy, without stifling restriction, on the contrary with some liberalisation, of the commercial interests operating there. Pitt and Dundas had set up a dual system, one which served India well till the Mutiny of 1857 required a complete overhaul. But it was a somewhat different dual system from that originally envisaged. The plan had been for the Board to control the Company, and in many routine matters that was how it actually did work. Dundas always paid lip-service to the notion. He wrote in July 1787 that 'we sometimes differ; and it is natural for them to feel now and then under the hand of Control, but we go on very well together. We take care always to keep within the powers with which the laws have vested in us.'[56]

But in high policy, the dual system came to consist of Dundas and a Governor-general supporting each other in everything important. This relationship of complete mutual confidence was just the one he had with Cornwallis. Both free of the Company's vested interests, they readily united against it. That alone gave them ascendancy over anyone else minded to interfere. The concentration of power matched a reality revealed in the course of reform, that change for the better in India needed guidance by a firm authority, enforcing higher standards of conduct yet restrained in its own absolutism. This was what Dundas brought about, and he could justly say: 'We never before had a government of India both at home and abroad working in perfect unison together, upon principles of perfect unity and integrity; these ingredients cannot fail to produce their consequent effects.'[57]

His own Indian exertions had a wider significance, for they represented processes transforming the science of government. The end of the eighteenth century saw growing concern for and interest in good administration, expressing itself also in disenchantment with aristocratic amateurism at home, as with corruption and oppression in the East. A rising politician such as Dundas was moved to draw up schemes for reform by studying, digesting, systematising and turning into rational policy options the mass of raw information produced by his everyday political activity. His claim to power rested on understanding of this detail and familiarity with the work of his departments: these, not broad acres, were in future to be the qualifications for high office. It was the emergence of the modern, professional public man as we know him, believing in orderly, efficient, reputable government as a practical necessity.

This was one consequence of Britain's growing up as a world power. The first, lost Empire in America had been in essence mercantilist. The second now in process of formation was perforce a trading rather than a colonising one, built on commercial outposts for the exploitation of resources which remained in the hands of alien peoples. India provided the model, and Dundas was to the fore in appreciating the economic implications. Partly through his Scottish background, and partly through daily contact with the practical problems, he was shaking himself free from a still widely prevalent mercantilism. Having accepted instead the principles of free trade (though in a limited sense compared with what was taken for granted a century later) he began to discern the outlines of Britain's future as the centre of an imperial system, with commodities from its outposts feeding industry and consumption at home.

Finally, he and others drawn into the novel imperial design represented forces at last making of Parliament something more than a medieval English institution, one where indeed narrow English concerns soon looked just as parochial as exclusively Scottish, Indian or, a little later, Irish ones. The development here paralleled that in the country at large as, in the trials of future years, a new greater British identity was forged.[58]

For Dundas personally, too, all this represented a qualitative leap forward. He had so far been a reasonably efficient electoral manager, a good Scottish Minister, a skilful parliamentary fixer. Such activities placed him at best in the higher ranks of the commonplace. With his Indian endeavours he had had, in a situation of extraordinary complexity, to apply liberal principles while making necessary concessions to the rankest jobbery; to raise the morality of government and standards of administration yet not to alienate vested interests; to promote Britain's advantage by reconciling it with the advantage of other powers; and to lay, with little more than rudimentary theories and unprocessed information, the foundations of a new economic system. He had balanced an enormous variety of claims and, by and large, he had kept people happy. Of course he did not get everything right – some parts of his structure had to be quickly altered, while others were never effective at all. Yet on the whole the new, sophisticated Indian machinery worked, and continued to work into the distant future. It was, to say the least, a political achievement of the first order.

How can one believe that, while thus promoting the good of India, he was glorying in the corruption and oppression of his native land? Amid his other labours, Dundas could easily have forgotten Scotland. But he did not. On the contrary, his career as a Scottish politician was just getting into full swing. His Indian involvement helped him here, though the extent to which it permitted him to extend his personal patronage has been exaggerated. More important was that it marked out, through his dominance of a crucial area of policy, his position at the centre of the Government. It was his general standing that made him the focus of the Scottish system too. No man eager for its favour could fail to note where the power really lay. Soon almost the whole Scottish elite, never backward in such matters, was scampering into Pitt's fold. Dundas in return accumulated the raw material of power, the offices and spoils to distribute to his sharp-set countrymen.

One hungry though eternally unsatisfied member of the herd, James Boswell, raised the subject while enjoying Dundas's hospitality in London in 1783, and asked his host why he consented to be 'a salesman for us, like cattle.' The reply came that 'it was better for the country, better for individuals not. For when all could scramble, they would have a chance to get more for themselves and their friends without regard to merit. Whereas an agent for government must distribute to the best purpose. He has a trust.' Four years later, when Boswell again inquired, Dundas almost appeared to be tiring of the business: 'He said that power was thought desirable on account of the patronage annexed to it; but that the uneasiness was much greater than the satisfaction for you had six or seven letters to write to people who were disappointed and probably had to give the office to one for whom you did not care, but that the government must be carried on.'[59]

Boswell, consistently passed over, became obsessive about patronage. He never paused to consider whether any personal defect might be to blame, but cheerfully expected sarcasm to do the trick for him. In that conviction, he even wrote an open *Letter to the People of Scotland*:

> Our country is at a miserable ebb, when its great and good families are totally indifferent about every public concern, and have so little spirit, even as to their private concerns, that they never advance, like men, to the fountain-head of government, but indolently or timidly suffer all to be done by some person who for the time is brought forward, as a minister for Scotland ... Yet I will do Mr Dundas the justice to declare, that, large as his power is, he has

not much abused it. He has, indeed, taken very good care of his relations! And why should he not? Though, to be sure, flesh and blood must feel his having put his young nephew over the heads of I know not how many of us, as Solicitor General. But I do not believe that he has been cruel, oppressive or vindictive!

except, he added with another side-swipe, in attacking Sir Lawrence Dundas's interest in Orkney and inducing Lord Auchinleck to manufacture votes in Ayrshire. This was mild compared with what Boswell, getting cold feet at the last minute, deleted from the proofs: 'Mr Dundas is not the lion. Ye lords and lairds and people of Scotland, attend! – Ye Lowland sheep, the Highland deer, why do you startle and fly? Don't be frightened! Come near him! Look at him! He roars indeed, and he roars admirably: but I tell you he is not the lion. He is only the jackal!'[60]

Given the character of the Scottish ruling class, where many were related and everybody knew everybody else, it was only too easy to impugn the motives for patronage. In fact people would probably have been more shocked if Dundas had not provided for his kin. He himself told Viscount Sydney, the Home Secretary: 'Our Scotch gentlemen beget such multitudes of children, it is a great satisfaction to me when I have an opportunity of relieving any of my old friends.' The business could still not always be conducted so amiably. Lord Breadalbane wrote bluntly in 1787: 'Unless the subjoined list of friends are immediately provided for, whom I have applied for at different periods since I came into Parliament, and for whom nothing has yet been done, my attachment for the present administration will be considerably diminished.'

Of course Dundas's choices were generally politic. Cockburn said of him: 'Too much a man of the world not to live well with his opponents if they would let him, and, totally incapable of personal harshness or unkindness, it was not unnatural that his official favours should be confined to his own innumerable and insatiable partisans.' Yet he 'was respected by the reasonable of his opponents, who, though doomed to suffer by his power, liked the individual: against whom they had nothing to say, except that he was not on their side and reserved his patronage for his supporters.' Even some of those opponents hoped against hope. The Whig, Lord Lauderdale, set out to ask a favour with a confession that he was owed none, yet 'in the belief that you have that sort of mind that likes fair, open and persevering conduct even in an enemy.'

There were, at the same time, real constraints on Dundas, as on the other managers, notably John Robinson and George Rose in England, who made something of a specialism out of this aspect of politics. They were providing the personnel for an emergent modern state, where efficiency was already at a premium, with no sure instruments for identifying it in people ostensibly qualified for an appointment. Such instruments were not indeed to be devised till William Gladstone reformed the civil service in the latter half of the next century. Meanwhile there was no choice but to rely on personal knowledge, connection or recommendation.

But Dundas took some care to distinguish between his personal and his official obligations. He wrote to Henry Addington:

You know enough of me to believe me when I say that I am not a person lightly to discourage merit or fair pretensions wherever I find them, but on the other hand if I find pretensions brought forward that are not founded and these supported in a manner which the departments of government, under which an officer must act, cannot consistently with their own dignity and authority countenance, I may be driven most reluctantly to dispense with services, which I am certainly disposed to avail myself of, because in doing so I believe I am essentially benefiting the public service.

His distribution of patronage still aroused suspicion, then as later. If far from democratic, however, government was not arbitrary. And authority was more widely diffused in the pre-modern British state. Dundas himself cautioned, for example, against overt political manipulation of the revenue's personnel: 'The appointments do not flow from the Treasury but the Commissioners of Excise, who must be furnished with some good grounds for acting upon in the change of an officer, otherwise they will get into a scrape.'

Moreover, the whole system was amenable to law. Burke had already in 1782 pushed through an 'economical reform', cutting down ministerial patronage: this in a bureaucracy already smaller, and therefore less venal, than that of any other European state. Dundas did comment that 'nothing was more hurtful to the country or a free constitution', yet the remark was not merely self-serving. He had to deal with real, not ideal, human nature, above all with the ambition – indeed the avarice, as he did not hesitate to call it – of the Commons. Somehow their personal interest had also to be turned to the representation of the country and defence of its liberties, in particular by the sustenance and control of an effective Ministry. Dundas feared the point was being reached where they could only be gratified with peerages, a reward more corrupting than civil office because it 'threw a great weight of influence into the hands of the King ... Nothing should be done to lessen the dignity and respectability of the House of Commons.' He later hinted that he had remonstrated with Pitt over the cheapening of peerages. Dundas's own view, surely prescient, was that a Government responsible to Parliament needed its own stock of favours to dole out, properly kept distinct from honours bestowed by the monarch. It explained observations apparently damning like this one to Grenville: 'There ought to be some such offices as those in question which ought to be sinecures and given as rewards in place of being looked on for the performance of duties.' He was obliged to use as best he might an existing system. He could and did not expect, however, that its operation would be superhumanly virtuous and altruistic.[61]

None of this yet precluded a conscious effort on Dundas's part to raise the standard of personnel. We have already seen him undertaking it in India. In Scotland, a historian of local government has found something similar – as well as a good example of his attention to detail, for the whole of it cost the Exchequer only £6000 a year. In the appointment of sheriffs, for instance, he would not allow the county sets to nominate their placemen, and demanded more than token qualifications. Instead of genteel amateurs, he sought bright young men who would rise to greater things, or else experienced practitioners worth a political reward. First in the larger counties, then in the smaller, those with no legal practice were denied appointment, even when they had powerful backing. If this meant that more sheriffs were non-resident, going on circuit from homes in Edinburgh, rational central government was also promoted at the expense of the noblemen in their localities.[62]

Again, we know just how Dundas proceeded with a vacancy in 1793 for a crucial post in the legal bureaucracy, the principal clerk of session. He had to consider eight candidates, supported respectively by the Duke of Buccleuch, by the Marquis of Tweeddale, by the Earl of Galloway, by the Sutherland family, by the powers of Perthshire, the Duke of Atholl and General Murray, by a group of gentlemen, including some personal friends, in the North-east. None of them was selected. The prize went to John Pringle, sheriff of Edinburgh, nominated by the Lord Advocate, who hardly required an incentive to keep in line – the reason was Pringle's 'recent public services', in other words, efficiency in the suppression of radicalism. The Dundases were everywhere and always on the look-out for talent.[63]

The same pattern emerges in Scotland as in India: not an excessive and rigid concentration of power, but a readiness to exploit the influence which central government could exert to enforce higher standards at subordinate levels. According to Thomas Somerville, Dundas

> was incessantly and disinterestedly active in meliorating the condition of all orders of men to the utmost extent of the influence which he derived from his official station … The augmentation of the salaries of the judges and officers of the Court of Session, of the stipends of the clergy, and of all the servants of the public in Scotland are chiefly to be ascribed to his influence and advice.

Of course it was politically beneficial for him to increase the size and wealth of the official establishment. But it is easy to forget, in times when the state does so much, the importance which patronage inevitably assumed in times when the state did little. It represented far and away the biggest item of business for Scottish government, and anyone conducting that government had necessarily to engage in it. A comment of Dundas's own confirmed how painstaking he was: 'I never made a promise in my life to any man. When I intended to serve a man, I waited till I could do it. I can also say that I never allowed a second day to pass without answering every letter addressed to me requiring one.' Even in 1798, when he faced an immensity of other concerns, his nephew Robert was still begging him to delegate: 'How can you allow such fellows to assail you? Turn them over to me, and unpleasant as the task is, I shall most cordially keep them at arm's length for you. Or if anyone ought to be admitted to you, I shall not fail to give him a passport.'[64]

What was the extent of the resulting influence? Dundas's papers overflow with applications for patronage, material hard to collate usefully. Some of it was summarised for him in 1801, however, when he started clearing his cupboards on what he assumed to be his retiral. A bundle of nearly 600 solicitations from the years 1784–90 was weeded out for destruction. In fact it escaped and found its way at length to the National Library of Scotland. How much of the business it contains is impossible to say; it does not include successful requests, nor any appointments made without written application, nor anything in India. The volume of cases here, at 100 a year, two a week, at least shows the minimum of what he had to deal with. This picture seems broadly confirmed by another surviving summary from 1807, though by then Dundas was out of office. That year he and his son dealt with 196 cases, of which 113 arose at home, including 27 inside Scotland, and 83 in India.

We are on firmer ground in defining the types of patronage at his disposal, for we have no reason to think the sample of 1784–90 unrepresentative. The most applications, 27 per cent of the total, were for the forces, about evenly divided between the navy, where his influence was direct, and the army, where it worked through his intimacy with the Commander-in-chief, the Duke of York. The next biggest group, of 19 per cent, was for posts in the civil administration. Then, at 14 per cent, came appeals for pensions, often from dependants of dead officials. About 9 per cent were for preferment in the Church and 6 per cent for appointments in the universities or patronage of literary works. Legal posts accounted for 2 per cent, as did requests for jobs in the colonies. Applications for peerages, or elevations within the peerage, were the subject of 1 per cent. The rest was miscellaneous.[65]

Dundas undoubtedly raised Scotland's share of patronage. After the turn of the century, with a population one-sixth of England's, she was getting, in value, more than one-quarter of official pensions and one-third of sinecures. Even then demand outran supply – 'at present I stand debarred from granting any more pensions on the Scotch establishment by a representation from the Chief Baron,' Dundas once reported. The general English view remained that Scots got too much, and Parliament was eventually to limit the amount available to them. The manager defended his system, however: 'I believe for a number of years back the small funds at the King's disposal in Scotland have been distributed with great purity and impartiality. They are given either to people of rank, with inadequate fortunes, to literary characters, or to females in urgent and needy circumstances.'

Nor, more widely, were his exertions always of direct political benefit. He was, for example, instrumental in winning sponsorship from the Prince of Wales for the Literary Fund, which he and others set up 'to relieve and support genius and learning in sickness, age and at the termination of life; and to preserve from distress the widows and orphans of those who have any claims on the public from literary industry or merit' – hardly the action of a sordid man. He did not personally profit from his patronage as he could have done, and as others did from theirs: it can scarcely be said often enough that he was never rich. Yet some things were hard to refuse. One William Armstrong, applying for a higher post in the West Indies, addressed him thus: 'I did myself the honour of writing you by the last August ships and at the same time sent a turtle which I hope arrived in good condition.'

If this was corruption, contemporaries found it hard to see. Not even critics of the system advocated the principles and methods of modern bureaucracy. On the contrary, they were fully persuaded of the value of patronage, which they themselves used when they could. The distinction they drew was between its justifiable and unjustifiable, or venal, uses. So long as patron and client alike took as their primary purpose not pecuniary reward but the promotion of the competent and eradication of the incompetent, then private influence and public duty could be compatible. The system was still by our lights hardly just, because the competent could be excluded for having the wrong or lacking the right political connections. Under it, all the same, the quality of administration did not wither, but flourished. Dundas had no other end in view.[66]

Patronage was extended not just to individuals. 'To you, therefore, Sir, this letter is addressed in the name of many of the principal citizens of Edinburgh, as to one who, they trust, has both the power and the will to serve his country,' ran the exordium to one grand design for embellishment of the capital. It could count itself lucky to possess a son in him. He piloted through five Improvement Acts between 1781 and 1790, for higher building standards, for a jail on Calton Hill, above all for an ambitious scheme of Robert Adam's, the South Bridge which would carry a roadway from the High Street across the chasm of the Cowgate to his magnificent new university. The original ideas were visionary indeed, with towering colonnaded buildings all the way along. Dundas strongly approved, and in February 1786 noted in dismay 'a good deal of conversation circulating abroad as if the town of Edinburgh was going to do the shabby thing in departing from the monumental part of Adam's plan.' But it proved just too expensive, and in the end the thoroughfare was lined with ordinary tenements and shops. Even on this more modest scale the scheme ran into financial trouble. Dundas promised to get extra funds for completion of the university in 1789, being made in return a Doctor of Laws. The money did not arrive, however, till after the Napoleonic Wars.

Since the plans were being altered anyway, Dundas took the opportunity of leaving his first mark on the city's topography. A modern observer of the bridge might be struck by the thought that it could more conveniently have followed a level course from the ridge of the High Street to the elevation beyond the Old College. Instead it dips before ascending quite steeply into Nicolson Street. This was because at the lowest point there stood Adam Square, long disappeared, where Lord President Arniston had his town house. With a level course, his outlook would have been blocked, and horses and carts would have been rumbling over his head. Dundas therefore arranged for the carriageway first to be led down to pass his door and only then allowed to rise.[67]

Patronage was indeed seldom a simple business, requiring little more than the necessary degree of subservience on the part of the client and cynicism on the part of the manager, from which neither could really lose. On the contrary, it might pose extremely complex political problems. One arose from Dundas's relations with the financial community of Edinburgh. He had incurred considerable debts there, both personal and pecuniary. But the obligations were mutual. The Royal Bank of Scotland was already in his pocket. In 1790 he became governor of the Bank of Scotland. That secured him all the financial clout he needed for his public purposes. According to Cockburn, the old banks were 'the conspicuous sycophants of existing power ... their favours and graciousness were all reserved for the right side.' Nor was this control confined to the capital. Glasgow, supremely enterprising in other ways, had failed to establish itself as a financial centre, so that Walter Scott could write of the 'bankers of Edinburgh, who are in general zealously loyal, and who hold the commerce of Glasgow and all the West in the hollow of their hand.'

The power thus vested in Dundas could be seen in his consistently thwarting the efforts at expansion by the third chartered institution, the British Linen Bank, which happened not to be under his thumb. A petition for leave to raise its banking capital once conveniently got lost in the Treasury in London. On the whole, however, Dundas's policy in the financial sector was the same as elsewhere, to unite the major Scottish interests round himself. Outside the public banks, he had a close association with William Ramsay of Barnton (who lent him £13,000 in 1786), but he tried also to woo the other potentate among the private bankers, Sir William Forbes of Pitsligo. He, however, resisted every blandishment, including a place on the town council, saying he was 'totally averse to all concerns with politics'. One reason became clear when, a few years later, he started turning up at Whig dinners.[68]

Financial patronage consisted mainly in carving up the business that was going. For more than a decade after 1784 the institutions were divided by a fierce dispute over how to do so in the remittance of public revenue. Proceeds of taxes were not, of course, retained at the Scottish Exchequer but sent south to the Treasury. The practice was for the money to be deposited with a bank in Edinburgh which in due course, after an interval of up to sixty days, carried out the transfer through its agent in London. Since the sums were large, the delay could be highly profitable.

Forbes's company had the lion's share of this business. Most of the rest went through the Royal Bank, of which Ramsay was a director. He was a peevish, rancorous man who could barely tolerate a rival's prosperity and now sought to blight it with an attempt to seize all the remittances. Finding that Dundas just would not listen to crude schemes for suppressing competition, Ramsay went over his head to Pitt. He wrote in July 1789 to repeat his complaints against Forbes and to insinuate that his own proposals had not received a proper hearing: 'I am almost convinced Mr Dundas never proposed the measure or even mentioned it to Mr Pitt, as I scarcely believe any Minister would be so imprudent and inattentive as not to prefer at once without hesitation the safest mode of remitting the public money if it was properly represented to him.' Dundas gave a private warning of trouble in store to Forbes, who generously replied that his own bank's particular interests should not be allowed to prejudice Scotland's general interests. This left the way open for the system to be amended.[69]

First, Dundas called for the facts. Inquiry revealed that, in 1789, Sir William Forbes & Co., remitting the excise from Edinburgh, handled £250,000. In addition, it received £90,000 from London in respect of the salaries of public servants in Scotland. The Royal Bank, to which were allocated the customs, land tax and stamp duty, remitted £170,000, a sum expected to rise with the yield from these. Finally, Ramsay's private firm took charge of £30,000 in revenue from the Post Office. Now that it was known these sums would be redistributed, others put in bids. The Bank of Scotland suggested to its governor that the two old banks should share the taxes between them. The British Linen Bank wanted some too. The Royal Bank stuck to its demand for sole charge of all public revenue, wheeling out its biggest gun, Buccleuch, to extol the size of its interests, the efficiency of its services, and the rocklike stability of a chartered as opposed to lesser institutions. There would be mutual advantages, his Grace hinted, if the state could deal with just one. What was more, the Royal Bank would undertake to remit promptly every quarter, and not exploit the lag of sixty days. It was all a little too plausible. Forbes warned that it opened the way for debauching of the currency, while the revenue services themselves judged that the risks of establishing a monopoly outweighed any conceivable advantage. After long deliberation, Dundas in 1796 apportioned the remittances four ways, equally to the two biggest public and to the two biggest private banks: not till 1810 did the poor relation, the British Linen Bank, get a fifth share. It was this episode that brought into existence the Committee of Scottish Bankers which, recently merged with its English counterpart, still survives.[70]

As for patronage abused, what took place during these years in the Church of Scotland has often been held against Dundas. He is supposed to have reduced its ruling Moderates to hirelings of his own, maintaining their ascendancy but in return for that political control of the Kirk's internal affairs which had never been conceded to him by William Robertson. Without the principal's moral fibre and intellectual distinction, his party is said to have lost its humane, progressive interests, rendering itself and established religion contemptible.[71]

We should not, however, forget the general evolution of Scottish politics. The Moderates' ascendancy had been a product of the interregnum between the Earl of Bute and Dundas. For twenty years they had governed the Church from within because there was no other way to govern it, competent external direction being simply unavailable after the Argathelians ceased to exercise it. Once Robertson had put himself in charge of an orderly and workable internal regime, he could with good reason ask the Crown to defer to him on ecclesiastical patronage, and it was happy to comply.

But now Scotland had, instead of strong leadership in the Church and weak leadership in the state, precisely the reverse. In place of Robertson's unique arrangement, something like the previous one re-emerged: this time in altogether more palatable form, for an at least conventionally pious Dundas shared none of the Argathelian contempt for the Kirk. He was broadly content for his influence to be mediated through a committee drawn mainly from the clergy of Edinburgh under a bureaucrat without pretensions of his own, John Drysdale, principal clerk to the General Assembly. In 1781, ministers outside this circle complained of 'the total negligence of administration', though they thought it had gone on 'almost ever since the accession of this King' – hardly a compliment to their lost leader. The deplorable result had been to allow 'a very great number of illiterate fanatics to slip in among us.'[72]

The popular party was indeed not downhearted. If still in a minority at the General Assembly, it could deploy there ministers more than a match for any Moderate, such as John Erskine and Sir Henry Moncreiff, both good orators holding prestigious charges in the capital. Among lay elders, Henry Erskine brought to their side the weight of a former Lord Advocate and present Dean of the Faculty. They pressed their advantage by raising again questions likely to embarrass the other side, notably lay patronage. Pamphlets of 1782 seemed to indicate a political undertone to the ensuing debate. In one, the system was held to reek of 'the spirit of unlimited monarchy and can only serve to increase the power of an aristocracy already too powerful, and to add to the system of corruption already far too prevalent … Many of the people have discovered their right, and have courage to set bounds to arbitrary power.' In that year's General Assembly and the two following, the Evangelicals proposed overtures on the subject, but without success.

They were firmly put in their place as soon as Dundas established himself by the parliamentary elections of 1784. In the General Assembly following, a confident lead to the Moderates was given by Robert Dundas, who thenceforth managed the Government's ecclesiastical business. They achieved something that had always eluded Robertson in his decades of power, winning a vote to drop the formal protest against the Patronage Act solemnly, if impotently, set on the record every year since 1712. But the High-flyers were only winged. Dundas constantly wrangled with them: after he once lost his temper and called them 'lawless banditti', he was forced to apologise for the discourtesy. And from time to time they won an encounter, as in 1789 when they defeated the candidacy of the arch-Moderate, Jupiter Carlyle, for succession to the principal clerkship.

Henry Dundas could live with all this. If his own inclinations lay with the Moderates, he had through his family's traditional allegiance many connections on the other side. Experience taught that both could be useful to the Government. For example, he rather preferred to Moderatism's bloodless abstractions the lusty preaching of the popular party. He was never going to allow it control of the Kirk, but accepted that proscribing it would be counterproductive. He knew ministers could be awkward customers, and wanted essentially to keep them all content: he told the Home Secretary that in his preferments he sought 'to make such a selection as the general body of clergy will acquiesce in the propriety of.' Thus the General Assembly was saved from sterile subservience. The 1780s should be seen rather as a period of transition in the Church when, at the end of a relatively independent phase, a new equilibrium was being reached between it and secular authority.[73]

Beside the routine tasks of management, there was during the 1784–90 Parliament a programme of Scottish legislation quite as full as that introduced while Dundas himself had been Lord Advocate. Though, of course, leaving the detail to his successor, Ilay Campbell, he continued to take a hand in what interested him.

He did so notably in action for the Highlands. Dundas was, we should recall, half a Highlander himself. The region stood second only to India in its perennial fascination for him. In starting to ponder its problems some years before, he arrived at an understanding, the first politician to do so, that everything there had been changed by the rebellion of 1745 and its aftermath. The old social and economic order had completely collapsed, requiring a deliberate effort to build a new one.

This was the practical, political expression of a general shift in attitudes. The Highlands, once just a nuisance to all outside them, were ever more widely prized, by the romantic for their beauty, by the literary as a cradle of the Ossianic noble savage, by the philosophical for their cultural contrasts, by the military as a recruiting ground. It was public gratitude for the Highlanders' gallantry in the American War that enabled Dundas to exploit the shift. He could, for example, act at once when a poor harvest in 1782 threatened the region with famine, and got a grant of £10,000 for distribution of grain by the sheriffs of the northern counties. That also gave him the proof of their precarious condition he needed to promote the legislation he had in mind.

The first item in his programme was perhaps little more than a gesture. In 1783 he repealed the Disarming Act (1746), thus reversing the ban in force since the rebellion on wearing the kilt and the tartan – though safe Whig landlords had never quite forsaken them on social occasions. Now they quickly became fashionable, even in the highest circles. George IV's fetching mini-kilt worn for his visit to Edinburgh in 1822 is still remembered. Less well-known is the fact that, as Prince of Wales, he had donned the garb of old Gaul at a masquerade as early as 1789 and 'during the evening, received the appellation of the Royal Highland Laddie. The prince is remarkably fond of Highland reels, which he dances with all the glee and ability of a native of the North.'[74]

An Act of 1784 might have seemed inspired by similarly romantic motives, but was altogether more serious in intent. In 1752 a swathe of estates from Stirling to Inverness, with others in the West and North – thirteen in all – had been confiscated by the Crown as a punishment for the Jacobite treason of their owners. Administered by commissioners (of whom Lord President Arniston was one), they were meant to become models of development to the rest of the region and to accumulate profits which could be used for continuous development. Disaffection could be tackled at its root, and the natives civilised by inculcation of hardworking, law-abiding, presbyterian values from the Lowlands. Yet the commissioners seemed on the contrary infected by Highland indolence. Their sluggish bureaucracy performed little better than all the other absentee landlords who let estates run down and lose money. The large public investment in them was, according to Lord Kames, 'no better than water spilt on the ground'.

Nobody really knew what to do till a new course was suggested by the fate of the Lovat lands. Simon Fraser, their *de jure* chieftain, had reluctantly been out in 1745. After his father's execution he was pardoned on account of his youth and inexperience, but without getting back his property. Later, he raised a regiment which fought with great courage at Quebec, where he himself was wounded. In 1774 he applied successfully for restoration of the estates, though he was displeased to find that their debts came with them.

On the strength of that, Dundas started lobbying for a general restoration. He persuaded the Treasury that this was the best way to be rid of an unwanted burden, and won agreement in principle from each of the successive Governments in which he served.[75] In 1783 he himself became a commissioner, in effect with a brief to wind the old policy up. The next year, he introduced a Bill to disannex the forfeited estates from the Crown. He reminded the Commons that after 1745 the Highlanders had been 'put under a kind of proscription and thereby disqualified from serving the state in any capacity.' He remembered how William Pitt the elder had ended this during the Seven Years' War by raising Highland regiments, with the words: 'I am above all local prejudices and care not whether a man had been rocked in a cradle on this or on the other side of the Tweed. I sought only for merit, and I found it in the mountains of the North.' Dundas called on the House to be guided now by the same generous sentiments. The dispossessed families had been atoning for the crimes of their ancestors – 'and there is not one of those families in which some one person has not since spilt his blood in his country's cause.' Dundas again stipulated, however, that if the estates were to be restored, so too should the debts as they had stood when the Government took over. Otherwise the heirs would be getting them back in better condition, and a premium would have been placed on rebellion. The return to the Exchequer (£90,000 in the event) could be used for a variety of public works. By contrast the estates, though valued at £9000 a year, were producing only £6700 gross and, after deducting for management and repairs, £4000 net. This 'is no extravagant boon that I ask for,' Dundas justly remarked. But he promised that it would please the inhabitants of the estates and discourage emigration.[76]

It was the first time Parliament had adopted a reform in the Highlands, as opposed to setting out to suppress rebellion or raise revenue. By it, according to the most eminent Gael, Adam Ferguson, 'the affection of all Highlanders [was] gained to the state and the King'. It represented also another retreat from control by the state, though the results were perhaps more symbolic than of direct or lasting economic benefit. But Dundas genuinely believed that his was the best way to reconstruct a sound fabric for a region which had suffered terrible damage. He could not have foreseen the catastrophe that would follow by the landlords' applying, in the clearances, a particularly extreme version of utilitarianism. In his view, the purpose of improvement was to reinforce, not destroy, the social order.

Dundas therefore wanted some agency still to pay heed to the needs of the region as a whole, though it would no longer be an agency of the state. Thus the Highland Society was founded in 1784, with the Duke of Argyll as president and Henry Mackenzie as secretary. Its membership, too, contained both landowners and literati, for it had more than economic aims. It investigated the authenticity of Ossian, in the process collecting many Gaelic manuscripts which were deposited in the Advocates' Library in Edinburgh. It published a Gaelic vocabulary in 1794, an Old Testament in 1803 and a full dictionary in 1828. It encouraged other cultural activities, such as piping. This stood in stark contrast to the earlier repression.[77]

But the first main task was to conduct exhaustive inquiries into the condition of the Highlands. Public-spirited private citizens had already taken the initiative. A certain John Knox brought out in 1784 his *View of the British Empire, more especially Scotland, with some Proposals for the Improvement of that Country, the extension of its fisheries and the relief of its people*. 'The situation of these people, inhabitants of Britain! is such as no language can describe, or fancy conceive,' he wrote. 'Upon the whole, the Highlands of Scotland, some few estates excepted, are the seats of oppression, poverty, famines, anguish and wild despair.'[78]

The basic problem he identified was that the people suffered under too many restrictions. As one example he gave the laws imposing severe quotas and duties on the importation into Scotland of rock salt. Their purpose was to protect local salters, who used the hopelessly uncompetitive method of evaporation from sea-water for a product which was markedly inferior. Without cheap salt, the High-landers could not cure fish, which they therefore did not bother to catch; they were at once deprived of food and work. A few used smuggled salt, though because the fish could not then safely be sold on the open market, trade was still ruled out. Thus all round Scotland, in seas teeming with fish, most of the boats catching it were Dutch. The situation was so patently absurd that a remedy had already been attempted in the form of fishing bounties. But, as Smith observed, the boats then went out to catch the bounty, not the fish.

After having further investigations carried out by the Treasury, Dundas took the matter up in Parliament in March 1785. A committee was appointed which at length agreed that the fisheries were 'clogged with too many unreasonable restraints'. Some were legislated away. Duties on fish caught by British boats for domestic consumption went. More customs houses were built on the western coast of Scotland for the convenience of fishermen, who were legally obliged to go to one to collect and register salt for curing, since it continued to be taxed. Greater bounties were offered, and public funds made available for other improvements.

To take advantage of them, a second semi-philanthropic body, the British Fisheries Society, was founded, again with Argyll as governor, and Dundas as one of the directors. It invited subscriptions to match the grants from the Government. They would be used to buy land and build villages with all necessary facilities for the fishing industry. Enough generosity was shown for three soon to be founded, at Tobermory on Mull, Lochbay on Skye and Ullapool in Wester Ross; a fourth would eventually be sited at Pulteneytown, next to Wick. Lochbay failed, but the others survived – even today, Ullapool thrives as a fishing port.

Construction of a road from Ullapool to Inverness marked the start of a further programme to open up Highland communications. Coastwise trade was encouraged by the building between 1793 and 1801, on Argyll's initiative, of the Crinan Canal. With settlements to accommodate them, and a safe sea passage, merchants could come from Glasgow to buy fish, instead of the fishermen having themselves to sail all the way round Kintyre to reach a big market. To aid navigation, the first Commissioners for Northern Lighthouses were appointed in 1786. Altogether, fishing now became viable as a full-time occupation, so that Highlanders no longer entirely depended on a subsistence economy. In 1787, only 5000 barrels of herring were landed in Scottish ports; by 1796, the number was 131,000.

That was the most successful result of the Government's effort during these years to find a definitive solution for Highland problems. It made a grant in 1789 to commission further studies, from which quite a precise economic analysis emerged. This rested on the view that the region had resources enough to flourish, but they had to be consciously exploited. Stress was laid, for example, on those that lay untapped in the fecund population: precisely the idea behind Dundas's measures against emigration. The corollary was provision of more employment on the spot. That, however, meant revolution in an economy where every family had fended for itself. In future they would have to specialise, to buy and sell from each other and to trade with more distant regions. They should therefore be brought together in settlements, where they would find a division of labour not merely desirable but necessary.

The Highlands were in sum to be treated as a living illustration of historical development, one where a painless passage from the pastoral to the commercial stage could be induced, with primitive, undifferentiated labour giving way to sophisticated specialisation. So vital did this task seem that it overrode considerations of public economy, as Dundas underlined: 'Although Parliament has been liberal in its grants for this object, its liberality has been amply repaid by the change which this, among other causes, has tended to effectuate in the manners and dispositions of the inhabitants of the North parts of Scotland.'[79]

The fruits of these efforts proved in the long run meagre, yet meanwhile there seemed no good reason why the Highlands should not follow the breathtaking, dauntless progress of the rest of Scotland. Glasgow, for example, got over with amazingly little dislocation the abrupt stop put by the American War to its mainstay, the trade in tobacco. The Government promised to help the merchants recover their debts through diplomatic efforts in the United States. But there was evidently spare capital enough for some to turn themselves almost overnight into manufacturers of cotton, the commodity which fuelled the next stage of the city's industrial expansion. Dundas also gave a helping hand. He arranged for part of the proceeds from the disannexed estates to be offered in a loan of £50,000 for completion of the Forth-Clyde canal. It had been started from the eastern end in 1768 but came to a halt in 1775 three miles short of Glasgow. Now the remaining stretch could be dug, so that by 1790 direct communication was opened between the West of Scotland and the North Sea.[80]

At Smith's prompting, the Ministry embarked on a general programme of commercial reform. Dundas, personally committed to it, kept in touch with the Scottish interests affected, notably with the chambers of commerce founded in Glasgow in 1783 and in Edinburgh in 1785, though he would ignore their advice if it was protectionist. He brushed aside objections to freer trade with France and Ireland, even when the Whigs (to Smith's chagrin) tried to exploit fears in Glasgow especially that the West Indian trade would be diverted to Irish ports. Protests came, too, from the Scottish textile towns. But Dundas declared that everybody could benefit from open markets without any special favours. George Dempster, the linen manufacturers' lobbyist, ruefully wrote to him: 'We have heard you are an enemy to all bounties.' Dundas also wanted fewer, simpler taxes, and not only for his powerful friends. Complaining to Pitt about the 'unequal and impolitic' excise duties on coal and salt, he said 'they are necessary to the lowest ranks of people, and I do not at present see any valid objection to the repeal of all taxes upon both these articles.'[81]

His liberalism was amply vindicated by Scotland's great prosperity in these years, with a rapid recovery from the recession caused by war. We can still see the conspicuous consumption that resulted, in the country houses or in the New Town of Edinburgh and its equivalents elsewhere. But much more must have been spent on further improvement in agriculture and communications. Most significant of all was the start of heavy capital expenditure in industry, as in the erection of large complexes of cotton mills, notably at New Lanark in 1786, or in technical innovations like the machine spinning introduced in the linen industry in 1787, and David Dale's application of water to the mule in 1790. There were then well over 200,000 spinners and weavers in Scotland: her first industrial proletariat.[82]

In legislation, a second target was the judicial system. Social and economic change again overloaded it. Proceedings grew in consequence slower and more uncertain, vitiating the virtues of Scots law. One particular problem (which perhaps persists to this day) lay in the quality of the Bench. Because of the rewards, then as now, in private practice, it could be hard to persuade the best advocates to become judges. Mediocrities had to be promoted instead, sometimes on partisan grounds. Here too, Dundas tried to impose higher standards. He replied, when Boswell cited his political merit in support of application for a gown, by refusing to

> admit that political merit of any kind is the proper road to judicial promo-
> tion. That opinion was one of the great foundations for thinking that the
> judges of Scotland were too numerous. If they were less so, such kind of merit
> would not be urged for such a purpose. If therefore Mr Boswell can satisfy His
> Majesty's servants that his promotion to a judge's seat would give satisfac-
> tion to the Bench, the Bar and the country, he will stand upon good ground,
> but any other is no good.[83]

Dundas believed he could effect little improvement without greater resources for a system run on the shoestring of £38,000 a year. But when he had suggested raising the judges' salaries to Lord North in 1779, and again in 1781, he was told that the money just could not be made available. What he and Lord Advocate Campbell now therefore proposed was that the number of gowns in the Court of Session should be reduced, through natural wastage, from fifteen to ten, with the salary left over to be divided among the rest. The pay of a Lord Ordinary would go up from £700 a year (rather less than the best advocates' earnings) to £1050 – though the comparable figure for an English judge was still £2400. The so-called Diminishing Bill, to enact these changes, was introduced in April 1785.[84]

For this eminently sensible measure Dundas and Campbell quite failed to win the necessary support. Instead they provoked a typical Scottish political row, in which much hot air was expended on the systematic misrepresentation of motives, while serious debate never got off the ground. Boswell, prompted by it all to write his *Letter to the People of Scotland*, exemplified the reaction: 'Scandal says Mr Henry Dundas has been applied to by some of the judges, who, after feasting at Bayll's French tavern, and raising their spirits high with wine, have formed the lofty wish of reverently paying their court to Regina Pecunia: – and Mr Henry Dundas (sometimes called Harry the Ninth), very willing to oblige those senators, has nodded assent.'[85]

By the time this appeared, Campbell had, rather badly, attempted to get the Bill a first reading and immediately run into fierce opposition. Critics claimed he needed the prior consent of the King for a measure altering an article of the Treaty of Union, that which guaranteed for ever the form and status of the Court of Session. The consent, once obtained, still failed to satisfy them, and an embarrassed Campbell eventually felt obliged to withdraw the measure altogether. Robert Dundas remarked: 'We did everything in our power to carry it through. But though the interest and influence of administration was at that time most intensive, and though every exertion was needed to persuade people of the necessity of some such change, our most steady and zealous personal friends even deserted us.'[86]

The Parliamentary resistance was encouraged by uproar in public opinion, not this time among the submerged masses, but among the Dundases' very own constituency, the electors in the counties. Henry quickly found that he was touching there a raw nerve burning with anxieties, less about the merits of the case than about Scotland's status in the Union. And he was doubtless surprised, as we might be, to find in her natural leaders such perturbation on that score eighty years after the Treaty and forty after the last rebellion against it.[87] Even abandonment of the Bill failed to calm their ruffled feelings. Meetings in the counties that autumn still buzzed with indignation. Nine passed resolutions against what Dundas had attempted. The one from Ayrshire said:

> The articles of the Union between Scotland and England cannot be infringed by the British Parliament, without the consent of the people of Scotland; because the number of members from Scotland being inconsiderable, compared with the number of members from England, those articles, upon the faith of which Scotland resigned her independency, if not immutable, would be nugatory.[88]

These were fine-sounding sentiments, but what did they mean? Who were 'the people of Scotland'? How was it to be ascertained whether they consented or not? What exactly was the procedure, if any, for amending the Treaty? The prevailing view seemed to be that the electors should act as its custodians. Kirkcudbrightshire said their agreement should have been publicly obtained. Inverness-shire claimed the Bill ought to have been submitted to them so that they could be 'satisfied of its utility to Scotland'. West Lothian declared it 'was a surprise on the country and disrespectful to the people, particularly to the landed interest, when no means had been used to apprise them of the design, and when there was no complaint of evil.'

All this might be interpreted as a resurgence of opposition to the doctrine of absolute parliamentary sovereignty, once articulated by Dundas's own father, though it was mild enough compared to what Americans and Irishmen had recently been saying. What seems rather to have been behind it was the first adverse reaction among the ruling class to the forces of assimilation. But if Scots did loudly lament the advantage taken of their poor, remote and helpless nation, they still did not attack the Union as such. They clearly assumed that it had come to stay, would indeed get closer. Their proviso was that the process of integration should somehow remain controllable. Even though many of them doubtless welcomed the more vigorous and enlightened leadership given them by Dundas (why else would they vote for him so solidly?) they were still giving him to understand that he must observe certain rules, and not play fast and loose with semi-independence unless the leaders of society were ready for change.

Dundas readily deferred to their sentiments. He conceded in 1786 that 'so great a prejudice went forth in Scotland against the proposition that the design was necessarily abandoned.' This was in the course of an announcement that the judges' salaries were to be raised anyway, having fallen so far behind the English equivalents. The increase was financed by a charge against the customs revenue and by a new stamp duty on Scottish legal proceedings. The Lord President would in future receive £2000 a year, the Lords Ordinary £1000.[89] All idea of general reform in the judicial system had for the time being to be dropped, but it would return to haunt the Dundas despotism.

Failure here may have contributed to Dundas's decision to decline succession
to his brother, when he died the next year, as Lord President. That move was
expected. The honour to the family of providing a third member to the office
would have been great. In many eyes, if no longer in his own, Henry was above all
a very good Scots lawyer who had done well enough in Parliament to bring within
reach the summit of his own profession. A definitive decision was put off,
however, by translating the Lord Justice Clerk, Glenlee, a close friend of the
Dundases. But he, aged 70, survived only two years. Now a choice could not be
avoided. No suitable candidate remained in the older generation. It had to be
someone more vigorous. Why not Henry?

He explained why not in a letter to Grenville in October 1789:

> There are many circumstances both public and private which prevent me
> from entertaining any wish respecting the President's chair. It was certainly
> for many years the ultimate object of my ambition, and I would not speak
> true if I was not to admit that I see it pass by me, both on occasion of the
> former and present vacancy, with considerable regret. It is a situation of
> great respect, and if the duties of it are ably and conscientiously discharged,
> it is a situation of great dignity and utility to the public service. I could not
> however accept of it at present without acting unfairly to the Government
> with which I am acting, and dishonourably to the pretensions of the present
> Advocate. You are a better judge than I can be of part of this proposition, but
> I am disposed to believe, without arrogating too much to myself, that I could
> not at present leave my share in the government of India without some
> inconvenience to the public service. But I speak with more confidence
> when I state that my secession from all public life at this time would be a very
> fatal step to the strength and hold Government has of Scotland. It is
> unnecessary to enter into the reasons, but it is a truth that a variety of
> circumstances happen to concur in my person to render me a cement of
> political strength to the present administration, which, if once dissolved,
> would, produce very ruinous effects.[90]

The historian Sir John Fortescue, not otherwise reliable on Dundas, read
between these lines and produced an admirable paraphrase:

> My dear foolish Grenville, at present I have the patronage of Scotland and
> of India; practically I govern both countries; you cannot get on without me.
> Of course it is very irksome for me to be besieged with requests and petitions
> whenever I go to Scotland, but in spite of my advancing years I bear up. Do
> you think that a pair of recluses, such as Pitt and yourself, with a stilted sense
> of honour and no knowledge of the world or of men, are a match for the great
> Whig magnates, with their control of rotten burghs, their great territorial
> influence and their commanding position as Lords-lieutenant? No, it needs
> men such as Henry Dundas to manage these matters. You cannot do without
> me, and I see no speedy remedy for it, for I have not the slightest intention
> of effacing myself.[91]

Instead, Campbell became Lord President, being himself succeeded by Robert
Dundas. This was the last point at which the course of Henry's life might have
changed. He was now irrevocably a politician.

The decision ought not to have surprised anyone observing how Dundas had unobtrusively amassed power and never, unless obliged to, let anything go. This was doubtless another reason why he had come to reject electoral reform, though, as we shall see from subsequent comments, he could have lived with it if necessary. He would sometimes acknowledge the demands for it still rising from within the Scottish political nation he expressly desired to serve. For example, in speaking against Pitt's motion on the subject in 1782 – to the theme that 'the constitution has existed for ages pure and it is not a proper time now to think of altering it' – he conceded that 'if any part of the representation wants a reform, it is that place from which I come.' When, to show approval of its author, he perversely supported the similar motion of 1783, he indeed averred that 'the granting so much to the wishes of the people will be to give a fresh infusion of fine blood to the constitution of this House'.[92]

In office, Pitt did not forget the matter, but brought forward a new proposal for England in 1785. It failed, Dundas now voting against. In a system where the doctrine of collective responsibility was barely formed, a Prime Minister even with real interest in a question had no choice but to leave it open inside the Government if his colleagues could not of their own volition reach agreement. Party discipline, too, was rudimentary. Pitt, personally popular and effective, could rely on a large following in the House over a wide range of measures. But it was still not a party that could be whipped. If it refused to accept a measure, there was nothing to be done. In that House, reform could simply not be carried.

Inside Scotland the agitation, after dying away during the crisis of 1782-3, rose again with the arrival of a Government apparently capable of action. Nominal franchises were still being created apace. Dundas himself wrote in November 1787: 'It is probable that the business of made votes must come to some eclaircissement soon, for it cannot with any propriety remain upon the present footing.' Meanwhile, the only remedy was through the courts. A test case that year yielded, though, at best an ambiguous verdict. Thurlow, who judged it on appeal to the Lords, warned the litigants they might be wasting their time: 'If it be a political object, and an honest object, to give to the land of Scotland its due weight in parliamentary representation, I am afraid that it is not to be obtained by a judgment of any court of law; but that resort must be had to Parliament to cure the great mischief that has happened to the constitution of that country.' The reformers yet persisted and at last in 1790 obtained, again from Thurlow, a favourable verdict. Its results will be followed in the next chapter.[93]

In the burghs, where matters had not improved either, a campaign for reform also now started up. Here too, legal action was tried, but test cases failed to enforce a residence qualification on councillors – notably in the corporation of Anstruther Easter, filled by all available members of the nearby laird's household, including his butler. Nor did it prove possible to impose financial control through the Court of Exchequer. Meanwhile, a series of letters to the press from one Zeno, otherwise a merchant of Edinburgh, Thomas McGrugar, denounced a system where people of little wealth or merit controlled not only the councils but also the parliamentary representation. He was indeed no democrat, urging a vote only for 'men in the middle ranks of life who generally constitute the majority of every free country'.[94]

This caused a stir in the capital, as in Glasgow and Aberdeen. Liberal advocates at Parliament House, Archibald Fletcher, Henry Erskine, John Clerk of Eldin, together with a judge, Lord Gardenstone, decided to see what they could make of it. Fletcher took upon himself to organise a convention of representatives from royal burghs. It met in two stages, in March and October 1784, with a standing committee deputed meantime to produce draft legislation. A pair of Bills was drawn up, one to govern parliamentary polls, the other to remedy local abuses, ending the councils' self-election and, it was hoped, the flagrant corruption and maladministration inside them. By itself, this would have created a more popular suffrage, since under it a wider body of citizens was to vote annually, on the same day, for every council in Scotland.

Although, at one session or another, delegates from fifty-two burghs attended, they made no headway. The Convention of Royal Burghs spurned the plaints. None of the Scots members at Westminster would listen. It was left to Richard Sheridan, the Irish Whig sitting for Stafford, to take up the cause, which he proceeded to do every year. With equal regularity his arguments were contemptuously dismissed by Dundas. 'The abuses are merely imaginary, and the Scottish nation does not feel them to exist,' he said on one occasion, and on another: 'A General Election in this country is never considered as a corrective of the morals of the people, but that is a species of dissipation which occurs but once in seven years. The Bill for the reform of the royal burghs provides for that scene of riot and drunkenness annually and therefore the honourable gentleman should have intituled it "A Bill for the Encouragement of Debauchery".' But he admitted privately: 'It would be easier to reform Hell'.[95]

By 1785 these flurries were encouraging the Scots Whigs to think that Dundas's various antagonists might yet be marshalled into a broader combination. They set up a political club in Edinburgh, demurely dubbed the Independent Friends, as a focus for it. William Adam worked hard to give it some electoral momentum. He had dealings with seventeen constituencies in the following years, but only in a handful did he make any progress. One supporter said the problems were

> owing to our party being in total want of anyone in Scotland to unite our friends in one common mode of exertion and in short to superintend and manage our politics, while the opposite party have the indefatigable manoeuvrer Dundas always at work, never missing the slightest opening for interference and too, too often successful ... Individuals unsupported had no chance against individuals supporting and supported.

This was not quite fair to his own side. Adam and Erskine did in 1788 compile a remarkable document, a *View of the Political State of Scotland,* listing every one of the 2662 electors in the counties, often with tips on how to canvass their votes: 'Major Alexander Turnbull of Ardo. Not rich. Requires some office, or other promotion.'[96]

Dundas was never complacent. On holiday at Dunira in August 1788, he warned Pitt: 'Our general politics for the next election look as I said to you very favourable, but it will be much more troublesome than I expected for our adversaries are indefatigable.' A couple of weeks later he wrote of the Whigs: 'I find them exceedingly awake in this part of the world, and whatever other effects it may produce, it will certainly have the effect of teasing me not a little … My great object is to secure friends with as few contests as possible, because I am well aware of the trouble, expense and embarrassment to which it naturally leads.' This strategy he was successfully preparing in the course of the Parliament, notably with his 'pacification' of the North-east. There he had thus far had no influence at all. But amid the confusion of its politics he discovered openings which he exploited with such superlative skill that he at length won the region over en bloc.[97]

The North-east had seen at the last election two broad alliances contending for control. One was headed by the Duke of Gordon, with Lord Kintore in tow; the other by the Earl of Fife, with Lord Findlater and, more loosely, Sir James Grant of Grant. A third force, the Moray Association, a grouping of independent gentlemen, had without binding itself to Gordon opposed Fife. At the polls, he all the same came off best, winning Banffshire and Moray, while the other seats went to untidy local coalitions.

Though Dundas was divided by no deep political differences from the Earl, they had in the past taken opposite sides on certain matters. He was therefore inclined to favour the Duke, a naive man and a poor one, whom he befriended to the extent of getting him a British peerage. In return Gordon grovelled, 'You have given me a new light totally in political matters, which I confess I was ignorant of … I am the very worst politician in the world.' Dundas may have been attracted rather by his remarkable Duchess, as much as Fife felt repelled: 'that horrid violent woman' and 'a perfect Divel', he called her. She was well known in Edinburgh, where as a child she had ridden through the streets on a pig. Her derring-do continued into adulthood. Later, in the French Wars, when the Duke raised the Gordon Highlanders, she and her daughters played recruiting sergeants, and stood in the market places with guineas between their lips. One rhyme ran:

> The Duchess triumphs in a manly mien,
> Loud is her accent, and her phrase obscene.

She seems altogether to have been Dundas's kind of woman, and they were soon on terms of bantering intimacy, if not more – she often appeared, scantily clad, in scurrilous cartoons. They certainly liked to get drunk together, and would sometimes drag Pitt along. She even inspired Dundas's one literary effort, of four lines:

> She was the mucklest of them aw,
> Like Saul she stood the tribes aboon;
> Her gown was whiter than the snaw,
> Her face was redder than the moon.[98]

Dundas was not one, however, to let personal feelings affect his political judgment. A by-election in Aberdeenshire in 1786 showed that Fife had lost none of the superiority established two years earlier. His man, George Skene of Skene, romped home against Gordon's candidate, James Ferguson of Pitfour. Dundas appreciated what this meant: these north-eastern seats could not be won, let alone be made safe, without the Earl, and other combinations might as well be ignored.

He was difficult to deal with, but if he could somehow be enticed into the Government's camp, it would be unbeatable in the region. The first step was to smooth over what misunderstandings he had with neutral connections, such as the Grants. A deal was done by which they would support each other in Banffshire and Moray. A tentative link was also laid across the great divide when the Grants were in turn persuaded to drop opposition to Gordon's candidate in Inverness-shire.[99]

Having prepared the ground a little, Dundas wrote to Grenville in August 1787:

> I am thus on my way to the North of Scotland on a visit to Sir James Grant, General Grant, the Duke of Gordon, Lord Findlater and Lord Fife. They are all very hostile to each other; and yet I am told that a visit from me may probably have the effect of uniting their political interests in such a manner as to co-operate for securing five seats in Parliament at the General Election in the interest of the Government.

He worked his charms well, and in a month had won them all over to an alliance, except the Duke. Now he showed how tough he could be. Gordon was brutally confronted with the choice either of acquiescing in the general arrangement, or else of being isolated by Dundas and politically extinguished. The reasoning in favour of the first was inescapable –

> The grounds of my opinion are: that, without committing the Duke of Gordon to anybody, it relieved him from a most expensive political warfare which no success could justify. Secondly, it gave him an opportunity handsomely and liberally to concur in obliging through me the families of Findlater and Grant, with whom his family must connect if they continue in opinion of not connecting with Lord Fife. Thirdly, these motives would have prevailed in deciding my opinion in any state of the election laws, but in their present extraordinary and unsettled state, I am adduced by this strong additional motive, a conviction that the issue of a contest could not possibly end better and may very probably end worse even for the Duke's immediate interest, and certainly much more, looking to the permanent interest of his family. Upon this others may differ; but it is my opinion and I must act on my own judgment.[100]

Under this battering the Duke naturally wilted, and the pacification went ahead with the concurrence of everyone. Its terms in the end explicitly covered four seats, though others were affected by it. Fife was to receive a British peerage, an honour which he obviously felt worth a considerable sacrifice of direct influence elsewhere. While he was to be left a free hand in Banffshire, his own seat of Moray, thus vacated, was to be restored to its previous patrons, the Grants. In Aberdeenshire, his man Skene would at the next General Election give way to Gordon's Ferguson. The weight of the whole alliance was then to be thrown behind removing the Whig, Adam, from the Elgin Burghs.

Apart from this pet project, Dundas had success after success at the by-elections of the Parliament.[101] In 1785 he backed a connection of Fife's, Alexander Brodie, in wresting Nairnshire from the Campbells of Cawdor, who were in opposition. In 1786 Dundas's own great-nephew, Sir Charles Lockhart Ross, taking advantage of

Whig confusion, snatched the Tain Burghs just relinquished by Fox on confirmation of his election for the city of Westminster. Next, he was able to nominate a
relation by marriage, John Hamilton of Pencaitland, for East Lothian after the
sitting member was enticed by a lucrative office into retirement. In 1787 he settled
his differences with the family of Wemyss, which since 1775 had helped to inflict
defeat after defeat on him in Fife. On a vacancy, he supported William Wemyss as
the new member, dumping without ceremony his own long-standing and afterwards irreconcilable candidate, John Henderson. In 1788, Clackmannanshire,
previously under the influence of Sir Thomas Dundas, fell to Henry's friends, the
Abercrombies of Tullibody. A distinguished independent supporter of Pitt, Lord
Adam Gordon, Commander-in-chief, Scotland, agreed on giving up politics that
the Government should name his successor in Kincardine.

A single setback marred the run of luck. Campbell's taking the Lord Presidency
in 1789 meant a by-election in the Glasgow Burghs. Through mismanagement
they were lost to John Craufurd of Auchenames, who had represented them,
finally in the coalition's interest, during the previous Parliament. The town
council of Glasgow, which voted in the minority against him this time, was so
furious that it refused to do business with him. That wrecked his renewed career,
which was over in months. In all, by-elections produced half-a-dozen net gains for
Dundas, with another four seats wrapped up for the next General Election.

So by the time it took place in 1790, he was in a formidable position.[102] The
centre of his power remained Edinburgh and its environs. He himself shifted to the
city, thinking representation of a capital now consonant with his dignity. Robert
Dundas was brought in for the county of Midlothian in his stead. To the south and
east all was his except the Haddington Burghs, controlled by the hostile house of
Lauderdale. Up the Forth, in West Lothian, John Hope of Craighall, into whose
family Dundas was soon to marry, swept aside the incumbent. In Stirlingshire, Sir
Thomas Dundas only just held on. Across the firth, Henry was not quite so strong.
Kinross returned, as usual, a mild Whig. In the Anstruther Burghs an arrangement
to bring into the Government's camp its eponymous patrons did not in the event
hold. Even so, Dundas controlled twelve of the region's sixteen seats.

In the North-east the pacification worked beautifully. Every constituency went
as planned, Banffshire to Sir James Grant, Moray to another Grant, Aberdeenshire to Ferguson. In the Elgin Burghs, Adam lost to Brodie, the member who was
vacating Nairnshire but failed to win the alternating county of Cromarty. As a
bonus, the Aberdeen Burghs, not included in the formal arrangement, were seized
from the Whig incumbent by one of Dundas's nabob friends, Alexander
Callander. Another, David Scott, his right-hand man in the East India Company,
was brought in for Angus. Continued alliance with Atholl's interest made certain
of Perth, both the county and this time also the burghs, where a relation of the
Duke's took over on the retiral of their long-serving independent, Dempster.
Dundas could therefore count on every member from this region.

In addition he made, for the first time, great inroads further north. In Orkney
and Shetland the same neglect on Sir Thomas Dundas's part as had almost cost
him his own seat delivered the islands, previously held by his brother, into the
Government's hands. He had already lost the Northern Burghs too, where he

formerly shared an interest with the Sutherlands; this family Henry had now wooed into returning for its county General James Grant, another party to the pacification. The sitting member for the Inverness Burghs, Sir Hector Munro, remained acceptable. In the county Dundas backed young Norman Macleod of Macleod, recently returned from India, on condition he made a pact there with Gordon. Caithness elected the independent Sir John Sinclair, who seemed all the same anxious to keep in with the Government, if only to promote his innumerable financial and commercial schemes. Ross alone remained in the Whig hands of the Earl of Seaforth, who gave refuge to Adam.

The Duke of Argyll provided a complaisant kinsman for his county, as did the Marquis of Bute for the Ayr Burghs. But in general, the elections in the West were, on account of wayward magnates, less predictable. Queensberry, a congenital weathercock, had twisted and turned so often as almost to ruin his interest. But since Buccleuch was heir to his title, Dundas bore with it all. In the county of Dumfries he supported, despite previous misdemeanours, Old Q's sitting member, Sir Robert Laurie. In the burghs he was able to bring in his banker friend from Edinburgh, Patrick Miller. The local arrangement in Dunbarton replaced a Foxite with Montrose's Pittite nominee, Sir Archibald Edmonstone. The Government held all the region's other seats except Renfrewshire, where a Whig defeated its candidate by just one vote. So despite some problems, matters here turned out rather well for Dundas.

In all, his advance was spectacular, his control now impressive. He could count on thirty-two more or less definite supporters, and a further seven usually reliable. The Whigs' attempts at a national organisation had crashed in ruins. Sir Thomas Dundas's interest was reduced from three seats to one. Adam had to flit from the Elgin Burghs to Ross. Erskine was unable, as he wished, to contest Fife, and could find no other remotely winnable seat.

By contrast, the peers' election proved a little troublesome. With thirty candidates, it was the most hotly contested ever. It also sharpened the old debate about whether their lordships should tamely accept the King's list (for some were clearly irked at the meteoric rise of the upstart Dundas), or assert a right to free election.

The vexed business of British titles had meanwhile generated a further complication, as to whether Scottish peers holding them, now entitled to sit by right in the Lords, could also be chosen as representatives. It was a question exercising both English noblemen objecting to the extent of executive power and Scots anxious for their share of official favour. When in 1786 the Duke of Queensberry and the Earl of Abercorn received peerages of Great Britain, the House declared that they had lost the representative status by which they had thus far been entitled to membership of it. In this vote, the Scots – in what Dundas called 'the maddest act … ever men were guilty of' – combined with the opposition, from whose ranks the two replacements, the Earl of Selkirk and Lord Kinnaird, were afterwards elected. Carried away, the Lords also renewed a standing order of 1709, application of which had grown lax, that recipients of British titles could not vote for the sixteen either. It created a real problem for the Government which, if too generous with them, might be unable to carry the King's list.

The heartened opposition made so bold at the General Election as to put up its own list. The normally decorous and expeditious electoral ceremony at Holyrood dragged on for nine hours, as their lordships wrangled about their respective rights to vote. While Queensberry and Abercorn were held to be disqualified, other British peers slipped through the net, not least the Prince of Wales as Duke of Rothesay. At the end of it only thirteen peers were indisputably elected, nine from the Government's and five from the opposition's list (Eglinton appeared on both). Six tied for the remaining three places. The dispute among them did not end till 1793. The House then seated one more from each side and ordered a fresh election for the last. Obviously, though, the doubts over voting rights had to be resolved. Dundas wanted them drawn as liberally as possible, and was ready to legislate to that end if necessary. The Lords themselves finally settled matters as he wished, and cancelled the limitations.[103]

Dundas had anyway established a convincing ascendancy in Scottish politics. It was a far cry from the days when his family had struggled to maintain a modest interest against the great Argyll. The present Duke was, as president of the Highland Society and holder of other honorific titles, a mere cog in Dundas's machine. It would have been inconceivable, not so long before, for almost the whole Scots nobility to be eating out of the hand of a minor laird, owing his position to his legal and political skills rather than to his acres.

He was besides a British politician of increasing importance, commanding great resources of patronage, playing a key advisory role in national affairs. The combination with his local dominance was what marked him out from all other notable politicians produced by Scotland since the Union. Lord Mansfield had reached a greater height in England, but without retaining any political base to speak of in his own country. The Argylls had lorded it in Scotland, while counting for little in the South. Dundas, in straddling both nations, reflected and advanced the integration of his own with the rest of the United Kingdom, just as he reflected and advanced the external expansion of a state which could no longer with justice be described as an English, but had to be called a British one.

In that state he also represented the new breed of professional rulers, sprung from stations well below the Whig oligarchy they were replacing, and aspiring to impartial efficiency in government. They could be liberals and even reformers, but were more usually of a conservative cast of mind, accepting the society they found rather than trying to remodel it. They took expediency as their watchword, not in the sense of being unprincipled but of having an open mind about pragmatic solutions. That was what distinguished them from the Whigs, or rather from what sticklers called Whig principles. During Pitt's first Government, justly called 'the years of acclaim' by his modern biographer John Ehrman, everything had gone wonderfully well for these people. As Dundas remembered it shortly before his death, 'the Minister of the day was in the zenith of his power and popularity, possessing the complete confidence of the King and the country, and advised by perhaps the ablest administration we ever had.'[104] The next decade would put them all on their mettle.

Notes

1. *Parl. Hist.* xxiv, cols 373, 473, 533.
2. SRO GD 51/17/117, 193; Campbell of Succoth Papers, TD 219/6/91.
3. NLS MS 63B, f.15; Laprade (1922), followed by Furber (1931), 203–5; WLC, Jan.18, 1784.
4. Brooke & Namier (1964), 470–513; a detailed study, of Berwickshire, is Sunter (1986), 133 et seqq.
5. Robinson (1985), 629; Burns, 36–7; WLC, Apr.13, 1784.
6. WLC, Apr.5, 1784; Large (1963), 669; Lowe (1978), 102 et seqq.
7. Wight (1784), 459; Fergusson (1960), 84 et seq.; McCahill (1972), 175–80.
8. Connell (1827), 9.
9. Chatham Papers PRO 30/8/157/2/351; Ditchfield (l981), 16 et seqq; McCahill (1981), 259, 263, 269.
10. Ferguson (1968), 237.
11. Dicey & Rait (1920), 313 et seqq.; Stanhope (1861–2), i, 246.
12. Wheatley (1884), iv, 10; Farington (1923), v, 162; Lonsdale Papers, LI/2/9.
13. Stanhope, Lady H. (1845), ii, 171; Wheatley (1884), iv,14.
14. Ehrman (1969), 131.
15. ibid., 426; Sinclair, Sir J. (1831), 109; Mossner & Ross (1977), 302.
16. *Parl. Hist.*, xxi, col. 401; Laing Papers, La. II. 419/8; Ehrman, 585.
17. SRO GD 235/9/9/11; Stanhope, Lady H., ii, 64, 100.
18. Laing Papers, La. II. 295; Anon. (1788b), 60; Scott, W.R. (1937), 302; Ferguson, 236.
19. SRO GD 51/5/628; Matheson (1933), 97; McWilliam (1978), 58–9, 320–1; Slater (1980), 238.
20. Dundas of Dundas Papers, NLS Adv MSS 80.1.10, ff. 29 et seq.
21. Mossner & Ross, 295.
22. SRO GD 235/9/7/6, 235/9/19/7, 235/10/22/7; NLS MS 1052, ff. 1–10; Bickley (1928), 124.
23. Cockburn, H. (1910), 13–14.
24. Campbell of Succoth Papers, TD 219/6/79; Trotter (1800), 2–7; Anon. (1811), 17.
25. Smith, N.L. (1953), i, 79; Rosebery (1891), 252.
26. Marshall (1976), 12; Bryant (1985), 23–40; Riddy (1989), 42.
27. Smith, A. (1976), i, 35, 91.
28. De (1961), 20.
29. Misra (1959), 5; De, 46, 83.
30. *Parl. Hist.*, xxii, cols. 1278 et seqq.
31. *Parl. Hist.*, xxiv, col. 1136; De, 140–180 passim.
32. Sutherland (1952), 391; *Parl. Hist.*, xxiii, cols 757 et seqq; Marshall (1968), 63.
33. De, 110, 181.
34. ibid., 209.
35. Sutherland, 398 et seqq; Misra, 30 et seq.
36. *Parl. Hist.*, xxiii, col. 1401.
37. Sutherland, 408 et seqq; Philips (1940), 14, 26–7; De, 209 et seqq; *Parl. Hist.*, xxvi, col. 150.
38. Buccleuch Papers, SRO GD 224/30/9/2; Ross (1859), 245.
39. *Parl. Hist.*, xxv, col. 1265; De, 379.
40. NLS MS 3387, 27.
41. *Parl. Hist.*, xxvii, cols. 132, 238; Misra, 34; Harlow, ii, 567; Philips,

51–61; Ehrman, i, 435.

42. Furber, 479–81; Philips, 438 et seqq.

43. Ross (1859), i, 237, 376; NLS MS 3387, 70; Harlow (1952), 171–2.

44. Quoted, Mill (1840), v, 31.

45. *Parl. Hist.*, xxv, col. 1069; xxvi, col. 1085; Carnall & Nicholson (1989), 1, 31.

46. *Parl. Hist.*, xxvi, cols. 87–9.

47. C. Cruse O'Brien (1989), 66; NLS MS 3387, 8; Buccleuch Papers, SRO GD 224/30/9/2; Burke (1963), iv, 315; NLS MS 16, f 20.

48. De, 269.

49. ibid., 248; Furber (1933), 56.

50. Wellesley Papers, BL Add MSS 12567, f. 85.

51. Dropmore Papers, BL Add MSS 58914. f.12; De, 267; Banerjea (1928), 29–30; Furber, 61–7; (1948), 34, 77, 106, 139, 149, 157; Harlow & Madden (1953), 13.

52. Fry (1970), 149.

53. NLS MS 1068, MS 3387, 68; SRO GD/51/3/23/1.

54. SRO GD 51/3/195; De, 391–7; Dropmore Papers, BL Add MSS 58914, f. 12, 59070, f.9; HMC, xiii, J.B. Fortescue MSS (1892), 268–9; Nightingale (1970), 50.

55. Forrest (1926), ii, 183.

56. Furber, 60.

57. NLS MS 3387, 8.

58. Sutherland, 57; De, 75; Furber, 62.

59. Lustig & Pottle (1981), 144–5; (1986), 152.

60. Boswell (1785), 8, 60; Lustig (1974), 250.

61. WLC, Aug. 8, 1786; WLP II, Nov.12, 1787, Apr.24, 1793; Cockburn (1856), 201–2; NLS MS 1074, f.159; JRL, 692/1048; Grant-Macpherson Papers, bundle 447, Aug.1, 1790; Sidmouth Papers, C1796/OZ 31; Boyle Papers, 9/49/42; Dropmore Papers, BL Add MSS 58915, f.112; Brewer (1988), 15.

62. Whetstone (1981), 7–8; Prof. Hannay Papers, SRO GD 214/650/4.

63. SRO GD 51/6/957; NLS MS 3834, ff.16, 20; Walker (1985), 332.

64. Somerville (1861), 316; Farington, v, 163; NLS MS 6524, f.199; SRO GD 51/5/423/2.

65. NLS MS 1078, ff.20 et seqq; JRL, 699.

66. NLS MS 12, ff.169–71; MS 1056, f. 21; MS 1042, 73–5; Campbell of Succoth Papers, TD 219/6/291; Warren Hastings Papers, BL Add MSS 29177, f.115; Brewer (1988), 74.

67. NLS MS 580, f. 330; SRO GD 235/10/36/25; Prof. Hannay Papers, SRO GD 214/653/3; Anon., (1785), 1; Youngson (1966), 113–17, 125; Catford (1975), 127; Fraser (1989), 73.

68. Cockburn, 252–3; Checkland (1975), 151–2, 157–8, 285; SRO GD 51/5/179.

69. Coleridge (1920), i, 280; Rait (1930), 98; NLS MS 17, ff.1–3.

70. Rait, 100–1; NLS MS 1058, f.20; NLS MS 62, passim; Hamilton H. (1963), 334.

71. Brown (1981), 44; Clark (1970), 211–16.

72 Dalzel (1793), xxxvi; Murdoch & Sher, 203; Benton (1969), 134.

73. WLC, June 2, 1784, Nov.13, 1786; Mathieson (1910), 109; Clark (1963), 120; (1970), 216–19; Bono (1980), 51; Cook (1829), 144; Meikle (1912), 67; Kay (1877), ii, 118 et seqq; Burleigh (1960), 306–7.

74. Horn (1968), 209 et seqq.

75. Ramsay (1888), i, 198; Smith A.M. (1974), 198 et seqq.; Macinnes (1988), 82.
76. *Parl. Hist.*, xxiv, cols 1316 et seqq; Edinburgh University Library Papers, DC I. 77, no. 71
77. Cheape & Grant (1987) 245.
78. Knox (1784), 122, 127.
79. NLS MS 6602; Dunlop (1978) 4, 20, 100, 128–9; Kapstein (1980), 148 et seqq; Munro R.W. (1979), 53–4; Youngson (1975), 120; PES, HE 151 (41) Coll. F, II, 3, i.
80. Lindsay J. (1968), 28; Hamilton H. (1954), 39; Devine (1975), 158.
81. Winch (1978), 7; NLS MS 653, f.1; *Parl. Hist.*, xxvi. col. 445; Chatham Papers PRO 30/8/157/2/317.
82. Dickson (1980), 153–4; Gayer, Rostow & Schwarz (1975), i, 7.
83. SRO GD 51/5/400/2.
84. SRO GD 51/5/396; Prof. Hannay Papers, SRO GD 214/650/4; Pottle & Wimsatt (1960), 325; Mitchison & Phillipson (1970),127.
85. Boswell (1785), 6.
86. Mitchison & Phillipson, 129.
87. Phillipson (1967), 167 et seqq.
88. NLS MS 12, f.4
89. *Parl. Hist.*, xxv, col. 1369.
90. Dropmore Papers, BL Add MSS 58914, f.53; HMC Fortescue, i, 534–5.
91. Fortescue (1911), 58.
92. *Parl. Hist.*, xxii. col. 1434; xxiii, col. 865.
93. BLY, Apr. 30, 1787; Seafield Muniments SRO GD/248/360/2/35; Beal (1812), 290; Bono (1980), 53.
94. ibid., 55.
95. ibid., 59–67; Christie (1962), 173–4; Porritt A.G. & E. (1903), 125; Keith (1916), 273; Meikle, 23 et seqq; Black (1963), 122–3; Gibson (1977), 77; *Parl. Hist.*, xxviii, col. 273.
96. Ginter (1967), 5; Adam (1887), 155.
97. Chatham Papers PRO 30/8/157/1/43 & 53.
98. NLS MS 8, f.1; Tayler A. & H. (1925), 186; Chambers R. (1896), iii, 243; Matheson, 129.
99. Seafield Muniments SRO GD 248/61/1/140.
100. Dropmore Papers BL Add MSS 59070, f.101; Furber, 210–2.
101. Brooke & Namier, 470–508, passim.
102. Sunter, 102–10; Thorne (1986), ii, 512–623, passim.
103. Fergusson Sir J. (1960), 36; Ditchfield (1981), 16–24; (1986). 309 et seqq.; McCahill (1972), 181, 189; Connell (1829), 9; Turberville (1958), 141; HMC Fortescue, i, 597; Buccleuch Papers SRO GD 224/30/9/2.
104. ibid., SRO GD 224/30/7/15.

5

'The French madness'

July 14, 1789, was a day of routine in the life of Henry Dundas, spent at the East India Company and at the House of Commons. He could rest on his laurels because, a week before, he had with plain speaking and witty barbs deflated the prolix Richard Sheridan in the latest debate on reform of the Scots burghs. Even when he at length heard about the happenings in Paris, he was not apparently much moved. No comment of his on the unfolding of the French Revolution is recorded till two years later, well after other Scots – Dr James Beattie, the Earl of Fife and even a Whig, Sir Gilbert Elliot – were sounding warnings. On the eve of war with France in 1793 he still discouraged counter-revolutionary provocation. This was how, the next year, he described the development of his views:

> What at first appeared to be a partial change from the ancient monarchy assumed an aspect so formidable to neighbouring nations that every man of a sober and deliberating mind took the alarm. It was not now a limitation of the ancient and monarchical form of government, but a conspiracy of the most profligate and ignorant people in the nation, against all the principles of society and religion, against all property, landed or commercial; and this conspiracy, too, formed in the centre of Europe, and threatening the subversion of every neighbouring government; a conspiracy made up of men equally destitute of principles and of property; who had everything to gain and nothing to lose by a general convulsion in Europe.

But, he implied, if excesses had been avoided, if the France of 1789 had imitated the England and Scotland of 1688, then he would not necessarily have been hostile.

There was nothing very original about these opinions. Yet the Revolution, more than anything else in his times, determined Dundas's historical reputation. In England, his campaign to contain the consequent outburst of radicalism is scarcely remembered – if at all, then as the standard precaution any Minister would have taken against rumblings of popular discontent. In Scotland, however, where he was no more severe, he has gone down as an ogre of repression. An interesting sidelight on where he actually stood inside the ruling circle was cast by a comment from one of his innumerable lady admirers, Georgiana, Duchess of Devonshire, also the sister of a colleague and clearly adept at winkling out what went on among Ministers: 'You are the only person I have met for a long time who has power, and yet seems to feel the necessity of not staking everything on coercion.'[1] In the mainstream of British historiography, which has seen him principally as author and executor of measures to counter the new France's external aggression, his character has been so vilified by military specialists as to have made it irredeemable by more sympathetic imperial scholars. Though to contemporaries he was a conspicuous success, posterity has treated him harshly. We must look afresh at the record.

The 1780s had established Dundas's political career; the 1790s saw it in its fullness. His greatest contributions came in Scotland, in India and in the struggle with France. The latter two were priorities, entailing as they did war and from time to time imminent danger to Britain or her interests; Scotland, therefore, if the basis of his power, could claim only the residue of his attention.

He relied there on his nephew and son-in-law, Lord Advocate and factotum, Robert Dundas. Before proceeding, it would be as well to introduce properly this second member of the Dundas despotism. Born in 1758 to the then Lord Advocate and Jean Grant, he was the eldest of four brothers, two destined for politics and two for the forces. Robert followed a well-trodden path, attending the High School of Edinburgh and being admitted an advocate in 1779. He diverted himself the while in the capital's clubs and in wooing his cousin Elizabeth. In 1787 he inherited Arniston.

He was not universally admired, his finer qualities being personal rather than professional. James Ferguson of Pitfour found one fault: 'The Lord Advocate should always be a tall man. We Scotch members always vote with him, and we need, therefore, to be able to see him. I can see Pitt and Addington, but I can't see this new Lord Advocate.' But face to face, he came across as a chirpy, genuine fellow. For the constituents of Midlothian he kept up his house's hospitable tradition, though obsessive hypochondria made him personally abstemious. He had once to be stopped from breaking up a dinner too early when the men present cried: 'Na, na, Mr Dundas, we're no a' slockened yet!' He was in general never so determinedly rough-hewn as others of his kin. His wife wrote to Lady Arniston the elder after his presentation at Court in 1786: 'His Majesty was pleased to pay the Solicitor a great many compliments of his having so little of the Scotch accent, and I am afraid he has been a comparison rather to the disadvantage of his uncle in that respect.' Henry Cockburn, a cousin, remembered him as a 'little, alert, handsome, gentleman-like man, with a countenance and air beaming with sprightliness and gaiety, and dignified by considerable fire: altogether inexpressibly pleasing'. Henry Dundas called him 'dear to me ... with a goodness of heart not always to be met with'; yet 'no circumstances will ever deter him from going forward directly and manfully in the execution of his duty'.[2]

For the following years one further happy familial circumstance may be noticed, Henry's remarriage in 1793. He had not, to be sure, practised celibacy since his first wife walked out on him. A wag composed this:

> What various tastes divide the fickle town!
> One likes the fair, and one admires the brown;
> The stately Queensberry, Hinchinbrook the small;
> Thurlow loves servant maids; Dundas loves all.

But for some time he had been seriously wooing Lady Anne Lindsay, daughter of the Earl of Crawford. It was a tangled affair. She, while not spurning Dundas, showed more affection for William Windham, a brilliant coming politician but also a confirmed bachelor. Her own brother reproached her for allowing the affair to drift, as she did till she was over 40: 'That man [Windham] uses you like a dog, and you use Dundas like one.'

The triangle was at last broken by Dundas's turning elsewhere. One night in the winter of 1792, 'after two extra bottles of claret', he proposed to Lady Jane Hope, elder sister of the Earl of Hopetoun. His was quite a powerful political connection: three brothers, two cousins and two sons-in-law sat in Parliament. She has been described as 'rather an elegant woman, possessing a figure over which drapery might be thrown with good effect. A gentle sad greyness pervaded her form, her dress, her manners, her mind.' Pitt once said, seeing her dressed in green, that she looked like a sickly sea-nymph. Some suggested that she bored Dundas, which was why he took to long, solitary walks when they were staying in the cramped lodge at Dunira; perhaps, however, he simply liked long, solitary walks. Their partnership may have been in large measure political, but the relations revealed by their correspondence seem tender enough, if companionable rather than passionate. At 30 Lady Jane was no chicken, and she could have had few illusions about him. Though childless, they stayed together till his death.

Lady Anne, however, was shaken by this sudden turn of events. Despairing of Windham, she married on the rebound a man much younger than herself, Andrew Barnard, indigent son of the Bishop of Limerick. She could still appeal to Dundas's feelings, at least in getting her husband a job: 'You owe me some happiness, in truth you do.' A place was found for him in the administration of the Cape of Good Hope, whence she continued a fond correspondence with her old flame. Dundas kept all her letters – perhaps both regretted, when it was too late, what might have been.[3]

As for politics, during the new Parliament's first months Dundas carried on in the same tasks as before. But soon a reconstruction of the Government brought him his big chance. Pitt had throughout acted as his own Chancellor of the Exchequer. One Secretary of State, at the Home Office, was his cousin, William Grenville, now elevated to the upper House to take over its official business from an increasingly capricious Lord Chancellor Thurlow. The other Secretary of State, at the Foreign Office, was the Duke of Leeds. Pitt thought little of him and had formed the habit, bad because bound to cause friction, of making extempore personal interventions in major matters of foreign policy. When, in the Ochakov crisis during the spring of 1791, he rashly risked war with Russia to safeguard Poland's interests, the indignant Duke resigned.

Grenville then became Foreign Secretary, and Dundas succeeded as Home Secretary. The office has seldom been held by Scots: he was the first since the reign of James VII and II. Pitt really wanted Lord Cornwallis for it, meaning to use Dundas only as a stopgap during the year or so he would need to inform the Governor-general and recall him from Calcutta. He told the King that he acted 'knowing that he can fully rely on him [Dundas] for the most cordial and efficient co-operation in business in the interval, and that he would with entire satisfaction quit to make room for Lord Cornwallis, retaining only the conduct of the business of India'.[4] The acceptance of Pitt's offer might have been thought demeaning by one of a less generous temperament. But Dundas set about his duties with a will – and lucky he did, for various circumstances conspired to prevent the further reshuffle ever taking place, so that he kept the job after all. Whether by design, or by the spontaneous exercise of his abundant energies, he soon consolidated his unexpected position at the top.

It doubtless helped that he at last began to get on well with George III, who admired his 'solid sense' and found him a more sympathetic listener than the frigid Pitt to tales of the royal family's numerous misdemeanours. Dundas gave guidance over the pecuniary embarrassments of the Dukes of Clarence and York, as well as over the annulment of an illegal marriage between the Duke of Sussex and Lady Augusta Murray, daughter of Lord Dunmore, who had served faithfully as last British governor of Virginia but had blood not blue enough to mix with Hanover's. The Prince of Wales, too, though a political foe, was on perfectly good personal terms with Dundas, and sometimes got drunk with him in return for financial tips.

He quickly made himself invaluable in Cabinet as well, maintaining an intimacy with his leader denied to most colleagues. In 1793 one insider wrote that 'the efficient Ministry is Pitt, Dundas and Grenville'. The simplest illustration of his position was the range of his responsibilities. The Home Secretary in those days dealt not only with British but also with colonial affairs. Dundas was landed besides with the administration of the war which broke out in 1793. He continued in addition to rule India and, with Grenville in the other place, took a hand in foreign affairs in the Commons. He was, apart from his chief, the only member of the Cabinet sitting there, so generally carried a heavy burden in debate.[5] The demands on him were altogether stupendous. But he bore them well, and Pitt cannot long have harboured doubts about his fitness for his station. In the following years the friendship and trust between them stood at their strongest.

Even so, from the Prime Minister's side it was unmistakably the trust of a leader in a faithful stand-by, sagacious and businesslike, content with full control of whatever was delegated to him. Pitt himself felt most at home in high policy, often casually leaving subordinates to worry over detail. Dundas graphically described the consequences for himself to Lady Anne Barnard, who attempted to transcribe them in the Doric: 'I often envy the rogue, while I am lying tossing and tumbling in my bed, and cannot sleep a wunk for thinking of expedeeshons and storms and bautles by sea and laund, there does he lay doon his head in his bed, and sleep as sound as a taup.' Or again, 'Pitt is perfectly good natured and affects nothing; he strikes out what he thinks is wisest and best for the good of the country, but he does not make himself responsible to himself for the results, and that is proof of his wisdom in my opinion, though I canna quite prauctis it.' Dundas, ever the realist, knew and accepted these limits. They did not require subservience on his part, for he could expect much in return: 'Mr Pitt, among the multitude of things which press upon him is at all times ready to accommodate himself to my call.' Nor did he hesitate to chide his chief, who was 'too humble not to call Dundas his friend'.

The Home Secretary's prime duty, then as now, lay in maintaining domestic law and order. Dundas it was who initiated the repression of radicals fired by the Revolution, soon organising themselves in clubs in London and elsewhere. Since English radicalism has been amply covered by other works, this volume will not go over the same ground, but in general confine itself to Dundas's measures in Scotland, which may be taken as representative.

It would yet be as well to note that the first disturbances with which he had to deal were the 'Church and King' riots in Birmingham. In July 1791, a drunken mob destroyed the houses of some radicals, including the dissenter and scientist, Joseph Priestley, when he provocatively celebrated the second anniversary of the storming of the Bastille. If the demonstration had a political character, it was conservative: a reminder of the ambiguities in popular sentiment. Dundas himself blamed economic problems and appealed to local magistrates to 'form some plan either by subscriptions or otherwise for the subsistence of people who will thereby be deprived of employment, for without the establishing of some system of that sort it appears to me that riots must inevitably take place.'[6]

His own attitudes had not yet hardened but, nothing if not thorough, he advised the Lord Advocate to take precautions in Scotland: 'If Government rested merely on its own strength, I should even in that case feel it incumbent upon it not to sleep over the evident signs there are of a very turbulent and pernicious spirit having pervaded numerous and various descriptions of persons in this country.' He suggested a proclamation against seditious writings, together with a ban on the entry of foreigners, and asked what the Scottish reaction was likely to be. 'Whatever is right to be done ought to be quickly done,' he added.[7]

It was the prelude to a period in Scotland usually depicted as one of deep and bitter conflict between the just claims of the people and the tyrannies of a repressive Government. This is a caricature. Before we come to questions about the nature of the popular protest, we should pause to recall that Dundas had for twenty years been administering Scottish affairs in a spirit far from immobilist. Reform was in the northern air not least because he had shown himself amenable to it, so long as it was sufficiently supported and sure to bring practical benefits. The premises were indeed conservative – seeking, rather than to emancipate the people, to place them under better paternalist rule – but they were not reactionary.

Dundas had vacillated over how far a wider franchise might be compatible with them. There was no simple answer because, at least in the counties, reformers were often conservative in motivation too: they aimed to secure the position of the old landed class. Nor did their brethren in the burghs want to bring in democracy, but to prevent abuse: they expressly condemned English demands for universal suffrage. In Scotland, agitations such as these came, broadly speaking, from within the political nation, even if sometimes from aspirant rather than from actual members. And Dundas's purpose in dealing with this political nation remained, as always, to unite it.

In the counties, a turning point seemed to have been reached in 1790 with Thurlow's judgment on a test case arising from a dispute in Aberdeenshire. The consequences were to affirm the truth of his earlier *obiter dictum*, that a rational suffrage would ultimately have to be restored by Parliament rather than by the courts. Yet the immediate effect was apparently to fulfil the heart's desire of the genuine freeholders, and prohibit faggot votes. As the ruling was applied, a franchise could not now be created for purely electoral purposes, but had to rest on some genuine interest in the land from which it derived, a point on which a claimant could also be interrogated before being admitted to a county's roll of voters. The *Edinburgh Advertiser* welcomed it as 'another great decision in favour of freedom' which would 'completely change the political interests of many of the counties … to the independent freeholders who have hitherto been outnumbered by parchment barons, it is of the greatest importance. It restores to them that respectable situation which the fictions of the law have so long deprived them of.'[8]

This was no hyperbole. In Inverness-shire at the following Michaelmas, 70 fictitious votes were annulled, pruning the roll to about 20. Simultaneously in Aberdeenshire, 53 electors were struck off, reducing their numbers by one-quarter. In Ayrshire the next year, James Boswell exerted himself to have 106 votes cancelled, nearly half the total. In Banffshire, the electorate fell from 108 to 39 by 1794. Decreases, if not so spectacular, were recorded in most Scottish counties over the next two decades. A renewed spate of manufacturing votes did afterwards swell the rolls again, though not on account of any complicity by the authorities, but of lawyers' cunning in finding novel loopholes in the electoral laws.[9]

For the moment, however, the purges raised again the problem thrown up when Dundas had been toying with reform in the 1770s, for they threatened to reduce the total Scottish electorate to an extent nobody thought desirable. The only way to maintain it at a reasonable size was to redefine the voting qualifications in a fresh statute: doubtless what Thurlow had in mind. This the government could and would not initiate without a consensus among the existing freeholders. A series of meetings to find one, starting in July 1792, culminated a year later in a national convention.

This assembly in the summer of 1793 was conscious of its serious purpose, and widely representative though almost free of gadabout radicals. That pillar of respectability, Sir James Montgomery, Chief Baron of Exchequer, chaired it. It naturally attracted a good attendance of Whigs, including Henry Erskine, Sir Thomas Dundas and his son Lawrence (who sat in Parliament for an English seat), Lord Daer, heir to the Earl of Selkirk, and the Revd Sir Henry Moncreiff. But the Government took a close interest too. Its delegation was led by the Lord Advocate himself, at this stage not at all ill-disposed to reform (though he would never, of course, have differed publicly from his uncle). William McDowall and Patrick Miller, members of Parliament for the Glasgow and Dumfries burghs respectively, also played a prominent part.

Consensus was the convention's keynote. While Norman Macleod of Macleod, already on this and other issues moving towards radicalism, claimed the Government's hand had been forced by the strength of feeling among electors, its wish to placate them was nothing out of the ordinary. More remarkably, the Whigs showed themselves willing to split the opposition for the sake of a deal the Dundases could accept. When Macleod moved that the franchise should be extended to all with property valued at £100 Scots, Sir Thomas Dundas countered with a successful amendment to set the figure at £400. Robert Dundas was delighted. In this favourable atmosphere, he had written to his uncle, 'the general voice of everybody, and your best friends, is for an amendment of the election law. So something ought and must be done.' The Lord Advocate was clearly distancing himself from the diehard conservatives, those who would have abolished faggot votes without liberalising the suffrage. The increasingly crusty Jupiter Carlyle, for example, warned Henry Dundas that a bigger electorate would 'perhaps open a door to bribery in the counties, where influence only has hitherto prevailed'.

A proper consensus also needed, however, explicit assent from the constituencies. The proposals were accordingly remitted to meetings there, which as usual would not be held till Michaelmas. It has been suggested that this represented some fiendish ploy by the Dundases to bring progress to a halt. Rather it was an absolutely standard preliminary to major Scottish legislation, and the only sensible way to deal with the interests at stake. Nobody could have known how soon the supervention of greater forces, hostilities abroad and more extreme radicalism at home, would drastically change minds. When Midlothian's meeting, for instance, was convened, it resolved that there should be no further action on electoral reform 'in the present situation of the country, at the commencement of a war, and when the minds of many members of the community are filled with the most delusive and dangerous doctrines with respect to civil government.' Without all this, though, it is not unreasonable to suppose that a moderately liberalising measure for the franchise might in due course have been widely endorsed. If Henry Dundas still needed convincing, he would probably not have stood out against a genuine consensus. As it was, the counties had to shift as best they could under Thurlow's judgment.[10]

The state of affairs in the burghs can be more summarily dealt with. There, too, reform was in the air, but in air politically thinner than the counties'. Despite Archibald Fletcher's efforts some years before, none but a handful of the largest burghs could generate a civic spirit or anything like an articulate public opinion. The rest were little more than villages sunk in rural idiocy, under cliques cringeing to local landed interests. The pressure for change was therefore limited, and even reformers clearly regarded it as a secondary issue – especially as popular election was in those days no cure for corruption. Only minor figures busied themselves in the matter, though again they included not just members of the political opposition but also others, such as Robert Cullen, closer to Dundas.

He and his nephew could hardly have deluded themselves about the burghs' condition. After Thurlow's judgment, however, it was not yet time to despair of a judicial remedy here as well. In the past, some councils had indeed been thus cleaned out. The Lord Advocate stressed the point to the Commons in April 1792: 'If any magistrate exacts taxes from, or dilapidates the property of the burgessses, he is amenable to the laws of the country; because there is a power in the Court of Session to inquire into and grant redress in such cases. In my official situation I have lent my name to such information and always will do so.'[11] In case of doubt, he brought in a Bill explicitly confirming the Court of Session's powers in this respect.

Since he merely abandoned the Bill on failing to find enough support, his may seem a feeble response. Still, we must never underestimate, for this century or the next, the obstacles at Westminster to the most minor Scottish legislation. They blocked the more effectively any wider reform. Besides, its advocates had not come up with a specific plan likely to impress Parliament with the need to intrude on the burghs' rights. These after all derived from the Crown and were guaranteed by the Treaty of Union. Nobody yet, certainly not the Dundases, took the cavalier modern view that the settlement of 1707 could be altered at whim. This was why, before legislation on the Court of Session in 1785, it had been felt necessary to obtain the sovereign's assent. Even then, resistance was such as to prevent any change. That could well have happened again. If numbers of the councils were venal, not every one was inconsiderable. Edinburgh, Glasgow and others might have caused a great deal of trouble had they been foolishly provoked by an attack on their rights, easily interpreted as an attack on Scottish rights generally. It was already being so interpreted by their collective mouthpiece, the Convention of Royal Burghs, a body with which the Government needed to co-operate for taxation and other purposes. But Dundas was not that foolish, and essayed no sweeping reform in advance of a consensus in its favour.

Recourse to self-help remained possible for the few burghs with a mind to avail themselves of it. Before long, an expedient was devised of passing private Acts of Parliament to set up so-called police authorities. These were elected bodies dealing with public order and sanitation, matters beyond the councils' competence, in every sense. Glasgow established one in 1800, Edinburgh in 1805 and others followed. The government was content for municipal improvement to proceed in this apolitical fashion.[12]

The broad picture we can draw from both counties and burghs is that efforts to reform specific abuses were continuous on either side of 1789. Having been conducted for two decades by liberal members of the elite, these efforts carried on under their own momentum into the era of the French Revolution. This does not mean that they were linked with it, still less caused by it, or that they had much in common with grandiose schemes of universal suffrage dreamed up by home-grown radicals. Robert Dundas could in one of his regular reports to his uncle write about the controversy over electoral law as well as a riot in Dundee without remotely suggesting a connection. It has been made too facilely, with the benefit of hindsight, by the historians of a supposed democratic awakening during this period in Scotland.

The usual contemporary assumption, at the outset anyway, was that the French were merely catching up with what Scotland had achieved a century before. The result, it was hoped, would rest on constitutional principles analogous to those of 1688 and 1707 that had made the Scots such a free and happy nation. Progressive intellectuals – Principal Robertson, Dugald Stewart and several professors in Glasgow – were especially keen to stress this. Hence the diverting sight of the Dundonian Whigs sending to the National Assembly in Paris congratulations on the triumph of liberty which, they were sure, would now work the same wonders in France as it had done in Scotland. Even Dundas, as we saw above, may have shared such sentiment for a while.

It followed that the French had nothing to teach the Scots. Though in Scotland defects in the political system might arise from time to time, they could not conceivably warrant its wholesale disruption. To remedy them was possible and desirable, but that had to be done in harmony with the broad commitment among the nation's leaders to progress in a shape and at a pace of their own choosing – if Scots had not taken change when they fancied it was foisted on them from England, why should they take it from France? Some applauded the French, but nearly all drew the line at emulating them. On this point the Dundases were in accord with reformers like the Whigs' agent, William Adam, or even Erskine, the future liberal martyr, who abhorred radicalism and called himself a 'strong aristocrat'.[13]

Dissidents in the elite were isolated and eccentric, not to say unsavoury, figures. Most notorious was the mentally unstable Macleod. Having failed in his revolutionary aim of persuading Dundas to get him a baronetcy, he retaliated by promoting social turmoil. When he crossed in pique to the Whigs, one called him

> a man the most universally disliked by all ranks I ever heard of, whose butterfly head is crammed with scraps and saws of political knowledge, picked up in ale-houses and fermented in debauchery and whose heart is the very sink of selfish insincerity and political depravity. In short, he is one of the ruffian spirits who confound the country with the Ministry and would rather ruin the former than not be revenged of the latter for refusing all that his overweening vanity thought his due.

It gave him the gall, after conflict broke out with France, to crawl back to Dundas with an offer to raise a regiment. The cool reply saw 'no necessity for resorting to those who disapprove of the war for their aid in conducting it'. Disowned by his family, Macleod became a laughing stock and spent his last years in drunken self-pity.[14]

Yet what of sentiment in the nation at large? There might appear to be a superficial likeness between the French doctrines and the egalitarianism native to Scotland. But whereas the former derived from the Enlightenment, the latter derived from theology, the two being in most respects antithetical. What preoccupied Scots was the equality of souls before God, a preoccupation translated as yet uncertainly into any social or economic programme of levelling. By this concept the most extreme presbyterians were indeed untouched, for their pietism made them passive in the face of authority, however fierce they might be in preaching the word. The concern, on the one recent occasion when the sense of equality had been roused in defiance of authority, was not social or economic. It was a protest against catholic relief. Here one can see the difference in the Scots' sense of equality, for political egalitarians would surely have sought to help a small, poor minority. Yet there could be no compassion for the stalking horses of Romanism, of the Antichrist who would crush true religion. One should note too that this mutiny did not breed a general rejection of authority: the people returned to their normal quiescence once they had successfully made their point. In 1779, it is clear, authority and equality could still co-exist in the way they had long done under the institutions and mentality of feudalism.

Traces of these survived. Certainly, the social stability characteristic of feudalism showed few signs of succumbing to novel antagonisms – for example, of class

– generated by progress. A sense of hierarchy came naturally to a country still overwhelmingly rural and agricultural, where traditional structures were barely beginning to come under strain. Scotland's tranquillity may therefore be primarily explained by her relative backwardness. If in the bigger towns it could be unsettled by merchants and manufacturers making fortunes, they usually tried to buy their way into the old elite rather than set themselves up as a rival force. Landowning thus still overlapped with capitalism, just as it did with the avocations of the professional pillars of society, lawyers and clergymen. The social authority assured by possession of land, together with the range of institutions through which it was exercised, went largely unquestioned till well into the next century. Few could or did resist it, the only considerable body being seceders from the Church, especially if they had also taken to new industrial occupations. But we should probe especially what the acceptance of authority offered to ordinary Scots at the critical points, those where tensions inevitable in an advancing society might have issued in alienation and disruption. Here they did not, if we may judge by the fact that Scotland remained much less violent than England right through this era.

One explanation that suggests itself is the greater security afforded by Scots law. Over more than a century it had been working as a social cement. This happened first, admittedly, in the elite, where it became an effective means of protecting life and limb, then of resolving disputes about property. Yet the benefits did not rest thus confined. The law also developed some protective functions for the people, for example, by allowing them to form combinations and by adjudicating on their wage rates. Where workers had advanced to the point of starting to assert rights, they did not have to strike, still less fight, for them. They could instead go to law.

The current law here derived from the verdict in a test case brought by the tailors of Edinburgh in 1762. It declared that the 'arts and manufactures which are necessary to the wellbeing of society must be subject to rules. This power has long been exercised by the magistrates of burghs and the justices.' Whether or not the obligatory appeal to days of yore was authentic, the courts repeatedly confirmed the judgment, permitting Sir John Rankine, institutional writer on the subject, to deduce the general principle that 'by Scots common law, every company is a distinct persona'. In other words, there was no need for combinations of Scots workers to establish their right to exist – as eventually had to be done by statute in England, where common law held combinations to be illegal.

Dundas was a firm supporter of the system. While still Solicitor General, he had in 1768 successfully defended the formation of a trade union by weavers in Paisley, and his part is recorded in later, similar cases.[15] Only once during his stewardship of Scottish affairs had there been a serious breakdown, when in 1787 the weavers of Glasgow went on strike against cuts in their wages, which they hoped the magistrates would intervene to prevent. Troops were called in to deal with the resulting disturbances, there being no police in Scotland, and during a clash they killed a few demonstrators. Though cowed, these workers could still secure a new table of wages by 1792.

Otherwise industrial relations were good. A recent study has shown both sides willing as a matter of course to resort to the courts for settlement of disputes. The judiciary, far from being the instrument of one class, was accessible to all: lawyers readily lent their services to humble as well as great. Conversely, all trusted that grievances would be impartially heard and dealt with, if not invariably in lower courts, where local political influences might distort the process, then certainly in the Court of Session. There the judges seemed conscious of how a regulatory function responsibly exercised could contribute to social harmony. In return, they won that general acceptance of their authority. Dundas said:

> Among the Scots a greater latitude and discretion is indulged their judges. But I affirm that this very circumstance it is that attaches the people to their laws. And I am bold to say, that there will be found fewer crimes to exist among them than in any other country in Europe, and that justice is administered among them with a degree of lenity and moderation, owing to this very discretionary power, not elsewhere to be paralleled.[16]

Apropos of law and order, it would be well to recall that Dundas was not, to borrow modern Tory terms, a hanger and flogger. He disapproved of corporal punishment, as of incarcerating people in hulks. In view of later events, what he wrote to Grenville in 1789 is interesting:

> I believe you will find nothing so good as transportation, and I cannot see any good reasons why in smaller offences, which are chiefly committed by boys or very young men, some plan might not be adopted to convert them into recruits for regiments situated in our colonies abroad, either in east or west; and after being inured to exercise and military discipline for a few years, they are very likely to lay aside their idle dispositions, and become good subjects.

As for hanging, it should be borne in mind that during the three decades to 1820, only eighteen executions were carried out in Scotland, against 1400 in England. The Scottish legal system was not inherently repressive or inhumane.[17]

Strangely, reformers regarded these marks of Scotland's legal independence as one of the worst features of the Dundas despotism. Daer explained to Charles Grey, the English Whig, after measures to control the radicals in 1793:

> As our courts of law found something of this to be necessary they instead of applying to the Parliament at London have taken upon themselves with a degree of audacity which can hardly be made credible to a stranger to make, under the pretence of regulating of courts, little laws (acts of parliament as they call them) materially affecting the liberty of the subject.

His sentiments were echoed by Scottish progressives into the next century.[18]

If, then legal authority generally enjoyed popular consent, how might it have started to break down? One view would be that it did not, at least not to a serious extent – Gilbert Elliot said: 'The idea of Scottish insurrections is certainly ridiculous to those who live in Scotland and know the truth.' On the other hand, in a literate nation, radical doctrines might be easily disseminated. Macleod wrote after the first repressive move, the proclamation against seditious writings: 'It set people of all ranks a-reading and as everybody in this country can read, the people are astonishingly informed.' Certainly the press flourished during these years, largely on news of French events and French opinions. In *The Annals of the Parish*, John Galt had his minister remark that 'men read more, the spirit of reflection and reasoning was more awake than at any time within my remembrance ... Cotton spinners and muslin weavers, unsatisfied and ambitious spirits, clubbed together and got a London newspaper. They were mightily in the habit of meeting and debating about the affairs of France.' Clearly also, to judge from frequent expressions of concern by the authorities, Tom Paine's *Rights of Man* must have had a wide circulation – it was even translated into Gaelic.[19]

Still, people sitting at home with a book were by definition not on the streets. Overt disaffection needed some specific spur. One scholar has stressed that its appearance in Scotland coincided with bad harvests, a rising cost of living and generally tougher economic conditions. Special resentment, he suggested, was caused by the elaboration of the Corn Laws in 1791. It set up an absurdly complex system to discourage imports and encourage exports, exaggerating volatility on the markets in a visibly inequitable way. It might have been taken as reflecting in politicians like Dundas a blatant bias towards their landed friends, except that it was not promoted by the Government. Pitt did, admittedly, commend it to the Commons as a reasonable compromise between the farmer's and the consumer's interest, speaking against Charles James Fox who wanted to make the scheme still more protectionist. No contemporary comment of Dundas has survived, though he wrote some years later of his

> very serious doubts how far the detail of legislative provisions upon the article of corn does not already go further than in policy it ought. Of this I am almost confident, that if Parliament is to interfere at all upon the subject, it ought to be by general rule and system and not by partial or occasional interference, which uniformly create alarm, and of course distress.[20]

So it is wide of the mark to blame him. True, the radicals were free traders, aiming to break what they saw as landlords' protectionism. Dundas, of course, subscribed to the same general principles, if not to that particular deduction from them; as a practical politician, he could not accept that simple-minded radicalism was an answer to anything. But he remained an economic liberal. He now tackled, for example, the peculiar Scottish problem of duties on coastwise trade, what Adam Ferguson called an 'absurd and oppressive tax'. Under a quirk of Scots law, all navigable waters were considered open sea, so that if a ship merely crossed the Forth it had to pay. The restriction could only damage the prosperity of places where maritime transport of goods in bulk was the quickest and easiest. Vested interests preserved such nonsense. Here, the Lothian coalmasters wanted to force local industry to use the output of their mines, and tried to exclude coal coming even from Fife, let alone from further afield. In fact the region's economy was growing so fast that demand for fuel far outstripped supply. When it had to be covered by English imports the cost to manufacturers became severe, exceeding any possible benefit from an unnecessary protection of mining. In 1790 the Lord Provost and the chamber of commerce in Edinburgh called for the main coastwise cargoes to be relieved of duty, stressing that there was no such imposition in England. Dundas agreed and in 1793 legislated the anomaly away.[21]

He had still been worried about a loss of revenue. Since the Union, extra revenue had been raised from Scotland mainly through the multiplication of excise duties – on beer, bricks, candles, cokes, glass, hides, molasses, paper, printing equipment, soap, spirits (home-produced and imported), tea, tobacco and wine, none of which had been taxed before. That made smuggling a major industry. Efforts at prevention being wasted, the Government was now trying to get rid of the incentive to smuggle by reducing the level and complexity of duties. It had in the event no need to fear for the revenue. In 1789, less than £300, 000 was raised in excise from Scotland. By the mid-1790s, this went up to nearly £400, 000. As so often, therefore, a cut in the rate of tax increased its yield. Yet Scots remained lightly taxed (which may, of course, have contributed to their prosperity). That figure represented only six per cent of the sum raised from England, while for the other principal levy, the ill-starred land tax, they were still managing to find only two per cent of the English total.

So there was no more than a temporary check to the impressive growth of the economy: in the decade to 1796 the total value of trade still rose by nearly 150 per cent. Prosperity could, of course, bring with it uncomfortable change, marked by rural enclosures and clearances, urban congestion and poverty. Dundas himself saw the trouble stemming from places where progress was at its most rapid: 'The great scenes of attempts to do mischief in this country are Edinburgh, Glasgow, Perth, Dundee, Montrose and Aberdeen. In a word I might have said all the towns where manufactures are flourishing, and in all those places they are flourishing to a degree beyond conception.'[22]

But the vague sense of unease was transformed only fortuitously into disturbances, and then almost a year behind the English ones. They began in Edinburgh on June 4, 1792, the King's birthday. In his pioneering work on the period, followed by all later historians, H. W. Meikle pinpointed them as the first outburst, after political tranquillity had reigned for nearly half a century, of what seemed to be deep popular resentment against the social order generally and against Dundas personally. They were thus a crucial event in the democratic awakening.

As a matter of fact, however, riots took place in the capital almost every year on this date, simply because it provided an excuse to hit the bottle and because Scotsmen on the skite were, as they still are, apt to misbehave themselves. In 1784, the Lord Provost of Edinburgh, John Grieve, had casually remarked to its member of Parliament, James Hunter Blair, that 'as it was the King's birthday, I was not without my fears and apprehensions of rioting as is usual on that day.' He went on to describe how the mob had been joined by the City Guard itself, obviously all blind drunk, in an attack against Haig's distillery at Leith, on the pretext, inherently convoluted but perhaps with a certain clarity to intoxicated brains, that the use of too much grain for whisky was raising the price of bread. The workers there, alarmed for their livelihoods, had defended the place with firearms, and one assailant had been killed. Archibald Cockburn, sheriff of Midlothian, arrived on the scene just in time to save a corn-merchant from being drowned by the rabble in the Water of Leith. The lucky man was Thomas, grandfather of William Gladstone.

Though the Lord Advocate himself called the riot of 1792 'very unexpected', it would still be hard to conclude that we are observing here, compared with 1784, some new and higher stage of Scottish political consciousness. The only difference was that Henry Dundas stood in for Haig's distillery. The mob this time chose as its target his family's residence in George Square, stoned it and burned him in effigy. He was absent in London, but his mother and other relations were dining inside. Two nephews, Francis Dundas and Adam Duncan, foolishly provoked the rioters by rushing out and attacking them with a golf-club and Lady Arniston's crutch. Forced to retreat, they presented their backsides for kissing before disappearing indoors. Luckily, the sheriff soon arrived and troops were called down from the Castle.

The crowd dispersed for a while, if only to go and beset the Lord Provost's house in St Andrew Square. Later on, doubtless inflamed by more drink, it re-assembled outside the Dundases' and goaded the guards with cries of 'Johnny Cope!'. Soon it began to hurl cobblestones, to a more frenetic chorus of 'Buggars, fire!' At length the soldiers obliged – they killed one man and wounded six others. Before retiring Lady Arniston wrote to her son: 'To say I was not a little frightened would be false, but I happily was supported by friends and expect a good night's sleep to remit my spirits.' Henry Cockburn observed years later that 'no windows could be smashed at that time without the inmates thinking of the bloody streets of Paris.' Still, he had not been in George Square on the evening in question, and it was perhaps understandable that the Dundases, at least, believed the threat real. Robert, so far relaxed about radicals, afterwards watched them like a hawk.[23]

Further incidents followed during the autumn and winter, though the immediate causes were usually non-political: one in Ross was about the threat of clearances, one in Lanark about enclosure, one in Berwickshire against turnpikes and tolls, one in Dundee against the Corn Law. Whether they were connected with the unrest in Edinburgh remains unproven, but the situation as a whole did offer a political opportunity for anybody minded to exploit it. It may have been no accident that, only seven weeks after the King's birthday, a Society of Friends of the People was set up in the capital, on the model of those which had already emerged in London. Active in the South were several well-born Scots, the Earls of Buchan and Lauderdale, Lords Daer and Sempill, who soon established contact between the two countries. In September, Dundas heard that a network of Scottish societies already had 300 members, including ordinary workers, whom they could attract because they set much lower subscriptions than their English counterparts.

Dundas thought he would make himself most useful to the Government by dealing in person with this, and returned to do so. He told the Lord Advocate: 'It would appear that they either wished to murder myself or to burn my house, for I was not two days arrived before notification of it was given in a very suspicious mode.' He set out to gather intelligence from those parts of the country where the Friends operated. The societies were penetrated by spies who, no doubt encouraged by the payment of piece-rates, duly produced a stream of long and lurid reports. At official prompting, supporters of the British constitution formed their own societies, while Henry Mackenzie led a band of hacks in churning out suitable propaganda. All public bodies of any standing were urged to send in loyal addresses to George III. More than 400 immediately did so, and many continued to at every excuse: by 1796 the King was sick of the sight of them, and ordered that they should be sent straight to Dundas without bothering him.

The Home Secretary's zeal could only with difficulty be restrained by his Prime Minister's increasingly urgent requests for a return to London, to which he at last yielded in December. There, too, he found the Government winning: ' The tide here is completely changed; all levellers are dropping their heads.' That assured him that he had not got his priorities wrong, as he insisted to Parliament:

> In Scotland I have been far from idle. With respect to my popularity in that country, I must own that I love popularity and that the odium created against me among my countrymen, from whatever pretence, has afforded me much uneasiness. During the last six weeks I have spent in Scotland, I was visited from every quarter, by the great manufacturers, by magistrates and by gentlemen from parts of the country where there are no magistrates, all expressing their alarm at the situation of the country and requesting the interference of the government to check a spirit which threatens such dangerous consequences.[24]

In fact the agitation in Scotland was far from over. Just as Dundas addressed the Commons, her radical societies were preparing to hold a convention. About 80 of them sent 160 delegates, hailing from 35 places in the central belt, though more than half came from Edinburgh. But conspicuous by their absence were nearly all those who had previously made a mark in reforming activity – even Macleod, though he was certainly a sympathiser. The only participants of the remotest political consequence, to the extent at least of being landowners, were Lord Daer and William Dalrymple of Fordell, leader of the delegation from Glasgow. Neither played such a part as the young advocate, Thomas Muir. He alarmed many with his intemperance and had to be restrained from reading an address transmitted by the seditious United Irishmen. Yet he was not the only one exhibiting a much fiercer radicalism than had been seen in Scotland before. Daer, for example, wrote an explicitly anti-unionist letter to Grey:

> Scotland has long groaned under the chains of England and knows that its connection there has been the cause of its greatest misfortunes ... We bartered our liberty and with it our morals for a little wealth ... Thinking we have been the worse of every connection hitherto with you, the Friends of Liberty in Scotland have almost universally been enemies to Union with England.[25]

It was not clear, though, that many of the delegates agreed. The majority affirmed their attachment to the constitution and rejected calls for manhood suffrage and annual Parliaments. Platitudes apart, their main object was apparently to present a united front with the Friends in London (who were obviously expected to do all the thinking and most of the work). For themselves, they could devise nothing more useful than to go on from Edinburgh and hold public meetings or organise petitions round the country, before meeting again to see what headway they had made. They made none, for France's declaration of war in February 1793 extinguished nearly all the remaining public or parliamentary sympathy for her Revolution.[26]

This was the inauspicious background to the Scottish Friends' second convention, which went ahead in April. It attracted 116 delegates from 29 places, most new to the agitation. They were also more extreme than the last lot. After some preliminary shilly-shallying, they openly espoused democracy. Most unhelpfully to themselves, they opposed the war too: considering that Britain had not started it, they presumably meant her just to submit to any demands the French might make. Ill-timed anyway, this convention was still more ineffective, isolated and frustrated than the previous one, managing neither to win support at home nor to co-operate with the English. Through their spies, the Dundases knew just what was going on, of course. They evidently took no great alarm and resorted only to mild deterrent action, such as prosecuting for sedition (and then often letting off) the printers of radical pamphlets.

They had already decided, however, to move against Muir, the most flagrant agitator. An attempt was made to arrest him in January, but he had fled. Having made his way to France, ostensibly in an effort to save Louis XVI's life, he was stranded there by the outbreak of hostilities. He took the chance to consort with Irish revolutionaries, notably with Wolfe Tone, who remarked: 'Of all the vain blockheads that I ever met I never saw his equal.'[27] Outlawed in his own country, Muir was foolhardy enough to return, by way of Dublin, and landed off an American ship at Stranraer. He was arrested and brought to trial in August. In what became a *cause célèbre*, the authorities were so anxious to convict him, and to exploit for the purpose every legal device, that they ended up, even with a strong case, damaging the reputation of Scottish justice.

The trial took place before Lord Braxfield, of late Lord Justice Clerk, who following normal practice in criminal causes himself selected the jury – and made rather too sure of its loyalty. Muir was accused of having given seditious speeches, having circulated *The Rights of Man* and having read out the treasonable address from the United Irishmen. If the first two charges were flimsy, he had no real answer to the third. He unwisely insisted on conducting his own defence, and not on the substance of the accusations but on a general political argument that there was nothing illegal in advocating reform. Still, it must be said that Braxfield, too, was happy to fight on the ground of Muir's choosing, uttering several notable *obiter dicta*, such as: 'A government in every country should be just like a corporation; and in this country, it is made up of the landed interest, who alone have the right to be represented.' Robert Dundas, leading for the prosecution, equally succumbed to political temptation in his address to the jury, of which Cockburn observed that 'great allowance must be made for the heat of a very excitable temperament'. He called Muir a 'demon of mischief … tainted from head to foot, and as unworthy to live under the protection of the law as the meanest felon.' When the accused was predictably found guilty, Braxfield handed down the ferocious sentence of fourteen years' transportation.[28]

Opinion at home and abroad was outraged. Fox said: 'God help the people who have such judges!' Even so, the same sentence was passed two weeks later on the Revd Thomas Fyshe Palmer, a unitarian minister in Dundee who had helped the Friends. At every turn the authorities clumsily contrived to convey an impression that injustice was being done. Legal controversy raged about whether sedition was actually an offence in Scotland (though of course the Court of Justiciary could declare new crimes), or transportation a legal punishment. The worried Dundases rather hoped Muir and Palmer would ask for clemency, without which, Robert wrote to his uncle, people would say 'your opinion was that the sentence and verdicts were either wrong or severe and that the conduct of the court is disapproved of'. But then the Lord Advocate himself made this admission to the Duke of Portland: 'Truth is that the Lord Justice Clerk was too violent and hasty in pronouncing sentence.' In the event neither Muir nor Palmer would co-operate, and clemency could not be spontaneously offered.

The argument over the legality of the procedure dragged on embarrassingly for months. Henry finally asked the Bench to give a collective opinion. In November he wrote to Robert expressing his anxiety 'that the judges will make their report with their first convenience, at the same time for their own sakes and for the sake of the law of the country, which must be upheld. I hope the report will be ably and scientifically drawn up ... If the judges' report expresses no doubt upon the subject, I will carry the sentence immediately into execution and meet their [the Whigs'] clamour in Parliament without any kind of dismay'. Robert replied a month later sending an elaborate defence of the verdicts for his uncle's use in public. Sedition was an offence at common law in Scotland and, unlike in England, 'our punishments are not in the case of the lesser offences [!] precisely defined, but are arbitrary, secundum arbitrium judicis'. Braxfield had therefore been quite within his rights in sentencing Muir.[29]

The Dundases were reassured enough to stage a third performance. The most radical fringe of the Friends, undeterred by growing public antipathy, decided on a final push, on a third, an all-British convention. They chose Edinburgh as the venue. There it met at the end of 1793, indeed with representation from all over these islands including, most provocatively, some United Irishmen. Robert wrote to Henry that he was keeping close watch on the proceedings 'and I hope they will not break up without doing something which will enable us to interfere'. One Irishman obliged by challenging the Lord Advocate to a duel. The law officers anyway moved in after a few days, dispersed the convention and arrested three of its organisers. They in their turn were condemned and transported.

That made six transportations in all. It was enough to sate the authorities, who now brought to an end the sequence of trials for sedition. Against later charges of barbaric harshness on the part of Robert Dundas, we might set Cockburn's assessment of him:

> Few could have exercised his half legal and half political office, in such times, without being excited into violence. But beyond a little frothy warmth and weak declamation at the bar, he had no tendency that way. If the times and foolish friends had ever provoked it, it would have been checked by his uncle's sense, by his own humanity, and by seeing that it was the curb, and not the spur, that his followers required. The true, and the very great, merit of both of these public officers is, that having nearly absolute power, they abused it so little.[30]

Only in a single case did the authorities go further and execute a radical. The victim, Robert Watt, exemplified the marginal nature of the movement. As a respectable merchant, he had signed on with the Dundases' swarm of spies, after commending himself by a warning that Lady Arniston should be discouraged from wandering round bookshops in search of seditious literature on which she could make tart comments to other customers. His special mission was to find out where Muir got his money. But Watt claimed expenses so exorbitant that he was dropped. Soured by this, he really joined the radical side and started concealing pikes in his house against the day of an implausible popular uprising. After they had been discovered during a routine investigation of something else, Watt was tried, found guilty and hanged in September 1794. Though the only Scots radical to be put to death during the revolutionary era, he was too potty and disreputable to appeal to later inventors of martyrs' cults.[31]

Radicalism now disintegrated – it was more or less finished, as we know in retrospect, for a good twenty years. Dundas acted, however, as though the threat remained palpable. If anything, he intensified the repression, exploiting the fevered atmosphere of war. He had the Act against Wrongous Imprisonment, Scottish equivalent of *habeas corpus*, suspended. He still sent spies into every gathering that could be reckoned remotely subversive. Cockburn remembered a general witch-hunt against anyone tainted with dissent: strikes were suppressed, workmen dismissed, tradesmen boycotted, even philanthropy was regarded with mistrust. The authorities deemed disloyalty among the well-to-do especially reprehensible. Mrs Archibald Fletcher said 'it was supposed that judges would not decide in favour of any litigant who employed Whig lawyers ... We were often at that time reduced to our last guinea'. Dundas fixed his own baleful eye on Erskine, who alone of the leading Whigs had refused to rally round the Government. Not only that, he continued to question its measures for internal security. He made a particular fuss about the Treason and Sedition Bills of 1795, introduced to clear up the legal controversies arising from the recent trials by declaring such offences indeed to be criminal in Scotland, just in case they were not so already. Erskine even blew on the embers of popular discontent. A nervous Robert Dundas noted with relief that he got nowhere in his efforts to sow disaffection from the new laws among shopkeepers. It was not only remarkably imprudent of him to needle the Ministry at its most sensitive point, but also grossly irresponsible, seeing that he opposed all political concessions to the people himself.

But, as Dean of the Faculty, this genial fool still held an eminent public position. In December several leading advocates circulated their colleagues asking whether his actions 'have been such as merit their approbation, or render him the properest person that can be found in the Faculty to represent them to the world'. A squib called him 'a demagogue in agitating the ignorant and giddy multitude'. In January 1796 he was voted out, and replaced by the Lord Advocate. Burns made a succinctly apt comment:

> Yet simple Bob the victory got
> And won his heart's desire;
> Which shows that Heaven can boil a pot,
> Though the Devil piss in the fire.[32]

This was another episode that has helped to gain Henry Dundas the reputation of bone-headed blimp. Assessments of his conduct during these years have usually stressed its expediency, arguing that whatever masks he had worn earlier now dropped to reveal the monster of depraved cynicism beneath. He had, though, always been conservative – if, like the best conservatives, ready to accept gradual change in the shape of reforms from above tending to strengthen the social fabric. Still, one effect of the threat to his conceptions posed in the 1790s was certainly to make him respond in kind. He saw himself as 'the main instrument of completely rousing the spirit and zeal of the country'.[33]

He did not merely react, however, but also reflected on what he felt called to defend. In common with most politicians of the age, he regarded himself as an heir of the Glorious Revolution, and in that distant and imprecise sense as a Whig at heart too. How could he justify himself by the values of 1688? The question was posed because the radicals claimed, for example, that their doctrine of natural rights logically extended and clarified the Revolution's heritage. John Locke, its theorist, had indeed said that government was created for the purpose of preserving the people's natural rights, which it must therefore recognise; if it did not, they were entitled to resist it.

Dundas countered that, while the people might have an ultimate right to resist an arbitrary tyrant, a general claim to an inalienable right of resistance would subvert all authority. When the Revolution took place, he told Parliament,

> the people were oppressed by the tyranny of the executive, and there was no question of their right to resist. But it was the resistance of the people, with the legislative branch of the constitution, contending against the executive … [Fox] has put an extreme case and asked, whether if the King, Lords and Commons were united for the purpose of depriving the people of their liberty, the people would not have a right to resist. There can be no difficulty in answering that question in the affirmative, because, in that case, there would not in fact exist any government at all. But I wish to put one plain question to the good sense of [Fox], which is, whether he really thinks it consistent with policy, or even with humanity, to hold such language to the people. The expediency of resistance is not a point which the generality of mankind can safely consider … Every ignorant man would conceive he had a right to resist everything which did not accord with his opinions, and the result might be shocking to humanity. Such language tends to bring all government into disgrace or, at least, to render it precarious.[34]

In other words, a right of resistance did exist, but could only be used in extreme circumstances and by the natural leaders of society.

Along with others, Dundas also arrived at a more general definition of what it was he wished to conserve against radical claims. The great principle of conservatism forged on the anvil of the revolutionary tumult was that of the organic society, a society not constructed according to some abstract scheme, but held together by traditional, mutual obligations, voluntarily accepted among its members. From Edmund Burke, its apostle, we can trace a succession which, passing through lesser, Scottish thinkers, led at length to Benjamin Disraeli, who by adapting these ideas to an age of mass democracy saved the Conservative party from the extinction that might then have awaited it.

Dundas's formulation of them ran like this:

> If ever there was a country in which these classes are united; in which, from the humblest cottager to the monarch on the throne, all ranks of society are

cemented and connected in one continuous chain, each giving assistance to the others, it is the country in which we live. The union of these orders appears from the connection between master and servant, landlord and tenant and above all from the innumerable charities that are everywhere established, from the parochial rates and from various other benevolent institutions, which will prove to the people that they are under the peculiar care of those whom Providence has placed above them. This very calumny against the higher orders of society forms part of that dangerous system, against which we are called to protect the country.[35]

The conservative defence of the existing structure was on the whole triumphantly successful, not least in Scotland. That ought to prompt the question of how important and dramatic this first radical outburst really had been in a hitherto politically tractable people. Scotland's history contained little preparation for a secular radicalism. Previous accounts, seeking its roots, have too glibly lumped it together with the reforming movements in counties and burghs, as part of a universal democratic awakening. But the more careful drawing of distinctions must cast doubt on whether, just because these activities were simultaneous, their aims could be taken as identical. Reformers, in contradistinction to radicals, owed nothing to foreign revolutionary inspiration. They were an indigenous movement strictly limited in scope. They did not seek sweeping constitutional reform, let alone a transformation of society. They showed next to no sympathy for radicalism, which impelled them rather into support for the Government.

While it would be idle to deny that more thoroughgoing doctrines did now, for the first time, appear in Scotland, the radicals were unsuccessful in rousing the masses with them. Strangely, no conscious appeal was made to that egalitarian streak which nearly all Scots inherited through their religion. The people had played the major part in the anti-papist agitation of 1779, and Burke posited a link between sentiment of that kind and Jacobinism. All one can say is that no such link ever became explicit in Scotland. The radicals themselves took care that it did not. Religion has often been of passionate concern to Scots, but has also too easily brought out their sectarian instincts. Aware of this, and of the difficulty of uniting older forms of protest with a new rationalist attitude towards reform, the conventions simply banned discussion of religious matters, 'because everything that tends to strife and diversion must be avoided'.

Nor did the radicals attract or apparently try to attract to their gatherings anybody at all from the great majority of the population, those living on the land. It was a significant oversight in view of Dundas's specific mention, when he reported back to Pitt from Scotland at the end of 1792, of the discontent 'among the lower orders of the people, whose minds are poisoned up to the point of liberty, equality and an agrarian law'. This last reference was to a project of social engineering which had so stirred the peasants of France that the overwhelmingly bourgeois National Convention purporting to represent them was to decree death for anyone formally proposing it. The idea had been culled by some diligent apostle of republican virtue from his Livy, who recounted how in 486 BC, with Spurius Cassius Vicellinus consul, a *lex agraria* had provided for equal distribution of land captured from Rome's enemies. In its modern imitation, the estates of all the French aristocrats, dead or fled, were to be similarly shared out. If, as Dundas seemed to suggest, the notion had been picked up in Scotland too, it was her earliest expression of that aspiration for land reform which would become so politically contentious in the next century, and which right till this one could awaken deeper emotions than any mere industrial issue. While it naturally horrified him, the radicals ignored it.

This may have been because the social origin of delegates to their conventions was on the whole confined to two groups: the lower middle class of artisans mainly from the old burghs of the East; and then the weavers, of whom it has been justly remarked that they were about the last people capable of winning power in contemporary circumstances. Together they might, however, plausibly be taken as a Scottish counterpart to the swelling ranks of the urban radicalism in England which one school of historians there has traced far back into the eighteenth century, and seen as a formidable force demanding constant response and reaction from the ruling elite. A parallel for the economic pressures underlying it might equally be sought, for example, in the bloody clash between the weavers and the forces of order in Glasgow in 1787. But this had remained an isolated incident. The West, too, though already seeing some concentration of the new industry, was notably under-represented in the conventions. The social dislocation arising from the Industrial Revolution would clearly be in large part to blame for the turbulence twenty years later, which did break out in the West. But during the 1790s, when trade fluctuated within tolerable limits, when many factories and mills were still sited in the countryside, and when we hear little of really degrading urban conditions, any distress was just as clearly not such as to drive people to desperation. The radicals' propaganda besides gave no special prominence to economic grievances.

In that case, the eruption of the modern type of radicalism in Scotland must be judged at the least premature, urbanisation being still limited, certainly too limited to generate a genuine mass movement or even to lay the intellectual foundations for one. The very fact of its taking its inspiration from across the border would here have been a handicap, since the Scottish masses were as yet scarcely anglicised. A radicalism as unfledged as this probably just could not identify the causes through which it might try to mobilise Scotland, and it could not learn better while it merely parroted ideas received at second hand from England or France. Whatever the reason, it stayed isolated and marginal, unable to broaden its appeal. Altogether, it scarcely shook the instinctive conformity and obedience of a loyal nation, which continued impervious to its influence and indifferent to its fate.[36]

Elliot's dismissal of fears about Scottish insurrections – 'certainly ridiculous' – might thus have been closer to the truth than Dundas's view. He, at any rate, took no risks. He thought it absurd (as indeed it was) to equate the British constitution, for all its faults, with the corrupt absolutism of the French *ancien régime*. What did concern him and his colleagues was that the collapse, in anarchy and terror, of the entire structure of the state in France had begun with the same sort of political clubs as now sprouted in Britain. They were justifiably appalled at a similar prospect at home, merely in consequence of mischievous fads and finicky grievances among rabble-rousing agitators or eccentric members of the ruling class. Severity, treating ostensibly innocuous associations like mortal enemies of the established system, counted in these circumstances as a sound political response, for it meant they were snuffed out before they ever had a chance of doing damage. Any harshness to individuals still paled in comparison with what happened in the France so admired by radicals. Since, through a display of the state's resolve to exert its authority, Britain was spared that sort of chaos and mayhem, success justified the tactics.

If a few were persecuted in Scotland, many more were emancipated in consequence of Dundas's efforts to rally all supporters of British constitutionalism. The two non-presbyterian religious minorities, the Episcopalians and the Roman Catholics, saw the penal laws against them lifted in 1792 and 1793 respectively. They then enjoyed the same freedom of worship and rights to property as everybody else.

The legislation had anyway scarcely been enforced against Episcopalians in recent times. But they were still officially ineligible for civil or military service in the state, and neither noblemen nor commoners could vote for parliamentary representatives. In fact a sect so long in decline was incapable of posing any threat, even if minded to. It was hard put just to maintain a clergy, which numbered about fifty, compared with 800 at the turn of the century; only diehard recusants could feel such an unattractive vocation. They continued to pray for the King, unspecified, and not for the Hanoverians by name right till the death in 1788 of Prince Charles, to them Charles III *de jure*. The primus, the Revd Abernethy Drummond, Bishop of Edinburgh, was a Jacobite but also a realist. He knew his flock would balk at recognising the succession of Charles's brother, Henry Cardinal of York. A meeting of the eight bishops resolved, with only two dissentients, that he had contracted engagements to the Pope which disqualified him as head of a sovereign state. The church then started to pray for George III. Drummond brought this to the attention of Dundas, who at once agreed to repeal the penal laws.[37]

In the light of experience, catholic relief would have appeared a more delicate matter. Yet this time it passed with no trouble. That the climate of opinion had changed so much in fourteen years might be hard to credit. But the enlightened elite was all along in favour of toleration: Abbé Paul Macpherson said 'it was perfectly ashamed of the barbarity and wild enthusiasm which had pervaded and blinded the inferior ranks of our countrymen'. Bishop Hay's successor, the Revd John Geddes, a familiar figure among the literati of Edinburgh, received from Dundas assurances that relief had not been abandoned for good.

The intolerance of the Scots at large seemed by now allayed. Economic growth had attracted papists into the central belt from the Highlands and from Ireland: if not popular, they were no longer utterly alien. War with France also made a difference, not only in reminding people of the military prowess of the catholic clans. Jacobin excesses awakened some sympathy for the persecuted French church – and the Scots seminarists, too, lost their college in Paris. The Comte d'Artois, one day to ascend the throne as Charles X, fled to Edinburgh and set up court at Holyrood (whence he came as an occasional guest to Arniston, giving its owner in gratitude a portrait of himself). Mass was regularly celebrated in the capital for the first time since the residence of the Duke of York, later James VII, more than a century before. It became quite a social attraction. In the Lowlands generally, priests had not been seen out and about for a quarter of a millennium. Now clerical refugees could be spotted on their way to give French lessons to the natives or, in time, to minister to prisoners of war.

Effective relaxation of the penal laws had started in 1783 with a legal ruling that a Catholic might succeed to and enjoy the lease of land. It was primarily a landowner's plight that led to legislation ten years later. The immediate family of George Maxwell of Munshes was threatened with dispossession on his death by the nearest protestant heir. An examination by Robert Dundas persuaded him that only repeal of the penal laws could with certainty save the estate. He moved quickly, introducing a Bill in April 1793 which completed all its stages in both Houses of Parliament within a month. In July the clergy took oaths of allegiance to George III, 'the final reconciliation between Scottish Catholicism and the House of Hanover'. A decisive contribution had come from Henry Dundas; compared with 1779, he had grown not only much more powerful but also much more experienced, taking care to consult Parliament and every interested party before expeditiously legislating.[38]

Scots Catholics had no stauncher friend, and this was not the last of his benefactions to them. They remained with few exceptions poverty-stricken, scarcely able to provide for their priests. Since loyal pastors would make for loyal flocks in a war where godless France was fighting their Pope as well as their King, Dundas wanted to help. From 1796 he had a secret subsidy of £1000 a year sent by the Treasury to the Scottish church: enough to run two seminaries, to pay two bishops £100 a year with £50 for co-adjutors, and still to leave a living wage for fifty priests. It was the Whig Government in 1806, supposedly committed to full catholic emancipation, that suspended the grant. This worked meanwhile its desired effect, by cementing the clergy's fidelity. One or two even served as secret agents on the Continent. Abbé Macpherson went on some pretext to Italy in 1812, but with the real mission of alerting Pope Pius VII to a plan to rescue him from captivity. It was only foiled when Napoleon removed the pontiff to France.[39]

Catholic relief was Dundas's answer to unrest in Ireland also, despite opposition from her protestant establishment. To Pitt, he stated 'the plainest of all political truths, that a country where a Parliament and a free constitution is allowed to exist, never can submit to the practice of three-fourths of the country being sacrificed to the whims, prejudices or opinions of the other fourth'. He was one of those in the Prime Minister's entourage working actively to alter that, and as early as December 1791 sent a specific plan to the Lord-lieutenant of Ireland, the Earl of Westmoreland. Because of the radical danger, he warned, a favourable ear must be lent to the Catholics' fair claims. Though nothing would be forced on Protestants, he thought they ran a bigger risk by intransigence than by offering the majority a 'moderate and qualified' enfranchisement; the penal laws should in any event go.[40] But Dundas understood the anxieties too, writing that change must come 'as it were insensibly to the Protestants, who have at present the monopoly of the government, and good things, and whose real fear is not, as they sometimes pretend, danger to the Protestant faith ... or, as at others, the restoration of the lands to the old Catholic proprietors, but the apprehension of losing the monopoly.' Elsewhere he declared simply that it was 'the wish of Great Britain to govern Ireland on a less corrupt system than formerly'.

The Catholics had set up a representative General Committee, which met from time to time in Dublin. Dundas appreciated that protestant immobilism could push it off the peaceful, constitutional path it was following. He wrote in January 1792 to Richard Burke, son of Edmund and the committee's agent in London: 'I cannot refrain from guarding you against what I think I perceive too much of in your letter, I mean an acquiescence in, if not an approbation of the propriety of Catholics having recourse to sentiments and measures of anarchy either separately or jointly with dissenters or any other description of persons in that part of Ireland where their interest is most prevalent.'

The impact of the French Revolution on Ireland lent urgency to these considerations. Dundas pushed, with rather more enthusiasm than Pitt, for generous indulgence to Catholics. At the end of 1792 they decided that a Relief Bill should be introduced into the Parliament of Ireland as an official measure. This awakened real alarm in the 'Irish Cabinet', the team of administrators at Dublin Castle. An Under-secretary, Edward Cooke, who by the standards of the Ascendancy counted as an out-and-out liberal, went over to reason with Dundas and Pitt in January 1793. He begged them to moderate their line, refrain from employing patronage to build up their own Irish party, guarantee the position of the Church of Ireland and above all concede that Catholics would remain excluded from the Parliament. They consented, yet only on condition that the franchise should be extended to propertied papists. Probably they had overstated their demands in the expectation of reaching just such a compromise. An Act was anyway then passed in Dublin on the agreed terms. Detailed drafting had been left to the authorities on the spot, but the main heads were undoubtedly Dundas's work.

The next year he was already discussing behind the scenes a still bolder plan – full union of Great Britain and Ireland, with further relief of the Catholics. How was the inevitable local opposition to be overcome? Dundas had the brainwave that Henry Grattan should be made Irish Secretary in the Cabinet in London. His colleagues were not so keen. The Lord Chancellor averred that 'no men here will hazard a convulsion of the government at such a time as the present, for the sole object of giving a little more or a little less influence to any particular set of men in Ireland'. While, in these highest circles, union was coming to be seen as the best of the available options, formidable practical difficulties forbade a premature move. One may note, however, that Dundas saw the solution in doing for Irish interests what he had already done for Scottish ones.[41]

A combination of religious and political loyalty was ever sure to warm his heart, and for good reason. At home in Scotland, ministers of the established Church were the main means of influencing public opinion, leaving aside a few subsidised newspapers of limited circulation. Dundas described to Pitt how he relied on the Moderates of Edinburgh:

The clergy through the different quarters of the country keep up correspondence with them and on most subjects take their key from them. From what I can learn the clergy with very few exceptions are all right in their dispositions. I hope to find it so, for perhaps if I was to name what circum-stance was of the most essential importance to the peace of the country, I would name the influence of the clergy over the people properly exercised. It is fortunate in the present moment that I have at all times been on the best habits with the clergy. From my first entry into life I have befriended and patronised them in all their concerns, and I have never yet found my influence fail with them when I had occasion to put it to the trial.[42]

Dundas had so far discovered nobody, however, who combined political loyalty with the sort of authority in the Kirk that Robertson had once wielded. The gap was now filled by Dr George Hill, principal of St Mary's College, St Andrews. He has often been branded as the man who organised the Church's entire subjection to the state, so that it became merely the 'Dundas interest at prayer'. Among the evidence adduced for this is the activity of those ministers who obviously did see themselves as anti-radical agents. The Revd Robert Ure of Airth, for example, wrote that 'in every case where matters of Government have been spoken of in the parish, large and populous though it is, there never appeared any seditious or improper tendency but I checked it.'[43]

As for Hill, his sordid sycophancy seems confirmed by the sentiment, uttered in the first flush of youth and presented with great glee by an earlier historian, that 'the true secret certainly for passing through life with comfort, and especially to a person in my situation, is to study the temper of those about him and accommo-date himself to them.' It was in 1786 that he came to the notice of Dundas who, without knowing him, recorded that he was 'of great abilities ... the ablest speaker in the General Assembly, and in the controversies which prevail there is the great champion in support of the law, good order and moderation in the Church.' Two years later, the politician was accommodated far enough to be elected chancellor of Hill's university. He did plenty of good turns back, especially in professorial appointments. At one point six out of thirteen members of the Senatus Academicus were relations of the principal – hence the proverbial popularity at St Andrews of psalm 121, 'I will lift up mine eyes to the Hills.' They dug themselves in there so well that they and the Cooks, another academic dynasty with which they intermarried, were to hold thirty-six chairs over the next century and a half.

Even so, the sleaziness of these arrangements can be exaggerated. Robertson, one may recall, had been a bureaucratic nepotist as well, but redeemed himself by his learning and by the quality of his appointments. Hill was in his own right a considerable Greek scholar and ecclesiologist. He personally revived theological studies among Moderates with his treatise, *Lectures in Divinity*, which became an approved text for students. And he without doubt raised the academic standard of his previously moribund university.

In the Kirk at large, Hill's weight was certainly brought to bear on the conservative side. But religious conservatism has its own characteristic emphases, and it implied for him a clearer distinction between the secular and the spiritual than had been drawn by the older generation of Moderates. In men like Carlyle, religious latitude and political rigidity appeared ever more oddly balanced, even to contemporaries – he was astonished at one General Assembly to be shouted down by his own side. Another of the old guard, Adam Ferguson, failed to get a post at St Andrews because of a critical reference from Hill, who found in him 'too great an aversion to the Church to accept of an office which would require him to resume the dress and station of a clergyman.' As an upholder of the Westminster Confession, the principal was against the Kirk's yielding, at least any further, to political authority. A German scholar has found that he had an outlook 'die für die Regierungsmacht Begrenzungen wollte. Zu einer Kreatur von Dundas wurde Hill nie ... Ein Funke des alten calvinistischen Ethos ist noch lebendig, and als etwa Dundas verlangte, die Pfarrer sollten von der Kanzel zu Spenden für den Krieg aufrufen, da widersetzte sich Hill.'[44]

In any case Dundas usually preferred, if possible, an emollient exercise of his influence which was bound in practice to limit it. We have already seen his readiness, as the price of unity, to offer some scope for the popular party. Again, just recently, Sir Henry Moncreiff had devised an ingenious scheme to raise ministers' pay, by which a parish would be left vacant for a year after the incumbent's death, the sum saved being shared among others. This won support from Moderates too and, after the General Assembly had given approval in 1790, it was the Lord Advocate who sought time to legislate along the lines proposed in 1793. Landowners generally came out against the plan, however, as they had come out against similar plans in the past, preferring to keep any savings for themselves. So the Bill was killed, but Henry Dundas promised: 'I will execute it, whenever the opportunity returns ... as a public mark of approbation to the body of the clergy in general.'

At that same General Assembly of 1790 the Evangelicals scored a bigger victory, when they persuaded it to approve their motion demanding exemption of Scots resident in England from the provisions of her Test Act. Dating from the reign of Charles II, it was meant to enforce religious conformity on those holding public office and thus forestall subversion of the state by dissenters. Obliging Scottish emigrants to take the test was denounced as a slur on the status of the Kirk: it being also established, its members could not logically be regarded as nonconformists even when they crossed the Tweed.

In practice the grievance was minor, and there existed no particular reason for raising it at this point. But a cavil both patriotic and syllogistic proved irresistible to Scots. Robert Dundas failed to keep the issue under control in the debate, during which Moncreiff got the better of him. The crucial intervention, in a negative sense, came from Jupiter Carlyle:

> The Test Act, instead of an evil, is a blessing. The Test Act has confirmed the Union. The Test Act has cured Englishmen of their jealousy of Scotsmen, not very ill-founded. The Test Act has quieted the fears of the Court. The Test Act has enlarged and confirmed the principles of toleration; so far is it from being a remnant of bigotry and fanaticism. The Test Act, Sir, has paved the way to office and preferment. The Test Act, Sir, for there is no end of its praises, is the key that opens all the treasures of the South to every honest Scotchman.

The effect of this ridiculous performance was to ensure a majority for the Highflyers' resolution.

Jubilant, they went on and petitioned for an amendment to the Act. Elliot, who sat for an English seat, agreed to put an appropriate motion to the Commons in May 1791. He could expect it to be negatived by the Government, but was not deterred from personally canvassing support. The result has been preserved and is notable as a rare indication of how opinion divided on a specifically Scottish question. Only half a dozen of the representation from Scotland were in regular opposition, but Elliot listed 14 of the 45 ready to vote with him (though not all did so) and 26 set against him. The unexpected dissidents were headed by Sir Adam Fergusson, a man of some weight on the ministerial side.

With national feeling aroused, the Dundases took care to argue that exemption was inexpedient rather than wrong in principle. Henry went around saying he personally favoured it – but, unable to win over the archbishop of Canterbury, he preferred not to stir things up. The debate was important enough to be chosen by Robert as the occasion of his maiden speech. He asked why the Test Act should have become a problem now, when it had been ignored since 1707: 'As to civil offices, few will say that the Scots are not admitted to their full share of them. Indeed, the reverse is much oftener insinuated.' The motion was easily defeated, but it showed that at home in Scotland the popular party could, by choosing its ground carefully, rally round itself sections of opinion wider than its own narrow, clerical ones. We may remind ourselves that Moderates formed only a minority of the clergy, so that their dominance depended on the support of the landed class, as lay elders inside the General Assembly and as patrons outside it.[45]

Other cracks in this support began to appear, for instance, in the vigorous evangelism of two exemplary lairds whose family had in the past intermarried with the Dundases of Arniston, James and Robert Haldane of Airthrey. Frustrated in a wish to witness in Bengal, they turned to missions at home. Their exertions in the Highlands inspired followers in Edinburgh, Glasgow and elsewhere to form missionary societies of their own. It was surely shabby of Moderatism to frown on this, as on other Christian endeavours not controlled by its bureaucracy. But a majority was rallied in the General Assembly to condemn missions. By the same means, a limit was placed on the numbers of chapels-of-ease, places of worship erected inside existing large parishes, often to cope with shifts in population, though in many Moderates' view as a pretext for accommodating churchgoers who disliked their minister. Even Sunday schools became objects of suspicion.[46]

Yet while Moderates ostentatiously presented themselves as pillars of patriotic order, it was getting hard to see in the High-flyers anything different. Members of the national Kirk, they had at bottom no interest in subverting establishments – if they had wanted to do that, they could easily have seceded. There was accordingly very little support among them for political radicalism. Nor, unlike in the struggle for America, did any question the justice of the war: one, the Revd William Porteous of Glasgow, was conspicuously bellicose. Adding to its loyalty a new flexibility and skill, the popular party kept on the right side of Dundas and was rewarded in its turn.

That did not, at the same time, stop it espousing devotionally a more intense evangelical outlook. Typical of this were the thoughts expressed by Thomas Chalmers, when in 1796, still a student at St Andrews, he precociously embarked on his preaching career: 'The Christian submits to the wanton exercise of extensive authority with a becoming patience and composure, and his love of order, harmony and peace often prompts him to forgo the advantages which would result from resisting the encroachments of power.' For sentiments of such lamblike mildness, a friend reported, 'we really thought our young companion in no little danger of being seized as one of the democrats and sent to durance.' They were yet markedly at variance in temper from the plebeian enthusiasm, or indeed bigotry, of the High-flying mentality in the past. Chalmers was an exemplar of its development and refinement. Evangelicalism grew elevated, in particular cases even aristocratic, and increasingly seductive to many for whom enlightened rationalism proved too arid. In this guise, it was poised to supersede the older Moderatism in the spiritual, the intellectual and eventually the social leadership of the Church.

Dundas, ever eager that his country should be well led, was in effect acknowledging the phenomenon. Pursuing in the face of the radical threat a unifying rather than a partial policy, he did not confine his favours to one side. This annoyed Hill. At the time of the Moderates' defeat over the Test Act, he described their situation to Dundas as 'very distressing'. Not only, he said, was the popular party as vigorous as it had ever been, but ready also to combine opportunistically with the elements of opposition among the lay elders, so that Erskine could now aspire to be 'the governor of our Church'. Hill glossed over the fact that the evangelical victory was largely due to the disarray of the Moderates, some of whom, notably William Robertson junior, voted with the other side.[47]

Anyway, Dundas took no notice. On the death of Principal Robertson in 1793, for example, he reallocated the money for royal chaplaincies so that their number could be increased from six to ten. Two of the new dignities were awarded to Highflyers, including their venerable leader, John Erskine. The erstwhile apologist for the Americans and scourge of the papists now called the people to arms and saw in Louis XVI 'a gentle and humane priest'. Moderates warned that such indulgence would produce a General Assembly of 'burgh elders raging with democratic zeal.' Hill reiterated that 'if the equalising of Court favour goes on, the Moderate interest will soon vanish from the face of the earth; and the Government may have more trouble than they are aware.' But Dundas continued to give the popular party a reasonable share of patronage. Analysis of livings in the Crown's gift has shown that evangelicals accounted for more than 40 per cent of presentees identifiable with one or other faction – though they were not so lucky further up the hierarchy, supplying but 30 per cent of the Kirk's permanent officials and 15 per cent of the Moderators. Still, they were clearly not being proscribed.[48]

Only of the dissenters' loyalty did Dundas entertain real mistrust: 'The established clergy are as well as I could wish, I would be happy if I could say the same with regard to those not of the establishment, or of the people under their charge.' They numbered 200,000, nearly a fifth of the population, a proportion daily increasing through eager proseleytisation. It testified to the vitality of the older, austerely Calvinist streak in Scottish presbyterianism which the ecclesiastical politeness of the age had never obscured.

As conscious heirs of the Covenanters, the dissenters despised Erastianism: the most otherworldly, the Anti-burghers, had a holy horror of all secular government. Yet none of the sects was seriously subversive, as Robert Dundas learned, if rather slowly. He had an agreeable surprise in 1795, at the height of his repression, when he was asked by their leading clergymen in Edinburgh for a confidential meeting, at which they assured him of their readiness to check radicalism in their congregations and, if necessary, among their own brethren. A few months later they got up a loyal address – the first time since the Original Secession that they had had a good word for the state. Later, the Lord Advocate was even more pleased to receive a second address from the Burghers, subscribed by seventy-four out of their 105 ministers: 'It has been with too much reason hitherto believed that the great body of these seceders, and the majority of their pastors, are as hostile to the state as to the religious establishment.'[49]

We have altogether seen that, within this establishment, the Dundases were not excessively partisan, but concerned in their usual manner to balance and unite. True, with Britain at war and Europe in turmoil, they would brook no preaching of subversion from the pulpit. Yet that did not by and large set them at odds with a clergy becoming on every hand more conservative. If it took loyal politics for granted, there was in its reviving spirituality, questing and fertile rather than servile and lifeless, ample compensation.

In any event, the Dundas despotism set wide the bounds of the intellectually licit, as it had to for the sake of Scotland's general development. During the 1790s the Scottish Enlightenment did flag somewhat. Some have therefore claimed that it flagged because of Dundas, almost that he personally did for it.[50] This is ludicrous. The Enlightenment remains a problematic phenomenon, and one problem is whereabout to set its departure and its terminus, a problem connected with the definition of which particular activities were enlightened. On the most generous interpretation, it started far back in the seventeenth century, and many are content to allow that it continued till 1832. How odd that it should promptly have expired at emerging from the dark depths of the Dundas despotism on to the sunlit uplands of the Whig millennium! Be that as it may, there would obviously have been within this broad span periods of greater and lesser vitality. Heights of achievement were scaled between David Hume's *Treatise of Human Nature* in 1738 and Adam Smith's *Wealth of Nations* in 1776, and never quite attained again, though that did not render negligible the later contributions.

But no sudden catastrophe can sensibly be posited for the 1790s. The Enlightenment was certainly undergoing a profound change. While older figures such as Lord Monboddo, James Beattie, Adam Ferguson and John Millar continued to write and publish, their successors turned away from polite, didactic works of what we today term social science. Instead they cultivated, on the one hand, novels, poetry and criticism or, on the other, epistemology, science and technology: a more literary literature and a more scientific science, as they have been called. It is all the same clear that they grew, partly of course in response to a developing external environment, out of earlier preoccupations. Such a change could anyway scarcely have been effected during a few months of firm government by Dundas.

Evidence for continuity comes also from where it mattered most, the universities. An influential account of them has advanced the opposite view, that they sold out to the hysterical illiberalism of this decade. John Robison has been named as an example. Professor of natural philosophy at Edinburgh, he published in 1798 his *Proofs of a Conspiracy against all the Religions and Governments of Europe*. This he thought to have uncovered while moving among freemasons in St Petersburg twenty years before. His reactionary extremism may, though, have looked as exorbitant to his own times as to ours. A leading Moderate clergyman said no notice should be taken of him, for opium has 'sadly disrupted' his wits. Nor was Dundas, himself a freemason, likely to have agreed in ascribing the world's ills to his brethren. Every age offers a deal of academic eccentricy and the views of one absent-minded professor must weigh less in judgment of the universities than the undoubted facts that they continued to grow in size, in intellectual purview and in reputation. They were indeed soon to exercise a decisive educational influence in the whole United Kindom. They proved, besides, attractive to the Whig section of the British ruling class. In the following years the future Lord Melbourne, Lord John Russell and Lord Palmerston all attended a Scottish university, and between them they were to govern Britain for most of the first half of Victoria's reign. Such pulling power would have been impossible if, during the period just before, the spirit of inquiry in Scotland had been snuffed out by official authoritarianism. Dundas, writing in 1801, drew his own conclusions:

> I have too great an interest in the prosperity of this country to admit any consideration whatever to enter into my mind in recommending professors to any university except what is truly best for the education of our youth in the sound principles not only of science but also of the constitution. Every professor in the universities of St Andrews and Edinburgh has been appointed for more than 20 years past either actually by myself or upon my recommendation, and I take the satisfaction to reflect that in not one instance have I been mistaken. Indeed the flowering state of those universities is the best proof of it.[51]

Dundas could anyway have had no interest in suppressing intellectual inquiry. He himself was a son of the Enlightenment. He had for years befriended its leading figures. It had brought honour and fame to his country, never for him a small matter. Despite the myriad of other calls on him, he continued to patronise literature and learning. Walter Scott, John Leyden, Archibald Alison, Adam Ferguson, Alexander Carlyle, Thomas Somerville, Sir William Jones, John Bruce, Henry Mackenzie were only the best known among the men of letters he personally helped. His enthusiasm for this role sometimes baffled more philistine colleagues. Soon after war broke out, on the death of the great Scots surgeon William Hunter, Dundas suggested to the Prime Minister that the state might acquire his anatomical collections. 'What!' said Pitt, 'buy preparations! Why, I have not the money to purchase gunpowder!'[52]

Dundas himself was quite the opposite of dogmatic or dismissive of new ideas. One may recall the enthusiasm with which he had embraced the political economy of Adam Smith, whom he indeed 'brought ... down from London a Tory, and a Pittite, instead of a Whig and a Foxite, as he was when he set out'[53]: this while Fox, reputedly the great reformer, blindly fought against commercial liberalisation. Even in the toils of his official duties, Dundas still throve on intellectual stimulus. Loving to solve practical problems, he constantly looked to specialist thinkers to cast fresh light on them; his papers are full of their ingenious schemes for this, that and the other. His own favoured mode of elaborating a policy was to write out all the various views of it, the differences among them and how they might be reconciled, often over many drafts and at inordinate length. This is tiresome for historians, but it does tell us something about Dundas's mind; that, if not always incisive, it was very receptive. To halt the production of ideas, in Scotland or anywhere else, could never have been to his advantage.

Besides, the Scottish Enlightenment had no time for political radicalism, and a glib association of the two is thoroughly misleading. The literati envisaged a society certainly progressive but also well-ordered, indeed hierarchical, by implication with minimal political influence from the masses. Not a single one showed the slightest sympathy for democratic notions. 'We had wonderfully few proper Jacobins,' Cockburn confirmed, though 'there were plenty of people who were called Jacobins.' Even then, the label was seldom pinned on intellectuals. Dugald Stewart made himself the most suspect, but the only molestation he suffered came in a private letter from two Lords of Session asking him to retract certain statements in his *Elements of the Philosophy of the Human Mind*. Undaunted, he defended them with vigour, and that was the end of the matter. The sole incident that might distantly be regarded as public, intellectual persecution was Erskine's deposition by the Faculty; and he, of course, had written nothing.[54]

The overwhelming impulse among the enlightened was to rally round the flag. A typical figure, Lord Monboddo, took advantage of a survey of *Ancient Metaphysics* in 1797 to remark that

> our government thus constituted has been of late so administered that, with the help of some of the nations in Europe, whom we put in motion, we have delivered Europe from those enemies of God and man, whose professed design it was to put down regal government and the present constitution in every country in Europe, and to introduce, in place of them, that ochlocracy (for it does not deserve the name of democracy) which prevails in their own country, and has joined to the most disorderly government impiety and contempt of all religion … Under such a government and with such a situation of our affairs, what should make any British man dissatisfied with our present government, and desirous of a change not only of the ministry, but of the constitution? Nothing that I can imagine except the contagion of the French madness: to prevent which our administration has used very proper means, and which I hope will be successful.

The Enlightenment, olympian, patrician, intellectual, universalising, belonged to a different world from the violent, populist, emotional, romantic age now being born.[55]

Political opinion, even among most of Dundas's erstwhile opponents, was overwhelmingly of the same mind. Well before radicalism came unwittingly to his aid, he had been intent on luring into his fold the few Scottish interests that remained outside it. In 1791 he was writing to Burke: 'I am certainly a party man and more so now than I ever thought of being. But my party principles have no mixture of rancour, and no public wish is so near my heart, as that the leading characters of the country should think soundly on all great constitutional points.'

Party, as conceived of in these times, was a notoriously deceptive term. Only the faction of Whigs in opposition bore any resemblance to what we should call a party, a group of people acting together on consistent principles as a means of attaining power, and claims have been made that to this end they had already set up quite a sophisticated electoral machine. Whether that was true or not, no equivalent existed on the Government's side, at least none in England. It is tempting to infer from the polarisation we are used to today that, because we might be able to see a reasonably cohesive body of Whigs, we ought also to be able to see a reasonably cohesive body of Tories. In fact even in the Commons there was no organised majority. Pitt had his own band of devoted followers, but they were not numerous enough for certain victory in parliamentary divisions. He could, of course, normally rely on the Scots; and since Dundas did methodically fix elections, he might be called a partisan in a way his leader was not. Pitt himself would a generation earlier have been called a Court Whig – he aimed to unite behind the King's Ministry everyone who sought effective administration on pragmatic principles. And he did often successfully appeal to many groups and individuals whom his Government was not in a position actually to control. He trusted not to any systematic management, however, let alone to whipping, but to the merits of his measures and to his own eloquence in advocating them.

If they could have been given longer to work, in other words if the 1790s had remained peaceful, Pitt might anyway have come to command an overwhelming national consensus. As things turned out, it was the Revolution, and fear of a replication here, that had the decisive effect. But the consensus thus formed stood on more conservative ground than Pitt (though not necessarily Dundas) would by nature have been inclined to choose, since all except a Foxite rump of the Whigs then abandoned constitutional reform. The only hope for it afterwards lay with the chance of that rump being one day called to office in place of the Pittites, a hope which looked extremely forlorn.[56]

In these circumstances, Dundas's 'public wish' to unite every politician of note in defence of the constitution was not unrealistic. It would, in particular, have been a tremendous coup for the government to win over Burke. It thought it had the chance to, now that he was also author of that classic statement of conserva-tism, *Reflections on the Revolution in France*. The chance came to nothing, but there were others on whom Dundas cast an interested eye. One was his old accomplice in warmongering against the Americans, Alexander Wedderburn, of late Lord Loughborough, who had been in opposition since 1784. Through him, Dundas hoped to reach still higher, to Portland, the sober leader of the moderate Whigs, a man alarmed by radicalism, belligerent towards France and on both accounts at odds with Fox. What was more, all the leading Scots still in opposition, Sir Thomas Dundas, Elliot and even Erskine seemed likely to follow the Duke (though the last in the event did not).

Residual differences on policy presented much less of an obstacle than the question of how, if at all, so many recruits were to be rewarded. Dundas wrote firmly to Loughborough in August 1792: 'The King's satisfaction in his present

Government, and the vigour which his Government feels itself in the possession of, totally excluded all idea of new arrangements ... Nothing can be farther from any well-informed person's mind in the present moment than the idea of a coalition arrangement.' By the end of that year the Prime Minister was anyway receiving the spontaneous extra support of Portland and friends, leaving only a remnant (of whom just three came from Scotland) in opposition round Fox.[57]

Despite what Dundas had said, Loughborough got the Woolsack when in 1793 Pitt at last lost patience with Thurlow. Yet not till July 1794 was a full junction with Portland effected. In Scotland, this ended organised Whiggery. Out of the bargain Sir Thomas Dundas won the peerage long coveted by his family (simply abandoning his electoral interests in Stirlingshire and elsewhere), while William Adam left Parliament for the English Bar. But the difficulties anticipated by Henry Dundas over sharing the spoils were now visited personally on him, for it was his job that Portland demanded as a personal reward.[58]

Pitt tried to compromise. The Duke should get a Home Office shorn of its duties in respect of war and the colonies. These, with their patronage, would be reserved for Dundas who thus, still in charge also of India, could justifiably keep the title of Secretary of State. Inevitably, this annoyed both. Dundas thought it foolish, because their intentions could not ultimately be concealed, that neither Pitt nor Portland had been frank enough with the other. The latter's camp remained intransigent, sneering that just for Dundas 'a new office was to be cabbaged out of the Duke of Portland's', for whom 'an obvious diminution of his credit and authority was to be proclaimed.'[59]

The problem was that Pitt did not believe Portland capable of conducting the struggle against France. He told Grenville how uneasy he was at the prospect of losing 'the advantage of Dundas's turn for facilitating business, and of every act of his being as much mine as his.' If he had to work out new arrangements with somebody else, 'I am sure the business could not go on for a week.' He proposed a modification, by which Portland as Home Secretary should get the colonies, but still not the war. Dundas, angered at being asked to make a further sacrifice, fell back on an objection he had advanced earlier, that military matters could not in the current circumstances be separated from the general work of the Ministry.[60]

He was being offered, he stated in no uncertain terms to Pitt, a non-job:

> I take it for granted you will this day explain to the King the proposed arrangements in your government – and you will of course state to him the accident which prevented the intended division of the Secretary of State's department. I therefore feel myself obliged to give you the trouble of a few lines to entreat that you will not mention, or more think of the idea you entertained of my being still a Secretary of State with a war department ... the idea of a war ministry, as a separate department, you must in recollection be sensible cannot exist in this country. The operations of war are canvassed and adjusted in the Cabinet and become the joint act of His Majesty's confidential servants, and the Secretary of State, who holds the pen, does no more than transmit their sentiments ... If you were to have a Secretary of State for War tomorrow, not a person living would ever look upon him or any other person but yourself as the War Minister.[61]

Pitt's response to this letter was immediate and anguished:

> I really cannot express to you the unease it has given me. I shall give up hope
> of carrying on the business with comfort, and be really heart-broken, if you
> adhere to your resolution … You must allow me to make a personal request
> in the strongest manner I can, that you will consent to continue Secretary of
> State in the way proposed. On public grounds, and for your own credit, I feel
> most sincerely convinced that you ought to do so, but I wish to ask it of you,
> on the strongest proof you can give of friendship to myself; and of that you
> have given me so many proofs already, that I flatter myself you cannot refuse
> this, when you know how anxiously I have it at heart.[62]

Dundas's personality was not a soft one, but this appeal from the lonely height
of power melted him at once:

> The letter I have just received from you has given me the most poignant
> concern. My only consolation is, that upon the premise of the letter I wrote
> to you this morning, you must be satisfied that neither the public service, nor
> your own comfort are at all concerned in the matter; whereas my feelings
> and public estimation would be deeply wounded by the conduct you suggest.

Still, he conceded, these objections might be overcome if the King would command him to do as Pitt asked. Thus was his face saved. The unmistakable depth
and sincerity of his leader's tribute to his abilities overcame, in a magnanimous
man, the blow to his pride which political necessity had struck. But, in a letter to
his nephew, there could be no doubt of the bitter taste it left: 'Here, then, I am still.
I must remain a very responsible Minister with a great deal of trouble, and without
power or patronage, all of which I have resigned into the hands of the Duke of
Portland.'[63]

Events had made it indispensably necessary to strengthen the Government.
The war was more than a year old, having been declared by the French on
February 1, 1793, soon after the execution of Louis XVI. That had worked them up
into a patriotic frenzy, so when Britain, Austria, Holland and Spain recalled their
ambassadors from Paris or made other protests, France resolved to fight them all.
Dundas and Pitt celebrated by going out and getting roaring drunk. Their appearance back in the Commons prompted the rhyme:

> I cannot see the Speaker, Hal, can you?
> What! cannot see the Speaker, I see two!

It was eleven days before Dundas addressed the House with suitable solemnity:

> We are going to war, because war has been declared by France, without a
> provocation on the part of Great Britain, in violation of the law of nations
> and contrary to the most solemn engagements of treaties. We are going to
> war to secure the best interests of this country, by effectually opposing a set
> of principles which, unless they are crushed, will necessarily occasion the
> destruction of this and every other country.[64]

But the Ministry's approach in the first months of combat remained one of
faintly irresponsible optimism, and many mistakes resulted. Without doubt Britain was ill-prepared, for neither Dundas nor any colleague in a militarily inexpe-
rienced Government had wanted to fight France. On the contrary, they had

viewed events there with complacency, assuming disorder would weaken her externally. They were later accused by Whigs of warmongering all along. If that had been true, then one would have expected them to make preparations. In fact no preparations took place. On the contrary, early in 1792 Dundas actually wrote that 'it is proper from the general prospect of tranquillity to make a reduction of the military establishment maintained for the general defence of the Empire'. Nor even in the files of the secret service, which he directed, is there a sign of heightened vigilance. They are incomplete for this last year of peace, but show that £5651 was spent between May and December – say an annual rate of £8500. In 1793, the first year of war, nearly £127, 000 was spent. A Government thus neglecting intelligence in the prelude to a conflict could hardly have been engaged in plans for it. The interesting list of personages on the payroll included an array of Scottish professors and French bishops, not to mention Burke, who received £21 on May 21, 1794 – though he was apparently to pass it on to a foreign refugee.

The government's main clandestine activity had been in talks with Charles de Talleyrand, who served as French ambassador for part of 1792, entirely directed towards keeping Britain neutral in case general hostilities should break out. Fearful for his own head, he now fled to London again. Pitt unwisely responded to the urgings of royalist émigrés and expelled him. A typically generous Dundas, hearing that his ship was detained and anchored in the Thames, invited him to stay at Wimbledon till he could depart. Talleyrand replied that he never wanted to set foot on English soil again. The expulsion was ordered under the Aliens Act, passed to impose control over the floods of refugees arriving from the Continent, some sent as spies by the French, and many genuine ones who were destitute. One needy case was brought to Dundas's attention by friends in Kirkcudbright, writing on behalf of 'an old acquaintance of your lordship's, the once beautiful and amiable Jenny Wishart and the widow of the brave General Westphalen', now 'in absolute want'. She was a daughter of the late Revd George Wishart, minister of the Tron church in Edinburgh and a stalwart of the Moderates, who had met and married her German soldier through English relations. Never able to resist an appeal from the fair sex, Dundas enabled her and her family to survive. Her grandchild and namesake, Jenny von Westphalen, was to become Mrs Karl Marx.

Amid the turmoil, the Government's assumptions about the coming struggle were not conducive to efficiency. Nobody dreamed it would last twenty years. Pitt was blithely certain it would be short, a mere interruption of peace. He believed the Jacobins incompetent as well as noxious: the chaotic finances and social disorder over which they presided would soon bring France to her knees. He thus paid little attention to the practical direction of hostilities. The mechanisms for it were woefully deficient. No General Staff existed, only an antique military bureaucracy headed by nonentities, first by Sir George Yonge, then by the Prime Minister's brother, known to his officials as the late Lord Chatham for his lethargy. And one thing the creation of a department for the war did not do was set up a unified command. It would prove in practice impossible for Dundas to stop Pitt or Grenville, let alone the King, committing forces independently. There were moments of inspired intuition in Britain's conduct of the struggle, but the more usual story was of muddle and misunderstanding, with Dundas and his long-suffering Under-secretaries, Evan Nepean and William Huskisson, picking up the pieces. Political rather than military in inspiration, the arrangement looked chaotic by contrast with the centralised military machine soon being driven from Paris.[65]

Dundas's strategic priority had from the start been the West Indies. The traditional school of military historians has usually dismissed this as an irrelevant diversion from the main aims of the war, but opinion has been changing – 'rational and ruthless' was the description of it in one recent study. Since Ministers reckoned on a short conflict the obvious course was for Britain, while safeguarding her own possessions overseas, to take as many as possible of the enemy's. These could then either be swapped against other advantages in a settlement or else held as compensation for any adverse change in the European balance of power. That kind of scope was just what the West Indies offered. But they were also, as Dundas put it, 'the first point to make perfectly certain'. Indeed it would hardly have been possible to treat as trivial or secondary the operations in a region where, it has been estimated, more than £70 million of the country's capital was invested. The British and French had been competing there over more than a century, for the trade, primarily in sugar, exceeded the Orient's in its profitability. Britain had gradually managed to gain the upper hand, though without crushing her rival, which retained valuable possessions from which a challenge could still be mounted. There was, in fact, no other theatre where British territories and interests were more plainly menaced unless an initiative was taken. This, anyway, was Dundas's reading of the situation, and the revolutionaries in Paris shared it. They too wanted to attack Britain in the West Indies, and started by fomenting rebellion among the slaves, who all over the archipelago had been excited by Jacobin doctrines spread from the French islands. Their royalist planters were so terrified that they sent to London begging protection. Here was the basis for an offensive of Britain's own.

Reinforcements were dispatched as soon as hostilities broke out, and in November 1793 a major expedition set off. Though, after dilatory preparation, it was still only at half the strength intended, its exertions were crowned with conspicuous success. It captured Martinique, St Lucia and Guadeloupe, reinforced the Spanish colony of San Domingo and finished in a flourish by taking Port au Prince, capital of Haiti, then the richest of all the islands. These prizes were certainly the best available. Seizure of them with such ease made it look as if the British might wipe the French out in the region. The mood in the Government at this juncture may be judged by what its most experienced diplomat, Lord Auckland, wrote to Dundas: 'I sometimes think that the crumbling to pieces of the French Empire will be too rapid and too complete, and so entire an annihilation of the old rivalry may enervate us.' Yet, for an advantage on that scale to accrue, peace had to come quickly. Unfortunately it did not, and to hold these distant acquisitions a ruinous price was exacted, in money and especially in manpower, since tropical disease decimated the troops. [66]

The impediment was failure in Europe. Dundas had stressed that, if Britain pursued a forward policy in the West Indies, then she would be unlikely at the same time to achieve much on the Continent. 'I could not,' he told Pitt, 'assent to appropriate any such share of the force of this country to any expedition on the coast of France as would interfere with the objects which naturally present themselves in the West or East Indies. Success in those quarters I consider of infinite moment, both in the view of humbling the power of France, and with the view of enlarging our national wealth and security.' In that case, however, Britain had to rely on her European allies, who turned out unreliable. An awkward dilemma faced her. Should she continue regardless with the struggle overseas, trusting that something would turn up to force the peace? Or should she, of her own strength, try to tilt the balance on the Continent? Dundas maintained that little difference could be made by the limited numbers of troops Britain might sensibly deploy there. But Pitt had from the outset felt obliged to offer some tangible help to a weak Holland under immediate threat, and sent the Duke of York with an expeditionary force to join the allies in Belgium. At first, even so, things seemed to go well. Dunkirk was besieged. Royalists rose in the South of France, and invited the British fleet into the main naval base of Toulon, then in the West, which they controlled for some months, defeating a republican force at Laval as late as October. Local patriots took over in Corsica, and eventually General Paoli would deliver his island to Britain as well.

Paris was by now in the grip of panic, anarchy and terror, which brutal measures by the Committee of Public Safety took months to master. The peril from the frontiers was meanwhile met through the desperate measure of a *levée en masse*, with the unlooked for result of creating the popular army as an instrument of modern war. Yet the allies quite failed, amid such confusion, to inflict a knock-out blow. The British performance proved as inglorious as any. Orders from London to seize St Malo, or some other suitable base on the western coast, were simply ignored by the commanders, so that no effective aid could be given to the royalists. The siege of Dunkirk was lifted, and at the end of the year the British were bombarded out of Toulon by the young Corsican general, Napoleon Bonaparte. The succession of scattered crises brought constant temptation to tap the forces massed for the West Indies, but the Government was afraid to draw off troops in the numbers needed to sway the contest decisively in any one continental theatre. Swithering between colonial and European purposes, Britain ended by succeeding in neither.

Retribution soon came with a marked turn for the worse in Europe. York took personal charge of a campaign in Flanders during the spring of 1794, only to preside over the collapse of that front. A French army beat the Austrians so soundly at Fleurus in June that they at once evacuated Belgium. The British abandoned their base at Ostend and retreated into Holland (this was the crisis that finally brought Portland and friends into the Government). Worse still, the advantage they had established in the West Indies threatened to slip after an engagement off Brest, when the French fleet, though battered, still got away and raced across the Atlantic to retrieve the previous losses. The conduct of the war had turned into a shambles.[67] The First Coalition dissolved, with Prussia, Holland, then Spain suing for peace. From the wreck only the alliance of Britain and

Austria was saved, in practice hardly a match for the formidably aggressive France emerging after the fall of Maximilien Robespierre.

This was the gloomy background to Dundas's becoming Secretary of State for War. In Europe, defeat loomed. He deduced that 'the whole attention of France ought to be directed to our distant possessions' – not the last time he accurately read his enemies' minds. Indeed their fleet was already reversing the position in the West Indies. It recaptured Guadeloupe, unleashing revolts of the slaves in the British islands of Grenada and St Vincent. Then another conquest, St Lucia, had to be abandoned to republican insurgents. Finally, an uprising took place in Jamaica too. Now it seemed that Britain might be the one to lose everything in the archipelago.[68]

Peace was the obvious way out, but the French would not give up on a winning streak, which carried through to 1795. Holland was at last abandoned to them with the recall of a now impotent British force, and in May they turned her into a puppet state, the Batavian Republic. That in turn posed imminent new dangers to Britain overseas. Dundas had written six months earlier to Grenville, when York was pulling out: 'If the French either by conquest or treaty get possession of the seat and instruments of the Dutch Government, and have their sense about them, their first act will be to send a French force on board the Dutch shipping to the Cape and take possession of it.' The security of the route to India had to be an absolute priority. On the authority of the Stadholder, William V, who fled to London, a British expedition promptly set out, forcing the surrender of Cape Town in September.

Dundas was worried about the other Dutch colonies too – 'if the French are directly or indirectly in possession of the island of Ceylon, the French Minister of War would deserve to lose his head if we kept our Indian possessions four years', he wrote. So an expedition from Madras was sent to Trincomalee, the naval base commanding the approaches to the Bay of Bengal. Further east, Malacca was snapped up. Dundas lost whatever friendly feelings he had once entertained towards the Dutch. We should never abandon these captured territories, he told the King: 'It is not the interest of Holland to wish for the restoration of the Cape of Good Hope and Trincomalee, unless she has in view to form connection adverse to the interests of Great Britain.' [69]

Control of the chain of Dutch stations was still not complete, however, till Colombo, capital of Ceylon, could be taken. The trouble was to find a force capable of it, when much of the army was dying in the West Indies and other operations were stretching manpower to the limit. To the rescue just at this point came the unlikely figure of Hugh Cleghorn, for the last twenty years professor of civil history at St Andrews. During travels in Europe he had befriended the Comte de Meuron, Swiss proprietor of a mercenary regiment in the pay of the Dutch East India Company, which employed it as the main part of Colombo's garrison. It occurred to Cleghorn that if these men could be transferred to British service, then the post would fall like a ripe tropical fruit into Britain's lap. He contacted Dundas, who jumped at the chance. Meuron, being mercenary, was easily satisfied with a fee of £10,000 and the rank of major-general (plus one of brigadier for his brother). He had now only to let his regiment know what he had done, though without revealing it to the Dutch. He was dispatched in person to make sure of a smooth transfer. To stop him vaingloriously spilling the beans on the way, Cleghorn went too.

From the coded reports he sent back to Andrew Stuart, the professor obviously took at once to a life of derring-do. En route in May 1795, he wrote: 'I cross the desert with as little concern as I would cross the Forth, for in truth believe there is no more danger.' At Alexandria he really entered into the spirit of the thing, asking the British Consul to bribe his Dutch counterpart for any official papers on their way eastwards or, failing that, 'to cause the person he dispatches to India to be attacked (but not murdered), his dispatches and letters to be seized.'

By July he and Meuron were on a boat to Jeddah:

We suffer from the numbers, noise and filth of the pilgrims; below the air is so confined that we can hardly breathe, and the stench of the bilge water has become intolerable. [But] the nights are worse for us than the day, and we have got a blind female passenger … who for at least five hours after sunset continues repeating and chanting without intermission passages from the Koran. She has taken her station immediately above our gallery and exactly opposite to my mattress. As there is no door to our cabin we cannot weaken the effects of a loud and shrill voice and we must submit to be disturbed as we cannot be instructed.

On arriving at Jeddah, 'first – the tenth part of our property was seized as due to the Custom house; second – we were robbed of all we possessed, and lastly had to pay near £200 for the privilege of carrying nothing away.' On departing in August, 'I was surprised and pleased to see marked on the mainsail the names of Sturrock and Stewart, Dundee. I little expected to find Angus canvas on an Arab ship.' Meanwhile its owner 'asked our permission to allow him a small state room near our cabin below for his wife, as far as Mocha. We thought it hard to refuse him, but instead of a wife he has sent on board four slave girls by whom our cabin is almost constantly occupied.'

Even after they reached India in September, the tribulations were not over. Cleghorn wrote of Meuron's strutting about as a general in Bombay: 'He should be kept as much as possible from the military society of this establishment and … immediately sent where his presence might be useful or his person and object should be lost in the more important business and conversation at Madras. He may cut throats at the head of his regiment, here he is only likely to cut his own.' At last they gained Colombo, where the regiment changed service, thus bringing the place into British possession in February 1796. Cleghorn returned home, but two years later was back as Ceylon's first Colonial Secretary, his career a fine proof of the infinite versatility of the Scottish Enlightenment.[70]

Meanwhile the war went on. With peace still refused by the French, the only British hope lay in such profitable colonial enterprises as remained available. The obvious place to salvage something was again the West Indies. Dundas used all his powers of persuasion to urge the Cabinet to a fresh offensive there, arguing that this was how Britain might most advantageously bring the conflict to an end. At length, in August 1795, his colleagues concurred. The result was certainly bold in conception. Despite the extreme pressure on resources, the expedition put together was the biggest ever to leave these shores. The command went to Dundas's old friend, and member for Clackmannanshire, Sir Ralph Abercromby. In October, he was ordered to make for Barbados, recapturing Guadeloupe and St Lucia on the way; he should then succour the depleted garrison of San Domingo, and if possible assault the Dutch colony of Surinam. But, amid the admirals' bickering, the fleet was still not ready to leave by the end of November, to Dundas's rage: 'I really feel it a disgrace to the executive Government of this country and to every branch acting under it, that an expedition determined on six months ago should not be in a state to sail seven weeks after the appointed time.' Then violent storms dispersed many of the ships. In January 1796, Pitt was complaining yet again of the 'repeated disasters, which tend to retard and weaken the expedition.'

The Government ought perhaps to have cut its losses at this point, but felt driven forward by the war's crippling burden on public finances. It feared them indeed to be near breaking point, so that only a spectacular success of some kind could ease the strain. Abercromby at last got away and during the spring about 30,000 troops straggled after him. But half were to die of sickness: with such appalling losses, and no chance of adequate reinforcement, Britain could after all do no more than make sure of what she held.[71]

The last months of 1796 saw a final brief offensive in the West Indies, though the acute shortage of manpower restricted its scope. It was prompted by Spain's declaration of war on Britain, which gave an excuse to seize her possessions. Abercromby captured Trinidad, but his repulse from Puerto Rico in May 1797 marked the close of the main conflict in this theatre.[72] It had ended in stalemate. British success in the original effort to win tradable advantages from a short struggle had for a time seemed to open up a much more alluring prospect – that she might strip France of the best part of her remaining overseas empire. This would certainly have been satisfactory compensation for defeat in Europe. But Britain had not managed it. At the finish, her offensive military capacity was exhausted by more than 20,000 deaths, with nothing more to show for them than an extended string of outposts requiring protection at a cost she could scarcely afford.

The war now entered a new phase, in which the main danger was a French invasion of Britain. Against it she had not the resources for more than a strictly defensive posture behind a naval blockade of the enemy's coastline. If unable to make peace, she had to brace herself for a much longer struggle. But that properly belongs to a new chapter.

Dundas's conduct of the war showed how central his imperial preoccupations remained. During the 1780s, India had demanded prodigious, but fruitful, efforts of him. They continued yet: indeed, he had thought of going to rule there himself. Lord Cornwallis, designated as Home Secretary in 1791, was unable to return in time to take up the post. When he did so two years later, Pitt just would not hear of sending Dundas to succeed as Governor-general in Calcutta.

In London, his dominance of oriental affairs anyway continued. He gathered, in his entourage of young politicians and academic advisers, soon to be supplemented by a professional staff at the Board of Control, what amounted to the nucleus of the legendary Indian Civil Service of future times. He became more content to leave detail to these subordinates, himself acting rather as arbiter among them. He loved to bring on his protégés, and several statesmen-in-waiting served a political apprenticeship under him: George Canning, William Huskisson, the Marquis Wellesley, not to mention William Dundas, younger brother of the Lord Advocate, whom Henry saw as the eventual inheritor of his Scottish interests. [73]

For his personal business with the Company, Dundas relied on the most tight-lipped of all his close aides, William Cabell, 'whom the torture would not compel to reveal anything'. Inside it, too, he had a faithful agent, David Scott. An impetuous man of limited judgment, he was also a warm, blunt Scotsman who had done well in life, much like Dundas himself, and the two became close friends. Born in Forfarshire, he had returned from Bombay in 1786 the acknowledged leader of the 'free merchants', engaged in the country trade, and rich enough soon to represent his native county in Parliament. He became through Dundas's influence a director of the Company in 1788, deputy chairman in 1795 and chairman in 1796–7.

In working at the Government's purposes from within, Scott naturally made enemies. They had combined to change the Company's rules so that a directorship could not be held simultaneously with one in a different enterprise – a move aimed directly at Scott, proprietor of his own trading house, which he had now, at least nominally, to give up. Then, during his term as chairman, ugly rumours circulated about his dabbling under Danish colours in illicit trade with the French, for which *prima facie* evidence was found on a seized ship. Scott exonerated himself to Dundas, but still had to defend himself publicly against the charges two years later. Though the dirty tricks helped to ruin his health, he was able to perform sterling service in breaking open the Company's charmed circle, bringing in new proprietors from among his own cronies, many of them Scots. They formed a steadily growing internal party of liberalisers which eventually was to play an important role in ending the Company's monopoly.[74]

In Indian policy, the problems of this decade were less daunting only than those of the last. The sub-continent, too, saw a renewal of war, which will likewise be dealt with in the next chapter. A major internal reform, the Permanent Settlement, was undertaken in Bengal. By this Dundas at last achieved another purpose he had had to abandon with his abortive Bill of 1783: the zemindars, as taxpayers to the Company, were henceforth reckoned outright owners of the land, the rate at which they paid being also fixed for good. The matter was of such extraordinary complexity that Dundas and Pitt had to closet themselves at Wimbledon for ten days in August 1792 to master it; its main burden, though, fell on Cornwallis. For Dundas personally, the prime task was renewal of the Company's charter, due in 1793.

Political circumstance had thus far obliged him to tolerate a more powerful Company than ideally he would have liked, and he remained a long way from his original aim of simply turning it into a non-monopolistic trading corporation. But he had learned to live with the current arrangement, even to see merit in its cumber. The old guard of the Company, though still touchy about its privileges, had ceased except in the detail of patronage to be a serious obstacle to him. His legislative framework and the steady infiltration of his own men gave him as much of a free hand as he needed. He later wrote:

> For the five first years after the institution of the Board, Mr Dundas frequently thought that he could have acted much better and have improved the affairs of India much more rapidly without the directors than with them. But further experience taught him that the pause and opportunity which frequently preceded great and important measures tended to mature them and to ascertain that they were not rashly adopted.[75]

Renewal of the charter did offer the chance of big changes if he wanted. The value of an antique, inefficient and unprofitable monopoly seemed all the more doubtful after a period of rapid expansion in the British economy from which the Company's Indian commerce had been excluded. Its intractable underlying deficits were screened only by the booming trade with China – 'the imposing facade of the millions brought in by the nabobs concealed an almost empty Exchequer'. It was really fit only for bankruptcy, but the consequences of that, in a troubled international situation, were too large to contemplate. Still, little stood to be lost by liberalisation and another close aide of Dundas's, Professor John Bruce, his son's former tutor and now historiographer of the Company, was set to work well in advance exploring the options.[76]

Amid these delicate considerations, however, nobody contemplated complete free trade: at stake was essentially a redistribution of India's spoils. A monopoly run by what was in effect an organ of the state struck Dundas as objectionable on principle, especially as others throve where it palpably failed. Not only free merchants in India, but also financiers and manufacturers in Britain managed to their profit to circumvent the restrictions by hook or by crook. The chamber of commerce in Glasgow, for example, passed a resolution saying that 'whatever good causes might have formerly existed, for continuing the Company's exclusive privilege, those causes no longer operate, because the enterprise and capital of individuals, and of companies of merchants [are] sufficient for carrying on trade to those distant regions'. Dundas, ever anxious to be on good terms with such people, could hardly resist their demands for the trade to be further opened up. Nor was the public at large likely to stand for mere confirmation of the *status quo ante*. On the other hand, the burden of running the war left little time for drastic reform which might provoke an open clash. And Dundas found, on consulting Cornwallis, that the Governor-general too was broadly satisfied with the existing mix. So a quick and easy settlement was what he went for, another empirical compromise between monopoly and regulation hedged round with safeguards.

Having come to an early decision, he set to work softening up public opinion. A big book, the *Historical View of Plans for the Government of British India*, was published under Bruce's name early in 1793. Some major catalogues, notably Harvard's, attribute this to Dundas himself, though it would seem unlikely that he had time for such a composition or for polishing the somewhat pernickety style. It could safely be concluded, however, that the professor acted as his amanuensis, for he was so employed on several later occasions when Dundas wished to air proposals without taking personal responsibility for them. Most of the works listed for Bruce in the bibliography below may thus have been dictated by his boss.

The plans put before parliament were anyway largely identical to those set out in the *Historical View*. It had recommended 'a system of Indian affairs, founded on the evidence of experience', since 'apparent incongruities in the domestic government of our Asiatic possessions have, in fact, been the source of their prosperity'. On the political side, Dundas now proposed a somewhat larger share for the Crown in a continuing joint administration. The main departure would be to formalise his unofficial role, with the creation of a post of President of the Board of Control, paid £2000 a year. In fact the whole Board was to be manned by a permanent, salaried staff rather than by politicians with too many other responsibilities.

The Company would, however, retain all its own patronage. This arrangement Dundas continued to respect scrupulously, as far as one can tell from his reply to a later supplicant: 'The whole appointments belong exclusively to the individual directors except two which they annually give to the President of the Board of Control. In addition to these two I reckon that on average, while I was head of Indian affairs, I received two more from individual directors, whom I had occasion to oblige in the course of my patronage in other departments.' Nor did he interfere with the actual disposition of personnel: 'I invariably refuse to recommend any person to a specific situation, leaving entirely to the Government abroad to promote them or appoint them to such situations as their merits and talents shall suggest to be proper.' And in telling Canning how he always referred legal appointments in India to qualified authorities at home, he showed a general attitude to patronage which must be described as exemplary: 'That is the shield I have found it absolutely necessary to set up to protect me not only from the indiscriminate corruption of those who consider all power as an instrument of aggrandisement, but also to protect myself from the danger of yielding to the temptations with which high political situations are constantly beset.'[77]

On the commercial side, the changes were bigger, though without fundamentally affecting the Company's position. Its administration and trade could still not really be disentangled and maintenance of the one implied maintenance of the other. The alternative, quite beyond the capacities of contemporary government, would have been to substitute a full-blown imperial administration with both political and commercial responsibility. 'A separation of the government and commerce cannot be made with safety either to the manufactures or the manufacturers of India,' Dundas himself wrote. At the same time he made a crucial distinction: 'The policy of continuing the exclusive trade of the Company rests on principles of expediency and political economy not totally, but in great measure distinct from pecuniary interests either of the East India Company or the public.' If, to prop up the ramshackle Company, some sort of privilege had to be maintained, at least it could be a 'regulated monopoly'.

What he meant by this was a suggestion he had received from David Scott. As Dundas later defined it to the Commons: 'My plan is to engraft an open trade upon the exclusive privilege of the Company.' He would oblige it to offer on its ships in each direction room for an annual 3000 tons of goods owned by private individuals, representing about one-third of the country trade or something over £300,000 in value. He reasoned that those goods could otherwise only enter international commerce through foreign ports, thus endangering the position of London as the great oriental emporium of the West and encouraging a possibly unhealthy outside interest in India.[78]

This provision was also the centrepiece of Dundas's latest scheme for matching the Company's debts to the fortunes of its servants, which had not so far been done through the country trade. The debts were gradually to be paid off through the increase in Indian commerce coming to London. With that prospect, funding them out of the City's resources ought to be easier. To facilitate it, new bonds would be issued, paying interest of five per cent, redeemable at home and aimed at two sorts of investors. The first, the financiers, found them attractive, since they were in effect guaranteed by the state. But the second, the Company's servants, unfortunately did not; they still preferred to run the higher risk, but also reap the higher returns, of the country trade they knew. And if they were not in practice to remit their fortunes by this new method, then the scheme broke down. The match of liabilities and assets thus never took place. As war again spread round the globe, the hope of a more solvent Company anyway proved illusory.[79]

That, however, lay in the future, and Dundas was sanguine when he submitted his scheme of renewal to the Commons in April 1793. He admitted that

> no writer upon political economy has as yet supposed that an extensive empire can be administered by a commercial association. And no writer on commercial economy has thought that trade ought to be shackled by an exclusive privilege. In deviating from these principles, which have been admitted and admired, I am sensible that my opinions have popular prejudice against them. But I am supported by successful experience.

After remarking that on its total trade with India, Britain could expect to run a surplus of £1 million a year, he went on:

> India, or the country in Hindustan governed by Britain, is in a state of prosperity unknown to it under the most wise and politic of its ancient sovereigns. The British possessions, compared with those of neighbouring states in the peninsula, are like a cultivated garden compared with the field of a sluggard … I am afraid to lay aside a means which has hitherto answered all the political and commercial purposes for which they have been employed.

He finished with a remarkably generous (and perhaps, given the gradual change in his own opinions, not entirely disingenuous) tribute to the Company. It had its effect, and he got his proposals through with little trouble.[80]

By his exertions Dundas managed the considerable feat, in time of war, not just of preserving but of expanding the Empire. The term meant to him primarily, of course, a worldwide trading system. One cherished aim of his cleaning up commerce in India was that it could then be expanded into China and lead to the development of a three-way trade. Eventually in 1791–2, Dundas was able to send under Lord Macartney the embassy to Peking he had long planned. Its instructions were to propose that, in addition to the opium which was already a major export from India, more woollens, cottons and bullion should be exchanged for Chinese goods. Heavy stress was to be laid on Britain's need for a secure depot, or at the very least for better facilities in Canton. Should the mandarins grow suspicious

Macartney was to assure them that Britain had no interest in acquiring territory. If they were to mention her record in India, he was to say that 'our situation in this respect has arisen without our intending it' because native rulers 'entered into cabals with other nations of Europe, and disregarded the privileges granted to us by different Emperors'. Finally, he was to investigate the chances of opening up Japan and Cochin China.[81] So, through diplomacy rather than force of arms, British commercial and strategic power would be extended over the whole Indian Ocean and Pacific.

This grand design also required some effort at formulating general imperial policies. On trade, Dundas remained liberal and tried to encourage Britain's several possessions to enter into commercial relations with one another. For example, at the Cape he lifted restrictions imposed on the Dutch settlers by their own East India Company. Though he never thought of Australia as more than a penal colony, he hoped it, too, might be brought within the system: 'It appears that the settlement in New South Wales is capable of affording material assistance to the Cape of Good Hope with supplies of coal and wood, two articles of very considerable importance to the colony and which are at present provided in this country at a very heavy expense.' He ordered an investigation into 'the prospect of a regular communication being maintained between the two settlements'.[82]

He took a different view of the Empire as a political entity. In India, he had the conduct of British subjects closely monitored. He effectively prohibited permanent residence there, for they were allowed out only under licence and urged to come home once their business was done. He constantly bore in mind the genesis of the United States. The peopling of colonies would irresistibly, he believed, create demands for autonomy, then independence, with disruption or loss of British commerce. Of the still largely empty Canada he wrote in 1792 that 'an ingrafted population' would bring 'a want of that regularity and stability which all, but particularly colonial, governments require' – this was, of course, a logical counterpart of his discouraging emigration. Where settlers were already present, he retarded political development. He supported the division of Canada into Upper and Lower provinces, to keep the British and French communities separate. At the Cape, the Dutch had their laws and rights guaranteed, but they lived under a benevolent military dictatorship offering them no representation at all. The second Empire was indeed geared to trade, and the idea of a global distribution of the native British stock would emerge only from the quite different assumptions of the third, Victorian Empire.[83]

The colonists of the West Indies alone enjoyed established political rights, through legislative assemblies dating from the earliest settlements. Planters or their partners in business at home were also present in force at Westminster. They pursued not autonomy, but their economic interest, above all in slavery. On this question the tide of public opinion had been turning, however, especially since William Wilberforce had taken up the cause of emancipating the wretched blacks in 1787. His first motion to end their importation from Africa was defeated in 1791. By the time he was ready to try again in 1792, he could count on support from both Pitt and Fox. Dundas had been instrumental in prohibiting not only negro slavery but also native serfdom in Scotland; though, to be sure, at no great

200   *The Dundas Despotism*

cost to anyone. The West Indian interest was, however, formidable and he
accepted that as a matter of practical politics some heed had to be paid to it, lest
the Empire be threatened in its wealthiest part.

When a series of debates on slavery was inaugurated at the beginning of April,
Dundas set out his view: 'The African trade is not founded in policy. The
continuance of it is not necessary to the preservation and continuance of our trade
in the West Indian islands. There is no mortality in that quarter which is incurable
and the human race may not only be maintained but increased in the West Indian
islands.' But, rather than immediate abolition of the trade, there should be

> regulations the most forcible and efficacious in order to promote the in-
> crease and encouragement of the breed of native negroes in the West Indies.
> My object is gradually and experimentally to prove the practicability of the
> abolition of the trade, and to provide the means of cultivation, to increase
> the population and to evince that all the alarms which are now entertained
> of danger from that measure are ill-founded.[84]

Two days later, Dundas returned to the subject, having been challenged by
Wilberforce to say what, in the light of his remarks, he actually proposed to do. He
replied that it was still for the abolitionists to bring in a Bill, which he would seek
to amend in the sense indicated:

> That the slave trade ought to be abolished, I have already declared. But I
> believe that any other than a gradual abolition will be attended with bad
> consequences to the public ... The co-operation of the legislators of the
> West Indian islands will be absolutely necessary to give effect to that mode
> of abolition which I conceive to be the most eligible.[85]

At length, after three weeks, he presented his own resolutions for a gradual
abolition. Even the greatest enemies of slavery, he pointed out, saw no practical
hope of ending the trade to our own colonies in less than five years – their
opponents said ten. He split the difference, and proposed a ban from January 1800.
On the other hand, the British trade with foreign colonies could be at once halted,
and this, he stressed, amounted to half the traffic of the last year. Equally,
foreigners would be forbidden to import slaves to our islands after October 1793.
With immediate effect, slavers would be obliged to transport equal numbers of
males and females. On an unspecified date, they would be limited to taking males
under the age of 20 and females under the age of 16. The aim of these two
provisions was to see if the planters could satisfactorily replenish their workforce
from natural increase. No new ships would be permitted to enter the trade, while
the numbers carried by existing slavers would be limited; their voyages were to be
notified to the customs, and a duty was to be paid. Offences under these regulations would be punished, but Parliament was to inquire into any commercial
losses. Finally, negotiations should be opened with other countries for a general
abolition.

The details strike us as grim and even shocking. But Dundas was widely praised
at the time for this work behind the scenes which resulted, through his habitual
thoroughness, in a deal offering something to everyone: a stop to a great part of the
trade at once, to the rest within a reasonable period, with allowance for adjust-
ment by those bound to be financially affected. Pitt, though an abolitionist, liked

what his colleague had done and suggested various amendments to maximise support. The Commons finally voted for the resolutions by a large majority. It was the Lords who refused to countenance any reform at all.[86]

Though now, at the height of his powers, Dundas could let his mind range over the five continents and the seven seas, still he had political ambitions for Scotland too. People might think the representation of this or that constituency mattered little to him, he would explain. But he had worked hard to build up his interest through his family, his friends, his favours for others, let alone his policies, and 'he was not fond of allowing it to be frittered away without his concurrence.' On the contrary, it was his special wish that the interest should engross the whole country, as he wrote after Parliament was dissolved in May 1796: 'It appeared to me upon a full review of the subject that if I came to Scotland and exerted myself thoroughly, I might be able to prevent the return of any one member for Scotland hostile to the government. The thing has never happened since the Union and the temptation was strong to make the experiment.'[87]

He very nearly succeeded. The main accretion of his interest came through those whom Portland had brought over with him to the Government. They were most numerous in that final bulwark of Whiggery, the peerage. In the election of the Scottish representatives, Dundas thus had a clear run. One recalcitrant, the Earl of Lauderdale, was overwhelmingly rejected. Three independents in the previous parliament, the Marquis of Tweeddale and the Earls of Breadalbane and Cassillis, were chosen again, but were all now in some degree working with Dundas.

In the elections for the Commons, too, he could bring overwhelming strength to bear. The last nests of resistance in his heartland of the South-east were being wiped out. In one, East Lothian, it was done by an alliance, covering the Haddington Burghs as well as the county, between Dundas and the formerly hostile Tweeddale, to the exclusion of the latter's brother-in-law, Lauderdale. It brought in candidates acceptable on both sides, Hew Hamilton Dalrymple and Robert Baird respectively. In hitherto stubborn Stirlingshire, too, the opposition dissolved when Sir Thomas Dundas took his peerage; the successor, Sir George Keith Elphinstone, was elected with Dundas's support. Clackmannanshire, alternating in place of Kinross-shire, fell to him through his friends, the Abercrombies of Tullibody. In the Anstruther Burghs he made his peace with the eponymous lairds, for one of whom his nephew William briefly acted as *locum tenens*.

In Perthshire he had always co-operated with the Duke of Atholl. On the death in 1794 of the previous member, the faithful and long-serving General Murray, the Duke had brought in a brother-in-law, Thomas Graham, whom Dundas distrusted. He thought instead to line up the other major connection in the county, Breadalbane's, behind his own son Robert: a quite unrealistic scheme, which people could scarcely credit when the news leaked out. In any event, Graham stayed, and proved loyal enough.

In the North-east the pacification still held, despite strains caused by the petulant Earl of Fife. At a by-election in Banffshire the year before, an association of independent gentlemen had been able to take advantage of the dissensions and return a candidate of their own. But the ministerialists rallied to regain the seat with William Grant at the General Election. In Inverness-shire the *soi-disant* revolutionary Macleod stood down and was replaced by an official nominee, John Fraser.

Further north, Whig defections again proved decisive. The Earl of Seaforth, previously patron in Ross of William Adam, sealed an alliance with Dundas by returning there the latter's great-nephew, Sir Charles Lockhart Ross. So it went also with the Sutherlands, who soon gave the Tain Burghs to William Dundas. So it went again in the alternating counties of Nairnshire and Bute, where respectively the Campbells of Cawdor and the Marquis of Bute came over, bringing in friendly members.

In the West the reconciliation of formerly hostile factions proved more delicate but no less successful. Only in the Dumfries Burghs had Dundas, through the Duke of Buccleuch, much direct influence, which he used in favour of his brother-in-law, Alexander Hope of Craighall. Ayrshire, always a complex constituency, was contested: the incumbent, Hugh Montgomerie, beat a conservative Whig, William Fullarton. Before the end of the year, however, Montgomerie succeeded as Earl of Eglinton, at which Dundas united the county behind Fullarton. In Renfrewshire the local Whigs followed Portland and the seat was secured for a Glaswegian nabob, Boyd Alexander. In Dunbarton the Duke of Montrose selected a member who rather quickly found himself unable to lend further support to the Ministry, at which he was replaced by the more compliant Alexander Smollett. Other magnates, the Duke of Queensberry and the Earl of Galloway, remained as awkward as ever, but one way and another they were just about kept in line. Old Q's member for Dumfriesshire, Sir Robert Laurie, had proved reliable enough and stayed on. Galloway was left a free hand in Wigtown, county and burghs, but yielded Kirkcudbrightshire to Patrick Heron, a firm friend of Dundas's.

Scotland was so well organised electorally that in the whole country just four polls took place. It did not necessarily follow that dissidence was being suppressed. Given the circumstances of a war almost universally supported by a patriotic ruling class, a high degree of unanimity could only be expected. It was no more than sensible of Dundas to exploit it. Mackenzie, his principal agent, wrote to General Grant, his main ally in the North-east, that 'it is always for the advantage of Administration to keep political interests from jarring'. So everywhere he had done what he could to bring them together to their mutual satisfaction.

Only in a handful of cases had he not quite managed it. The contest in Ayrshire we have already dealt with, while another in Dunbarton had no political significance. In Berwickshire and the Stirling Burghs, the two seats attacked by the opposition, it was beaten off with ease – literally so in the latter, where the campaign culminated in the Battle of Kinghorn, a bloody struggle to liberate kidnapped councillors. On petition, the victory of the Government's candidate, Andrew Cochrane, was triumphantly vindicated at Westminster against Fox in the evidence given by its agent, 'Lucky' Johanna Skinner, hostess of a local inn.[88]

Yet in two other seats Dundas was thwarted; even at this peak of his electoral career his power had limits. The Dysart Burghs, a venal district in Fife, had in 1790 chosen Charles Hope, now his brother-in-law. But Hope's hold was tenuous, for two of the four councils were Whig and he had won only by the casting vote of the burgh where the poll took place. The office of returning burgh rotated, and this time it would go to one hostile to him. Hope, finding the obstacle insuperable, did not bother to stand again and left the seat to the opposition.

The second defeat was remarkable indeed. Forfarshire had been held since 1790 by David Scott of the East India Company. He, if anyone, ought to have been impregnably safe, with his intimate connections in Government and his infinite resources of patronage. Yet he had to stand down as well, to Dundas's mortification: 'The pictures of ingratitude which the county has exhibited are not to be paralleled even in all my political experience.' Scott was just far too busy to attend to his constituency. Moreover, he was being undermined by his own agent there, Sir David Carnegie. The latter harboured the ambition of getting the attainted earldom of Southesk restored to himself, which would be much easier with a parliamentary seat. Till 1790 he had indeed had one, the Aberdeen Burghs, whence Scott had helped to eject him. How they afterwards came to co-operate in Forfarshire is unclear: though, in the cosy Scottish political world, mere electoral skulduggery was not always a bar to otherwise sociable relations. In any event, Carnegie announced he was going to put up himself. Scott at first wanted to fight back. But this would have demanded much time and effort, when Dundas badly needed him in London. He therefore gave in and took the venal Perth Burghs instead. The supple Carnegie, thus returned unopposed, vaunted himself as an independent but gave a good deal of support to the Government afterwards. The case yet furnished proof, contrary to the usual assumptions, of how dangerous it could be to take a Scottish electorate for granted: constituencies were not simply to be bought, but had to be won.[89]

Still, Dundas had indeed won forty-three seats and failed only by a fluke in the other two. At any rate, he saw the disappearance of a coherent opposition in Scotland. If he needed more consolation, he could draw it from the fact that this time he also acquired quite an interest in England (the extent of which can only now, with publication of the relevant volumes in the *History of Parliament*, conveniently be traced).

Several Scots occupying English seats belonged to Dundas's entourage – notably his son, as well as another relation by marriage, William Nisbet, and a nabob and banker of Jacobite stock, James Strange, about to wed Henry's widowed daughter Anne. The last brought into the circle his partners in business: John Agnew, the brothers John and William Petrie, and William Stirling. They formed the core of a still wider association of Scottish interests linking the City and India, including Walter Boyd, John Callander and Mark Wood. A more personal connection of Dundas's was with Lord Dalkeith, who as Buccleuch's heir could not sit for a Scottish seat but took one provided by a relation in the South. Safe English havens were otherwise found for old friends such as John Fordyce and Andrew Stuart, as for Dundas's private secretary, William Garthshore. Finally there were miscellaneous Scottish hangers-on: for example William Drummond, an itinerant philosopher from St Andrews, or Andrew Strahan, son of the renowned printer in London of the works of the Enlightenment.

Their seats were usually rotten boroughs in southern England – Berwick being the one place where Dundas's interest spilled directly over the border – either purchased by themselves or supplied by him. A favourite was Weymouth and Melcombe Regis, which together returned four members, two on the Johnston-Pulteney interest (victorious in the infamous contest of 1768 for Cromartyshire) and two on the Government's, with the nomination often given to Dundas. In six Parliaments from 1790, Scots accounted for half the representation of these English boroughs almost as far from the border as could be. Dundas's Anglo-Scottish following this time amounted to a score or so, which together with double that number from home made them a force to reckon with. He did not, like a great nobleman, absolutely control them. But they formed an effective phalanx of self-interest. No wonder Londoners ruefully recited to themselves a verse of psalm 75: 'Promotion cometh neither from the east nor from the west, nor yet from the south.'

Inside Scotland, the result of the election was clear. The manager's perfected skills had rallied almost the whole ruling class round him in a way never before equalled: the rump could only be perverse, thus negligible, or up to no good, thus deserving of persecution. Dundas, for all his faults, may yet perhaps be admired at this climax of his career, as political master of his homeland, protector of the United Kingdom and pioneer of the Empire. Fortune would not again be so kind.

Notes

1. NLI, 54A/83; *Parl. Hist.*, xxxi, col. 411; Matheson (1933), 156; Brims (1983), 58; Danzinger (1988), 72.
2. Cockburn H. A. (1910), 151; Bickley (1928), i,14; Omond (1883), 219, 247; Adam (1888), 117; Lovat-Fraser (1916), 49; SRO GD 235/9/18/3; WLC, Dec. 12, 1987; Malcolm (1942), 135.
3. Anon. (1795b), 212; Matheson, 156, 171–2, 180; Granville (1916), i, 470; Wilkins (1901), 11.
4. Aspinall (1962–3), i, 539; Chatham Papers PRO 30/8/101/29.
5. NLI, 55/182; Chatham Papers PRO 30/8/157/1/124; Anon. (1795b), 7; Matheson, 220; HMC Fortescue Papers, ii, 396; Bickley, loc.cit; Aspinall, ii, 39, 106; (1963–71), i, 124; Ehrman (1967), 457; (1983), 185.
6. Dropmore Papers, BL Add MSS 58915, f.92; Matheson, 154.
7. NLS MS 6. f.50; Thompson (1931), 259.
8. Ferguson, (1957), 102 et seqq; Thorne (1986), i, 72.
9. Ferguson, 106; Thorne, ii, 513–590, passim.
10. Anonymous (1792c), passim; Home Office Papers SRO RH 2/4/66/313; Hughes (1956), 27; Gallin (1979), 136; Lee Papers NLS MS 3464, f.96; Bono (1980), 74; Miscellaneous Fragments, BL Add MSS 41567, f. 187.
11. *Parl. Hist.*, xxix, col. 1203.
12. Omond, 178; Cunninghame Graham Muniments SRO GD 22/315/6; Pryde (1960).
13. Thorne, iv, 28–30, 652–3, 707.
14. ibid., 504–8; WLP I, Feb. 28, 1793.
15. Fraser (1987), 52; Marwick (1967), 5–6.
16. Fraser (1985), 33 et seqq; (1987), 39–56; *Parl.Hist.*, xxxi, col. 62.
17. Dropmore Papers, BL Add MSS 58914, f.63; HMC Fortescue, i. 556; *Parl. Hist.*, n.s. vii. col. 1205.
18. Home Office Papers SRO RH 2/4/66/254.
19. Hughes (1956), 31–3.

20. Mingay (1989), 209–10; *Parl. Hist.*, xxix, cols. 98–102; Warren Hastings Papers, BL Add MSS 29177, f.255.
21. Wilberforce (1897), 91; Campbell (1985), 103–4; Edinburgh University Library Papers, DC I. 77, no. 71; NLS MS 14, ff.27–8, 40–1, 83, 87; Whatley (1987), 94; Brims, 231–41.
22. WLC, Nov.12, 1792; Chatham Papers PRO 30/8/157/1/144; Brims, 136; Meikle (1912). 74; Campbell & Dow (1968). 114–5; Gallie (1979), 59.
23. Hunter Blair Papers, June 5, 1784; Miller (1975), 9–11; Home Office Papers SRO RH 2/4/63/79; Meikle (1910), 21 et seqq; (1912), 83; Nicholson (1895),10; Logue (1979), 134; SRO GD 235/10/2/4.
24. Meikle, 84; Furber (1931), 83; *Parl. Hist* , xxx, cols. 45, 48; Home Office Papers SRO RH 2/4/64/364; HMC, ix, J. J. Hope Johnston of Annandale MSS (1897), 132.
25. Hughes (1956), 23; Brims, 255.
26. NLS MS 7, f.17; Brims (1987), 248.
27. Holland Rose (1911), 177.
28. Cockburn (1888), 173.
29. NLS MS 6, f.65; MS 1051, 68; SRO GD 51/17/117; *Parl. Hist.*, xxx, col. 1490.
30. Cockburn, 90, 237; (1856), 151; Furber, 56.
31. Home Office Papers, SRO RH 2/4/76/107; Gallin, 202–6; Furber 82, 88.
32. Richardson (1875), 66; NLS MS 7, f.78; Anon. (1796), passim.
33. Black (1963), 232; Furber, 94.
34. *Parl. Hist.*, xxxii, col.467.
35. Noble (1987), 145; *Parl. Hist.*, col.338.
36. WLC, Nov.12, 1792; Chatham Papers, PRO 30/8/157/1/144; Lenman (1981), 103; Rose (1984), 113 et seqq; Brims (1989), 58; (1990), 40 et seqq; Devine (1990), 53–60.
37. Lawson (1843), 336; Mather (1977), pp.540 et seqq.
38. Sher, 294; Scottish Catholic Archive, Scottish Mission Papers 5/2; Cooney (1983), 13–6; Raleigh (1921), 299; *Parl. Hist.*, xxx, col. 766; Anderson (1965), 165.
39. Scottish Catholic Archive, Scottish Mission Papers 5/3/10; Meikle, 196; Thompson (1927), 236.
40. Hardwicke Papers, BL Add MSS 35919, f.42; Harlow (1952), i, 632; Chatham Papers PRO 30/8/157/1/72; Feiling (1938), 220.
41. NLI, 54/15, 47, 54A/74; HLH, bMS Eng 1327(1); Minto Papers, NLS MS 11048, f.297; Bickley, i, 36; Burke (1967), vi, 470; vii, 3, 33, 349; Malcomson (1978), xvii, 242.
42. Chatham Papers PRO 30/8/157/1/144.
43. Brown (1982), 8–9; Mathieson (1916), 108; Voges (1984), 106; (1985), 145.
44. WLC, Nov. 13, 1786; Meikle, 227; Mathieson, 102; Cant (1970), 99; Voges (1984), loc.cit.; Maciver (1977), 6; Benson (1969), 141.
45. Carlyle Bell Papers, NLS 23765, f.60; Meikle, 67–9; Minto Papers, NLS MS 11203, ff.159–76; *Parl. Hist.*, xxix, col.495.
46. Kay (1877), ii, 118 et seqq; NLS MS 8, f.21; Cook (1820), 164.
47. Ditchfield (1980), 37 et seqq; Burton (1860), 552; Clark (1970), 216.
48. Clark (1963), 148, 157; (1970), 219; Mathieson, 109; Donovan (1987), 312; Meikle, 195; Chatham Papers PRO 30/8/157/1/144.
49. ibid., 30/8/157/1/154; NLS MS 8, ff.203–6; Home Office Papers SRO 2/4/ 83/195.
50. Sher (1985), 319; Fontana (1986), 11.

51. Pelham Papers, BL Add MSS 33108, f.450; Morrell (1971), 43–51
52. Lovat-Fraser (1902), 360.
53. Winch (1978), 7.
54. Cockburn (1910), 73–4; Veitch (1854–60), lxxi–iv.
55. Monboddo (1795), iv, 199–200; Hanham (1964), 20; Nairn (1977), 118 et seqq, 140.
56. Burke, vi, 428; Ginter (1967), passim; Thorne, 328.
57. Ditchfield (1986), 309 et seqq.
58. SRO GD 51/1/17/3; Burke, vii, 192; Ilchester (1908), i, 102.
59. Ehrman (1983), 411–2; Stanhope (1879), ii, 56; Aspinall (1962), ii, 222; HMC, xv, Earl of Carlisle MSS (1897), 720–1; NLS MS 10225, f.52.
60. HMC Fortescue, ii, 595–7.
61. NLS MS 10225, ff.47 et seqq; SRO GD 51/1/24/1.
62. SRO GD 51/1/24/2.
63. SRO GD 51/1/24/3, 51/17/227 & 229; NLS MS 10225, ff.52 et seqq; Aspinall, loc.cit.; Ehrman (1983), 270.
64. *Parl. Hist.*, xxx, col. 378.
65. Home Ofice Papers SRO RH 2/4/65/78; NLI, 54/50; WLP I, secret service files 1792–5; LC, undated Papers [but 1793] & Jan.28, 1794; Fulford & Strachey, ii, 344; Glover (1963), 15; Cobban (1971), 236.
66. Bathurst Papers, BL MS loan 57/107; Auckland Papers, BLH, Nov.9, 1793; Anstey (1978), 309; Duffy (1987), 18–19, 369–70; Benians, Newton & Rose (1940), 45–6.
67. Duffy, 125.
68. ibid., 170; Corbett (1913), i, 148.
69. HMC Fortescue, ii, 645; Corbett, ii, 215; Aspinall (1962), ii, 454; Spilhans (1966), 170–2.
70. Neil (1927), passim.
71. BL Add MSS 40102, passim; Duffy, 159 et seqq; *Parl.Hist.*, xxxii, col. 467; Fortescue (1906), iv, 479; HMC Fortescue, iii, 166.
72. Corbett, i, 233; Duffy, 198 et seqq.
73. Ehrman (1968), 465.
74. Minto Papers, NLS MS 11140, 22; Canning Papers, bundle 77; De, 420; Furber (1948), 302, 339; Philips (1951), xix, 104, 168; Parker (1985), 197 et seqq.
75. NLS MS 1062, 87.
76. Harlow (1952), ii, 224, 486; Tripathi (1956), 3, 26–7.
77. WLC, Oct.9. 1797; Buccleuch Papers SRO GD 224/30/4/25/3; Canning Papers, loc.cit.; Bruce (1793), 265, 595.
78. Philips (1940), 66 et seqq; (1951), xv; Tripathi, 27–36.
79. Ingram (1970), 6.
80. *Parl. Hist.*, xxx, cols. 660–85.
81. Harlow & Madden (1953), 46; Harlow, ii, 486.
82. Walker (1963), 181; NLS Acc 8017.
83. Bumsted (1982), 79; Cowan (1961), 14; Benians, Holland Rose & Newton, ii, 24.
84. *Parl. Hist*, xxxix, cols. 1105–9.
85. ibid., cols.1174–6.
86. ibid., col. 1206; WLP I. Feb.5, 1792.
87. Thorne, iii, 542, 638.
88 Grant-Macpherson Papers, bundle 447, June 7, 1795; Kay (1877), 403.
89 Sunter (1986), 134–45.

6

'British purposes'

Henry Dundas, aged 54, was starting to turn his thoughts to a time when his labours would be over. He told Sylvester Douglas, a recent recruit to his circle of Scots cronies: 'I think I might now look to a peerage.' When before long the tetchy Lord Grenville made one of his periodic threats to resign, Dundas dropped eager hints of a desire to replace him as the Government's main spokesman in the House of Lords, having 'lost the pleasure of hearing himself speak in the House of Commons'. He became ever more depressed as 1796 went on and remarked to Sir John Sinclair, who celebrated Hogmanay with him at Wimbledon: 'I hope that this year will be happier than the last, for I scarcely recollect having spent one happy day in the whole of it.'[1]

An immense burden of work, which he was yet singularly reluctant to lighten, took its toll of his constitution. He would never be in really robust health again. In 1798 he wrote: 'I hope I shall be able to weather it all, but in truth I am overdone, and unfortunately have got into a habit from anxiety of not sleeping at night.' Two years later, his doctors diagnosed a weakened heart. They advised him to eat and drink less manfully, to take exercise and laxatives and to avoid stress. He retorted that he would not 'interrupt the pleasures or the business of my life, by an anticipation of a misfortune I have no means of preventing ... If I am to ride at all, I must ride either fast or slow as the inclination of the moment suggests; and if I speak at all, I must make the exertion which the moment calls for, without thinking my physician is, or is not, listening to me.' There followed, however, a showdown with Lady Jane Dundas. As he reported it to William Pitt, she complained 'that in place of relaxing my hours of business, I had rather increased them, so as to give her much less of the real intercourse of my society than she used to have.'[2]

Already he had asked George III if he might be relieved of responsibility for the war and confine himself to Indian affairs. The King replied that this could not be done without the consent of the Prime Minister. Dundas had evidently omitted to consult him beforehand, a clear sign of their deteriorating relations. Now he wrote to his chief: 'The more maturely I consider the business, the more I am satisfied I ought not to lose this opportunity of retiring with credit.' Pitt, as ever, refused to hear of it. Dundas agreed to stay on for the duration as Secretary of State for War. But he did cease to be Treasurer of the Navy, exchanging the post for a sinecure of equal value, that of Lord Privy Seal for Scotland, relinquishing also the Scottish signet to his son.[3]

This valedictory discouragement and weariness arose above all from the beating the British had taken at the hands of the French. They clearly gained the ascendant during 1796, sustained by an array of allies (most forced into submission), able to choose at leisure in which new theatre to mount an offensive. After the surrender in October 1797 of the Austrians, Britain's last remaining friends on the Continent, she could look for nothing more there. She was obliged rather to be constantly on guard for her worldwide interests – though outside Europe, admittedly, she had so far had not a bad war.

According to Sir John Fortescue, author of the standard *History of the British Army*, the blame for this situation ought to be laid squarely at the door of Dundas, whom he depicted as utterly clueless in military matters and incapable of the simplest tasks of organisation: worse still, he was a Scotsman. The last he could not help, and the military inexperience may be conceded too – it is not in itself a disqualification for the political conduct of hostilities. On the charge of incompetence, it must be said that Dundas was not by nature an incompetent man. He made his share of mistakes, but the weak position he had inherited on becoming Secretary of State for War was to a large extent already beyond his power to change. It had arisen from a variety of factors, from the country's lack of preparation at the outset, from a misreading by the Government as a whole of the severity of the task then facing it, from the feebleness of its allies. Yet it certainly had to take the blame for not pursuing with firmness clearly identified objectives.

This was not, however, for want of any such objectives, as Fortescue's diatribes contended. His criticism of the higher direction of the war rested almost entirely on departmental orders issued to commanders in the various theatres and on the operational results which followed. But to appreciate what was going on, one really must retrace the decision-making process and try to understand the motivations of those engaged in it. Here as elsewhere, the sometimes irrational role of personalities should never be underestimated. At least, compared with the American conflict, there was this time relatively little interference from the King. Chastened by his previous experiences, he had become less aggressive, less confident of his ability to supervise a world war, more acquiescent in the expedients of his senior Ministers. Among them, whatever the formal allocation of duties, job-sharing was the norm. In fact three men directed the struggle: Dundas, a realist interested primarily in the Empire; Grenville, a precisian captivated by the concert of Europe; and, trying to mediate their increasingly bitter quarrels, Pitt, closer in outlook to the former, in character to the latter, but coming to value Grenville's judgment above that of Dundas.

This vexed and unsettled the man left in the minority. What exasperated him most, though, was the fretful niggling brought out by Pitt and Grenville in each other, which found release in their bouts of impulsiveness. Dundas later told how he was

> apprehensive of a disposition in [Pitt] which I have often had occasion to check, an overeagerness to run at the object immediately in contemplation. When in war his hopes and confidence are sanguine beyond all reason; and when aiming at peace, there is no sacrifice which at times he has not been ready to make for the attainment of it. He is either in a garret or in a cellar.

But with all his faults there are a thousand honourable and amiable qualities in him, and it is impossible for me to separate myself in affection from him. There was no such reserve of goodwill to soften collisions with Grenville, whose 'cold, distant and undecided' nature Dundas years afterwards still recalled with repugnance.

He, by contrast, was the least opportunist, the least likely in crises to fall for hasty, ill-judged expedients. His nerve showed itself notably steadier when things kept going wrong in Europe, and he refused to be deflected from the colonial campaigns he wanted to fight. Still, the net result was a lamentable lack of cohesion in the war effort, with the three leaders devoting more energy to arguments with each other than to planning with their military experts. The chain of command being anyway so loose, it was incessantly tugged one way or another by conflicting interventions. Tactical misdirections repeatedly undermined any consistent strategy.[4]

A second source of discord was the choice of strategy. To Dundas's mind, Britain's war ought above all to have been economic. And since she was a worldwide trading nation, her European interests would have to take their place among other priorities. But this evaluation was never fully accepted by his colleagues, who from the outset yielded to the urge, fed by both the allies and by their own interventionist instincts, to deploy British forces directly on the Continent. This was not to say that Pitt underestimated Britain's dependence on trade for her prosperity. But in the period of his closest personal involvement in foreign affairs during 1790 and 1791, he had pursued a forward policy in Europe, and once a general war broke out had at once committed troops there. As for Grenville, he showed himself the most emphatic on the point that it was revolutionaries that had to be combatted, rather than mere competitors. 'In the establishment of the French republic', he warned, 'is included the overthrow of all the other governments of Europe.'[5]

It has been proposed that we should read into these differences an ideological rift between Whig and Tory – Whigs being (originally because of an attachment to Hanover) more interventionist, Tories less so.[6] But nobody then thought it out or argued it in those terms. Dundas would have been surprised to hear that his attitude arose out of any disaffection from Hanover. He would surely have pointed rather to his own acquirements as a son of the Scottish Enlightenment, and in particular as a student of political economy. In the third book of *The Wealth of Nations*, Adam Smith had elucidated the advantages of foreign commerce, transferring to the international scale his teachings on the utility of a division of labour and of a free exchange of goods. He also noted the tendency of European wars to ruin it, and of colonial enterprise to make it flourish. Still, the proposition is of use in serving to show that Fortescue swallowed whole the Whig interpretation of geostrategy.

It blinded him, amid his tendentious and unseemly libels against Dundas, to the deep, genuine disagreement among Ministers. This had already been revealed by the events of 1793–4. Indeed it reflected a dilemma Britain faced in just about every war she fought during the eighteenth century. One choice she had was to join, as the English had intermittently done since the middle ages, in their continental cousins' general mêlée on land. But after accumulating territories and interests in the Americas and the Orient, and perforce devising the naval means to defend and extend them, she had acquired a second choice, of fighting maritime wars. Here she assumed a basically defensive stance against the enemy (nearly always France) and relied for victory on economic pressure coupled with the military operations of her allies. She might thus compensate for the inevitable handicaps of an insular country in competition on land, for she had then the possibility of offsetting overseas any shifts in the European balance of power.

This position, novel and unique among the nations, had the advantage of marrying with the avocations of a seafaring race, and so of buying security more cheaply and efficiently than the construction of fortresses and maintenance of standing armies would have done. Moreover, Britain might replace or even augment the resources necessarily expended on fighting. The navy could not only protect existing channels of trade but also open up new ones, sustaining seaborne traffic, domestic industry and revenue. Commercial wealth and naval power thus nourished one another.

The benefits Britain derived from this strategy had, however, forcibly struck the rulers of France after her disasters during the Seven Years' War. They were free to counter it because it did not, after all, aim to knock her out or even reduce her militarily, except perhaps in the long run by the economic pressure. So, as the only way to contain Britain, they had afterwards exerted themselves to build up their own strength at sea, while avoiding entanglements on the Continent. That had paid off handsomely during the American War, when the French led the combination of European navies which did most to beat Britain. She afterwards saw no choice but to redouble her maritime efforts. In the ten intervening years of peace, re-establishment of her command of the seas had remained the essential of her foreign policy, political and economic.

Dundas's views on strategy are known in detail from his extensive published correspondence with Earl Spencer, First Lord of the Admiralty.[7] In it he held that the renewal of war between France and other European powers was no reason for deviating from the course set after 1783: Britain should still concentrate on the struggle at sea. He had at first reluctantly gone along with his colleagues' differing view, at least to the extent of trying to make them envisage their continental enterprises as the mere landward components of an essentially maritime master-plan. He wrote in April 1793:

> When Great Britain was compelled to take a part in the war with France by the unprovoked outrages of those exercising the government of that country, it must have been in His Majesty's contemplation to connect his operations on the Continent as much as possible with the operations of the fleet. The naval strength is the national strength of Great Britain, and it requires some cogent reason to procure the approbation of the people of this country to the application of its strength in any other direction.[8]

But with continual reverses in Europe, Dundas's opposition hardened. He reasoned from the inescapable fact that Britain had only one-third of France's population. Since her commitment of manpower to the navy was necessarily great, her army could only ever be small, too small to have any hope of conducting successful campaigns against the French, let alone of conquering and occupying their territory. That had been quite beyond her even when she was contending, earlier in the century, against their relatively limited numbers of purely professional soldiers. How much more quixotic it was when they had mobilised their whole nation and fired it with revolutionary zeal. Dundas said to Sir Gilbert Elliot in 1794: 'If France is completely united and fascinated with the madness which at present reigns there, I am afraid to conquer them is impossible.'[9]

What followed was that France would again have to be defeated on land by a European coalition, and that its armies should assume the main burden of continental hostilities. While joint expeditions might be contemplated, Britain's most useful contribution would come not from her meagre supplies of men but from her ample resources of money. When preparing a fresh attack in the West Indies in 1796, Dundas wrote that operations like this were

> at all times in the reach and within the means of this country to accomplish
> ... whereas, we have constantly amused ourselves and trifled away the time
> in forming fancies about splendid expeditions to act with men who did not
> stand in need of such aid, who, I truly believe, are infinitely better without
> it and who would have found no difficulty in forming as many armies as they
> pleased ... if we had directed their hopes and expectations solely to that object.

European coalitions were, of course, formed and subsidised by Britain, though they repeatedly foundered. A long war needed, it turned out, not just the generosity on Britain's part but the will on her allies' too. If the will was wanting, Dundas can hardly be blamed.[10]

In his view, what role should in any event fall to his own country was one which no other could fill. From the security afforded by command of the narrow seas, which held even when France's subjugation of the allies left her free to attempt invasion, Britain should 'protect the essential interests of commerce and navigation'. She would thus be neutralising the one threat to her own ability to sustain the struggle: 'Home will take care of itself. But whatever feelings anybody in ordinary wars may entertain on that point, there can be little doubt that in the present war, and under its present circumstances, there can be no real injury done to this country but in its distant possessions.' With this duty efficiently discharged, moreover, Britain could even go on the offensive and exploit her maritime strength by damaging the enemy in every way possible, seizing his outposts, ruining his commerce, sapping his naval resources – as Dundas put it, 'the way to defeat France is to take all her colonies and to destroy her trade.' He eventually defined the struggle quite simply to Parliament as one 'in which we are contending for colonial interest with France'.[11]

Other historians than Fortescue have queried the value of dispersing scanty forces to seize territories sometimes of little immediate value. But the margin of error on the opposite side, had Dundas done what Fortescue wished, would surely have been greater. Strikingly, when the historian defined British war aims at the outset, he mentioned all these matters only in subordination to the two he set at the top, the integrity of the Netherlands and the maintenance of an effective barrier between them and France. These were the assumptions of a soldier-scholar regarding the struggle on land as primary: hence the severity of his strictures when he could not see our boys thrashing their foes on various foreign fields.

There is nothing new in soldiers and politicians falling out over how to fight wars, even at a century's remove from each other. The soldier's purposes are military, but only one element in the politician's wider calculations. The scholar's purposes are to introduce some structure into the chaos of historical reality. Fortescue pursued them with a Whiggish zeal to impose on the development of warfare his teleology, which he wished to reach its end in the scientific direction of mass armies, such as revolutionary France had inaugurated. Dundas's real crime lay perhaps in his not fitting neatly into the scheme. It was easy for Fortescue to appreciate with the benefit of hindsight what indeed Dundas never grasped, that these French Wars were changing profoundly the nature of all wars, at least of all wars on land. But he did grasp what eluded Fortescue even with the benefit of hindsight, that Britain's recent history had just as profoundly changed her position in the world, so that her wars were not to be fought in the same way as others'. That held true till the cataclysms of the twentieth century.[12]

The situation facing Britain after 1796 put the maritime strategy decisively on trial. At the point where the narrative was interrupted in the last chapter, the struggle in Europe had been lost. The British embarked on negotiation with the French which continued into 1797, when the latter brutally broke it off. Dundas felt little regret, for he was loth to relinquish for the sake of peace any of the latest conquests. Indeed he hinted he would rather resign than give up the Cape and Ceylon. The French, on the other hand, were under no great pressure to settle. As the talks drifted, they became convinced that Britain had nothing to offer that they could not get by continuing to fight. They even persuaded themselves, on the strength of fanciful reports from spies and from traitorous British radicals, that the population was yearning to rise against its rulers and oppressors. They were therefore eager to try an invasion.

The first attempt had come in Ireland at Christmas 1796, when their fleet had descended on Bantry Bay but was scattered by storms. The next target was a second Celtic nation. In February 1797 a force actually landed on the Welsh coast, though it was easily overwhelmed. A plan existed for the third Celtic nation too, as appeared from the hand of no less a personage than Wolfe Tone, who communicated it to the French: 'On peut maintenant avec autant de facilité qu'en Irlande débarquer nos 15,000 hommes à Leith; ces 15,000 hommes sont plus que suffisants pour se rendres maîtres de tout le pays entre Edimbourg et Glasgow, pays actuellement entièrement dégarni de troupes', an observation certainly well-informed.[13]

Nothing came of these ventures, but the strain on British nerves and resources remained intense all through the first half of the year. Since the country was wholly dependent for safety on its fleet, its plight began to look desperate when mutinies broke out at Spithead and the Nore that summer – 'a bomb burst over our heads when we were least thinking of it', in Dundas's words. Yet the French could not sustain their threat. If they were to come, they needed more ships than they had. To supply the deficiency, they looked to two recent allies, Spain and Holland. At the critical point, these were crippled as naval powers by British victories at Cape St Vincent and Camperdown, achieved respectively by Admirals Sir John Jervis and Adam Duncan, the latter Dundas's nephew by marriage; such was the country's relief that both were awarded viscountcies. Mastery of the narrow seas was thus held, and the French were thwarted.[14]

Any threat to British naval supremacy arose rather, and paradoxically, from developments on land, a matter to which it will be necessary to recur. Napoleon Bonaparte had meanwhile smashed the Austrians along the Rhine and launched his brilliant conquest of Italy – one of the reasons why Spain had entered the war on his side. In respect of the maritime strategy, this increased the naval forces ranged against Britain and turned almost the whole northern seaboard of the Mediterranean into a hostile one. That in turn endangered, if it did not render untenable, the British position there, which rested on occupation of Corsica.

Grenville, believing Britain had to cut her losses somewhere, demanded that she should quit not just that base, but the whole theatre. Dundas opposed him furiously, writing to Spencer that this

> amounts to a distinct confession that whenever France and Spain are at war [with Britain] we must abandon all connection with the Mediterranean and in truth with the whole South of Europe … The measure of not abandoning the Mediterranean is in my opinion so essentially connected with the present and future naval strength and glory of the country, that it ought to be preferred to every other service whatever which does not necessarily involve the security of our distant possessions.

We could, he went on, no more afford to forsake the Mediterranean than the Channel or the East and West Indies. Nor did he concede that Britain needed to, but asserted that through efficient deployment of ships she could control them all. Grenville, however, was the one who carried the Cabinet, winning the support of Pitt and even of Spencer, usually Dundas's ally. For him, it was the biggest defeat to date.[15]

He had vainly staked a good deal of his political capital. He had done so because he was sure that the French, left unchallenged, would try through Egypt to seize the overland route to India – a scheme which their rulers had indeed kept on their agenda ever since the Seven Years' War. With it they would imperil Britain's eastern Empire; at the least, they might force her to an adverse peace. So when Napoleon started massing troops at Toulon early in 1798, Dundas was at once alerted. 'Did the instructions to Lord St Vincent mention that Egypt might be in the contemplation of Bonaparte's expedition?' he asked Spencer in June after counter-moves were belatedly set in train: 'It may be whimsical, but I cannot help having a fancy of my own on that subject.' He even paid oblique tribute to a mind moving on the same lines as his: 'If it is actually destined for Egypt, it appears to me to be a masterly stroke and, if successful, would be attended with very pernicious consequences to the interest of this country.'[16]

He was right. Napoleon sailed to Malta, took it and proceeded straight to Alexandria. The British rushed every possible ship eastwards but the fleet, commanded by Admiral Horatio Nelson, could only follow a good three weeks behind. It was a measure of the alarm felt that another squadron was sent out on the immense journey round the Cape to intercept the French, should it be necessary, in Arabian waters. In August, Dundas wrote to Spencer that, assuming Bonaparte had made good his landing, there is no price too dear to be paid for it, if by any means that army could be rooted out of Egypt, and its further progress prevented. I am always in hopes we shall hear of Nelson doing something brilliant with regard to the fleet, as it is so far good and will gratify the feelings of the country, but neither that nor any other success will compensate to the country in reality for the misfortune it has undergone by the French with a large army getting possession of Egypt.[17]

The intuition was again astounding, for almost at once news arrived of Nelson's smashing victory at Aboukir Bay. Napoleon was for the time being marooned by the Nile. Dundas breathed a huge sigh of relief in a letter to Spencer, confessing that the difficulty and expense of defending India from direct French attack would have 'rendered it very doubtful whether this country was equal to it either in point of inclination, or ability.' His colleagues were forced to admit that he had been right all along, at least in asserting that Britain could still deprive France of control in the Mediterranean if she wanted to – it was now possible to go on and blockade Malta, as well as occupy both Sicily and Minorca.[18]

This signal success at long last for British arms spurred other powers to re-enter the war. Austria, Naples, Portugal, Prussia, Russia and Turkey successively did so, in the Second Coalition. Dundas remained unimpressed. In a long memorandum on the strategic situation, put to Pitt in December, he cautioned against a premature belief in the defeat of France or a trusting reliance on fair-weather friends:

> I am afraid that a new continental system, or an old again reverted to a burdensome expense, may stagger the confidence of the country in its own resources, and produce many of the prejudices and doubts which we have already encountered and overcome. At the moment we feel every shilling expended is for British security and British purposes.

He complained that previous subsidies for allies had been wasted. Since a correspondingly greater exertion had then been required of this country, it would justly protest at having to go through the same again. He pointedly reminded his chief that we had already spent a vast amount on re-establishing superiority in the Mediterranean: members of the coalition should be told that this was as much subsidy as they were going to get. We had no need to pander to them because, even in fighting on alone, we had yet defended ourselves and, what was more, restored our commerce. We should not be seduced by the prospect of an early peace before we were certain of safeguarding our own interests.[19]

Once again, though, Dundas's warnings against European entanglements were ignored. During 1799 the coalition began to make headway by means of concerted offensives. The Government responded not just with subsidies, but also with a fresh British expedition to the Continent. The chosen target was the Netherlands, thought to be yearning for liberation from the French yoke. There Russia and, more questionably, Prussia were supposed to mount with Britain a joint invasion. Dundas had the deepest misgivings. It was his responsibility to select the command for the British force, but when he wrote in June to offer it to his favourite general, Sir Ralph Abercromby, he warned that Prussia might fall by the wayside because she was 'corrupted and weak'. A month later he told Grenville that he did not count on a welcome from the Dutch either, or anyway think much could be achieved so late in the campaigning season.[20]

The British share of the enterprise, as originally conceived, was to seize the island of Walcheren, lying between the mouths of the Maas and the Scheldt, from which both could thus be blockaded. Foremost in Pitt's and Grenville's minds, however, were operations not at sea but on land. They intended indeed a full-scale campaign in the interior of the Netherlands. On this point Abercromby's reservations seemed as great as Dundas's. He stressed that it would be feasible, if at all, only through close co-operation with large contingents of the allies, so far not greatly in evidence. His friend, thoroughly disquieted, held things up by exhaustive discussion of logistic problems. Pitt and Grenville continued to insist, however, on the political necessity of the expedition.

In the middle of August, Dundas gave up trying to dissuade them and abruptly told Sir Ralph that he would have to sail right away. If he could not take Walcheren he should go on to Den Helder, at the tip of the province of Holland to the north of Amsterdam, and to Texel, which between them commanded the entrance to the Zuider Zee. If these proved too strong, he should proceed to the Ems: 'Details have been avoided, wishing to leave entirely to the judgment of Sir Ralph the direction of the movements of his army according to the intelligence he can procure on the spot.'[21] Obviously, amid the delay, a clear objective for the expedition had been lost, and Dundas cannot be exonerated. Not that his commander showed much more enthusiasm – when his 24,000 troops eventually disembarked at Den Helder he reported back: 'We have succeeded, though success hardly justifies the attempt.' It turned out that a clearer definition of objectives would not have made much practical difference, though some initial successes were achieved. With British control of the main waterways, the Dutch fleet was captured early in September. Other allied forces moved into the Netherlands, as into Lombardy and Switzerland. For a while it seemed touch-and-go with the French defences.

But the difficulty for the British of sustaining continental campaigns was soon visited on them with a vengeance. Unseasonably stormy weather disrupted transport of reinforcements and supplies to them. So far from breaking out of the bridgehead, they found themselves bogged down in the face of ever stronger counter-attacks. By mid-September Dundas thought the situation 'very awkward', especially as there was no sign of the Dutch turning against the French. On the contrary, a combination of their forces cornered the British, threatening defeat in the field unless these either inundated the country or withdrew. Hurriedly arranging an armistice, they got out, though they could at least take the Dutch fleet with them. Dundas was scathing about the Grenvilles who had 'induced the British Government to conceive that the force of the United Provinces was loud in calling for our assistance and that we were sending an army to Holland not to make a conquest, but to aid a revolution. You will recollect,' he bitterly remarked to one of his generals, 'how far there was any such co-operation as we had been led to expect.' In the event it was not only a setback for, but the end of any serious activity by the coalition, which dissolved in morose squabbles.[22]

The French, on the other hand, found a new lease of life. They had proved more than a match for a revived combination of enemies, and soon got a new leader too. In October, Napoleon slipped past the British ships patrolling off Egypt and regained his own country. A month later, he staged the coup d'état of 18 brumaire and set himself up as dictator. Dundas accurately warned the Commons:

> In one point, no doubt, the Jacobinical government is at an end, in point of form; but in substance and essence all the other qualities of the revolutionary government are as much in force at this moment as they were in the days of Barrère and Robespierre ... Form and substance are all now concentrated and consolidated in the hands of Bonaparte, and the government stands with a military despot at its head, with unlimited power and authority.[23]

Napoleon fulfilled both French and foreign expectations by launching at once into vigorous attacks on his continental foes, of which Austria remained the chief. Inside a year, with a crushing victory against her at Marengo, he established complete military dominance in Europe. This gave him the chance to attempt some challenge to British naval supremacy, though not with his own fleet. Instead, he cajoled the minor powers he had knocked out of the war into the Armed Neutrality, with the purpose of mutual support in resistance to the British blockade of French ports. It marked the start of Napoleon's long and strenuous effort to wage an economic war of his own.

Britain's expedients, in the face of this renewed aggression, seemed exhausted. Her own territory and most of her colonies were in practice unassailable. But resources for successful initiatives elsewhere simply did not exist: the ones tried, at Ferrol and Cadiz, turned out utter fiascos, causing much tension between Pitt and Dundas. To strike against the enemy, the British were reduced to futile attempts at promoting a counter-revolution through what remained of an opposition inside France. When they tried again to negotiate, they could find no means of compelling Napoleon. On the contrary, by continuing to harrow Austria, he meant to make Britain disgorge some of her conquests in order to procure better terms for this last ally. The British Cabinet remained hopelessly divided all through 1800: some, like Dundas, still hoping for energetic prosecution of the war; others ready to concede whatever it might take to get a settlement, starting perhaps with cessation of the struggle overseas; others again not knowing what to do. The fact of the matter was that Britain could make neither peace nor war.[24]

The hiatus may be filled by bringing into the picture that constant object of Dundas's solicitude, India. There, his policy of the last ten years had rested on an assumption that peace was necessary, not only for security but also for profit. War would naturally undermine these objects, or at least demand other methods of attaining them.[25]

India was at first remote from the main theatres of conflict, so that the early effects were felt only on her trade. Dundas had always taken it as a rule that one way to get round the East India Company's wasteful and inefficient monopoly was to ensure that no system of colonial exclusion operated in its territories: if foreigners had the capital and made no trouble, they should be free to enter the commerce. Since this ran counter to the example set by other countries in their possessions, as by Britain in her first Empire, the wisdom of the policy did not go unquestioned. Complaints against it now grew louder, for much of the extra Indian business generated by the war went to traders from neutral countries, especially Americans. The aggrieved directors of the Company asked Dundas in 1798 to stop them trafficking with Europe. The authorities in India, too, thought it might be better for the duration to close down all foreign factories.

Dundas and David Scott were inclined to treat such notions as monopolist special pleading. But in wartime they could not feel so keen on an open trading regime either. It might divert from Britain business that she needed, and perhaps encourage a political interest in India by the foreigners venturing there. Dundas still balked at excluding them, and in the end did not do so. Fears for security might be justified, but they could not be met by inviting restoration of the old rackets. He told the directors, to their intense annoyance, that they must still treat redemption of debt as the first priority for their spare capital, since otherwise the high rates of interest prevalent in wartime would worsen the Company's long-term position.[26]

If neither they nor foreigners could safely be allowed to expand their Indian business, an alternative would be necessary. The obvious one was to look to growth of the private trade in British hands. The charter of 1793 provided for some of this to be carried in the regular traffic between London and India. But the Company had proved unco-operative, offering space only at awkward seasons and high cost. Though a few individuals profited, as a means of repatriating large amounts of capital the scheme was not working. The directors told Dundas that if he was so worried he should force the people in India to remit their fortunes home. He rejected the notion out of hand: 'I totally disapprove of attempting to accomplish this by penal restrictive statutes. All such have ever been, and ever will be, nugatory, when resorted to for such a purpose. Trade can never be regulated or directed by any other certain rule than the interest of those concerned in it.'

Instead, in 1796 he put forward another bright idea from Scott. The monopoly had hitherto included the financing and building of all ships for the Indian trade – activities invariably carried out in Britain and, under such a protectionist regime, inefficiently. For example, since it was too much trouble for the directors to develop exports from home, they would send out their new vessels empty or laden only with bullion. The proposal now was that trade to Britain should be opened to ships constructed in India, which would also be a useful deployment for the private fortunes of the Company's servants. Since the shipbuilding market there was a free one, its products would probably be cheaper and better too.

The directors made their usual mighty fuss, complaining that this would take away trade from them. Dundas calmly tried to demonstrate that the volume of their own shipping could not be affected: 'If you fix the capital you mean to apply to investment, and accurately direct your servants to provide that investment, there can be no occasion for any extra shipping. Your investment and shipping will correspond accurately together, and your commerce be systematically conducted.' They should, he sharply advised them, look not to regulation but to 'the exercise of a judicious and well-devised system of commercial policy'. Even so it proved in the event only possible for him to break the closed ring of British shippers who dictated the cost of freight to the Company, which then fell somewhat. A prohibition, with only minor exceptions, on ships built in India was successfully maintained by the directors for as long as their monopoly lasted.[27]

In the light of all this it may seem strange that Dundas felt able in 1800, near the end of his Indian career, to assure the chairman, Sir Stephen Lushington, that he wanted the Company's trading monopoly to continue. The existing system had blended Britain's commercial and strategic purposes and served them so well 'that the maintenance of the monopoly of the East India Company is even more important to the political interests of the state than it is to the commercial interest of the Company.'[28]

Had the erstwhile liberal been at last fully captured by the monopolists? The liabilities could, of course, cut both ways: at a time of dearth in Britain after the bad harvest in 1799 Dundas was able more or less to order the Company to import more foodstuffs. He had anyway never thought expediency a dirty word. And the existence of the monopoly, with vast resources of money and influence to defend its privileges, was an inescapable political fact with which he had perforce to come to terms. He did not concede anything to the monopolists beyond what was bequeathed to them by history. All the same, he had at no time been able to contemplate a comprehensive and direct assault on them. As a pragmatist, he wished no more than to feel his way forward, always deferring to public and parliamentary opinion, and taking opportunities for action as they occurred.

Dundas knew there was also a price to pay for this prudence. The monopoly could be identified as the basic cause of malfunction in the economy of Bengal which otherwise, as Adam Smith had remarked, possessed everything requisite for rapid economic advance. Since such advance was not actually taking place, the British in their turn did not make as much out of their connection with India as they might have done. Through reform, she had ceased to be pillaged. Moreover, since the loss of America she had been, even amid a spreading network of tropical outposts, the axis of a British worldwide trading system, far and away the chief source of raw materials both for Britain and in lieu of exchanges with third countries. But as a market she left a great deal to be desired.

If of little value as an agency of economic development, though, the Company still served as a means of political control in India. Its absence would, Dundas believed, lead to

> the worst kind of adventurers taking root in that country ... No principle ought ever to be tolerated or acted upon, that does not proceed on the basis of India being considered as the temporary residence of a great British establishment, for the good government of the country, upon steady and uniform principles, and of a large British factory, for the beneficial management of its trade.

Till alternative means appeared, the maintenance of British hegemony required a degree of indulgence to the Company, and its privileges could only be dismantled insofar as this entailed no political risk. Thus a *modus vivendi* between Dundas and the monopolists was necessary, indeed useful.

The caution and economy of Dundas's methods ought not, however, to obscure the boldness of his conceptions. In fact he had found considerable freedom to attack the system's weak links, the abuses which monopoly invariably threw up.

They gave him the excuse to devise piecemeal remedies encouraging the greater efficiency that would serve everyone's interest, including on occasion the Company's. As he delicately and cryptically put it in a letter to Lushington, 'if anything can endanger the monopoly it is an unnecessary adherence to points not essential for its existence.' This was a euphemism for saying that the monopoly had not remained, and should not remain, intact. Looking back to 1784, one can see how far it had been eroded. Oriental commerce, though still dominated by the Company, was now much more diverse. Treaties with various foreign countries had formalised their part in it. It had been opened to British private traders and to some Indian shippers. In effect any *bona fide* merchant could enter it. These new interests, granted recognition and legitimacy, also thus gained the chance to extract more concessions in future.

Altogether, Dundas's liberalising policies were a means rather than an end. He did not intend to pursue them as an article of true faith. He believed them justified because they matched the comparative advantages of a maritime, and increasingly of a manufacturing, nation. An open trading system global in compass was ultimately the best way to enrich and thus secure the country at its centre. As these advantages accrued, further erosion of the monopoly would be accepted with equanimity by all but the most blinkered of its beneficiaries.

At the end of Dundas's Indian administration, the monopoly was already becoming a hollow one, tolerable till the circumstances arose in which it could be ended altogether. Having irrevocably set that process in train, he was happy that the Company should crumble in its own time, doing whatever good it could meanwhile, conscious that he might never himself see the finale. He also made sure that the process could not run out of control. Thus Dundas, architect of this second British Empire, the Empire of trade, proved yet unwilling to leave its development to the impersonal operation of iron laws, as in the utilitarian ideal. His was an Empire with a purpose, and consciously directed to that purpose. It was indeed the first of the great imperialist systems.[29]

War would further these processes. This may seem paradoxical, when a cornerstone of Indian policy since 1784 had been the maintenance of peace, to which the legislation of that year gave every possible statutory reinforcement. In particular, it provided that the British authorities in the East might neither take up arms against nor even conclude a treaty with any native prince, except if London consented. They were only to interfere at all should a European power take one side, in which case they were to take the other.

The power in everyone's mind was, of course, France. She now possessed only a minor commercial, and no political, presence in the sub-continent. But she continued to cultivate relations with Britain's greatest foe there, Tipu Sahib, Sultan of Mysore. He came of a house which had continually vexed and often scared her. He himself was a dangerous man, fierce and wily well above the normal run of Indian rulers. Dundas said, 'I own I never look with very sanguine expectations to the continuance of peace in India while Tipu lives.' The British had set out confidently in their last conflict with him, in 1784, to seize lands containing the sources of exports which they particularly wanted for trade with

China. It had ended rather with the presidency of Bombay ceding territory to him. Neither Dundas nor Cornwallis could believe this had settled the score. Beneath the facade of irenic impartiality adopted by the Governor-general towards the native states, he in fact did what he could to undermine Mysore and abet her enemies. Dundas supported him, in private and in public: if a further military confrontation was inevitable, it would only be sensible to set matters up so that Cornwallis's superior abilities could next time weight the balance in Britain's favour.

It was equally unlike Tipu to await her convenience. He carried on his intrigues, backed where necessary by force, all through the rest of the decade. In 1789 he turned on the small and defenceless state of Travancore. The British rushed to its aid, unleashing the Second Mysore War. For a year the sultan bested the army of Madras, till the Governor-general took the field in person, marching on his capital, Seringapatam. Tipu promptly cut off the British force's supplies and obliged it to retreat. Cornwallis had apparently struck too soon, and Dundas in some alarm sent instructions to seek a compromise. The Governor-general yet persisted. After more thorough preparation for the campaign of 1792, he forced his way through till his troops stood under the walls of Seringapatam, from which the sultan had not the strength to dislodge them. Thus Britain could dictate the terms of peace, obliging Tipu to hand over half his territory, a large indemnity and two of his sons as hostages. Still, he was left as ruler of Mysore, and bitterly plotted revenge.

Only now could Cornwallis lay down his office and return to London – though too late to join the Government. Pitt refused to let Dundas change places with him, and no other suitable public figure at home could be found for the succession in Calcutta. It therefore went to Sir John Shore, his predecessor's principal aide. He was dull though correct, but altogether far too nervous and irresolute for the job. He had spent his whole career in the service of the Company, the directors of which strongly favoured his appointment. Yet they deluded themselves if they imagined it would bring any shift in the balance of power. Dundas just worked instead through the men he put into the subordinate presidencies, Lord Hobart in Madras and Jonathan Duncan in Bombay. It was still an unsatisfactory arrangement, for Shore predictably quarrelled all the time with both, especially with Hobart, a rancorous soldier who wanted to renew a forward policy in India. In his apparent countenance of such notions, Dundas showed the growing prevalence of his political over his commercial priorities. But he was too far away to smooth the differences between Shore and Hobart. Their clashes on practical policy waxed so violent that in 1796 the two of them had to be recalled.[30]

Dundas wanted to send Cornwallis back for a second term, but his services were meanwhile required elsewhere. He chose instead a member of the Board of Control, Richard Wellesley, Earl of Mornington in the Irish peerage, who on becoming Governor-general was granted the British title of Lord Wellesley. With his French wife and brood of illegitimate children, he cut a raffish figure. But he was clearly a manic-depressive, by turns euphoric and despondent, hyperactive and lethargic, altogether difficult to work with. He showed himself especially touchy about rank, and waxed furious at being rewarded in 1799 for his services to date only with an Irish marquisate – what he called his 'gilt potato'. He was scarcely mollified by being made, in addition to his political office, Commander-in-chief in India the next year.

This did, however, acknowledge that under him conquest again became explicitly the centrepiece of policy there. Given Dundas's desire to keep trade open, a military solution was doubtless inevitable for the problems of security created by France's resurgent ambitions, evinced in her attention to Egypt. Alexander had marched overland to India, so why not Napoleon? As soon as the French expedition set sail from Toulon in 1798, Dundas sprang into action, sending embassies to win support in Constantinople and St Petersburg, urging the Turkish pasha at Baghdad to reject any overtures, making contact with the Shah of Persia, planning to seize the island of Perim at the entrance to the Red Sea and dispatching reinforcements of men and money to Calcutta. If belligerence was needed to hold what Britain had in India, then belligerent she would be.

Wellesley's view was cooler, not to say cynical. He well knew that Tipu had made contact with and offered co-operation to the French through the governor of their colony, Mauritius. But he did not believe it at all practicable for them to intervene in the East. Regardless of what Napoleon did, the Governor-general meant to go to war anyway, on whatever local pretext was available. Feeding Dundas's fears, he implied in his reports home that Tipu was about to attack the British. In fact they were about to attack him. Wellesley, securing his flank by an alliance with Hyderabad, launched a ferocious assault on Mysore in the spring of 1799. Within three months the Scottish general, David Baird, stormed Seringapatam, and on taking possession of its citadel came across the sultan's corpse.

The elimination of this most formidable foe only whetted what the Governor-general called his own 'voracious appetite for lands and fortresses'. Over the next few years he annexed several minor states. He brought the entire Carnatic under the Company's administration. He forced Oudh to cede territory. He reduced the Peshwa of the Marathas, after the battle of Assaye, to a puppet. For good measure, he had Ceylon proclaimed a crown colony, and drew up plans to conquer Java. Britain then entirely dominated, where she did not directly rule, the whole of India up to the northern bounds of the Deccan, and controlled the surrounding seas. It was not the French but the British ambitions that had proved resurgent. And these had been indulged to an extent not seen since the days of Robert Clive.

As for Dundas, he had apparently allowed Wellesley's aggressive instincts to run away with them both. Yet their correspondence does show him trying to exercise restraint: 'The military force must not be too much divided nor expended in hunting petty rajas among the jungles.' And while he willingly acquiesced in the crushing of Mysore, he did not give the Governor-general a free hand against the Marathas, the Carnatic or Oudh. He also put his foot down when Wellesley asked for the power to overrule his council at will, and dismissed out of hand his demand for control of the Company's appointments to India. But the most pointed advice could be blunted at a distance of 8000 miles. Dundas constantly stressed the financial pressures: 'My present creed with regard to India is that nothing new is to be attempted without weighing well every rupee it will cost.' If strapped for cash, however, the Governor-general would just seize the bullion sent out for the Company's investments and spend it on his wars.[31]

Worldwide conflict had anyway altered the context of Dundas's policies. He could justify territorial acquisition in India on the same grounds as he justified it elsewhere – 'The French have for a long time been deprived of all their colonial resources, and of all their commerce,' he boasted to Wellesley. Beyond that, the aggression solved cleanly, if brutally, some problems that had dogged even the reformed British administration. It settled for good the balance of power, at least in the West and South of the sub-continent. Britain's previous neutrality among the native princes had not in fact maintained a balance, nor in any way mitigated the prevailing Indian anarchy. France was under a standing temptation to exploit it. To such an intractable complex of problems British supremacy actually offered the simplest answer. Wellesley in effect demonstrated this, and Dundas was not disposed to quibble. As a matter of fact, the Orient turned out Britain's most successful theatre of war. Not only were the native powers subdued, but all traces of French influence were swept away and the eastward sea-lanes were secured. These certainly represented worthwhile aims, amounting to a good deal more than aggrandisement for its own sake.[32]

Yet had not Dundas also plainly compromised a policy which he had never ceased to advocate for a quarter of a century, that Britain's supremacy in the East should eschew oppression? The fact remained, however, that even when her armies overthrew native rule and substituted British administration, little change was forced on indigenous societies, which after submitting were still left to go their own way.

Dundas himself had no aims for dominion beyond imposing whatever control was necessary for prosperity and security, expecting Indians on that account to be reconciled to it. He positively opposed the transmission to them of European values. He would not let British subjects settle in India: they were to trade and leave. He rejected the establishment of a college in Calcutta to offer a Western education, for he thought 'such an assemblage of literary and philosophical men would indulge themselves in political speculation and thus degenerate into a school of Jacobinism which, in India, would be the devil.' If the British felt obliged to meddle, as in devising the Permanent Settlement for Bengal, they yet tried as best they could to respect customary law and social habits. The same attitude prevailed towards religion, the aspect of India most alien and often most repulsive to Europeans. Dundas simply ignored the schemes of Charles Grant, a born-again Christian and aspirant chairman of the Company, for evangelising the natives. Again, he laid down these principles for dealings with the native monarchy at Kandy in Ceylon:

> Our great care must be to do nothing by force or concussion of any kind, but if by conciliation and fair treaty we obtain a substantial right of interference in the Government of Candia, our great attention must be to improve the happiness of the people and prosperity of the country. The sword must be exclusively ours, and the civil government in all its branches must be substantially ours, but through the medium of its ancient native organs.

To counter any impression that Dundas may have been losing his grip in India, one need look no further than what happened after he left the Board of Control. With that firm restraining hand removed, the directors immediately rose up against Wellesley, who had always unnerved them; his cavalier seizures of their bullion were the last straw. All through the reforming legislation of the last two decades they had clung on to their formal right to initiate the recall of a Governor-general, subject to the Ministry's consent. And at last in 1805, when he was far away from his own capital besieging Delhi, they exercised it. In due course, a new Government at home complaisantly concurred. Thus Wellesley's administration ended, and with it the second great expansion of the British territories in India: not before time, since by then official credit in Calcutta was exhausted and the army unpaid.[33]

The conclusion must be that Wellesley was able to pursue his policy because Dundas gave him his head, a fact the former must have appreciated, for his papers reveal towards the latter none of the bitter contempt and impatience he often showed others. Dundas had, during his stewardship of Indian affairs, worked with a succession of Governors-general whose outlook and activity varied. His own part was not necessarily inconsistent or weak, but on the contrary sensitive to the variety. In this case, he clearly valued the energy, intelligence and originality of Wellesley, and was prepared to put up with his touchiness. From the outset he had accepted that the people on the spot were the best judges of which particular measures to take, while he could sensibly do no more than determine the general framework for them. It was not a perfect, but a political solution: and Dundas always trusted first to his political judgment. 'We must look rather to what is practically best, than to what in theory we think so ... We must legislate and regulate public affairs not on the hypothesis that the instruments of government are always to be the ablest, the purest and the best of men, but we must take mankind according to the general run of human nature, some better some worse, some able some less able,' he had somewhat wearily commented on Indian affairs.[34]

Yet on the whole his administration of them had proved brilliantly successful. His practical policies were shrewd and realistic. And he adroitly conceived the means by which they could be vigorously executed. John Bruce, or perhaps Dundas himself, had written in the *Historical View* in 1793:

> The relation subsisting between Great Britain and its Asiatic dominions is ... a new event in the history of mankind. As a political phenomenon it has been the wonder of foreigners, more particularly when they adverted to the circumstances, that the seats both of our eastern dominions, and of our trade, are distant from us at nearly half the circumference of the globe, and that we have discovered the political secret of maintaining our sovereignty, by an administration that is local, discretionary and prompt; and yet of ingrafting by it, on Asiatic institutions, degrees of the mild maxims of British government and laws.

Whatever has been said of him by the rest, imperial historians have accorded him golden opinions. The Indian scholar, Barun De, saw him as the man who decisively determined the economic, if not always the political, character of future British policy overseas. To another, he was 'the presiding genius of the new empire'.[35]

It is time, after this Indian digression, to round off the narrative of the war, and of Dundas's influence on its course. The interval of peace which was at last to come in 1801 resolved an extended stalemate. Britain remained free, behind her natural and man-made defences, of the mastery established by the French over western Europe. On the other hand, she had mastered the Orient so far as she needed, and safeguarded the maritime route thither. The one blemish in such a tidy division of global control was that the enemy straddled the overland route with the army left by Napoleon, after his escape, in occupation of Egypt. To all appearances, this isolated force could do little harm, and might perhaps have safely been allowed to moulder by the Nile. Dundas held a different view. He noted that the French had not set out merely for the sightseeing. They had taken 40,000 soldiers, together with numerous scientists, scholars and officials. As he saw it, they aimed to establish a colony on the land-bridge between East and West, posing a permanent and potentially mortal danger to the British Empire.

However cogent Dundas's chain of reasoning, he still found it hard to persuade his colleagues. Grenville had always thought commitments in Egypt 'useless and expensive'. Historians have matched this obtuseness. Yet Egypt was indeed an acid test of the maritime strategy. This had not yet provided a satisfactory answer to the question of whether Britain could really accept the rise to absolute European domination of a hostile power, trusting to naval supremacy to defend herself and her interests. With her resources too stretched to permit successful direct intervention on the Continent, she could involve herself there only by the indirect means of subsidising allies. Such payments had, however, been ineffective in helping them to withstand the enemy. Now the triumphant French enjoyed interior lines of communication to critical points on the periphery of the European land-mass and beyond.

They had already once obliged Britain to abandon the Mediterranean. With Egypt then left exposed, it was open to them to circumvent British mastery of the oceans by striking overland at the Orient. Should they permanently occupy Egypt, Dundas feared Britain would have no real means of stopping an eventual advance on India. Even if it did not come to that, the French would have the chance to bring the trade of the Orient through the Red Sea and the Mediterranean to Marseille, a much safer and cheaper route than the one round the Cape. It would then have been proved that the maritime strategy could not adequately defend Britain and her interests. The implications would have been enormous. They would have required Britain, whether she liked it or not, to intervene with her own forces in all future wars in Europe in an effort to prevent its domination by one power. She would have had to become, as during earlier times, a direct and active participant in the struggles for hegemony on the Continent. The whole of British history during the nineteenth century might have been changed.

Apart from the general argument, there were particular circumstances prompting Dundas to press for an early Egyptian expedition. Britain's exhausted allies, the Austrians, had already sued for peace, and by their intermediation she made clear to Napoleon that she was ready for it too. He responded, offering to cease his own operations on land if Britain would do the same at sea, in other words, agree to a naval armistice and abandon colonial warfare. There could be no plainer admission of how much it perturbed the French. If, however, the olive-branch was spurned, they would renew the assault on Austria, which they then seemed bound to crush.

Pitt felt the offer should be accepted. Dundas predictably dissented:

> Separate negotiation without a naval armistice is the best line we can follow for bringing the war to a safe and not disgraceful conclusion, and Providence seems to interfere to prevent our adopting any other. Entertaining this opinion, I have no uneasiness with respect to the footing on which we shall meet the enemy, except what arises from his being in possession of Egypt ... I have watched with increasing concern the unavailing efforts made by the Turks to drive him from that province, and coupling the weakness of that ally with the disasters of our other allies on the continent, and the direction of British politics during this campaign, I own I have seen with great alarm the necessary moment of negotiation draw near.

Dundas thus believed it vital to get the French out of Egypt as a preliminary to treating with them. To throw the same object into the negotiation might require the sacrifice in exchange of some captured points of strategic importance, such as the Cape or Ceylon, which he was intent on keeping.

But a war-weary Government could not easily summon up the will for this fresh trial of strength in a distant country whence no imminent threat was posed. Dundas kept doggedly at it. He wrote, for example, to Pitt in September 1800: 'I am impressed by the danger of delaying action. The importance of expelling the French from Egypt is obvious; for it is clear that Bonaparte will subordinate every object to the retention of that colony. The danger to India may not be immediate, but it must be faced.' After surveying the alternative needs of our allies, he went on: 'By our subsidies and naval help we have borne our fair share in the Coalition. Further efforts in that direction will be fruitless. We must now see to our own interests. By occupying all the posts of Egypt, we can coop up the French and force them to capitulate. Action must not be postponed for any consideration whatever.'

Still no further forward a month later, he desperately took it on himself to relieve his colleagues of any collective responsibility by declaring he would answer for the enterprise personally. On that understanding, opposition was withdrawn. Dundas then had to go again over all the same ground, and resort to the same expedient, in order to persuade an equally unwilling King. He consented with 'the greatest reluctance' and with the scarcely encouraging thought that Egypt 'must prove a burial ground ...to as great an extent as San Domingo. I am therefore not surprised that Lord Grenville and Mr Windham [Secretary at War] have dissented from the measures'. Dundas averred that he was not downhearted 'by those difficulties to which characters of less energy or less standing than your own allow themselves to yield'. This was in the course of a letter offering the command to his dear old friend and political ally of twenty years' standing, Abercromby, courageous author of such military success as Britain had enjoyed in the West and now a relation too, since the marriage a year ago of his son to Dundas's favourite daughter, Montague.[36]

The plan of attack which they worked out was an original one. For the first

time, it exploited the fact that an oceanic Empire in possession of widely distributed strongholds could surprise and disconcert an enemy with mutually reinforc-
ing attacks from different quarters. Egypt was to be taken by a pincer movement.
The larger part, under Abercromby, approached through the Mediterranean. He
landed early in 1801 and within a couple of months won a decisive victory, though
also a glorious death, at the Battle of Alexandria. The second force came from the
East, from Trincomalee, whence it was somewhat grudgingly let go by Wellesley,
who had assembled it for an expedition to the Dutch East Indies. Its arrival
persuaded the French, still hanging on in the interior of Egypt, that further
resistance was useless. That summer they surrendered and were expelled. With
them went for ever their country's hopes of dominion in India.

Meanwhile, Nelson had beaten the enemy fleets at Copenhagen. On land and
at sea, the war finally seemed to have turned again in Britain's favour. George III
rode out in person to Wimbledon to toast the Minister who had dared to stand up
to him, and been vindicated:

> I desire to drink to the health, the happiness and the prosperity of the
> inhabitants of this house, and of everybody connected with them, and
> particularly of the man who proposed and carried into execution the
> expedition to Egypt, for in my opinion when a person has been perfectly in
> the wrong, the most just and honourable thing for him to do is to acknowl-
> edge it publicly.

It may be instructive to compare Fortescue's views:

> Equally culpable with Bonaparte's proceedings in Egypt were those of Henry
> Dundas ... The more the matter is examined, the more shameful appears the
> careless neglect with which the two forces from the Mediterranean and from
> India were hurried to Egypt ... Dundas, true to his nature, ordered the troops
> upon an errand which, according to all human calculation, should have
> ended certainly in failure and possibly in disgrace ... Let not, therefore, the
> Egyptian expedition be taken as in the slightest degree atoning for his
> previous faults, for it was dictated by precisely the same ignorance, folly and
> presumption as had inspired all his previous enterprises.[37]

Enough has been written in these pages to demonstrate that Fortescue's
description of the war as run by Dundas was viciously partial and distorted. It is
perhaps the moment to give the politician the chance to state a coherent case of
his own, something which the soldier-scholar never allowed despite the abundant
materials for it. Dundas did so in a speech to the Commons in March 1801. This
was certainly, in one sense, an effort to set the record straight at a time when he
feared a parliamentary inquiry into the many setbacks and especially faults in
execution, not all caused by him, over which he had nevertheless presided. He
could not have been expected to put other than the best construction on his own
motives and actions. Anybody is free to differ, but if Dundas truly was a man of
ignorance, folly and presumption then one might expect his account in some way
to have betrayed it.[38]

The central part of the speech concerned the principles on which Britain
should wage war. Considering that she was an island, not populous enough to build
up large armies for campaigns in Europe, and that her strength depended on trade,

the primary object of attention ought to be, by what means we can most effectively increase those resources on which depends our naval superiority ... Navigation and commerce are inseparably connected, and that nation must be the most powerful maritime state which possesses the most extensive commerce ... We ought, as early as we can at the commencement of a war, to cut off the commercial resources of our enemies, as by so doing we infallibly weaken or destroy their naval resources ... Upon the possession of distant and colonial commerce the extent of our trade must in a great degree depend. It is therefore as much the duty of those entrusted with the conduct of a British war to cut off the colonial resources of the enemy, as it would be that of the general of a great army to destroy or intercept the magazines of his opponents ... Exertions of that nature ought to admit of no limitation, except what may arise from the necessary reserve of force to be kept at home for the security of the United Kingdom.

Dundas then proceeded to show that this war had in fact been conducted according to such principles, listing the acquisitions: in 1793 Tobago, St Pierre and Miquelon, Pondicherry and part of San Domingo, in addition to which the French fleet at Toulon had been destroyed; in 1794 Martinique, Guadeloupe, St Lucia, other West Indian islands and Corsica; in 1795 Malacca, Ceylon and the Cape of Good Hope; in 1796 Amboyna and Banda [in the Molucca Islands], Demerara, Essequibo and Berbice [Guiana]; in 1797 Madagascar, where the French settlement was wiped out, and Trinidad; in 1798 Minorca; in 1799 Surinam, Goree [Senegal], Curaçao and Malta.

He continued:

Our naval successes are not solely owing to the unparalleled skill and valour of our commanders, and the decided superiority of our fleets; but they are likewise in a great degree to be attributed to the measures which have been taken to annihilate the naval resources of our enemy. And what are those measures, other than the capture of their colonies, and the consequent annihilation of their navigation and commerce?

Since in every conflict, particularly with continental powers, we could not help losing markets, the seizure of the enemy's colonies might also compensate.

By our successful exertions in the course of the war, we have provided markets for the export of the produce and manufactures of Great Britain, more than a substitute for the markets of Europe ... The true way of viewing the exports of those conquered colonies is to consider them as an acquisition of additional markets, and not merely as a substitute for old ones.

He showed that, in the 1790s, exports to old and new colonies grew by £3.2 million, compared with an increase of £2.9 million in exports to the European countries still open. Though, he added, we had pursued the general strategic principles more successfully than in any previous struggle, we had suffered from our inconsistencies and from our allies' disunity. Thus we had not finally destroyed the French threat.

That was the nearest Dundas came to admitting his tactical mistakes. But in any long war such mistakes are inevitable. Indeed, the two go together: a war would only be short if one side or the other had not just a clear grasp of the strategic possibilities but also faultless means of realising them. For a variety of reasons, such means had eluded the British. The military machine had certainly had its deficiencies. But, as much as anything else, the problem had lain with Dundas's inability to win over his colleagues to his strategic view amid so many demands on the country's resources at so many points, in a worldwide conflict, where it seemed indispensable for those resources to be applied. If he himself from time to time lost sight of an absolutely clear order of priorities, he was not alone in that: he would anyway have had difficulty in imposing one when Pitt and Grenville were trying to set their own. He had, for example, simply to fall in with, and direct as best he might once it was under way, a scheme such as the expedition to Den Helder, about which he harboured deep reservations. Dundas was on that occasion, as on others, proved right in his contention, disputed by Fortescue, that Britain could not fight France on land with any expectation of winning. True, she did later embark on the successful Peninsular War, of which Dundas also disapproved once it started to move away from the seaboard. But Britain was victorious there because it was a sideshow for Napoleon, of relatively little concern as he set off on the course which would lead him to Russia and ultimate defeat.

Dundas held that the biggest strategic contribution Britain could ever make to that ultimate defeat would be not with her army but with her navy. His argument here was not unimpeachable in detail, as others than Fortescue have pointed out. The flaw lay less in its effect of diverting British soldiers from feats of arms on the Continent than in its over-estimation of France's dependence on colonial possessions and commerce. She was not a Spain or Holland, but much more self-contained and self-sufficient. The capture of her West Indian islands, for example, obviously did not cripple her navy. But the essence of Dundas's view, that command of the seas should determine British conduct of war, proved sound. It was the means by which, first, Britain successfully defended herself. Then, by keeping France's fleets bottled up in port, it frustrated any operations she might have contemplated away from the European land-mass. Finally, it allowed trade not controlled by her to flourish, to her detriment.

In combination, all this meant that at least one of France's foes could never be knocked out of the war. So resistance to her was kept alive, till the time came when a continental coalition potent enough to beat her might at last be formed. Britain on the whole prospered anyway. She emerged from the titanic struggle with Napoleon in 1815 as the one colonial power of any importance, with a mastery that had meanwhile spread from the North Atlantic to all the other seas. Since 1780 her trade had more than doubled, while her enemy's had actually declined. Without this, she would have been unable to feed her own people, or her allies with the subsidies which helped to keep them going. If those conditions had not been fulfilled, the war might well have been lost. Dundas's strategy was vital to their fulfilment.

Thus war, which determined foreign and imperial policy, conditioned domestic policy as well. It caused two big problems, of money and of manpower. Its expense was already by 1796 financially embarrassing the Government, while bouts of nerves in the City of London shook even the soundest houses. One plight especially close to Dundas's heart was that of Boyd, Benfield & Co., a merchant bank which had risen meteorically since its establishment a few years earlier by Walter Boyd, a Scots crony of his as well as the leading international financier of the age, and Paul Benfield, wealthiest of all the Arcot Squad. They had rendered vital help in raising the loans needed by Britain and her allies to carry on fighting. But now, having lost their entire business in countries subjugated by the enemy, they faced insolvency. The firm's failure might, as Pitt and Dundas were distraughtly aware, precipitate a general financial crash, with consequences that did not bear thinking about. In the normal course of events, either Parliament could have been directly requested to authorise a rescue with public funds, or else the Bank of England would have been asked to arrange the necessary accommodations. This time the Prime Minister feared, however, that any open move would only bring on the disaster he sought to avoid.

Dundas found the way out. One morning in September he summoned Charles Long, a secretary to the Treasury of legendary discretion, and launched on a detailed explanation of why it was vital to help Boyd, Benfield. He then handed over £40,000 in notes to the bemused mandarin and told him to return to his office, where he found a jittery Boyd waiting with a pile of securities to the same value. Swapping them for the money, he scuttled off back to the City to settle the most pressing claims on him in cash. It had been drawn from the Bank of England on Dundas's personal authority as Treasurer of the Navy. Though the securities were good ones, and the advance was shortly repaid, that did not alter the highly irregular nature of the deal. The accounts neither of the Government nor of Boyd, Benfield revealed anything about it. Since the firm nevertheless went bankrupt a year later, the facts were not to emerge till parliamentary investigation into Dundas's management of public expenditure in 1805. Still, it must be recorded that the Commons absolved him, passing a motion

> that the measure of advancing £40,000 to Messrs Boyd & Co upon unquestionable securities which have been regularly discharged was adopted for the purpose of averting consequences which might have proved highly injurious to the financial and commercial interests of the country; and although not conformable to law appeared at the time to be called for by the peculiar exigencies of public affairs.[39]

If an immediate crash had been averted, the crisis rumbled on, and was bound to do so as long as the war continued. When in 1797 the French cut short the preliminaries for a peace, Dundas said 'it was obvious that their plan could be nothing else than to ruin this country by a procrastinated contest which in the end must prevail against us through the medium of public credit hurt by immense loans.'[40] He and Pitt were now caught in a vicious circle – the less money they had, the less chance there was of victory, and the less chance there was of victory, the less likely they were to get money. That was why, when France went on to proclaim total mobilisation and girded herself for an attempt to invade Britain, they poured most of their remaining military resources not into defence but into what has been regarded as a pointless new expedition to the West Indies. It was a desperate attempt to forestall the difficulties by raising the stakes, to buy a strong negotiating hand with a financially reckless bid for victories before the money ran out. And since it achieved nothing much, it did indeed all but exhaust the Government's credit. When the bills came in, something had to give.

What gave was the gold standard. Confidence in a domestic monetary system sophisticated for its time rested on the undertaking by the Bank of England to pay the precious metal against its notes to the bearer on demand. The mere thought of this guarantee usually sufficed in any crisis to calm the agitated. It did not suffice, however, when in March the French force landed on the Welsh coast, for all anyone knew, as the van of a full-scale invasion. Wild financial panic ensued, with a frantic run on the banks. If the authorities had honoured their normal obliga-tions, they would soon have had no gold left. The Government therefore issued an order in council forbidding the Bank to make further payments in specie, an order that remained in force till 1821.

The tremors were felt far away in Edinburgh as well, and even in the surround-ing countryside, whence people came flooding into the city's counting-houses to get rid of their notes. The secretary to the Bank of Scotland at once urged his directors to stop redeeming this paper, but they were too overwrought to act. He therefore sent post-haste to Dundas begging him to force their hands: or else to provide the £3 million that would be needed to meet all prospective claims. Knowing, of course, what was about to happen in London, Dundas complied. In a communication to the Committee of Scottish Bankers he made clear that 'there was no choice left but to follow the example of the Bank of England, and suspend further payments in specie,' as Sir William Forbes noted it. He reported back that 'the conduct of the banks of Edinburgh, as well as those of the country, who all did the same thing, has been very generally approved of by intelligent persons. The withholding of specie, however, for small change, has occasioned a very great ferment in the minds of the lower classes.' The Scottish banks asked for their position also to be regularised by some official instrument, but Dundas did not get round to it. The suspension, though technically illegal, was never contested in the courts. That the banking system nevertheless remained sound may be gauged by a singular fact. While it was off gold, the Bank of England's notes fell to a discount, yet those of the Scottish chartered banks always circulated at par. John Fordyce reminded his patron of 'the great advantage which the country draws from having different banking houses instead of having all the business transacted by one great bank'.[41]

In Britain generally, the authorities' action at least produced the intended effect of staving off financial collapse. But during a recession which followed in 1799 and 1800, the inflationary consequences of abandoning the gold standard proved severe. Much hardship resulted; though in Scotland, for example, it was perhaps rather among people on fixed incomes, such as ministers and schoolmas-ters, than among the workers, who could exploit shortages of labour to raise their wages.

Taxes, too, rose to unheard of levels. One result was to make Scots still slower to pay them. In 1797 a parliamentary committee on finance discovered that in Scotland their collection cost three times more than in England. It was not so much a matter of evasion as of extreme inefficiency, or at any rate of reluctance to disgorge their balances, on the part of the collectors. They were found to owe more than £190,000 to the Exchequer, £100,000 of it accounted for by the estate of a Receiver-general who had died two years earlier. In total, less was being remitted than when the system had been set up in 1708. The committee demanded a 'radical cure', to no effect whatever. The Dundases continued to view their countrymen's frugality with indulgence: Robert ingeniously devised abatements and allowances for them against the new income tax. The amount they paid turned out in consequence ludicrously small. In 1806, Scots' assessed incomes totalled £1.8 million, against £36.6 million for the unfortunate English and Welsh.[42]

Though the financial system survived in 1797 only on desperate expedients, the British economy was at this point performing well enough to cope in the short term with monetary difficulties. Despite some painful turns of the trade cycle still to come, the long-term trends stimulated production, generating the high profits needed for the further industrial investment and agricultural improvement that saw the country through. Even when shortages threatened, Dundas would not abandon his liberal principles: 'A free trade will find its own level, and always ensure a proper supply. A foreigner has expressed great surprise how, without any regulations, the market of London could be supplied with provisions, and he was answered by an intelligent person, that it was because there was no regulation that the supply was so good'. When Warren Hastings sent in from his retirement a plan for controls on the distribution of food, Dundas briskly retorted: 'Whatever the wisdom of Parliament has interposed for the regulation of provisions or the supply of the market, it has tended rather to increase than diminish the evil.'[43]

Besides furnishing labour for a still growing economy, Britain had to be garrisoned. Her stretched military resources contrasted starkly with those available to France from the *levée en masse* on a population three times greater. At the outbreak of hostilities Britain had had 9000 in the army and 15,000 in the navy. These figures had meanwhile tripled or quadrupled – but there were more than 850,000 Frenchmen under arms. Could a war be sustained against such hordes? At any rate, the need for more men was acute.[44]

An unquenchable flow of ideas for finding them, above all in his homeland, came from Dundas. He put it to the chiefs that they might revive the custom of calling out their clans. He circularised the nobility with the thought that game-keepers might be given more specialised training in the use of fowling pieces, so that they could serve as sharp-shooters in case of invasion. A modern writer, not by nature a well-wisher, has ascribed to Dundas an 'inspired energy in military administration' on account of his astonishing record in raising Scots regiments. The population was one-sixth of that in England and Wales. Yet during the 1790s, out of 60 regiments of fencible foot and 46 of horse raised in Great Britain, Scotland produced respectively 37 and 14. During the wars, 50,000 Scots served in the non-regular, defensive forces.[45]

These were the answer to providing security without starving the economy of manpower, and Dundas experimented with three different types. One was the fencibles, in favour of which, he recorded, Scots had a 'particular prejudice'. They were raised by individuals such as large landowners, often from among their tenantry. Permanently embodied and ready for action, they were by the same token expensive. Another drawback was the customary limitation on their service to one area, for most were assured that they would not have to cross the border. Since the fencibles were trained, however, Dundas was eager to entice as many as he reasonably could into the regular forces. He proposed the establishment in different parts of the country of depots and bases for 'skeletons of regiments' returned from service abroad: 'In order to fill up these skeletons a portion of each of the fencible infantry corps should be induced to enlist in them ... Although many of the privates would be very raw men, still they would be serving under a set of officers all or most of whom had been on actual service.'

A second type was the volunteers, civilian part-time soldiers, often gentlemen, who got arms from the Government but provided their own uniforms and other equipment. Dundas defined their function as 'to preserve the internal tranquillity, and to repel foreign invasion, or rather raids on the coast of Scotland'. They were cheap, but slow to mobilise and obviously restricted to a single locality. Edinburgh had such a regiment, of which the 735th member, with service dating from July 1, 1795, was Henry Dundas. It consisted, he later recalled,

> of men of property and character ... The confidence of the whole of this part of the United Kingdom has rested on the conviction that in consequence of the awe inspired by the respectability and unremitted energy of this corps, the seeds of sedition and disaffection would not be permitted to grow again in the metropolis of Scotland.

The third type was the militia. It differed from the others in not being voluntary. It was raised rather by compulsory ballot, a method naturally unpopular with those eligible. Because recruitment thus required little time or money, the militia was all the same attractive to the authorities. Hitherto Scotland, unlike England, had had none – though it will be recalled to what lengths the enlightened literati had once gone to equip the nation with this virility symbol, and how disgusted they were when a Government nervous of rebellious Scots refused to oblige.[46] By 1793 those old fears seemed stilled, and the Ministry was ready to pass a Militia Act for Scotland too. Even then, at the last minute, it got cold feet about arming too many of the workers. The only part of the planned measure to go through was the innovation of appointing Lords-lieutenant to the Scottish counties. Their powers included organising a militia, so that the scheme could be revived at any time. Still, when in 1796 Dundas tripled the size of the English one, he told his nephew: 'You might be overrun with half a dozen invasions before a Scottish Militia Bill could be agreed upon, formed, passed and put into train for execution.' The next year, perturbed at Scotland's defensive nakedness under the continuing threat of invasion, he decided he could wait no longer.

Perhaps it was just national perversity that brought more resistance to this than to any other of the Government's military measures. According to Adam Ferguson, the resort to 'compulsory statute' left 'an impression of servitude' which provoked popular ire. But it was not as if Dundas moved precipitately. He first set up an advisory committee of the Lord Advocate, the Duke of Buccleuch and Lord Adam Gordon, the Commander-in-chief. They in fact cautioned that 'a Militia Law would now be felt by the country as if the Government took advantage of the laudable spirit which has shown itself to introduce an oppressive measure, that of forcing men to be soldiers, to which the lower ranks of the people have the most rooted dislike.' Officers would besides be hard to find and great expense would be incurred: it was all rather too much trouble for a modest force. Instead, they advised, Dundas should use powers available under the Volunteer Act if he wanted more local defence. His son reported that there was even opposition during a private meeting of landowners at Dalkeith House. While he supported his father, he felt 'considerably staggered'.[47]

Dundas did not believe, however, that there existed any reservoir of willing recruits so far untapped. Some compulsion would therefore be necessary. He drew up legislation which authorised the raising, by a quota on each county, of 6000 men to serve for the duration, though not outside Scotland. A list of those eligible was to be compiled by the schoolmaster in each parish. He would have to inscribe all fit men aged between 18 and 23 except if they were married with two children; also exempt were sailors, apprentices, articled clerks, parish constables, ministers, schoolmasters, professors and men serving otherwise in the forces. At the same time, anyone chosen could get out of his service by finding a substitute or paying £10 to hire a volunteer. In practice, then, the burden was to fall on hale young fellows of the labouring class, perhaps the least inclined to accept it meekly.

Dundas got his Act through with no trouble. But when it came into force in August 1797, 'Scotland went stark mad', in the words of Sir Gilbert Elliot. Not only were those in the targeted group aggrieved at the high probability of being picked. They also feared, since no limit of time was placed on their service, that they were in effect being conscripted, most likely to be sent out of Scotland. Riots began in Berwickshire in the middle of the month and rapidly spread as far as Aberdeenshire. They bore especially hard on the hapless schoolmasters, who were often beaten up for their pains by gangs of youths. Dundas, noting simultaneous resistance in widely scattered places, blamed Jacobin agents – an absurd idea, though a few radicals certainly exploited the situation as far as they could. He fulminated from the South against the irresolution of the Scottish authorities: 'If they do not execute the law they may give up all idea of being ever able again to rear a proper internal defence for that part of the United Kingdom'; they should 'declare in the most positive terms their determination to execute the law without delay, and to bring to exemplary punishment any person who shall in any manner be accessory to the resistance to the execution of it.' As for gentlemen, 'they are much mistaken if they think their barnyards or anything else will be safer by timidity in taking care of themselves and their property.'

When the time came for the balloting at Tranent, then as now a wretched mining village in East Lothian, a military detachment, from the Cinque Ports and Pembroke Dragoons, arrived to parade itself and daunt the locals. The latter muttered sullenly over their drinks in the ale-houses then, having fortified themselves enough, sallied forth to shout, swear and throw stones at the soldiers. These, after enduring it for an hour, ran amok. Twelve people were killed including two women and a boy.[48]

In London this violent repression won the approval of the Home Secretary, the Duke of Portland. But in Edinburgh, Robert Dundas deplored a 'very unfortunate affair'. He added: 'It does not occur to the Duke of Buccleuch, Lord Adam Gordon and others now here how it is possible to coerce the whole of Scotland, if unfortunately the spirit and example already shown should carry along with it every county and district.' Pressed by alarmed local authorities, the Solicitor General, Robert Blair, had the balloting temporarily suspended in Lanarkshire and Stirlingshire. But Henry Dundas, too, at once accepted the need to defuse the situation. Though he would not be deflected from his object, he also turned to persuasion, suggesting that notices should be posted on church-doors, with an appeal to the nation's honour and an explanation of how mild the terms of engagement really were. Still, he also sent 1400 troops across the border. The prompt application of both carrot and stick brought the trouble to a speedy end, except for some messy legal proceedings. Actions were raised against the soldiers responsible for the massacre, which the Lord Advocate had to exert himself to impede. He countered with an attempt to prosecute some of the rioters, but abandoned it when juries refused to convict.

The episode has been represented as showing Dundas at his worst: bringing in by compulsion an unpopular and oppressive measure, arbitrarily denying legal redress for the results. But the necessity of it can scarcely be doubted, and was reflected in his strength of purpose. At the same time, he had kept himself well enough informed to appreciate the difficulties, which in fact he approached with some caution. He probed the limits of what public opinion would accept, rapidly adapting the execution of his policy to what he learned. He shrewdly identified the decisive moments, and was thus able to judge with niceness how and when to bring into play his own vigour and determination. It was altogether a fine example of Dundas the politician at work. By mid-September, his nephew could write that 'the threatened rebellion vanishes away rapidly.'[49]

It was tempting for Dundas (as for later historians) to posit a link between this and the previous unrest. The French, too, indulged in wishful thinking about the strength of radicalism in Scotland. They made so bold as to designate a Directory to rule the country after their conquest, headed by Thomas Muir and Norman Macleod; but the first would die in 1799, and the second was a drunken wreck. In reality little connected reluctant militiamen with revolutionaries. Next to nothing could be made out of the trouble by a new subversive group which now emerged – or rather did not emerge, for the recent repressive laws banned open association by radicals.

The United Scotsmen were somewhat unconvincingly modelled on the nationalist United Irishmen across the North Channel, with whom they maintained contact, as with a third group, the United Englishmen. Their organisation rested on an elaborate network of secret committees, lent cohesion by the fact that the membership was concentrated among weavers. Robert Dundas reported to his uncle in May 1798 that 'the system of United Scotsmen has ... been proceeding more extensively than I could have believed'. Still, for a movement said at one stage to number 10,000, they were remarkably elusive. All the Lord Advocate had to show in the way of hard facts was that, while he had been busy on investigations round Glasgow, four ringleaders at Ayr and Perth had given him the slip. The authorities did later capture, try and transport one Dundonian weaver. But the

United Scotsmen's ability to inflame the people at large was patently minimal. Even so, in official papers at least they survived in some form till about 1802.[50]

The only real domestic danger came from Ireland. It was dramatically underlined by the events of 1798, with a French landing and native uprising there. But Dundas saw in this an opportunity. He wrote to Spencer: 'If the rebellion can be speedily got under ... the thing in Ireland may be of the happiest consequences to that country'. The answer he had long proposed to her state of endemic revolt was a union with Great Britain, accompanied by catholic emancipation.[51] Though these ideas, shared by Pitt, were far from popular, it was Dundas's conviction that their time had come. They animated a speech of his to the Commons in February 1799 which was much admired and which he himself reckoned his finest parliamentary performance. Its message was that a union would benefit both Great Britain and Ireland, more so than ever in current circumstances. He conveyed it through an extensive survey of Scotland and the course of her affairs since 1707, with the implication that the Irish could in their turn expect the same advantages.

Dundas began by admitting relations had been unhappy. Enemies had exploited that, and been foiled only by repeated British interventions on the sister island. To be well-run, any nation needed the mutual confidence of governors and governed, but the 'melancholy truth' was that Ireland did not enjoy it. The right remedy was for the British Parliament to restore peace and confidence. It would do so by assuring equal privileges and freedoms to the peoples of both islands in an 'incorporating union', just like that of Scotland and England. The Protestants, secure as part of a majority in the whole United Kingdom, could then lay aside their suspicions, while Catholics could aspire to the same rights as others, knowing that one Government for all three nations would be free of Irish animosities. 'I have no hesitation in maintaining that an incorporated Parliament, partly English, partly Scotch and partly Irish is much better calculated for the management of the affairs of the British Empire than separate Parliaments in England, Scotland and Ireland.'

For proof, he turned to his own country:

> I, as one of the 45 Scotch members, can, in the face of the 513 English members, freely discuss and watch the interests of Scotland. The Parliament, thus constituted by the Union, has not deprived Scotland of any of the privileges enjoyed previously to its incorporation with England. The Union has increased the privilege of the Scotch members: for, instead of confining their deliberations to the affairs of Scotland, they are empowered to take part in discussions respecting the affairs ... of the whole British Empire.

He recalled Lord Belhaven's famous philippic against the Union in the old Scots Parliament which had painted an apocalyptic picture of the nation's destiny. Dundas showed each of his predictions to have been false. Though in 1707 the people had feared for the Kirk, 'that very national Church [is] so firmly secured in all her privileges that it is very likely she will continue to possess them unimpaired for ever.' As for the nobility, 'if the Union has had a tendency to break asunder the bands of feudal vassalage which prevailed to too great an excess in that country, wise and virtuous men will not be disposed to consider this as one of the evil consequences.' Again, 'I see the burghs, instead of being desolate, are most of them ten times improved in population, in industry and in wealth.' Confounding fears for the judiciary, 'I see no such violation or alteration of the municipal law of Scotland, which is as purely administered now as it was before the Union took place.' Belhaven had forecast that old soldiers would be beggared, yet 'I do see nothing but the most liberal rewards and provisions made for the Scottish as well as the English hero.' He had warned that crippling taxes would make drink impossibly dear, 'yet the increase of excise in Scotland, since the time of the Union, is certainly no proof that the point of prophecy has been fulfilled; or that water has become the beverage of the people of Scotland.' Instead of agricultural depression, 'now I do see the mere ploughman enjoying treble wages and treble comforts, while his master, the farmer, instead of his corn spoiling on his hands, for want of sale, reaps such profits from its immediate sale, as enable him to live almost upon an equal footing, in point of every social enjoyment, with even the heredi-tary landed gentleman, the possessor of the soil itself.' Finally, with an observation that won a lusty cheer, Dundas said 'the pretty daughters of the Scotch nobility and gentry, so far from petitioning for husbands, bear at the present moment a very high premium in the hymeneal market of the English aristocracy!'

And he concluded:

> When gentlemen pretend to think lightly of the sacrifices of Scotland compared with those of Ireland, let them recollect that Ireland has not for many centuries been free or independent of England, but that Scotland never was completely subdued or under the control of England; that Scot-land gave up, what Ireland cannot give up, an independent Parliament of King, Lords and Commons; and that Scotland gave up, what Ireland cannot give up, an independent and separate Crown. The Scots undoubtedly surrendered these honours at the time with reluctance, and evinced the greatest hostility to the Union, until experience made them acquainted with its blessings.

The speech was important as Dundas's only lengthy treatment of Anglo-Scottish relations. The unionist who claims a pride in Scotland, in her historic traditions as in her present progress, has become a character of somewhat uncon-vincing cliché in the intervening two centuries, often a figure for the anglicising toady. But we would be rash to see anything of the sort in Dundas. At the turn of the nineteenth century, the amalgam of Scottish and British patriotism was still an innovation – partly his own – and not yet compromised or jaded. True, the depth of his personal commitment, to the one or to the other, was never put to the test, for there existed in his time no real conflict between Scottishness and the Union. This was in large measure because all the national institutions which the Treaty of Union took such trouble to safeguard were still intact and firmly under indigenous control. He meant to keep them that way. Indeed, he had reclaimed lost ground by seeing that natives were appointed to some of the country's most senior offices, such as those in the Court of Exchequer and in the command of the armed forces, invariably held by Englishmen since 1707. One side of his Union was certainly a Scotland for the Scots. The other, as has often been observed in these pages, was a United Kingdom and an Empire fully opened up to them.

His consolidation of the Scottish interest might seem to sit strangely with, for example, his efforts to undermine the Indian one in the imperial capital. But a comparison of his work there for Scotland and India is once again instructive in demonstrating how his influence was essentially moderating. A political animal, he did not at all object to political interests being fashioned and articulated, not at least up to any point where they palpably deformed the body politic as a whole. At his entry into public life, the Indian interest had been too strong, the Scottish one too weak. He skilfully corrected the malfunction of both.

On his terms, the bargain counted by any standards as an excellent one for the Scots. It was surely not exorbitant of him, given the political assumptions and arrangements under which he operated, to exact by way of reward his hegemony in the domestic Scottish structures, and to keep it immune to any reform, or rather to any large reform, which he found inimical. Since no better method of running Scotland had been hit upon, what suited him anyway suited the political nation. It sat easily with the conservatism of both, the more so because that conservatism was patriotic too. Though Dundas had proved himself no immobilist, the fact of something having been guaranteed for the nation in 1707 would always be a touchstone for policy with him, to an extent unimaginable during the century-and-a-half since Governments at Westminster have taken the Union to mean anything they want it to mean. Rejecting reform in favour of preserving the Treaty meant respecting Scotland's semi-independence. When reform did eventually end the Dundas despotism, other survivals of the old Scotland could not long withstand the assaults from a centralising British state convinced of its own superiority.

The political nation seemed at any rate in accord with the sentiments Dundas set out in his speech, though a few protested that admission to the Union of an Ireland with catholic voters might pose some threat to the protestant establishment in its older members. Only in one instance did it provoke the thought that this was an occasion for looking again at the settlement of 1707. Sir John Sinclair wrote privately to Dundas expressing astonishment at a report that Ireland might be given 100 representatives in the Commons and thirty-two in the Lords. He went on: 'It must be acknowledged that [Scotland] is neither so fertile nor so populous; the revenue is also less; but if Scotland had been a separate kingdom with an independent legislature, its population and revenue must have been much greater than at present.' Here, then, was one knowledgeable public figure apparently less than impressed with the Union's benefits. Whatever the condition of Scotland, it 'cannot possibly justify so vast a difference between the representation of the two countries'. He suggested five extra Scottish seats in the Commons, three for the alternating counties, one for the universities and a separate one for Glasgow, with Paisley taking the place in its former district. But he did 'not wish to bring the subject forward, unless the claims of Scotland are well founded in point of principle, and likely to be successful.' This would no doubt have been the general view, and nothing more was heard of the matter.[52]

Ireland it was that now precipitated the crisis of Pitt's Government. He agreed with Dundas that the events of 1798 clinched the argument for union, and at once started drawing up practical proposals. In April 1800, in a masterpiece of oratory, he introduced them to the Commons. For the moment successfully resisting pressure to declare his hand on emancipation, he saw his Bill enacted in two months, against an opposition never mustering more than fifty-eight votes. But he again moved fast after it came into force on January 1, 1801. As soon as the Parliament of the new United Kingdom met three weeks later, Pitt got the leading members of his Cabinet to confirm an earlier agreement among themselves, reached without the King's knowledge, that they should proceed straight to a measure for emancipation.

Dundas was of course a party to this. All through their career together, he and his leader had taken care to buttress the consensus in favour of their many innovations by elaborate deference to the sensibilities of the ruling class. For once, they now miscalculated. Everyone could, of course, appreciate their desire to win Irish Catholics for the Union and thus, not least, for continuation of the war against France. But that still did not outweigh the general conviction that a prime function of any Government, however enlightened, was to defend religious and political establishments – and certainly not to sacrifice them to a creed which conspicuously opened Ireland to alien and subversive influences, and might do the same in the whole United Kingdom. It soon became clear that the number so minded among Pitt's usual supporters in the Commons was large, and in the Lords probably preponderant. The decisive resistance came, however, from a deeply disquieted George III. Egged on by intriguers such as Lord Chancellor Loughborough, the King declared himself bound to refuse his assent to emancipation by the oath taken at his coronation for maintenance of the protestant religion.

Things already looked black when, on January 28, Dundas went to a royal levee at St James's and found his monarch in testy mood. The King at once launched into a diatribe against emancipation: 'I shall consider every man who supports that measure as my personal enemy.' Dundas, if anything yet more deeply committed to it than his chief, would not cave in. Instead, he tried to blind the King with science, arguing that the passage of an appropriate law in both Houses of Parliament could in effect set aside the oath, for it bound him only in his executive rather than also in his legislative capacity. George III would have none of it, retorting that he was absolutely prohibited from allowing Catholics in Parliament and in any high office of state, or from endangering the protestant establishment in any other way. Finally be exploded: 'None of your damned Scotch metaphysics, Mr Dundas!' Afraid that his spluttering sovereign might go mad again if further pressed, the Minister allowed the interview to come to a rapid end.

The King remained implacable, leaving Pitt no choice but to resign – as he did, in tears, some days later. To colleagues he stressed it was a purely personal decision, which should not involve them. On the contrary, he urged them to stay and serve under the new Prime Minister, Henry Addington, promoted from Speaker of the Commons. Yet it was clearly a matter of principle rather than personality, and most soon followed him out. Dundas had said: 'If men in office hold opinions different from those of their sovereign, I do not say they ought to give their opinions up. But if the sovereign can find other servants who will undertake to conduct the government without this sacrifice, he has certainly the right to appoint and make use of them.' He handed in his seals on March 17.[53]

Though he had long claimed to covet leisure, Dundas seemed unready for it. He continued as caretaker at the Board of Control until the summer. In June he was still writing to Grenville that he had just got the latest financial accounts from India, and 'if they are complete or in sufficient order to be reduced into the shape of a budget, I am afraid I cannot be so shabby as to turn my back on it, even out of office.' Some days later he did present this budget to the Commons, but as a swansong, 'doing my last duties to India'. The period of transition anyway proved useful for Lord Castlereagh, his eventual successor at the Board, with whom he established cordial relations, cemented through correspondence and holidays together at Dunira. Their communications were so copious as to justify a conclusion that Dundas remained the *eminence grise* of Indian policy for another five years. He struck an avuncular tone, advising Castlereagh to be cautious and pragmatic: some European power or other was bound to dominate India and it happened to be us, but we should not take for granted 'the anomalous and complicated circumstances to which we are indebted for our existing pre-eminence'. In these private letters, too, he felt free to reveal his true sentiments on the Company, 'that they will ultimately fail in their competition with individuals from the continent of India', so that the monopoly was doomed.[54]

One man for whom he could do nothing was David Scott. Dundas had just unwisely prevailed on him, ill from overwork and unpopular in the Company though he was, to serve a second term as chairman. He barely outlasted his patron. The monopolists launched a furious assault on him when in the autumn he put forward a new scheme for opening the trade with India to ships built there. Dundas advised him that since his view of the subject 'happens to be directly opposite to those of the great majority of the court of directors and proprietors, you cannot, from the moment the discussion in Parliament begins, remain chairman of the East India Company.' He added, however, that Scott should not leave before, but continue his necessary labours. And when the moment came, he ought to state his reasons openly rather than hide behind the excuse of his health. In September he did resign as chairman, and some months afterwards as a director. Devastated by the loss of his wife a year later, he died 'broken and wretched' in 1805.[55]

To Dundas the Company showed itself more gracious. It offered him an annuity of £2000 a year, the same as the salary he had been drawing. He declined, on the grounds that the King had just awarded him the Privy Seal of Scotland. 'The emoluments of it I trust will be adequate, with due economy, to the moderate scale of expense compatible with the system of retirement I have long planned for the concluding years of my life.' As usual, he was prone to quite absurd miscalculations about money, and before long had to accept the Company's generosity after all. In other respects, too, his retirement was to turn out considerably more eventful than he reckoned.[56]

Notes

1. Bickley (1928), i, 81, 107; Sinclair (1831), 106; Sinclair of Ulbster Papers, SRO RH 4/49/2. f.421.
2. Laing Papers, La.II.500, Apr. 30, 1798; SRO GD 51/9/209; Chatham Papers, PRO 30/8/157/2/274.
3. Minto (1874), iii, 38; Aspinall (1962), iii, 343–4; McCahill (1978), 143–4; Clerk of Penicuik Papers SRO GD 18/3335.
4. Fortescue (1906), iv, passim, especially 73 et seqq; SRO GD 51/1/556/14; BL Add MSS 40102, f. 120; Speirs Papers, box 25, bundle 8, July 28, 1806; Richmond (1946), 175; Philips (1940), 101;
5. Petrie (1954), 45–6; Benians, Holland Rose & Newton (1940), 40, 164; Burne (1949), 260; Duffy (1987), passim; HMC, J. B. Fortescue MSS (1892), iv, 273.
6. Black (1988), 476.
7. Corbett (1913), passim.
8. ibid., i, 239.
9. SRO GD 51/1/25.
10. Auckland Papers BL Add MSS 34450, ff.166 et seqq; WLC, Mar.31, 1796; Thorne (1986), iii, 640; Baugh (1987), passim.
11. *Parl. Hist.*, xxxiii, col. 582.
12. Fortescue, iv, 72, 149, 865; Duffy, 297 et seqq.
13. Woods (1974), 108 et seqq.
14. Matheson (1933), 245; Corbett, ii, 233; Sidmouth Papers, C1799/ON 1.
15. Charles-Roux (1910), 28 et seqq; Corbett, ii, 321.
16. ibid., 239, 448; Wellesley Papers, BL Add MSS 37274, f.30; NLS MS 14839, f.1.
17. Corbett, ii, 16; iv, 186.
18. SRO GD 51/1/772/1.
19. Fortescue, iv, 433.
20. Dunfermline (1861), 144; HMC Fortescue MSS, v, 206, 215.
21. SRO GD 51/1/713.
22. HMC Fortescue, v, 323, 334; Matheson, 273; Boyle Papers, 9/49/42; WLC, Oct. 6, 1808; Mackesy (1974), 180, 318–9.
23. *Parl. Hist.*, xxxiv, col. 1242.
24. SRO GD 51/1/17/18; BL Add MSS 40102, f.75.
25. Embree (1962), 159.
26. Roberts (1929), 261; Philips (1940), 103; Tripathi (1956), 49, 92; NLS MS 1062, 7, 39; MS 1066, f.163.
27. Embree, 171; Marshall (1968), 99; Ingram (1970), 9.
28. Melville (1813), passim.
29. JRL, 692/1572; Embree, 159.
30. *Parl. Hist.*, col. 1322; SRO GD 51/3/328/1; VPL, Oct. 11, 1793, Jan. 10 & 31, 1794, July 5, 1796.
31. NLS MS 1062, 15; WLC, June 13, 1798; CPL, Wq091.92 W459; ALM, July 11, 1800; Wellesley Papers, BL Add MSS 37275, ff.204–5, 207.
32. Furber (1933), 7; Philips (1951), xx; Ingram, 206; Wellesley Papers, BL Add MSS 37274, f.312.
33. Philips, loc.cit.; Ingram, 6; NLS MS 1062, 23.
34. Ingram, 294; Butler (1973), 72, 83.
35. Wellesley Papers BL Add MSS 37275, f.186; Perera (1933), 30; Bruce (1793), 6; De (1956), 75; Benians, Holland Rose & Newton, 167.
36. SRO GD 51/1/526, 548/3, 744/19 & 33, 776/1, 777/1, 778/1 & 3; BL Add

MSS 40100, f.298; WLP I, Oct. 5, 1800; Chatham Papers PRO 30/8/157; HMC Fortescue, vi, 37; Dunfermline, 251; Hoskins (1928), 44: Mackesy (1984) 142, 159, 162.
37. Bickley, i, 233; Fortescue, iv, 865.
38. *Parl. Hist.*, xxxv, cols. 1070 et seqq.
39. BLH, 14; *Parl. Debates*, v, app.; 45 George III, cap. 78; Cope (1947), 233–8, 300, 356–7.
40. Duffy, 296; Buccleuch Papers, SRO GD 224/30/4/11/1.
41. Rait (1930), 108–12; BLH, 15.
42. SRO GD 51/5.255; NLS MS 57, ff.224–6; Ward (1954–5), 299, 306; O'Brien (1988), 5.
43. *Parl. Hist.*, xxxiii, col. 823; Warren Hastings Papers, BL Add MSS 29177, f.255.
44. *Parl. Hist.*, xxx, col. 1247.
45. Prebble (1975), 270; McCahill (1978), 20; NLS MS 3834, f.27; HMC Laing MSS (1925), ii, 646; Laing Papers, La.II.500, Mar. 7, 1798.
46. WLP I, Jan. 1804; WLC, Sept. 26, 1802; Logue (1974), 37 et seqq; J. Fergusson (1934), 230; Meikle (1912), 148; *Parl. Hist.*, xxxi, col. 89; Anon., (1795a).
47. WLP II, Dec. 29, 1792; WLC, Aug. 2, 1802; NLS MS 5, ff.101–2; MS 7, ff.154–7; Chatham Papers PRO 30/8/157/2/345; Western (1955), passim; Robertson (1975), 145; Sher (1989), 262.
48. Logue (1979), 78 et seqq; HO SRO RH 2/4/80/1 & 186; Laing Papers, La.II.500, Sept. 3, 1797.
49. Home Office Papers SRO RH 2/4/80/248 & 81/131; Logue, 108; Western , 18.
50. Meikle, 188 et seqq; Murray (1978), 212; Elliot (1982), 144–5; SRO GD 51/5/432/2.
51. Corbett, i, 357; BL Add MSS 40100, f.2114.
52. *Parl. Hist.*, xxx, cols. 345–65; NLI, 55/94.
53. Mackintosh (1835), i, 170; Bickley, i, 147; Parl. Deb., ix, 256.
54. HMC Fortescue, vi, 22, 26; *Parl. Hist.*, xxxv, col. 1456; CPL, Wq091.92 M497, passim.
55. SRO GD 51/3/109/13; Thorne, v, 107.
56. SRO GD 51/3/107.

7

'A person of great merit'

The events opening the year 1801 had, beyond the decisive break they brought in Henry Dundas's career, much wider consequences. Scotland was dumbfounded. A stable and vigorous administration, which here had endured for a quarter of a century, suddenly seemed to have vanished. Henry was followed out in May by Robert Dundas, who exchanged the post of Lord Advocate for the apolitical one of Chief Baron of Exchequer. Robert Blair, the Solicitor General, went on to the Bench. Soon David Scott quitted the chair of the East India Company too. Truly an era was ended. Henry Brougham caught the mood:

> Strange sight! hateful and perplexing omen – a Ministry without Pitt, nay, without Dundas, and an opposition leaning towards its support. Those who are old enough to remember that dark interval may recollect how the public mind in Scotland was subdued with awe, and how men awaited in trembling the uncertain event, as all living things quail during the solemn pause that precedes an earthquake ... For a while, all was uncertainty and consterna- tion, all were seen fluttering about like birds in an eclipse or a thunderstorm; no man could tell whom he might trust; nay, worse still, no man could tell of whom he might ask anything ...

'But such a crisis was,' he added,

> too sharp to last; it passed away; and then was to be seen a proof of Mr Dundas's power among his countrymen, which transcended all expectation, and almost surpassed belief, if indeed it is not rather to be viewed as an evidence of the acute foresight – the political second sight – of the Scottish nation. The trusty band in both Houses actually were found adhering to him against the existing Government; nay, he held the proxies of many Scottish peers in open opposition![1]

In London, by contrast, the change would prove more profound and lasting. With most senior colleagues joining Pitt in resignation, a very strong Ministry was broken up, to be replaced by a very weak one. Major political connections dissolved, notably that between Pitt and his cousin, Lord Grenville, who despite this intimacy with a leader of somewhat different kidney had remained at heart an old Whig oligarch. Released from that bond, he could embark on a rapprochement with Charles James Fox in the reconstruction of Whiggery.

For the time being it was the instability that struck and worried people. To Pitt, Dundas forecast bluntly, even before Henry Addington's Government was inaugurated, that it would prove unequal to the situation, and 'crumble to pieces as soon as it is formed.' While some mutual friends had stayed on in office, they did so 'with the utmost chagrin and unwillingness,' sure that the administration must 'soon be an object of ridicule'. They 'feel a degradation in the first Ministry of the country having been selected from a person of the description of Mr Addington, without the smallest pretensions to justify it, and destitute of abilities to carry it on.'[2]

While, for public consumption, he and others going out said they would sustain Addington, their contempt for him led them at once into hostile intrigues. Dundas first pushed the Duke of Portland as an alternative. Yet within weeks he drew up a plan to bring back his old chief and most of their colleagues, rejuvenated by one or two rising stars such as Lord Hawkesbury. In the only acknowledgment of recent events, Addington was to be thrown the sop of the Home Office. Dundas realised this would hardly satisfy George III that he was not simply restoring a Government he had just ousted. It should therefore also undertake, for the rest of the reign, to maintain the exclusion of Catholics from Parliament and high offices of state, though lesser disabilities might be lifted.[3]

Apparently unaware of Dundas's plots, of which this was just the start, most insiders assumed he had bid adieu to public life. Sylvester Douglas, now Lord Glenbervie, noted gossip that his real motive was not the catholic question but fear of an inquiry into his conduct of the war. His resignation would have defused demand for one, and 'having hitherto failed in obtaining the King or Pitt's consent to this he has hit on the present mode of obtaining his end … Dundas has rather encouraged the explosion, in order to get out of office on public grounds, and so make his terms, and as safe a retreat as he can.' The rumours grew so insistent that he himself felt obliged to declare to the House of Commons in March that nothing but Ireland had actuated him. Glenbervie offered sound advice: 'He should return to Dunira, because he cannot afford to live elsewhere'.[4]

If that would have been Dundas's wisest course, two things impeded it. His yearning for a rest did not prove very durable, as his cabals, not to mention his lingering at the Board of Control, testified. Then Addington, wittingly or not, fed this reluctance to disappear from the scene. Aware of his Ministry's fragility, he ostentatiously wooed Dundas for the sake of the Scots members' votes. Not only was he consulted, flattered and normally deferred to in everything concerning Scotland and India, but the administrative routine of both countries was besides entrusted to his proxy and nephew, William. Glenbervie could not believe he would rest content with this: 'God help them. Are they so inconsiderate as not to see that he cannot govern India and Scotland without remaining in Cabinet?'[5]

William, who may now be introduced as the next member of the Dundas despotism, was Robert's brother, third son of the second Lord President Arniston. Born in 1762, he had been sent to Westminster School. Alone of the family, and to his uncle's distaste, he thus acquired an English education, which he continued at Oxford and at Lincoln's Inn, before practising as a barrister. To his countrymen this would have accounted for the differences between him and Robert, who was always popular. By contrast, William struck Glenbervie as 'a tall, stiff, affected coxcomb – perhaps with more parts, but offensively important and assuming.' The sharp dissimilarity gave rise to stories that they had been begotten by different fathers, 'which my recollection of the mother's reputation might perhaps confirm.' Be that as it may, William himself did not appeal much to women – not till he was over 50 could a suitably complaisant heiress be found for him.[6]

In his career he had so far been wholly the creature of Henry, who fixed his return to Parliament for the Anstruther Burghs in 1794 and the Tain Burghs in 1796. He made himself useful, piloting through some minor Scottish Bills, becoming an expert on, indeed a stickler for, procedure and quite often acting as the Government's teller. In 1797 he was appointed to the Board of Control, in a move which Pitt told the King would be 'peculiarly flattering and gratifying to his uncle, would afford him an assistant at the India Board on whose diligence and judgment he could rely, and would bring forward a person of some parliamentary talents.' George III found in him 'the appearance of a man of sense' and made him a privy councillor in 1800. It was arranged that he should stay on at the Board after the departure of Henry, who seemed for the present to rate him above his own son, hinting broadly that William should in due course take over management of the family's electoral interests.[7]

He now lacked only a Scottish office, but there was nothing both suitable and vacant. Inside the political structure at home, the Dundases were instead represented by their relation, Charles Hope of Granton, who succeeded as Lord Advocate. He came of a collateral line to the Hopes of Hopetoun, one of whom, Lady Charlotte, he had moreover married. Since she was the sister of Lady Jane Dundas, he might fairly be counted as a fourth member of the despotism. He cut a far more dashing figure than most Scots lawyers. He unnerved Henry Cockburn, who called him 'the tongue of the [ruling] party, and in the van of all its battles ... His great defect, both as a speaker and as a public man, consisted in want of tact, and this arose from the warmth or rather the heat of his temperament ... Though possessed of superior abilities, and every virtue, he was often felt to be unsafe.' A modern writer has captured him still better:

> He was a tall, handsome lawyer, a stubborn Tory with a stentorian voice that was less effective in court or Commons than it was on St Ann's Yards, where he wore a cocked hat and crimson sash as Colonel of the Edinburgh Regiment of Gentleman Volunteers. Holiday soldiering delighted him as much as the subtleties of the law.[8]

In office he was high-handed, and conceded after stepping down that it had required a degree of temper and forbearance he found hard to command. For example, in 1803 he put an undisguisedly irregular request to the post office at Glasgow to censor the letters of some Irish residents: 'But I make it in my official capacity as His Majesty's Advocate, and on my own responsibility, and I have already acquainted Lord Pelham [the Home Secretary] with this step.' He also told Pelham that he had ordered interrogations of suspect Irishmen landing in Scotland: 'Does your lordship wish that they should be sent back to Ireland in custody, or shall we deal with them as vagrants and turn them over to the navy?' In mitigation it could only be pleaded that Hope shared the authorities' general nervousness about subversion after the renewal of war with France. Nor did he seem quite certain that the Scots were true-blue:

We are here remote from the centre of public affairs, and from all those scenes which serve so powerfully to rouse the spirit of the people in England, especially in the vicinity of London. The very presence, I may say, the personal acquaintance of the King, which so great a number of the English have, gives an enthusiasm to their loyalty which cannot be felt by those who never saw their sovereign.[9]

Hope all the same asked for trouble. In the end he got it over his treatment of a farmer in Banffshire, one Morison, who sacked a worker for attending drill with the volunteers. The Lord Advocate, though unable to intervene directly, ordered the sheriff to lock Morison up if the French landed and not free him without an official warrant. This came to the ears of Samuel Whitbread, a priggish young Whig in the Commons, where he moved in June 1804 that such conduct had been oppressive, illegal and contrary to Hope's professional duties. He responded in kind with a speech which became the *locus classicus* for a statement of the Lord Advocate's powers under the system of semi-independence.

Patronising Whitbread from a very great height, he said:

> Whatever opinion he, who knows me not, may entertain of my official conduct, a charge of injustice or oppression was never before coupled with the name I bear ... They who judge of the office of Lord Advocate for Scotland by a comparison with the dry, formal office of Attorney-General in this country have indeed formed a most erroneous opinion ... I wish that I could within any reasonable compass define its duties, and then I could answer the House that though extensive, almost beyond conception, they would afford me ease and retirement, compared with the endless succession of duties which now successively pass under my review.

Before 1707, the Lord High Chancellor, Lord Justice General, Lord Privy Seal and Lord Advocate had formed the Scottish administration, but the first three offices had disappeared or lost their powers, which thus devolved on the last. All the lower grades of the public service in Scotland looked to him, so that 'it may be said that he possesses the whole of the executive government under his particular care.' Such claims might sound extravagant to English ears but, despite the Union, 'Scotland is still to all intents and purposes a separate kingdom. Its laws, its customs and its manners have undergone no change. In the application of general Acts much local explanation is required, and therefore the Lord Advocate of Scotland must frequently act on his responsibility.'[10]

This history of the Dundas despotism here arrives for the first time on ground which may truly be termed Tory. Neither Henry nor any other of his kin had ever used the name of themselves. And though Hope did not either, the tenor of his remarks on the prerogatives of authority and on the conservative character of Scotland was unmistakable. Later they were held up in horror by Whigs as exemplifying everything most evil about the *ancien régime*. But on the occasion itself one of their leaders, Lord Moira, thought Whitbread's motion (which was lost) a political mistake: 'They make war unnecessarily on a powerful connection ... Morally, they have not sufficiently examined their ground. The Lord Advocate, though somewhat intemperate, is an useful and energetic servant of the Crown.'[11]

The attacks anyway had no obviously adverse effect on the administration of Scotland by William Dundas and Charles Hope, under their patriarch's watchful eye. Now with few distractions in the way of British and imperial responsibilities, the despotism could revert to a busy programme of Scottish legislation. On the domestic front these years have been dismissed as 'an era of political immobilism'. But the mood of the moment among the governing class was perhaps better captured by what Walter Scott, certainly no friend to wanton innovation, wrote in January 1802:

> There never was a period in the history of this country apparently more favourable to the improvement of its laws than that in which we are now placed. The pressing and peremptory duty of national defence swallowed up till lately every lesser consideration and our legislators thought as little of amending our laws where they might be imperfect as a sailor would of painting his cabin during a hurricane. But as we are now I hope safely moored for some time ... there is surely no reason why a thorough repair should not take place were it only to fit us to weather the next gale.

One Scottish Act put up schoolmasters' wages for the first time since 1696. Another expanded the militia. After a year of its operation, however, Colonel Sir James St Clair Erskine, member for the Dysart Burghs, wrote in to complain that except in the North the number of balloted men who actually served was exceedingly low. The vast majority preferred to pay the £10 penalty for hire of a substitute. Of the 5600 soldiers newly raised, only 400 were principals, and in the whole militia, now numbering 10,000, less than 1000. The Government was therefore really imposing a tax to finance the normal bounty for anyone who joined the forces. It was an unfair tax, too, since the better off tended to be ineligible for service in the militia anyway. The result was to make an administrative maze of recruitment, which now in some cases cost 25 guineas a man. Dundas agreed that it might instead be better to increase the volunteer forces, or even introduce compulsory part-time military training for all youths between 18 and 21 years of age.[12]

Three other measures dealt with the Highlands. Those of the 1780s, innovative though they had been, were clearly not fulfilling the hopes reposed in them. Some new master-plan seemed necessary. The man commissioned to draw it up was Thomas Telford, the outstanding civil engineer of his time, who had been born on the Duke of Buccleuch's estates in Dumfriesshire, apprenticed as a stonemason in Edinburgh and had since made his reputation with a series of major projects in England.

The first task the Ministry gave him was to think up fresh ideas for economic development. Telford wrote two reports on this. One concerned what became known as the Caledonian Canal, up the Great Glen, linking the western Highlands to the North Sea. Completed in 1822 it was, as a piece of construction, a work of genius – but still an economic failure. The other report comprehensively detailed the region's need for roads and bridges, and was indeed the blueprint for its modern system of communications. They were built in 1810–20 at a cost of £470,000, half of it from the Government.[13]

Telford's second task was to find out why emigration continued despite official discouragement, and to suggest more effective measures. In 1802, a year when 4000 people left, Alastair Macdonald of Glengarry wrote to the Home Secretary voicing a familiar fear: 'If the Government or the legislature do not speedily interpose, the Highlands will be depopulated.' The Dundases had already put their own pundit, Henry Mackenzie, on to the problem. His account of it indicated how distant the sentiments in their circle lay from the brutal commercialism now commencing its Highland reign. He recalled that the earlier phase of emigration had followed from destruction of the clans, and of the historic social system. Its place was filled by an impersonal cash nexus. Worse, the population had increased beyond the capacity of the country to feed it.

Now an underlying discontent was being aggravated, by agents encouraging emigration for profit, by fear of the Militia Act and by the introduction of sheep. Some 'general political effects', Mackenzie continued, could be expected from this situation:

> It tends evidently to dissolve all connection between the great landed proprietors and the body of the people, it turns the domains of the latter into a mere chattel, productive only of so much money to the proprietor without influence or attachment even from the few inhabitants who occupy them. It may thus be considered as tending to increase the propensity to a mere trading and manufacturing community.[14]

Telford then reported independently that emigration could be controlled, at least to the extent of preventing net depopulation. Some administrative restrictions had been in force since 1801. Hope bolstered them with legislation two years later. The declared purpose of his Act was to end hardship on voyages across the Atlantic by setting minimum standards of equipment and victualling for the ships. But, in his words, it was intended

> to prevent the effects of that pernicious spirit of discontent against their own country, and rage for emigrating to America, which had been raised among the people ... by the agents of Lord Selkirk and others, aided, no doubt, in some few cases, by the impolitic conduct of the landholders, in attempting changes and improvements too rapidly.

The measure pushed up the cost of a passage and by that alone emigration was stanched.[15]

The double aspect of this markedly interventionist policy – what I shall venture to call the Tory approach to Highland improvement – was still being recommended in official papers two decades later. As a matter of fact, however, it did not work. In expecting the same spectacular success from application to the Highlands of methods used earlier for economic development in the Lowlands, it hopelessly underestimated the problems of soil, terrain and climate. Nor, since the application was not coercive, did it overcome some reluctance among Highlanders to co-operate. Above all, it was just unable to cope with their soaring population. There had always been demographic safety-valves to ease the strains in the Lowlands, through migration to the towns, through the growth of rural villages, through rising levels of employment from more extensive agriculture. Nothing of the kind relieved the Highlands. At the time of Dr Webster's census in

1755, the population of what are now known as the seven crofting counties had stood at about 250,000. When it reached its peak in the 1840s, it was over 400,000. Such congestion made it impossible to deter emigrants, especially as North America offered them unlimited land on freehold. A fundamental aim of this Tory approach proved, if well-intentioned, impracticable.

It was as much as anyone could do to provide for those who stayed behind. The Dundases had early on noted with alarm the temptation to go for radical remedies. Robert was already writing to his uncle in 1792 to deplore the spread of sheep-farming, 'a measure very unpopular in those Highland districts where sheep are not yet introduced, as it tends to remove the inhabitants of these estates from their small possessions and dwelling houses.' In fact, with their own policy now faltering, they could not stop much more drastic structural changes being imposed on a helpless people by what may be called the Liberal approach to Highland improvement – in other words, the clearances. Its Whig theoretician, Selkirk, undaunted by open disapproval from the authorities in Edinburgh, came out strongly for forced emigration in his *Observations on the Present State of the Highlands of Scotland* (1808). Its first major practitioners were the Sutherlands, soon to forsake their connection with Henry Dundas and rejoin the opposition. [16]

From his retiral in 1801 the despotism depended not so much on any programme of policies as on Dundas's relations with the Government. In his low opinion of the current one he considered, like many others, that Addington was just keeping the prime ministerial seat warm for Pitt. The great man, however, far from conspiring to return to it, sat lightsome on the back-benches. When pressed, he urged all to support the Ministry. He evidently calculated that for now he had nothing to gain by making its life impossible. But these private thoughts he kept to himself; the days were anyway gone when he would freely have confided in Dundas. Malcontents thus had to take Addington seriously.

His first business was peace. It had soon became clear, though, that Britain could not buy a settlement cheap. Conquests would have to be forfeit. Dundas, ever intransigent in dealings with France, fiercely opposed this. Only three months after leaving office, and almost with the air of one who had never done so, he addressed Addington directly:

> A rumour has repeatedly reached me of late that there was existing among His Majesty's Ministers an indifference about the Cape of Good Hope and an idea that it was not to the interests of this country. God forgive those who entertain or propagate such an opinion. Be the authority for it what it may, I will pledge myself to prove it is a most damnable error ... I am asking no secrets nor do I wish to receive any, but the mere surmise of the possibility of such a fatal step is enough to induce me to enter my solemn protest against it. [17]

Dundas was not thanked for his advice, nor encouraged to give more, and in the summer retired grumpily to Scotland. It was there in October that news reached him, by Pitt's own hand, of the terms agreed with France in the Treaty of Amiens. They included restoration of the Cape to the Dutch, together with abandonment of Malta and other stations. Still, his old leader averred, the bargain was not so bad. Dundas retorted that 'the only wise and friendly thing I can do is to impose upon myself silence … The surrender both of the Cape and Malta I confess is more than I have brought myself even to suspect. The only consolation I have is that my time of life gives me some chance to escape being a witness to the calamitous consequences which in my judgment must result from such a conclusion to the contest.'[18]

In private Dundas was anything but silent, venting his wrath to all who would listen. He scribbled furiously to the Prime Minister to accuse him of having 'irremediably damaged the security of the most important interests of the British Empire.' He let fly at greater length to Grenville, protesting that the Cape was essential to India's security, and Malta to our pre-eminence in the Mediterranean. He would never give his vote for such a peace. Yet he was averse from going into opposition, and had found contentment enough in his farm and plantations. So he might prefer to renounce politics altogether, not wanting to end his public life in open conflict with Pitt. Undecided on the right course, he tarried in the North till March 1802. Then, back at Westminster, he did after all support the Treaty, while still deploring the capitulations. This, on May 13, turned out to be his last speech to the Commons.[19]

Dundas always accommodated himself to realities and, the peace apart, did not stand on overtly bad terms with Addington. Once he had brought himself to accept that Pitt was definitely out for the present, he could treat the successor quite cordially; during the months just spent in Scotland, he gave the Prime Minister the use of his house at Wimbledon. As for political matters, they had in most respects a working partnership. On India, Dundas was anyway an invaluable counsellor. And even on the Scottish affairs which he naturally regarded as his preserve, he professed himself ready to enter into ample consultations. Here, unfortunately, Addington was not altogether content with the minor role thus allocated to him. Perhaps he expected, like earlier Prime Ministers, that the Scots would simply fall in behind him: the alternative had been the utmost confusion in their affairs, to their country's visible detriment. This expectation may have risen as the time approached for the country to go to the polls again – in fact Parliament was to be dissolved in June.[20]

But it reckoned without what Dundas had wrought in the last twenty-five years. The Scots factions had been forged under him into a much more coherent interest which could not simply be overlooked. One thing on which it insisted was that, in electoral business and the associated patronage, the English should not interfere. This would now be put to the test. Dundas's task had, of course, anyway become more delicate. Since 1784, the Government's and the Scottish manager's purposes had been identical. Now, if they were not exactly opposed, they ran at least the risk of conflict. The risk materialised when Addington, who badly needed to expand his personal following, did indeed meddle north of the border. Dundas reacted ferociously. He sensed that, out of office, he could not continue to exert the same magnetic force on his compatriots' loyalties. Moreover, there was no longer, as with the war in 1796, any great issue round which the voters could rally to him. In his and the Ministry's astonishingly successful performance then, fickle but opportune local circumstances had also played their part. But if Dundas and the magnates had been at one in martial ardour, that did not alter a jot the fact that they, not he, controlled a number of the seats that had taken him from an adequate to an overwhelming Scottish majority. This imposing facade of national unity had since come to look decidedly rickety in several parts.

In Aberdeenshire, for example. Dundas at last broke with that born curmudgeon, the Earl of Fife, who meant to back an opposition to the aged and faithful ministerialist member, James Ferguson. At the other end of the country, he quarrelled with the equally truculent Earl of Galloway, without whom he could barely hold the south-western seats. A new Duke of Hamilton, succeeding in 1799, was a Whig; his interest dominated Lanarkshire, and threatened the Linlithgow Burghs. On the change of Government, the Dukes of Argyll and Montrose had indicated that their loyalty lay with the King's Ministers rather than with Dundas.

Against these and others, he now had to jockey for electoral advantage. One awkward case was Wigtownshire, where he had so far operated a typical scheme for the alternation of interests, between a kinsman of his, Andrew McDouall, and Galloway's son, Colonel William Stewart. The latter had been returned in 1796, but the Earl now wished to renege on the agreement and put him in for a second consecutive term. Both sides appealed for support from Addington. He consulted Dundas, who treated this courtesy as an affront. The reply might have been addressed to an especially obtuse schoolboy:

> It would take a volume to explain to you all the particulars respecting the county of Wigtown necessary for you to know before you could answer the colonel's letter … It is not the characteristic of a gallant soldier to take you by surprise, but it is perfectly worthy the intriguing trickiness of the Earl of Galloway. He has already tried it upon me, but in vain. In short, it is impossible to decide upon any particular election in Scotland without at the same time taking under consideration the other political interests with which it is complicated. This is particularly the case with regard to the south part in which the county of Wigtown is situated.[21]

Similar difficulties ramified. In Fife the sitting member was Sir William Erskine, selected in 1796 as a compromise between the interests of Wemyss and Dundas. The latter, Erskine suspected, meant now to supplant him with one of its own, John Hope. To forestall this move he declared his adherence to Addington. In Stirlingshire the incumbent, Sir George Elphinstone. commander of the fleet which had conveyed the Egyptian expedition, was about to be rewarded with the title of Lord Keith. Dundas thought it fitting to replace him by a brother of the dead hero of Alexandria, Sir Robert Abercromby, who was having to vacate Clackmannanshire because it did not return this time. But Montrose, whose local interest was paramount, had a different idea: he fixed on Sir George's nephew, Charles. The duke being also a member of the Government, he was in a position to get his way. Addington wrote a stiff letter to Dundas asserting his preferences in both constituencies. The retort was unyielding, and without the slightest degree of respect to a Prime Minister: 'Nothing, I am bold to assert, but the grossest misrepresentation could have induced you to write such a letter. In the case of Fife, the misrepresentation is so perfectly atrocious as to be perfectly ridiculous. If, under these circumstances, you choose to proceed in the line of conduct your letter points at, the consequences must rest with you, not with me.'[22]

But the imminence of the election concentrated their minds. During the visit to London, Addington invited Dundas to call – though he was not disarmed enough, even as they buttered each other up, to give anything away. He reported to his son:

> After the explanations I secured from Mr Addington both as to public matters, and as to any personal misunderstandings between us, I really did not feel myself at liberty at the moment to pursue any line of conduct that could be interpreted as a coldness or indifference to the support of the King's Government, more especially when Mr Pitt, contrary to my decided opinion of what is right, ... remains in the awkward and undefined state he now is.

Having thus shown himself obliging, 'I shall certainly continue to take the same charge of our Scottish affairs as I used to do'. Before he set out northwards for his electioneering he had another visit at Wimbledon from George III, who wanted to satisfy himself about the reality of the reconciliation. On being assured, he 'was so pleased with [Dundas] that he told him he must keep the government of Scotland in his hands.'[23]

With this royal seal of approval, Dundas could run a smooth enough campaign which left his position after all little changed. His strength lay, as ever, in the South-east. Dundases still monopolised the city and county of Edinburgh. The latter had been occupied by Henry's son and heir, Robert, since being vacated by the Chief Baron a year before. The other Lothian seats were held by a pair of his many brothers-in-law, the East by Charles Hope of Waughton (not to be confused with the Lord Advocate), the West by Alexander Hope of Craighall. But beyond this innermost circle some setbacks occurred. In Fife, Dundas backed down, leaving Erskine to be returned unopposed. In Stirlingshire, he ran Abercromby against Elphinstone and lost. Here, then, the Government clearly beat him. It picked up an extra supporter in the Haddington Burghs, where his arrangement had juggled the interests of Dalrymple and Lauderdale (which really meant Tory and Whig). It was the latter's turn this time but the candidate, Thomas Maitland, cocked a snook at Dundas by also winning independent endorsement from Addington. Elsewhere, the Whigs retained the Dysart Burghs, and through the alternation of Kinross-shire gained a seat.

The North-east presented fewer problems than would have been expected from the squabble with Fife. The latter's candidate went to a poll with Ferguson in Aberdeenshire and was defeated. Otherwise the dispositions dating from the pacification held. Even Sir David Carnegie in Forfarshire could hardly claim any longer to be in opposition, and had more trouble from grumbling constituents than from the Government.

In the Highlands, the Dundases' performance was more mixed. For Sutherland, their alliance with the eponymous magnates brought in William. But other interests asserted some autonomy. In Orkney and Shetland the incumbent, Robert Honyman, had become estranged. In the alternating county of Caithness, the wayward Sir John Sinclair was returned. In Inverness-shire a new member, Charles Grant, had as a director of the East India Company good relations with the manager, but was also a man of obsessive moral rectitude, priding himself accordingly on political independence.

In the West, ever precarious for Dundas, the aristocracy proved unruly. Argyll and Hamilton returned Whig kinsmen for the counties under their control. In the seats in contention between Dundas and Galloway, they clashed fiercely. For the county of Wigtown, McDouall beat Stewart; but the Earl was able to bring his son in for the burghs at a by-election the next year. In Kirkcudbrightshire, Galloway set another son on Dundas's sitting member, Patrick Heron, who won narrowly but was unseated on petition. So the honours were more or less even. In Ayrshire, William Fullarton, previously backed by Dundas despite his mild Whiggery, was another who sought to safeguard himself with support from Addington. The manager ruefully left alone a difficult and expensive constituency. Soon afterwards, however, Fullarton demanded of the Ministry a colonial appointment in reward for his defection. He was fobbed off with the far from exalted post of first commissioner for Trinidad. He accepted it on the understanding that he could remain in parliament, and was assured that indeed it did not disqualify him. Then Dundas investigated and found to his glee that it did. At the subsequent by-election, he returned Sir Hew Dalrymple Hamilton, the displaced member from East Lothian. In the Dumfries Burghs, he secured the return of Lord Advocate Hope. Otherwise he held steady.

Earlier biographers have seen these polls as distinctly loosening Dundas's grip. But surely they rather proved his underlying strength. If some of the marginal elements in his coalition now fell away, this was no more than the hazard of politics, only to be expected with him out of office. On the whole, he fought off reimposition of electoral control from London. Once the petitions, by-elections and other manoeuvres were over, he could for the rest of the Parliament count on a following of thirty-two members. Of the remainder, a mere four were loyal primarily to Addington, and just three Whigs had found a seat. No more than six could be counted, on the widest definition, as independent. Dundas did not achieve a walkover as in 1796. Yet still only a handful were systematically hostile to him. The peers, too, after heavily defeating another candidature from Lauderdale, remained fairly solidly loyal.

Dundas had said to Pitt beforehand: 'Don't let them suppose that the means by which it is in my power to bear up the King's Government in this country are of a nature to be dissolved by the breath of any Minister.' With that assertion vindicated, he could afford to affirm his amity towards Addington, reporting: 'The success has been very complete, although the democratic interest has been more alive and active than I have known for many years past'. Giving way to a little pardonable exaggeration he added that, despite the troubles, 'a more steady and attached representation never came from Scotland'.[24]

Addington was obviously impressed too, because he replied at once with the offer of a viscountcy. One might have thought this a matter entirely for rejoicing at Dunira, whither Dundas had once again withdrawn. But beneath his triumphalism he clearly still felt some unease, and the offer brought to a head a debate in his circle about how its interest was best going to be secured under any future adverse circumstances. Some months before he had told his son that while a peerage 'has been invariably the object of every other statesman as the final reward of his labours', he did not especially want one. Yet he had also to weigh up that outside Parliament he would inevitably be less of a leader and electoral manager for Scotland, and thus a loss to 'that body of personal and political friends who now look up to me as their common adviser and protector'. His son's response was cautious. He asked especially if the family had the money to support a prospective ennoblement. They decided to consult Buccleuch and Hope.

The question was evidently still unresolved when Addington's letter arrived. Dundas at first wrote back to accept the offer. But a mere hour or two afterwards he sent a second note asking for a delay, on the excuse that he wanted to ensure a smooth succession to his own parliamentary seat and had some Indian business to clear up. He went on:

> I have no personal wish whatever for a peerage. My period of life, my dispositions and especially the very limited state of my income are powerful considerations with me in wishing for complete retirement from all public concerns ... I desire distinctly to be understood as yielding to the opinions of others, who conceive that my remaining at all in public life is essentially connected with the preservation of the strong political interest which has been collected and consolidated in the course of so many years, and is thought to be of use in upholding the general interest of the Government.

The conflict between his supposed longing to leave politics and his friends' entreaties to stay would become a decidedly hackneyed theme of Dundas's during the remaining decade of his life. He now procrastinated for four months, doubtless also to see whether Addington could cope with his mounting problems – for the time being he could. So, with the family's anxieties stilled and with Hope ready to swap his provincial constituency for the capital, Dundas became on Christmas Eve, 1802, Viscount Melville and Baron Dunira. For his new arms, he chose the appropriate mottos of Essayez and Quod Potui Perfeci.[25]

The King had been barely gracious in the matter. On granting the warrant, he remarked to Addington that he 'hopes it will keep that gentleman quiet, and that he will not enter into captious opposition that does no credit to some members of the House of Lords.' Pitt showed himself still sourer, telling his confidant, George Rose:

> that he was beyond measure surprised at it; that he had not heard one syllable from him on the subject since they parted early in the summer; that he had indeed had no letter from him for some months; but what was most extraordinary, that when he last saw him, Mr Dundas had stated to him a variety of reasons why it was impossible for him to accept a peerage.

The comment must have been disingenuous, for Pitt had long known of Dundas's wish to retire and could not have doubted that ennoblement would be his proper reward.[26]

Pitt was probably irritated rather at the Ministry's resort to such expedients to shore itself up. Personally, it irked him that Addington, while still sycophantically playing his pupil, often ignored his advice. Politically, he thought it disastrous that spending on defence had been cut to the level of peacetime. This may ostensibly have followed his own principles of sound public finance, but the treaty between Britain and France could clearly provide no more than a breather while they summoned their strength for a fresh bout of fighting. By the spring of 1803 they were allowing themselves to be dragged into a dispute over the occupation of Malta from which neither apparently much wished to extricate herself, so that war seemed unavoidable. Appalled at Addington's short-sightedness, Pitt had for some time ceased to offer even informal parliamentary support to the Government, but secluded himself in the country. His followers, sure that renewed hostilities would bring him back to power at once, showed no restraint in mocking and goading the Prime Minister. In fact, Pitt did not greatly approve. He believed that any change must carry public opinion, not to speak of the King, with it. For preference, therefore, Addington would have to go of his own accord rather than be felled.

But he was the less likely to do so while people held out straws for him to grasp at. Melville's contortions were widely viewed with distaste – Sir Gilbert Elliot, now Lord Minto, said: 'He is another eel and winds about too much to be followed or much attended to.'[27] Such strictures in no way inhibited him. He went to London again early in 1803, to make his debut in the Lords and sound off once more against abandonment of the Cape. Rumours ran that he was about to replace the First Lord of the Admiralty, Lord St Vincent, an unreasonable tyrant who had made himself highly unpopular in the navy by harsh enforcement of discipline and a drive against corruption; he was also a Whig who at the outset had been against the war. Melville's flag-waving caught the current mood much better. Nothing came of it, but he clearly enjoyed the stir he caused.

Beyond that, what exactly was he after? It may be interjected that this interlude, with a weak Government inevitably fostering cynicism, did no great credit to British politics. But Melville's conduct was not worse than many others'. If his playing up to the Prime Minister sat oddly with a low opinion of the man, the Whigs for their part would gleefully bolster his majorities to settle old scores. Melville was going on two assumptions. First, he believed that Addington could not simply be thrown out, but would somehow have to be included in any new Government. Otherwise it would be wantonly weakened just when (presumably on declaration of war) it needed as much strength as possible; besides, the King would be most upset. Secondly, Melville knew well enough that he could not alone save Addington, but would come in, if at all, with Pitt – and Addington indeed was interested in Melville not for himself but as a bait for Pitt. If both assumptions were right, they could lead to a good, strong, broad administration, but one still facing a major problem: who was to head it? Pitt could surely not serve under Addington, while he would be humiliated by having to serve under Pitt.[28]

In these circumstances, Melville saw himself as the natural go-between. On his visit to London he bent the Prime Minister's ear. During April they devised a compromise which they hoped would appeal to Pitt: that in a new Government he and Addington should enjoy equality as Secretaries of State under the premiership of the latter's brother, Lord Chatham, the lethargic 'late' Lord Chatham once in charge of the War Office. At the end of the month, Melville rode down to Walmer Castle on the coast of Kent where Pitt, as Warden of the Cinque Ports, liked to sequester himself. They dined together cordially enough. But when afterwards the guest broached the subject of his visit, the host turned frigid. Refusing even to let Melville get into his stride, he made clear he would have nothing to do with the scheme. 'Really I had not the curiosity to ask what I was to be,' he later told William Wilberforce.[29] Despite the snub, Melville manfully kept talking and managed to extract a full statement of Pitt's views on the political situation.

These he wrote up the next day, had corrected by their author and sent to Addington. Pitt, the report said, did not wish to return to office and was ready, as he had been ever since 1801, to support competent and successful Ministers from the back-benches. But in foreign and financial policy, he did not consider the present Ministers competent and successful. If the country had not been faced with a crisis, he would have publicly attacked their 'fatal errors'. As things stood, he preferred to stay where he was, out of politics. Melville went on:

> I did not conceal from him the idea you mentioned of his returning to a share the Government, with a person of rank and consideration at the head of it perfectly agreeable to him, and I even specified the person you had named. But there was no room for any discussion on that point of the subject, for he stated at once, without reserve or affectation, his feelings with regard to any proposition founded on such a basis.

In the British system, 'there should be an avowed and real Minister, possessing the chief weight in the council, and the principal place in the confidence of the King. In that respect there can be no rivalry or division of power.'[30]

Rose acidly commented after this was passed to him to read: 'It is difficult to decide whether the impudence of Mr Addington or the baseness of the messenger is most to be admired.' That was unfair. On Melville's assumptions, his had been a reasonable attempt to satisfy both Addington and Pitt. In any event, the message he had taken to Walmer was clearly intended to open a negotiation: he would otherwise scarcely have bothered to compile an exhaustive report on the response. No doubt he would have avoided offending Pitt if he had been more certain of how to approach him. But he was unsighted here surely not by any baseness of his own but by the carapace of conscious inscrutability which his old leader had put on.

Pitt could anyway not have been that offended, for he allowed a personal meeting with the Prime Minister to be set up in London three weeks later. There it emerged how far Melville erred in his assumptions. If Pitt saw advantage in not discarding Addington altogether, he would tolerate no question-mark over his own authority in any Government containing them both. His conditions were indeed not modest. Lords Melville, Spencer and Grenville, together with William Windham, were to be brought back into the Cabinet. How would room be made? Why, by a 'general sweep' of Addington's supporters. Addington must himself, moreover, recommend the changes to the King, who would of course have to concur entirely. The terms were too humiliating even for him to accept. A few days later, Pitt softened a little, writing that they should be taken not as definitive demands, but as a response to approaches made to him: 'My only motive has been the desire of endeavouring to prevent any possible misunderstanding with respect to what has passed.' Melville advised Addington to write an equally conciliatory reply. But no further progress could be achieved, and he returned thwarted to Dunira.[31]

A stronger Government thus proved unattainable for the present. The declaration of war which followed certainly did not diminish the need for one. Even a year later, however, nothing had been resolved. By then, in the spring of 1804, Napoleon Bonaparte was camped with the Grande Armée at Boulogne, awaiting the chance to ferry it across the Channel. In Britain's peril, with the King intermittently mad again, Addington simply would not do. But the question of the succession was now further complicated by the prospect of a Regency under the Prince of Wales. He would naturally favour the Whig cronies who had through their years of unemployment milled around his residence at Carlton House to drink and plot with him. Yet they too accepted that in the circumstances they should not hog power. Grenville especially urged them to rise above narrow partisanship and join with Pitt in an irresistible onslaught on a now impossible Ministry.

It was typical of Addington's luck that he blundered at this juncture into a quarrel with Melville, the closest he had to a friend outside the Government, over the trivial matter of that year's list of Scottish pensions – a matter not, however, trivial to Melville himself, who had drawn it up. As it made its way through the official machine it was considerably altered, probably by William Dundas in his offhand way. When Melville received it back in this state, he exploded. Unable to get over the imputed insult, he was still spluttering in indignation about it six months later.[32] William Dundas prudently resigned from the Ministry while the going was good.

Of course, Melville anyway kept in touch with all the conspiracies in London. He had a most useful informant on the Whig side in Moira, the Commander-in-chief, Scotland, an Irish peer married to a local heiress who was cutting a popular figure in Edinburgh. He passed on through Hope some hearsay from Carlton House: that, if the King's insanity persisted, Addington was likely to try throwing in his lot with the prince. He, however, would spurn any such ploy, and certainly seek a new Prime Minister. The Whigs, supposing Pitt did take part in a broad Government with them, would prefer a neutral head, possibly Moira himself (though he demurred). Melville passed back the intelligence that Pitt was also in favour of a broad Government – if by no means sure that one could be formed – in which he would settle for the Exchequer so long as his position of effective leader was acknowledged. This correspondence proved most useful in fostering fellow feeling among previous adversaries: 'Beware of the Post Office when you and I … correspond on critical points or in critical times,' Melville cautioned Moira.[33]

In April, he sent a message urging Pitt that the moment had come for him to replace Addington, though with the curious rider that it should be accompanied by 'suspension of all political animosities, and a collection of all the talents, vigour and experience of the country in one general mass of energy and action.' Even now, Melville's generous though vain hope was that a broad Government could still find a niche for the tottering Prime Minister. For himself, he had successfully negotiated every hazard besetting his path back into office. Pitt assured him he was indispensable, and said he might have the Board of Control with the management of Scotland, a not unduly burdensome combination.[34]

So, with the prospect of jobs for them all, the country's great men concerted their opposition to the Ministry, and Melville hurried to London to be in at the kill. Dundas zealously whipped the Scottish members who, as Moira noted, obediently flocked southwards to deliver 'a thundering blow against Addington'. Only the hapless Lord Advocate hesitated. As now the sole representative of the despotism actually serving in the Government, Hope could scarcely attend Parliament for the express purpose of bringing it down. Deeply embarrassed, he just went on circuit in Scotland. He explained his conduct afterwards to Addington, apologising that 'my resignation would have thrown the public business into great confusion, and ... my retiring from office would only have left me at liberty to vote against you.'[35]

At Westminster the tension rapidly mounted. Fox put down a motion criticising the state of the country's defences. He lost by fifty-two votes, but this was such a drop from the Government's habitual majorities as to represent a moral defeat. Pitt then took up the attack, and in perhaps the bitterest speech of his career violently denounced in particular St Vincent's conduct at the Admiralty. This time Addington's majority dwindled to thirty-seven. The writing on the wall was too plain for him to ignore. He went to George III, who proved lucid enough to accept his resignation on the last day of April.

There was now no nonsense about a neutral head. Summoned at once, Pitt did, however, set about redeeming obligations to those who had joined him in a so far opportunistic alliance. He indeed wanted to govern with the best men of all parties, including both Grenville and Fox. But the King simply could not stomach the latter. Fox, with disinterested generosity, still urged his supporters to serve, but they refused. His similar plea to Grenville and friends likewise fell on deaf ears. Pitt was thus left with a narrow Government, very much a second best in his eyes. He would face not just a small minority in opposition but a host of lost friends as well as inveterate foes: a sorry contrast with his situation during his best years.

Indeed he had trouble keeping Melville, the sole figure of the first rank remaining to him. When the Cabinet was being put together, Pitt proposed him as First Lord of the Admiralty: 'The King told Mr Pitt there were two or three persons, naming them, whom he could not forgive, for voting with Mr Pitt against him' (in other words, against Addington's Ministry). One was Melville, who 'had given the King the most positive and unequivocal assurances that he would never oppose His Majesty's Government. That assurance was given at his lordship's house at Wimbledon, when the King was there at a grand review in the summer of 1802, and was repeated in most distinct terms when his lordship took leave that year to go to Scotland.' Thus did royal chickens come home to roost. The King relented, but Melville still had foes enough – St Vincent and the Whigs whispered that under him 'the Board of Admiralty and everything connected with it would be filled by Scotchmen.' [36]

He was a little hesitant himself, after confessing to his wife what they faced:

> Upon stating the circumstances to Lady Melville she was alarmed at the proposal. The house at the Admiralty was unfurnished, and a very great outlay was immediately necessary for the purpose, and for our re-establishment in many particulars. The income of the Admiralty was inadequate to one-third of its necessary annual expenditure. The prospect was speedy and certain ruin.

Pitt promised, if after a year they were out of pocket, to have the salary raised or at least any expenses reimbursed. A mere two months later, Melville said he could not wait. So £1500 was added to the £3000 he got as Lord Privy Seal of Scotland, backdated to 1801: it meant, apart from the increase, a windfall of £5000. Even then, his term as First Lord cost him by his own reckoning £7000, which he could certainly not afford.[37]

But power, not money, was what he craved, and at the Admiralty he had it again. It was extended through rewards for his entourage. William Dundas became Secretary at War, in charge of the finance and expenditure of the army, and proved himself in his turn an unfailing provider of fresh recruits. Melville's protégé and great-nephew by marriage, George Canning, became Treasurer of the Navy. The family was more or less running the war. Matters were just as cosily arranged in Scotland. Hope shortly went on to the Bench, to be replaced as Lord Advocate by Sir James Montgomery of Stanhope, son of the man who, after taking the same office thirty-eight years before, had used his patronage to give young Henry Dundas a first chance in politics. One observer wrote: 'The late arrangements have disappointed everybody miserably, except the House of Arniston and its dependencies.' Even a friend, John Ramsay of Ochtertyre, remarked: 'The Dundases seem to aim at a monopoly, which is not very wise. They are determined to make hay while the sun shines.'[38]

There were for some months to come occasional further blasts of regal disapprobation too. But George III also wrote, inimitably, to Melville of 'the pleasure he feels at seeing him again in his service and in a department where his activity and enmity to novelty must be very useful.' Nor did the appointment go unnoticed on the other side of the Channel. A British spy in France masquerading as an Irish revolutionary brought it up when granted an audience with Napoleon, who delivered himself of this sentiment: 'The First Lord of the Admiralty is a person of great merit.'[39]

Melville soon confirmed these golden opinions. The navy he found in a 'weak, enfeebled and inefficient state.' This was a matter of vital national concern. Napoleon tarried at Boulogne so as to be instantly ready, at any opportunity, to convey the Grande Armée across the Channel. To do so, he would have to command the narrow seas for just a relatively short time. The British fleet needed to show unremitting alertness and flawless organisation to counter the threat. If it no longer did so, that was largely because of its demoralisation by the previous First Lord, though nothing untoward had thus far followed.[40]

Melville set methodically but vigorously about correcting the failings. The first thing was to draw up for the ships at his disposal a rational scheme of deployment. 'Soon after I came to the head of the Admiralty', he later wrote,

> I made it my business to examine by every means in my power the state and condition of the various ships in commission, as also those likely soon to be so, and after having got all the information I was able, I made out a distribution of the whole fleet upon a very comprehensive scale, meaning as fast as circumstances would enable me to get the arrangement gradually accomplished and adhered to with as little variation as possible.

The country at large was scarcely less alarmed than in 1797, but Melville soon felt certain in his own mind that any attempt at invasion could be defeated. Against it he devised a triple shield: blockade of the enemy's posts; control of the narrow seas; and means of resistance along the coasts. Protection was even provided for Scotland too, after complaints of its inadequacy, though by the cheapskate method of arming fishing boats; their crews were dignified with the name of 'sea fencibles'. He found out that the Grande Armée could probably not put to sea except over six tides, something even the French had neglected to calculate with precision. In that case their flotilla might be broken up before it ever got properly under way. While he would not guarantee, to himself or to anybody else, that no hostile troops might be landed by surprise, he did not doubt that his navy could cut off the supplies and reinforcements they would need for a decisive victory. It occurred to him that he could demonstrate to the French once and for all the vanity of their designs by running fireships into the harbours and destroying the transports. He himself sailed across to stand off Boulogne and observe an experiment on these lines – the nearest he ever got to going abroad.[41] In his plans, he never ceased at the same time to stress the clamant need for more ships. A French invasion 'cannot be accomplished against a decided naval superiority consisting not only of a large fleet of ships of the line, but of innumerable small cruising vessels. Such was our state when I left the Government. I wish to God that there existed at present anything that had the most remote resemblance to it.' That general restoration of the navy was what he saw, beyond immediate defensive precautions, as his great task. St Vincent had carried economy to extremes. In a country weary of inflation and taxes, this would have been commendable for a prolonged peace. But after a mere temporary ceasefire it might prove disastrous, especially as Spain and Holland, the two other major naval powers, soon joined France against Britain.[42]

But the state of the shipyards, short of men, materials and money, was dire. And racketeering, despite St Vincent's obsessive attempts to stamp it out, remained rife there. The worst fiddles involved traffic in timber, which was very scarce and expensive. Contractors still ordered it and dealers supplied it for patently unnecessary purposes, so that it could then be sold on at a still higher profit. Typically, Melville at once abandoned checks on irregularities, provided he could prise open the bottlenecks in supply. Previously, even maintenance had stretched the yards' capacity – and he was especially worried by the quality of his ships, warning one admiral about to take a command: 'I am inclined to suspect that many are in a state only to be broken up.' Now enough timber miraculously appeared to repair, over the next eighteen months, two-fifths of the fleet. It was supplemented by rapidly opening up a new trade with Canada, to the benefit of Highland emigrants who could work the forests there.[43]

On Melville's taking office, the navy had afloat eighty-one ships of the line (the generic name for the bigger classes), which he thought nowhere near enough. St Vincent had ordered, on behalf of the previous Government, only five new ones from its own, the so-called King's yards, and taken delivery of none. A further five were ordered and delivered from commercial shipbuilders, known in contemporary parlance as merchants' yards.

Melville decided he had to rely on these latter. He put through them orders for ten ships of the line, together with more than fifty frigates, cruisers and other smaller vessels equally necessary for raids, patrols and transport. The trouble was that merchants' yards, operating in a market, were in current conditions much more expensive, and the navy's budget increased from £12 million to £19 million while Melville was in charge. His critics clamoured that he was abetting swindlers. He retorted: 'When I inquired into the state of those five ships of the line, so ordered to be built in the King's yards, I found that not even the keel of any one of them had been laid down. ... It would have been a dereliction of my public duty not to have looked to some other source of supply from which the navy might be kept up.' The means were again surely less important than the ends, for the number of vessels launched during Melville's term at the Admiralty was higher than in any similar period of the navy's history. By the summer of 1805, Britain boasted 105 ships of the line on active service and five others almost of the same standard. That autumn she would have 120, including twenty-six new ones.

Of these, eighty were deployed round Europe, most on the dreary and arduous duty of blockading: twenty-four rode off Brest alone. This meant that the French, Dutch and Spanish fleets, though together bigger than the royal navy, were useless because they could not get out of harbour. Britain then ruled effortlessly the rest of the world's oceans. A mere four ships controlled the Caribbean, where the French now had no squadron, while one at Halifax (Nova Scotia), two at the Cape, two at Rio de Janeiro and one off India otherwise sufficed. This situation was what Melville hoped to exploit with a restored fleet. There was, it bears repetition, no chance of challenging Napoleon on land. The trouble to which Britain had put herself with the navy thus offered the only chance of resuming an offensive war, in contrast to the purely defensive one which the previous Government had left the country equipped to fight. Now that the fears for the country's defence had been stilled, Melville declared to the Lords, the fleet should not confine its operations to blockade but go on the offensive. It could then, rather than await movements of enemy ships and trail along behind them, establish such a supremacy that it would be ready to meet them whenever they went.[44]

Dramatic events now vindicated him. In March the French had at last suc-ceeded in an attempt to break the blockade, when Admiral Pierre de Villeneuve escaped from Toulon. This was in part a feint to draw off British squadrons from the Channel, on the shores of which Napoleon's legions waited yet. But Melville already suspected that his opportunity for crossing was past, that he had given up all real hope of an invasion and would instead deploy his naval resources to some other end. The French, in the First Lord's view, would be better directing their attacks away from the British mainland, at colonies in particular. Having surveyed the options open to them in a memorandum to Sir William Cornwallis, com-mander in the Channel, Melville wrote that 'any of the objects I have mentioned would be more likely to annoy this country, in some of its essential interests, than any desperate attempt they may meditate of an attack on any part of the United Kingdom, against such a superiority at sea as we possess.' So he remained calm, and ordered his squadrons to keep station. An exception was of course made for that under Horatio Nelson, commander in the Mediterranean, who set off in pursuit of

Villeneuve. He made first for Egypt, thinking this an obvious target to the French. In fact they had gone to the West Indies, carrying moreover – one can only marvel again at Melville's intuition – a force capable of seizing all British outposts there. Nelson at length realised the mistake and, without bothering to wait for orders, hurried after them. So redoubtable was his reputation that on news of his arrival in the Caribbean the French at once turned back. By great exertion, he came up close behind them, though not fast enough to stop them slipping into Spanish ports.[45]

Here Villeneuve disposed not only of his own but also of the squadrons which Spain had kept cowering in harbour. He thus by happy chance assembled a combined force apparently more than a match for any that Britain could concentrate in those waters. With it, he was ordered to break the blockade decisively and re-establish control of the Mediterranean, which the British in chasing him had left almost unguarded. In Paris and London, everybody realised that one of the war's turning points might be at hand. Nelson, exhausted after more than two years at sea, had gone home for a rest. Pitt summoned him to say he must be ready to sail again in a few days' time: 'I am ready now,' he replied. Torn from the arms of the broken-hearted Lady Hamilton, he hastened with his fleet to Cadiz, whence Villeneuve prepared to lead out the French and Spanish ships. Nelson, after making sure they had all cleared, engaged them on October 21 off Cape Trafalgar. By inspired tactics he cut their line and in three hours captured or destroyed more than half of them. This smashing victory was to settle the naval war for the duration. Never again would Napoleon dare to challenge us at sea. That meant Britain could not be defeated, even while she and her allies were still a long way off defeating France. The great captain, canonised now by a valorous death, had been an untiring importuner at the Admiralty for ever more vessels to deploy in his equally untiring offensive actions. Melville had highly approved and done whatever he could to satisfy these demands. The efforts had gloriously paid off. He could fairly claim – a claim acknowledged on every hand – to be the man who made Nelson's triumph possible.

He was at Dunira when news of it came, sent personally by Pitt. Melville replied in exultation:

> The guardian angel of Great Britain never fails to interpose at moments the most critical, and where such interposition is least looked for ... The disasters on the Danube [inter alia, Napoleon's victory at Ulm] require some antidote more powerful than we had almost ever required at any former period, and the one which has arrived exceeds what the most sanguine wish could have almost desired ... I am aware of the kindness of your allusion to the ten months' administration of the navy when I presided and the consequences of it at the present moment.

As for the fallen hero, 'his death is enviable beyond expression ... Such a brilliant end following such a series of brilliant services places his name beyond the reach of caprice, envy or malevolence.'[46]

The last remark was doubtless pointed. The reader will have gathered that Melville was no longer at the Admiralty. The proceedings which led to his impeachment were under way, not on account of any failings as First Lord, or in any other of the higher offices he had held. In his own words, 'little did I conceive that I ever should be the object of attack as Treasurer of the Navy.'

People had noted during the political intrigues of 1803 and 1804 how anxious Melville was to secure the Admiralty. The ambition, so rumours ran, had much to do with St Vincent's poking his nose into malpractices and frauds, including some in the Treasurer's office. Pitt's stinging invective during the attack which had brought down the last Government seemed to have made something snap in its First Lord's mind. He sat down at once to write his *Memoirs of the Administration of the Board of Admiralty*. The tone of this work could only be described as demented. Written in the third person and published anonymously (though promptly withdrawn because of the libels it contained), it allowed the author to refer to himself *passim* as 'the great Chief' or 'the greatest seaman that ever existed'. Its flavour may be sampled from this description of how the fleet was saved on his coming into office: 'Upon one temper, the constitution of a single mind, and the firmness of a single wrist, depend sometimes the fate and glory of an Empire. The Earl of St Vincent demanded, and the King's Cabinet consented, to measures of vigour and decision.' After much further ranting and raving – 'The flagitious hands of the Minister have invaded and usurped the powers and privileges of parliament! ... The very sanctuary of the Constitution has been profaned and rifled by the sacrilege of the Treasury!' – he came at last to the subject of his hated successor:

> We denounce and proclaim the high crime and misdemeanour of the Viscount Melville, formerly Treasurer of the Navy, in withdrawing from the Bank of England, contrary to the law (st.25 of the King, c.31) the money issued from the Treasury for the service of the Navy; and in converting the use of it to his own profit, at the hazard of his personal solvency.[47]

Melville's Act of 1785 had certainly not cleared up the financial shambles in the navy. This was a failing on his part. Was it also the consequence of high crime and misdemeanour? Before being sacked, St Vincent had set up a commission of naval inquiry to work on that very question, among others. Such parliamentary investigations were often carried out with the main aim of scoring partisan points. The commission's chairman was Admiral Sir Charles Pole, a dull and naive creature of the Earl's, aided by Ewan Law, one of Addington's loyalists, the other three members being officials. Its political colour could not thus be mistaken. In fact it never did much more than try to put flesh on St Vincent's charges, without troubling to master the evidence or consider alternative views. The absence of objective interpretation accounted for basic weaknesses in the case at length made against Melville.

This was how the commissioners started off:

> We issued precepts to the Treasurer of the Navy, for an account of the state and deposition of the balance of public money, with which he stood charged on the 31st of December in each year from 1786 to 1802 inclusively; that we might judge of the propriety of the public money left in his hands, and see whether the balances, unappropriated to the public service at those periods, were in the Bank of England, as required by the 25th of his present Majesty, cap.31.

The most obvious reading of the Act, which converted the Treasurer's from a private to a public account, was indeed that it required him to keep all unspent money at the Bank and forbade its use for any other purpose. This had, it appeared from the admittedly chaotic accounts, not happened. During nearly every year under investigation, Melville had had standing in his name at the Bank a sum lower than the unspent budget of his department. The deficit rose from £65,000 in 1784 to £105,000 in 1785, fell to £50,000 in 1790, rose again to £75,000 by 1796, and finally disappeared by 1800. Where had the money gone?[48]

The commission spent from June 1804 to January 1805 trying to find out. Melville, it must be said, was quite unco-operative. When written questions were submitted to him, he often declined to respond for the reason, valid in law yet hardly inspiring confidence, that he was not compelled to incriminate himself. As his first published biographer put it,

> a Minister, who had clung so tenaciously to the office of Treasurer of the Navy, who had destroyed all the papers throwing any light on the case against him, as soon as the Naval Commission was appointed, and who refused to answer questions on the ground that his replies would be prejudicial to the public interest, could not complain if an ill construction was put upon his conduct.

The commissioners therefore turned elsewhere. Melville's chief subordinate, the Paymaster of the Navy, emerged as the key figure in the drama. Alexander Trotter was a fine example of that never popular character, the Scotsman on the make: even the benevolent Walter Scott called him a scoundrel and villain. His origins were not humble and he had good connections in the City of London, including a brother who was a partner in Coutts Bank. Even so, he had done exceptionally well out of what was, by any standards, a modest career in the civil service. On a fortune of £50,000 he had now retired to a fine estate, Dreghorn, at the foot of the Pentland Hills with a splendid view northwards over Edinburgh. He had thus established himself in a degree of financial security which eluded his boss.[49]

Trotter did not possess a well-ordered mind, and had conveniently forgotten or had never known many details raised in the questioning. But once he resolved his own confusions, he still came across as an unrepentant witness:

> When first called upon to account for these deficiencies, [he] said he could not precisely explain the cause of them: but afterwards acknowledged that he had been in the practice of drawing money from the bank in large sums, and lodging it in the hands of private bankers, previously to its being issued to the sub-accountants for the public service.

At length he confessed to drawing sums of £10,000 to £20,000 without specific authorisation, and placing them with Coutts. 'That practice, he states, was introduced about the year 1786 with the knowledge and approbation of the Treasurer,' because it made easier the payment of small sums especially – sailors' widows would not always know what to do with a draft on the Bank of England.

A dubious administrative short-cut began to look considerably more heinous when the commissioners went on to interrogate a partner in Coutts, Edmund Antrobus. He revealed that Trotter had five accounts: one as paymaster dealing with the Exchequer; an account in his own name where public and private monies were mixed; a second account of the same nature; a further private account containing mainly public money; and an account in trust for the estate of one Adam Jellicoe. The public money had not been left dormant in them either. It had been invested in Exchequer and Navy Bills, been lent on the security of stock and been used by Trotter in a personal sideline of discounting. He had bought large blocks of shares in the Bank of England and the East India Company. He had deposited £25,000 at four per cent with Mansfield, Ramsay & Co. in Edinburgh. On occasion, he had placed £100,000 a day in his accounts – once, in April 1795, £1 million. Over the whole period he had paid into them £6 million drawn from the Bank of England.[50]

Trotter first claimed that the resulting perquisites were understood as compensation for the 'exceeding smalless' of his salary – till reminded that a rise in 1786, following on the legislation, was specifically granted in lieu of them. So he could only insist that the public had never suffered loss or delay: 'I had every right to regard myself as banker rather than accountant to the state, and as banker I discharged my liabilities to the uttermost farthing.' Again, 'of a sum exceeding £134 million which, under the regulation of the Act directing the money to be issued to the Bank, was put under my direction … not one penny remains in my possession.'[51]

He also contended that the commissioners misread the law if they thought it prohibited the paymaster from transferring public money to a private account:

> To make every individual payment of each department of an extensive office by such drafts [on the Bank of England] could never be the intention of the Act, nor were such payments ever attempted to be so made by me or by my predecessor or successor in office; accordingly, sums were drawn by me from the Bank in gross to form funds for the satisfaction of such payments, of the amount of which I, as representing the Treasurer, was left exclusively to judge.

He had made no secret of these or other transactions, which were known to his superiors and everyone else concerned.[52]

The commissioners, in going back to Melville, ignored this challenge to the terms of their inquiry – unwisely, for it would be important. They sought only to establish that the funds, on their way from the Bank to the eventual beneficiaries, had been diverted to different purposes. Melville had conceded as much in his written testimony, though declaring himself unable to give a complete account:

> During a great part of the time I was Treasurer of the Navy, I held other very confidential situation in government, and was intimately connected with others. So situated, I did not decline giving occasional accommodation from the funds in the Treasurer's hands to other services, not connected with my official situation as Treasurer of the Navy. If I had materials to make such an account as you require I could not do it without disclosing delicate and confidential transactions of government, which my duty to the public must have restrained me from revealing.[53]

Needless to say unsatisfied with this, the commission summoned Melville personally in November to be examined under oath. At first, even on his direct responsibility for Trotter's methods of operating, he was cagey: 'If it is meant to ask whether I ever gave any direct authority to the paymaster to use the money in the manner above-mentioned, I should certainly say No: but I have no hesitation in saying that I believed and understood that he did, and never prohibited him from doing so, and I believe it was so understood by others at different times.' That hardly cleared up the point, to which the commission recurred in a later session:

'Did you authorise the paymaster, in or about the year 1786, to draw the money applicable to naval services from the Bank and lodge it in the hands of a private banker?'

'I cannot precisely fix the time. But I am certain that I did permit Mr Trotter to lodge any money drawn from the Bank in his private banker's hands during the period it was not demanded to the purposes for which it was drawn.'

'What circumstances induced you to give such permission to the paymaster?'

'An opinion in which I still adhere: that if the whole monies necessarily drawn from the Bank in pursuance of orders from the competent boards were lodged in the hands of a respectable banker, under the control of the paymaster, ... that it would add more facility to the conduct of the business of the office, in the multitude of small payments to be made, than if the money were deposited, according to the constitution of the office, in an iron chest.'

His interpretation of the Act thus coincided with Trotter's. Except for purists, most contemporaries would actually have found it hard to disagree that this practical arrangement was perfectly reasonable, even if it did not go strictly by the book. Moreover, in those times Ministers routinely employed, and let others employ, unspent public money for private purposes. Well after this furore Can-' ning, for example, did so when Foreign Secretary in Portland's Ministry, as did the Duke himself. Nobody apparently thought anything of it. The prohibition of such practices in respect of naval money alone would therefore have been anomalous. The commissioners might have moved on to a more productive line of questioning if they had tried to pin Melville down on what he knew of the money's destinations after its deposit in Coutts. They had already discovered his subordinate's transactions on the side. They had at the same time Melville's own claim that the non-naval uses of the funds were too confidential to be disclosed. They may thus have deemed it useless to pursue the matter with him, or perhaps they preferred to leave his obstruction and sarcasm to speak for themselves, to insinuate in effect that he and Trotter were referring to the same thing. But it was surely a mistake on their part to concentrate so exclusively on the intermediate ground and the merely circumstantial evidence to be gathered there, while neither making absolutely certain of their legal basis for proceeding, nor refining their discoveries into explicit, actionable allegations.[54]

The commissioners' report on Melville, the tenth they had issued, came out in March 1805. It found that his part did not end with some vague overall responsibility: 'The money issued for navy services was used to a great amount for the purposes of private emolument: and this circumstance leads us to observe that if a Treasurer of the Navy derive profit from the money issued for navy services, he becomes upon principles of equity a debtor to the public, and is accountable for such profit.'

They rejected the view that the Act of 1785 had not prohibited this: 'Our duty requires us to add that the withdrawing of public money from the Bank of England in the manner and for the purposes before related was, in our judgment, a disobedience to the law.' And though they did not accuse Melville of lining his own pockets, they concluded that he deserved censure for 'devolving his emolument' on Trotter. Altogether, 'the public money has been unnecessarily put to hazard, and that in defiance of the precautions taken against it by the legislature.'[55]

This was damning. Pitt would say: 'We can get over Austerlitz but we can never get over the tenth report.' The Government was indeed far from strong enough to ride out easily such aspersions on a senior Minister. They at once caused a split in its ranks. The most hostile to Melville was Addington who, created Viscount Sidmouth, had at the previous New Year been brought into the Cabinet in the hope that his followers would supply the extra votes needed for a secure majority in the Commons. But he remained semi-detached. Taking now the chance to settle at least one old score, he threatened to resign again should his colleagues resolve on defence of Melville. If they did not, Pitt retorted, the Ministry would anyway be destroyed. A piece of feminine gossip may cast light on his loyalty. Lady Bessborough, an intimate of Lady Hester Stanhope, wrote that the Prime Minister himself might recently have faced financial disaster, 'had not Lord Melville been able to lend a large sum entrusted to his care ... This money was repaid, but there were other large sums gained by successful speculations and appropriated to the same use.' We may in any event accept that Pitt was not the sort to leave an old companion in the lurch, a man whom he knew to be generous and careless rather than avaricious, doubtless lax in this case but surely not culpable.[56]

Regardless of personal feelings, the Prime Minister faced a major crisis. He risked his Government's collapse whatever he chose to do, whether to brazen it out or to sack Melville – though he certainly preferred the former course. Sidmouth had the sense to see this, and now sought some means of felling the First Lord without forcing Pitt's hand. He demanded that the whole matter should be submitted to the judgment of the Commons, in the form of a proposal for a parliamentary inquiry to determine the validity of the charges. Melville himself acquiesced, and the Prime Minister was glad to have some response ready when the vain and venomous Whitbread put down a motion of censure.

It was called on April 8, with Sidmouth's proposal as an amendment. The debate went on all through the night. Melville did not lack able defenders, including Canning, Castlereagh and Pitt himself – whose speech, lasting an hour, was ominously punctuated by murmurs and laughter, however. The most telling intervention came from Wilberforce. He intensely disliked Melville for having, as he believed, obstructed suppression of the slave trade: another Bill to that end had been defeated shortly before. Whatever his motives, they were clad in spotless morality, and the House sat up and listened when he warned of dire consequences if it turned a blind eye to this case. That was, one might say, the moment when in public life the exalted ethical tone of the nineteenth century was first struck. Melville had, of course, himself been at pains to curb the Old Corruption. But, too much the child of a bygone age, he would be the first victim of a new.

Wilberforce was said to have swayed forty votes. And at the division on the amendment, the Ayes and Noes stood each at 216. It was a small tally for such a dramatic, fateful debate. But many of the Government's normal supporters had left the chamber, unwilling either to follow Pitt in this or openly repudiate him. Mr Speaker Abbot sat 'white as a sheet' for ten minutes before giving his casting vote against an inquiry. Whitbread's motion was then carried without further division. The Speaker's normal rule would have been to vote in such a way as to keep the question open. Abbot explained afterwards that, the substantive motion being one of censure, on alleged irregularities violating an Act of Parliament, he could not see it in effect rejected. But he emphasised that his decision did not imply a belief in Melville's guilt. That helped little in the stress of the moment. One member noted how 'Pitt immediately put on the little cocked hat that he was in the habit of wearing when dressed for the evening, and I distinctly saw the tears trickling down his cheeks.'[57]

Melville had no choice but to resign. His chief came to see him at the Admiralty later in the morning

> overwhelmed and depressed by all that had happened. I reminded him that I was not the first person, either in ancient or modern times, who had fallen a sacrifice to the violence of party spirit, and that although I laid my account with much distress and disquietude to my family and friends, I knew myself sufficiently to be certain it could neither break my spirit nor humble my pride.

The King too, on receiving the resignation, confessed himself 'much grieved'.[58]

The whole Government rocked. Fox hoped 'Lord Melville would be only the first removal of a lost and disgraced administration.' The Grenvilles tattled about the Prime Minister: 'The first idea of his friends seems to have been that he must go out; but the difficulty of taking the step without its implicating him in all the disgraces of Lord Melville's resignation seems at present to make the step impossible.' They eagerly spread rumours of a fresh rift between the two: 'Rose and some others of Pitt's confidential friends, when talking together, do not spare Lord Melville, whom they describe (and probably truly) as having put the seal to the ruin of Pitt by the scrape he has got into ... Lord Melville, four days ago, said to a common friend of his and Pitt, "do you not think that Pitt should go out upon this"; you must not repeat this, but I know the fact.' Nor, according to Thomas Creevey, was recrimination lacking on the other side. He wrote of the Prime Minister's 'dolorous, distracted air. He betrayed Melville only to save himself, and so the Dundases think and say.' Even Napoleon took the chance to stir things up, and instructed a subordinate: 'Faites faire un petit pamphlet sur l'affaire Melville pour montrer l'immoralité de M Pitt et du gouvernement anglais.'[59]

With Melville's ministerial career indisputably over, it was unpleasant to see how vindictively Whitbread pursued him long after this main object had been gained: the enemy was not just to be defeated, but dishonoured. Returning at once to the attack, he demanded Melville's dismissal from the Privy Council. The Government resisted intense pressure on this for a month but then, at the victim's own urging, gave in. George III thought these proceedings 'unbecoming the character of Englishmen'.[60]

Yet Whitbread, in frenziedly pressing home his advantage, did not have things all his own way. When he successfully moved towards the end of April for a select committee on the tenth report, the Commons stipulated, at Pitt's suggestion, that the remit should be restricted to matters not the subject of legal proceedings. The Prime Minister hoped that at least the most sensitive questions could be removed from an overheated political arena into a cooler judicial one. Three days later the House again followed his advice in voting for a civil suit against Melville and Trotter. It would allow the Attorney-general to recover any profits they had made at public expense, in the process of which, perchance, the affair might die away. Early in May, Canning could remark: 'Opposition have overrun their game – and we shall stand after all, though we have yet an awkward day or two to weather.'[61] Indeed, Whitbread was not easily outflanked. If there had to be judicial proceedings, these too he might dramatise, not to say politicise. It could be done by impeaching Melville, and by trying to render explicit what might be read into the tenth report, that Trotter's revealed transactions and Melville's secret dealings were the same. He drew up corresponding articles of impeachment in the form of a motion called on June 11. The accused was beforehand heard in his own defence at the bar of the Commons.

Melville set out to answer the charge that he had evaded legitimate questions. He had not realised till he saw the tenth report that the commission, when examining him, knew of Trotter's accounts at Coutts. So only now was he able to respond to allegations arising from them. He had meanwhile written to the commissioners on the point of whether he had derived profit from the monies at his disposal. He rejected their assumption that he personally had supervised the public accounts in which irregularities were alleged: 'They were no accounts of mine, nor am I party to them. They contain a variety of sums issued nominally to me, which never came into my hands.' He was thus simply not in a position to confirm or deny the details of Trotter's impossibly confused mixture of public and private transactions, which indeed would never have permitted him to know if there were any profits. The report had been made without receiving his explanations. And he asked why impeachment was necessary at all when the Attorney-general had now been authorised to proceed in a civil suit.

Turning to the charges proper, he summed them up thus:

> Mr Trotter did, at various times, under pretence of naval services, and by a manifest evasion of the Act, draw from the bank, and invest in Exchequer and Navy bills, and lend upon security of stock, and employ in discounting private bills, and in the purchase of Bank and East India stock, large sums of public money for the purposes of private emolument, and in doing so he acted with my knowledge and consent, being my private agent ... Mr Trotter, so acting as my private agent, did occasionally lay out £10,000 or £20,000 in those transactions for my use and benefit.

But, he retorted,

> I never knew that Mr Trotter had drawn any money, for the purposes of private emolument, in manifest evasion of the Act. I never knew that he had invested any money in Exchequer or Navy Bills. I never knew that he had lent upon the security of stock. I never knew that he had employed any

money in the discount of private bills. I never knew that he employed any
public money in the purchase of Bank or India stock.
Besides, 'every sum advanced to me by Mr Trotter, in any shape, or on any
account, has been repaid to the uttermost farthing, and … I am indebted upon the
treasurership in question not one single mite, either to him, or to the public.'

He still did his best for Trotter too. The paymaster had, he said, commended
himself by zeal in making sure that seamen got all the money to which they were
entitled. This was why Melville had put him in charge of day-to-day financial
transactions with the Bank of England. 'I shall never refuse him the justice of
acknowledging that, under his management, the pay office of the navy was
conducted, for a period of 14 years, without one payment being a moment
delayed at the Treasurer's office, and an account of no less than £134 million has
been closed without the loss of one farthing having arisen to the public'. Accordingly, if the charges meant that he had allowed Trotter to use money privately,
there was no proof of them. If they meant only that the sums had been put into
Coutts, the relevant legislation was not violated. And these were far from the
same thing.

The object of the Act, he again stressed, was not to prohibit what he had been
doing, but to convert the Treasurer's account from a private into a public one, so
that he could close it on leaving office and avoid payments to and from it carrying
on for years. Out of it, many small sums were disbursed for which it was impractical
to use drafts on the Bank of England. Trotter had followed correct procedure in
transferring large amounts from there to Coutts and employing them as necessary,
a practice which had continued well after Melville gave up the treasurership.
He might have interpreted the Act wrongly, but that was hardly grounds for
impeachment: 'I certainly never felt it to be a clandestine or mysterious arrangement … I meant no concealment in the transaction.' If Parliament had wanted to
prohibit the practice, it could easily have done so.

So why had he been evasive in his answers to the commission? He had
responded only in general terms because he knew that the money was sometimes
used for different purposes, unaware that questions on this point were going to be
turned to his disadvantage. On realising it was necessary, he had explained at
once. The question of whether Trotter had employed the money for public or
private objects merely confused matters. And Melville maintained that he ought
not to have disclosed non-naval transactions. 'During the whole period in which
I was Treasurer of the Navy,' he went on,

> I was, at the same time, the confidential adviser of government in every-
> thing relating to the administration of the affairs of Scotland, or supposed to
> be connected with the general interests of government in that part of the
> kingdom. In that capacity, every person must readily perceive the imposs-
> ibility of being so, without having recourse to the expenditure of occasional
> sums for the purposes of government … It is impossible that those purposes
> should be detailed, without both great public and personal inconvenience.

He denied, moreover, that he held on to the treasurership after he became a
Secretary of State because he wanted the money. The record would show that he
had repeatedly tried to divest himself of various offices in order to concentrate on

the affairs of India. Only the country's needs and the King's commands had compelled him to a different course.

Finally he averred:

> My fame, not my fortune, is the object of consideration with me ... This is
> not such a conclusion as I had hoped for, and as I think I had a right to
> expect, to a long and laborious life, devoted to the service of my country. But
> I feel within myself a strength and fortitude of mind adequate to every
> suffering I have undergone, or by which I may still be harassed. My enemies
> are mistaken if they suppose that my spirits are easily to be broken down by
> any exertions in their power ... I despair not, even in my own time, to
> receive ample justice from my deluded country; this is, however, not the
> period to enter upon that theme. But I feel the consciousness of my own
> rectitude deeply implanted in my breast, and I shall descend to my grave
> with the heartfelt satisfaction that, however the shafts of severity and
> cruelty may be levelled against me at the present moment, the future
> impartial historian will be able to hand down my name in the list of those
> who have strenuously and, I hope, not ineffectually exerted, during a long
> life of public service, their unremitting endeavours to promote the welfare
> and the dearest and most essential interests of their country.[62]

Melville then withdrew, leaving the House to another long night of fraught debate. This time it had before it two separate motions. The one was for impeachment. The other, again inspired by Sidmouth, provided for a criminal prosecution. Pitt confidently expected both to be defeated, and proved right about the first when, at six o'clock in the morning, it was voted down by 272 to 195. What he had not foreseen was that the opposition, sensing an opportunity, would then go into the lobbies with Sidmouth and friends. Together they carried the second motion by 238 to 229. Abbot, knowing his House, commented that the Pittites had a standing strength of about 230, so must be beaten when three other parties combined against them: a junction of Fox, Grenville and Pitt had done for Addington; now a junction of Fox, Grenville and Addington had done for Pitt.

But one of Sidmouth's entourage thought Melville had done for himself:

> There is good reason to believe the vote of prosecution would not have been
> carried if Lord Melville had not spoken in his own defence ... The indiscre-
> tion and indeed arrogance with which he told the House of Commons that
> no human power should compel him to give any account of the sum of
> £10,000 which he had disbursed in Scotland about the year 1786 from the
> cash in the navy pay office disgusted the House so much ... It was indeed
> considered an avowal of the principle that a Minister might apply the public
> money (not secret service) at his own discretion, and afterwards positively
> refuse to account for it.[63]

Overtaken by a second disaster, the furious Prime Minister remonstrated with Sidmouth, whose importuning and threats had anyway become thoroughly tiresome to him. But not much else could be done against the turncoat: it was above all necessary to limit the damage. What concerned Pitt most at this juncture was that the relatively innocuous civil action, adeptly plucked out by him as a compromise from the distracted machinations of April, had now metamorphosed into a much more perilous criminal one. To that, he thought, (and Melville agreed) impeachment would actually be preferable, for the peers were more likely than the courts to acquit. The Prime Minister therefore essayed an audacious gamble. Three weeks later, in a thin House right at the end of the session, he slapped down a motion to reverse the previous decision and vote the impeachment after all. Melville's own son was put up to propose it, which he did in a notably brief and nervous performance. Impeachment would be tedious yet 'most befitting the situation and rank of the person to be tried, and best calculated to promote the ends of justice. It is the mode Lord Melville himself wishes for. I do not wish, unaccustomed as I am to speak in public, to trouble the House with any more observations.' Though carried, the motion aroused a storm of protest. Sidmouth resigned in outrage at such sharp practice. It was a measure of the man's essential silliness that a manoeuvre which, a short time earlier, would have ruined the Government now had no effect at all. Few, however, still bothered to conceal their partisan motives. It was said that Canning and the younger Pittites had cheerfully gone along with a stratagem which they knew would rid them of Sidmouth, more detestable in their eyes than a Whig. Even Minto, from the opposition, commented: 'The whole of this inquisition seems too much the effect of party rancour, and so venomous against Dundas personally, that I don't sympathise with it.'[64]

The immediate pressure on the Ministry then eased when Parliament rose for its long recess. Whitbread, called on after all to substantiate the articles of impeachment, set himself to that immense labour, going over the infinite complexities of the evidence yet again, though finding little new. Melville retreated to Dunira, but went down before the end of the year to idle his time away at Bath and elsewhere: poverty forbade use of the house at Wimbledon, which he had to rent to his protégé the Earl of Aberdeen. His son kept him informed from London about the investigations. Lord Hopetoun offered him £10,000 towards his legal expenses, while one R. K. Dick, of Sylhet in Bengal, wrote offering £5000 more.

The prospects were still not reassuring. Lady Bessborough probably reflected a general mood in Pitt's circle when she noted during November that though Melville

> never dreamt, I doubt not, of embezzling the public money, and his fault is on the contrary extravagance and carelessness, yet he has been so careless in borrowing it continually without any account that it will be very difficult to disprove the allegations against him. It was a most unfortunate transaction to be brought before Parliament, for there are many things which may have been necessary to carry on Government in time of difficulty which may be known and winked at, but if once brought before Parliament must be reprobated and punished.

Meanwhile, the Prime Minister struggled on through the final winter of his life, with no remedy in sight for his political weakness. He was, to be sure, gladdened by the tidings of Trafalgar. But against that Austria's humiliations at Ulm and Austerlitz heralded the collapse of the Third Coalition, formed only the previous July.[65] He and Melville last saw each other at Bath in December. Soon afterwards, Pitt's health rapidly deteriorated. He died on January 23, 1806, utterly worn out.

William Dundas recalled: 'I lived with him for the last two months almost every day, and he could with difficulty find half an hour for air and exercise, being the slave of all his colleagues who in their turns pressed so upon him and exhausted his day.' Lord Fitzharris added: 'I have ever thought that an aiding cause in Pitt's death, certainly one that tended to shorten his existence, was the result of the proceedings against his old friend and colleague Lord Melville.'

Melville had not deluded himself with hopes of a recovery. Even so, the news devastated him. Lord Wellesley observed: 'Lord Melville's affliction today is not to be described.' Aberdeen wrote on the morrow: 'Lord Melville breakfasted with me this morning on his return from Bath. He embraced me with tears and for some time could not speak.' Lady Hester Stanhope remembered that 'I could not cry for a whole month and more, until one day Lord Melville came to see me; and the sight of his eyebrows turned grey, and his changed face made me burst into tears. I felt much better after it was over.' His wife, too, recorded that 'to me in every way this misfortune has been dreadful, for Lord Melville's sufferings have been such as I never witnessed before – this loss of sleep alarming and the constant agitation of his mind such as made all medicine ineffectual.' One drastic remedy was rejected by both: 'She feels as I do a great reluctance to my beginning to take laudanum. There is no getting rid of it again.'

To sincere grief was added the fright of losing his greatest champion in his own political armageddon: 'Mr Pitt's death appeared to be a mortal blow to my cause, and left me totally in the hands of my enemies.'[66] Worse still, those enemies now took power as, euphoric euphemism, the 'Ministry of All the Talents'. Grenville's and Fox's Whigs formed its mainstay. They were joined by some independent Tories under the egregious Sidmouth. The Pittites went into opposition. There still being no majority in the Commons, an early election was bound to follow; but that story must be left till the next chapter.

The impeachment was formally presented to the Lords as its first ordinary business in the new session of Parliament, the day before Pitt's death. Melville replied that 'he was in no way guilty of all or any of the articles of impeachment, exhibited by the Commons, … which he was ready to prove on a proper opportunity being afforded him by their lordships' right honourable house.' At once, the managers of the impeachment started flexing the political muscle they had just acquired. In an effort to harden up their evidence, they introduced a Bill indemnifying potential witnesses for offences they might have committed under Melville as Treasurer of the Navy, if they would consent to testify against him.[67]

The minute picking over of his books thus made him extremely nervous. So much is obvious from correspondence with his son, extracts from which are here published for the first time. Having returned to Bath, he wrote

> I confess to you that if these papers are to be produced, I mean that which contrary to the truth contains the statement of the Iron Chest [the internal accounts of the Treasurer's office] and my being debtor to it, it would be better to stop the trial by pleading guilty. While the whole rests upon Trotter's verbal statement, there is room for many explanations from him, which would be of no avail if my name is produced to a paper confessing

myself debtor to the Iron Chest. If Trotter tells the truth he will explain that he never meant it in that view but merely as a vidimus of what in the event of my going out of office I would be obliged to repay him. I never would have allowed it to go out of my hand if it had been to bear any such construction as would now be put upon it. In fact the paper contradicts the evidence for it includes in it the very sum of £20,000 borrowed from him and for which I paid him interest. Although I know myself I never paid any attention to those accounts, and in reality never scarcely looked at them, still everything I could assert to that effect, every explanation Trotter could give, and every argument which the ingenuity of my counsel could advance would be unavailing against a plain document of that kind, on which people would plainly rest and never give themselves the trouble of thinking more upon the subject. Seeing the matter as strongly as I do and which I could enforce with many other considerations I cannot see any good to arise from putting it into the hands of my solicitor or anybody else ... Beware of pressing Trotter harder than he is disposed to, especially till the part as to himself is decided, for you may depend upon it whatever he communicates to my counsel, the confusion of his ideas will lead him to communicate to the Managers, and consequently you will lose all the benefit of any good disposition he may have.[68]

As the preliminaries to the trial dragged on, Melville sought relief of his frustration by joining battle for public opinion, so far not on his side. He kept urging his son to spread the word, perhaps from Parliament, about the true state of his affairs. He complained of the

belief that I had robbed the public of great sums of money and that I was wallowing in wealth. My accounts ... contain irresistible proof that I have all my life been poor, that it never was an object with me to be otherwise, and that I am at all times greatly in debt and was paying large sums annually in interest and annuities ... Compare that with the means I had of being otherwise, if I had ever acted upon the plan laid to my charge.

His income was £4000 a year, of which half went to service debts. He thus had at his actual disposal a mere £2000, 'and it is only by perfect seclusion at my farm at Dunira I have the prospect of living with any degree of comfort.' Except for Hopetoun's contribution to his expenses, he later added, he would have had to abandon his own cause and plead guilty. Both Robert and William Dundas appealed to the Commons to expedite the proceedings, and not pauperise a man who had done, no matter what else, essential service to the country. This pleading had some effect, for even Whitbread conceded that 'a love of money was never imputed to him by me or any man.'[69]

The trial at last opened on April 29, amid huge public excitement, in a Westminster Hall thronged by notables. Presiding was Lord Chancellor Erskine, brother of Henry Erskine, the luminary and martyr of Scots Whiggery: no friend, then, to the accused. But Melville had shrewdly engaged as his senior counsel another Whig, William Adam, ebullient, popular and confident of acquittal from the outset. In the full light of day the prosecution's case did look rather weak. Only the first of ten articles charged Melville with corruption. The rest concerned

Trotter, so far arraigned of nothing. Typically, Whitbread set out his case with a scoff – 'Scotland bowed down before this idol' – but that was his last good line. It all grew a trifle boring, amid the rehearsal of evidence heard dozens of times before, and the erection by Melville's lawyers of a maze of technicalities. On the defence put forward by his junior counsel, Thomas Plumer, a joke ran the rounds: 'It was plumber's work, hot and heavy.' The accused also carried himself better than under previous tests. One of the glittering ladies who came to see and be seen said his 'conduct is highly dignified; no man in such a predicament could be more so. He is steady and respectful to the House, actively employed with his counsel, and betraying no marks of anger or want of patience to the most severe language.' The audience thinned as a sense of anticlimax set in. On May 4, Adam said to friends outside: 'He is as clear as the sun – nothing could be plainer, and anybody must think so.'[70]

That was even before the principal witness, Trotter, had testified, which he did for the next three days. Over the months of repeated interrogations, he had entrenched himself in his position, admitting that he personally had made money, but denying that Melville knew. So long as he could effectively defend that, as he could, it was most unlikely that Melville would be convicted. In the final speeches on May 17, fifteenth day of the proceedings, Plumer had the best of it, showing that no law had been broken: and it was breaches of the law (rather than motives, corrupt or not) that were at stake. Even the Whig grandee Lord Holland, thought 'the trial was miserably conducted by the Commons. Though there were five or six lawyers among the managers, the articles were so ill drawn that it was difficult to ascertain to which act of Lord Melville each respectively referred.' Another Whig, Henry Cockburn, was blunter: 'The charges against Lord Melville were groundless, and at last reduced to insignificancy.'

The House, in its judicial capacity, now adjourned till it was to vote on June 12. Meanwhile, some points of law were referred to a panel of judges. They resolved to Melville's advantage the most basic questions, whether it had been illegal for Trotter to draw public money from the Bank of England and put it into private accounts, or to profit from the money while it lay otherwise unused. They thought not, so long as his ultimate intention had been to employ it for naval purposes. That clinched the matter. On the appointed day, Melville was acquitted of nearly all charges by comfortable majorities: only on two dealing directly with Trotter's alleged embezzlement were they small. Thus ended the last impeachment of a British Minister.[71]

Melville sent the glad tidings to his daughter Ann at Madras:

> The party spirit continued unremitting to the last moment. Five Cabinet Ministers voted on the day of decision, all of them against me, but I prevailed on every point ... I'll be obliged to stay here for a few weeks chiefly with the view of resuming the society of many friends from whom I have separated myself for these 15 months. After that I return to Scotland, where I much long to be.[72]

Scotland meanwhile rejoiced. 'The Land of Cakes has really gone crazy,' Minto said. The Chief Baron told his wife: 'It would have done your heart good to have witnessed what I have done yesterday and today, the universal joy of all persons here on your father's acquittal. I really could hardly get along the street, being stopped by every person I met.' The town council of Edinburgh, truckling to the Talents, tried in vain to discourage celebrations. As soon as the news arrived, 500 exultant supporters of Melville organised a very drunken public dinner, for which Walter Scott specially composed a ditty, one of his lesser poetic achievements:

> Come listen, brave boys, and I'll sing as I'm able
> How innocence triumphed and pride got a fall.

When the great man returned to his capital in July, Scott wrote: 'His journey too has been very flattering to his feelings – nothing but huzzaing and cheering in almost [all] the towns they had occasion to pass through.'[73]

Melville was, of course, guilty all along. He was guilty not as charged, for, in the impenetrable mass of cryptic evidence, his accusers simply did not know where to look. But he certainly was guilty of malversation, and on his own admission. The reader will recall how depressed he had been at the beginning of the year in Bath, when anxiously following the investigations through correspondence with his son. One of his letters complained of the

gross impropriety of prying into my whole private affairs, under the cover of being the managers of an impeachment for a particular object ... I have been thinking how far the examinations might not lead to a discovery of any of those secret political purposes which I have declared my determination never to disclose. But I don't think they can unless something may appear in Mr Robert Dundas's books, accounts or letters connected with the Stirling district of burghs. Probably that may not be the case, and in general I should suppose nothing could appear, for in the expenditure to any extent on those political purposes, it was mostly done through Mr Mitchelson or Mr Walter Ross, both of whom are now dead, and although a third person employed pretty extensively on one occasion is still alive, it is impossible there can be any clue to lead them to a discovery of him, and any remittances to Scotland for those purposes are so blended with the expenditure of my private affairs, I don't believe any discovery can be made from the accounts of any of my three confidential men of business whom I have at different times employed ... If you have never yet done it you may give a hint to Mr Le Blanc [one of his lawyers] not to suppose that the sums I refused to disclose any account of arose from what is properly called secret service. That may be true as to England, but in Scotland it was electioneering purposes, chiefly at the dissolution of Parliament in 1784 and occasionally at after periods.[74]

The reader will surely be struck, as the author was, by the insouciance of Melville's remarks, the absence of any hint of shame or guilt, or of any expectation that his son – beyond doubt an honest, upright man – might be shocked at what he revealed. Are these not the lineaments of a creature inured to villainy, rotten to the core? Still, we must be wary of applying here the yardsticks of our own age. The probity of modern British public life is high, if not without its ups and downs. Yet these standards did not descend to us intact from an ancient constitution. They had to be built painstakingly – today's cannot be traced back beyond the middle of the Victorian era. Melville played a part in helping the country attain them, especially through his insistence on sound and efficient administration. But he was a transitional figure. Immediately behind him stood the Old Corruption. After him came a new rectitude, to the giddiest heights of which he was too worldly to aspire. He shared some of the attributes of both. By 1806, however, he was a figure from the past. Political behaviour which in his youth had been taken for granted became before his death the object of moral outrage. Fallen politicians often say that their only crime was to have been caught. Though formally acquitted, Melville might have said the same, for the stain on his character proved indelible.

Notes

1. Brougham (1839), 231.
2. SRO GD 51/1/61, 195/1.
3. BL Add MSS 41102; Feiling (1938), 223, 339.
4. Bickley (1928), 156, 159, 162; *Parl. Hist.* xxv, col.1104.
5. Aspinall (1962), iii. 503.
6. Bickley, 124, 126.
7. Chatham Papers PRO 30/8/104/2/342; Aspinall, ii, 1621, 1623; iii, 2180.
8. Cockburn (1856), 152, 154; Prebble (1975), 452.
9. Home Office Papers SRO RH 2/4/88/237, 243 & 255; Omond (1888), 209.
10. *Parl. Debates*, ii, 1804, cols. 797–803.
11. Lenman (1981), 114.
12. Bickley, i, 290; NLS MS 1810, f.65; Grierson (1932), i, 127; HLH, bMS Eng 1327(12); WLP I, Aug.11, 1803.
13. Thorne (1986), iv, 229, *Parl. Papers* (1803–4a), 15–7; (1803–4b), iv.
14. SRO GD 51/5/52/4.
15. Home Office Papers SRO RH 2/4/87/53, 89/140; Hunter (1976). 24–5.
16. *Parl.Papers* (1827), 14–5; Home Office Papers SRO RH 2/4/64/2544; Logue (1979), 63.
17. SRO GD 51/1/556/2.
18. SRO GD 51/1/556/7.
19. SRO GD 51/1/556/9, 10, 14, 17; HMC J. B. Fortescue MSS (1892), vi, 56; Sidmouth papers, C1801/0Z 102.
20. Pellew (1847), i. 405.
21. Sidmouth Papers, C1801/0Z 103; Thorne, ii, 587–8.
22. ibid., 538, 583.
23. SRO GD 51/1/195/2; Harcourt (1860), i, 123.
24. BL Add MSS 38737, ff.12, 17.
25. SRO GD 51/1/195/2; Aspinall, iv, 65.
26. SRO GD 51/1/64/9.
27. Aspinall, loc.cit.; Harcourt, i, 516.
28. Minto (1874), iii, 266.
29. Wilberforce (1868), 262.
30. Canning Papers, bundle 31; SRO GD 51/1/63/7; Stanhope (1879), iii, 110 et seqq.
31. Harcourt, ii, 31; HMC Fortescue, vii, 151.
32. Pellew (1847), ii, 118, 122.
33. SRO RH 2/4/15/1.
34. Mahon (1852), 5, 10, 17, 22, 27, 31, 33.
35. SRO GD 51/1/78/9: Aspinall (1963–71), iv, 533; Thorne, iv, 229.

36. Harcourt, ii, 123; Aspinall, iv, 159, 215; Buccleuch Papers, SRO GD 224/30/4/25/3/1.
37. SRO GD 51/1/195/28, 212/1.
38. Romilly (1905), 23; Horn (1966), 153.
39. Aspinall, iv, 178; NLS MS 1043, f.65.
40. Londonderry (1851), viii, 44; SRO GD 51/1/979/1; WLC, June 10, 1804; LC, Oct.16, 1804.
41. Melville (1810), 3.
42. Lloyd (1950), iii, 82; Holland Rose (1911b), 511; James (1859), iii, 304.
43. Marcus (1971). ii, 246; Bumsted (1982), 191.
44. *Parl. Debates*, iv, col. 21; v, col. 81.
45. James, iv, 86; Holland Rose (1904), 101; NLS MS 7199, f.88.
46. NLS MS 14837, ff.82–92; LC, July 14, 1804; Leyland (1899), ii, xxxv, 366; Schom (1990), 169.
47. SRO GD 51/1/64/7; Aspinall, iv, 300; St Vincent (1805), ii, app. 11.
48. *Parl. Papers* (1805a), ii, 127.
49. ibid., 128.
50. Lovat-Fraser (1916), 104; Coleridge (1920), ii, 212–7; NLS MS 786, f.3.
51. Aspinall, iv, 310 et seqq; *Parl. Papers* (1805a), ii, 139.
52. ibid., 141, 148, 239.
53. ibid., 150; Coleridge, ii, 213.
54. ibid., 216; Tenth Report, ii, 210.
55. ibid., 149, 191.
56. ibid., 148, 150, 157.
57. Granville (1916), ii, 45.
58. Maxwell (1903), 34; Thorne (1986), v, 564; iii, 5; Aspinall, loc.cit.
59. ibid.; HMC Fortescue, vii, 257, 259; Maxwell, loc.cit.
60. *Parl. Debates*, iv, col. 608; Chatham papers. PRO 30/8/104/2/441; Aspinall, iv, 324.
61. ibid. 313–21; Ferguson (1968), 268.
62. *Parl. Debates*, v, cols. 249–89.
63. Aspinall, iv, 334–6; HMC Fortescue, vii, 278.
64. *Parl. Debates*, v, col. 61; Holland (1852), i, 204; Minto (1874) iii, 382.
65. Aspinall. iv. 339; BL Stowe papers 374; SRO GD 51/1/87–8; Granville (1916), ii, 136.
66. Thompson (1931), 278; Maxwell (1903), i, 33; Wellesley (1914), i, 190; Balfour (1923), i, 42, 45; Stanhope (1845), ii, 79; NLS Acc 9140, Feb.17, 1806; SRO RH 4/15/8/6.
67. *Parl. Debates*, vi, col.22.
68. NLS Acc 9140, Jan. 30, 1806.
69. ibid., Feb. 13, Mar.14, 1806; *Parl. Debates*, vi, cols 542, 550.
70. Granville, ii, 190, 193; Holland, i, 233; Cockburn (1856), 203; Farington (1923), ii, 236; HMC C. Wykeham Martin MSS (1909), 422.
71. *Parl. Papers* (1805c), passim; Farington, iii, 328; Fulford & Strachey (1938). i, 77; Liverpool Papers, BL Add MSS 38359, ff.59–65.
72. SRO RH 4/15/8/6.
73. Minto, iii, 385; SRO GD 235/10/18/238; Lockhart (1837), 106 et seq; Grierson, i, 305, 312.
74. NLS Acc 9140, Feb.7, 1806.

8

'The want of former consequence'

Lord Melville's travails inevitably loosened his grip on Scotland. Various hostile interests tried to seize the political opportunity thus presented to them. But as an opposition they were disjointed, being bound – if at all – by no more than their connections in London. There, however, a more coherent Whig party was in process of reconstruction. Its origin can be traced back to 1794, to the fright then taken by the conservative Whigs under the Duke of Portland which induced them to cross over to William Pitt's Government. The rump left round Charles James Fox remained consistently critical of the war and consistently in favour of parliamentary reform, so heralding two great liberal causes of the nineteenth century. It was still only one among several factions in the House of Commons rather than the pole of a party system. Even when Lord Grenville, after his break with Pitt, converged with these Whigs, they amounted while the French Wars went on to little more than an unpopular clique under the wing of the Prince of Wales, himself scarcely a progressive. Though they might well have been dissolved by some accident, they did manage to stick together. And it was in contradistinction to them that the governing factions gradually adopted the otherwise redundant label of Tory. While many more splits and deviations occurred, this was the starting point for the further development of party in Britain.

In Scotland the process looked formally somewhat more advanced, if only because she had just one governing faction, Melville's. He meant with his machine to engross, and reward, the entire political nation. He had proved hard to resist. There were Whigs north of the border, but of little account: the eccentric ex-Jacobin 'Citizen Maitland' (now consenting to be known by his proper title, Earl of Lauderdale), Henry Erskine and William Adam, none of them in Parliament. One or two noble families, such as Minto, had inherited an older Whiggism based not so much on ideology as on aristocratic personal politics, on mere faction therefore: a new Duke of Hamilton had recently sided with them, and soon the houses of Argyll and Sutherland would do the same. But faction was something most Scots condemned. It said a good deal about the condition of the native Whigs that their most influential figure since the turn of the century, with whom even Melville felt obliged to treat, had been an Irishman, the Earl of Moira.

The one important force to which a properly liberal label might with justice be attached was the *Edinburgh Review*, launched in October 1802. It attempted something beyond the ken of any eccentric aristocrat, the forming of opinion.

It was the first real ancestor of modern serious journalism, clever, probing, irreverent. And it brilliantly identified a gap in the market occupied by a rising middle-class readership which wanted to learn about and judge events for itself, rather than swallow what officialdom deemed fit for it. The *Review* was in Henry Cockburn's words 'an entire and instant change of everything that the public had been accustomed to in that sort of composition ... The learning of the new journal, its talent, its spirit, its writing, its independence, were all new; and the surprise was increased by a work so full of public life springing up, suddenly, in a remote part of the kingdom.'

Its authors were a circle of young Whig lawyers, pupils of Dugald Stewart, despairing of success at the Tory Bar. Francis Jeffrey was the editor, Henry Brougham a prolific contributor, and several of them went on to distinguished careers, though often in London. The scale and speed of their success were astonishing. It raised them to a British prominence where they could not be readily persecuted by the establishment in Edinburgh – in fortunate contrast to the older generation of Scots Whigs, who accordingly gave the parvenus no encouragement whatever. But these were sensible enough, at their outset anyway, to avoid blatant partisanship. Even Melville occasionally cast an eye over their screeds. He once wrote to the Earl of Aberdeen: 'Have you seen the late Edinburgh Review? ... There are many things in it acute and worthy of attention, and perhaps more so as coming from a person rather attached to those who are the authors of the Bill [for legal reform]. His name is Jeffries, a gentleman at the Bar here.'[1]

In the short term the Scottish political situation was more obviously altered by the advent at Westminster in February 1806 of the Ministry of All the Talents. Its talents were not used to much effect. It flaunted commitments to peace, reform and catholic emancipation. But while Fox was against, Grenville was for the war; and he had on his side a patriotic population increasingly convinced it was in a fight to the finish. The struggle with Napoleon therefore continued. On reform, most Whigs were just hypocritical, knowing that only the existing system gave them a real chance of power. The sincere minority did not much like being reminded of its earlier radical sympathies. Equally, the Whigs in effect abandoned the Catholics' cause. In Scotland, their performance was accurately summed up by Walter Scott: 'So here are people who have stood in the rain without doors for many years, quarrelling for the nearest place to the fire, as soon as they have set their feet on the floor.'

The Government contained two schools of thought on how to tackle Melville's interest, vulnerable on account of the impeachment. Fox and his followers were eager for a direct assault, a purge of the manager's cronies and a systematic electoral offensive. Erskine, belying a reputation for heroic amiability, wrote to his leader that he expected a 'just retribution to individuals'; there need not be a 'rigid system of expulsion' but it had to be demonstrated that the old order was gone. Alas for him, those of like mind formed only a small and shunned minority. A plain laird like John Ramsay of Ochtertyre could write: 'The people esteemed Jacobins are now in power and their conduct is as inexplicable as their principles.' In fact they lacked even the minimum of acceptable personnel required if they were to eject Melville's creatures and repopulate his apparatus with their own.[2]

By contrast, Grenville and his followers, essentially old Whig oligarchs, were more inclined to take Scotland as they found her. Why, after all, should her members of Parliament not sustain this Ministry with the same docility as they had sustained so many other weak ones in the past? These hopes rose when, almost as soon as it took office, William Dundas made contact. The approach came in a letter to Thomas Grenville which, he told his brother, was worthy of attention despite 'an evident tendency in it to stipulate for an unlimited continuance of the old influence, that is of the Melville influence'. A meeting confirmed this: 'He could certainly be made useful enough, if he really would act bona fide individually; but I own I fear that he naturally must look to keeping up a Scotch party, at the head of which he would naturally find himself. At all events it is useful to show by communication with him that there is at least no spirit of proscription to that class.'

But Dundas was acting alone, and overreaching himself. He had no job and needed one. He knew the Sutherlands, patrons of his seat, were going to back the Talents. He began openly supporting them himself, and in his usual rashness was free with assurances that the rest of the Scots, if left alone, would prove amenable. He had a doubtless genuine concern about the dangers of their being forced into permanent opposition. For the *raison d'être* of the Dundas despotism was government. All its leaders, Melville especially, recoiled from systematic hostility to His Majesty's Ministers. This was not, however, a problem that William Dundas could solve single-handed, at least not when dealing with an administration impeaching the head of the clan. 'I do not think the course he intends to follow, or that he has pursued, is wisely determined,' wrote his cousin Robert, Melville's son.[3]

As it happened he and Charles Hope had set out on the same quest, though they had the sense to keep it secret. They aimed to avert the Talents' wrath by winning Moira's good offices. They thought they might ultimately detach him and other less radical Whigs from Fox (whom the Earl was known to dislike) and free them to combine with the Pittites. But the immediate purpose was to give Moira a strong claim to the management of Scotland, resting on an assurance of co-operation from a majority of her members. Robert Dundas wrote that if events 'shall bring us into a more intimate connection with your Lordship than the tone of the new administration renders practicable at present it will afford us from many motives, both public and personal, the most sincere gratification.' In token of their goodwill they undertook, despite the impeachment, to avoid attacks on the Government. They had but three conditions: that they should not be bound to support its measures; that they should not be required to act against other Pittites; and that they should not be subverted in Scotland.[4]

This was all very well, but Moira counted as a minor Whig. The plan would only work if a senior Minister was brought in on it. That had to be Grenville. He was responsive to an approach from Moira. But Melville thought best to tread warily with his old antagonist, whom he besides could not forgive for failing Pitt in 1804. His son warned it was no time for picking at old wounds: if means were not found to make the stratagem succeed, they might as well go over into open opposition. The father wondered if Grenville was really prepared to stand up to Fox in Scotland: 'It is certainly not possible to form an administration more hostile to me than it is, and I am afraid all you now do is giving yourself a great deal of unnecessary trouble … I suspect Lord Moira totally overrates his influence in any quarter.' Rapprochement would carry big risks – promotion of Lauderdale and Erskine was fair enough, but Melville feared that in power they could not be stopped from 'all the violence they may find necessary for the gratification of the blackguard and disreputable trash which forms what has been formerly the Jacobin and is now called the Prince's party in Scotland.'[5]

Moreover, a mutiny among the native Whigs could be relied on once the moment came for Moira to show his hand. Dundas tried to strengthen it by surveying opinion among the sitting Scots members, who obliged with enthusiastic disclaimers of any desire to oppose the Ministry. For a while it almost seemed as if his terms for a truce might carry conviction. He reported to his father as the administration was being put together: 'There is a great dissension among them on Lord Moira's demand of Scotch patronage; Lauderdale is outrageous, and the matter was still in dispute last night.' But in the end the native Whigs were just not prepared to collaborate with the Dundases in however indirect a manner, not even with William, let alone with Robert.[6]

Robert then wrote: 'Decided hostility seems to me the only honourable course. From the reply which I understand was made to William, with regard to the administration of Scotland, I am clear that Lord Lauderdale is there to be absolute. A more tyrannical and violent Minister we shall not have been blessed with since a century ago that we had a Duke of that name to rule over us.' Melville concurred, forecasting that official Scotland would not put up with a democrat, and forbidding further approaches to him. William won for his pains only the furious wrath of his uncle, who never trusted him again. For the first time, however, he formed a real respect for Robert: his exertions had failed, but his intentions had been good and his methods politic. Father and son commiserated with one another and agreed they had done the best in impossible circumstances.[7]

The hardliners among the Whigs seemed to be getting their way. Lauderdale was granted the Great Seal of Scotland, and with it nominal control of patronage. Erskine embarked on his second stint as Lord Advocate. The post of Solicitor General went to John Clerk of Eldin, a colourful, all too colourful character, an able advocate, a coalmaster, a talented painter, but irascible, drunken and lecherous; there were apparently legions of servant girls in Midlothian whom he had pursued hirpling into the woods and terrified into submission. Some famous stories of the Scots Bar originated with him. What Lady Elizabeth Grant of Rothiemurchus called his 'truly hideous' countenance was owed to a picturesquely broken nose: the result, he boasted, of having in his cups studied 'Clerk upon Stair'. One day he arrived in court so hungover that he started pleading his client's guilt instead of innocence. According to Lady Elizabeth,

> at last he was made to understand the mischief he was doing … and then turning to the judge resumed the address thus, 'Having now, my lord, to the best of my ability stated my opponent's case as strongly as it is possible for even my learned brother' – bowing to the opposite counsel with a peculiar swing of his short leg – 'to argue it, I shall proceed point by point to refute every particular advanced.'

Cockburn passed this verdict on the new administration:

> It was very unfortunate for the progress of sound opinions that Scotland was unavoidably put under the charge of persons so little qualified to turn the power thus given them to the best advantage. Personally Erskine was excellent; liberal, judicious and beloved. But he was married to Clerk who personally was also excellent but officially crotchety, positive and wild; and domineered over the softer nature of Erskine by mere obstinacy. Lauderdale, who from his position ought to have controlled his inferiors, had neither of these qualities himself. He was then, as he had been before, and as he continued to the end, an able, agreeable and signally, almost ostentatiously, wrongheaded man. It may be doubted if he was ever right in his life … There was some merit, however, in the skill with which he usually relieved the wearisomeness of perpetual error by being wrong on the worst grounds.[8]

Much Scottish business thus passed by default to the English Home Secretary, Earl Spencer. It was a crucial development, for it coincided with the formulation of other doctrines which the Whigs were to turn into policy when they at long last had a real chance to, after 1832. Along with reform, retrenchment, peace, toleration and many other worthy causes, a distinct approach to Scottish government took its place in the canons of Whiggery. Scotland was to be governed not by a Scot, as had been the rule since 1707, but by an Englishman relying on Scottish advisers. After the smoke of this particular battle cleared, Hope noted: 'The language of the [Whig] party now is, that they hope in God never to see another Minister in Scotland. I suspect that Lords Grenville and Spencer, having unexpectedly got rid of their engagements to Lord Moira, have been very glad of the opportunity of resuming the patronage of Scotland – and have given a repulse to Lauderdale.'[9]

Even at this first trial the system had little to commend it, for the Talents succeeded in nothing. Lauderdale and Erskine set out with touching public spirit to prove their credentials not just as jobbers but as zealous reformers. In rapid succession they announced plans to raise ministers' stipends, to revise the Poor Law, to liberalise the tenure of landed property, to repeal the Test Act and, most important, to reform the legal system, with a particular view to improving the speed and quality of justice in the Court of Session. This was something for which Melville also saw the need and, since his abortive project of 1785, had intermittently made his own suggestions.

The Government's were to go much further than any of them. In typical Whig fashion, the *Edinburgh Review* had been harping on about the authoritarian spirit of the Scots law and judiciary, which it attributed ultimately to Rome. It prescribed remedies imported from England. But because the English never systematised their law in the way that the Romans and the Scots had, there was no coherent example to follow. All that could be proposed was piecemeal tinkering: the reform of structures here, the alteration of procedures there, the introduction of juries just about everywhere. The eventual result would be a mess, robbing Scottish jurisprudence of its integrity and elegance but putting nothing as good in its place, nor even curing it of those practical defects which hindered the citizen's access to expeditious and certain justice.

Grenville himself sponsored the Bill embodying the Ministry's proposals early in 1807. They were dauntingly complex, providing for a division of the Court of Session into three chambers with an appellate court above them. The details need not detain us. Suffice it to say that the Bench was horrified at a measure 'subversive of the constitution of the court, and of the fundamental laws of the country. contrary to the Act of Union and in violation of the Claim of Right.' Melville was shorter with it – 'a daring and abominable job'. The principal modern authority has agreed that this was one of the most remarkable documents in Scottish legal history: 'It was proposed to remodel the Court of Session on the lines of the courts of common law in England.'

The Faculty of Advocates thought the issue so crucial that, as on similar occasions in the past, it held its own debate. Baron David Hume, nephew of the philosopher and professor of Scots law at the university of Edinburgh, praised the prudence of the English when contemplating reforms of their own: 'But observing this rule of conduct for themselves, as they uniformly do at the present day, it is, I must say, very strange, and somewhat hard, that they prescribe just the opposite rule for us.' Scott condemned 'Anglomania – a rage of imitating English forms and practices.' Surprisingly, even Jeffrey entered objections, protesting that 'the Union is a treaty betwixt Scotland and England. Its sole object is to prevent the usurpation or encroachment of the latter country.' On the vote, the Faculty divided almost equally. Approval of the measure was largely confined to the senior Whigs, those closest to the administration, though they were followed by numbers of venal hangers-on. More remarkable was that the opposition included not only the Tories but also the junior Whigs. Nobody rejected reform in itself. This was, however, just too crude. In its favour Grenville could not even rally all his own supporters, and few were sorry when the Ministry fell before the Bill could pass.[10]

Scots at large were as ever more interested in men than in measures, and especially in how far the purge of Melville's clients would go. The Talents established a committee on it, consisting of Lauderdale, Moira, Erskine, Lord Douglas, heir of Hamilton, and the Marquis of Stafford, husband of the Countess of Sutherland and William Dundas's patron. They drew up a blacklist of sixteen officials to be removed, and ten more to be put on good behaviour. But this, like many committees, may well have been a device for postponing action. Melville's acquittal, leaving him again free to defend his interest, provided another pretext for caution. Dismissals and appointments anyway needed the sanction of Spencer, with whom the Dundases enjoyed good relations. Grenville also promised them that he wanted no purge in Scotland and would reject advice amounting to that. Moira, too, intervened to prevent some sackings. These three, Robert assured his father from London, had a low opinion of Lauderdale and meant to thwart him.

The new Scottish manager showed little determination to surmount the obstacles put in his way. Supporters in the country clamoured in vain for favours from him. Two wrote in to say they were 'sorry to find you so extremely backward in answering letters, or yet of recommending friends, though solicited thereto in the most supplicant manner, by connections of your very best constituents.' Another remarked on 'an apathy in the conduct of administration which is wonderful'; yet another, months later, that 'Ministers are still in the same dormant state respecting Scotland in spite of all Lord Melville's friends are doing to irritate them.'[12]

All this was an inauspicious background to the Talents' decision in November 1806 to go to the country in an effort to secure themselves. Even so, from the Dundases' side the prospect looked none too bright either. Melville confessed he was 'not in a very good state to encounter the bustle of a new election'. It was the second time he had had to fight without official backing. Now indeed he was in direct opposition, and the strain told. He had already gloomily worked out how it might affect his chances, reckoning he could return 22 of his own members, against 10 for the Government and 13 others. This no doubt tempered his enmities – he even thought of offering Edinburgh to Erskine, who was having trouble in finding a seat, 'if he would come to a clear understanding upon it and not interfere in the interior of town administration or politick.'[13]

In their turn, Scottish politicians and voters were confronted by starker alternatives than last time. Then they had still been able to follow the Dundases without repudiating the Ministry. Now they had to choose. The Whigs were eager to seize their first opportunity in decades of making decisive gains. If by some chance they won a majority at Westminster it might well, nourished on the resources of the Treasury, prove durable. Scotland would in that case face new realities, and opposition would have turned out a bad bargain. Such calculations led several sitting members towards the Talents, and offered them openings for attacks elsewhere. Yet Melville's interest remained obviously superior to any single rival's.

In the South-east a core largely of his own family held the Lothians steady for him. He had, when Edinburgh was vacated the year before by Hope's elevation to the Bench, fitted in his son-in-law, George Abercromby. With him now able to remove to his native Clackmannanshire, Melville entrusted representation of the capital to yet another of his brothers-in-law, Sir Patrick Murray. The Border counties, too, were solidly his. But elsewhere he suffered setbacks. Two local interests, the Elphinstones in Stirlingshire and the Anstruthers in their pocket district of burghs, went over to the Government, taking their constituencies with them. The Whigs, though losing Kinross-shire because it did not return this time, held the Dysart Burghs and made three gains. In the Haddington Burghs, Lauderdale consolidated his hold. Having accommodated Erskine for a few months before the election, he now gave the seat to young William Lamb, just graduated from the university of Glasgow and one day to be Prime Minister as Lord Melbourne. At a third attempt on the ruinously expensive Stirling Burghs, Sir John Henderson won. The biggest upset in this region came in Fife, where William Wemyss, a former ministerialist member selected to come back and replace the retiring Sir William Erskine, was defeated by a Whig.

In the North-east, under Melville's control for twenty years, he met reverses still more severe. The incumbents in Moray and Perthshire defected to the Talents. William Adam gained Kincardine. In Forfarshire, the equivocal Sir David Carnegie had on his death in 1805 been replaced by a decided Whig,

William Maule. He now held the county, while his brother took the Aberdeen Burghs. With the Earl of Fife's help, the Government won the Elgin Burghs too. That left only the Perth Burghs (where Sir David Wedderburn had succeeded the late David Scott) and Banffshire (retained by William Grant in a contest with Fife's nephew) safe for Melville. But to his intense delight, a cliffhanger in Aberdeenshire ended in the victory of his trusty James Ferguson by two votes over a Whig.

The situation was just as dire in the Highlands, where the magnates deserted en masse. The Sutherlands had already done so, taking in their wake the Tain Burghs and their own county, which William Dundas continued uneasily to represent. The Duke of Argyll and his pocket constituencies now followed the same path. In Bute, the Marquis, and in Nairnshire, Lord Cawdor rejoined the Whigs after a period of estrangement, again returning members of that party. The whole region sent back only two who might be reckoned friendly to Melville, Charles and Francis William Grant in Inverness, county and burghs respectively.

Nor did respite come in the West. Again, magnates' movements were decisive. Through the influence of the wayward Duke of Queensberry and the Earl of Selkirk, the Lord Advocate found a billet in the Dumfries Burghs. The Earl of Galloway also supported the Ministry. One of his sons won Kirkcudbrightshire on its ticket, though another, in the Wigtown Burghs, remained hostile. Hamilton held Lanarkshire for the Whigs, while Argyll revived his interest in Dunbarton to take the county for them. Sitting members in Ayrshire and Renfrewshire deserted Melville. He then remained in control only of Dumfriesshire, of Wigtown, county and burghs, and of the Glasgow Burghs.

He could therefore count firmly on just 18 members, though perhaps five independents were not altogether ill-disposed to him. The Ministry might reasonably rely on 22, of whom 13 were Whigs. The estimate here is more unfavourable to Melville than any in other sources. But these have not fully taken into account the extent to which men previously elected on his interest decamped; there were still plenty of Scots ready to support the Government whatever its colour. He confessed himself shocked at how the 'great aristocratical interests' had acted: 'It is a matter of real surprise to me that so many people of that description should so completely forget their own and the interests of their country as to give way to all the upstart and democratical interests.'[14]

It could therefore have been no surprise that the peers' election turned out badly too, not least because the Talents bought support by distributing British titles. But there has been some disagreement about the precise results. Of the sixteen representatives sitting at the dissolution, seven were returned; among the newcomers, young Aberdeen was a protégé of Melville's. One scholar has accordingly ascribed to him continuing control of half the representation. But again, it ought not to be taken for granted that a peer elected once on Melville's interest was thereafter exclusively committed to it. Lauderdale (relieved by one of those British titles of the need to stand himself) assiduously canvassed everybody, including apparent enemies. In consequence, fifteen of those chosen came from a King's list drawn up by him, the exception being Aberdeen; though he too was intensively wooed, and certainly had not burned his boats with the Ministry. That led a Whig hostess to an equally erroneous conclusion: 'The Scotch peers' elections have gone well. Lord Melville was cruelly disappointed: he expected to carry four, and only carried Lord Aberdeen.'[15]

The truth of the matter seems to be this. Several of Melville's candidates were indeed rejected, but Lauderdale had skilfully balanced his ticket so that a good proportion of his nominees were equally acceptable to the other side. Such was opinion in the aristocracy that it simply would not have been feasible to construct a representation entirely hostile to Melville. A number of his friends were at the same time prepared to give conditional support to the Talents. He himself had reckoned that the men on his list 'will suffer from those peers who in general wish us well ... giving some detached votes to some of those candidates who are on the ministerial list ... All those who are countenanced by or secure their mandates from Government act as a party, whereas our friends exercise in many instances their own partialities or other connections.' What Lauderdale in fact arranged was an exact division of the representation between himself and Melville. It might thus plausibly be argued that the Scots peers' older tradition of helping to form a party of the Crown had survived their years of attachment to a particular manager. The conditional nature of their support was revealed rather by the interesting fact that they stayed on in Edinburgh for a day after the election to debate another of the Talents' reforming schemes, that the sixteen should be chosen for life and the rest of the peers be left free to stand for the Commons. They overwhelmingly rejected it.[16]

In the United Kingdom as a whole the elections brought the Government gains, but not enough to survive. It fell within a few weeks of meeting the new Parliament. In March 1807, the Duke of Portland once more became Prime Minister, twenty-four years after his first term. He was able to bring together most of the factions fallen apart since 1801. Their alliance would dominate British politics for the next two decades. Opposition dwindled. Fox was dead, Grenville aloof, Grey gone to the Lords, Sidmouth too compromised to be a danger. The Talents' hard-won advances were immediately reversed when Portland went straight back to the country, to be returned with a majority of 200. For Melville, who had urged this course on him, it was quite like old times. Walter Scott found him 'at work with election business from morning to night and I think will give a good account of the returns.'[17]

Melville at once recouped some of the more spectacular of his late losses. Fife was handed to Wemyss without a contest. Another crony, General Alexander Campbell of Monzie, retrieved the Stirling Burghs, thanks to a personal intervention by Melville at his most incorrigible. After all that had happened, he could still in the heat of the hustings bid his son: 'I wish ... Huskisson [now secretary to the Treasury] would not forget the note I sent to him about a supply of secret funds. I have this morning been obliged to pledge my own credit for £300.' But even here in the South-east there remained a core of Whigs which he could not crack. In the burgh districts of Anstruther, Dysart and Haddington, as in Stirlingshire, they held on. They even made two gains. Into the Linlithgow Burghs, Melville had in 1806 placed his nephew by marriage, Sir Charles Lockhart Ross, after shifting him from the county of Ross where he had been a most unsatisfactory member. He had not improved here, and was beaten by a Whig. Adam stood in his own alternating county of Kinross, but being returned again for Kincardine too, chose to stay there, leaving this to a friend.

Things went better in the West. Melville won back Dunbarton with Henry Glassford, a merchant prince from Glasgow, and the Dumfries Burghs with Sir John Maxwell, against whom Erskine did not even bother to stand. In Renfrewshire a turncoat, William McDowall, came to heel. Another in Ayrshire, Hew Hamilton Dalrymple, was to Melville's enormous satisfaction driven out by one of his young legal protégés, David Boyle. Galloway, that perennial thorn in his flesh, had meanwhile died. The successor to the earldom supported the Government, and made sure that his brothers sitting for Kirkcudbrightshire and the Wigtown Burghs did the same. That left to the Whigs only Lanarkshire under Hamilton and the Ayr Burghs under Argyll.

In the North-east Melville ejected other renegades from Moray and Perthshire. transferring Francis William Grant to the first and bringing in Lord James Murray for the second. James Farquhar regained the Aberdeen Burghs from their Whig. The one in the Elgin Burghs was beaten by Archibald Campbell Colquhoun, designated as the new Lord Advocate. In this region too, however, a nucleus of opposition survived with Adam in Kincardine and Maule in Forfarshire.

In contrast, over much of the Highlands hostile magnates, led by Argyll and Sutherland, still held sway. William Dundas was retained for the latter's county only on condition of his neutrality, but it was too much for him and he resigned the next year. A local opposition also kept hold of Orkney and Shetland. Melville's grip on the region had in fact permanently slackened, and he was obliged to rely on friendly independents such as Charles Grant in Inverness-shire and Sir John Sinclair in Caithness.

One way and another, he can be reckoned to have returned twenty-nine members, a considerable success after the previous debacle. Yet the Whigs, virtually annihilated only a few years before, also did well to hold thirteen seats; there were three independents. Melville had hoped for better, after finding in the campaign that public opinion was overwhelmingly behind the Government. He blithely apologised that 'from the constitution of our burghs and sheer habits on occasion of elections, the popular voice does not operate with equal effect as in England'. Among the peers, however, he triumphed. At the advent of Portland's Ministry, eight of the sitting representatives (in other words, Lauderdale's half of the total) had gone into opposition. A single one, Selkirk, now survived, while five who had lost their seats in 1806 came back. They and the rest were nominated by Melville. His success, he crowed, was 'very complete – I never doubted it the moment they felt the importance of acting in concert.'[18]

This only raised in more acute form, though, a question that had taxed the Government even before going to the polls: what, if any, part was he to play in it? His son contended in the Commons that 'the acquittal in the impeachment, from which Lord Melville did not shrink, left him as clear of imputation as if he had never been accused.' However that might be, he was aging, clearly past his best and, whether justly or not, branded by his trial as a figure from the bad old days of

British politics. It set him apart from that new generation, now coming into power, which espoused the higher ideals of the nineteenth century. On the other hand, he represented a revived Scottish interest which it would be difficult to pass over. Above all, he himself wished to be fully vindicated. To his mind, full vindication could mean only one thing – office.

The frustrations he then suffered brought out the worst side of his character. He became more and more withdrawn, untrustworthy, unpredictable, self-pitying, irascible, callous even to family and friends, more and more repulsive in fact. The condition was exacerbated by continued heavy drinking, against which doctors warned him in vain, and even more by poverty; the cost of the trial had, despite help, been ruinous. His influence on events was strictly circumscribed by the fact that he could barely afford to attend Parliament. 'I can, by persevering in the attention and economy I now pursue,' he wrote from Dunira, 'continue to live in one place, but a double residence is literally impossible.' This naturally isolated him: 'My son … is the only person in Government with whom I have any communications,' he told a correspondent. Once, when he did manage to London, he bumped into the Bishop of Lichfield, who recorded: 'I saw Lord Melville the other day. He looks older and, I thought, like all unplaced statesmen, feeling the want of former consequence.'[19] His shrunken influence formed a sorry contrast to his aspirations. He hinted to the King that he would like to go back to the Admiralty. All he got was readmission to the Privy Council, a recompense so meagre that he wanted to refuse it till dissuaded by his family.

An offer instead came to Robert Dundas. He at once asked Melville to be completely frank with him and say if he still genuinely sought a ministerial post for himself. Dundas assumed that not to be the case, but if he was wrong, or if his father felt excluded by Portland, or in any way neglected, then he would not accept. Melville responded sourly, but with no apparent ambiguity: 'The present Ministers have clearly manifested a disinclination to be officially connected with me; I have the same feeling in regard to them.' He would even, he declared a couple of months later, wash his hands of Scottish jobbery:

> Eagerly bent as I am both from inclination and necessity to live a life of retirement and the enjoyment of my family, a few friends and my farm, I look forward with horror to the situation of what they call Minister for Scotland, in which there is no room for the exertion of any real talent I may possess, and one is liable to the perpetual annoyance of hungry or greedy beggars beating at your door and disturbing the quiet and repose of your life … It was always my intention as soon as possible gradually to have got rid of the whole trouble of it. [20]

The Dundas despotism was thus, it seemed, to be devolved on Robert. In these troubled times he had been its loyal servant, but also a moderating influence and honest broker. They were the qualities he would bring to the *ancien régime* in Scotland for as long as it yet lasted. Since he was now embarking, at the age of 36, on his ministerial career, it may be time to catch up with his story since those experiences as a long-suffering student at Göttingen.

He proceeded to the universities of Edinburgh and Cambridge, afterwards to Lincoln's Inn. But he inherited no interest in the law, and never practised. Indeed it was unclear what he might do, except lounge around like many young men of his age and class. In 1792, after he had been packed off on a second continental tour, his father wrote disapprovingly: 'I trust this present excursion may put him more in the habits of punctuality than he formerly practised.' He at length took Robert on as a private secretary, at which he would work for seven years. It was thought useful that he should be in Parliament. He was chosen for Hastings in 1794 then for Rye in 1796, but gave no maiden speech. The same year he made a good match with an English heiress, Anne Saunders, who had an income of £3000 a year. It seemed at first that he might be forced to assume her name in order to get the dowry. He was most reluctant to do this, and compromised by officially calling himself Robert Saunders Dundas, though in his signature he always dropped the middle name. As part of the settlement with her trustees, he became the owner of Melville Castle. But the financial curse on his family did not spare him, and this security was to prove impermanent. In 1797 he did some soldiering. After he had been briefly posted to Ireland, his father wearily noted: 'It would not suit my son, I am afraid, to undertake a military life.' As late as 1799, when weighing up whether to go to the Lords, he remarked that Robert was 'not ambitious and had not turned his thoughts to political pursuits, so that his exclusion from the House of Commons would not disappoint any views of his.'[21]

All this changed, however, when he was at last able to escape the stifling weight of paternal solicitude and win some independence. It happened, not before time, when he was 30. On his father's retiral in 1801, he himself became a Scottish politician. He took custody of the signet and was elected to succeed his cousin and namesake as member for Midlothian. Before long, even Melville could say: 'My chief comfort is that my son is getting on so fast in the confidence and goodwill of the country, I think he will soon save me a great deal of disagreeable trouble.'

His conduct during the events following Pitt's death, in contrast to the opprobrium attracted by William Dundas, left no doubt about Robert's political future. He was industrious but sociable, a keen sportsman, a loyal friend; he remained all his life on close terms with two schoolmates, the Earl of Dalkeith and Walter Scott. The latter described him thus: 'Though not a literary man, he is judicious, clairvoyant and uncommonly sound-headed, like his father.' Cockburn, too, wrote that 'he had fully as much good sense, excellent business habits, great moderation and as much candour as, I suppose, a party leader can practise' – which was perhaps an improvement on his father. Lord Liverpool, the Prime Minister under whom he later served, called him 'an excellent man of business'.[22]

Dundas also followed in his father's footsteps by being called in 1807 to the presidency of the Board of Control, though without a place in Cabinet. Still, in a famous comment, Scott wrote: 'His effectual interest must be in Scotland, and no-one can carry Scotland that has not the command of the Board of Control, which is in a manner the key of the corn-chest ... All our live articles of exportation are our black-cattle and our children, and though England furnishes a demand for our quadrupeds we are forced to send our bipeds as far as Bengal.' Incidentally, an interesting sidelight on the Dundases' long dominance of Indian affairs was cast during a parliamentary debate in 1813, when William boasted that a majority of the British resident in India were Scots. Another member added that they outnumbered the English by two to one.[23]

Robert Dundas's predecessor, Lord Castlereagh, had tried to restrain the aggression of Lord Wellesley, the Governor-general whom he inherited, and did nothing to prevent his recall in 1805 at the instance of the East India Company. An interregnum followed. Under the Talents, Scots were still intent on monopolising Indian administration. Lord Minto took charge of the Board and Lord Lauderdale asked to be sent to Calcutta, though the appalled directors vetoed him. So, *faute de mieux*, Minto went out instead. He was a moderate Whig, with whom the Dundases enjoyed good relations. His appointment, which could have been cancelled by Robert, was allowed to stand, and these two worked together ruling India for the next five years.[24]

It was not as if Dundas felt entirely satisfied: 'Lord Minto writes a good deal more than is necessary, but ... he does not produce efficient measures.' Though the Governor-general lacked the sense of proportion to know a vain project when he saw one, this was a period of relative tranquillity, and the Board could reassert its authority after Wellesley's excesses. It did not, on the other hand, permit any great reduction in Britain's oriental military commitments, since India still counted for something in the balance of world war. A Europe dominated, after the Peace of Tilsit, by an alliance of France and Russia remained almost barren of opportunities for the British. Only Napoleon's outrageous conduct towards his ally Spain, where he deposed the king and installed a puppet regime, permitted them a fresh continental intervention in support of a popular uprising there. Melville, true to his principles, warned against moving the expeditionary force into the interior from the ports it first occupied. He was less than his judicious best in disapproving of the generalship shown by Sir Arthur Wellesley, later the Duke of Wellington. While confidently predicting Napoleon's downfall, Melville still held Britain would do most to hasten it through economic, or in effect imperial, warfare. He urged the opening of trade with South America, possibly by taking outposts such as Buenos Aires, now that the Spaniards were not in a position to prevent it. He was delighted at the recapture of the Cape of Good Hope in 1806. On this view of strategy, Britain's guard in the Orient could not be relaxed.[25]

Dundas's special concern was that Napoleon might exploit his Russian alliance to turn eastwards again. 'I cannot bring myself to doubt that the overthrow of the British power in India is one constant object of his hostile ambition,' he wrote. Though the dangers proved exaggerated, he put in train several counter-measures. He ordered Portugal's factories in India and China, which she could not defend, to be peacefully taken over. In 1811 Minto led in person a similarly pre-emptive occupation of the Dutch colony of Java. The same year the French stations on Mauritius and Reunion were seized. A mission was sent to conclude a treaty with the Shah of Persia, where agents of Napoleon were believed to be intriguing. And Britain entered into friendly relations with the native princes of Kabul and Lahore. With these successes, Dundas declared, 'the British interests and trade in the East Indies will be secured against any hostile attempts in a more substantial manner than at any period of our history.'[26]

What further military enterprises could not do, though, was reverse a sharp deterioration in the company's financial position resulting from earlier ones. It grew critical as the Continental System closed off Europe to oriental goods. With only a meagre Indian market for British manufactures, trade stagnated. Dundas summed things up thus to his father:

> The Mahratta Wars [after 1802] were honourable to our arms, but ruinous to our finances, and the territorial acquisitions we have made, whatever may be their value in point of military security, are most burdensome in point of expense. … There is now no alternative between an effective and decided parliamentary interference in support of the credit and resources of the Company, or struggling on for a few years longer with increased dangers and increasing difficulties.

A solution was already suggesting itself to him: that the Company's monopoly on Indian trade, the great obstruction to more vigorous commerce, should at last be ended. This decisive step was more than Melville had ever dared take, though he agreed, when the idea was put to him, that the time had come. He still counselled caution, warning especially against any move by the Government to acquire more Indian patronage and generally against harsh, gratuitous attacks on the Company. Not only the logic of a new arrangement but also the vested interests had to be borne in mind.[27]

The sagaciously moderate Dundas did not mean, however, to drive the Company out of business. When he disclosed his intentions to Minto too, he declared indeed that he was ready to help it. But he added that there would be no support for such help in Britain without 'adequate concessions on the part of the Company in the monopoly of their trade'. For himself, he would offer no succour to a system such as the existing one, unprofitable not just to those excluded from it but even to those included in it. Minto demurred, arguing that the Company could do better, though unable to say quite how. Dundas was actually in an unassailable position to enforce his will because its charter again fell due for renewal in 1813. He did not therefore hesitate to take a strong line: 'Unless [the directors] concede much, and indeed all that is essential, their charter will not be renewed, and the other advantages held out to them will not be granted.'[28]

But he still went to great lengths to create a consensus in favour of his chosen course. With his own mind about the basic direction of policy made up, he could start detailed preparations five years in advance. He took the chair of a parliamentary select committee which was to publish a series of reports, together presenting a survey of the entire Indian system since its creation in 1784. They predictably concluded that commercial liberalisation was the way to remedy such defects as had emerged. The progress of this work brought a response in public opinion. A cry for freedom of trade went up from the manufacturers of England and especially of Scotland, where they resented confinement of the Indian traffic to London. Petitions of protest came from Glasgow, Edinburgh, Paisley, Kirkcaldy and Kilmarnock: by 1812, about 130 had been sent from every part of Britain. The Company also now contained a growing faction of free-traders, to whom Dundas gave his support in elections of directors. And he took care to placate those of his countrymen among the proprietors, notably the formidable clan of Grants, who were not naturally inclined to approve of what he was doing.

The monopolists thus found themselves scarcely capable of formulating a coherent response to the rising public debate. They themselves opened the door to radical reform when they were forced to petition Parliament for financial aid in 1810, shiftily asking for this to be dealt with separately from questions of the monopoly – 'not a very efficient communication in a great work of retrenchment and reform', Dundas commented with rare acidity. The next year he was ready to put his own definitive proposals to the Cabinet, in good time for legislation in the session of 1812–3. It was a skilfully contrived package. Indian trade would be fully opened, yet the Company's monopoly on Chinese traffic was to be maintained. Its army would be gradually merged with the Crown's, yet the existing system of government in its territories was to be guaranteed: inside India, commerce would altogether at last be strictly divorced from administration. In return for all this, assistance was to be granted.[29]

By the time Parliament did renew the charter in these terms, Dundas was gone from the Board of Control. But he can fairly be called the architect of the measure. Though the dismantling of the Chinese monopoly had to wait till the next renewal in 1833, in essentials the last major institution of mercantilism was overthrown, and Britain could embark untrammelled on her great century of free trade. Scotland was jubilant, Glasgow in particular. One of its merchant princes, Kirkman Finlay, sent a ship to Calcutta as soon as he heard the news. It had been for a comparative novice like Dundas a fine political achievement. He had proved bolder than his father, and just as skilful in dealing with opposition. India made his reputation too.

Only on one point had the legislation been significantly amended against the Government's wishes. A clause was inserted that 'it shall be lawful for the Governor-general in council to direct that … a sum of not less than one lakh rupees every year shall be set apart and applied to the revival and improvement of literature [viz., in English] and the encouragement of learned natives of India' so that those 'now engaged in the degrading and polluting worship of idols shall be brought to the knowledge of the true God and Jesus Christ whom he has sent.'[30] This was a victory for the phalanx of evangelical members, dubbed the Saints, who were coming into the House and gathering round William Wilberforce, their harbinger and mentor. So far their attention had been largely confined to particular philanthropic causes such as the abolition of slavery. But they were now reaching a position where they could have a wider influence on imperial policy. They intended the new British Empire to be a confessedly Christian one, bent on civilising through conversion the pagan millions over which it held sway.

The Dundases did not agree with this. On the contrary, as British rule in India had expanded, their administration at both ends took the sensible line of not interfering in religion, conscious that its power relied in the end on acquiescence by the masses. Indians, inured to misrule, had most of them long given up worrying who was actually set over them, provided they were not offended in their immemorial customs. The Company sought to ingratiate itself in this respect. Military bands were allowed to take part in Hindu and Moslem processions. In 1802, when news of the Treaty of Amiens reached Calcutta, an official party went to give thanks for it at the Kali temple.

The odd example of insensitivity revealed the danger in any different conduct. In 1806 new disciplinary regulations were issued to the sepoys, the Indian soldiery, requiring them to shave off their beards, adopt a new style of head-dress and stop wearing caste-marks. A serious mutiny immediately erupted at Vellore near Madras, among men who thought they were about to be forcibly converted to Christianity. It was partly in response that the Company instructed Minto in 1808 to halt the activity of evangelical missions and ensure toleration for native religions.

Despite protests at home, Dundas refused to intervene. He had just received a request from Charles Grant to abolish a tax levied on pilgrims to the statue of the Juggernaut at Cuttack. It was used to pay for the upkeep of the cults there and so, Grant argued, for the horrible ceremonies accompanying them. Dundas replied: 'Much may be done towards putting a stop to such abominable cruelties and sacrifices ... by the prudent interference and management of the local Government, with the aid of the most enlightened of the priests; but I am very averse to any orders to that effect being sent from hence.' It was not his policy to encourage idolatry, but he thought the tax helped the authorities to keep things quiet. 'No man has the right to make another happy against his will,' he added. He then wrote to Minto: 'I have said distinctly that I consider any concurrence of this Government, as a Government, in schemes for the conversion to be inadvisable, because I know that it would not be safe.' By 1811 he was prepared to go further, and in public, announcing his suppression of an evangelical tract circulated in India 'containing animadversions of the most severe nature on the religion and customs of the natives ... It is the substratum of British government in India to uphold the laws and usages of the natives.'[31]

Underlying this attitude were the easy terms on which an older generation of empire-builders had lived with the strange and often repellent customs of India. Out there, many had gone native in their private lives. The emergence of the Eurasian community was one result, for on the whole the British felt little sense of racial apartness. The best did not want to disparage or destroy local culture. It fascinated them, and their role in its preservation and appreciation, as by Sir William Jones and the Asiatic Society of Bengal, was of the first importance.

Melville had encouraged and patronised such men, holding that Indians were to be left to themselves rather than turned into sham Europeans. His view had been shaped by the Scottish Enlightenment, with its open-mindedness, its tolerance, its empirical acceptance that societies were to be found in different stages of development and should be left in freedom to follow their own evolution, not wrenched out of one course into another. This sane and liberal outlook was about to yield, however, to a new one arising primarily from the rapid progress in Britain of evangelical religion. Its motives, to improve man's lot in this world and save his soul for the next, cannot be disparaged. But, as a matter of fact, it did often replace open-mindedness with self-righteousness, tolerance with didacticism and empirical acceptance with dogma and coercion. And this could lead to a belief that the religious and moral superiority of individual Christian men was tantamount to the racial superiority of Christian peoples. These were not notions which the Dundases, father or son, ever entertained.

'Scotland must be his effectual interest,' Scott had said of Dundas, but he was as yet, with so much else on his mind, only spasmodically involved in her affairs. If some of his compatriots started looking to him for direction it suited Melville, who was able thus to brush off importunities: 'I have no correspondence with any public department and therefore it is only through my son that I can have the means of serving any friend.' In fact Dundas deferred to him, taking care not to touch his innumerable sore spots. Sir John Sinclair thought this left a hiatus: 'there is properly speaking no Minister at present for Scotland'. Nor could subordinates easily fill the gap. Lord Advocate Colquhoun was described by his patron, the Duke of Montrose, as 'most distinguished for his zeal, and forwardness, in resisting Jacobinical principles of all kinds'. Melville still did not like him and trusted him with nothing. But the Solicitor General, David Boyle, commended himself by his piquant electoral victory, by his debating skills and by his sound advice.[32]

The basic question for Scottish government was still how its normal business should be carried on without a manager in Cabinet. The normal business consisted, of course, above all in patronage. It emerged that Dundas did not share his father's, let us say robust, view of jobbery. In pulling such strings as he yet held, he could be almost apologetic, for instance to Minto: 'I trust that your lordship will not deem me very obtrusive in soliciting occasionally your good offices or favourable notice towards servants under your government; parliamentary and other connections render such requests sometimes unavoidable on my part, and I can only promise that they shall be as seldom as possible.' To the Commons he declared: 'As for the great official influence which has been imputed to me ... I have only to state distinctly that I never exercise it.' Yet he did not hesitate to intervene if he saw abuse. He ordered all the Company's servants in India who had purchased appointments to be dismissed and sent home – 'the measure is severe, but unavoidable'. By character and inclination, Dundas was evidently more comfortable with the rising standards in public life than his father could ever have been.

That was all very well for India, but in Scotland the Chief Baron warned him not to be so independent of judgment, but rather 'to take the opinions of such friends as the President, the Justice Clerk and myself on any arrangement'.[33] Melville was besides, despite his disclaimers, clearly intent on regaining full control of Scottish patronage. He repeatedly warned how difficult things could get for the Government if it should not concede this, and blustered that he would abandon the whole business unless it did. An English observer wrote: 'Melville is more than ever Minister de facto in Scotland, and ... a year's fasting has so sharpened the appetites of his followers, that not a chaise is to be got on any of the roads which lead to Dunira, so numerous are the solicitors and expectants that attend his court.' After the General Election, all Whig office-holders had been removed (so much for the evil of purges). Curiously, young Cockburn found himself promoted to advocate-depute, and at Melville's, not the Lord Advocate's behest. The bold reviewer shamefacedly explained in later years: 'The place was offered, and its acceptance urged on me, solely from family connection.'[34]

The banished Whigs yet exerted an oblique influence for they had, in desperation to bolster their interest, almost drained the sources of patronage dry. That hardly deterred Melville's clients, but he could not ignore it: 'During the late administration I am informed that pensions to the amount of £4000 per annum had been added to the pension list of Scotland, and therefore if great circumspection is not used on the subject, there may be a deficiency in the funds to answer the present establishment.'

Parliament soon showed that it had had enough of insatiable Scots, Whig or Tory. In 1810 it passed an Act 'for preventing excess and abuse' in Scottish pensions. The measure was deliberately designed to ensure that old Scots pensioners would die off faster than new ones could be created, so that the expenditure would be reduced by the ravages of time to an acceptable level. Not more than £300 was to be awarded to anyone, and the annual increase in the value of the list for the whole country would be limited to £800, till its total was cut from the current level of £36,000 to £25,000 – by past standards, real drouth. Worse threatened to follow, for a select committee investigated sinecures in Scotland and found that £20,000 a year in salaries could easily be saved. If there were to be rewards in future for faithful Scots, they had to come cheap. That was perhaps why Dundas raised with Portland the grievance that no peer had in the last twelve years been granted a British title, except for four promoted all at once by the Talents. With special reference to electoral prospects, he warned that 'unless some disposition is shown to confer favours ... the interest of the present Government among the peerage of Scotland and their immediate connections will be materially shaken.' This plea, or threat, fell on deaf ears.[35]

With a slackening in the flow of patronage from above, loyalty from below thus immediately turned turbid, and this at a time when the Scottish system as a whole was starting to be questioned. The resurrected Whigs had been hypocritical and cynical in their own exploitation of it. Yet they had at least aired the alternative of an anglicising spring-clean, lent intellectual weight by the *Edinburgh Review* and not easy to pillory as Jacobin. The Scottish political nation was certainly mercenary, but also in general well-educated, with the leisure and inclination for public pursuits. It could be made receptive to the idea that Scotland, in standing guard over her interests, would be ill-advised to continue relying on the sacredness of a Treaty signed a century before. And dogged institutional inertia became harder to justify as everything else in the British constitution was scrutinised on criteria of utility and efficiency. The notion entered even Scottish heads that problems might be solved by other means than more patronage.

Thus, for example, the legal reform left unfinished by the Talents was not just dropped. This Government produced its own, less drastic and more respectful of local sensibilities, though the legislation was still entrusted to the English Lord Chancellor, Eldon. He proposed to divide the Court of Session into two chambers. In the original draft, the first was to consist of seven judges under the Lord President, the second of six under the Lord Justice Clerk, representing therefore a reduction in their number. This in itself proved offensive, and an amendment was accepted maintaining the time-hallowed tally of fifteen. It did not compromise the aim of greater efficiency, for the court's capacity would still be doubled. Not only was justice at home to be expedited, but procedures were also introduced to cut down appeals to the Lords. On the vexed question of trial by jury in civil causes, an inquiry was to be set up. Even this limited concession to the reformers' favourite fancy nettled Melville, who roused himself to go to London and speak against it. It passed, but the inquiry was then packed with foes to the idea, including Melville himself, the Chief Baron of Exchequer and the Lord Advocate. They did at length come out in favour of an experiment with juries, but in terms so lukewarm that nothing ensued for some years. One may add that this package fell far short of remedying the system's defects.[36]

The universities were another pillar of society which seemed, despite their excellence, increasingly weighed down under tradition. Here patronage generated the particular problem of pluralism, by which a clergyman held a chair concurrently with a living outside. Once a pleasant perk for the more erudite Moderates, it was becoming a necessity. Since 1784, through a series of unconnected executive and judicial actions, professors' real incomes had fallen, a trend recently intensified by inflation. The universities could do little about it because of the increasing inadequacy of their own revenues; the Government had already been obliged to make up deficits at Aberdeen and St Andrews. The revenues were largely composed of teinds, the medieval episcopal taxes put to this better use after the Reformation. The Church, exerting itself to meet the nation's needs, now made many other calls on them, especially to raise the ordinary clergy's stipends. So the remuneration of professors was squeezed, and pluralism offered a way of helping them to cope.

But it caused as many problems as it solved. To outsiders it appeared to be fossilising the old clerical domination of the professoriate. This was hardly sensible when the universities had expanded well beyond their function of training candidates for the ministry, and were giving a wider range of students instruction in more specialised, especially scientific, disciplines. Pluralism thus also became a stick with which to beat the Moderates, who had for decades engrossed most of the chairs along with other offices in the Church's gift. These they tended to regard as their own, despite the Dundases' efforts to ensure a reasonably equitable distribution. The popular party, which could anyway no longer be dismissed as a gang of ignorant bigots, had won its share of promotions. In general, though, evangelicals were not greatly interested in becoming professors. They believed rather that ministers ought to serve parishes, from which duty pluralism was a dereliction: better that the professoriate should be laicised.

The friction of economic and pastoral pressures was generating a good deal of heat. In 1805 the chair of natural philosophy had fallen vacant at St Andrews. Dr Hill wrote to Melville proposing for it his brother-in-law, the Revd James McDonald, minister of nearby Kemback. The appointment, he said, would be of political importance by demonstrating his hold on the university to a band of Whig professors who had won a majority at one college and sought to challenge him. The alleged Whigs had, of course, themselves been installed through the usual official channels, so one may guess that Hill was, as ever when eager to get his way, laying on the politics with a trowel. In fact they too wrote in, asking 'whether our professorships are to become the birthrights and marriage portions of the present rulers and their connections'. The very fact of the appeal was interesting; they would hardly have bothered if they had thought it a waste of time. When

Melville took Hill's advice, they pursued the matter through the courts, and at length had McDonald's election set aside. Here was another limit to the powers of patronage.

A still livelier controversy followed over the chair of mathematics at Edinburgh. The contenders were a Moderate clergyman from one of the city's churches, Thomas MacKnight, and a lay mathematician, John Leslie, with Thomas Chalmers as an also-ran. MacKnight flaunted his intended pluralism. Since he was not going to give up his parish, his appointment would increase the Moderates' representation in the Senatus Academicus without reducing it in the presbytery. The High-flyers resolved not to let them get away with it. Thus Leslie, a Humean sceptic, was agreeably surprised to find lining up behind him not only Whigs and literati but also clergymen of the popular party – indeed there were Moderates who conceded that he was the better candidate. The town council, which held the patronage of the chair, chose him. MacKnight's backers only made themselves look churlish when they tried to persuade the General Assembly to condemn this.[37] It was a big defeat for the Moderates, and has been represented, on no evidence at all, as a slap in the face for the Dundas despotism too. But nobody knows what Melville thought. His kinsman Cockburn stated quite definitely that clerical domination of the universities was the basic question at stake, and Melville had never declared himself in favour of clerical domination as such.

During these years the Kirk was thus trying both to defend its old status and to respond to new demands, all on severely strained resources. That may explain why, for example, protests against lay patronage notably failed to ignite; odd, when they had flared up so fiercely in the preceding period, as they were to do again in the following one. But everybody from the Dundases to the evangelicals apparently regarded this as a closed question, even in particular cases which could have reopened it.

The parish of the Canongate had two livings, to the first of which the Crown presented, to the second of which the magistrates elected. When a holder of the first died in 1808, the magistrates asked for the holder of the second to be promoted in his place. They would then as usual choose the other, so that all at once the church would acquire two elected ministers. Dundas dismissed the idea out of hand (though he did not, as has been claimed, reject election in itself). He replied that 'it would be only an indirect mode of depriving the Crown of its rights of presentation for the purpose of transferring it to the parishioners'. Melville was full of praise for his son's handling of the matter. On the general issue of lay patronage, he noted that 'the question is now very much at rest, and has been accomplished very much by the wisdom and moderation of the Crown in the exercise of presentations belonging to the Crown.' He advised Dundas to look for clergymen 'not much engaged in either the ecclesiastical or political intrigues of the day, and to discover such a person it will always be preferable to avoid any avowed reference to meetings or consultations of the people at large.'

Further dispute, here and elsewhere, may have been avoided because all sides saw the growing difficulty of attracting to the ministry the well-qualified, let alone the well-born. For the Moderates, that precondition of their regime, a socially and economically secure clergy, was no longer guaranteed. Hill warned that, unless stipends were raised, the decline in the clergy's status 'would render them contemptible, and the Church would soon be supplied only out of the lowest orders of the people. It is a branch of political wisdom to save the established clergy from this degradation'. The High-flyers for once would have agreed, at least in part. They might not have shared his horror of the lowest orders, but they were not vowed to poverty either. And as matters stood, some ministers plainly lacked the income to perform their duties properly. Despite a long-standing promise, Melville had done nothing about it.

That was doubtless why the Talents had seized the chance to devise a plan for more frequent increase of clerical stipends. It still did not serve to establish good relations between them and the Kirk. Here too, they were excessively eager to get their own men into influential positions, and to this end interfered more blatantly than Melville had ever done. There was much indignation about this at the General Assembly of 1806, when Hill clashed bitterly with Erskine. He in any event found no more time to deal with stipends than with the rest of his reforming schemes.

The General Assembly of 1807, which followed soon after the change of Government, tried to make sure the matter would not be dropped. A proposal for at least a committee on it was put forward. Hill objected: given his own views, not a commendable move. Probably he disliked not the idea so much as the collaborators of the Talents he descried behind it; like too many men past their heyday, he was becoming full of petty animosities. He even asked Melville to use his influence and quash the move. The response was intended rather to cool things down – the heritors paying the stipends, Melville felt sure, would never 'be adverse to countenance the fair pretensions of the clergy.' In fact there was a good deal of acrimonious debate between the two groups. After echoes of it reached Parliament, the Government at last consented in 1810 to a grant of £10,000, allowing a minimum annual stipend of £150 to be set in regular parishes (not chapels-of-ease). There were 172 of them, nearly one-fifth of the total, needing supplement. This was hardly lavish, but it eased the worst problems.[38]

Another result was the damage done to Hill's position, largely by himself. Even some Moderates now saw him as a divisive influence. The ministers of Edinburgh in particular grew so disgruntled that their leader, Dr Henry Grieve, frankly voiced their complaints to him. Their party had grown visibly disunited, and in his view the major reason was 'an unfortunate relaxation of that confidence which, we presume to think, ought to subsist betwixt you and your clerical connections in this city.'[39] A gap opened up between two schools of Moderatism, centred respectively on St Andrews and Edinburgh. The former was to all intents and purposes immobilist, the latter more receptive to political and intellectual change – simply because, as the metropolitan presbytery, it had to be.

A counterpart was perceptible in the attitudes of the Dundas despotism. Robert the elder, Chief Baron of Exchequer, had turned blimp: 'The popular party in the Church, like the opposition in the state, are infinitely more assiduous in measures ... and by applying through every possible channel they have, in the case of every vacancy of a church in Scotland, succeeded as often in putting in clergy of their way of thinking, that many presbyteries ... are now gradually converted into wild presbyteries, and uniformly send to the Assembly members of that description.' Robert the younger, president of the Board of Control, was more ready to acknowledge new realities: 'It is rather too much to expect that in all cases whatever, where the Crown is patron ... the patronage of the Crown is to be bestowed from no other motive and with no other view than to uphold what is called the Moderate party in the Church of Scotland.'[40]

For this Robert, however, there could be no really independent discretion while the position of his father, sulking at Dunira, was still to be resolved. Both professed themselves unhappy at the Government's weakness, which they ascribed to, among other things, their own lack of influence in it. For Melville, the only answer was his recall. He assumed this to be as blindingly obvious to others as to himself. He told the Chief Baron in February 1808 that 'if the proposition is not too long in coming and comes in such a manner as alone can induce me to listen to it, you may rest assured, however reluctantly I may give up my present happy retirement, I will most undoubtedly do it and sit down to business again with all the alacrity I am possessed of.' In his wishful thinking he even betook himself to London that spring: 'I cannot walk the street or go into a company without being asked on what day I am to resume my situation at the Admiralty Board.' He had an interview with Eldon, who conceded that the Ministry could not last, but offered the crafty advice that Melville would position himself best by avoiding hostility to it meanwhile. He was delighted: 'I certainly entertain no doubt that the time is fast approaching when I shall be called upon to accept some prominent part in Government.' Still, nothing happened immediately, so he retired home to await events.

Another year passed. Early in 1809 Dundas made so bold as to send a reminder to Portland, in the form of a warning that few of his countrymen could be expected to attend and support the Ministry in either Commons or Lords. The only response was a minor reshuffle which took Dundas as Chief Secretary to Ireland and held out nothing to Melville, though he may have been content to await a major reshuffle.

Both remained restive. Dundas declared his new job 'neither very agreeable nor personally convenient'. He confessed to 'an hereditary hankering after Indian concerns, and a proper Caledonian maladie du pays'. Like his father before him, he anyway found it hard to tear himself away. As late as June he told the Lord Lieutenant, the Duke of Richmond: 'I have not yet been provided with a successor at the India Board, and I must of course remain till the next ships are dispatched ... Your Grace has found me hitherto a very inefficient Secretary.' These discontents he would take out on the Irish, still seething with lawless discontent. 'We are not quite right in our senses in this country,' he wrote to Richmond after finally arriving in Dublin, 'and I have no doubt you will also concur with me at thinking that forbearance and concession are not the weapons with which Jacobins and traitors ought to be fought.' Nor was he much placated by his main parliamentary business, to pilot through a Bill for the draining of Irish bogs.[41]

In London, little attention had so far been paid to the Dundases' grumbles, but now the Cabinet deputed Eldon to find out exactly what lay at the bottom of them.

Robert's response was cryptic: 'Unless some steps are taken to have the public business carried on in a manner more suited to the times in which we live, and to the state of the country, you must not reckon upon the support of many persons on whom you have hitherto relied,' he descanted. He laboured the point that absolute identity of the Government's and of Melville's interest should not be taken for granted either. Some sort of crunch did then come: 'It will be impossible for me to continue in office if there is reason to suppose that the next session will commence and be carried through under the same system as the last.'[42]

Dundas did not 'presume to suggest a remedy' but private communications with his father show that they actually wanted George Canning to become Prime Minister. And, as almost a Dundas himself, what a natural choice he made! He was besides a young man of consummate talents, already Foreign Secretary. Who could tell? Perhaps he was a new Pitt, to whom they could repeat the trick of attaching themselves early and so secure their position into the distant future. And Canning, too, saw himself as the man to succeed a Portland on his last legs.

They had been in cordial contact, often over patronage, ever since the Government's formation. Melville, during a further visit to London, noted a 'long and unreserved conversation' with Canning in January 1809. He mainly vented his ideas on the conduct of war in the Peninsula, but also used the opportunity to pass on his reply to a recent inquiry from Portland, whether he could not see his way to giving the Ministry some open support in the Lords. He said he could not, because 'so many measures must come under discussion which it is impossible for me either to approve or defend', and then 'it could be imputed to me that I was giving my countenance to the views of a factious and intemperate opposition'. But almost at once he felt he had been too negative, and asked his son to make clear to Canning that a change of political circumstances might also work in him a change of mind.

Canning responded to the signals, and soon they were in close consultation. In June he had an interview with Robert Dundas at which they went over the contenders for the succession and agreed on ruling all the others out. They met again in July, when Canning was assured that if he provoked a crisis in the Government by resigning, then Dundas would go too. Even so, neither side was fully confident of the other. Canning thought the Dundases rather too fearful of sticking their necks out. They were dismayed at his insistence that Castlereagh, now Secretary of State for War, should be excluded from a new Cabinet. Rigid conditions were, they thought, unhelpful in a fluid situation. Little progress had thus been made by the time Robert Dundas was sent off to Ireland, which put a stop to these contacts. He never found the chance to act on his 'conditional notice to quit', for in September the Ministry was overtaken by an extraordinary crisis.[43]

Canning's courting of the Dundases turned out to have been just one thread in a broad skein. He believed his time had come. Reverses in Spain, culminating in Sir John Moore's heroic retreat and death at Corunna the previous winter, offered the chance to thrust aside Castlereagh, who might stand in his way. In March 1809, Canning had forced matters by privately telling the Prime Minister that he would resign himself unless his rival was moved. A jittery Portland sought support for this from the King, Eldon and others – evidently the Dundases knew what was afoot too. Only vacillation and subterfuge resulted. Castlereagh stayed in the dark right through the summer. When inevitably he found out, he challenged Canning to a duel. Both survived, but they could not possibly continue serving together. That meant the end of the Government. Nor indeed could either be called to take over. Portland stepped down regretted only to the extent that he apparently had to be succeeded by the uninspiring Spencer Perceval, Chancellor of the Exchequer. And the building of a workable Ministry would clearly be even more wearisome than usual.

Dundas, in Dublin when the crisis broke, left immediately for London. He was among the members of the administration who did not at once resign, and now thought he ought not before the situation clarified. This headless body faced three problems. It had first to keep itself together so as to form the continuing core of a Government. Dundas, among the most prominent of the junior Ministers, was reckoned vital to that. Perceval pressed him to stay, promising promotion to Castlereagh's vacant post. Dundas replied that he did not particularly want it, but would be guided by his father. Their second problem was to decide if they really were going to accept Perceval as leader or find someone else. Connected to this was a third problem, of broadening an incoming Government's base in the Commons.

With the components of the old administration at daggers drawn, some thought of bringing in the Whigs. Dundas advised that at most they should approach Lord Moira, and certainly not Grenville or Grey; to them the King was in any case bound to object. His colleagues apparently hoped that he would take up the delicate task of negotiation, doubtless through his contacts from 1806, but he declined. With nobody else willing to bell the cat, there was little choice but to abandon any idea of a broader Government. For himself, Dundas said that 'provided a strong and efficient Government is formed, and the King is not delivered over, bound hand and foot, to the last administration [the Talents], including the Jacobins, I shall be satisfied'. This was clearly a modification of his previous position put to Portland, that the Ministry's base should be broadened. He justified it to Huskisson on the grounds that the failure to do so had 'not been from any unfairness or illiberality'. Now the outgoing administration 'ought to fight the battle till the sense of Parliament shall be decidedly against them, and they are compelled to represent to the King that they are unable to carry on his Government'. Unfortunately, he omitted to say the same to Canning.

Dundas did, however, sedulously consult Melville, who even commented 'how wonderful a coincidence of opinion has taken place between him and me at the distance of nearly 400 miles from each other.'[44] That changed abruptly after Perceval at last received the King's commission in October. He repeated his offer to Dundas who, though ready to accept, wished with wonted candour to let the Prime Minister know that he would really have preferred a Government under Canning. He further stipulated that he would have to ask his father's approval. Perceval, writing to Dunira to second this request, called such conduct 'plain, straightforward, determined, open, manly and honourable in every possible respect'. He added that he would have given Melville something had he not been assured that nothing was wanted. In any event, he hastened to explain, with both

Canning and Castlereagh out, his Ministry would have to rely on the Commons' independent members: the very ones who, having swung the votes for impeachment, were unlikely to tolerate Melville's presence in the Cabinet now. What he could offer instead was an earldom. But the well-meant frankness of this letter deeply offended its recipient, who replied in a barely civil manner denying any aspiration to high office or higher rank.

The mask dropped when Melville wrote to tell his son of the exchange:

> Perceval states in terms very kind and flattering to you, your acceptance of the seal of the War Department. But if I have not misapprehended the import of your letter to me on the subject [seeking approval], I conceive he does so in more unqualified terms than the transaction warrants. I confess on that subject I entertain very great anxiety. You must at the present moment consider what is best for your private and political character, never forgetting that you are connected with a great and powerful interest, which has long wished, and that too very recently, for my return to office as essential to their having any confidence in the administration at a period when it was stronger than it is likely now to be. I cannot take it upon me to predict what may be their feelings on the present occasion.

Those importunate friends were at him again! He anyway preferred his son to return to the Board of Control: 'It may perhaps occur to yourself that the same feeling against the appearance of a compromise which induces me to refuse the advancement in the rank of peerage should operate with you to avoid, if you can, an advance in the progress of your ambition at the present moment.'[45]

Dundas, meanwhile in Dublin clearing his desk, found the letter waiting on his return to London. He told Perceval at once: 'It is impossible not to perceive an altered and a more frigid tone, and though it is a matter of little moment to me personally, it is not a state of things which on public ground can be viewed with indifference. There is only one course for me to adopt.' That course was set out in an immediate reply to Melville – 'to decline accepting either the War Department or any other office.' He went on:

> As an individual member of Parliament I shall persevere in the support I have promised, as long as I can do it without discredit, but I must decline for the present all connection with those interests which have hitherto adhered to you, because unless support was to be hearty and cordial, I should be dealing most unfairly with the Government, if I were to hold out to the latter any expectation of real and substantial aid from that quarter ... There is one point on which in justice to myself I must endeavour to undeceive you – I mean your allusions to the 'pursuit' and the 'progress of my ambition'. I must positively and decidedly disclaim any such motive on my part and have only to assure you that you have no ground for the insinuation of my having been actuated by such a sentiment.[46]

The correspondence now degenerated. Melville reflected on Perceval's comments with heavy-handed irony: 'I am flattered by the idea that my services are duly appreciated, and that it would be of importance if I would serve again.' Yet, he fumed, 'it is found inexpedient to admit my service, because it would be offensive to a coalition of Methodism and Jacobinism in the House of Commons.' When his son's letter arrived he exploded: 'It is no practice of mine to insinuate.'[47] The breach soon threatened to become irreparable, and the halls of Arniston rang with hard words. Its laird, the Chief Baron, wrote imploring his cousin not to step down from his post, still less from Parliament or public life: 'I should consider your refusal of it indeed as almost breaking up all connection betwixt us.' He had, he said, stopped his own wife from interfering, but Anne Saunders Dundas was now wading in. They should really all show a little more understanding and forbearance, and avoid irrevocable steps. So violent were these quarrels that their echo even reached Perceval and the King. An abyss loomed before the Dundas despotism. If father and son were to go their separate ways, where would it all end? Without a Dundas in office, perhaps without a Dundas in politics, the despotism must crumble.[48]

There could be but a single outcome. It was for Melville to abandon the impossible demand that Robert Dundas should sacrifice his prospects to those of his father, who in truth no longer had any. At last he climbed down. The experience had been painful, but 'I express my earnest wish that you would consider all my letters to you as never having been written and act solely on what may be the dictates of your own judgment and the feelings of your own honour, exclusive of any consideration respecting me. I shall direct my own steps the best way I can.'[49]

The brutal demonstration of his impotence still failed to impress itself fully on a man no longer capable of seeing beyond his personal frustrations and resentments. In order to mollify him, it was settled that Dundas should after all go back to the Board of Control, but now with a place in Cabinet. Even this Melville tried to obstruct. He got Hope to write and complain once more how insulting the Prime Minister's letter had been. Dundas coolly replied: 'You must not judge the public feeling in England on that point by the meridian of Edinburgh.'

His troubles were not over, for now Canning also complained of having been 'hardly used'. The Dundases had encouraged him to force a crisis, then failed to honour their undertaking and follow him out of office. Robert squirmed:

> Do you imagine ... that all those who would adhere to my father or myself in Government or in opposition on any sound and rational principle of public conduct would also follow us for no better reason than because we choose to indulge our private partiality in your favour, and to harass the King and disturb his Government by joining in a controversy for official pre-eminence?

Canning sarcastically rejoined that they had spent the last year doing just that. At any rate, it was now established that they were not going to become Canningites as they had been Pittites. While working relations could in due course be restored with Canning, profound trust never would.

It proved altogether a hard winter for Dundas. Early in 1810 the correspondence between his father and the Prime Minister was leaked to the press. He felt so embarrassed that he again offered to resign, since he could not guarantee an end to these incessant pinpricks: 'It is come to a crisis in which I must either break off altogether all political connection with him and endeavour to attach to the present administration as large a portion as possible of his friends in Scotland, or I must act inconsistently with my duty to His Majesty's Government.' Inquiry revealed, however, the unalluring prospect that three-quarters of Melville's followers in the Commons were likely to stick with him. It was then Perceval's painful part to disclose that investigation had uncovered Melville himself as the source of the leak. In quiet fury, Dundas wrote: 'I cannot help suspecting that you are little aware of the precipice on which you stand, and I doubt if there is any person who has ventured to put it to you. Whatever step I may feel myself compelled to take in the matter shall at least be with your eyes opened to all the consequences both public and private.' Melville would certainly not look very good, he went on, if the whole business was broadcast. The old man still seemed unrepentant but, being again on a visit to London, was at least induced to see Perceval in an effort to patch up their differences. It would be idle, however, to pursue these matters further. Melville had finished himself, and it was a pity he could not accept the fact with more dignity. For Dundas, it had all been a harsh lesson in the vicious and ruthless side of politics, for which he in future showed a marked distaste.[51]

After making some speeches in the Lords, Melville returned to Dunira. He showed every sign of wishing to stay there for good and devote himself to rustic pursuits. 'I am very anxious,' he wrote to a lady of his acquaintance,

> to establish pheasants here; the more so, as last year I had almost accomplished it, if an abominable polecat had not in some way discovered, got into the pheasant-house, and in one night destroyed the whole lot that were ready to be turned out. I am determined, however, not to be discomfited by a polecat having, in the course of my life, got the better of so many other mischievous vermin.'

To his son he remarked in January 1811: 'Among other causes of aversion I have at going to London is the disagreeable feeling I have of being exposed to the urgent demands of tradesmen and shopkeepers which I cannot immediately answer.'

Spring came, and he was still at Dunira when he heard in May about the death of Robert Blair, Lord President of the Court of Session since the reorganisation in 1808. Blair had been a friend of his youth, an original member of their old club, the Feast of Tabernacles. He was also a next-door neighbour of the Chief Baron at the house in George Square where Melville stayed in Edinburgh. They had thus remained on close terms, and he was deeply affected. Some extra intelligence greatly excited him – that Henry Erskine would seek the presidency. It was usual for vultures to gather at once round any official corpse, and Colquhoun intimated that he wanted the job too. Melville hurried to Edinburgh whence he wrote to his son, in the portentous style of his last years: 'My mind as yet is not at leisure to deal with any feelings of sorrow which agitate me personally on the present melancholy occasion. It is totally absorbed in the contemplation of the calamity which has befallen my country and the deep affliction which overwhelms the family of my friend.' This contemplation did not stop his then launching into an extended discussion of the judicial reshuffle which must now take place.

Nothing set Melville's pulses racing like a bit of jobbery, but no particular bit had quickened him so much for ages. He went down to dine with Hope at Granton, where both agreed that the idea of promoting Erskine was a 'fantastical fancy'. Up betimes the next morning, he wrote another long letter to his son on the subject, among others, of young Cockburn's allegiance to the Whigs: 'Nobody can give me a reason how it began or why it continues.' Perhaps he should be made sheriff of East Lothian, and that would cure him; should he decline, 'it would show to everybody that it was not the fault of government, if such party nonsense was set up in the faculty'. He added that he was just about to see Blair's solicitor, and hoped to hear details of the will. He had so much business that he expected to stay in Edinburgh at least another week.[52]

What he meant was a little scheme of his own, to put Boyle, the Solicitor General, into the president's chair over the Lord Advocate's head. The Chief Baron wrote to Dundas that the idea was scandalous: 'Your father's mind is prejudiced against Colquhoun, and to gratify private antipathies or dislikes in so public an arrangement as the irreparable loss of Blair has occasioned is I hope impossible' – the Lord Advocate 'must and ought to be the president'. The next day was a Sunday. Melville attended church and walked home with Henry Mackenzie, another neighbour in George Square, talking of dead friends and past times. That evening he went down to Arniston with his daughter Elizabeth.[53]

She may now take up the story:

> He spent all Monday, the 26th, with me and the children, and seemed much gratified by riding about the place all the morning, and walking with me in the evening. Next morning he desired Anne [a daughter] to give him his breakfast early, previous to his going to Edinburgh. The president's funeral was to be next day, the 28th. Contrary to my usual practice I felt an irresistible desire to be up in time to see him before his departure. I did so, and he flattered me with hopes of returning Thursday or Friday.[54]

Scott can fill in the final details of what happened in Edinburgh:

> Lord Melville wrote a most affecting letter to Mr Perceval recommending Mrs Blair to the protection and generosity of the public to whom her husband has rendered such eminent services. In the evening he made his visit to the disconsolate family whose house is next door to the Lord Chief Baron's, then his residence. Upon his return he supped with the Chief Baron who did not remark anything particular in his appearance. As he undressed to go to bed he directed his mournings to be prepared for next day when the funeral of the president was to take place, and at the same time said 'I lie down satisfied for I have done all the painful duty which friendship exacted from me.' … In the morning he did not ring at his usual hour of seven for he always rose early and his servant becoming alarmed entered his room about eight and found him dead and all remains of vital heat quite departed.[55]

He must have slipped away peacefully soon after retiring. He had authorised the opening of his body, and the surgeons found the wine from his last meal had not even entered the bladder. He was very obese. His liver looked no better than it ought after years of heavy drinking. The arteries of his heart were narrowed, with walls hard as stone, and this had clearly led to his death. He was laid to rest on June 8 in the family's lair at the old kirk of Lasswade, near Melville Castle, the funeral being private.[56]

Official Edinburgh and, beyond it, the Scottish political nation were stunned at their loss. Here the mourning was doubtless genuine: monuments were erected to the departed statesman, streets named after him. And, if one discounts for the purpose of striking a balance the opinions of both bosom friends and virulent enemies, contemporary judgments of him were generally favourable. Cornwallis, for example, a great public servant and a close collaborator though not a crony, said: 'I never met with a more fair and honourable man.' Adam Ferguson. disappointed of patronage in his latter years, still thought that Melville had taken 'leisure to do good as well as to struggle for power'. The chaste Wilberforce could not forgive his sins but, recalling how after the impeachment Melville had stopped him in the Horse Guards and shaken his hand, commented that he 'was a loose man; yet he was a fine fellow in some things. People have thought him a mean, intriguing creature; but he was in many respects a fine, warm-hearted fellow.'[58]

Not least for the light cast on the Scots' changing comprehension of their past, the later history of Melville's reputation makes an interesting study in itself. It sank under the influence of the Whigs who at length defeated the Dundas despotism, and who were able to implant their own account of the era in the Scottish mind. Yet Cockburn could say that Melville 'was the very man for Scotland at that time, and is a Scotchman of whom his country may be proud. Skilful in Parliament, wise and liberal in council, and with an almost unrivalled power of administration, the usual reproach of his Scottish management is removed by two facts, that he did not make the bad elements he had to work with and that he did not abuse them.' The memorialist later imagined a scene in Elysium, with a political debate among Edinburgh's dead luminaries. He gave Melville the most agreeable part, to 'represent all sides: defending the old system as natural for Scotland in the last age and the new in this'. Brougham, too, inhibited by no ties of blood, yet owned that he was 'a steady and determined friend, who only stood the faster by those that wanted him the more … void of all affectation, all pride, all pretension; a kind and affectionate man in the realms of private life'. With such testimonies, it was no surprise that his personal reputation stood high well into the Scots Liberal hegemony. At the end of the century, G. W. T. Omond, an eminent advocate and in his spare time a very competent scholar, wrote from the family's papers a history which, within his chosen limits, could still be scrupulously fair.[58]

That became steadily less possible after the work of the second school of modern Scottish historiography during the early 1900s. H. W. Meikle and W. L. Mathieson were good historians to whom Scotland is still indebted for pioneering studies. But they and others were also, as far as one can gather, typical Edwardian Liberals, with little inherent sympathy for Melville. He was inevitably cast as a villain by Meikle's concentration on radicalism; and Mathieson just could not remain objective about him, descending at times into pure invective. Meanwhile, Sir John Fortescue exerted himself to ruin Melville's military reputation. There were professional protests at the more grossly unjust aspects of this portrayal, though no systematic refutation. Melville did later appear as a hero of Vincent Harlow's imperial histories; but Barun De's positive appreciation remains an unpublished thesis. Little known to non-specialists, their work has not restored his standing.

Two biographies made use of the muniments at Melville Castle, before these were broken up and sold. Holden Furber's, insofar as it concerned Scotland, was weighted heavily towards electoral politics, giving a lop-sided view of its subject. Cyril Matheson's, if valuable on many points of detail, could not see the wood for the trees. Modern Scottish historical studies started up again in greater earnest after the Second World War without fresh original work on Melville, which dispersal of the papers made difficult. The initial *summa* of these efforts, William Ferguson's volume in the Edinburgh History, could thus scarcely avoid taking a dim view of him, reinforced by the author's own evident dislike. So it has gone on, despite caveats entered by John Dwyer, Alexander Murdoch and Richard Sher. Arriving from North America without the native prejudices, they have sought to show that in certain particulars there might be something to say for the old devil after all.

They still could not rescue him from the Caledonian pandemonium, where bad Scots go, though perhaps he was well out of a pantheon containing Mary Queen of Scots, Prince Charles Edward Stewart and John Maclean. By the time Alistair Campsie's novel, *The Clarinda Conspiracy*, appeared in 1989, Melville's reputation had become a dustbin into which any accusation could be shovelled. Artistic freedom is to be defended always and everywhere, but Campsie wrote articles in the newspapers claiming he had represented historical truth as well. Others may have dismissed Melville as a mere knee-jerking reactionary and anglicising toady; the novelist was now able to reveal the ultimate depths of his unredeemed depravity, as paranoid, alcoholic, drug-addict, cuckold, impotent and murderer (of Robert Burns, no less).

Those familiar with Scottish historiography will perceive that Melville was being mythicised, cast into a limbo where objectivity would be not just redundant but even undesirable. It would suffice to recognise in him the monster, ogre, renegade, enemy of the people and the nation. But we might pause to recall the words of Castlereagh, who had here no axe to grind, and who returned wonderingly from a visit to Dunira:

> Lord Melville … had a partiality for Scotland such as might not have been expected in a man of his standing in the world, with views of mankind which might be supposed to do away with particular prejudices of this kind. But it was not so, he felt for Scotland all that partiality that has been remarked as a characteristic of the people of that country.[59]

No attempt has been made here to hide his faults: indeed, new ones have been revealed. I have preferred, however, to look at him not as a bogeyman, nor yet as a misunderstood paragon, but as an effective politician. Politics certainly has to find room for deep thinkers, such as, in this age, Edmund Burke. It must also find room for public spirit and high integrity, of the sort that William Pitt the younger exemplified. But politics would scarcely be possible at all without the practical men, those who appreciate that the choice usually lies between evils, who strike the bargains and push through the measures that make political systems work, and who take the punishment when they do not. Without them the deep thought, public spirit and high integrity would go for nothing. Dundas was one of these. This is not to say he was devoid of principle, or that he did not sincerely seek the public good. But he contributed most in what he was best at, this third aspect of political activity which it would be foolish and unjust to despise.

A supremely versatile man, he left his mark in many places. His work in India was his greatest achievement. Linked to his vision (not too strong a word) of Empire was also his more controversial war effort, for which the case has at some length been set out above. He anyway takes a rightful place as one leader of a pivotal generation in British politics, which gradually, and not yet always thoroughly, shook itself free of the political trammels of Whiggery and the economic trammels of mercantilism. If sometimes only in intuition, these people realised that Revolution principles could not be cited as the automatic answer to every problem, that new means had to be conceived by which Britain could meet the demands of a new age. Scientific government and economic liberalisation in a setting of social order were their aims. It is remarkable how successful they proved in an era of chronic external crisis.

Where, in this great scheme of things, do we fit Melville's preoccupation with Scotland? His flexibility on the inheritance of 1688 did not extend so fully to that of 1707. But we must recall the nature of the Union in its first decades, about which historians no longer delude themselves or their public. A typical recent contribution makes comments like this: 'England's relationship with Scotland and Ireland in the ... early eighteenth century was classically imperial. The policies of the English government gave the law to the other kingdoms ... From an English point of view, Scotland was an alien country.'[60] Melville overcame this unhappy legacy, not by throwing in his lot with the English, still less by retrogressing into patriotic self-pity. He did what came naturally to him: he realistically appraised a political problem then solved it, forging the fragmented Scottish interests into a stronger force and welding them to the centre of power in London.

In the nature of the case, compromises had to come, and the system he left remained imperfect. But the net result was to raise Scotland from helpless subordination. No longer did English government give the law. On the contrary, Scots might, if not without difficulty, win themselves a hearing, win themselves attention, even win themselves action. It was crucial that Dundas could convincingly present himself as much more than a narrowly Scottish politician, the first since the Union who could. In his generosity, he helped Irish, East Indian, West Indian, a whole range of different interests as much as he helped Scottish ones.

He was indeed a unionist and imperialist, if the terms are not anachronistic, and found his natural arena at Westminster. But Westminster, in his conception, was not properly dominated by small-minded English attitudes and concerns. On the contrary, he intended that all those interests should there attain a legitimacy of their own. John Brewer has recently shown how the growth of the British state during the eighteenth century was matched by the rise of lobbying on behalf of such interests needing to appease and harness its power for their own ends. In response the state at least aspired to impartiality and efficiency in dealing with them. Though he drew attention above all to the commercial ones, it may not be unreasonable to extend the paradigm to others which felt a common bond. And what common bond is more powerful than nationhood?

There were two national interests, Scotland's and Ireland's, with which the

British state was obliged to grapple at close quarters. Both had long advanced claims essentially particularist. In the new conditions, these came to be balanced by demands that both should share more of the economic rewards and political privileges enjoyed in England. Thus the desire for a truly British state arose as much from the periphery as from the metropolis, undercutting the English arrogance that would gladly have held the two smaller peoples down.[61] There was, however, an instructive difference in the outcome. Ireland's interests never, despite the exertions of Melville and others on their behalf, attained complete legitimacy. They remained in essence alien interests to which English government gave the law. Scotland, on the other hand, passed through a strait gate which changed her entire relationship with England. Largely, though not exclusively, the achievement was Melville's. On the strength of that, the Empire could be justly dubbed British, not English.

The emergence of a British identity was doubtless a complex phenomenon, but we can point to elements which Melville may have contributed. One was the widening of Westminster's horizons. A second was that the Union's benefits came to be more equally apportioned. This was especially true of, thirdly, the spoils of Empire: while the English bemoaned favouritism to his countrymen, they profited from his luring them into the imperial mission. Fourth, the wars fought under vigorous leadership, if not engendering British patriotism, did raise it to new heights, displacing the older, specifically Scottish one – displacing also, by the way, the radicals' alternative vision of national identity and freedom. Unlike in France and some other countries, in Britain conservatives appropriated patriotism.[62]

An answer now appears to the question raised at an early stage in this work about the nature of Melville's political activity and its relation to the world of the Scottish Enlightenment which formed him. It clearly would be implausible, after all that has been related above, to read him as a country ideologist, in the way that Dwyer and Murdoch have tried to do. Probably during the last winter of his life he wrote to Lord Londsdale a long memorandum which, however it was meant, certainly looks like a sort of political testament. The crucial passage ran:

> We have ... been gratified to see rich, independent and respectable commoners taking an active part in the concerns of the country, and in a constitutional mode superintending the affairs of the country and watching over the conduct of executive government, but whatever speculative men and idle theorists may think or say, I believe no rational man, with a practical understanding, ever entertained so wild an idea, as to suppose that the balance of the constitution could ever last long, if the executive government lost its paramount interest in the popular branch of the constitution ... Unless the monarchical and aristocratical parts of the constitution unite in the formation and support of a Government competent to withstand the rapid approaches of democratical and revolutionary combinations, they will feel the catastrophe when it is too late to prevent it.[63]

It is a document of classic conservatism, clearly concerned with the authority of the state, not with the autarchic elitism that would be expected of civic humanist values.

But in Britain, or rather in Great Britain, the state never strove towards the kind of absolutist authority it attained in the other multinational monarchies of Europe. It resorted in achieving unity neither to force nor to the sweeping rationalist reform of institutions. Unity instead came peacefully, without up-heaval, in the evolution of a shared culture, in the distribution of proceeds from a burgeoning commerce and (of particular relevance here) in political manage-ment. This set common purposes for the national elites, from which they were diffused downwards through the chains of dependence in contemporary civil society. The development was not altogether symmetrical, for the identity of the junior partner needed special consideration to avoid submersion by the senior one. And as befitted the Caledonian antisyzygy, the methods were somewhat contra-dictory. On the one hand, the power of the central state was circumscribed, by keeping the English at arm's length. On the other, the central state was colonised and its opportunities were exploited with as much gusto as those in any distant imperial outpost.

Still, partners were what Melville made of Scotland and England. The terms of such a relationship are worth marking. It requires joint responsibility in all undertakings, not necessarily in mutual affection, but certainly in mutual respect. It surely cannot demand, as the Whigs thought, conscious effacement of differ-ences, still less the domination or absorption of one partner by the other. Given that relationship as the end, the means to it adopted by Melville may appear in a kinder light. In fact the only ready means he had to hand were a more elaborate and efficient network of patronage. This has often seemed shameful to a nation which prides itself on being composed of men of independent mind. But was it so different from the system which Scotland has wished on herself in the course of the twentieth century? Yes, there are differences: for one, that the system today deploys resources which make those of the Dundas despotism look puny; for another, that to gain them Scots have turned themselves from partners into supplicants.

Notes

1. Cockburn (1852), 131; Aberdeen Papers, BL Add MSS 43227, f.128.
2. Thorne (1986), i, 87; i, 309; Horn (1966), 237.
3. HMC J. B. Fortescue MSS (1892), viii, 35, 43; SRO GD 51/1/195/16–17; Thorne, iii, 653.
4. NLS Acc 9140, Feb.10 & 12, 1806; Thorne, iii, 642.
5. NLS Acc 9140, Feb. 2 & 3, 1806.
6. ibid., Feb.4, 1806; SRO GD 51/1/195/5–10.
7. SRO GD 51/1/195/9–10, 14 & 90/5; NLS Acc 9140, Feb.23 & 28, 1806; Grierson (1932), i, 279.
8. Duckham (1970), 128; Grant (1988), ii, 101; Kay (1877), ii, 441; Cockburn (1856), 200; Cockburn (1932), 90.
9. NLS Acc 9140, Feb.16, 1806.
10. Phillipson (1967), 180–2; WLP I, wrongly attributed to 1804; RHL, ii, f.272; WLC, July 17, 1808; Anon. (1807b), 20, 35, 155; NLS MS 12, ff. 62, 77 et seqq; Campbell of Succoth Papers TD 219/6/470.
11. SRO GD 51//1/195/18–9; Speirs Papers, box 25, bundle 8, July 28, 1806.
12. Thorne, 86; Fergusson (1882), 439; Patrick (1973), 157–8.

13. NLS Acc 9140, Feb.8, 1806; Lonsdale Papers. LI/2/11; Thorne, iii, 709: Matheson (1933), 378.
14. Seaforth Muniments, SRO GD 46/4/17/16.
15. Ilchester (1908), ii, 1919; Chamberlain (1983), 95–7; SRO GD 51/1/119.
16. Aberdeen Papers BL Add MSS 43227, f.64; Chamberlain, 98; Large (1963), 677; (1986), 241 et seqq; McCahill (1978), 161.
17. SRO GD 51/1/119; Grierson (1932), i, 361.
18. Aspinall (1962), v, 358; Turberville (1958), 472; Boyle Papers, 9/6/15; WLC, May 8, 1807.
19. *Parl. Debates*, ix, col. 649; NLS MS 1052, f. 126; SRO GD 51/1/131; Cochrane Papers, NLS MS 2573, f.14; HMC Wykeham-Martin MSS (1909), 425.
20. SRO GD 51/1/195/25–6.
21. NLS MS 14839, f.67; MS 8, f. 222; Boyle Papers, 9/6/21.
22. Auckland Papers, BL Add MSS 34443, f.207; SRO GD 51/1/66/7; GD 51/11/20; Chatham Papers PRO 30/8/157/2/343; Aspinall, v, 405.
23. Thorne, iii, 645 et seqq; Huskisson Papers, BL Add MSS 38737, f.10; Grierson, i, 123; Cockburn (1856), 216.
24. Scott (1894), 157; *Parl. Deb.*, xxvi, col. 1099; Liverpool Papers, BL Add MSS 38245, f.133.
25. SRO GD 51/1/743/5; GD 51/1/520/9.
26. NLS MS 1063, f.123; Minto Papers, NLS MS 11302, ff. 1 et seqq; 11283, ff. 181, 259.
27. Tripathi (1956), 113; Kumar (1983), 817; SRO GD 51/1/195/42; GD 51/1/139; NLS MS 14839, f.172; MS 1064, f. 158; Philips (1940), 153.
28. NLS MS 1063, f.60; MS 59, f.141; Minto Papers, NLS MS 11340, ff. 63 et seqq; MS 11302, ff. 25 et seqq; Parker (1985), 197.
29. NLS MS 1063, ff.20 et seqq., 60, 65; JRL, 692/1810; *Parl. Debates*, xvii, col. 225; Grant (1813), 150; Dodwell (1929), 458.
30. *Parl. Debates*, xxvi, col. 788.
31. Ingram (1956), 33 et seqq; Tripathi, 217; Embree (1962), 249; Philips, 161; Minto Papers, NLS MS 11283, f.315; *Parl. Debates*, xix, col. 467.
32. ElibankPapers SRO GD 32/25/89; Mitchison (1962), 207; Thorne, iii, 377.
33. NLS MS 1063, ff.36, 68; *Parl. Debates*, xvi, col.23.
34. Maxwell (1903), i, 85; Cockburn, 214, 228.
35. *Parl. Debates*, xvii, app.4, xcviii; SRO GD 51/1/136/1; Macleod of Geanies Papers, NLS MS 19301, f.136; Rose (1810), 59.
36. Ferguson (1968), 269; Omond (1883), 224; Willcock (1966), 253; Cooper of Culross (1958), 343; Paton (1958), 54; Phillipson (1967), 234–45.
37. Clark (1960–3), 179 et seqq; Morrell (1975), 63 et seqq; Furber (1931), 298.
38. Cockburn, 203; Brown (1982), 24; NLS MS 17, f.37; WLC, Apr.27, May 27, 1808, Mar.11, 1811; Cook (1820), 131–2; Clark, loc.cit. & in Mitchison & Phillipson (1970), 216; Clark (1963), 135; Benton (1969), 136; *Parl. Papers* (1810).
39. STA MS 4706; Cook, 189, 200; Matheson (1916), 107; Clark, loc.cit., Smith (1987), 51–2.
40. Cook, 164; Matheson, 112; Clark, 219; NLS MS 59, f.93; MS 14838, f. 16; SRO RH 4/15/1; SRO GD 51/1/136/2–3; GD 51/1/347/5, 10–11, 22.
41. NLI,55/268–70; Buccleuch Papers SO GD 224/30/7/9; Liverpool Papers, BL Add MSS 38571, f.134; Aspinall, v, 257, 301.

42. NLS Acc 9140, June 22 & 24, Nov. 2 & 3, 1809; Buccleuch Papers, GD 224/30/7/7.
43. SRO GD 51/1/146/1; GD 51/1/195/86; GD 51/1/349/35; NLS Acc 9140, Sept. 14, 15, 17, Oct. 24, 1809; Canning Papers, bundles 31, 34.
44. NLS Acc 9140, Oct. 5 & 8, 1809; NLI, 55A/331.
45. Spencer Perceval Papers, WLP, Oct.11, 1809; NLS Acc 9140, Oct. 15, 1809.
46. ibid., Oct. 11, 16 & 20, 1809.
47. ibid., Oct. 22, 1809; Aspinall, v, 422.
48. NLS Acc 9140, Oct. 23, 1809.
49. ibid., Oct.31, Nov.4, Dec.12, 1809, Jan.15, 1810.
50. ibid., Apr.14, 15, 17 & 28, 1810; Canning Papers, bundles 34, 34a; Thorne , i, 90.
51. Mure (1853), iii, 376; SRO GD 235/10/22/38.
52. NLS MS 9, ff.101–7.
53. ibid., 111–7; Thompson (1927), 144.
54. SRO GD 51/1/117/323.
55. Grierson (1932), ii, 516
56. NLS MS 547, 459–60.
57. HMC Wykeham-Martin, 405; Edinburgh University Library Papers, DC I. 77, no. 71; Wilberforce (1868), 266.
58. Cockburn, 202–3; (1874), 164–5; Brougham (1839), 230.
59. Farington (1923), vii, 19.
60. Hayton & Szechi (1987), 241–3.
61. Brewer (1988), 14, 251.
62. Cunningham (1989), 65.
63. Buccleuch Papers, SRO GD 224/30/7/12.

9

'The best-conditioned country'

Nothing more plainly illustrates the first Viscount's utter cluelessness in personal finance than a memorandum which he drew up at some time during his last years:

> Lord Melville will die possessed of a respectable landed property of his own creation. This has not been done without considerable expense. From this and other unavoidable causes he will leave debts, but he has made such a disposition of his affairs, no demand against him will exist six months after his death.

Quite what he could have meant must have been a mystery to the family and executors who, after driving back from his funeral on a fine morning along the verdant valley of the North Esk, met at Melville Castle to hear his will and examine his papers. What they learned only deepened the gloom of the gathering. The debts stood at £65,000. Nothing but the rents from Dunira, not more than £1000 a year, could be applied to their repayment. Unless that property was sold – a step all wished to avoid – even the settlement on Lady Melville would be impossible. She existed for a while on the £2000 realised from her late spouse's wine-cellar. Her stepson eventually managed to cobble together an annual income of the same amount from various sources, making up himself any deficiency. It was a relief when in 1814 she remarried.[1]

Heroically, the second Viscount resolved to pay off every penny of the debts himself. The decision was to cripple him financially for years ahead – the interest alone amounted to an annual £3500. A friend pitied his 'many privations and pecuniary embarrassments'. By 1815 he felt he had to jettison Dunira, but a group of well-wishers saved it for him, offering £20,000 against his life insurance. He even thought of selling Melville Castle, till he found he could not get a good enough price for it. Though he limited his outgoings to £7000 a year, by 1820 the combined total of his own and his father's debts was £90,000 and still rising. Drastic action became unavoidable. His wife's remaining English estates were disposed of, and in 1823 Dunira finally went to a kinsman, Sir Robert Dundas of Beechwood. These two transactions brought in about £125,000, which sufficed to stabilise the position. But Melville, like his father, was always a poor man. Unlike his father, he did not think he could spend freely anyway, which must be borne in mind when comparing their political careers.[2]

Considering how he had been treated, Melville's filial piety was heroic too. He encouraged, after naval officers raised a subscription, that body of Edinburgh's citizens which wanted a fitting monument to his father. A column similar to Trajan's in Rome was thought proper. Much argument ensued about where it should be placed.³ Two sites initially favoured were in the middle of Melville Street (where the second Viscount's own statue would eventually stand) or of Coates Crescent (nowadays occupied by William Gladstone's memorial). The second recommended itself especially because this westward extension of the New Town would on completion be 'much superior, by all accounts, to the Place Vendôme at Paris or the Forum of Trajan at Rome'. But Lord Advocate Colquhoun, equally abused by the dead statesman, called it 'a stain on the memory of Lord Melville to send his monument into banishment, by placing it at Coates'.

In 1817 the town council decreed it should be built on the northern point of Calton Hill, but then realised that would block the observatory's outlook. A committee was appointed to report back, and suggested St Andrew Square or Picardy Place at the head of Leith Walk. The latter was ruled out because a column there could not have been seen. Meanwhile, inhabitants of the square were objecting. Somebody mooted the compromise of placing the statue not in its middle but on its western side facing George Street. After debate, however, the conclusion was reached 'that it could only with propriety be put in the centre of the square, from which, if placed at a side, it would have the appearance of having been excluded'. During 1819 the projectors ruminated over a site at Leith Docks, the bottom of the Mound, the cross of George and Frederick Streets, various spots in Queen Street, on Corstorphine Hill, Salisbury Crags, the Castle Esplanade, even Arthur's Seat, because 'every sailor, when he walks the deck of his ship in Leith Roads, and in the Firth of Forth, is entitled to a view of this monument and to consider it peculiarly his own'. Finally, the centre of the square seemed least exceptionable after all. The column, 132 feet high, designed by William Burn, was completed in 1827 and topped with a statue by Robert Forrest, the whole at a cost of £8000.

Problems presented to the new Viscount Melville by his political inheritance demanded a quicker solution. The first was the judicial reshuffle occasioned by the death of Lord President Blair. Melville now felt free to pursue his own scheme, the nub of which was the succession of Robert Dundas of Arniston, Chief Baron of Exchequer. Uniquely, that would have made the third generation of their family to sit in the chair of the Court of Session. A further advantage was that William Adam could then be promoted Chief Baron: he needed the money, deserved reward for leading a successful defence in the impeachment and would have symbolic value as a conservative Whig drawn anew into the network of patronage. Urging this arrangement on his cousin, Melville added that 'it would enable Adam to put down, or at least to keep in order, a parcel of shallow-pated reviewing reformers at Edinburgh, who were meddling in matters which they did not understand, but were doing much mischief'.⁴

Unfortunately, the Chief Baron did not relish this high honour. A martyr to hypochondria, he replied that he thought he was dying – 'but let me recover or not, let me live one or ten years, in health or in misery, now I must decline the presidency'. He wrote as an afterthought that the only thing remotely likely to persuade him would be a peerage: he was after all head of the house of Arniston.

Melville duly applied to the Prime Minister, only to be sent away with a flea in his ear. Spencer Perceval retorted: 'I feel great objection to the introduction of a notion that distinction on the Bench in Scotland should afford a claim to a seat in the House of Lords when the man in question would, by necessity of attending to his judicial duties, be rendered physically incapable of giving the House of Lords the advantage of his knowledge or his presence'. Besides, 'I should not know how to explain ... that the peerage would diminish the risk to his health.' Elsewhere, he was ruder: 'The Chief Baron's health it seems is improved so far that, provided that strengthener of nerves, a British peerage, could be promised, the danger which otherwise his constitution might apprehend from the change would no longer be alarming!!' Dundas therefore obtained nothing. Retreating to Arniston he survived, to his surprise, another eight years.[5]

So Melville's ploy came to nought. Like his father, he was wary of promoting Colquhoun, a fellow anyway so prickly that he had refused to communicate since finding he was not the first choice for the presidency. Deeply embittered, he would take it out on his Solicitor General, Alexander Maconochie, with such vehemence that the latter almost challenged him to a duel. Melville warned Colquhoun that any repetition would lead to his dismissal, and eventually shoved him sideways into the harmless sinecure of Lord Clerk Register. For now, it seemed the best of the available options that Charles Hope should become Lord President, a change reluctantly made because of his excellent supervision, as Lord Justice Clerk, of the criminal judiciary. In his new post, where he served till 1841, he was an even more magnificent presence. To his old one the rising star, David Boyle, succeeded.

After these and other moves, the Bench offered four vacancies. Melville gave two to Whigs. He wrote that because of

> the folly of the Scotch Bar ... in setting themselves forward as political characters and very important personages in that respect, it has been difficult at all times to exclude political feelings and predilections from our courts of justice. Since party animosities have somewhat subsided, as they have for several years, I have done my best ... to extirpate those notions from our courts, and to bring the Opposition portion of the Bar to a more decent and restrained system of political conduct than used to be their practice during the fever of the French Revolution and even at later periods.[6]

Melville later said he had not found that 'a certain degree of proper (and prudent) liberality towards political opponents was prejudicial to my interest'. He was not, though, ingenuous about it. He had conspicuously passed over Henry Erskine, who went into a penurious retirement, consoled only by his garden and his violin. He refused to promote anyone associated with the *Edinburgh Review* 'because it does not appear to me that they have proper judicial heads' and because they had been too eager to woo rising advocates for Whiggery – the apostasy of young Henry Cockburn evidently rankled yet. 'This attraction, however, is on the decline,' Melville believed, 'and there are many fine young men coming forward of a subsequent growth who have not been inveigled and whom it is our bounden duty to protect and encourage wherever we shall find them with prominent professional claims.' Still, reconciliation was his rule. Non-partisan patronage did its share in improving the judiciary. Lord Eldon thought Melville handled these matters better than his father.[7]

Such commendations were useful in London, for the position of a new Scottish manager was bound at first to be a little precarious. Moreover, by the middle of 1811 the Whigs were again knocking on the doors of government. George III had recently descended into the final bout of insanity from which only death was to release him. The Prince of Wales became, with some limitation of the royal prerogatives, Regent. Following the Hanoverian tradition, he had all his life been at odds with his parent, thus a focus for the expectant Whigs. But they had realised few of their hopes. Now, given the King's great age and the prospect that the Prince would soon assume full powers, their future appeared brighter than ever before.

Their chance seemed to arrive with another extraordinary turn of events in May 1812 – the assassination of the Prime Minister inside the very Palace of Westminster. This made necessary a further laborious reshuffle. Those left in office looked for leadership to Lord Liverpool, during the last three years a good, efficient Secretary of State for War. But the House of Commons as a whole, conscious that Perceval had never overcome his Government's weakness, passed a resolution calling for a stronger one. It appended a recommendation that any such would have to act on two specific principles, a review of catholic emancipation and a more vigorous prosecution of the struggle against Napoleon. This implied an opening to either or both of the most important factions in opposition, to the Whigs who espoused the first principle, and to the Canningites who espoused the second. George Canning, chafing at his exclusion since the crisis of 1809, declared himself in accord with the House's judgment, as did one or two Whigs such as Lord Moira. But their leaders, Lords Grenville and Grey, felt they could not compromise previous commitments to peace, as the resolution seemed to require. The remaining Cabinet relished alliance with neither lot.

The Prince's attitude was crucial. Expected to call on the Whigs, he in fact ditched them. Rather, he just refrained from backing Grenville and Grey, so that they passed up their opportunity, their last for twenty years. His idea for bringing the two sides of the House together was instead to find them a neutral leader. He hit upon Lord Wellesley, who had continued a distinguished if controversial career since leaving India, and had only recently stepped down as Foreign Secretary. But in practice he could do no more than lamely seek support among the incumbent Ministers, who had already made clear their own preference. He might have been able to offer them a reunion with his friend Canning. But they could just as well arrange that for themselves, and were better placed to make any deal acceptable to Lord Castlereagh, his mortal enemy, who had taken over the Foreign Office.[8]

Liverpool's confident retort to the expedients thus bandied about was that he and his colleagues would neither serve under Wellesley nor even discuss with him the Commons' resolution. Melville alone excepted himself from this blank hostility, for he still wished to see Canning in the Government. The latter sounded him privately to see if something could be salvaged. Melville answered that, while rejecting Wellesley too, he went along with the two principles, though 'I think it improbable that any consideration which the Government can give to the subject of the restrictions on the Roman Catholics will enable it to propose such a system as will wholly satisfy their claims, and at the same time afford that degree of security to the Protestant Establishment which is generally felt to be necessary.' On the strength of that, he might be regarded at this stage as the Ministry's most liberal member.[8] In fact he always remained, like his father, tolerant in religion. He now stated to the Lords that 'we cannot have in our contemplation the continuing for any long period to withhold the repeal of the remaining disabilities', and repeated this sentiment over the years.[9]

Melville's conduct may have been honest, but gave an impression that he was a weak link in the chain holding the headless Cabinet together. An observer claimed: 'The Prince may have him when he likes'. Wellesley and Canning tried again, the latter writing: 'Your objection is so much more limited in its nature than that of your colleagues in general ... that, having thus no public ground on which to rest your refusal, I cannot help hoping you will reconsider it.' When this still did not work they evidently calculated that his stubbornness was born only of irresolution, and thought to scare him out of it by tempting William Dundas with hints of office in his cousin's stead. He had already told them, following the Commons' resolution, that two-thirds of the Scots members would support a Government led by them, and anyway oppose one containing Whigs. But at that stage it did not occur to him that he and Melville might split. Now, in response to the promptings, he intimated that he would be available after a seemly hiatus to join Wellesley and Canning and so 'preserve a strong and effective interest' in Scotland. He seemed to rule out any intermediary role, however – 'I know nothing of what Lord Melville and his colleagues intend.' [10]

The Prince kept up the pressure also, trying to pin individuals down on why they would not come to terms with Wellesley. He in his turn targeted Melville, to whom he guaranteed a place in Cabinet whatever befell. His cajolery went too far. Melville bluntly told him that his wiles could not produce a strong administration: if they brought movement on the catholic question, or supplanted Castlereagh, most Ministers would resign anyway. These successfully maintained a united front. Having had no joy after a month, the Prince conceded that they should all stay on under Liverpool. The new premier was less talented than some of his colleagues. But with a cool head, hard work and common sense, he held together broad-bottomed Governments through all the strains of war then peace, of repression then liberalisation, for fifteen years.

Nor did Liverpool prove ungenerous once he had established that he could not be dictated to. On his own terms he too actually would have liked Canning in the Cabinet, for his Ministry remained vulnerable, especially in the Commons. It so happened that nearly all its senior members sat in the Lords, Castlereagh being the sole exception of note. But he was a nervous speaker, and only the brilliantly eloquent Canning could ensure the Government's invincibility in debate. How, though, were two men who had tried to kill each other to be brought together on the same front-bench? To say the least, neither would willingly subordinate himself to the other. Melville, as the Minister closest to Canning, was deputed to find out what the response might be to a proposition. He returned with a demand for an explicit promise of the 'lead' on the Government's side. Liverpool turned Canning down flat. The latter was still overplaying his hand, and drew back too late: Castlereagh had by then made clear he would not tolerate him in any event.[12]

A different way for the Ministry to strengthen itself was by going to the country, which it did in the autumn of 1812. Liverpool, now at peace with the Prince, had little trouble in winning a majority. For Melville, the test was more crucial. Since, indeed before, his father's death, the opposition in Scotland had grown more active. At a by-election in 1810 in Renfrewshire, held for the Government since 1796, dormant Whig interests had suddenly pulled themselves together and regained it. In Ayrshire the next year, following Boyle's elevation to the Bench, his previous opponent had tried again, gone to a poll against the official candidate and narrowly taken the seat. Heartened, the Whigs were organising in several other constituencies.

Nine counties were to be contested, more than at any General Election since 1790, and five burgh districts. Not only did the opposition stir, but squabbles also broke out among ministerialist factions, something the first Viscount Melville would surely have taken trouble to avert. If the net result had been bad for the Government, it might have finished the second Viscount. As a matter of fact, he did quite well, and the colour of the Scottish contingent in the new Parliament turned out not much different from that in the old.[13]

It was in the Dundases' heartland of the South-east that the Whigs, organised by John Clerk of Eldin, showed themselves most boldly. They attacked the very citadel of the despotism, Midlothian itself. After Melville himself had gone to the Lords on succeeding his father, no suitable member of his family was available as candidate. He therefore turned to a close ally, Sir George Clerk of Penicuik, who at the by-election in July 1811 crushed his opponent, Sir John Dalrymple. The latter, however, impudently came back to renew the challenge now. The county, Cockburn wrote, 'had immemorially been a mere appendage of the House of Arniston, as completely as Edinburgh, or one of the Arniston farms ... It would be vain to make any modern man comprehend the indignation excited by this first interference with the hereditary monopoly.' Even in France, 'on y a vu le premier signe d'une ère nouvelle. Aux élections de 1812, le fait que Sir John Dalrymple eût osé briguer, comme candidat Whig, le siège de Midlothian, considéré comme le fief de la famille de Dundas, avait déjà paru caractéristique.' There was anyway some discontent with Clerk, reckoned callow and subservient to Melville. Sensationally, Dalrymple lost by only ten votes.

Scarcely less audacious was the assault led by Gilbert Elliot, heir of Minto, on Roxburghshire. The family had long had an interest there, usually overborne by the Duke of Buccleuch's. But the Duke's candidate this time, Alexander Don, was little known, having been a prisoner in France, and scarcely a match for the son of an Indian Governor-general. So Elliot won, though only to succeed to the peerage two years later, at which Don was returned unopposed. Elsewhere, Whigs kept control of the Dysart and Haddington Burghs, while in the Anstruther district the latest eponymous laird could maintain his independence. The sole representative of the junior Whigs to stand, in the Stirling Burghs, was the relentless reviewer,

Henry Brougham. He lost with credit, and narrowly enough to dispute the return. The petition was, though, shamefully mishandled by Clerk of Eldin.[14]

The Ministry hit back by taking the Linlithgow Burghs with Sir John Riddell and Stirlingshire with Sir Charles Edmonstone, the latter ending a dominance by Whig, or covert Whig, interests which had lasted since the days of Sir Lawrence Dundas. East and West Lothian continued to be occupied by Hopes. The Dundases' own dissensions were healed by the election of William for Edinburgh, with Buccleuch supplying the necessary finance. The new member described the choice of himself as 'the most suitable and as coming nearest to what was wanted ... with the duke's money and my father's [not, note, my uncle's] name'.[15]

The Whigs maintained their new strength in the West. Thanks to magnates' interests, they were safe in Argyll, Bute, Lanarkshire and the Ayr Burghs. And they held, in the face of official counterassaults, their recent gains in Ayrshire and Renfrewshire. The Glasgow Burghs made a truly popular choice of Kirkman Finlay, the city's Lord Provost and the first native Glaswegian to represent it in seventy years. He was highly independent, though more inclined to support liberal than conservative causes. All other seats in the region were the Government's.

The North saw a further victory for the opposition with the reappearance, after an Indian career, of Sir James Mackintosh. This 'Whig Cicero' had once won notoriety for springing to the defence of the French Revolution against Edmund Burke. He was invited to sit for Nairnshire 'grâce à l'appui du thane [sic] de Cawdor'.[16] In his eagerness, he got himself adopted before qualifying, and for a year the seat was occupied by a *locum tenens*. On the other hand the Sutherlands, who disposed of their own county and the Tain Burghs, were moving back into support for the Government and brought in quite friendly members, James Macdonald and Hugh Innes. Also co-operative were the nabob father and son, both called Charles Grant, who had converted Inverness, county and burghs, into a fief of their own.

In the North-east, the old order was more or less fully restored. The Whigs suffered their major casualty here, when Adam was obliged to give up Kincardine on account of financial troubles. His successor, George Drummond, a kinsman of Melville's, would in time suffer the same fate. But for the present the inheritance from his banking family proved ample enough to build a castle in the constituency and buy the votes he needed to win. William Maule, secure in Forfarshire, was now the only Whig in a region otherwise entirely controlled by the Ministry.

Despite some successes, the opposition achieved no net gain. It once more returned thirteen members, against twenty-nine usually supporting the Government, and three independents. Melville commented: 'Our elections on the whole have gone on well, and better than we expected.' The peers proved docile, the Earl of Selkirk being the one Whig to retain his place. Neither at the polls nor over the subsequent behaviour of parliamentarians did the new manager have or seek the same control as his father.[17] Still, he had surmounted his problems and generally handled his succession smoothly. He would hold his interest together sufficiently to give him the weight he needed in London till difficulties of a quite different order overtook the Dundas despotism.

In London too, Melville continued to win plaudits. He was now offered the Governor-generalship of India in succession to Minto, but declined. Instead Moira went and, as Marquis of Hastings, was to perform excellently in the post. An observer still wrote:

> I wish they had sent Lord Melville. He is a quiet worthy man, of a moderate but sound understanding – very laborious and initiated from his early youth into all the mysteries of Indianism. Besides he would take care to have decent people about him, and Moira will be surrounded from the moment be puts foot on shore by all the low, profligate, rapacious wickedness that the place ... affords – to say nothing of the cargo he will export with him.

But Moira also commented that 'it is a pity to have the grace of the measure frittered away through ... intrigues of the Board which baffle the kind dispositions of Lord Melville.'

He, in his unassuming way, steadily entrenched himself in the Ministry. From the recent turbulence he had emerged, once more following his father, as First Lord of the Admiralty. A few months later he was sounded about going back to the Board of Control, in order to make room in the Cabinet for Canning. Nothing came of it. When the same move was again mooted in 1816, Melville could just refuse, such was the strength of the position he had meanwhile built. Coolly he told the Prime Minister: 'Circumstances have altered in a material degree, and without troubling you with my reasons in detail, some of which are of a public and others of a private nature, I shall only say that I feel great repugnance to the change at present.' And that was an end of it.[18]

One might suppose that the Admiralty in this final phase of the war was a relatively undemanding post, requiring no more than efficient administration to maintain Britain's naval supremacy while she waited for the continental powers to assemble a winning coalition against the Emperor Napoleon – though a long wait it turned out to be. William Dundas, appointed a Lord of Admiralty and acting as his cousin's spokesman in the Commons, indeed boasted: 'We have a naval power equal to check the combined fleets of the world, and even capable of overwhelming them.'[19]

But Melville took little for granted. The nation's exertions brought shortages everywhere, not least of manpower. A sign of this strain on resources was rising public protest against the depredations of press-gangs. It reached such a pitch in Glasgow that the magistrates were moved to dispute whether Scots law allowed impressment, and freed some men who had been seized. The First Lord sternly wrote: 'I am yet to learn that the authority of the Lord High Admiral to require the services of all seafaring men ... does not extend to the Clyde and to Scotland as well as to all other parts of His Majesty's dominions, or that the law in that aspect is different or ought to be differently administered in Scotland and in England.'[20]

Warned by this and other difficulties, Melville conducted during his first winter in the job an exhaustive examination of the navy. The results, committed to paper in February 1813, were not altogether reassuring:

> Since the decisive battle of Trafalgar, the enemy has not been able, or has not ventured to push out to sea a single squadron of his ships of war with any hostile purpose. He has not however been inactive in naval preparations.

The possession of the ports of Holland and of Italy has more than doubled his former means of naval equipment and naval resources ... The extent to which he has availed himself of these important resources, since the year 1805, compared with our own means of keeping up an efficient fleet, will afford a tolerably correct idea as to the period of time, when we may expect him to have advanced to a state of readiness to oppose to us an equal naval force, at least as to the number and magnitude of ships. That period is not very far distant.

During those years, the First Lord reckoned, France had launched 60 vessels, against Britain's 53. At such a rate, she would achieve superiority by 1816, when the two fleets would possess respectively 108 and 99 ships of the line. It looked therefore as if the royal navy would have to commission more.

But why should Britain worry, Melville rhetorically asked, when previous conflicts had shown that she could maintain her supremacy against the combined fleets of France, Spain and Holland? The trouble was that ships now remained seaworthy for a shorter time, often for only four or five years against ten to fifteen formerly. He gave two reasons. First, most were built in merchants' yards (as 40 of the 53 had been) which could not get hold of enough suitable material, especially of seasoned timber. Secondly, blockading buffeted them: 'The present war has totally changed the character and system of naval warfare. It is blockade on our part, and a state of rest and preparation on that of the enemy.' Again, an increase in shipbuilding, especially at the King's yards, was the obvious answer. The Cabinet welcomed this impressive paper. Enough action was taken to ensure that the British fleet did keep the upper hand till the end of hostilities. The First Lord then reflected with relief on how different the outcome might have been.[21]

He and his navy had above all had to remain vigilant. Inevitably some lapses occurred, especially after a threat arose from a new direction with the outbreak of war between Britain and the United States in 1812. Guarding the long Iberian seaboard in particular was always difficult, and impossible once the surrounding waters were invaded by swarms of adventurous American privateers. They steered clear of convoys, which now had to be formed as far away as the Cape, but individual merchantmen fell prey to them in alarming numbers. Melville met sharp criticism when he refused to counter by detaching warships from the more important stations of the Channel, North Sea and Baltic. He retorted: 'It must inevitably be the case when the whole force of an enemy is devoted to privateers, that our entire fleet, wherever stationed, cannot prevent the capture of some of our merchant vessels.' But, he added, we had caught 200 of those privateers, and avenged our own losses by taking 900 American commercial ships, with 20,000 seamen, into detention. Even so, 'America having no fleet, there can be no splendid victories obtained'.

Things then turned more awkward with the involvement of General Lord Wellington, British commander in the Peninsula. From his Portuguese headquarters he made an official complaint in the summer of 1813 that naval protection for his theatre was inadequate. The First Lord patiently offered to accept the blame, so long as it was appreciated that the fleet could never respond to every demand. It was unreasonable to expect that each merchant vessel should either have protection the moment it was ready to sail, or should be able to sail safely without protection: 'so great is the number of transports, so extended their services, that the whole Channel fleet would not suffice for protection of this nature.' He preferred to avoid a public fuss about the practicalities of adding to the navy. Faster construction faced genuine obstacles, and legislation would be needed to procure men for a bigger fleet, men who in any case might be wanted for the army: 'I must scramble on as well as I can with the means in my power, and resort to these extreme measures only when they are manifestly unavoidable.'[22]

Wellington refused to be mollified. From whatever cause, he carped again and at greater length, he was not getting the help he needed, to wit: there were no ships of the line off northern Spain; supplies had been delayed for lack of convoy; the blockade of San Sebastian, under siege by the British, did not work; the squadron there was undermanned; attacks from the sea were impossible; French coastal trade had not been cut off. Melville did not mince his words this time, but bluntly told Wellington that he had no understanding of naval warfare: 'I will take your opinion in preference to any other person's as to the most effectual mode of beating a French army; but I have no confidence in your seamanship or nautical skill.' It was rare for the First Lord to get angry, but a comment to one of his admirals indicated how greatly this exchange had annoyed him: 'Neither Lord Wellington nor those who are employed on the coast appear to have the least conception of what is physically practicable by ships and boats and seamen, and to be strongly impressed with the usual complimentary notion that they can do anything.'[23]

Wellington was indeed being intemperate, for the Peninsular War actually showed to good effect how maritime power could sustain military operations too. Those he so brilliantly conducted would not have been possible without British command of the sea, the strategic mobility that it offered, the communications it allowed among different sectors of a difficult terrain, the supply and reinforcement it ensured. With all this, the struggle could be carried on despite France's superior strength on land.[24]

Still, the British in Spain, if resourceful and valiant, made a relatively minor contribution as other European powers now gathered the armies to strike a decisive blow at Napoleon following his disastrous retreat from Moscow. In the battle of the nations at Leipzig in October 1813, they at last crushed him. It was then only a matter of time before the league of Emperors and Kings pressed him back on to the frontiers of France, broke through, forced him to surrender Paris and abdicate. For Britain more than two decades of continual fighting seemed by the spring of 1814 to be over; though the real peace would only come after Napoleon, having escaped from his first exile on Elba, was beaten at Waterloo more than a year later.

Melville took charge of arrangements for Napoleon's captivity, instructing Admiral Keith, who received the fallen Emperor on board the *Bellerophon*, that he was not to go ashore, send or receive communications, and that his suite should be limited to four or five: 'Napoleon Bonaparte is to be considered and addressed as a general officer.' It was the First Lord's secretary who suggested St Helena for the second exile, and the First Lord's message that broke to Napoleon the news of his fate:

> It would be inconsistent with our duty to the country and to His Majesty's allies if we were to leave to General Bonaparte the means or opportunity of again disturbing the peace of Europe, and renewing all the calamities of war: it is therefore unavoidable that he should be restrained in his present liberty to whatever extent may be necessary ... The island of St Helena has been selected for his future; the climate is healthy, and its local situation will admit of his being treated with more indulgence than would be compatible with adequate security elsewhere.

In August, Melville announced to Castlereagh that Napoleon was 'gone off apparently in good humour.'[25]

Peace of course changed radically the frame of the Admiralty's operations. Other countries still had a few overseas possessions; Britain emerged from her victories as the only real colonial power. And while this trading network dispersed her expensive naval resources, it was also to be the basis of her worldwide commercial and industrial dominance. At the Congress of Vienna, she insisted on keeping the Cape and the others in the strategic chain of ports – Mauritius, Trincomalee and so on – leading to India. She even toyed with the idea of retaining Java, though she eventually tossed it back to the Dutch. That did not mean giving up an eastward extension of the chain. Singapore was acquired in 1818. The First Lord took a personal interest in the foundation of settlements in northern Australia, including Fort Dundas on Melville Island; it was intended as a commanding military post and mercantile station to suppress piracy and offset Dutch influence in a region thought to offer lucrative trade.

He also directed resumption of the search for a shorter route by sea to Asia in the opposite direction, by a North-west passage. He sent Sir John Ross on a voyage through the Arctic archipelago in 1818, and Sir William Parry on a series of them in the following years: Melville Island and Melville Peninsula were named along the way. In 1819, Sir John Franklin led an overland expedition from Hudson's Bay to the mouth of the Coppermine River beyond the Arctic circle, then back along the northern coast of Canada – a journey of 5500 miles from which the survivors returned in 1822. These were a product of the First Lord's scientific interests. But he certainly hoped, if here in vain, for an economic benefit. The Empire remained, as in his father's vision, a commercial one. There was no acquisition of territory beyond the trading posts, no advance in military occupation. Absolute command of the seas after all rendered such exertions unnecessary.[26]

As a matter of fact, however, the country could not continue making the same prodigious efforts as in wartime to sustain that command, not with £800 million of public debt and the prompt onset of recession. 'There can be no question that our first object ought to be the husbanding our pecuniary means', Melville wrote, 'and I feel that necessity so strongly as to have been and to be still quite ready to cut down without compunction every expense that can safely be spared.' And so, 'I am much more in the habit at this office of saying no than saying yes.'[27] Somehow naval supremacy would have to be bought cheaper.

The First Lord examined the prospects with his usual care. A possible target was to reduce the establishment to the level of 1792, the last year of peace. But closer examination showed this could not be done, for Britain's commitments had everywhere grown. In the Mediterranean she had acquired a base in Malta, and would have to protect its communications from the pirates of Barbary. The outposts of St Helena, the Cape and Mauritius needed cover, while the abolition of the slave trade, since 1807, would have to be generally enforced along the coasts of Africa. South America had earlier been closed to all but Spanish or Portuguese vessels; opened by the independence of its several nations, that continent too required a naval safeguard for merchant ships, which might in time have to be extended to the Pacific littoral. Melville reckoned that 100 ships of the line would still normally be essential.

This was his opening bid for negotiations in Cabinet. The cuts on which it decided at the end of 1815 looked by comparison extraordinarily savage. Just forty-four ships of the line were to be left in commission, while 216 vessels of various types would be laid up and one-third of the sailors demobilised. In fact, this was merely the Treasury's wishful thinking. Such drastic economies proved quite impracticable. The next year still saw 101 ships of the line in commission, and the total was only slowly pared. The target would never be met. As for manpower, the First Lord actually boasted in 1819 that 'so far from the naval establishment being reduced, the number of seamen now employed is greater than in any previous peace.' But he did suspend exercises of the fleet, run down installations, sell or scrap superfluous vessels. Moreover, in the first ten years after the war only twenty-six new ships of the line were launched, and Parliament complained even about them.[28]

There was a further problem. The British had been as deeply shocked as the French had been impressed by the Americans' swashbuckling successes at sea during the war of 1812–14. Their privateers' threat was just about contained, but their navy – all three ships of it – came off better in its skirmishes with the royal one, for these vessels were nearly one-third superior in dimension, calibre of guns and size of crew. A new seafaring nation had attained, quite unnoticed, superior naval technology. As the restored Bourbons rebuilt France's fleet, they emulated it. Britain was anyway stuck with the many ramshackle ships hurriedly constructed to get through the war. A survey in 1817 found that less than half could be expected to last more than five years. The country thus faced the daunting task of modernising the navy wholesale with new models and classes, besides paying enormous sums for the repair and maintenance of older ones.[29]

This was not a palatable prospect, and Melville could bring himself only reluctantly to confront it. In 1813 he had rejected such modernisation 'merely because there were three American vessels of unusual dimensions', and poured scorn on the idea of 'building ships which would be fit only to cope with the American navy.' He promised to do something about defects in British design, yet maintained: 'In the modelling of vessels the French and other nations are superior to us, but in the execution we are superior to them.' By 1815 his line had modified: 'It has always been the system of the British Admiralty to adapt our ships to the nature of those with which they have to contend. But it cannot be supposed that the whole system of our navy can at once be changed in order to meet a few American frigates of a larger size than any vessels that have ever gone under that name.' By 1819 he was facing the truth: 'I concur in the propriety of this country building ships on a scale similar to those with which our navy may have to contend. It is the duty of the legislature to maintain, on any emergency, that naval supremacy which the country has acquired.'[30]

Melville has been accused of blind conservatism in naval matters. But no First Lord could in such conditions dismiss innovation out of hand, not at least any tending to raise efficiency. 'A sufficient union of scientific knowledge and practical experience' was his declared aim. The fleet first needed well-constructed, easily manoeuvred ships that would withstand long battering from the high seas. It was thus essential to improve naval architecture which in Britain, as Melville confessed to Parliament, had not been of the best. He therefore patronised a school devoted to it, and rejected such proposals for economy as that the larger vessels should every one be built to a standard design, 'checkmate against all further improvements (much needed) in the models of our ships'. As for other novelties, he was intrigued when his rascally cousin, Thomas Cochrane, sent him a secret plan for the use in battle of smoke-screens and poison gas generated by naphtha and potassium. He thought the smoke-screens fine, but had misgivings about the gas (though it would eventually, in 1855, be used to great effect at the siege of Sebastopol).

It was the admirals who most hated new-fangled inventions. In 1813 Marc Isambard Brunel, originally a refugee from France, hired a steamship which till then had merely plied with trippers back and forth from London to Margate, and showed it could safely tow vessels of war in adverse winds and tides. When he begged to bring this to the attention of the naval authorities, their official response was that it would be 'unnecessary to enter at present into the consideration of the question as to how far the power of the steam engine may be made applicable to the general purposes of navigation.' As a matter of fact, Melville did not share this view, but was still obliged to be tender of his subordinates' prejudices in favour of sail.[31]

He always bore in mind that running the fleet was not just a technical but a political task. Since the First Lord (unlike the army's Commander-in-chief) sat in the Cabinet, the state and its senior service had to be familiar with and sympathetic to each other's requirements. This was eased by the fact that the Board of Admiralty contained both professional sailors and politicians, who could reach their own understandings behind closed doors, free from parliamentary or public pressures. By the sailors Melville was regarded as a thoroughly reliable representative of their interests, by the politicians as one who could be ruthless when he had to. The net result was that his navy found itself comparatively coddled. After 1819, the Cabinet gave up the struggle to make further cuts, and would usually accept his estimates on the nod.[32]

Scottish expectations of Melville had somehow to be fitted in with these burdens in Whitehall and Westminster. It did help that Scots still thronged to join up with the fleet. A critic complained that his administration of it was 'one perpetual job', he himself a man 'who made the patronage of the Admiralty instrumental to governing Scotland'. Indeed this patronage represented, more than ever under the restrictions imposed elsewhere, a sizable share of the total available. The First Lord could spend days on end meeting queues of officers who sought to improve their prospects of promotion. His correspondence, too, overflows with applications and replies to them.

This was time-consuming, but it would be unnecessary to conclude that Melville's influence on Scottish patronage generally was let slip in some involuntary way, as has been suggested. He kept separate in his papers his 'Scotch Appointments', memorandums of notes on the subject sent to the Treasury. The only complete year for which this record has survived is 1819, when he dealt with forty-eight cases. That implied, if the figure could be taken as at all typical of the volume of such business, that it ran at about half the level dealt with by his father. The obvious reason was not any dereliction on Melville's part, but the pruning of the Scottish establishment which anyway continued apace. Even so, forty-eight annual appointments in a small country would still amount in the long run to a most powerful influence. That Melville assumed he had a double authority seemed clear in a note of 1818 to the Prime Minister: 'I have acted towards you in regard to applications from Scotland very much in the same manner with those from the navy ... and have stood between you and importunities from various quarters.'

His own interventions were indeed ubiquitous. In 1817 he recommended the Earl of Dalhousie as Governor of Canada. He was the channel of perennial efforts by sundry Scots nobles to have themselves raised to the British peerage. The law officers demanded a higher salary through him. Bills for the construction of Calton Jail in Edinburgh and prohibiting houses on the southern side of Princes Street passed with his blessing, as did financial aid for the capital's observatory. When requested to by the novelist John Galt, Melville solicited support from naval officers for the Caledonian Asylum. In May 1819 he asked the Prime Minister for a grant to set up a ferry across the Tay at Dundee, matching those already financed on the Forth and so completing a route to the North-east. The next month he applied for money to repair academic buildings at Aberdeen. That winter he seconded an appeal from the town council of Glasgow for docks to be built at the Broomielaw in order to provide work for unemployed weavers. Then he nominated William Alison, Scotland's great pioneer of reform in public health and the Poor Law, for the chair of medical jurisprudence at the university of Edinburgh. The following spring he proposed the rumbustious John Wilson, known to the literary public by his *nom de plume* of Christopher North, for its chair of moral philosophy. And so on, and so on, and so on – there could be no doubt of Melville's omnipresence in Scottish patronage.[33]

He took special trouble over the most important areas of internal administration. The representatives of the state in the country at large were the sheriffs. Melville was concerned to preserve the exercise of their office from meddling by the powerful. He declared himself 'decidedly adverse to the nomination of a sheriff in Scotland on account of local interests or connections, or local recommendations', for 'the sheriffs in Scotland, being judicial officers and in that respect unlike the sheriffs in England and Ireland, ought to be selected on professional grounds as advocates, and not merely as local patronage.' Thus he ruled that nobody related to or proposed by the Sutherlands could be appointed in their county. The only general exception he admitted was that Highland sheriffs should be chosen from those who knew Gaelic. In 1817, on a vacancy in Argyll, he insisted that the candidates should be 'constantly resident and accustomed to its people and language', deprecating the fact that 'the Lord Advocate wishes that some Saxon Lowlander should be appointed.'[34]

Melville was similarly determined to maintain high standards in patronage of the Church, despite the 'very limited' influence he professed to enjoy. Here he elaborated quite a detailed set of rules for the different cases coming before him, regularising the procedures in a way his father had never bothered to do, though he always claimed to be merely following established administrative practice.

A minister was conventionally nominated for a Crown living by the local member of Parliament, but Melville would only regard him as a channel for the wishes of the heritors, whose recommendations he nearly always accepted. Certainly he would not foist anyone objectionable on them. Only if they disagreed was he prepared to judge for himself of the candidate's suitability, even then preferring to be guided by the choice of a resident majority. He explained why to Buccleuch:

> Nobody knows better than yourself how necessary it is for the welfare and good order of a country parish in Scotland that the minister should if possible be on good terms with the heritors, as well as with the rest of the parishioners, and how injurious it would be, both to the state and to the interest of religion, if the reverse was generally to be the case. The Crown and the heritors have the same object in view, and therefore as a general rule the former is sage in acceding to the recommendations of the latter.

If ever he did yield to other pressures, he told the Duke of Montrose, 'the Crown would be a public nuisance and a most mischievous promoter of discontent in religious matters, instead of being, as I verily believe it is, the most conscientious and useful patron in Scotland', especially important since the number of livings in its gift was so large a proportion of the whole. As for other lay patrons, he did not believe it worth his while to interfere with them: 'in most cases it would be unsuccessful, and it is always an unwise and imprudent intermeddling in a person in my situation in Scotland.'[35]

It naturally followed that he saw no scope for popular election – 'an indecent proceeding as well as injurious to the public interest'. He noted with evident horror a case where a congregation tried to make its own choice regardless: 'Meetings had been held in the church which was extremely crowded on such occasions, and where long debates took place, as well as voting as to who should be minister.' He refused to accept the result, and asked the heritors to come to a private understanding among themselves. Yet in a dispute at Dunfermline, where no statutory rights were in question, he instructed the Lord Advocate not to appoint 'a person who though respectable as an individual might be extremely disagreeable to the parishioners'.[36]

Except for making sure his rules were kept, Melville evinced little desire to control the Kirk's internal politics. He did remark that the General Assembly was 'by no means to be neglected and ... might be troublesome'. But between its factions he remained impartial, so that a presentee's allegiance to one or the other formed no bar to preferment. In 1817 he himself received Thomas Chalmers, the rising star of the evangelicals, and later gave him the chair of moral philosophy at St Andrews – even though the situation 'requires not only talent, but solidity, and I should be afraid that he might sometimes be eccentric'. Nor would he pander to the Moderates, as George Hill had found out when he sought to ingratiate himself with the new manager. The Chief Baron advised that 'the whole system of the university of St Andrews has been, since the Hills attained their influence there, to make it an asylum for their family and dependents, without regard to merit of any sort'. Hill's nominations, he added, had latterly been turned down even by the first Viscount – a practice which the second continued. Perhaps that was one reason why the university delayed three years before electing him chancellor in succession to his father. When it did, he at once proposed that the whole outfit should be moved to Dumfries, where it could increase its revenue by attracting students from the North of England. On Hill's death in 1819, his crony, the Revd John Lee, confidently expected to take over as an agent for official patronage. Melville spurned him.[37]

Perhaps he felt obliged to involve himself to such a degree because in Scotland he could not count on able lieutenants. In particular, he found the Lord Advocates during these years unsatisfactory. Few regretted it when he got rid of the unpopular Colquhoun, said to care 'for no communication except between his pocket and the Exchequer'. Some doubts were entertained too about the obvious replacement, Maconochie, though he had been a favourite of the elder Melville, who declared that 'any trivial frailties he may possess will wear away as he advances in knowledge of the world'. But his own father was on the Bench as Lord Meadowbank, he had married a daughter of Lord President Blair and was already serving as Solicitor General. Altogether his succession was irresistible. Promoted in 1816 and brought into Parliament for an English seat while awaiting a Scottish vacancy, he shortly proved himself a very bad choice.

When everyone else failed, there was William Dundas. He indeed pettishly complained that 'my relation, who leaves to me all the correspondence and daily attention, is only sometimes active and awake'. His humour was not improved by dealings with other senior Ministers: 'It is very sad and weary work to get those men to do anything, and though often sick of their delay, I am obliged to forget, and begin again.' This was surely a just desert for one who so stoutly defended sinecures, as representing 'the rights of the Scottish people, the remnants of their ancient monarchy, the memorial of their pride as an independent nation'. Under his supervision the list of Scottish pensions also remained overcharged, despite the Act of 1810. Since Dundas too spent much of his time at Westminster, he relied for local information on an agent in Edinburgh, James Denholm, a tall, suave hatter on the North Bridge. But standards tended to fall further down the political scale. After an irregularity in his re-election to the town council in 1817, an attempt to overturn it through the courts had to be bought off for £1100. The business was doubtless tedious to him as well, but the pair of them found ways to relieve it: 'where his face was only red, that of his friend, the Rt Hon. William Dundas ... was literally purple.'[38]

The problem with Scottish patronage lay not in any neglect by the Dundases, but in the hostile attention it still attracted from Parliament. At a time when ferocious cuts were being made in expenditure of all kinds, back-benchers especially busied themselves in digging up examples of unjustifiable waste. One by one, cherished but decrepit Scottish institutions were bound to topple under this pressure. An early victim, for example, was the mint at Edinburgh, which went in 1817 at a saving of £1200 a year, having produced no coins for more than a century. While Melville publicly asserted that the Scots 'have a fair right to expect that their great offices of state, as stipulated by the articles of union, shall be maintained', he also conceded that 'other offices, which are not of that national description, must be subject to the same economies as those in England'. Privately he confided to Hope that there was a 'great risk of being beat in detail, office after office' on the votes for money, unless members could be convinced that it was well spent.

Unfortunately, some zealous Englishmen talked as if the whole Scottish establishment consisted of sinecures, and took little care to discriminate between them and posts serving a useful purpose. 'It is rather hard that our criminal jurisprudence is to be surrendered to the stupidity of those reforming economists in the lower House,' Melville once complained. The Chief Baron, too, had to protest over a measure tampering with his responsibilities: 'The nature of the offices and of the duties performed in them seems to have been entirely misunderstood by those who have framed this Bill: that they are in many respects essentially and radically different from those of the same description in the Exchequer of England.'[39]

This latter comment pointed to a second pressure bearing on the system, for compliance with English norms. If the old Scotland was not just to be swept away, she had to be renewed. Compared to the reforms which his father had routinely undertaken, however, Melville proved inactive. During his management remarkably little primary Scottish legislation was passed, and virtually none by him. He almost boasted to his colleague, the Home Secretary: 'There is no part of the United Kingdom that has prospered more than North Britain for a century past, with the exception of a small mistake we made in 1745, and I have no relish for experimental changes by wholesale.'[40]

Melville relied instead for influence on his shrinking stock of patronage and on improving the administration. Able and innovative in the latter, he still could not make it a convincing substitute for reforms. They came instead on the initiative of others. As a matter of fact, Whigs were the ones generating most of the proposals. Their purpose was often to anglicise, in which they were abetted by English parliamentarians moved in equal measure by ignorance of and antagonism to Scotland. And since no coherent official alternative was on offer, Ministers were sometimes persuaded to respond.

For instance, the sole major legislative innovation during these early years of Melville's management was the introduction of trial by jury in civil causes, copied from England, to supplement hearings before a judge sitting alone. It had long been urged by Whigs as a panacea for deficiencies in Scottish justice. But it rent the logical division between criminal and civil jurisdiction, the first dealing with violations determined by the state (so that offenders had to have the security of a jury against its wrath), the second dealing with disputes between citizens (for resolution of which nothing more was needed than impartiality and learning in the law). Still, the proposal had won support, had been considered and half-heartedly endorsed by an inquiry, and in 1815 was put into a Bill brought forward by Lord Chancellor Eldon. He provided not for a general introduction of the jury in civil causes, as Whigs wished. It would be confined rather to a special court set up for an experimental period, presided over by commissioners, not judges, and empowered to decide only specified types of case referred there by a Lord ordinary.

Melville still did not like it, arguing with Clerk of Eldin that on account of
> the preference justly due to our own system of law, secured to the people of
> Scotland by solemn compact at the Union, I think that any proposal to
> innovate upon that system should be received or adopted with great caution
> and only with a thorough persuasion that the scheme, whatever it may be,
> has something intrinsically better to recommend it than its novelty, or than
> a desire for experiment which might perhaps with more safety be left alone.

To Parliament he complained that benefits predicted from earlier reforms had not materialised, certainly not in reducing appeals to the Lords, which had multiplied. He was angry at a provision for the court always to have on it one English lawyer, supposedly to keep the machinery in order. William Dundas forced an amendment that all appointments after the initial ones should be of Scotsmen. With that solace, the Bill passed. An outstanding problem of patronage was incidentally solved at the constitution of the new Bench. 'Why is the Jury Court like the Garden of Eden?' quipped Erskine. 'Because it was created for Adam.' The unemployed William Adam became its first chief commissioner.

Pace the Dundases, the experiment was judged enough of a success for the court to be given a permanent existence, with wider powers, by a further Act of 1819. Instead of trial by jury being available only on reference, it was now made obligatory for assault, defamation, breach of promise and seduction. Enthusiasts later had this principle extended to some types of action, such as those for damages arising from personal injury, which even in England were heard by a judge sitting alone. But the court, with its alien principles, would disappoint the hopes reposed in it. Not in the event permanent at all, it was merged into the Court of Session in 1830.[41]

That would be one result of stringencies afterwards imposed on the Scottish judicial establishment too. For oddly, in this era of rigorous public economy it now attained its greatest extent. There were the 'Auld Fifteen' in the Courts of Session and Justiciary; the latter also had a nominal head, the Lord Justice General, a sinecure currently held by Montrose. Then there were five judges in the Exchequer, four in the Consistorial Court and another in the Court of Admiralty. The post of chief commissioner in the Jury Court was additional. Filling all these Benches proved in itself a problem for a conscientious manager. When his cousin, the Chief Baron, died in 1819, Melville wrote: 'As the Scotch Bar has to supply 16 judges for the Courts of Session, Justiciary and Jury trials, who ought to be, and always are if possible, advocates of eminence and considerable practice, I assert ... that the supplying of 16 proper persons for those judicial situations is very difficult and scarcely practicable.' Thus he felt obliged to set an Englishman over the Exchequer.[42]

It still did not readily sink in among Scots that the old expectations were no longer going to be automatically fulfilled. 'The Athenian Tories,' a satirist wrote, 'are perhaps the most place-devoted race in the British dominions. Office is their god.'[43] The trouble was that an apparatus of patronage built by and for the lairds of the eighteenth century no longer answered to the requirements of uniting and controlling a Scottish political interest. The social order was changing. It had, in the Enlightenment's great days, seemed immutable, hallowed alike by religion and philosophy. Even the wars had not obviously disturbed it. But when the country's tremendous martial exertions came shuddering to a halt in 1815, the dire economic consequences roused deep alarm. Now, social differences once taken for granted began to appear intolerable. Social problems, which had scarcely figured in the cerebrations of the literati, patently required urgent thought and action.

The new forces generated in these economic cycles could be hardly comprehended by a political system vesting its rights in feudal superiority of land. Once, there had been no clear distinction in Scotland between landowners and capitalists. Land alone could yield capital on a scale needed for industrialisation, much of which took place in the countryside. Now it shifted. Glasgow's great wealth, first accumulated from trade in tobacco, waxed fabulous through the merchants' blockade-busting in Napoleonic Europe. It offered the resources for development of an enormous industrial complex along the Clyde. Textiles were long established, together with the horrors of the factory system. This primary activity was spawning ancillaries, in foundries, engineering and chemical works. Local production of iron and coal would soon burgeon too. But the gentry turned indifferent or hostile to the development. For in its new forms it obviously altered social relations: paternalist, hierarchical structures gave way to the impersonal cash nexus of manufacturer and employee. In textiles, the small weaving settlements of the East, often founded by local lairds, paled in significance beside the vast satanic mills of the West. In mining, the blue-blooded coalmaster retreated before the joint stockholder. The participation of the old elite in metal manufacture, and in other heavy industries marking the second stage of the industrial revolution, was to be negligible. It failed to maintain its economic leadership, which passed instead to bourgeois capitalists.

The governing circles were not blind to all this. Walter Scott noted how 'manufacturers have been transferred to great towns where a master calls together 100 workmen this week and pays them off the next with far less interest in their future fate than in that of as many worn-out shuttles'. But political implications were only reluctantly acknowledged. The first Viscount Melville had always kept on good terms with the merchants of Glasgow: his last public distinction was honorary citizenship of the town in 1810. To his son, Finlay's victory in the election of 1812 – clearly an assertion of commercial interests – still came as a surprise and a shock. Nor were the Tories alone in their obtuseness. A Whig hostess, Lady Elizabeth Grant of Rothiemurchus, could disdainfully describe such Glaswegians as 'no longer the cadets of the neighbouring old county families, but their clerks of low degree shot up into high places'. As to why in the capital's serious politics the Lord Provost found no place, he was 'a tradesman of repute among his equals, and in their society he was content to abide'.[44]

But political implications were certainly there. One thing the Government had never had to worry about since the 1790s was reforming pressure from the periphery of the ruling circle. The richest of the upwardly mobile had continued to buy their way into it. The rest had accepted official propaganda that the constitution would be best left just as it was till the dangers of revolution and war were past.

That had not, though, put a stop to political thinking. The huge success of the *Edinburgh Review* attested to it. Scott wrote in scorn that the authors 'have a great belief in the influence of fine writing and think that a nation can be governed by pamphlets and reviews'. But without doubt they served to create a junior Whiggery markedly different in spirit from the nonchalance of the aristocratic senior school. It offered serious analysis of the country's condition and plausible proposals for improving it. It also made a conscious appeal to public opinion: in the capital an observer found that 'one cannot stir a step without stumbling over troops of confident, comfortable, glib, smart young Whigs'. The message ran that it was the duty of enlightened reformers to seize the leadership of the forces for change, guide and restrain them, and keep them orderly.[45]

This did demand a response. Scott himself acknowledged as much when in 1808 he set up a rival publication, the *Quarterly Review*. But on social questions it held to a tame line in defence of landowners' privileges, too congenial to the establishment to lend it much impact. A real conservative counterattack came only with the foundation of *Blackwood's Edinburgh Magazine* by William Blackwood in 1817. In contrast to the anglicising enthusiasms of Francis Jeffrey and friends, it vigorously espoused Scottish interests, and when necessary would criticise the Government on that score: it apparently originated the idea that, if London was Rome, 'Edinburgh might become another Athens'. It also defended the country against the city, the North against the South, rugged yeomen against pallid intellectuals. While it sang the praises of social hierarchy, it did so in the cause of maintaining a sense of responsibility at all levels. Its luminaries were John Gibson Lockhart, later the biographer of Scott (his father-in-law), and John Wilson, Melville's choice for the chair of moral philosophy at Edinburgh. Other men of letters who regularly contributed were John Galt and Thomas de Quincey, together with a lawyer, Archibald Alison, brother of the medical pioneer.

Though the Whigs thus by no means dominated political discourse, the Government continued to complain of a bad press. It now embarked on something it had long routinely done in England, the subsidising of newspapers. It was prompted to by the successful launch in 1817 of the first liberal one, *The Scotsman*. The law officers arranged financial guarantees for two Tory rivals, *The Beacon* in Edinburgh and *The Sentinel* in Glasgow. Both were editorially robust to the point of scurrility, and correspondingly accident-prone. *The Beacon* was soon closed down on the grounds that it implicated Ministers in the publication of libels. The same fate befell *The Sentinel* after one of its contributors, Alexander Boswell, son of the great biographer, was killed in a duel with James Stuart of Dunearn, whom he had insulted in its columns; this despite the fact that Boswell was an expert shot and Stuart had hardly fired a gun in his life. He told Cockburn that 'he was never more thunderstruck than when on the smoke clearing he saw his adversary slowly sinking down'.[46]

The honours in the war of words were otherwise more even, certainly in journalism and reviewing. In the novel this was if anything a Tory era, with Walter Scott, John Galt and James Hogg the leading figures. It is thus hard to take seriously the picture painted by Cockburn of overwhelming Whig ascendancy in letters. The Government, seeing well enough that reforming sentiments could no longer easily be branded unpatriotic or subversive, actually worked hard to retain support among the middle-class readers of political literature. The very fact of this competition helped to make partisanship respectable in Scotland, however, in a way it had never been before.

The better part of valour for conservatives was to divert attention away from constitutional issues to political economy, which Whigs had made their own. Some of its most fulsome advocates adopted, with the *Edinburgh Review*'s approval, an attitude to the weakest members of society verging on the brutal: witness the Highland clearances, most organised by liberals, and repeated efforts from the same quarter to tighten an already parsimonious Poor Law. But the alignments in this intellectual battle proved complex. The progressive side, too, included some with reservations about complete freedom of the market. Robert Owen, who was starting to become politically active in the opposition, indeed founded his experiment at New Lanark on precisely opposite principles. Posterity has called it socialist, but more striking were its paternalism and lack of democratic tendency. This was perhaps why, according to Owen himself, the first Viscount Melville had 'promised to aid him in his attempts to improve the condition of the lower orders'. The second Viscount Melville undertook to go and inspect New Lanark, though it is unclear whether he ever did.[47]

Owen's concern for the welfare of the working class was in any event widely shared by conservatives. *Blackwood's* damned political economy as insane, on the grounds that free markets sundered the bonds of mutual protection and loyalty in the old order. The answer proposed was a new alliance between a benevolent gentry and the downtrodden workers against utilitarian reformers and their industrialist friends. But while this analysis could have been a scientific one, it was more often couched in political language, if indeed it did not degenerate into polemics or romantic historical whimsy. Another stalwart of *Blackwood's*, W. E. Aytoun, afterwards a Tory nationalist and professor of rhetoric at Edinburgh, chose satiric verse as a suitable vehicle for advocating protectionism:

> Barley from Mecklenburg, grain from Polonia,
> Butter from Holland, American cheese,
> Bacon gratuitous,
> Cargos fortuitous,
> Float to our shores with each prosperous breeze.
> What need we care though a desperate peasantry
> Prowl round the stackyards with tinder and match?
> Blandly we'll smile at such practical pleasantry:
> Downing Street's not surmounted by thatch.

Still, the grasp of the social situation in the Scottish press, as an ensemble, left nothing to be desired. And the focus, in pursuit of a remedy, on the formation of bourgeois opinion demonstrated in itself how important, and how self-conscious, such opinion was becoming. The paradox in Scotland, of course, lay in the fact that the vast majority of the bourgeoisie was disfranchised. How could it be treated as politically responsible yet denied political responsibility? At any rate, even before the peace it was beginning to speak up for himself. Especially in Edinburgh, it made its presence felt at a series of gatherings on such worthy subjects as slavery, the income tax and plans for the North Bridge. Its rulers at first affected hauteur. The Chief Baron reported in 1814 'a shabby meeting, consisting of enthusiasts and hot opportunists of the most inconsiderable class and description'.

But such public spirit, once aroused, could not be diverted from the economic and social distress soon so evident in Scotland. Often this was bound up with rapid, almost ungovernable urbanisation. The appalling state of administration in the burghs, deplorable enough thirty years earlier, then looked quite indefensible. The census of 1821 would show Edinburgh with a population of 138,000: yet still it was ruled by a self-elected, self-serving clique of twenty-five councillors. Thus the movement for reform revived, under its original, evergreen leader, Archibald Fletcher. By the winter of 1817–8 it could organise some activity in twenty-eight royal burghs, including all the largest.[48]

This came in response to the discovery at Montrose of an electoral irregularity which enabled reformers to win a judicial ruling that the council was improperly constituted. A new one then had to be chosen by the whole body of burgesses: it would also have the right to draw up a more democratic sett. The Government faced the disquieting prospect of a repeat wherever any similar misdemeanour could be exposed. On Montrose, Maconochie wrote that 'the clamour which would have been excited all over the island and probably in Parliament, by keeping the power of electing to the municipal offices in the burgh close, in opposition to the unanimous wishes of the whole parties concerned, would have been so great that it was better to concede the point in discussion'. He noted with derision the efforts to widen the loophole, 'as if the law officers ... were prepared to recommend similar changes in all the corporations throughout Scotland than which, I will venture to say, nothing was farther from being contemplated. Much clamour, however, will be the result, and I have become extremely alarmed that by wishing to avoid one pretext for exciting the minds of the people I have afforded another.'

Publicly the Government refused to admit that there could be wider repercussions. It was driven into staking the absurd claim that the councils of royal burghs were not in any way accountable, even to the courts, and could not be reformed, even by the Crown in exercise of its prerogative. But behind the scenes Maconochie was asked to draw up a report on what might be done. He surveyed the arguments, pointing out that the Convention of Royal Burghs had in practice altered setts: a power to do so was therefore to be presumed. Having thus in effect confessed to itself that it had no case, the Government could only rely on legal hair-splitting to impede further actions. But it was unable to prevent two more burghs, Aberdeen and Inverness, emulating Montrose.

In fact Melville did not himself see how, or why, piecemeal reform of the burghs could be stopped. As patron of Edinburgh, one of his first moves had been to pilot through in 1812 a wider Police Act for the city, after a shocking outbreak of drunken proletarian violence, the Tron Riot, at the previous New Year. He had improved arrangements for law and order, already handed over from the town council to a board of commissioners, and was currently extending their powers in a new measure. He wanted besides to offer some remedy against malversation, and asked the Lord Advocate to see to it. Maconochie, however, failed with the Bills he then brought forward in two successive sessions.

The Commons were far from satisfied. The agitation inside Scotland had been brought to their attention by the Whig member for Lanarkshire, Lord Archibald Hamilton. He called forth a typically orotund defence of the existing system from William Dundas, who owed more than most to it. Hamilton's notion of reform, he declared

> is nothing less than to strike down the constitution of Scotland ... . This system has received the sanction of time and the seal of ages. It is at no particular abuse, but at the whole of the chartered rights of Scotland that the motion is aimed ... I have no ambition to give to Edinburgh or Glasgow the benefits of a Westminster election ... The people of Scotland are a sedate, religious people, not easily moved, but if once roused, let the House beware of them! [49]

In fact the Government, bankrupt of other expedients, gave in to Hamilton's demand for an inquiry two years later. During it, Whig diligence uncovered some amazing facts. At Forfar an idiot had been elected councillor, but the courts decided they could not interfere on grounds of his incapacity if the magistrates had willingly chosen him. Perhaps the most notorious regime in Scotland was that of Alexander Riddoch in Dundee. It had lasted forty years by dint of his filling the council with his creatures. According to the town clerk's evidence, they had 'in general been weak old men, who fancied 'they had been chosen for their wisdom, and that the office conferred a distinction on them, or raw ignorant young lads from the country, who could be easily managed, or individuals under such personal obligations to the leader, as would ensure their support to all his measures.' Dundas's argument from chartered rights could in his time still be taken seriously. But what price chartered rights granted to people like these? What price ancient institutions of which the main duties were perforce, if to be carried out at all, transferred to others? Urban administration in Scotland was manifestly moribund and contemptible, shamefully inadequate to the problems it faced, and a Government so failing in its duty as to pretend otherwise could only damage itself.[50]

In its stale habits of patronage it was even less fitted to respond to demands from the Scottish people at large. They now found expression in a radicalism far more formidable than that inspired twenty years earlier by the French Revolution. Then it had been largely confined to the capital, to humble artisans of the sort anciently patronised by the Court and later by the cultural elite, or to small towns in the East where some industry developed early; too narrow a base for success during the generally prosperous decade of the 1790s. But now the whole country was plunged into a series of horrific recessions affecting an industrial population meanwhile grown much bigger, above all in the West. There indeed everything appeared on a scale Scotland had never known before, not only the swings of the economic cycle but also the reactions to them, not only the social upheaval but also the danger.

A crisis had for some time been brewing amid the strains of wartime, the high inflation and the restrictions on trade in Napoleonic Europe. Then, coinciding with the final phase of the conflict, came by ill chance a series of poor harvests and by deliberate action of the Government a new Corn Law. All caused much hardship. There followed a sharp deterioration in the hitherto by and large harmonious relations of capital and labour in Scotland. The legal provisions conferring a right to the local regulation of wages, with appeal to the courts in case of dispute, had helped to maintain them. This may have been offensive to fanatical political economists, but few graced the Scottish ruling class. The Combination Acts, passed at Westminster in 1799–1800 to ban trade unions, had been ignored north of the border. A still nationalist Bench said it could not understand or apply statutes drawn up entirely according to English concepts. No native principle declared combination inherently illegal, at most only a civil wrong. Even after Scots law hardened, prosecutions under the Acts remained rare, not least because, as the Lord Advocate would say in 1819, 'in none of the cases of simple combination which came before me was I satisfied that the masters were entirely without blame' – a sentiment that would have struck his English counterpart as extremely odd.

But little else of an essentially equitable system was to survive the changes now imminent. Scots law also moved with the times, and the times held political economy to be scientifically true. The first sign of its operating on the judges' minds appeared in a civil case against some paper-makers of Edinburgh in 1808. The Court of Session then, as it was entitled to do, declared combination a new offence at common law (in other words, by virtue of native vigour, not statute). Meadowbank explicitly rested his judgment on the principle that 'a measure of this kind destroys the freedom of the market'. The new offence had yet, however, to be precisely defined, and for some years introduced confusion into the law. In 1811 a cotton-spinner from Glasgow was found guilty of it. But Hope, passing sentence, charged it as an aggravation that there was no need for combination when, by way of an alternative, wages could be fixed. He implied therefore the continuing validity of the regulatory system.[51]

This was seized on by workers' leaders, engaged in several trades on a struggle to maintain living standards. The best organised were the weavers, self-conscious enough to have sustained since 1808 a national union, the Scottish Weavers' Association. They tried to activate the old law by formally requesting the Lord Provost of Glasgow to convene the magistrates for the purpose of fixing higher wages. He sought to evade the issue by urging on employees and employers a settlement outside the legal framework. When the latter refused to co-operate, forty of them were sued by 1500 weavers.

In June 1812 the Court of Session ruled that these indeed possessed the right they wished to exercise and directed the magistracy to enforce it, which was at length done by accepting their demands. But no way could be found of obliging the employers to pay, except through the wearisome and expensive process of following to its end the litigation against each of them. From this point the law ceased to help the weavers. When their patience and money ran out, 40,000 of them struck work in November. The Government bided its time for three weeks, then charged the ringleaders with criminal combination – the first time any such action had been brought in Scotland. The strike continued till February 1813. After its collapse, the accused were tried and imprisoned or, if they had fled into England, outlawed. The weavers' union shortly disintegrated. To add insult to injury, Parliament at once set about repealing the laws on regulation of wages.[52]

The whole exercise thus turned out a disaster for this vanguard of the proletariat. They had not merely failed to assert their legal rights, but lost them; they were not merely beaten, but humiliated. It was a crucial turn of events. These sturdy, independent craftsmen had little remotely revolutionary about them, but surely represented rather what paternalists ought to have wished from an educated working class. Yet just as such aristocrats of labour began to attain a social and economic standing which might plausibly merit translation into a political one, the Scottish state blankly refused to countenance their claims and treated them instead as no more than a radical canaille. Nor was history to vindicate them. They afterwards struggled tenaciously but in vain against falling prices for their goods and competition from machines. Within a decade or two their craft disappeared. If the law would no longer protect them, or allow them to protect themselves, little hope could be held out to any other group.

Once the equitable laws were gone, it did not prove possible amid severe economic dislocation to find a substitute. The Government was itself moved to attempts at alleviating the distress, for example with a scheme mooted in 1816 for a general agreement in the West of Scotland on reducing wages rather than destroying jobs. The workers 'although suffering privations and diminished comforts ... would be prevented from acquiring habits of idleness and of becoming burthensome or mischievous members of the community'. It came to nothing. The Scottish state had in effect abandoned any role in the labour market, and could in future at most only act as a referee in its contests. With the end of the native tradition, workers had no recourse but to the criminalised unions. The bias in the system was now towards strife rather than conciliation, and the industrial strife would often entail political strife.[53]

From 1815, the Scottish radicals promptly set about organising themselves, under the stimulus of correspondence with those in England and visits from their leaders. A network of local reforming societies sprang up, reviving the demands of the 1790s. But there was among them a new and more extreme element, reflecting the workers' desperation amid much terrible need. Some contended that only physical force could bring about a transformation of society, so that the war of one class on another had for the first time in Scotland to be taken seriously. An apparently profound alteration in attitudes, previously unsuspected by the landed elite, struck Melville when he tried to raise corps of volunteers in the industrial areas against the radicals: 'Officers have ... found, to their astonishment and mortification, that they could not trust those on whom they had depended for loyalty and attachment; I allude to artisans and persons of that description and that class of life. Your shepherds and hill peasantry are as yet, thank God, of a very different description, not only physically but morally.'[54]

Amid this growing nervousness on the part of the authorities, Maconochie assumed responsibility for law and order in Scotland at the end of 1816. He obviously intended that his parliamentary debut, early in the following year, should be an occasion to remember, and played the palace at Westminster with the assurance of one who knew he could make his audience's flesh creep. No nonsense of an innocuous maiden speech for him! Instead, promising to be a scourge of the radicals, he moved for a banning of their societies and a fresh suspension of the Act against Wrongous Imprisonment. At the climax he read out a secret oath which he said they were taking in Glasgow, and which called for the establishment of democracy by violence if need be. His performance did make a great impression, and the House at once voted the repressive measures he asked for.[55] In fact Maconochie was a fool.

One reason for his fuss was that he did not dispose of enough police to investigate and control what was going on. Glasgow's, established in 1800, had a strength of only 123, most of them employed in such work as clearing snow or repairing smashed street-lights. Little of value could be found out till a diligent detective, Andrew McKay, was drafted in from Linlithgow. He had discovered that weapons were being made in secret and hidden when he apparently became suspect to the radicals. He was replaced by the head of Edinburgh's police, Captain Brown, who went westward 'disguised as a reformer'. More information came from Alexander Richmond. Originally a weaver at Pollokshaws, he had been one of the leaders of the strike in 1812. An intelligent and articulate man, he so impressed Jeffrey and Cockburn when he went on trial that they afterwards gave him the money to start up his own business. Through his widening contacts he at length met the Lord Advocate. In his immature, melodramatic way, Maconochie disclosed what he chose to call a state secret: that there was in Scotland a plot against the Government, which would pay to find out who was behind it. Richmond accepted the offer. It was probably he who reported the text of the oath read out to the Commons.

With his new powers, Maconochie ordered the arrest of four radicals, though the evidence against them personally amounted to very little. 'The circumstance of their having been engaged in a conspiracy to procure annual Parliaments and universal suffrage by physical force was deemed sufficient ground for charging them,' he uneasily explained. When they were tried, their Whig counsel suggested with some success that the whole thing had been rigged. Public opinion swung behind the accused, and the jury was obviously reluctant to convict. None received a sentence heavier than six months' imprisonment. Maconochie had had a case, not an open-and-shut case but a case all the same, which he entirely mishandled and allowed to be pilloried as the product of agents provocateurs. He confessed himself 'mortified', and his effort to show a stern face to the disaffection only backfired and damaged the Government.[56]

The last straw came in a quite different context, with his conduct at the General Assembly of the Church of Scotland in 1819. As Hope described it to Melville, Maconochie on entering told a friend he was going to claim his privilege, without making clear what he meant. Approaching the throne, 'he then sat down and clapped on his hat – and this on the ground of the privilege or supposed privilege which the Lord Advocate has of pleading before the Court of Session with his hat on ... He has made himself such a laughing stock that it really makes one quite ashamed to have patronised him – and I am quite clear that he must cease to be Advocate.' The death soon afterwards of the Chief Baron offered a pretext. Maconochie fondly expected to succeed him at the Exchequer, and thought the mere judge's gown offered him instead a 'degradation'. But he had no choice. His assumption of the same judicial title as his late father had borne gave rise to one of the best Scottish legal jokes. An advocate whom he one day pedantically taxed with the difference between 'also' and 'likewise' allowed enlightenment to spread over his features, then retorted: 'Ah! your lordship's father was Lord Meadowbank. Your lordship is Lord Meadowbank also, but not likewise.'[57]

Meanwhile, after a brief economic revival, recession deepened again, to reach its nadir in 1819. Parliament passed the repressive Six Acts in response to a wave of demonstrations and riots which culminated in the Peterloo massacre. But trouble on that scale was confined to the South, and Scots commonly congratulated themselves on escaping the worst. A level-headed Melville wrote: 'Though I have no doubt that there are persons in Glasgow and the other manufacturing districts of the West of Scotland whose political views are as mischievous as any of those in Lancashire and elsewhere in England, and though it may be proper and necessary to take all due precaution to frustrate their designs ... I have no apprehension of any general disturbance.' He remained sanguine even when trouble did break out in the West during September. In January 1820 he could still comment: 'I should hope it may be subdued without any violent excesses or any formidable attempt at insurrection. I have never felt any other alarm on the subject than what might arise from the country not being sufficiently alive to what was going on. It appears now to view the matter as it ought, and of course the great body of the nation are quite prepared to resist and put down the disaffected.' The *Edinburgh Review* itself remarked that 'during the outrageous proceedings of the mob, nothing could exceed the temperate, conciliatory and even kind demeanour both of the magistrates and the military'.[58]

But when the authorities thought to clinch matters in February with the arrest of twenty-seven Glaswegians on charges of rehearsing an uprising, they produced the opposite of the intended effect. On April 1, posters appeared in the western towns signed by a committee for organising a provisional government. They called for a general strike and a popular revolt. Troops hurried to Glasgow, where fighting broke out on April 5. The same day fifty men set off from the city to seize the Carron iron-works. Soldiers met them near Falkirk in the Battle of Bonnymuir. A few were killed and the rest taken prisoner: three were eventually hanged. These small affairs were later dignified by the name of the Radical War. But they did frighten Scotland. Never before had this tranquil country emulated England with an armed rebellion of industrial workers.

Even then, the authorities kept cool. The new Lord Advocate was Sir William Rae, previously sheriff of Edinburgh, described by Hope as 'of conciliatory manner and frank and open temper', and by Melville as 'a most judicious adviser'. Whig intellectuals of course lampooned him as just another dim and incompetent reactionary. In fact in his own county of Lanarkshire he had been voting for their friend, Hamilton. That progressive circle anyway saw nothing much wrong with repressing radicals. Lord Archibald's brother, the Duke of Hamilton, declined to chair a meeting of them in Glasgow. Thereupon, Scott reported, 'they wrote to him that they saw he was flinching from what he himself had begun and that since he would not come to them they were resolved to come to his house ... and burn it about his ears': his Grace was 'terribly frightened'.

By contrast Rae, as soon as he heard of the violence in the West, predicted: 'This will end in nothing', despite 'the undue alarm which seems to pervade both the magistrates and the military commander in Glasgow.' He went there himself, and remained unimpressed: 'Although we have had abundance of false alarms, all has continued quiet in Scotland ... I am satisfied that the radical gentlemen are completely frightened, and that we shall have no opportunity of bestowing on them any of that description of chastisement which I came here in the hope of seeing inflicted.' He rebuked the town council for a lack of energy against the disorders, yet for the most part showed a good sense of public relations, tempered justice with mercy and struck shrewd plea bargains with radical prisoners and their counsel. His own forensic approach was rigorous by Scottish standards: 'I may notice it as an occurrence almost unprecedented in state trials that in the course of those now concluded not one juror has been challenged by the Crown and not a single person offered as a witness who was either a spy, a socius criminis or liable to the most remote suspicion in any point of view.' [59]

The scale of the trouble was undeniably modest, and its significance lay rather in a more general effect on Scottish politics. The Government had won the Radical War, and workers learned that violence would neither intimidate the middle and upper ranks of society nor gain support among them. In that sense, despite its wider potential base in an expanded proletariat, radicalism was more isolated than it had been even in the 1790s. Scott recalled 'when the same ideas possessed a much more formidable class of people, being received by a large proportion of farmers, shopkeepers and others, possessed of substance.' The effect was to make the working class recoil from this isolation, to fall back from militancy on self-improvement through respectability: in other words, from physical to moral force.

This was truer to its traditions. Scots workers had long shown an independent spirit, in eagerness to better themselves through education and in readiness through religious dissent to work out their own salvation free of the establishment. This venerable presbyterian egalitarianism could now be made compatible with the recent secular radicalism, industrial society offering scope for its development in a way that the overwhelmingly rural Scotland of old could not. A moderate spirit endured among that majority of the proletariat which was neither crushed nor radicalised, but did its best under an economic order which, if slowly and painfully, would bring a real rise in living standards. Common values were not entirely lost in Scotland, and continued to be shared up and down the social scale. Workers, however, would have to wait longer to attain their political aims.[60]

It was still remarkable how little of all this found reflection inside the political nation. At the dissolution of Parliament in 1818. Melville blandly wrote: 'Our electioneering prospects are tolerably fair in this country. I do not expect that we shall be worse off than in the last Parliament and shall probably be better'. A relatively high number of contests took place, for new loopholes discovered in the law had allowed the creation of faggot votes to start up again. The national electorate increased by one-fifth in the course of the decade, and at its end was larger than before Thurlow's judgment of 1790. Melville discussed doing something about it and 'establishing by Act of Parliament a regular and equitable system for ascertaining the fiars in this country'. He thought that it would require a clear expression of support from the landed interest, as from both Houses of Parliament, and that the initiative had therefore better come from outside the Government. Nothing happened. In any case most of the new voters seemed to be on his side, for his position at the polls was now consolidated where it was not actually improved.[61]

In the South-east, for example, previously dissident elements came back over to the Ministry. The Anstruthers, patrons of the eponymous burghs, did so, and were zealous enough converts to offer their district to Maconochie, then to Rae. Kinross-shire, not previously safe, elected a Graham of Kinross who supported the Government, and when he died the next year elected his son on the same ticket against opposition from the other major local interest, represented by Charles, a son of William Adam. For his new man in Berwickshire, Melville found a Whig defector, Sir John Marjoribanks, formerly member for Bute. The opposition was now secure only in the Dysart and Haddington Burghs, yet made attempts on two other districts. In Linlithgow a ministerialist was elected at the General Election, but died in 1819. At the by-election Owen, who had built up some influence in the town council of Lanark, masterminded a victory for the opposition; it would, however, be reversed the next year. In the notoriously corrupt Stirling the official candidate returned in 1818 was unseated on petition by the loser, a brother of the Earl of Rosebery, though again his tenure lasted only a few months.

The North-east also offered a picture of stability, except for a spectacular gain by the opposition. This came with the election in the Aberdeen Burghs of Joseph Hume, the only radical ever to wend his way through the unreformed Scottish electoral system. It happened because Montrose, one component of the district, now had a popular sett, and a second, Aberdeen, was on its way to getting the same, if for the present disfranchised while awaiting the legal judgment. The others were delivered to Hume by Maule, who sat on as Whig member for Forfarshire. But all else in this region remained in the Government's hands.

The situation in the Highlands was as ever more confused. The region had in effect slipped from the Dundases' control, but nobody else took over the whole. The Sutherlands. with two seats at their disposal, were now normally supporting the Government again. The Grants became more firmly attached to it: Charles younger, succeeding the elder as member for Inverness-shire, was soon appointed Chief Secretary for Ireland. Melville declined to intervene in a contest in Ross but the winner, Thomas Mackenzie, supported him anyway. Other seats were held by independents. Caithness elected George Sinclair, heir of Agricultural Sir

John, as wayward and eccentric as his father. In Orkney and Shetland, where politics remained local, the victor was George Dundas, a grandson of Sir Lawrence, still hostile to his kinsman of Melville. In Cromartyshire, a formerly loyal interest turned its coat with a new member. Argyll continued to return a Whig Campbell.

In the West the Government made gains. From the Glasgow Burghs, Kirkman Finlay was obliged to retire in favour of the more reliable Alexander Houstoun. In Ayrshire, where there had been a brisk creation of votes, the incumbent Whig surrendered without a contest to the official candidate, James Montgomerie. That left to the opposition only three safe seats, in Lanarkshire, Renfrewshire and the Ayr Burghs. Altogether one may reckon that the Government could count on thirty-four supporters in the new House of Commons, the rest being a mixed bag of Whigs, radicals and independents.

The peers saw a large turnover because of retirals, and half those chosen were newcomers. In reply to one aspirant, the Viscount of Arbuthnott, Melville disclaimed any wish to control the proceedings: 'Your lordship has adopted a very erroneous notion of the interference of Government in the election of the 16 Scotch peers, if you suppose that we have nothing more to do than select any individuals whom we may choose to nominate, and afterwards to call upon our friends to support them. Such a course of proceeding would give just offence to the peerage of Scotland.' Nevertheless, the representation remained congenial to him. Selkirk, the sole Whig sitting in the previous parliament, resigned. But two new ones, the Duke of Roxburghe and the Earl of Rosebery came in, together with the doubtful Marquis of Tweeddale. Another Whig, Lord Belhaven, won a by-election in 1819. But the great majority still supported the Government.[62]

Altogether, then, Melville had clearly established a stable regime, in itself a magnet to lesser interests. The core of seats held by various hostile elements since the Ministry of All the Talents was gradually being squeezed. No wonder the Prime Minister called Scotland 'the best conditioned country in the world'. Official control did seem more vulnerable to local coups, of a kind which the elder Melville had always nipped in the bud. But these scarcely represented the deeper forces stirring in the nation which would render the old methods of management inadequate. When George III died only eighteen months later, it would have taken a bold man to predict that, in the course of the new reign, the Dundas despotism would crumble.

Notes

1. SRO GD 235/10/10/3, 10/18/175; GD 51/11/42, 11/35/1.
2. SRO GD 235/10/17/65–75; GD 51/16/62–3; Lonsdale Papers, LI/2/158.
3. Walker (1821), passim.
4. NLS MS 9, f.119.
5. ibid., ff.141, 145–9; Thorne (1986), iii. 645.
6. SRO GD 51/5/483/1, 507/3, 684; Home Office Papers, SRO RH 2/4/121/400.
7. Liverpool Papers, BL Add MSS 38269, f.306; 38278, f.83; Peel Papers, BL Add MSS 40312, ff. 89–96; Boyle Papers, 9/14/16, 9/31/2–7.
8. Wellesley (1812), passim; (1914), ii, 98.

9. Holland (1905), 137; Wellesley Papers, BL Add MSS 37297, f.9; Canning Papers, bundle 61; Fry (1987), 27; *Parl. Debates*, xxiii, col. 865; xxxi. col. 683.

10. Wellesley Papers, BL Add MSS 37296, f.402; Canning Papers, loc.cit.

11. Aspinall (1938), i, 90–1, 102, 108–9; NLS Acc 9140, May 28, 1812.

12. ibid., July 18 & 19, 1812; Melville (1931), 79–80.

13. Thorne, i, 94.

14. Cockburn (1856), 273; Halévy (1912), 110.

15. Thorne, iii, 653.

16. Halévy, loc.cit.

17. NMM MS 9441, MEL 101; Home Office Papers, SRO RH 2/4/94/365.

18. SRO GD 51/2/437/20; WLC, Feb.8, 1816; Romilly (1905), 176; Aspinall (1938), i, 242–3; Petrie (1954), 228.

19. *Parl. Debates*, xxvii, col. 871.

20. SRO GD 51/2/1046/2.

21. NLS MS 1045, ff.94 et seqq, f.116; Fulford & Strachey (1938), i, 14; Glover (1963), 8

22. NLS MS 1046, f.204; *Parl. Debates*, xxix, col.11; Wellington (1868), vii, 419; viii, 144.

23. Original Letters, NLS MS 3420, ff.125–6; Martin Papers, BL Add MSS 41367, f.34; Gurwood (1844), vii, 700; Hamilton (1903), ii, 352, 354, 363; Marcus (1971), ii, 352–8.

24. Original Letters, NLS MS 3420, f.124; Martin Papers, BL Add MSS 41367, f.79; Marcus, 359.

25. Petrie, 218; Durdans Books, NLS MS 10218, f.16; SRO GD 51/2/1081/6, 18.

26. Weld (1848), 410–14; Crouse (1934), 26–9; Barnard (1962), 193; Parry (1963), 26–7, 124; Graham (1965), 41, 59; Kennedy (1976), 128–9.

27. Boyle Papers, 9/31/9; Bowles (1854). 45; Bartlett (1963), 16, 20, 33; Cookson (1975), 119.

28. SRO GD 51/2/555/1; NLS MS 1044, ff.157 et seqq; WLC, Feb. 28, 1818; *Parl. Debates*, xxxix, col. 1162; Cookson, 32.

29. ibid., 146; Bowles, 32.

30. *Parl. Debates*, xxvi, col. 183; xxxi, col. 735; xl, col. 1033.

31. WLP I, memorandum of 1816; *Parl. Debates*, xxix, col. 911; Bartlett, 37, 207; Beamish (1862), 142; Twitchett (1931), 155–7; McCleary (1947), 2.

32. Cookson, 31–2, 147.

33. Dalhousie Muniments SRO GD 45/3/330; GD 51/1/182, 5/749/1, 7, 129, 220; NLS MS 9, f.276; NMM MS 9441, MEL 102; Liverpool Papers, BL Add MSS 38276, f.354; 38277, f.243; Renwick (1912), x, 519; Fulford & Strachey, i, 219; Youngson (1966), 88, 135; Gibson (1985), 10.

34. SRO GD 51/5/749/2, 94, 102, 334; Home Office Papers, SRO RH 2/4/ 118/478.

35. Seaforth Muniments, SRO GD 46/4/17/57/183; SRO GD 51/5/686/1, 749/1, 89, 120, 749/2, 2, 258, 457, 465.

36. SRO GD 51/5/684; NLS MS 9370, f.3; Peel Papers, BL Add MSS 40317, f.18.

37. STA MSS 4513, 4517; SRO GD 51/5/749/2, 99; Home Office Papers, SRO RH 2/4/104/330; Lee Papers, NLS MS 3433, ff.248, 273; MS 3434, ff.262, 271; Cook (1820), 246; Maciver (1980), 1; Brown, (1983), 110, 164; Brown, (1988), 153.

38. NLS MS 10, f.13; SRO GD 51/17/74B, 2/437/10; Boyle Papers, 9/8/8 &

41, 9/24/17; J.P. Wood Papers, NLS MS 3105, f.69; *Parl. Debates*, xxii, col. 1159; Laurie (1925), 179; Grierson (1932), iv, 370.

39. Cookson, 127; Murray (1974), 51.
40. HO SRO RH 2/4/129/329.
41. Thorne, iii, 35; SRO GD 51/5/496; *Parl. Debates*, xxix, cols.1004, 1086; xxx, col. 585; *Edinburgh Review*, xxi, 104–5; Smith (1961), 73 et seqq; Paton (1958), 54; Willcock (1966), 255; Murray (1974), 51.
42. Liverpool Papers, BL Add MSS 38282, f.326.
43. Mudie (1825), 182.
44. Renwick, x, 75; Grant (1988), ii, 42–3, 103.
45. Lockhart (1819),·149; Aspinall, ii, 540.
46. Fetter (1960), 85 et seqq; Cockburn, 368; Roach (1970), 339–40.
47. SRO GD 51/1/198/27/10; GD 51/5/749, 441.
48. Liverpool Papers, BL Add MSS 38258, f. 139; *Edinburgh Review*, xxx, 511 et seqq; *Blackwood's Edinburgh Magazine*, iii, 107.
49. *Parl. Debates*, xl, col. 186.
50. NLS MS 10, ff.47 et seqq, 70; Home Office Papers, SRO RH 2/4/118// 454; *Parliamentary Papers*, 1819, vi, 375; 1820, iii, 58; Omond (1888), 255; Ralston (1980), 41 et seqq.
51. McCulloch (1823–4), 322; Gray (1928), 340; Straka (1985), 128 et seqq.
52. Richmond (1824), passim; Roach, 13.
53. Home Office Papers, SRO RH 2/4/110/417; Marwick (1967), 5 et seqq; Murray (1978), 208 et seqq; Fraser (1985), 33 et seqq; Straka, 140.
54. Letters to Scott, NLS MS 3890, f.250.
55. Thorne, iv, 514; *Parl. Debates*, xxxv, col. 729; Roach, 75.
56. Home Office Papers, SRO RH 2/4/116/49. 117/268; Roach, 76, 80–1, 84– 8, 118, 135.
57. NLS MS 10, ff.160 et seqq; Thorne, loc.cit.
58. NLS MS 1054, f.1073; SRO GD 51/2/609; Home Office Papers, SRO RH 2/4/126/627; *Edinburgh Review*, xxxiii, 219.
59. NLS MS 10, f. 156; STA MS 4712; Home Office Papers, SRO RH 2/4/ 131/313, 135/163; Mackay (1866), 46; Omond, 258–60; Grierson, vi, 16.
60. Grierson, v, 467.
61. STA MS 4558; Home Office Papers, SRO RH 2/4/121/400.
62. SRO GD 51/1/197/54.

10

'A very hollow dependence'

As its first political consequence, the accession of George IV dissolved Parliament. A return to the polls could not have been expected to produce results very different from those so shortly before. In the South-east of Scotland, the Government if anything recovered ground. The opposition was turned out of both burgh districts it had gained at by-elections meanwhile. In the one, Linlithgow, the Lord Provost of Glasgow, Henry Monteith, defeated Robert Owen, now standing in person. In the other the new member, Robert Downie of Appin, crowed to Lord Melville: 'I appear to have accomplished what few men would have attempted and perhaps still fewer have succeeded – that is, destroyed, for the present at least, the Whig interest in the Stirling district of burghs.' Even in the district of Haddington, under the house of Lauderdale a stronghold of opposition for twenty years, the Ministry had won control in two of the five councils. The victor there, Hew Dalrymple Hamilton, was a relation by marriage of the Dundases. But he had been a thorn in their flesh ever since his entry to the House of Commons in 1795, having repeatedly crossed the floor in quest of a peerage; in a precarious seat he would prove more amenable to Melville's wooing. Yet the balance of parties was also finer than of old in the adjacent East Lothian, where the sitting member, Sir James Suttie, beat off the Whigs by a single vote. Still, their only safe constituency in the region was the Dysart Burghs, held by Sir Ronald Ferguson of Raith. His brother challenged for Fife when the serving member, General William Wemyss, handed over to his son James, but was soundly beaten.

On the other hand the western Lowlands were stable, with the opposition holding three seats, the Ayr Burghs, Lanarkshire and Renfrewshire. In the last the Government might have had a chance if its manager had been willing to relax his undoubtedly high integrity for mere electoral advantage. Some wealthy merchants from Glasgow were keen to have a go at toppling the county's Whig incumbent and merrily manufactured franchises to that end – the electorate had doubled in ten years. They put it to Melville that a few judicious promotions in the navy would do their vote no harm. He replied:

> I cannot consent either in regard to Renfrewshire or any other election contest to enter into any compact on that subject. The giving way in one instance to that sort of demand would produce similar demands from a hundred other quarters where contests might be carried on, and a compliance with

them would be most injurious to the naval service and discreditable to that department of the Government.

So the efforts came to nothing.[1]

In the entire North of the country, Melville's grip had visibly slackened, largely because of unruly magnates. The Duke of Argyll remained committed to opposition. So did the families in control of the alternating counties of Bute and Nairnshire. The Sutherlands, patrons of two constituencies, were capricious though for the time being well-disposed to the Ministry. It was sure of just three members, Charles Grant the younger and George Cumming in Inverness, county and burghs respectively, and Thomas Mackenzie in Ross. Orkney and Shetland fell to a new local coalition whose victor, John Balfour, usually supported the Government too.

Its glaring weakness this time was the collapse of the arrangements which had so long pacified the North-east. As ever, the house of Fife caused the trouble. James Duff, the fourth Earl, had come in as a ministerialist for Banffshire in 1818, though Melville entertained deep suspicion of his loyalty. What Fife wanted most was restoration to his family of the British peerage granted in 1790 to his uncle, the second Earl, but then lost because he had no sons. An obvious path to this goal lay through rebuilding a decayed electoral interest. That inevitably entailed upsetting the existing dispositions, which in the course of time had come to be run by Grants, either the chiefs of the clan, recently succeeded to the earldoms of Seafield and Findlater, or the nabobs. The upshot was a feud of Duffs and Grants. It brought at Elgin a confrontation between 2000 of their tenants, with violence just averted by the exertions of the sheriff and the clergy. Fife's men kidnapped a bailie and put him on a boat for Brora in an attempt to alter the balance in the town council. It was still the Grants' candidate, Archibald Farquharson, that won.

Melville's personal interest suffered a disaster in Kincardine. The previous member, his spectacularly profligate kinsman George Drummond, had been forced to abandon the seat, along with his castle, wife and children. Two ministerialist candidates then took the field, only to let a Whig slip home between them. The winner was a relative of William Maule, whose influence now stretched all the way from his own seat of Forfarshire to the Aberdeen Burghs, still occupied by his protégé Joseph Hume.[2] Melville was blamed for not having taken a firm grip on the situation. He lamely explained that he had been unwilling to offend either of the unlucky contenders. His father would never have countenanced anything of the kind.

Even so, the Ministry could count on thirty Scots in the new Parliament, with another five more loosely attached. The Whigs were making no net progress at all.[3] And they sustained loss in the peers' election. The manager, his previous disclaimers notwithstanding, did send round a King's list. From it fourteen were elected, Lords Rosebery and Belhaven alone hanging on in opposition. Melville had specified that he wanted rid of the Duke of Roxburghe, who duly forfeited his place.[4]

With its electoral position confirmed, the Government reckoned that a new reign also offered the chance to restore the reputation of the monarchy and of the constitution in general. The finally tragic figure of George III, 'an old, mad, blind, despised and dying king,' had been no great object of loyalty. And though the heir could, along with his brothers, also be called by Shelley 'princes, the dregs of their dull race, who flow through public scorn, mud from a muddy spring', George IV was in fact a cultured man anxious to do well and make amends for his past.

One part of it immediately came back to haunt him, in the person of his estranged, not to say hated wife, Caroline of Brunswick. Since 1813 she had lived in scandal abroad. Now she meant to claim her rights. She certainly did not lack gall, writing as she approached the Channel that she 'desires that Lord Melville will be so obliging as to order one of the royal yachts to be in readiness at Calais to convey Her Majesty to Dover'. He politely promised to ask the King. Yet fickle public opinion swayed in her favour. On her landing – without Melville's help – crowds marched through the streets of London under banners bearing the legend, 'The Queen's guards are the people'. It was, of course, quite impossible for George to concede anything. On the contrary, he now brought against her a Bill for divorce on the grounds of immoral conduct.

Curiously Melville, not otherwise inclined to rock any boats, harboured reservations about it. When Ministers decided to have the matter out in August 1820, he was still hurrying down from his holidays in Scotland. He told Lord Liverpool on arrival that he 'was both surprised and annoyed at finding from you in one or two conversations that the Cabinet were quite decided on the question of divorce', and went on to raise various quibbles. The fact of his being personally uxorious, as well as something of a stickler for legality, perhaps explained this stance. It confirmed his place among the Government's liberals; another of them, George Canning, president of the Board of Control, resigned over the matter. In the face of wide popular protest, egged on by Henry Brougham's scathing parliamentary oratory, the Bill had anyway to be dropped. The problem of the Queen was solved by her death a year later, a few days after being restrained by force from an attempt to enter Westminster Abbey and be crowned with her husband.[5]

Melville's relations with George IV did not suffer. To mark the coronation, the King created four new Knights of the Thistle, of whom one was to be the First Lord of the Admiralty. The offer must have surprised him, for he asked cautiously: 'Has your Majesty mentioned it to Lord Liverpool?' To which came a classic royal retort: 'Lord Liverpool be damned! I offer it you, will you take it or not?' He took it.[6]

It occurred to the King that one way of polishing his image would be to show himself among his subjects: his father, even when able to, had scarcely ever moved beyond St James's and Windsor. In 1821 the King went to Ireland and Hanover. He planned for the next year to attend a congress of the allied powers in Vienna, from which his Ministers were most anxious to dissuade him. So it came about that, initially as a diversion, a trip to Scotland was mooted – though the idea had been put to him already by Melville and Walter Scott. Up to the last minute there was some doubt which of these journeys the monarch would actually undertake, complicated by the question whether his mistress, Lady Conyngham, should accompany him. She might do for Vienna, but was thought likely to offend the northern kingdom's stern morality: she finally fell victim to a diplomatic illness. And if Scotland was indeed to be the destination, what should the sovereign see?

One plan was for him to pass through both Edinburgh and Glasgow, before calling on the Duke of Montrose at Buchanan Castle and the Duke of Atholl at Blair Atholl. Much to Melville's relief His Majesty settled for something simpler, and stayed in the capital for 'one and twenty daft days' during August 1822.[7]

Scott set with zest about organising the visit, but such was the burden that Melville often had to take a hand too. He was to be found, for example, advising the principal of St Andrews: 'I think there would be considerable awkwardness in a joint address from all the four universities; it would look like clubbing their loyalty to make up a sufficient quantity of it.' Or again, to one Bailie Macfie, on the arrangements after the King's disembarkation:

> Though I at present do not recall the precise grounds on which the magistrates of Leith were not assigned a special place in the procession, I presume it must be because their powers and functions are not similar to those of all the other magistrates who are included in the procession, and because it would have been nearly out of their jurisdiction as soon as it began to move.

While he did not discourage Scott's 'celtification', he grew a little nervous at the thought of hundreds of Highlanders in Edinburgh, armed to the teeth. He therefore wrote advising Atholl to leave his private army at home: 'I think we have fully as many of the Gael, real or fictional, as is prudent or necessary.'

When the time came, however, all went well, despite the rain and fog often provided by Edinburgh for visitors at this season. The King's route from Leith to Holyrood on August 15 was lined by vast crowds. Two days later he appeared at a levee in Highland dress, complete with fetching flesh-coloured tights under his mini-kilt. This appealed to his female admirers: 'Since his stay is so short, the more we see of him the better', said Lady Saltoun. He was surrounded by cronies from London who, despite tenuous claims to the tartan, kilted themselves too. One, a former Lord Mayor, was taken as the object of his devoted loyalty by an enthusiastic Scot 'who kneeled to kiss the fat Alderman's hand, when, finding out his mistake, he called out "Wrong, by Jove" and rising, moved on undaunted to the larger presence'. So it continued, with the monarch commuting from Dalkeith Palace, where he was the Duke of Buccleuch's guest, to a succession of evocative events. He also paid a private visit to Melville Castle, in which Sir Robert and Lady Peel were accommodated by the Viscount.[8]

He, his earlier misgivings fully dispelled, wrote afterwards to his sovereign:

> When your Majesty announced your intention to visit Scotland, Lord Melville had no doubt that the people of that country would not be deficient in dutiful respect to your Majesty; but he did not anticipate to its full extent the determined and deep-rooted monarchical feeling which evidently pervaded the great body of the people. Lord Melville is sensible that your Majesty has been exposed to considerable trouble and inconvenience in undertaking the voyage; but he is firmly persuaded that your Majesty's visit will be attended with important public benefit.

Scott had already voiced a hope that the jamboree would unify Whig and Tory. No doubt it was on Tory terms that he and Melville expected unification to take place.

The one thing to mar George IV's stay was the arrival halfway through of the dreadful news that the Foreign Secretary, Lord Castlereagh, unbalanced by the burdens of office, had slit his throat. It required yet another reshuffle of the Cabinet. For twenty years, that had always caused problems. Liverpool's constant aim was to emulate Pitt in forming non-partisan Governments of the broad bottom, embracing all except a disgruntled few. Though urbane and conciliatory, the Prime Minister yet never found it easy to blend ambitious rising talents with those he already disposed of. A further problem was that too many members of the Cabinet still sat in the House of Lords, depriving the front bench in the Commons of weight and experience.[9]

Liverpool's difficulties would have been solved if, say, he could have called simultaneously on the brilliant services of Canning and Peel. Though they were rivals, there seemed no other reason why this should not be accomplished. Yet over a whole decade it proved uncannily difficult to bring off. Canning had been excluded at Castlereagh's insistence in 1812, when Peel came in as a strong-willed Irish Secretary. Only two years after Canning took the presidency of the Board of Control in 1816, Peel decided to resume his independence and enjoy a spell out of office. At Canning's departure over the royal divorce, the Prime Minister was again left without either.

A fresh chance of including both opened when Lord Sidmouth, for nine years a reactionary Home Secretary, told Liverpool in the summer of 1821 that he wanted to retire. The Prime Minister thought to replace him with Melville and put Canning in the Admiralty. Though the incumbent First Lord did not wish to move, complaining to his secretary that he was being 'kicked upstairs', he considerately agreed. In his case the King was ready to concur, but made clear that he would not have Canning back. The position was then further complicated because Peel, offered the Board of Control, set his sights higher and demanded either the Home Office or the Exchequer. Now Lady Liverpool died, indisposing the Prime Minister himself at a crucial juncture. On his return to business, he was still more insistent on having Canning. But five of his colleagues caballed and agreed that 'there was no reason for readmitting Canning to the Cabinet, except to prevent his becoming a rallying point for the dissatisfied friends of Government'. Melville, one of this group, was the key to the situation, for his complaisance had created the opening. Now he changed his mind and declared he would not take the Home Office after all, so that Canning had to stay out. Instead the post went to Peel, against whose claim to it Melville had earlier urged resistance.[10] He was never skilful or consistent in these personal high politics, or comfortable with the naked ambition displayed. In any event he did not believe, as a loyal gentleman, that Liverpool should be permitted to impose unwanted Ministers on the King.

Now, in the summer of 1822, Castlereagh's suicide started the bother all over again. Canning's claim to succeed to the Foreign Office, where he had served his ministerial apprenticeship as an Under-secretary in the 1790s, then as Secretary of State in the Duke of Portland's Government and even as ambassador to Portugal in the interim, would anyway have been hard to overlook. And the Prime Minister was more determined than ever to bring him in. But as usual, things could not be so simple. Canning had meanwhile accepted a consolation prize and agreed to go to India as Governor-general. The King was anxious to hold him to it, and to appoint the Duke of Wellington as Foreign Secretary. Liverpool could only get round that by winning the other Ministers' support for his preference. He pressed them. 'I should not oppose such a proposition if others deemed it on the whole the most advisable', Melville awkwardly replied. This was a coded reference to the question of whether Peel would exercise a veto. He did not, however, so Canning joined the Cabinet again.

He was in fact increasingly to dominate it during the next five years, despite growing distrust of his character among the rest. Melville, for example, shared many of his opinions and would work closely with him, notably in deploying the navy to deter European intervention in the former Spanish colonies of South America on behalf of their legitimate sovereign, Ferdinand VII. From his correspondence with Canning, where they cracked private jokes about their colleagues' foibles, it would appear that their relationship was of the easiest and happiest; though when eventually put to the test, it would break. Still, Liverpool's astuteness should not be underestimated. With the crises of the previous decade subdued, he was steadily shifting his Government in a more liberal direction, while holding a skilful balance not only between old and new but also between conservative and progressive. Certainly with both Canning and Peel, and later with William Huskisson and Frederick Robinson in the Cabinet, it contained an array of talent to outshine easily the opposition in the Commons. [11]

In the Cabinet Melville just stayed contentedly where he was, having declined for a second time the vacant Governor-generalship of India.[12] With one brief interval, the rest of his ministerial career would be spent at the Admiralty. His conduct of it in these years has been the subject of severe stricture, as from this naval historian: 'Lord Melville's retrograde proclivities were only too well-known, and therefore nothing in the shape of reforms or improvement could reasonably be expected during his time of office; expectation was not disappointed … The administration of Lord Melville was the era of donkey-frigates, overmasted sloops and coffin gun-brigs.' That judgment was largely built up round a minute from members of the Navy Board who 'felt it as their bounden duty, upon national and professional grounds, to discourage, to the utmost of their ability, the employment of steam-vessels, as they considered that the introduction of steam was calculated to strike a fatal blow to the naval supremacy of the Empire.' [13]

Such a silly statement must demand further investigation, given that Melville was not by nature a silly man. For one thing, the offending quotation concerned only a proposal for a steamer to convey mail between Malta and the Ionian Islands. Its pompous tone, out of all proportion to this triviality, was owed to a stuffy naval bureaucrat. For another thing, the Navy Board did not act as a channel for Melville's personal opinions. He was not hostile to steam. He knew that commercial steamships had been successfully running on the Clyde since 1812. He was privately informed, through scientific interests keeping him in close touch with technological developments at home and overseas, that the French Government had under active consideration the building of a steam-driven navy with shell-guns by means of which, its experts said, it might gain command of the seas from

Britain. And he could not have missed the fact that his wayward cousin, Thomas Cochrane, was as a freelance admiral soon cutting up the Turkish fleet with three steamers acquired for the service of the insurgent Greeks.

The First Lord obviously knew of their potential. In 1824, when he judged the time right to put his Prime Minister in the picture, he declared: 'I believe we are only in the infancy of our skill or knowledge in regard to the applications of those vessels to the purposes of naval warfare.' He later added: 'With our command of machinery and fuel, we ought to out-steam all Europe.' In other words, he well realised that steam must eventually benefit Britain as the most industrialised country, with more coal and iron than wood.[14]

Still, prudence was not misplaced either, as Melville had learned from his thorough investigations after the approach from Marc Isambard Brunel in 1815. An experiment then, of putting a steam-engine in an old surveying schooner, showed that a smaller and less clumsy mechanism would be required for use in naval vessels. Only slow progress had since been made towards producing reliable engines at reasonable cost. It was thus not till 1821 that the First Lord felt it worthwhile to coax his navy into chartering its first small steamer. In 1822 he had another, the *Comet*, constructed and launched just in time for some favourable publicity as an escort to the royal yacht on the Scottish visit: so nervous was the Admiralty that it obliged the contractors to provide the crew for the engine-room, in case of explosion. In 1823 he took a bigger step forward and ordered steam-engines fitted to a number of the ten-gun brigs used for coastal protection. In 1825 he asked Messrs Bolton & Watt to reserve for the fleet's use some engines of eighty horsepower, and authorised them to start building for the same purpose engines of 100 horsepower. By the end of the decade, the navy was just about getting used to the new technology. Before leaving the Admiralty, Melville remarked that 'we could find employment for several more steam vessels than we possess'.[15]

The pace of innovation may have been leaden. But the Government's prime duty lay not in running flightily off after every novelty proposed by scientific enthusiasts, rather in maintaining British naval supremacy – which counselled caution. It rested much more on the seamanship of her officers and men than on the sometimes deficient quality of her ships. Steamers would lessen that advantage, for though independent of wind and tide they were in every other respect inferior to sailing vessels. It was thus unwise for Britain to rush into technological advance, setting out in effect to scrap her fleet and start again. In competition to build a new one she could have no edge over any other country. An innovator would almost be bound to make technical mistakes; this argument was precisely the one used by the French Admiralty, after commissioning its own first steamer in 1818, against the abandonment of sailing ships on the stocks. All the naval powers similarly hesitated. In the end, of course, the dominant one could expect to make up and reverse any temporary loss of superiority, simply because it already had in place the facilities and expertise to construct ships faster. Britain could therefore afford to watch and wait. Ever since, her naval security has rarely depended on the most advanced shipbuilding methods, but rather in following another's lead with something better.

Melville was thus no fool in concentrating on conventional armaments. He found himself subject anyway to overriding economic constraints, not only from his colleagues but also from the Commons, all too eager to howl down spending proposals: the navy's greatest rigours were in fact yet to come, after he handed over to a Whig in 1830. Within those constraints he could first restore the quality of the fleet, sacrificed during the war to quantity, by reimposing earlier standards of shipbuilding. In 1825 he was able to boast to Parliament: 'If you were to take any period in our history and compare it with the present, you would select the latter as that period in which the greatest number of ships are to be found in a sound state, and likely to last long.'

Then he had to face the question whether Britain should construct larger vessels than ever before, so as to match the latest in the United States and especially in France: with bigger guns and greater firepower they could potentially break blockades. Though he has been condemned with hindsight for frittering away resources on older models, it was not a simple question. Britain, more than any rival, had to have a versatile navy – the demands in the Channel, the Atlantic or the Mediterranean were quite different. She therefore also needed many smaller ships. Easier to build, maintain and man, they were often better suited to the demands of a far-flung trading empire, and not just a product of conservatism: 'Other powers build ships for temporary purposes,' Melville said, 'but the ships of the British navy are intended to go through a course of service which other navies never contemplate.'

Priorities thus had to be set. As a matter of fact they did admit, by 1826, a programme of construction responding to the challenge from the United States and France. Melville then ordered ten ships of the line as big as the *Ohio*, pride of the Americans, and afterwards a new class of more powerful frigates. By 1829 the royal navy could again outgun anybody. At the Admiralty as elsewhere, Melville was constantly aware of the risks of acting precipitately. His policy as a whole had to be nicely judged. It cannot be claimed that his judgment went wildly astray.[16]

Caution also remained the hallmark of Melville's Scottish administration, though here it would answer less well. Amid the nation's headlong progress the Dundas despotism stayed true to its ethos, that the laird should be benefactor to a well-disciplined community. Revolutionary radicalism had after all been crushed at Bonnymuir. New people's champions could themselves be anti-radical: men like the Revd Henry Duncan, originator of trustee savings banks, who combined evangelical religion with a belief in workers' education and self-improvement, all within a conservative vision of social harmony. Moreover, the economy underwent in this decade an improvement, interrupted by recession only in 1825–6 and 1829. Capital still had the upper hand of labour. The latter's activities were partly driven underground till the repeal of the Combination Acts in 1824 by the efforts of Joseph Hume, but since they had scarcely been enforced in Scotland, that made little difference. While reformers did not believe trade unions could withstand free markets, in better times a shortage of industrial workers anyway became normal: hence the child labour and the large shifts of population, including the first great tide of Irish immigrants. Under such conditions the proletariat could still raise its standard of living.[17]

Evolutionary radicalism posed by definition only a long-term threat. The battle for the mind of the middle class was far from over. The eclat of the King's visit certainly outshone the Whigs' earnest meetings, pamphlets and petitions. Whether a soothing celtic twilight could assuage respectable citizens' desire for a vote was an altogether different matter. In the mean time the Government faced little political challenge, but from 1820, Scott reported, Whig lawyers took up regular contact with the 'democratical party'. Nearly all the democrats were anxious after the bloody episode of the Radical War for a peaceful settlement, on whatever terms they could get. Despite Tory efforts, Whigs seemed the best associates and leaders, and in their reciprocal sympathy Scotland had the makings of her later Liberal hegemony.

Still, this was already a decade of reform too. Except on the constitution, the Government proved far from immobilist. But the spirit of the times was reflected imperfectly in Scottish politics, with public debate often bogged down in captious detail over the merits of outworn institutions and offices. The sweeping economies and anglicisation proposed by the Whigs offered at least a clear-cut response. Melville countered only with extremely reluctant concession, and was seldom prompted to positive action of his own. This would not be enough.

The manager reached the age of 50 in 1821. With at that stage no reason to suspect that his regime was in sight of its end, he took care for the succession. His own sons were still too youthful: the eldest was in the army, the second in the navy, and though both dabbled later in politics neither would ever acquire a taste for it. The new laird of Arniston, another Robert Dundas, was of an age to enter Parliament and might have expected to represent Midlothian. Unfortunately the seat had been held since 1811 by Sir George Clerk of Penicuik. Dundas considered taking over in 1820, but somehow it seemed ungracious to shove Clerk aside without good reason: recently appointed a Lord of Admiralty by Melville, his career was just beginning to flourish. So Dundas held off, a decision the family was to rue. A cousin, Robert Adam Dundas, issue of Philip, youngest son of the second Lord President Arniston, did choose a political career. He sat first for an English seat, later for Edinburgh in place of his uncle William after beating, at the last unreformed election in 1831, the Whigs' Lord Advocate, Francis Jeffrey. Ejected the next year, he had again to pursue his ambitions in the South. There he became one of the sternest protectionists and at length, under the Earl of Derby in 1852, a member of the Cabinet. But in the early 1820s he was unready for public life.

So it was on another sprig of the Dundases' broad family tree that expectations flourished, namely on John, son of Lord President Hope. In 1820, aged but 26, he was made joint deputy keeper of the signet, which caused 'a little bit of rebellion' among his legal colleagues. In 1822 he became Solicitor General (with Dundas of Arniston as an advocate-depute), very early promotions to these promising positions being a feature of the despotism. Tory lawyers sang to mock Whig jealousy:

> Oh! the Toga, the dear, delightful Toga!
> Charming dress
> Of old Dundas.
> Solicitor's silk Toga! [18]

Henry Cockburn commented: 'His advance gave great alarm to the liberal party ... for he was then looked forward to as the person who was likely to have charge of our public affairs; and if Toryism had lasted he probably would have.' Hope was like his parent too excitable for the memorialist's taste – 'political animosity was never so bitter as it then was in Edinburgh, and no head but a very solid one could safely engage in its conflicts. But from the first he was drawn into the heat of the bad scenes ... and in all these was received as the rising man of his party.' Yet Scott was bowled over:

> decidedly the most hopeful young man of his time; high connections, great talent, spirited ambition, a ready elocution, with a good voice and dignified manners, prompt and steady courage, vigilant and constant assiduity, popularity with the young men, and the good opinion of the old will, if I mistake not, carry him as high as any man who has arisen here since the days of Hal Dundas. He is hot, though, and rather hasty: this should be amended.

Melville himself said Hope was 'very promising and likely to fill high offices in Scotland hereafter with credit ... I have more reliance on the son's discretion than the father's.' But he also insisted that a Solicitor General could not sit in Parliament, since the Crown Office's business required one law officer always to be available in Edinburgh.[19]

For the rest, however, the resources of patronage, life's blood of the Dundas despotism, still drained away. Not even the family was spared indignity. Melville rejected a niece's request on behalf of her husband: 'Any influence I may have in the disposal of offices is not to be exercised exclusively according to my private inclinations or for the benefit of my relations.' William Dundas, now a harmless old claret-soaked buffer, had to justify his sinecures to the carping Commons, after a Whig claimed they were worth £7000 a year. This was, he retorted, a gross exaggeration. For example as Lord Clerk Register, since 1821, he had been held personally accountable for the most trivial details of his department's work: 'So far, indeed, has this been carried, that the insertion of George III, instead of George II, produced an action in one case, in which I was compelled to pay damages of £400; and in another, the bare omission of a word cost me £300. The office is not, therefore, without duty and responsibility.'[20]

A fortiori, the rest of Scotland could not be spared. The Act of 1810 at last exerted an effect. Melville told Scott: 'In the distribution of a sum so limited as the Scotch pension fund, what is given to one person is withheld from another, who perhaps may be starving.' The establishment continued to be cut back, often at the instance of Whigs who easily persuaded English parliamentarians that it consisted solely of sinecures. Excesses there might have been in the past, but some economies were false – public services needed a certain minimum of staffing if they were to run at all. When in 1823 the post of Scottish deputy postmaster general was suppressed, Melville protested: 'Whatever may be the extent of the storm in the House of Commons, there will be a much louder one in Scotland if they are to be left without some superintending local authority to whom they can appeal in the daily concerns of that department.' He stressed that he did not mean it to become a sinecure: 'I find by today's post that Lords Home and Kellie, and half the inefficient peers and commoners of Scotland are candidates for the office, and I admit that if it were to be bestowed on any such persons, or even on the ground of charity to Lord Caithness's family, it had better be abolished.'[21]

But no appeasement could halt the attacks. In 1823 the whole Scottish Boards of Customs and Excise were summarily eliminated, a move defended by Cockburn on the grounds that they had been nests of corruption. It was casually assumed that the functions could be centralised in London. But, Melville soon wrote to the Chancellor of the Exchequer, 'I have observed for some time past in your London revenue boards a strong propensity on the ground of contraction and consolidation to set aside laws and institutions in the North they don't understand, but without the aid of which they cannot in that part of the kingdom perform their duty to the public.' By the end of the decade he could only despondently contemplate 'the many influential interests in Scotland who are pressing for the crumbs and remnants of the few offices which are now left at our disposal'.[22]

Scott feared for the political effects: the gentry would stick by Melville, 'for they are needy, and desire advancements for their sons, and appointments and so on. But this is a very hollow dependence, and those who sincerely hold ancient opinions are growing old.' That showed itself even at Westminster, where Lord Archibald Hamilton came in 1825 within a few votes of securing a first reading for a Bill to extend the franchise in the counties. Persuasively, if luridly, he described how he kept his seat only by outdoing the Lord Advocate in the manufacture of votes. Still, in this class of constituency the suffrage was relatively rational, and not markedly more iniquitous than in others furth of Scotland.[23]

No such apology could be made for the burghs. The Government did tinker a little with them. It hit on an idea that the failings lay not so much in the setts as in the fact that, through a series of disconnected legal rulings, burgesses had in effect lost the right of redress against malversation. After defeating an attempt at a remedy by Hamilton, Rae brought forward in 1823 a largely similar measure allowing corrupt councillors to be called before the Court of Exchequer. But it remained a dead letter. Another to enforce residence on magistrates was withdrawn.

Pressure mounted from outside Parliament too. In 1823 the Whigs got up a petition, attracting 7000 signatures, for a better form of representation in Edinburgh. They argued that since the capital had a member to itself the method of electing him could be improved without affecting arrangements elsewhere. Early the next year a corresponding Bill was moved by James Abercromby, connected to Melville by marriage but a Whig and member for an English seat. It failed by only twenty-four votes, a close enough shave to prompt his making a second attempt in 1826. To this William Dundas replied in his usual blustering fashion: 'The design which it openly manifests is to beat down the charters and extinguish the existing rights which have lasted for ages ... After these articles of Union, so solemnly ratified, is England now to violate them? Is the richer country to turn upon the poorer? The stronger upon the weaker? I cannot believe that England would be guilty of such injustice.' But Scott said: 'The whole burgher class of Scotland are gradually preparing for radical reform – I mean the middling and respectable classes; and when a burgh reform comes, which perhaps cannot be long delayed, Ministers will not return a member for Scotland from the towns.'[24]

The shortest answer to Dundas's humbug came in the stream of reports from parliamentary committees investigating the burghs. They appalled contemporaries much as they might tickle the modern reader. One wretched fellow on whom legislators turned their searching gaze was George Lyon, innkeeper and provost of Inverurie. He had a sideline in regularising, for a small consideration, clandestine marriages (the legal term for those not duly conducted by a minister of the Church of Scotland). Drinking parties would follow – the cost of which, between 1804 and 1817, had each year almost equalled the entire revenue of the burgh. The committee hauled over the coals the wretched town clerk:

> 'Was bailie Lyon, the chief magistrate, in the practice of fining people for clandestine marriage?'
> 'Yes, he was.'
> 'Can you tell whether these proceedings were intended to check the irregularity in the burgh, or for what purpose?'
> 'I could not say what he meant by it, but I know he fined the people; but what it was for I could not say.'
> 'Were those fines in consequence of complaints made to him as a magistrate?'
> 'I never knew any complaint made to him.'
> 'Then how were they brought before him?'
> 'They just came themselves.'
> 'Did the bailie confine those proceedings to people residing within the burgh?'
> 'No, there were some came from Aberdeen, and different parts of the country.'
> 'Do you mean to say the people came from different parts of the country to be fined by the bailie?'
> 'They came with the intention to be married.'
> 'What became of those fines?'
> 'He put them in his pocket.'[25]

Perhaps there would have been no great harm if the abuses had been limited to petty fiddles. In fact, major economic interests could be involved. An example arose in Edinburgh, where Melville himself noted 'the public inconvenience, to say nothing of the personal and constant plague arising from an inefficient and unsafe magistracy'. The capital faced bankruptcy from huge debts run up in the course of spending £300,000 on improvement to the port of Leith, necessary to maintain its trade against competition from other eastern harbours. The councillors decided they had to find some way of milking Leith's commerce. They thought to set up a joint stock company, owned by themselves, with the power to charge dues in the port at a rate enabling the debts to be serviced. This rate, the merchants of Leith could see, would ruin them.

Both sides appealed to Melville, who sought a compromise. To the Leithers he agreed that 'persons immediately interested in the trade of Leith should take precautions to secure themselves against any injurious consequences which they may justly apprehend'. But he said it was unreasonable to demand that the docks, which were after all the council's property, should be disposed of without its consent, for example, to a board of trustees. To the Lord Provost he was less agreeable: 'The complaints of the merchants and ship owners of Leith on the want of such local controlling authority have appeared to me not only far from groundless but substantially well-founded. The superintendence of the town council of Edinburgh may have been sufficient when the trade of Leith was unimportant in point of extent; but something more efficient is now indispensable.' The council had already given up powers over police, he noted, so could not claim that any principle was involved with docks and harbours. His eventual proposal would be to vest control of them with commissioners drawn in equal numbers from the capital and its port. The unfortunate but predictable result was deadlock, broken only when Edinburgh did go bankrupt in 1833. Melville helped with a revision of the arrangement by which the Government cancelled some of the debt and rescheduled the rest, but then was empowered to nominate members who on a new commission would hold the balance between the two sides. It was one example of how, after reform, appeal to central authority became necessary in intractable Scottish disputes.[26]

That might have been forestalled if, during the 1820s, Melville's administration had shown itself ready and able to seize the political initiative – the bar presumably being that this might have entailed a more coherent policy of reform. The *ancien régime* thus had little defence against parliamentary censure, abetted by the Whig fifth column at home. It proved as often destructive as constructive, inevitably when consequent on forensic investigation of palpable abuse. All Melville really did in response was try to introduce a spirit of inquiry more neutral and objective, for example by setting up the first royal commissions on specifically Scottish affairs.

One in 1824–5 reviewed the legal system, with special reference to procedure and appeals. It was no forum for wild radicals. The sixteen members, including none of the system's vocal critics, were chaired by the Lord President. Yet intellectually the establishment hardly contested any longer the Whigs' cry that the law was the fountainhead of Scottish authoritarianism. Melville had already yielded further to their nostrums, introducing ballots (subject to peremptory challenge) for criminal juries, previously chosen by the judge. He also patronised more Whigs, raising John Clerk of Eldin to the Bench in 1823, then three others. Outcasts no more, a succession of them were elected Deans of the Faculty, culminating with Jeffrey in 1829. He could have been stopped but the Solicitor General told Melville:

> It is not expedient to exclude Mr Jeffrey. He is personally very popular. His splendid genius and his almost unrivalled attainments render him an ornament to the profession, in the business of which he has acquired reputation equal to the fame of his literary talents and acquirements. The Bar in general feel proud of ranking among their number a man of such splendid talents. But for his political opinions there can be no doubt that the distinction would be conceded to him without scruple.[27]

The Whigs' general influence grew accordingly. Peel took the chance, while escorting the King on his visit, to consult the judges on a notion he had conceived of amending Scots practice where it was 'totally different from English practice, and rather repugnant to English feelings'. He asked them, too, what they thought about the Lord Advocate's powers. They pronounced themselves happy, but the *Edinburgh Review* seized the opportunity to publish a long attack on the office by Cockburn. A classic of Scots Whiggery, it ranted on about quite unrelated matters, the native vigour of the law and the impossibility of criminal appeals to the Lords. But it objected especially that

> the Lord Advocate is the organ of the Administration in which he acts on matters purely political. It is from this that the principal dignity and influence of his office is derived. He is not only the professional adviser of the Crown in legal affairs, but he necessarily obtains and holds his position solely on condition of his supporting the interests of the party that promotes him; and in order that he may do so the better, it is quite well known to everybody whom he may have occasion to address or act with, even in his proper official character, that he engrosses a very large share of the most effectual patronage ... So far as we know, there is no one man armed with so great a power in any Government professing to be free in Europe; and certainly there is no other within the sphere of the British Constitution.

Moreover, the

> mixture of general political superintendence with undefined legal rights makes it difficult to say what privileges he has not, or at least will not be held to have, whenever a particular case occurs in which it is necessary to answer a complaint by reference to the nature of his situation ... The Lord Advocate is the Privy Council of Scotland, the Grand Jury of Scotland, the Commander in Chief of the forces of Scotland, the guardian of the whole police of the country, and ... in the absence of higher orders, the general management of the business of Government is devolved upon him. [28]

This polemical farrago was not in itself taken seriously. Yet it remained undeniable that some defects of the system now ran so deep as to require more drastic treatment than any thus far contemplated. To these the royal commission addressed itself. The most serious was the backlog of appeals to the Lords, which really made it begin to look as if their jurisdiction in Scotland might have to be ended. Melville said they would need three years, sitting every day, to get through just the Scottish causes before them, let alone the English and Irish ones. Statistics collected by the commission showed that, between the two periods of 1763–93 and 1793–1823, the annual number of cases coming into the Court of Session had gone up by 38 per cent, to nearly 3000, while the annual number of appeals to the Lords had risen by 67 per cent, to more than 1000. To a mere handful did this recourse make any difference. Most were deserted for one reason and another before coming to judgment, but only after taking up on average two days of their lordships' time. The commission proposed a number of remedies. First, to speed things up within Scotland, oral pleading was largely to replace written papers at all levels. Then the judgments of the Court of Session were to be made final in the pettier causes. Finally, its internal structure would be altered so as to increase its capacity for appeals, with an Inner House of two divisions, each with four judges, taking disputed decisions from an Outer House of five permanent Lords ordinary.

All this was put into the legislation of 1830 by which the Court attained more or less its modern shape.

That might have brought more immediate benefits if at the same time the establishment had not been savagely pruned. At a stroke, eighteen judicial offices were abolished. The Bench in the Court of Session anyway suffered a reduction of two from the traditional total of fifteen. But then the Jury Court was merged into it. The Court of Admiralty had already been deprived of jurisdiction in prize, in what one authority called 'a particularly offensive example of the tendency of certain influential interests to regard the English courts as important and the Scottish as local and limited'; it too was now eliminated. The powers of the Consistorial Court were drastically reduced. The Court of Exchequer was halved in size. With the exception of the last, which survived till 1856, all these other tribunals would be quickly abolished after the Whigs came to power. By 1836 there were only thirteen judicial posts altogether in Scotland, half the figure of twenty years before.[29]

Sluggish concession to reform for the present, incapable of averting violent change once the *ancien régime* broke down, was also the Kirk's lot. In the 1820s its internal politics remained much as ever. Melville was far from impressed with the ruling party: 'the Moderate gentlemen in the Church ought to be more alert in their parish duties and more active, if they expect to be upheld.' Yet he was also wary of their High-flying rivals, whom he sometimes found 'carried away by a degree of religious zeal very much at variance … with substantial justice and even with Christian charity'. In fact they were moving into an intellectual and spiritual ascendancy which was bound to have its effects.

At the crest of the rising evangelical wave rode the imposing figure of Thomas Chalmers, officially recognised in 1823 with his appointment to the chair of moral philosophy at St Andrews. He himself sought no upheaval in the Kirk. Indeed he has been called a Tory, though his thought did not fit into neat political categories: a colleague said that 'he is by no means a violent party man – if he be a party man at all'. Karl Marx labelled him an 'arch-parson', however, which has been enough for progressive academics of our own day to heap scorn and contumely on him. They have singled out his alleged 'complete inability to understand the industrial working class and the difficulties under which it laboured'. As a matter of fact, he had done what few progressive academics would think of doing and gone to minister to the industrial working class for four years of his life.

He was in truth an acute critic of the new, rootless, volatile society round him. What he shared with conservatives (*Blackwood's*, for example, recognised the affinity) was a belief that out of the impersonal, though necessary, operation of the laws of political economy a sense of community had to be salvaged. Scots were now divided not just physically, in urban or rural localities, but morally and culturally too. Their country was thus increasingly marked by lack of community, antagonism among classes being the clearest sign of it. Chalmers saw the need of reform, but in much more than the constitution. He said of the people: 'It is our belief that through the medium not of a political change in the state, but of a moral and personal change upon themselves, there is not one desirable amelioration which they might not mount to.' Such change would according to him be best worked by the Kirk, which was entitled to call on the state to remove obstacles in its path.[30]

And in his opinion the state tolerated patent evils. One, for example, was pluralism, which indulged slack and worldly clergymen. He set about making strenuous objections when instances came to his notice. These Melville waved aside. In a case at St Andrews, he answered:

> I believe that a regulation to prohibit in future pluralities to that limited extent (if the living is in the same town) would be attended with injurious consequences to the Church; but whatever may be said on that point, I can have no doubt of the injustice of attempting to carry it into effect by a direct invasion of the rights of the Crown, and of every patron in Scotland, and in opposition given to presentations in individual cases, instead of meeting the question as one of a general nature to be settled by the supreme judicature of the Church, or if necessary by Parliament.

He would as a rule protect 'the rights of patrons and of legally qualified presentees from being capriciously invaded by any of the subordinate authorities of the Church'. Such rebuffs made Chalmers bitter against Melville, previously his benefactor, for a 'most blasting and deleterious effect, both on the interests of literature and the Church. He is Chancellor of our university, and by his corrupt and careless patronage he has done us a world of mischief.'

This was no mere personal fixation, however, but reflected wider discontent. It emerged publicly in 1823 when the Revd Duncan Macfarlane, principal of the university of Glasgow, was presented as a minister to the city's cathedral as well. The presbytery rejected him, and only after appeal to the General Assembly could he be inducted. The assembly itself saw in 1826 a fierce attack on pluralism. It was joined even by some Moderates, and just defeated by organisation of the lay elders' votes. Support came from outside the Kirk too. Contrary to what Cockburn has told us of utter political subservience in the town council of Edinburgh, one evangelical Lord Provost, Walter Brown, tried to ensure that in its patronage it did not countenance pluralism. That was indeed how Chalmers, flouncing off from St Andrews, got the chair of divinity at the university in 1827; all the Moderate contenders were held to be disqualified by occupying charges in the city. Who can say whether these episodes did not plant in his mind the idea that the underlying system of patronage, rather than just pluralism in itself, was the essence of the Church's problems, with such fateful consequences in later years?

Others of the popular party were already picking at that old sore. A minister in the capital, the Revd Andrew Thomson, had founded a Society for Improving the System of Patronage, by which he meant in effect abolishing it.[31] And he had a political point, for the Solicitor General warned Melville in 1824 that the 'fanatical party' was about to gain a majority in the presbytery of Edinburgh. The Crown, he went on, must take care

> to prevent that party by the command of the principal presbytery being able to give a tone and assure a lead among the other presbyteries. There is hardly anything which could occur which will tend more to shake the influence of the Moderate party in the Church or tend more directly to increase the influence of the High party (whose leaders have always made their Church

politics subservient to their determined and violent party politics) than the ascendancy of the latter in the metropolitan presbytery.

Otherwise, however, Melville tried to continue his father's policy of quietly placating the evangelicals. One of their greatest aspirations was a programme of Church extension. The term meant building new places of worship to ensure adequate provision of clergy, and of the education and welfare they supervised, for a burgeoning population, especially in the towns. Here too there were obstacles. Most heritors declared themselves unwilling or unable to spend the necessary money. Parliament, when asked in 1819 and 1820, also refused to do so. The next year Melville called a conference of political and ecclesiastical leaders to consider the matter. But the only general scheme of endowment they could agree on was for the Highlands and islands, where kirks had long been few and far between. It was decided thirty new ones should be constructed there at a cost of £180,000, to be met by parliamentary grant. Yet this merely glossed over the most fundamental problems. They lay not in the North but in the central belt, where little extension took place before the late 1830s. So it proved impossible even for the Church, with its ready access to Government, to realise without great delay and difficulty its schemes of social improvement, limited and conservative as they were.[32]

In the same context, a great debate was going on about the poverty which formed such an obvious and distressing feature of the new industrial society. Scotland had a Poor Law, dating in part from the middle ages, which urgently required modernisation. The Kirk was involved here because money to help the needy came through parochial assessments, rates levied not compulsorily but at the discretion of heritors, and distributed by ministers. Only about a quarter of the parishes raised them, though this fraction had doubled since the turn of the century. Over that period, however, the able-bodied unemployed had become by a series of legal decisions more or less excluded from benefit. The spirit of the times approved. A complimentary report by the Lords in 1817 had said: 'The Scotch have uniformly proceeded on the principle that every individual is bound to provide for himself by his own labour as long as he is able to do so, and that his parish is only bound to make up that portion of the necessaries of life which he cannot earn or obtain by other lawful means.'[33]

Some advanced thinkers held that this principle of parsimony could be extended, indeed that Scotland might in effect abolish poverty if only she got rid of the Poor Law. Chalmers in particular was convinced that both donors and recipients would be done far more moral good by their own efforts than by legislative compulsion. He had set about proving as much in the prelude to his professorial career. For four years, from 1819, he took charge of a parish in the East End of Glasgow, one of the very worst in the country, the sort of place where civilised society seemed to be breaking down. On its behalf he opted out of such relief as was legally available. Instead he, his elders and his congregation endeavoured, through acquainting themselves with the spiritual and physical state of every family, to cure distress by inspiring those who could afford it to spontaneous charity and those who were in need to self-help. A residue of the irredeemably destitute was supported. But for the rest, the community succoured itself without obligatory transfers of resources. Controversy started then and has continued ever since about the worth of the experiment. Perhaps Chalmers's main aim was to demonstrate that an established Church could still rise to national problems. And he may indeed have confirmed that presbyterian values – sturdy independence, hard work, thrift, temperance and piety – were not doomed in an industrial society.[34] But an effect on practical policy was harder to discern. The scheme worked more or less while he retained his charge but ended after he left and, though tried, was never successful elsewhere. Better remedies were, however, slow indeed to come.

Nor were they sought very hard by the Whigs, his main allies in campaigning against the Poor Law, which they too thought bad for the lower classes. In 1819 Thomas Kennedy of Dunure, member of Parliament for the Ayr Burghs, had introduced a Bill to abolish any appeal by an individual against the refusal of his parish to grant relief. While it failed, a judicial ruling of 1821 did most of its work for it, stipulating that such appeals could only go to the Court of Session, so that legal recourse became practically impossible for the poor. In 1824, Kennedy tried to widen this breach with a Bill allowing heritors in any particular parish to cease paying a rate provided they themselves took on relief of the existing paupers. After they had made such a decision, no new assessments and no appeals were to be permitted: relief would in effect become voluntary. So drastic a scheme aroused fierce opposition. Cockburn wrote that 'the whole fools of the kingdom are up against the poor Bill', noting that Melville and the Lord President were especially hostile. It turned out during the Commons' debates that the fools also included Hamilton, on the Whigs' own side. Hearing it said the measure would be a boon to the poor, he observed that the poor themselves thought it a great grievance. William Dundas seconded him, predicting they would most likely be left without any resources. For the Government, Rae stressed how little support the Bill had won in Scotland and urged Kennedy to withdraw it.

This he did, but his friends would not leave the matter alone. Rosebery, the Whig peer, proposed in 1828 that the period of residence in a parish required of any individual to qualify for relief should be raised from three to seven years. Melville saw through him: 'The sole object of this Bill is to prevent the influx of the poor Irish into Scotland. This mode of legislating is contrary to the spirit of the Act of Union, and is unfair and invidious.' He objected 'because it is the first attempt to introduce a different species of legislation for different classes of His Majesty's subjects. I contend that the natives of England and Ireland have a right to enter Scotland.'[35]

In another matter touching the Kirk's interests Melville responded with a second royal commission, set up in 1826 to investigate the universities. There, ever since they had gone beyond their original function of training the ministry, clerical control had been in retreat before secularism. All remained besides financially straitened, in particular able to offer only meagre salaries and pensions. This encouraged pluralism too, and professors often outstayed their useful intellectual life. Melville himself disapprovingly noted the clergy's 'passion for engrossing all the chairs they can'.

But he had so far steered clear of reform, not only on educational grounds. It was, for example, a strange fact that Scotland still boasted no chair in the science of political economy which she had invented. In 1826 a proposal was made to endow one at Edinburgh. John Ramsay MacCulloch, the favoured candidate for it, was distinguished as editor of *The Scotsman* and author of the classical theory of public finance. But he was otherwise almost a parody of the earnest, humourless side of the national character: *Blackwood's* pilloried him as the Stot, a 'sour, surely, dogged animal'. Worse, he was a Whig. Now John Wilson, Tory professor of moral philosophy, reminded everyone that it was actually his duty, as it had been that of his predecessor, Dugald Stewart, to lecture on political economy. Unfortunately, he had never done so (and Stewart only rarely). In return for a promise to repair the omission – which Wilson hardly honoured – the authorities fought off establishment of the chair. 'The only real obstacle is Melville,' MacCulloch noted, 'but I believe that will be found insurmountable, and that consequently the project will for the present fall to the ground.' The endowment went instead to the new university in London, and MacCulloch with it. This was perhaps the first occasion on which Scotland let slip something of her ascendancy in British higher education.[36]

Such conservatism was only a part of the deeper troubles now apparently threatening the system and its enormous international prestige. But Scots were genuinely proud of it, and feared that too radical an overhaul might diminish one of their few advantages over the English, whose own universities were manifestly inferior. Against this background, the royal commission's work has been seen by the philosophical historian of the 'democratic intellect' as the first attack on it, from which the later decay followed. He was, though, certainly wrong to ascribe this to Tory, anglicising influences (terms anyway not interchangeable, rather the reverse). If too many noblemen sat on the commission, Melville himself complained – 'though it contains names enough, it might have been foreseen that the working gentlemen in it are very few.' The same note made clear, however, that the burden of the inquiry fell on an inner group of eight, of whom only three, including the chairman, Lord Aberdeen, the Lord Advocate and the Solicitor General belonged to the Tory establishment, the others being a Canningite, Lord Binning, two Whigs, Lord Rosebery and George Cranstoun, and two academics, Thomas Taylor and George Cook. So they covered the political spectrum.[37]

They went thoroughly into the administrative and financial problems, but also paid surprising attention to the generalist curriculum. It was not clear why. In defining the terms of reference, Melville showed no special concern on the point. He himself once objected on generalist grounds to establishment of a chair of conveyancing at Edinburgh: 'Lectures on the general principles of the laws of nations, or of Rome, or of Scotland are fit and proper subjects of instruction in such a seminary of learning; but to descend from such a level to lectures on writering is really an insult to the university.'[38]

Nor did many of the commission's witnesses attack the curriculum. Even Jeffrey, praising the universities as an ornament to Scotland, advised it to leave well alone. In England learning was confined to the few, he said, but in Scotland open to the many. As one in three schoolmasters went through higher education, it touched the masses too: 'It enables relatively large numbers of people to get – not indeed profound learning, for that is not to be spoken of – but that knowledge which tends to liberalise and make intelligent the mass of our people.' While English learning was prone to lose itself in detail, Scottish learning was always general and philosophical, not at all superficial in giving an elementary grounding in first principles. It thus represented a genuine cultural value.[39]

The commission, in publishing its conclusions in 1830, accepted the argument, though still with what looked like an apology to English preconceptions: 'While the universities in Scotland are intended and well fitted to embrace the youth of the highest ranks of society, their institutions have in no respect been framed or modified with reference to the means, or pursuits, or habits of the aristocracy. The system is that of a general plan of education, by which persons of all ranks may be equally benefited.' In principle, it did not wish to change this: 'We should consider it to be one of the greatest misfortunes which could be inflicted on Scotland, if, with the view to improvements of one description, any material bar should be opposed to the full participation of the benefits of university education by all whose means and prospects can render such education of the smallest use to them.'[40]

Even so, it did then propose reform of the curriculum. For a degree in arts it wished to reverse the traditional order of priorities and have the first two sessions devoted to classics and mathematics, the third to logic and mathematics, and only the fourth to moral and natural philosophy. From this, however, the two academics dissented strongly. It happened that such revisions to the curriculum had long been adopted at Marischal College, Aberdeen, so the change was not as radical as all that. The universities in any event felt a need to move with the times, and especially to fit Scots to compete outside their own country, not least for the opportunities which the Dundas despotism had opened to them. Academic training was as a matter of fact more specialised in England, and at her universities heavily concentrated on the classics and mathematics. To shift Scottish learning the same way, without sacrificing what it had always considered essential, could be equally taken as a reasonable reform of, rather than a crude attack on, the native tradition. Still, no consensus proved possible, with the result that the recommendations were shelved. Thomas Carlyle, for example, expected them to affect only the exercise of patronage. Thinking to apply for the chair of moral philosophy at St Andrews, he wrote that the 'professors, electors to this office, boast much that they have amended their ways, and under the terror of the late royal commission, who knows but the Melville interest may have ceased to be omnipotent there'. Perhaps action was inhibited by the very thoroughness of the commission's job on such a comprehensive and complex report. Melville himself concluded that student discipline and variation in the standard of degrees were the worst problems. He later commented, however, that 'all those suggestions have ever since remained without any practical result, the whole object having apparently been too weighty for any administration to meddle in.'[41]

Scottish qualms about reform, especially under an anglicising rubric, did not always bring mere stalemate. In the most notorious case they took the shape of what has been seen as bizarre and atavistic nationalism. It was mobilised in defence of the banks, which had never before figured as Scots totems. The prime mover here was Scott, in the letters he published in 1826 under the pseudonym of Malachi Malagrowther. His polemic was directed against a scheme for tighter regulation after a financial crisis which caused eighty banks in England to fail, though only three in Scotland. The reason identified by the Treasury was their excessive issue of paper. It therefore proposed, and secured the Cabinet's approval for, a ban on notes of £5 and under, except those from the Bank of England, and not only in England, but in Scotland and Ireland too.

This misread the Scottish situation. English banks were rendered unstable by, among other things, the state of English law. In Scotland, on the other hand, freedom from misguided restriction had allowed the development of a perfectly sound financial structure, able to weather all the storms blown up from the South. This was indeed generally acknowledged. Public confidence in the system had grown so complete as to allow bank-notes to displace gold almost entirely in the country's circulation. And two-thirds of them were in denominations of less than £5. Their suppression would in the short term cause a savage monetary contraction, and in the long term damage the banks' ability to serve a great variety of the country's needs through a wide network of branches. Greater conformity to English practice seemed scarcely a worthwhile exchange.

It took an extraordinary purblindness in Melville to overlook all this. He did admit to no deep understanding of the issues, observing vaguely that the substitution of paper for gold was somehow inconvenient, and that perhaps Scotland had too many banks. The basis of his position was really no more than this: 'It is difficult to assign in principle any reason why if the measure is proper in England, it would not be equally proper in Scotland.' Others in London jested that Scott only took up his cudgels as a bankrupt who needed the financiers' help. This was no answer to the furious reaction generated in Scotland by his thunderous attacks, and evidenced by 500 hostile petitions to Parliament: 'Men of all parties threw aside their differences, and men of all ranks forgot their inequalities, to raise one unanimous outcry against the threatened introduction of gold at the expense of paper; and merchants, manufacturers, bankers, shopkeepers, and even artisans, joined heart and hand to resist the innovation.' From the South it genuinely looked as if the protest might get out of hand. John Wilson Croker, the Irish man of letters who doubled as secretary to the Admiralty, noted: 'Lord Melville certainly felt his administration of Scottish affairs was sweepingly attacked, and the rest of the Government were astonished to see the £1 note made a kind of war cry which might excite serious practical consequences.'[42]

In vain did Melville blame Scott for 'the inflammatory tendency of his letters, ... the gross misrepresentations to be found in every paragraph and almost every line of them, ... his insulting taunts and unfounded attacks on the present Government.' In vain did he try to put his own motives in a better light, claiming he had wanted to leave Scotland alone till persuaded that the reform was in her interests – 'not for the sake of uniformity, which no-one ever dreamt of as a reason for such a change'. In vain did he point out that she belonged, after all, to a Union: 'The people of North Britain who have lately come forward have either overlooked it altogether or have thought, as a matter of course, that England was bound to submit to every inconvenience and loss which Scotland might think fit to impose on her.' In vain did he get Croker to strike back with letters written under the Scottian pseudonym of Edward Bradwardine Waverley: 'No year has passed without some moral approximation of Scotland and England, and the result is national degradation? – public distress? – retrogradation in wealth, happiness and honour? No, but a five-fold increase in every species of prosperity'.[43]

In the end the Government just had to give in. Application of the law to Scotland was delayed, then dropped. William Dundas, at last officially conceding the value of her banking system, proposed to the Commons a face-saving inquiry, one so limited in its terms of reference as to ensure that it would disturb nothing. Melville then told the Lords: 'All the banks in that part of the kingdom view the present Bill with the utmost alarm. Their system might, perhaps, ultimately appear to be bad. But until that fact is established, I think no alteration should be attempted.' With this surrender. the two protagonists could be reconciled. Scott recorded later in the year: 'Lord Melville and I met with considerable feeling on both sides, and our feuds were forgotten and forgiven.' And so said Melville: 'I regret most extremely what has happened; but it is past, and though it cannot be recalled, Sir Walter shall find that it will not have diminished, even in the most trivial degree, the great regard I have ever felt for him.'

Malagrowther's letters have proved of enduring interest, well beyond the dispute which gave rise to them, because they also seized the opportunity to survey the condition of Scotland. What she had to put up with then may seem minor compared to what has sometimes happened since. The common strand lies in Scott's depiction of a Union changing to her detriment, so that she could no longer defend herself against assimilation to her more powerful partner. This has resonated in the modern rediscovery of her nationhood. Of the recent commentaries, a number would even like to claim Malagrowther as a posthumous member of the Scottish National Party. His was indeed nationalism of a sort, though its nature cannot be entered into here. Suffice it to say that Scott also believed Scotland had better become 'an inferior sort of Northumberland' than tamper with the settlement of 1707. A weightier interpretation has been offered by Nicholas Phillipson, in an article of 1969, who saw it all as 'a fuss about nothing', by which 'Scott gave to middle class Scotsmen and to Scottish nationalism an ideology – an ideology of noisy inaction.'

This case rested on a view of the affair as something essentially trivial. But the preservation of the old Scottish banking system, even though only for another two decades, ought not to be thus belittled. At the time of writing Phillipson was evidently unaware of the interest already shown by Friedrich von Hayek, and afterwards excited among his followers, in this example of spontaneous liberal order generated free of control or interference by the central authorities of the modern state. The economic analysis need not detain us. The point is rather that in monetary policy too Scotland enjoyed at least a semi-independence, if not more. It had worked all through the last century, and was proving its resilience in the more difficult and unstable circumstances of an emerging industrial economy. It did now come under attack from centralising pressures, but their triumph was by no means inevitable. And though Scotland eventually gave in to them, that did not mean she had fought over a triviality.

Phillipson's analysis also suffered because two decades ago the Scottish political historiography of the 1820s scarcely existed. He may not have been fully aware either how all-pervasive the assault on the old Scotland must have seemed to contemporaries. He anyway did not take it seriously: 'We look with interest,' he wrote, 'to Scott's evidence for this general contempt' of England for Scotland, and dismissed what he found as 'hyperbole'. The prospective suppression of small bank-notes may have been only a detail of the whole picture. Yet enough has been recounted in these pages to show it was not a hyperbolic representation of that whole. Nor could it have been far-fetched to assert that Scotland might, with will and leadership, defeat conscious measures of assimilation. She did, after all, defeat this one.

Hence, surely, Scott's efforts to inject into mere resistance to change some deeper national purpose, and his harking back in his journal to a period when that purpose had been manifest: 'Ah! Hal Dundas, there was no truckling in thy day!' He expanded on the theme elsewhere:

> Scotland is fast passing under other management and into other hands than Lord Melville's father would have permitted. In points of abstract discussion, quickness of reform, etc. the Whigs are assuming an absolute and undisputed authority. Now here was a question in which the people might be taken absolutely out of their demagogues, and instead of that our members strengthen the hands of these men with ministerial authority to cram the opinions of these speculative economists down the throat of an unwilling people, as they have crammed a dozen other useless experiments already.

Scott came back once more to this in a retort to Croker:

> Depend upon it, that if a succession of violent and experimental changes are made from session to session, with Bills to amend ills where no want of legislation had been at all felt, Scotland will, within ten or twenty years, perhaps much sooner, read a more fearful commentary on poor Malachi's Epistles than any statesman residing out of the country, and stranger to the habits and feelings which are entertained here, can possibly anticipate ... Scotland, completely liberalised, as she is in a fair way of being, will be the most dangerous neighbour to England that she has had since 1639 ... If you unscotch us, you will find us damned mischievous Englishmen ... under a wrong direction, the most formidable who ever took the field of innovation. The late Lord Melville knew them well, and managed them accordingly. Our friend, the present Lord Melville, with the same sagacity, has not the same advantages. His office has kept him much in the South; – and when he comes down here, it is to mingle with persons who have almost all something to hope or ask for at his hands.

The first part of this sally was wildly off target, for only in the most improbable circumstances could Scotland endanger England. The better point was an oblique one: namely that, as things stood, Scots were yet to be unscotched. In other words, while there was still some way to go towards assimilation, the process could be halted, or at least limited. The English might push it forward out of sheer careless indifference, the Scots Whigs in full awareness of what they were up to. The efforts of neither need be decisive in destroying that Scotland for the Scots postulated by the Dundas despotism at its zenith. If, however, the very political leadership of Scotland was to acquiesce, then all would be lost. Malagrowther meant to stop it acquiescing. We shall see in the rest of the chapter how Melville responded.[44]

There was evidently no need to worry about the electoral effects at least, even though Parliament would shortly be dissolved. Yet Melville's management of the polls in 1826 did have a decidedly erratic air about it, perhaps reflecting some strain and loss of self-confidence. The Government was still capable of bringing its influence forcefully to bear. But it also made astounding mistakes.

In the old Parliament, the Whigs had held only one safe seat between Tweed and Tay, the Dysart Burghs. Their influence was apparently declining in the region. Two veterans of opposition, the Earl of Lauderdale and Sir Hew Hamilton Dalrymple, member for the Haddington Burghs, had recently in effect come over to the Ministry. This allowed it to contemplate a systematic strengthening of its local position. Sir Hew now retired in favour of a loyal kinsman, Adolphus Dalrymple. An alliance was cemented with the Earl by giving his cousin, Anthony Maitland, the official nomination in Berwickshire. In these circumstances it was extraordinary that East Lothian, where both patrons had influence, should have turned Whig. Its sitting member, Sir James Suttie, petty and senile, had survived in 1820 by a single vote against Lord John Hay, brother of the Marquis of Tweeddale. He returned to fight again, easily outshone his adversary and took the county, the first time in forty years that it had slipped from the Dundases' grasp.

Then Lord Advocate Rae lost the Anstruther Burghs, in rather obscure circumstances. His challenger, John Balfour of Whittinghame, would show himself a firm Tory in the new Parliament and afterwards: indeed he was the grandfather of a Conservative Prime Minister. A nabob, he had used his fortune to buy up lands in East Lothian and Fife. That brought him to the notice of the venal burghs round the kingdom's shores, and he was able to build an interest in two of the five composing the district. Taking advantage of dissensions in a third, he snatched victory at the poll. Melville just looked on; it is inconceivable that his father would in such a case have remained neutral. Rae cast pathetically about for another Scottish constituency. He could not scramble back into the Commons for a year, and then in the Treasury's English pocket burgh of Harwich.

Less remarkable only because it did not come off was the opposition raised to William Dundas in the town council of Edinburgh, still smarting from Melville's snubs over the harbour at Leith. The Lord Provost, William Trotter, declared his rival candidacy as a 'mere protest', but then found surprising support from the trades. Here, however, the young Tories intervened decisively. Dundas of Arniston described to his uncle how 'Hope and I saw at once that despatch was the only remedy … I went straight to the Provost; he came into the room shaking and trembling and clearly ashamed of himself. The general tenor of the intervention was that he felt he was pledged to uncle William and the seat was in his hands'. Still mistrusting the terrified Trotter, Dundas probed further and found that eleven of the council's votes were engaged to him: 'I have more than reason to suspect that it was not without the Provost's knowing it, and that he would not have been sorry had the seat been forced upon him.' Still, in the capital even an abjectly failed revolt was an astonishment.[45]

In the North-east the opposition had also been contained to just two safe seats, Forfarshire and the Aberdeen Burghs. Kincardine, which the ministerialists ought not to have lost in 1820, was regained simply by their uniting behind a new candidate, Hugh Arbuthnott; the incumbent Whig did not bother to stand again. The Government's interest in the region was otherwise upheld by clan Grant, which had three members elected this time: Francis William in Moray and the nabob brothers, Charles and Robert, in Inverness, county and burghs respectively. But they were under constant sniping from the Earl of Fife, obsessed with rebuilding enough influence to get his family's British peerage restored. All he had so far to show for his efforts was an agreement with the Grants, reached after the battle in 1820, to name alternately the member for the Elgin Burghs. On this, however, they now thought to renege, by offering the district with their support to Robert Adam Dundas. Melville would not hear of it, and wrote with ostentatious warmth to the Earl: 'I regret those frequent collisions in your part of the country and I must do your lordship the justice to say that in fairness they ought not to be ascribed to you.' There was thus no choice but to leave a clear run to Fife's brother, General Alexander Duff. Undaunted, the Grants carried the battle to his own constituency of Banffshire, where they put up a candidate, John Morison of Auchintool. Though comfortably beaten, he tried his luck with a petition against the return. While the case was going on, Fife got his British peerage and abandoned the seat to his rival.[46]

Further north, Melville was unusually successful. The alternating county of Cromarty chose a member friendly to him, Duncan Davidson. An unexpected victory came in Caithness, for half a century in the pockets of the independent Sinclairs of Ulbster. George, their candidate this time, shared with his father Sir John not only scholarly interests but priggish earnestness too. His reforming views had so angered Melville that he organised a ministerialist coup in favour of James Sinclair, from a different branch of the family: which showed what he could do if he wanted. The other major Highland interest was the Sutherlands'. They remained attached to the Government, but still brought in for their county a scion, Lord Francis Leveson Gower, who favoured reform. In Orkney and Shetland, always a local contest, the Whigs won again with George Dundas, of the collateral line hostile to Melville. Even so, the Ministry had advanced in this region.[47]

The West proved more stable, with one change in the parties' positions. It was, however, an amazing upset. Kirkcudbrightshire, not normally a hotbed of subversion, fell on a single vote to Robert Ferguson of Craigdarroch, a devotee of reform ever since his involvement in the agitation of 1792. Then, during a career at the English Bar, he had actually been imprisoned for trying to help a radical client escape justice. After restoring his reputation and fortune in India, he had returned home with his liberalism intact. He was just the sort the Dundas despotism execrated, but it could not now stop him.[48]

Still, it suffered little net change in its parliamentary strength. Against eleven Scots members committed to opposition, a good thirty still normally voted with the Ministry, even if the steadiness of some would become questionable. Nor did the representation of the peers shift much; though Tweeddale, elected in 1820 on the King's list, really had to be counted with the Whigs this time, joining two others, Rosebery and Belhaven.

The stability proved deceptive, for the crisis of the Dundas despotism was at hand. In February 1827, Liverpool had a stroke from which it soon became clear he could not recover. The Government of the broad bottom he had kept together with urbanity and moderation for fifteen years was not to recover either. Who would succeed? Canning, the strongest candidate, felt his time was at last really come. But the deep distrust of him among numbers of his colleagues had not been allayed by a foreign policy espousing altogether too many progressive causes. What was more, he promised at home to grasp the nettle of catholic emancipation.

On this most contentious of issues, Liverpool had taken care to maintain an even balance in his Cabinet between the two factions conventionally labelled 'Protestants' and 'Catholics'. One of the latter, Lord Maryborough, brother of the Duke of Wellington, demonstrated this in a memorandum he drew up in 1823. For emancipation, he named himself, Melville, Canning and three others, six in all. Against it were likewise six, mostly older men, but including Peel. Wellington was stated to be undecided but tending to be against, Liverpool undecided but tending to be for.[49] The Prime Minister thus made sure that among his closest colleagues it remained an open question, on which no common position was sought. That in turn kept the Government as a whole from pitting itself against the great parliamentary opposition to emancipation, or the probably still greater opposition in the country.

Melville, who was after all a presbyterian in an anglican Cabinet, had never hidden his hereditary commitment to toleration. In 1821 he declared to the Lords:

> Under any Government, particularly one like our own, the exclusion of a considerable proportion of the population from rights and privileges enjoyed by others must be attended with risk ... If any people are told that such as they are they must remain – that whatever talents, whatever industry they might exert, it is all in vain, for a boundary is put to their rank in society – surely it is not in human nature but that such language must produce irritation in a high degree.

He promised that if a measure for relief was brought forward he would personally supervise its extension to Scotland, where a 'spirit of liberality' prevailed on the subject.

As one insider wrote, these opinions 'quite coincide with Canning's'.[50] It was strange, then, that Melville should now have been canvassed, amid the buzz of speculation in the political salons, as the man to stop Canning. In the middle of March 1827, Croker dined with Peel and noted: 'I feel that he is quite indisposed to serving under, not Canning he says, but a Catholic premier. He would like the Duke [of Wellington] or Lord Bathurst, or even Lord Melville. I observed to him that Lord Melville was a Catholic.' The First Lord's moderation, on this as on every other question, commended him over those high Tories as one who might hold the Government's factions together. Wellington concurred. Recording his conduct after the crisis was over, he explained, in the third person, that he would have served in a Government with Canning 'if any steady man had been put at the head of it; Lord Bathurst or Lord Melville would have satisfied him. He wanted rather a person of the same opinion on the Catholic question with himself should be Prime Minister, but he would not have separated from his colleagues on that account, as is proved by his mentioning Lord Melville.'

Unfortunately the Duke omitted, in advance of a quite different resolution, to vouchsafe his view to Canning, to the latter's great subsequent annoyance. He might conceivably, if Wellington had been more open, have fallen in with the suggestion, still hoping to fight another day or meanwhile to exercise control from behind the scenes. Melville would then indeed have become Prime Minister. Did he himself believe it could happen? He later claimed to have been in the dark about the manoeuvres, but cryptic references in the surviving documents indicate that he might at least have sounded his colleagues out.[51]

The moment anyway passed. The King, seeing no prospect of agreement on anyone else, did send for Canning in April. He, in construction of his Cabinet, naturally turned first to his outgoing colleagues, though it seemed clear that the Protestants would not serve. Melville let the whips know that he was of a like mind: 'notwithstanding his opinion on the Catholic question he never could belong to any Government which Canning might ever wish to form, to the exclusion of his Protestant colleagues.' In other words, he was really objecting to the end of Liverpool's balancing act. It seemed a feeble sort of sticking-point for one of his convictions. It anyway sounded somewhat different when he elaborated it to Canning a few days later, on being sent an invitation to remain in office. Melville, without by his own account referring to the rest of his colleagues, agreed to stay on provided that the new Cabinet should hold the same principles and be composed of the same persons as Liverpool's, and that he personally was required to give no pledges on emancipation. The next day he asked to see Canning and did, repeating his terms and saying he thought Peel would not join – but that he still would do so if Peel was the only defector.

That night most of the old Cabinet dined together, though Wellington and Peel absented themselves. Melville accordingly went next morning to speak to them, and found that neither would join. One observer thus savagely described his visit to the Duke: 'Lord Melville, poor weak man, is goose enough to consult him – and gets such a decided answer that he too must go out.' It was at the least odd of him, one of the Ministry's liberals offered now a presumably not uncongenial tack in political course, to let the balance of his mind be tipped against it by Wellington, who counted as the arch-reactionary.

Such, however, was the formal reply which Melville sent to Canning that afternoon:

> I told you yesterday that, as far as I was concerned, I should willingly contribute my assistance in the administration which His Majesty has directed you to form, provided you could keep Lord Liverpool's Government together ... I have only today learnt that the separation is to an extent of which I was not before aware, and I really feel that I could not do justice to your Government if I were to continue in office. I regret the result most sincerely and deeply.[52]

Melville thus went along with the five other members of the Cabinet and the majority of junior Ministers who deserted Canning. The Prime Minister was forced into uneasy coalition with the Whigs – and even then only with their conservative wing, for the more radical joined the high Tories in opposition.

Whatever his actual part in events, Melville was most anxious to put his preferred version on the record. In May, he addressed the Lords on the outcome of the crisis:

> The members of His Majesty's late administration, who have resigned their official situations, have been charged with conspiracy. For myself, I declare distinctly, and on my honour, that from the hour of Lord Liverpool's illness down to the hour of his resignation, I did not have the slightest communication of any kind or description with any of my colleagues regarding the formation of a new administration.

He then rehearsed what had happened, though certainly not in every detail, before going on: 'I hope therefore that it is quite clear that I have not acted in concert with anyone. In fact it was not possible, in the nature of things, that any concert or conspiracy whatever can have existed.' But when he had heard that Wellington and Peel were resigning,

> I immediately determined to follow their example: notwithstanding that, on the question of catholic emancipation, I pursue a different course from them … I must say (feeling, as I do, the highest respect for the talents of the First Lord of the Treasury) that still the change from the Government of Lord Liverpool was a change for the worse.

In July Melville told Scott a barely credible tale that the Prime Minister would have sacked him anyway.[53] None of the old Cabinet, he added, had suspected Canning might outwit them by turning to the Whigs (except Wellington, who apparently charmed the information from Ladies of the Bedchamber). Since it was an obvious counter, which they surely could have acted to forestall, Scott found this statement strange. Melville

> allowed the truth of what I said and seemed to blame Peel's want of courage. In his place, he said, he would have proposed to form a Government disclaiming any personal views for himself as being premier or the like but upon the principle of supporting the measures of Lord Castlereagh and Lord Liverpool. I think this would have been acceptable to the King. Mr Peel obviously feared his great antagonist Canning and perhaps threw up the game too soon. Canning said the office of premier was his inheritance – he could not from constitution hold it above two years and then it would descend to Peel. Such is ambition!

Melville admitted elsewhere that he had been badly thrown off balance: 'My case was somewhat peculiar, and I had only a few hours to decide on the line which I should follow.' But, he insisted, 'I have greatly rejoiced ever since at finding myself where I am, instead of being entered among a strong faction, with whom, though on good terms personally, I have never had any connection'.[54]

His resignation could not all the same be regarded as other than a stupendous mistake. English Tories had a point in standing firm on the catholic question, since Canning's answer to it threatened the Church represented by their party.

But this was of no consequence in Scotland. There, the issue had to be maintenance of the King's Government, as ever with the unity behind it of all the most
able and loyal in the nation, leaving to faction only the disaffected. That from its
outset was the Dundas despotism's rationale. Melville, by going into opposition on
a partisan matter, destroyed the rationale. With Canning he in truth had no
disagreement, merely quibbles. To place them above the integrity of his Scottish
system was a miscalculation so gross as to bring its rapid collapse.

Cockburn said Melville's move 'was viewed first with stupid dismay, and then with
abuse of his want of skill by those to whom the idea was unbearable'. He himself
claimed that 'almost all the great leading interests are on our side'. As a matter of
fact the Scottish ruling caste just could not abdicate en masse along with him.
William Dundas let Canning know that 'far from applauding Melville's course he
deeply and bitterly deplores it'. Rae would not resign as Lord Advocate, nor Hope
as Solicitor General. The latter wrote that they 'were placed in an embarrassing
situation. We separately formed the opinion – that we ought not to resign – an
opinion in which we were strengthened by every consideration applicable to Lord
Melville's interests and confirmed by every statement we have seen of the grounds
of his resignation – as not affecting us, I mean.' Sir George Clerk, who owed his
seat in Midlothian to the Dundases, not only opted for Canning but accepted a job
from him. For a man under his obligations this was thought unpardonable, and
when he stood for re-election he found it difficult to justify. Still, the Dundases did
not oppose him for fear of letting in a Whig on a split vote: 'An amnesty has been
granted to rats,' said Lady Melville.
    These defections from the heart of the despotism were followed by others, by
Galloway in the South-west and by both the Duffs and the nabob Grants in the
North-east: Canning promptly and astutely awarded Fife his British peerage while
offering Charles Grant the presidency of the Board of Trade. It would be hard to
say just how many among the run of Scottish members joined them, given the
paucity of recorded divisions under a short-lived Government. In all it may be
that, including Whigs, Canning could count on sixteen Scots in the Commons.
The peers were more solidly against him, only three rallying round on a crucial
division in June. He called this 'unprecedented', being evidently one of those who
assumed they would support any Ministry. He found he had not much to offer
against the 'threats and promises ... prodigally held out by Lord Lauderdale and
Lord Melville to all their brethren of the Scotch peerage; and as appears by the
result, only too successfully'. But a month later the Solicitor General reported that
he had been working on Lord Hopetoun because of his 'station in Scotland and
extensive influence which he might have very injuriously exerted'. He was won
over, and perhaps in time would have gathered in his other parliamentary
connections too. It really was looking as if Melville could not carry his political
constituency with him. [55]
    Who in these uncertain circumstances was to be put in charge of Scottish
patronage? Scott thought that the Whiggery of 1806 was come again and that
Lauderdale would be the man, not reckoning with the perversity that kept him in
opposition. A more obvious choice was Binning, heir to the Earl of Haddington.

He had sat for various English seats since 1802, initially with the encouragement of the first Viscount Melville, his relation by marriage (Binning's mother was yet another of the innumerable Hopes of Hopetoun). Moreover he had for twenty years been a Canningite, though his leader regretted his 'indolence and shilly-shallyness'. He too saw himself as the perfect choice, and put it about that Scottish patronage would be his.

He presumed too much. Cockburn wrote: 'Canning had in his ignorance proceeded on the notion that this was the established system for the Government of Scotland, and had consented to "let Lord Binning have Scotland".' Whigs chorused objections, and it was a sure sign of a precarious Prime Minister that he felt obliged to heed this minor Scottish faction. He took it out on Binning, who sent a pained reply explaining that there had been 'great anxiety as to the hands into which the business would fall', and that 'a long tried friend of your own would afford a satisfactory solution to that anxiety and doubt'. The Whigs were indeed insisting on a return to 1806, with Scottish affairs run from the Home Office. They positively rejoiced at the thought of an Englishman as Minister for Scotland, and an end to 'the horrid system of being ruled by a native jobbing Scot'. Binning vainly maintained the contrary: 'It is nonsense to imagine that a Minister of this country can manage Scotland without consulting someone – that someone will infallibly be the person to whom people will address themselves.' He also disputed the Whig claim that fairer distribution of Scottish offices in recent years was due to Peel and Liverpool: 'This I believe to be most unjust to poor Melville. I know it to be unjust to Solicitor General Hope.' It was still the Whigs' advice that Canning took, asking his Home Secretary, Lord Lansdowne, to oversee Scottish policy directly, aided in the finer points by a couple of native advisers, Kennedy and Abercromby.[56]

The Prime Minister made this arrangement with some satisfaction. He not only eliminated the Scottish manager, but also put the First Lordship of the Admiralty into abeyance. Its functions were assigned to the Duke of Clarence as Lord High Admiral, an ancient office resurrected for the purpose. With the heir-presumptive to the throne roped into his Ministry, Canning might reasonably hope to last two reigns. Even if he fell, his successor could hardly sack the Duke, and Melville's return would be thwarted: 'Of this his friends boasted as a coup de maitre, inasmuch as it at once shut the door against Lord Melville's return, and so punished him'. Scott went to see how things stood with 'my very old friend, this upright statesman and honourable gentleman, deprived of his power and his official income which the number of his family must render a matter of impor-tance. He was cheerful, not affectedly so, and bore his declension like a wise and brave man.'[57]

In August 1827, a month after that was written, cruel fate killed Canning and conjured up a new political crisis. The King called on Lord Goderich who, as Frederick Robinson, had been an able, reforming Chancellor of the Exchequer. One of the Tory minority who stayed on in April, he now hoped to bring back the rest. Rumours ran of an offer to Melville. But he replied from home, when a friend inquired:

I have told Peel that being comfortably deposited here, I have no wish to return to public life. If circumstances should arise to render it a matter of duty to obey any such call (which I think improbable), I must of course submit and obey it, and at any rate I feel that it might be injurious in some respects if I promulgated to the world that I meant permanently to abjure office. I observe in the newspapers that Lord Goderich has invited me to join his administration. I have not yet received the invitation, but if it comes it will be easily answered! [58]

Similarly rebuffed elsewhere, Goderich had to give up the King's commission in January 1828 before ever meeting Parliament. Briefly and tantalisingly, the prospect of a Ministry under Melville again took shape. Croker, privy to all the political gossip, noted: 'They have a report that it is intended to place Lord Melville nominally at the head. This would appear to me quite monstrous if I did not recollect my conversation with Peel last year, in which he said he would serve under Melville.' He could see some sense in setting up his old boss as peacemaker among the factions, 'but what is to become of Peel's speeches and pledges about the head of the Government being protestant? Besides, the country will not bear a man of straw; and Melville himself, though not bright, has too much good sense to undertake it. The difficulties are very great, but this expedient will not solve them.'[59]

The King could only turn back to the high Tories. He asked Wellington and Peel to form a Ministry, at first in coalition with the Canningites. When the Duke told Melville, he replied: 'I am ready to lend my assistance in the Government you are forming; at the same time, I wish you distinctly to understand that I am not at all anxious for office.' The message was coded: for indeed it would prove awkward to sack Clarence, and Melville had no wish to share naval responsibilities with him. So he returned, after fifteen years, to the Board of Control, but without a seat in Cabinet. Wellington did have a great many more claims for preferment than posts with which to satisfy them, and Melville was merely part of the balancing act. Even so, his loss of status was unmistakable. He wrote, however: 'The arrangements in the Government, though not perfect in all respects, have on the whole been judicious ... With regard to myself the India Board is unquestionably the situation which suits me best.'[60]

There was still no promotion for him when Wellington, realising that reunion with the Canningites had been a mistake, got rid of them after a couple of months. The occasion was an amendment to the Corn Laws proposed by Charles Grant. It split the Ministry, with Melville taking the liberal side: 'It will be very strange, when all the trammels are removed, if the manufacture of corn shall be the only one in the kingdom in which no improvements shall take place.' A compromise was cobbled together, but the Canningites decided to go anyway, and Wellington did not try to stop them. It was thus a depleted Government that faced its coming battles.

The biggest would be over catholic emancipation, given a priority which few expected. Most assumed that Wellington meant to bury it for the foreseeable future. In fact he soon satisfied himself that the balance in Parliament had swung in its favour, that the Cabinet would agree to it, that it must therefore come and that his duty was to see to its coming with as little upheaval as possible. These were the concurring opinions at Melville Castle, as reported by its mistress:

> Lord Melville holds that the Catholics will cease to be Roman when they cannot allege that their spiritual and worldly interests are divided ... At all events it appears to me that the effect of the [anti-catholic] policy has been to put the Protestants and the Tory party in the wrong, and make that sedition which used to be loyalty and to have turned the only men in the Tory party who are of capacity to govern into Whigs.

But Melville's liberalism here was, like his father's, unrepresentative of Scots. He commented: 'The opinions of the great majority of the most intelligent in Scotland are in favour of the measure. I admit that the majority, in point of numbers, may be the other way.' Catholics still formed only a small minority, at least of natives. It was reckoned that their enfranchisement would benefit a single peer and just about a dozen freeholders. As soon it was mooted, 250 hostile petitions arrived from Scotland, most from town councils, while many clergymen preached against it. On the opposite side was ranged almost the entire political establishment, from the Whigs right across to Melville's circle (Robert Adam Dundas, sitting for Ipswich, being one of the few exceptions). By April 1829, Wellington and Peel had their legislation safely through. But in alienating the highest Tories, they made certain that their Ministry could not endure.[61]

Melville's own work in it was humdrum. Since his last stint at the Board of Control, a series of able Indian Governors-general had stolen the limelight from it. This went on, for arriving in Calcutta almost simultaneously was one of the greatest of all, Lord William Bentinck, who set his Government on an actively liberalising, westernising course. Melville found little to contribute but efficient administration of the routine business at home. The Board had a larger staff nowadays, so that it was easy to delegate. Many of the problems remained only too familiar: 'If the statement prepared by Lord Melville's directions respecting the finances of India be a correct one', Peel told Wellington, 'the East India Company is not very far from insolvency.' There was also, as ever, the wearisome patronage. Melville wrote to an importunate Duchess of Atholl: 'When I state to your Grace that I shall not have any patronage, civil or military, for a twelvemonth to come, you will at once perceive that it would be improper in me at present to make any promises, or hold out any expectations as to what may or may not be in my power to do next year'.

The only major political question was on what conditions the Company's charter might again be renewed in 1833. Melville saw no good reason for maintaining the last vestige of its monopoly, in the trade with China. On the other hand, he favoured continuing the existing system of Indian government, cumbersome though it was. It at least spared Parliament a great increase in business bound to follow if the Crown ruled India directly. These were the terms on which renewal would be granted but, as before, Melville was by then gone from the Board.[62]

He stayed only seven months. In the autumn of 1828 Wellington managed what he was itching to do and got rid of Clarence. The plump prince was too used to throwing his weight around, and forever telling the First Sea Lord, Sir George

Cockburn, where to send the fleet. The Admiralty Board, supposed to be independent in operational matters, could not work under nonstop royal interference. Melville, deputed as spokesman for his colleagues, wrote 'assuring Your Royal Highness, and ... earnestly entreating you to believe, that unless you adopt as a positive rule from which you will on no account, and under no circumstances deviate, that all official orders and instructions of every description which Your Royal Highness may be pleased to issue, shall pass through the regular channel of your council and public secretary, great confusion and great detriment to His Majesty's service must ensue.' He then had 'a most violent scene with him', at the climax of which an apoplectic Clarence resigned. Melville took the Admiralty and its place in Cabinet again, not without reluctance, after Wellington assured him he could think of nobody else. Lord Ellenborough, his successor at the Board. said 'he does not like the change at all, nor does the navy'. But the Lord-lieutenancy of Ireland, which he declined in December, was evidently still less to his taste.[63]

Several thought Melville had lost his touch. Scott noted: 'He is a terrible dawdle in certain matters which is wretched policy.' Ellenborough too, after watching him perform in the Lords, concluded that 'our management under Lord Melville does not answer'; in Cabinet he was 'surprised by Lord Melville's inertness'. A dreadful episode occurred in Scotland, on a vacancy for the lucrative office of Chief Baron of Exchequer. Rae, after eleven years in harness as Lord Advocate, quite reasonably expected it. Melville passed him over in favour of his Whig nephew, Abercromby, whom even Lord Grey called a 'perfect humbug'. Regard for the opposition was doubtless more necessary than ever, but this went too far. The Solicitor General wrote: 'The treatment of the Advocate is scandalous, I think it the very harshest and most unfeeling thing any Government ever did ... The cry against Lord Melville is louder and more general than any ever raised in my time as to any public or personal matter.' The manager himself brushed Rae's protest aside, claiming it was nothing to do with him: 'You must often have heard me deprecate any separate or personal influence in Scotland, which must in many circumstances be an encumbrance rather than an advantage.'[64]

His management seemed in his own mind already over. Unlike the Whigs, however, he did give some thought to how it might be replaced. In November 1829 he wrote to Peel of

the inconvenience frequently complained of by the natives of Scotland, particularly the members of Parliament, that there is no special officer or office in London for the transaction of the business, Parliamentary or otherwise, of that part of the Kingdom, though in fact from the dissimilarity of our laws and institutions, such an establishment is even more necessary than a similar office for Ireland. It has hitherto devolved chiefly on the Lord Advocate, most improperly and inconveniently for the public service.

He had in mind a junior Minister in the Home Office. But the case was essentially the same as that which brought the creation of the Scottish Office, under a Scottish Secretary, more than half a century later.[65]

Meanwhile, however, the Dundas despotism had its electoral swansong to sing. In June 1830 the death of George IV dissolved Parliament. It was not a moment the Government would have chosen. Times were hard, above all for agriculture. In England, especially the South, the distressed population was driven to violence against its landlords, though little of the trouble spilled over into Scotland. Then a new revolution in France dethroned the Bourbons once again, sending Charles X to resume his exile at Holyrood. It inevitably awakened memories of forty years before, and the atmosphere of the General Election was tense. Through vigorous manipulation of its interest the Ministry actually gained seats. Large swings against it in the popular English constituencies seriously weakened it all the same.

In her own increasingly unpredictable way, Scotland mirrored the general pattern. The Government did maintain control of the South-east, where its only clear defeat came in the notoriously corrupt Stirling Burghs: the incumbent Downie, self-proclaimed destroyer of the Whigs' interest there, was ejected by one of them. The alternating county of Clackmannan brought back George Abercromby, another of Melville's Whig nephews. But there were compensations. In East Lothian the sitting member Hay, after starting off in opposition, had recently taken to voting with the Ministry; Melville recognised this by declining to back a challenger. The Dysart Burghs returned Lord Loughborough, heir of Rosslyn, whose family had long been in opposition but now also, faced with the actual prospect of reform, recoiled; at the end of his career Loughborough was to be among the highest of Tories. In Fife, the incumbent Wemyss moved in the opposite direction. Though elected on and giving support to Melville's interest, he accepted the need for constitutional change and would vote for the Reform Act of 1832. So there were in this region eleven Tories, two Whigs and three waverers.

Mixed results came from the West too. Lanarkshire, under the control of the Hamiltons since the turn of the century, was deserted by its sitting Whig for the safer seat of Renfrewshire. It then fell to a rival Tory interest represented by Charles Douglas. Yet the opposition was well enough organised to make a serious attempt on two constituencies which ministerialists only just held. In Dunbarton, Lord Montagu Graham, son of the Duke of Montrose, won on a casting vote. The same happened in the Glasgow Burghs, where the incumbent Archibald Campbell of Blythswood beat off Kirkman Finlay, now a reformer. Two counties, Dumfries and Wigtown, elected liberal lairds, John Hope Johnston and Sir Andrew Agnew respectively, who while not hostile to the Government were also to support reform. The opposition retained two other seats, the Ayr Burghs and Kirkcudbrightshire. This region thus returned six Tories, three Whigs and two waverers.[66]

The North-east proved more stable, if not entirely so. Most constituencies were safe for the Ministry, while one, Maule's in Forfarshire, was safe for the opposition. A fierce battle took place over the Perth Burghs, complicated by the temporary disfranchisement of corrupt Dundee. Blatant irregularities in the election of a Tory, John Stuart Wortley, caused the poll to be declared null and void. When it was held again in January 1831, the Whigs put up as their candidate Jeffrey, now Lord Advocate. By dint of highly unreformed behaviour (kidnapping of some councillors, imprisonment of others for bogus debts and further enjoyable nonsense) he then won. In the Aberdeen Burghs, Hume chose after twelve years not to stand again, but removed to the popular English constituency of Middlesex. He was replaced by Sir James Carnegie of Southesk, son of the late Sir David whose political cavortings had been primarily aimed at getting lifted the attainder on his family's peerage. They continued in the new generation: Sir James, while meaning to support the Government, still had to appease his rather radical district, and was thus 'actually turning liberal'. In the Elgin Burghs, the sitting representative of Fife's interest, General Duff, had gone over into opposition with the Canningites; he maintained himself now. Altogether in this region we might count five Tories, two Whigs and two waverers.[67]

In the Highlands, where the Dundas despotism had long broken down, it returned just two members. In Bute, Lord Advocate Rae again found a Scottish seat. In the Inverness Burghs, John Baillie of Leys drove out, with generous help from the Treasury, the sitting Canningite, Robert Grant, who took refuge in England. In the county, Melville personally organised a similar assault on Robert's brother Charles; but it failed, and he survived to become president of the Board of Control in a Whig Cabinet. Elsewhere, both Argyll and Orkney were safe for the opposition, which gained an extra seat by the alternation of Nairnshire. The sitting member in Ross, James Stuart Mackenzie, was one of those Tories moving in favour of reform. So was Lord Francis Leveson Gower in Sutherland, who eventually went back to the Conservatives, but his family's factor, James Loch, chosen this time for the Tain Burghs, would gravitate permanently to Liberalism. We should reckon for the region two Tories, four Whigs and three waverers. For Scotland as a whole their respective strengths were 24, 11 and 10. Though reduced, Melville's interest yet held a majority – and some waverers did normally vote with the Ministry. Almost all the representative peers were still his.[68]

In London the Government staggered on till November, when it was narrowly defeated on a trivial question. It had anyway lost the strength and will to continue. Peel took very much amiss the conduct of young Henry Dundas, heir of Melville, who never spoke, served only by a silent vote and absented himself from the division which finished his father's ministerial career. 'Can I personally regret the end of such a Government?' Peel asked.[69]

It was also the *coup de grâce* for the Dundas despotism, which Thomas Carlyle described as 'having become noisome in the nostrils of all men'. The Whigs came in, afire with reforming zeal. The next year they went to the country again, seeking a specific mandate for a wider franchise. They won it, though narrowly, from Scottish electors too. If not without difficulty, Reform Acts for Scotland and England could be passed during 1832. At the first General Election under a new suffrage the Scots Tories were all but swept away. Even before the parliamentary battles subsided, Melville had resigned himself to the inevitable:

> If the English Bill should be rejected, it does not follow that some alteration may not be adopted with regard to the Scotch representative system … So far am I from thinking that the system in Scotland does not require amendment that I have been for several years endeavouring to carry measures for its improvement. I must protest, therefore, against being classed

with those individuals who approve of the Scottish system in all its parts, though I am not inclined to go the length of the wild propositions which are so hastily advanced on every side.

In Scotland the Reform Act was, however, botched. It succeeded neither in curing major abuses of the old constitution nor in creating a new one which satisfied popular demands. And it could not be easily amended afterwards, since the channels for Scottish measures provided previously by the system of management were just shut down. Perceptive reformers soon repented of it. Good government in Scotland was to become more imperative as economic and social advance quickened in the Victorian era. Whigs, complacent at the outcome of their tinkering, viewed the problem with indifference. Indeed, as fanatical advocates of Parliament's absolute sovereignty, they stood by while it wrought irreparable harm to what Scots had preserved under the Union. The law, for which Whigs had a silly contempt, degenerated. The Church suffered the catastrophic Disruption. The universities were forced towards conformity with their inferior English counterparts. Not till half a century had passed did Scotland find means to arrest the havoc.

Melville, meanwhile, had an active and not unduly political retirement. He was not past helping to draw up the circular which showed Conservative agents how, through exploitation of loopholes in the Whigs' slapdash legislation, faggot votes might still be made. But when Peel formed a brief Ministry in the winter of 1834–5, he wrote to his former colleague: 'I do not go through the vain ceremony of inviting you to return to the King's service, because I know that appeal would be unsuccessful.' To which came the reply: 'You judged me correctly as to my wishes in regard to office. When I quitted it in 1830, it was really and bona fide (and to say the truth without regret) in the intention of never returning to it.' Even so the battered Scots Tories continued to look to Melville till, later in the decade, a new Duke of Buccleuch and the Earl of Aberdeen were ready to take over the leadership.

Perhaps this continued aristocratic dominance inhibited the revival of Scottish Conservatism in and by the bourgeoisie. But Melville and his entourage were not natural partisans. He took the old-fashioned view that they had no business impeding the King's Government (though it was a pity he had not acted on that in 1827). He therefore refrained from attacking Whig Ministries just for the sake of it. The high Tories, he commented, 'disgust all really loyal and well-intentioned conservatives who look only to the stability of the monarchy and preservation of the constitution'. As chancellor of St Andrews he wrote to the Home Office when the post of principal fell vacant: 'I shall act with any respectable Whig who may be appointed to the situation, and you know enough of me to be tolerably certain that his politics would be no obstacle in that respect.' He espoused till his end some liberal causes. In the crisis over the Corn Laws in 1846 he argued against 'the uselessness of what is called "protection of British agriculture" … I believe and expect that the agriculture of the United Kingdom, especially in the greater part of Scotland and Wales, will receive a wholesome stimulus by removing the incubus of protection: but with our rapidly increasing population, I do not expect that the price of corn generally will be reduced.' He therefore followed Peel when the question split his party, even though that killed it off in Scotland till it could be reconstituted on a fresh basis at the end of the century.[70]

Melville preferred to work now as a disinterested elder statesman. Cockburn wrote: 'Though withdrawing from London and its great functions, he did not renounce usefulness, but entered into every Edinburgh work in which it could be employed with respectability.' With no power, he seemed to become more popular. So many institutions were anxious for his services that he turned into something of an institution himself. As he once described it, 'Lord Melville, the chairman of the Prisons Board began to deliberate with Lord Melville, the governor of the Bank of Scotland as to whether it might not be convenient for the said bank to advance the money [for new buildings] and save us all further trouble.' General tribute was paid, by the way, to his work for prisons, in which he shared his father's enlightened attitudes on penal policy. Some would not be out of place today. He sought an 'alteration in our law as to the description of punishment usually inflicted on boys, and frequently repeated, most injuriously as affects their future reformation, probable or possible' – there would be 'no satisfactory results from any establishment which does not involve the future destination or employment of the lad'. He wanted 'a radical reform, which in this case I advocate, of the disgraceful receptacles (with few exceptions) called "prisons" in Scotland'.

Melville was also highly gratified to be put in charge of the royal commission which reported in 1843 on the Poor Law. By then the old one was about to break down because a disrupted Kirk could no longer administer it. But rather than sweep it away (for example, with a more voluntary system), he sought to preserve the best of the parochial structure in a fresh guise. So he proposed that an agency of the state should oversee arrangements which in every other way remained local. The report was followed in 1845 by the legislation that remained the basis of welfare in Scotland till the establishment of modern social security. A new national Board of Supervision had few positive powers, yet could still exert pressure to raise the standard of provision. Melville himself would have preferred something stronger. He acknowledged, however, that 'it was very desirable … if possible, to let the country feel that they must make adequate provision for those who are legally entitled to it, but also to take the country along with us, by allowing them to do it in their own way, provided they do it effectively'. In any case, many more parishes were soon levying a rate, and expenditure on relief greatly increased. If the problem of poverty was hardly solved, at least an effort had been made to enliven a distinctive Scottish system and ethos, rather than resorting to the usual ruthless anglicisation of the Whigs.[71]

It would be pleasant to record that Conservatives consistently followed that line. But they otherwise notably failed to do so during their one extended term of office in mid-century, under Peel from 1841 to 1846. That was when the Disruption took place, to which Melville responded mainly with the wringing of hands. He and the Prime Minister came into closer contact over the Banking (Scotland) Act, 1845. With this Peel fulfilled an old ambition and destroyed what monetary independence remained in Scotland, which he chose to regard still as a threat to stability in the whole United Kingdom. The means he employed were onerous indeed: the banks were obliged to back with gold any increase in their circulation of notes beyond the current level. What he offered in exchange was to suppress competition. New entrants to the banking business were forbidden altogether to issue notes, handicap enough to halt abruptly the vigorous expansion which the system had undergone since its victory in 1826. Now it was cartelised, in due course fossilised: no new banks would be founded in Scotland till the 1980s.

Those of the time acquiesced, but perhaps their true views came out in Melville's effort only a year later to regain some of their lost freedom. He proposed a union of the three chartered institutions, in effect into a Scottish central bank. So long as it operated under the same regulations as the Bank of England, he argued, it would have a far better effect than anti-competitive legislation. Since Scots sought and found prudence in their bankers, 'I have no doubt that the same feeling of confidence would follow the new establishment, and would materially assist in pursuing the same course – to the great advantage of the public generally. and also, really and truly, of all other banking establishments in Scotland whose affairs might be conducted on a similar principle of safety'. Melville tried to enlist political support in various quarters, but Peel's response was so dusty that he abandoned the idea. It was already too late to preserve, let alone extend, the autonomy of Scottish institutions.[72]

For himself Melville, if somewhat gouty, remained in good health and good spirits, even after losing his wife, right till his own death in June 1851, soon after his eightieth birthday. He was buried beside his father at Lasswade. Cockburn penned this obituary:

> He deserved ... unanimous public trust by plain manners, great industry, excellent temper, sound sense and singular fairness. Though bred in the bad old school of Scottish Toryism, and not a bad scholar in it, while that school was uppermost, his chief merit is that, as it went down, he neither got sulky nor desperate, but let his mind partake freely of the improvement of feeling which its decline implied. He stuck to his old politics, and his old political friends to the last, but not in their greater follies; and in candour and liberality became as good a Whig as a Tory can be.[73]

Presumably no back-handed compliment was meant. The Dundas despotism had in fact provided government considerably more effective than anything ever to come from Whigs. In its prime, it without doubt found the right formula for ruling the Scotland that had entered into an incorporating Union. It filled in all the administrative gaps left by the Treaty itself. It subdued aristocratic faction. It passed power to those fitted by ability and loyalty for enlightened leadership. This power was exercised with restraint because exercised within a still robust and respected framework of traditional institutions. 'Power is always intoxicating,' the first Viscount Melville had confided to the young Canning. But it is time finally to admit that the Dundas despotism, though making a fine title for a book, was in truth a misnomer.

More than that, good Scottish government redressed the Union's imbalance. It could safeguard Scotland's interests, while opening to her opportunities more splendid than have ever come the way of any other small, stateless nation. An unfair electoral franchise was meanwhile a slight price for Scots to pay, as a great

French historian agreed: 'L'exclusivisme de leur patriotisme explique dans une large mesure que l'Ecosse se soit résignée à un régime électoral monstrueux: ce régime est un des moyens qu'elle emploie pour marcher à la conquête de l'Angleterre.'[74]

Why then, when the Dundas despotism passed away, did it go unmourned? If stumped for an answer about Scotland it is always as well to look to the Caledonian antisyzygy, the principle that, whatever may be asserted of Scots, the opposite may be asserted with equal force and truth. It has already just been left as a contradiction that they had been simultaneously holding at arm's length a more powerful British state while colonising and exploiting it. But this in time brought them face to face with a wider dilemma constantly to recur in their relations with that state. Scots are obliged to be conservatives in order to guard a nationality for which the state itself has in latter days offered few formal guarantees. Yet so much of the finest in the spirit of their nationality, its self-improving energy, its intellectual rigour, its idealism and its democracy, drives them into being progressives. The product in the national condition is at best divine discontent, at worst calamity brought on through the clash of irreconcilables.

Modern Scotland's first experience of this followed quickly from the debacle of the Dundas despotism. Perhaps some deluded themselves that native institutions could survive in their former integrity under the new dispensation. After all, the old one had gratuitously inhibited its own rejuvenation. It had neglected to extend itself from the aristocracy and landed gentry to the commercial and manufacturing interests, let alone to the people; though a conservative appeal to both, resting in the one case on granting property its due, in the other on acceding to the claims of evangelical religion, ought not to have been impossible. It must have made a difference if, say, the captains of industry and Chalmers's votaries had alike been shepherded into the Tory fold. The failure to seize such opportunities has in justice to be laid at the door of a jaded second Viscount Melville, for surely his father's keener political instincts would not have permitted them so casually to pass. And that might have offered a basis for Scottish management to weather the rampant factionalism by which, from 1827, the unreformed system at Westminster signalled its collapse from within. The first Viscount had in his own time steered a shrewd course through similar squalls, and still come out on the right side.

There was indeed no inescapable reason why the Whigs should have been handed Scotland on a plate, to dismember. With greater confidence and energy in the old elite, some limit might have been set to the effrontery of their claims that everything Scottish was antiquated and reactionary, everything English modern and liberal. Because it was they, the victors, who as usual wrote the history, the extent of the damage they wrought has been obscured. But what they set out to do was eradicate native traditions in politics and public life, and confine the distinctively Scottish to the kailyard. Their notion of progress would eventually prove too much even for a Scotland which had joined them in fighting the constitutional immobilism of the *ancien régime*. The nation would at last call a halt. All that must, however, be the subject of another book.

The new structure then devised for the state in Scotland, with the establishment of the Scottish Office in 1885, might be seen as a compromise between those contradictory alternatives which the people had by turns rejected. Means to institutional conservatism were restored and, with legislative mechanisms which admittedly took long to perfect, it would not for the future be possible to confuse reform with indiscriminate wrecking. Congenial at the same time to central authority, the structure in fact resurrected a sort of Scottish management. An essential difference, however, lay in the fact that under the Dundas despotism the historic Scottish institutions had yet enjoyed a degree of internal autonomy, a vestige of the sovereignty derived from erstwhile nationhood, in short a semi-independence: all of which helped Scotland to think of herself as England's partner. In contrast, new Scottish institutions have often been created by and certainly derive their authority from a modern British state notoriously recognising no sovereignty save its own, and imputing dependency to everything under it, so that indeed Scotland thinks of herself as dependent.

It is above all this debasement in ethos and moral condition that marks out to her loss the Scotland of today from the earlier one. It ill behoves us, therefore, to accuse the Dundases of authoritarianism or corruption. At their best, they were in their politics an integral part of the endeavours that gave the nation its one era of genuine historical importance and claim to imperishable fame. Even at their worst they did well, on infinitely fewer resources, what modern Secretaries of State for Scotland have done with fitful success, providing for the few their power and riches, for the many a tolerable contentment. It would be high praise to say of any among these epigones what Cockburn truly said of Henry Dundas, that he was 'well calculated by talents and manner to make despotism popular'.[75]

Notes

1. SRO GD 51/1/198/9/31, 26/43.
2. NLS MS 11, ff.28,39; Sunter (1972), 190.
3. NLS MS 2, f.31.
4. SRO GD 51/1/198/14/19; Large (1963), 678.
5. SRO GD 51/2/437/13; WLC, May 28, June 1, 1820; Liverpool Papers, BL Add MSS 38287, ff.21, 37.
6. Maxwell (1903), ii. 27; Aspinall (1941), 69.
7. SRO GD 51/1/214/45, 5/749/2, 32; Aspinall, 83; Prebble (1988), passim.
8. SRO GD 51/5/749/2, 40, 67; Prebble, 215; Grant (1988), ii, 166.
9. SRO GD 51/2/645/4; Aspinall (1938), ii, 539–43.
10. Jennings (1985), i, 186; Aspinall (1947), 58–64; Bamford & Wellington (1950), i, 82. 94.
11. SRO GD 51/2/437/19; Canning Papers, bundle 77.
12. SRO GD/51/2/437/20.
13. Briggs (1897), 8–20.
14. Liverpool Papers BL Add MSS 38299, f.36; Bartlett (1963), 202.
15. Bartlett, 199; Lewis (1948), 119–20.
16. WLP I, Feb.22, 1823, Mar.2, 1825; WLC, Nov. 8, 1830; Liverpool Papers, loc.cit.; *Parl. Debates*, n.s. ii, col. 529; xii, col. 591; Bartlett, 33–7, 207; Lewis, loc.cit.; McCleary (1947), 12–25; Bourne (1967), 31.
17. Ramsay (1927), 306–36; Gray (1928), 343; Marwick (1934–5), 87 et seqq; Straka (1985), 128 et seqq.
18. Omond (1883), 264; Cockburn (1932), 106; Brash (1974), xlviii.
19. SRO RH 2/4/15/11, 155; Peel Papers BL Add MSS 40304, f.38; Lockhart (1902), viii, 145.

20. Trotter Papers, NLS MS 20269, 592; *Hansard,* 2nd series, xxiii, col. 958; 3rd series, col. 1186.
21. Letters to Scott, NLS MS 3901, f. 179; Liverpool Papers, BL Add MSS 38296, f. 56; Cockburn (1856), 464.
22. SRO GD 51/5/722, 17/77, 266.
23. Grierson (1932), viii, 469.
24. *Parl. Debates,* n.s. xv, col.169; Ferguson (1984), 291.
25. *Parl. Papers,* (1821), 8, 37–8; Connell (1827), 524.
26. SRO GD 51/5/603/2, 612; 51/5/623; 51/5/749/2, 375; Lenman (1977), 151–2.
27. NLS MS 1057, ff.207 et seqq; *Blackwood's Edinburgh Magazine,* xv (1824), Phillipson (l967), 61.
28. Omond, 283; *Edinburgh Review,* xxxix, 363–76; Prebble (1988), 272.
29. SRO GD 51/5/525/1, 537/3; *Parl. Papers,* 1824, x, passim; *Parl. Debates,* n.s., xi, col. 1428; xii, col. 711; Phillipson, 286; Cooper of Culross (1958), 343; Paton (1958), 54; Smith (1961), 72–6; Willcock (1966), 255, 261; Murray (1974), 51.
30. SRO GD 51/5/749/2, 457; Campbell (1961), 139; Nisbet (1964), 153–4; Cage & Checkland (1976), 45; Maciver (1980a), 1; McCaffrey (1981), 43; Cheyne (1985), 3; Brown (1988), 147.
31. SRO GD 51/5/749, 325; NLS MS 1057, ff.72 et seqq; Hanna (1851), ii, 497; Cockburn (1874a), 152; Craven (1956), 127, 195; Maciver (1977), 15; (1980b), 223 et seqq.
32. NLS MS 11, f.79; Maciver (1977), 136–51; Smith (1981), 123.
33. *Edinburgh Review,* xxxix, 322.
34. Home Office Papers, SRO RH 2/4/102/447; McCaffrey, 33; Murdoch & Sher (1988), 138.
35. Cockburn (1874b), 100–3; *Edinburgh Review,* xli, 229; *Parl. Debates,* n.s., xix, cols. 1034, 1369; Campbell & Dow (1968), 151; Mitchison (1974), 59; (1979), 207; (1988), 261, 265; Cage (1981), 119; Whatley (1987), 127.
36. *Blackwood's Edinburgh Magazine,* xii, 337; Napier (1877), 45; Fetter (1960), 88; Chitnis (1986), 126–7.
37. Davie (1961), 3–5; SRO GD 51/17/75, 178.
38. SRO GD 51/5/7492/2, 135; Clark (1969), 284.
39. SRO GD 51/5/749/2, 325; Grierson, vii, 165; Davie, 26 et seqq; Davie & Ritchie, 211 et seqq; Anderson (1972), 199.
40. *Parl. Papers,* (1831), 9.
41. ibid., 90; Sanders (1970 –), iv, 304; NLI, 55A/403.
42. SRO GD 51/5/386/1–3, 537/3, 51/17/75. 42; Home Office Papers, SRO RH 2/4/15/11, 133; Lockhart (1837), vi, 269; Wellington (1867), ii, 209.
43. Lockhart, vi, 249, 271; Phillipson (1969), 181 et seqq; Croker (1972), 10.
44. Letters to Scott, NLS MS 3902, f.133; *Parl. Debates,* n.s. xiv, cols. 1358, 1384; xv, col. 215; Lockhart, vi, 325; Grierson, viii, 400, 468.
45. NLS MS 2, f.79; Home Office Papers, SRO RH 2/4/15/11, 135, 139–40; *The Scotsman,* June 14, 1826; Harris (1989), 15–6.
46. SRO GD 51/5/749/2, 446; *The Scotsman,* June 17, July 5, 1826.
47. SRO GD 51/1/198/6/16–27; NLS MS 641, ff.251 et seqq.
48. Lee & Stephen (1908), vi, 1228.
49. Scottish Catholic Archive, Scottish Mission Papers 5/20/7.
50. *Parl. Debates,* n.s., v, col. 353; xviii, col. 1579; Temperley (1925), 427.
51. ibid., 420; Jennings (1885), 365; Wellesley (1914), ii, 167–8; Aspinall (1937), 55.

52. Peel Papers, BL Add MSS 40317, ff.195 et seqq; Temperley, 524; Aspinall, 84, 128; (1938), iii, 218; Parker (1891), i, 488.
53. Aspinall, 147; Anderson, 326.
54. Boyle Papers, 9/12/19; *Parl. Debates*, n.s., xvii, col. 483; Anderson (1972), 327.
55. NLS MS 2, ff.111–3; SRO GD 51/17/77, 4; Canning Papers, bundle 74; Cockburn (1856), 446; Omond (1887), 343; Aspinall (1937), 173, 205; Large (1963), 678; (1986), 241 et seqq.
56. Lonsdale Papers LI/2/11; Aspinall, 203; Cockburn (1874), 153–4; Thorne (1986), iv, 126–7.
57. Cockburn (1874b), 153–4.
58. Aspinall (1941), 92.
59. Jennings (1883), i, 404.
60. Boyle Papers, 9/9/54; Aspinall, 92; Wellington (1867), iv, 188; Fulford & Strachey (1938), i, 198; Kitson Clark (1964), 31.
61. Cochrane Papers, NLS MS 2271, f. 93; Peel Papers, BL Add MSS 40599, f.78; *Parl. Debates*, xxi, col. 545, xx col. 1418; Machin (1963), 190 et seqq; Muirhead (1973), 26 et seqq; Brown (1988), 154.
62. SRO GD 51/17/777, 17; Wellington (1867), iv, 632; Colchester (1881), i 219; ii, 137.
63. SRO GD 51/17/77, 100; Wellington, iv, 628, 657; ,v, 320; Fulford & Strachey, i, 220; Colchester, i, 218; Bamford & Wellington (1950), ii, 225.
64. NLS MS 11, ff.200–4; Home Office Papers, SRO RH 2/4/15/11. 193; Peel Papers, BL Add MSS 40317, ff.217 et seqq; Grierson, x, 498; Colchester, ii, 41, 137; Omond, 349; Thorne, iii 15.
65. SRO GD 51/17/77, 338.
66. Smith (1850), 170.
67. *The Scotsman*, July 28, 1830.
68. NLS MS 2, f.158.
69. Gash (1961), 658.
70. NLS MS 2, f.175: STA MS 4746; Peel Papers, BL Add MSS 40403, f. 249; 40407, f.247; 40408, f.97; Aberdeen Papers, BL Add MSS 43237, f.126; 43426. f.242; Kitson Clark, 145; Parker (1891), ii, 271; Gash (1953), 354–5; Hutchison (1986), 13.
71. NLS MS 642 f. 299; Ellice Papers, NLS MS 15013, f.161; Ferguson (1948), 194 et seqq; Levitt & Smout (1979), 173–4; Crowther (1990), 271.
72. Peel Papers, BL Add MSS 40601, ff.297–303.
73. Dalhousie Muniments SRO GD 45/14/574, 629/3, 14 & 17; James Skene Papers, NLS MS 20467, f.43; STA MS 4713; Cockburn, ii, 265 et seqq.
74. Canning Papers, bundle 77; Halévy (1912), 111.
75. Cockburn (1856), 59.

Chronology

1742   *Henry Dundas born.* Walpole falls. *Robert, Dundas's brother, becomes Solicitor General.*

1743   2nd Duke of Argyll dies, succeeded by brother, Ilay.

1745   Jacobite Rising.

1746   Scottish Ministers dismissed and office of Scottish Secretary abolished.

1747   Heritable jurisdictions ended.

1748   General Election. *Lord Arniston, Dundas's father, becomes President of Court of Session.*

1753   *Arniston dies.*

1754   General Election. Newcastle's Ministry. *Robert, Dundas becomes Lord Advocate*

1755   Webster's census.

1756–63   Seven Years' War: British conquer Canada, expel French from India.

1760   Accession of George III. *Robert Dundas becomes Lord Arniston and President of Court of Session.*

1761   3rd Duke of Argyll dies. General Election.

1762   Bute's Ministry. Start of Douglas Cause.

1763   Bute resigns. *Dundas qualifies as advocate.* William Robertson becomes principal of Edinburgh University.

1766   *Dundas becomes Solicitor General; marries Elizabeth Rannie.*

1767   Edinburgh New Town started.

1768   General Election.

1770   North's Ministry.

1771   *Robert, Dundas's son born.*

1772   Ayr Bank crash. Warren Hastings becomes Governor-general of Bengal.

1773   Regulating Act for India.

1774   General Election, *Dundas member for Midlothian.*

1775   *Dundas becomes Lord Advocate.*

1776   Adam Smith's 'Wealth of Nations' published. American Declaration of Independence. Emigration from Scotland banned.

1777   *Dundas becomes joint keeper of signet.*

1778   *Dundas divorces.* Riots force him to drop catholic relief. France enters American War.

1779   *Dundas sole keeper of signet.*

1780   General Election. Pitt the younger enters Parliament.

1781   Surrender of Yorktown.

1782   North falls. Ministries of Rockingham, then Shelburne, in which *Dundas is Treasurer of the Navy.* Tipu Sultan becomes ruler of Mysore.

1783   End of American War. Fox-North Coalition dismisses *Dundas.* On its fall, Pitt takes office and *restores him.* Ilay Campbell becomes Lord Advocate.

1784   General Election, won by Pitt. India Act sets up Board of Control. *Robert, Dundas's nephew, becomes Solicitor General* .Forfeited estates restored. Kirk abandons annual protest against Patronage Act.

1785   Diminishing Bill fails. Hastings returns from India.

1786   Cornwallis becomes governor-general of India.

1787   *Lord Arniston dies, Dundas declines to succeed him.*

1788   Death of Prince Charles Edward Stewart. Hastings impeached.

1789   French Revolution breaks out. *Robert, Dundas's nephew, becomes Lord Advocate.*

1790   General Election, *Dundas member for Edinburgh.* Thurlow's judgment against faggot votes. Burke's 'Reflections'.

1791   *Dundas becomes Home Secretary.* Canada Act.

1792   Reign of Terror in France, war with Austria. In Scotland, radical agitation, national convention on county franchise, religious disabilities start to be removed.

1793   Louis XVI executed, war with France. Scottish sedition trials begin. East India Company's charter renewed. Permanent Settlement in Bengal. *Dundas becomes President of the Board of Control. He marries Lady Jane Hope.*

1794   French conquer Belgium. *Dundas becomes Secretary of State for War. Robert, his son, enters Parliament.*

1795   Prussia, Holland, Spain make peace with France: end of First Coalition.

1796   British seize Cape and Ceylon. General Election: *Dundas's greatest victory.*

1797   Wellesley becomes Governor-general of India. Napoleon conquers Italy. Invasion scare, financial crisis, Militia Act.

1798   Irish rebellion. Napoleon's expedition to Egypt, cut off by Nelson's victory at Aboukir Bay.

1799   Second Coalition formed. Helder expedition fails. Napoleon returns to France. Tipu defeated and killed at Seringapatam.

1800   French victories at Marengo and Hohenlinden end Second Coalition.

1801   French expelled from Egypt. Union of Great Britain and Ireland. Pitt falls, *Dundas resigns all offices.* Addington's Ministry. Charles Hope and *William Dundas* manage Scotland.

1802   Peace of Amiens. General Election. *Dundas ennobled as Viscount Melville.* 'Edinburgh Review' first appears.

1803   War renewed.

1804   Addington falls, Pitt returns, *Melville to the Admiralty.*

1805   *Melville impeached and resigns.* Third Coalition. Trafalgar establishes British naval supremacy. Wellesley recalled from India.

1806   Pitt dies. Ministry of All the Talents, Lauderdale and Erskine manage Scotland. General Election. *Melville acquitted.* Minto becomes Governor-general of India.

1807   Portland's Ministry. General Election. *Robert, Melville's son, President of the Board of Control.* Archibald Campbell becomes Lord Advocate. Treaty of Tilsit.

1808   Peninsular War starts. Court of Session reformed.

1809   Perceval's Ministry.

1810   Acts to limit Scottish patronage and to set minimum stipend in the Kirk. Hope becomes President of Court of Session.

1811   *Melville dies.*

1812   Labour troubles in West of Scotland. Liverpool's Ministry, with *2nd Viscount Melville at the Admiralty.* General Election. War with US. Napoleon invades Russia.

1813   New charter for East India Company permits free trade and missions.

1814	Napoleon defeated.
1815	Waterloo, peace in Europe.
1816	Economic depression. Alexander Maconochie becomes Lord Advocate.
1817	Scottish sedition trials.
1818	General Election.
1819	Sir William Rae becomes Lord Advocate.
1820	Death of George III. General Election. Radical War.
1822	George IV visits Scotland. John Hope becomes Solicitor General.
1823	Royal commission on Scottish judiciary.
1826	Royal commission on Scottish universities. 'Malagrowther's Letters'. General Election.
1827	Liverpool resigns. Canning's Ministry, which *Melville refuses to join*. New Whig scheme of Scottish management.
1828	Ministry of Wellington and Peel, *Melville at Board of Control, then Admiralty*.
1829	Catholic emancipation.
1830	Ministry resigns, *Melville retires*. General Election brings Whigs to power, with Francis Jeffrey as Lord Advocate and Henry Cockburn as Solicitor General.
1832	Reform Act.
1833	Scottish burgh reform.
1843	Disruption of the Kirk.
1845	Banking (Scotland) Act.
1851	*Melville dies*.

Bibliography

1. Melville Papers, held in the following archives (with abbreviations used in the notes)

Ames Library of South Asia, University of Minnesota	ALM
Baker Library, Harvard	BLH
Beinecke Library, Yale	BLY
British Library	BL
British Library of Political and Economic Science	PES
Cleveland Public Library, Ohio	CPL
Houghton Library, Harvard	HLH
John Rylands Library, Manchester	JRL
Library of Congress	LC
National Library of Ireland	NLI
National Library of Scotland	NLS
National Maritime Museum	NMM
Rhodes House Library, Oxford	RHL
St Andrews University Library	STA
Scottish Record Office	SRO
Van Pelt Library, University of Pennsylvania	VPL
William L. Clements Library, University of Michigan	WLC
William L. Perkins Library, Duke University	WLP

2. Other manuscript sources

Abercairney Muniments, SRO
Aberdeen Papers, BL
Advocates' Manuscripts, NLS
Airlie Muniments, SRO
Auckland Papers, BL & BLH
Bathurst Papers, BL
Blackwood Papers, NLS
Borthwick Papers, NLS
Boyle Papers, Kelburn, Ayrshire
Buccleuch Papers, SRO
Campbell of Succoth Papers, Strathclyde Regional Archive
Canning Papers, West Yorkshire Archive
Carlyle Bell Papers, NLS
Chatham Papers, PRO
Clerk of Penicuik Papers, SRO
Cochrane Papers, NLS
Cockburn Papers, NLS
Cowie Collection, NLS

James Cumming Papers, NLS
Cunninghame Graham Muniments, SRO
Dalhousie Muniments, SRO
Dropmore Papers, BL
Dundas of Dundas Papers, NLS
Durdans Books, NLS
Edinburgh University Library Papers, general series
Elibank Papers, SRO
Ellice Papers, NLS
Erskine Murray Papers, NLS
Fergusson of Craigdarroch Papers, SRO
Gordon of Invergordon Papers, SRO
Grant-Macpherson Papers, Ballindalloch, Banffshire
Haldane Papers, NLS
Hamilton of Pinmore Papers, SRO
Hamilton-Dalrymple of North Berwick Muniments, SRO
Professor Hannay's Papers, SRO
Hardwicke Papers, BL
Warren Hastings Papers, BL
Hunter Blair Papers, Blairquhan, Ayrshire.
Huskisson Papers, BL
Home Office: Scotland, Correspondence, PRO & SRO (microfilm)
Innes of Stow Papers, SRO
Laing Papers, Edinburgh University Library
Lee Papers, NLS
Liston Papers, NLS
Liverpool Papers, BL and Duke University
Letters to the Lord Advocate of Scotland in the Year 1745, NLS
Lonsdale Papers, Cumbria Record Office
Lynedoch Papers, NLS
Maclaine of Lochbuie Papers, SRO
Macleod of Geanies Papers, NLS
Mar and Kellie Papers, SRO
Martin Papers, BL
Minto Papers, NLS
Miscellaneous Fragments, Letters and Papers, BL
Miscellaneous Papers, SRO
Murray Papers, NLS
Nelson Papers, BL
Newcastle Papers, BL
Nisbet-Hamilton Papers, SRO
Ord and Macdonald Papers, NLS
Original Letters, NLS
Paul Papers, NLS
Peel Papers, BL
Pelham Papers, BL
Spencer Perceval Papers, Duke University
Robertson-Macdonald Papers, NLS
Royal Bank of Scotland Papers
Saltoun Papers, NLS
Scottish Catholic Archive
Letters of Scott, NLS
Letters to Scott, NLS

Writings and Notes of Sir Walter Scott, NLS
Scott of Harden Papers, SRO
Seafield Muniments, SRO
Seaforth Muniments, SRO
Sidmouth Papers, Devon Record Office
Sinclair of Ulbster Papers, SRO (microfilm)
James Skene Papers, NLS
Small Purchases, NLS
Speirs Papers, Houston House, Renfrewshire
Stowe Papers, BL
Stuart Stevenson Papers, NLS
Sutherland Papers, NLS
Trotter Papers, NLS
Walker of Bowland Papers, NLS
Wellesley Papers, BL
Wilberforce Papers, Duke University
Windham Papers, BL
J. P. Wood: Life of Henry Dundas, Lord Melville, NLS
Yester Papers, NLS

3. *Printed sources, and unpublished academic theses*

Adam, Sir C. E.: *View of the Political State of Scotland, 1788* (Edinburgh, 1887).
Anderson, R. D.: 'Scottish University Professors 1800–1939 – Profile of an Elite', *Scottish Economic and Social History*, vii, 1987.
Anderson, W. E. K. (ed): *The Journal of Sir Walter Scott* (Oxford, 1972).
Anderson, W. J.: 'David Downie and the "Friends of the People"', *Innes Review*, xvi, 1965.
Anstey, R.: *The Atlantic Slave Trade and British Abolition 1760–1810* (London, 1978).
Arniston, Dundas, R., Lord: *Law Tracts* (Edinburgh, 1777).
Auckland, William, Lord: *Journal and Correspondence* (London, 1862).
Australian Encyclopaedia, The (Sydney, 1983).
Anonymous: *Heads of a Bill for correcting certain Abuses with respect to the Qualifications of Freeholders in that Part of Great Britain called Scotland* (Edinburgh, n.d.).
: *A Second Letter to the Author of the North Briton* (London, 1763).
: *A Warning against Popery drawn up and published by order of the Associate Synod* (Edinburgh, 1778).
: *A Memorial to the Public in behalf of the Roman Catholics of Edinburgh and Glasgow* (London, 1779a).
: *A Narrative of the late Riots at Edinburgh and a Vindication of its Magistracy* (London, 1779b).
: *A Narrative of the Debate in the General Assembly of the Church of Scotland, May 25, 1779* (Edinburgh, 1780a).
: *Calumny Detected* (Edinburgh, 1780b).
: *Scotland's Opposition to the Popish Bill* (Edinburgh, 1780c).
: *To the Public* (Edinburgh, 1780d).
: *An Address to the Landed Gentlemen of Scotland* (Edinburgh, 1782a).
: *An Address to the Landed Gentlemen of Scotland upon the Subject of nominal and fictitious Qualifications* (n.p., 1782b).
: *Observations on the Laws of Elections of Members of Parliament* (Edinburgh, 1782c).
: *Remarks on the Bill which was intended to be brought into Parliament in 1775, for annulling nominal and fictitious qualifications* (Edinburgh 1782d).
: *A Letter from a Member of the General Convention of Delegates of the Royal Boroughs* (Edinburgh, 1784a).

: *An Address to the Burgesses and Heritors of the Royal Burghs of Scotland, on the present imperfect and arbitrary systems of election established in the burghs* (Edinburgh, 1784b).
: *A Letter to the Right Honourable Henry Dundas on the proposed Improvements in the City of Edinburgh* (Edinburgh, 1785).
: *Observations on the Fishing Trade* (n.p., 1786).
: *An Illustration of the Principles of the Bill proposed to be submitted for the Consideration of Parliament, for correcting the abuses and supplying the defects in the internal government of the royal burghs* (Edinburgh, 1787a).
: *Historical Accounts of the Government and Grievances of the Royal Burghs of Scotland* (Edinburgh, 1787b).
: *Journal of the Rt Hon. Henry Dundas* (London, 1788a).
: *The Album of Streatham, or Ministerial Amusements* (London, 1788b).
: *Report of the London Committee for conducting the Application to Parliament, for regulating the internal government of the royal borough in Scotland* (Edinburgh, 1789).
: *An Address to the Landed Gentlemen of Scotland upon the Subject of nominal and fictitious Qualifications* (Edinburgh, 1792a).
: *A Letter to a Friend in the Country, wherein Mr Paine's Letter to Mr Dundas is particularly considered* (London, 1792b).
: *Meeting of County Delegates* (n.p., 1792c).
: *Heads of a Bill for altering and amending the Laws with respect to the Qualifications of Freeholders in that Part of Great Britain called Scotland* (Edinburgh, 1793a).
: *A Friend of Order: A Few Plain Questions to the Working People of Scotland* (Edinburgh, 1793b).
: *A View of the Establishment of the Royal Edinburgh Volunteers* (Edinburgh, 1795a).
: *Rolliad* (London, 1795b).
: *Trial of David Downie, for high treason* (Edinburgh, 1795c).
: *Printed Documents connected with the Election of Dean of Faculty in January 1796* (n.p., 1796).
: *An Exposure of the Persecution of Lord Melville* (London, 1805).
: *Life of William Pitt, with biographical notices of his principal friends* (Philadelphia, 1806).
: 'Proposed Reform of the Court of Session', *Edinburgh Review*, ix, 1807a.
: *Substance of the Speeches delivered by some Members of the Faculty of Advocates* (Edinburgh, 1807b).
: *Biographical Sketch of Henry, Lord Viscount Melville* (Edinburgh, 1811).
: *Monody on the late Lord Melville and the late Lord President Blair* (Edinburgh, 1811).
: *Authentic Correspondence and Documents explaining the Proceedings of the Marquis Wellesley and of the Earl of Moira in the recent Negotiations for the Formation of an Administration* (London, 1812).
: 'Burgh Reform', *Edinburgh Review*, xxx, 1818.
: 'The Recent Alarms', *Edinburgh Review*, xxxiii, 1820.
: 'Considerations on the Expediency of the Law of Entail in Scotland', *Edinburgh Review*, xliii, 1826.
: 'Parliamentary Representation of Scotland', *Edinburgh Review*, lii, 1830.
: 'The State of Public Feeling in Scotland', *Blackwood's Edinburgh Magazine*, xxxi, 1832.
: 'Slavery in Modern Scotland', *Edinburgh Review*, clxxxix, 1899.
: *Edinburgh 1329–1929* (Edinburgh, 1929).
Arnot, H.: *Act and Testimony of the Ladies of Edinburgh against the Popish Bill* (n.p., n.d.).
: *A Letter to the Lord Advocate of Scotland* (n.p., 1777).
: *The History of Edinburgh* (Edinburgh, 1779).
Arnot, R. P.: *A History of the Scottish Miners* (London, 1955).
Aspinall, A. (ed.): *The Formation of Canning's Ministry* (London, 1937).
(ed.): *The Letters of George IV* (Cambridge, 1938).

: *Lord Brougham and the Whig Party* (London, 1939).
(ed.): *The Correspondence of Charles Arbuthnot* (London, 1941).
(ed.): *The Diary of Henry Hobhouse 1820–1827* (London, 1947).
(ed.): *Three Early Nineteenth-Century Diaries* (London, 1952).
(ed.): *The Later Correspondence of George III* (Cambridge, 1962).
(ed.): *The Correspondence of George, Prince of Wales* (London, 1963–71).
Bailyn, B.: *Voyagers to the West* (New York, 1986).
& Clive, J.: 'England's Cultural Provinces – Scotland and America', *William and Mary Quarterly*, xi, 1954.
Balfour, Lady Frances: *Life of George, 4th Earl of Aberdeen* (London, 1923).
Bamford, F. & Wellington, Duke of (eds.): *The Journal of Mrs Arbuthnot 1820–1832* (London, 1950).
Bannerman, P.: *An Address to the People of Scotland, on ecclesiastical and civil liberty* (n.p., 1782).
Baring, Mrs H. (ed.): *The Diary of the Rt Hon. William Windham* (London, 1866).
Barnard, M.: *History of Australia* (Sydney, 1962).
Barrow, G. (ed.): *The Scottish Tradition, essays in honour of R. G. Cant* (Edinburgh, 1974).
Bartlett, C. J.: *Great Britain and Sea Power 1815–1853* (Oxford, 1963).
Baugh, D.: 'British Strategy during the First World War in the Context of Four Centuries – blue water versus continental commitment', in Masterson (1987).
Beamish, R.: *Memoir of the Life of Sir Marc Isambard Brunel* (London, 1862).
Bence-Jones, M.: *The Viceroys of India* (London, 1982).
Bewley, C.: *Muir of Huntershill* (Oxford, 1981).
Banerjea, P.: *Indian Finance in the Days of the Company* (London, 1928).
Bell, A.: *Lord Cockburn, a bicentenary commemoration* (Edinburgh, 1979).
: *Sydney Smith – a biography* (Oxford, 1980).
Bell, R.: *Treatise on the Election Laws* (Edinburgh, 1812).
Benians, E. A., Holland Rose, J., & Newton, A. P. (eds): *The New Empire*, vol.ii, *Cambridge History of the British Empire*, (Cambridge, 1940).
Benton, W. W.: 'The Ecclesiology of George Hill 1750–1819' (University of Edinburgh, Ph.D. thesis, 1969).
Bickley, F. (ed.): *The Diaries of Sylvester Douglas, Lord Glenbervie* (London, 1928).
Black, E. C.: *The Association – British extraparliamentary political organisation 1769–1793* (Cambridge, Mass., 1963).
Black, J.: 'The Tory View of Eighteenth-Century British Foreign Policy', *Historial Journal*, xxxi, 1988.
Bono, P.: *Radicals and Reformers in Late Eighteenth-Century Scotland, an annotated checklist of pamphlets and documents printed in Scotland 1775–1800* (Rome, 1980).
Book of the Old Edinburgh Club (1908–).
Boswell, J.: *A Letter to the People of Scotland* (London, 1785).
: *Life of Johnson* (Oxford, 1924; first published, 1791).
Bourne, K.: *Britain and the Balance of Power in North America 1815–1908* (London, 1967).
Bowles, Vice-admiral: *Pamphlets on Naval Subjects* (London, 1854).
Brady, F.: *Boswell's Political Career* (New Haven and London, 1965).
: *James Boswell, the Later Years 1769–1795* (London, 1984).
& Pottle, F. (eds.): *Boswell in Search of a Wife* (London, 1957).
: 'So Fast to Ruin, the personal element in the collapse of Douglas, Heron & Co.' *Ayrshire Collections*, xi, 1973.
Brash, J. I.: *Papers on Scottish Electoral Politics 1832–1854* (Edinburgh, 1974).
Braxfield, Robert Macqueen, Lord: *Information for Archibald Earl of Eglinton* (Edinburgh, 1777).
Brewer, J.: *The Sinews of Power – war, money and the English state 1688–1783* (London, 1988).

Brickle, M. S.: 'The Administration and Management of Scotland 1707–1765'
    (University of Kansas, Ph.D. thesis, 1972).
    : 'The Pelhams versus Argyll – a struggle for mastery of Scotland 1747–1748', *Scottish Historical Review*, lxi, 1982.
Briggs, Sir J. H.: *Naval Administrations* (London, 1897).
Brims, J. D.: 'The Scottish Democratic Movement in the Age of the French Revolution'
    (University of Edinburgh, Ph.D. thesis, 1983).
    : 'The Scottish Jacobins, Scottish Nationalism and the British Union', in Mason (1987).
    : 'The Covenanting Tradition and Scottish Radicalism in the 1790s', in Brotherstone (1989).
    : 'From Reformers to "Jacobins" – the Scottish Association of the Friends of the People', in Devine (1990).
Brock, W. R.: *Lord Liverpool and Liberal Toryism* (Cambridge, 1941).
Brooke, J. & Namier, Sir L. (eds.): *The House of Commons 1754–1790* (London, 1964).
Brotherstone, T. (ed.): *Covenant, Charter and Party – traditions of revolt and protest in modern Scottish history* (Aberdeen, 1989).
Brougham, Henry, Lord: *Historical Sketches of Statesmen in the Time of George III* (London, 1839).
Brown, C. G.: 'Religion and Social Change', in Devine and Mitchison, R. (1988).
Brown, S. J.: *Thomas Chalmers and the Godly Commonwealth in Scotland* (Oxford, 1982).
Browning, O.: 'Adam Smith and Free Trade for Ireland', *English Historical Review*, i, 1886.
Bruce, J.: *Historical View of Plans for the Government of British India* (London, 1793).
    : *Review of the Events and Treaties which Established the Balance of Power in Europe and the Balance of Trade in Favour of Great Britain* (n.p., 1796).
    : *Report of the Events and Circumstances which produced the Union of the Kingdoms of England and Scotland* (n.p., 1799).
    : *Report on the Negotiation between the Honourable East India Company and the Public, respecting the renewal of the Company's exclusive privilege of trade, for 20 years* (London, 1811).
Brunton, F. & Haig, D.: *An Historical Account of the Senators of the College of Justice* (Edinburgh, 1836).
Bryant, G. J.: 'Scots in India in the Eighteenth Century', *Scottish Historical Review*, lxiv, 1985).
Bulloch, J. & Drummond, A. L.: *The Scottish Church 1688–1843* (Edinburgh, 1973).
Bumsted, J. M.: Sir James Montgomery and Prince Edward Ireland, *Acadiensis*, vii, 1978.
    : *The People's Clearance – Highland emigration to British North America 1770–1815* (Edinburgh, 1982).
Burke, E.: *Correspondence* (Cambridge & Chicago, 1963–8).
Burgess, R.: 'Perpetuities in Scots Law', *Stair Society*, xxxi, 1976.
Burleigh, J. H. S.: *Church History of Scotland* (Oxford, 1960).
Burne, A. H.: *The Noble Duke of York* (London, 1949).
Burton, J. H. (ed.): *The Autobiography of Dr Alexander Carlyle of Inveresk 1722–1805* (Edinburgh & London, 1860).
Butler, D. (ed.): *Coalitions in British Politics* (London, 1978).
Butler, I.: *The Eldest Brother – the Marquess Wellesley* (London, 1973).
Butt, J. & Ward, J. T. (eds.): *Scottish Themes – essays in honour of Prof. S. G. E. Lythe* (Edinburgh, 1976).
Butterfield, H.: *George III, Lord North and the People 1779–1780* (London, 1949).
Cage, R. A.: *The Scottish Poor Law 1745–1845* (Edinburgh, 1981).
    (ed.): *The Scots Abroad – labour, capital, enterprise 1750–1914* (London, 1985).
    & Checkland, E. O. A.: 'Thomas Chalmers and Urban Poverty', *Philosophical Journal*, xiii, 1976.

Campbell, A. B.: *The Lanarkshire Miners* (Edinburgh, 1979).
Campbell, A. J.: *Two Centuries of the Church of Scotland 1707–1929* (Paisley, 1930).
Campbell, R. H.: 'The Church and Scottish Social Reform', *Scottish Journal of Political Economy*, viii, 1961.
: 'The Economic History of Scotland in the Eighteenth Century', *Scottish Journal of Political Economy*, xi, 1964.
: 'The Scottish Improvers and the Course of Agrarian Change in the Eighteenth Century', in Cullen & Smout (1977).
: *Scotland since 1707 – the rise of an industrial society* (Edinburgh, 1985).
: 'The Landed Classes', in Devine & Mitchison (1988).
& Dow, J. B. A.: *Source Book of Scottish Economic and Social History* (Oxford, 1968).
& Skinner, A. S.: *Adam Smith* (London, 1982).
: *The Origins and Nature of the Scottish Enlightenment* (Edinburgh, 1982).
Campsie, A.: *The Clarinda Conspiracy* (Edinburgh, 1989).
Cannon, J.: *The Fox-North Coalition* (Cambridge, 1969).
Cant, R. G.: *The University of St Andrews* (Edinburgh & London, 1970).
Carlyle, A.: see Burton (1860).
Carnall, G. & Nicholson, C. (eds.): *The Impeachment of Warren Hastings* (Edinburgh, 1989).
Carter, J. J. & Pittock, J. H. (eds.): *Aberdeen and the Enlightenment* (Aberdeen, 1987).
Cater, J.: 'The Making of Principal Robertson in 1762', *Scottish Historical Review*, xlix, 1970.
Catford, E. F.: *Edinburgh, the story of a city* (Edinburgh, 1975).
Chamberlain, M. E.: *Lord Aberdeen, a political biography* (London, 1983).
Chalmers, G.: *Caledonia* (Paisley, 1887).
Chalmers, T.: 'Statement in regard to the Pauperism in Glasgow', *Edinburgh Review*, xli, 1824–5.
Chambers, R.: *Biographical Dictionary of Eminent Scotsmen* (London, 1875).
(ed.): *The Life and Works of Robert Burns* (Edinburgh & London, 1896).
Charles-Roux, F.: *Les Origines de l'Expédition d'Egypte* (Paris, 1910).
Cheape, H. & Grant, I. F.: *Periods in Highland History* (London, 1987).
Checkland, S. G.: *Scottish Banking, a history 1695–1973* (Glasgow & London, 1975).
Cheyne, A. C.: *The Practical and the Pious, essays on Thomas Chalmers* (Edinburgh, 1985).
Chitnis, A.: *The Scottish Enlightenment* (London, 1976).
: *The Scottish Enlightenment and Early Victorian English Society* (London, 1986a).
: 'Agricultural Improvement, Political Management and Civic Virtue in Enlightened Scotland – an historiographical critique', *Studies on Voltaire and the Eighteenth Century*, cclxv, 1986.
: 'The Eighteenth-century Scottish Intellectual Inquiry – context and continuities versus civic virtue', in Carter & Pittock (1987).
Christie, I.: *The End of North's Ministry* (London, 1958).
: *Wilkes, Wyvill and Reform* (London, 1962).
Clark, A. M.: *Sir Walter Scott, the Formative Years* (Edinburgh & London, 1969).
Clark, I. D. L.: 'The Leslie Controversy 1805', *Records of the Scottish Church History Society*, xiv, 1960–3.
: 'Moderatism and the Moderate Party in the Church of Scotland' (Cambridge, Ph.D. thesis, 1963).
: 'From Protest to Reaction – the Moderate Regime in the Church of Scotland 1752–1805', in Mitchison & Phillipson (1970).
Cleveland, C. L. W. Powlett, Duchess of: *Life and Letters of Lady Hester Stanhope* (London, 1914).
Cobban, A.: *Aspects of the French Revolution* (London, 1971).
[Cockburn, Henry, Lord]: 'The Office of Lord Advocate of Scotland', *Edinburgh Review*, xxxix, 1823–4.

Cockburn, Henry, Lord: *Life of Lord Jeffrey* (Edinburgh, 1852).
: *Memorials of his Time* (Edinburgh 1856; 1910).
: *Journal* (Edinburgh, 1874a).
: *Letters chiefly connected with the Affairs of Scotland 1818–1852* (London, 1874b).
: *An Examination of the Trials for Sedition in Scotland* (Edinburgh, 1888).
Cockburn, H. A.: Edinburgh Clubs, *Book of the Old Edinburgh Club*, iii, 1910.
: *Some Letters of Lord Cockburn, with passages omitted from the Memorials of his Time* (Edinburgh, 1932).
& Cockburn, Sir R.: *Records of the Cockburn Family* (Edinburgh & London, 1913).
Colchester, Lord (ed.): *A Political Diary 1828–30 by Edward Law, Lord Ellenborough* (London, 1881).
Coleridge, E. H.: *Life of Thomas Coutts* (London, 1920).
Colley, L.: 'Whose Nation? Class and national consciousness in Britain 1750–1830', *Past and Present*, cxiii, 1986.
: 'Radical Patriotism in Eighteenth-century England', in Samuel (1989).
Colston, J.: *The Incorporated Trades of Edinburgh* (Edinburgh, 1891).
Connell, A.: *A Treatise on the Election Laws in Scotland* (Edinburgh & London, 1827).
Cook, G.: *Life of the late George Hill* (Edinburgh, 1820).
Cookson, J. E.: *Lord Liverpool's Administration – the crucial years 1815–1822* (Edinburgh & London, 1975).
Cooney, J.: *Scotland and the Papacy* (Edinburgh, 1983).
Cooper of Culross, Lord: 'The Central Courts after 1532', in *Stair Society* (1958).
Cope, S. R.: 'The History of Boyd, Benfield & Co, a study in merchant banking in the last decade of the eighteenth century' (University of London, Ph.D. thesis, 1947).
Corbett, J. S. (ed.): *Private Papers of George, 2nd Earl Spencer 1794–1801* (Navy Records Office, 1913).
Cosh, M.: 'The Adam Family and Arniston', *Architectural History*, xxvii, 1984.
Couper, W. J.: *The Edinburgh Periodical Press* (Stirling, 1908).
Cowan, H. I.: *British Emigration to North America* (Toronto, 1961).
Cowan, R. M. W.: *The Newspaper in Scotland* (Glasgow, 1946).
Craig, M. E.: *The Scottish Periodical Press 1750–1789* (Edinburgh & London, 1931).
Craik, Sir H.: *A Century of Scottish History* (Edinburgh & London, 1901).
Craven, J. W.: 'Andrew Thomson 1779–1831, leader of the evangelical revival in Scotland' (University of Edinburgh, Ph.D. thesis, 1956).
Croker, J. W.: *Two Letters on Scottish Affairs* (Shannon, 1972).
Crouse, N. M.: *The Search for the North West Passage* (New York, 1934).
Crowther, M. A.: 'Poverty, Health and Welfare', in Fraser & Morris (1990).
Cullen, L. M. & Smout, T. C.: *Comparative Aspects of Scottish and Irish Economic History 1600–1900* (London, 1977).
Cunningham, H.: 'The Language of Patriotism', in Samuel (1989).
Daiches, D.: *James Boswell and his World* (London, 1976).
: *Scotland and the Union* (London, 1977).
(ed.): *A Companion to Scottish Culture* (Edinburgh, 1981).
: *The Scottish Enlightenment*, Saltire Society pamphlet, new series, viii, 1986.
Dalzel, A.: 'An Account of the Author's Life and Character', in Drysdale (1793).
Danzinger, M. K.: '"Horrible Anarchy" – James Boswell's View of the French Revolution', *Studies in Scottish Literature*, xxiii, 1988.
Darrach, J.: 'The Catholic Population of Scotland since the Year 1680', *Innes Review*, iv, 1953.
Davie, G. E.: *The Democratic Intellect* (Edinburgh, 1961).
: *The Scottish Enlightenment*, Historical Association, general series, no. 99, 1981.
Davies, G. & Ritchie, L. A.: 'Dr Chalmers and the University of Glasgow', *Records of the Scottish Church History Society*, xx, 1980.

De, B.: 'A Note on the Melville Manuscripts in the National Library of Scotland', *The Indian Archives*, x, 1956.

: 'Henry Dundas and the Government of India, a study in constitutional ideas' (University of Oxford, Ph.D. thesis, 1961).

de la Torre, L.: *The Heir of Douglas* (London, 1953).

Devine, T. M.: 'Glasgow Colonial Merchants and Land, 1770–1815', in Ward & Wilson (1971).

: *The Tobacco Lords* (Edinburgh, 1975).

(ed.): *Lairds and Improvement in the Scotland of the Enlightenment* (Glasgow, 1978).

(ed.): *Conflict and Stability in Scottish Society* (Edinburgh, 1990).

: 'The Failure of Radical Reform in Scotland in the Late Eighteenth Century – the social and economic context', in Devine (1990).

& Mitchison, R. (eds.): *People and Society in Scotland, i, 1760–1830* (Edinburgh, 1988).

Dewar Gibb, A.: *Law from over the Border* (Edinburgh, 1950).

Dicey, A. V. & Rait, R.: *Thoughts on the Union between England and Scotland* (London, 1920).

Dickinson, H. T.: *Liberty and Property – political ideology in eighteenth-century Britain* (London, 1977).

Dickson, T.: *Scottish Capitalism – class, state and nation from before the Union to the present* (London, 1980).

Ditchfield, G. M.: 'The Scottish Campaign against the Test Act 1790–1791', *Historical Journal*, xxiii, 1980.

: 'The Scottish Representative Peers and Party Politics 1787–1793', *Scottish Historical Review*, lx, 1981, and in Jones & Jones (1986).

Dodwell, H. A. (ed.): *British India 1497–1858*, vol. iv, *Cambridge History of the British Empire* (Cambridge, 1929).

Donaldson, G.: 'Scottish Devolution, the historical background', in Wolfe (1969).

Donovan, R. K.: 'Voices of Distrust – the expression of anti-Catholic feeling in Scotland 1778–1781', *Innes Review*, xxx, 1979.

: 'Sir John Dalrymple and the Origins of Roman Catholic Relief 1775–1778', *Recusant History*, xvii, 1984.

: *No Popery and Radicalism – opposition to Roman Catholic relief in Scotland 1778–1782* (New York & London, 1987).

: 'The Popular Party of the Church of Scotland and the American Revolution', in Sher & Smitten (1990).

Doubleday, H. A. & Howard de Walden, Lord (eds.): *Complete Peerage* (London, 1932).

Drysdale, J.: *Sermons* (Edinburgh, 1793).

Duckham, B. F.: 'Life and Labour in a Scottish Colliery', *Scottish Historical Review*, xlvii, 1968.

: *A History of the Scottish Coal Industry* (Newton Abbot, 1970).

: 'English Influences in Scottish Coal', in Butt & Ward (1976).

Duffy, M.: *Soldiers, Sugar and Seapower – the British expeditions to the West Indies and the war against revolutionary France* (Oxford, 1987).

Dunbabin, J. P.: *Rural Discontent in Nineteenth-Century Britain* (London, 1974).

[Dundas, J.?]: *A Letter to a L-d of the S-ess-n* (London, 1710).

Dunfermline, Abercromby, J., Lord: *Lieut-Gen. Sir Ralph Abercromby, a memoir* (Edinburgh, 1861).

Dunlop, J.: *The British Fisheries Society 1786–1893* (Edinburgh, 1978).

Durie, A. J.: 'Lairds, Improvement, Banking and Industry in Eighteenth-Century Scotland', in Devine (1978).

Dwyer, J.: *Virtuous Discourse – sensibility and community in late eighteenth-century Scotland* (Edinburgh, 1987).

Dwyer, J. & Murdoch, A.: 'Paradigms and Politics – manners, morals and the rise of

Henry Dundas 1770–1784', in Dwyer, Mason & Murdoch (1982).

: 'Henry Dundas revisited but not revised', *Studies on Voltaire and the Eighteenth Century*, cclvi, 1988.

Dwyer, J., Mason, R. A. & Murdoch, A.: *New Perspectives on the Politics and Culture of Early Modern Scotland* (Edinburgh, 1982).

Edwards, O. D.: *Burke and Hare* (Edinburgh, 1980).

Ehrman, J.: *The Younger Pitt – the years of acclaim* (London, 1969).

: *The Younger Pitt – the reluctant transition* (London, 1983).

Elliot, G. F. S.: *The Border Elliots and the Family of Minto* (Edinburgh, 1897).

Elliot, M.: *Partners in Revolution* (New Haven & London, 1982).

Embree, A. T.: *Charles Grant and British Rule in India* (London, 1962).

Emerson, R. L.: 'The Social Composition of Enlightened Scotland – the Select Society of Edinburgh 1754–1764', *Studies on Voltaire and the Eighteenth Century*, cxiv, 1973.

: 'Lord Bute and the Scottish universities 1760–1792', in Schweizer (1988).

Encyclopaedia Canadiana (Toronto, 1977).

Eyre-Todd, G.: *History of Glasgow* (Glasgow, 1934).

Fagerstrom, D. I.: 'The American Revolutionary Movement in Scottish Opinion 1763–1783' (University of Edinburgh, Ph.D. thesis, 1951).

: 'Scottish Opinion and the American Revolution', *William and Mary Quarterly*, xi, 1954.

Farington, J.: *The Farington Diary* (London, 1923).

Fay, C. R.: *Adam Smith and the Scotland of his Day* (Cambridge, 1956).

Feiling, K.: *The Second Tory Party* (London 1938).

Ferguson, A.: *The History of the Proceedings in the Case of Margaret, commonly called Peg, only lawful sister to John Bull* (London, 1761).

Ferguson, T.: *The Dawn of Scottish Social Welfare* (London, 1948).

Ferguson, W.: 'Electoral Law and Procedure in Eighteenth and Early Nineteenth Century Scotland' (University of Glasgow, Ph.D. thesis, 1957).

: 'Dingwall Burgh Politics and the Parliamentary Franchise in the Eighteenth Century', *Scottish Historical Review*, xxxviii, 1959.

: 'The Reform Act (Scotland) of 1832 – intention and effect', *Scottish Historical Review*, xlv, 1966.

: *Scotland, 1689 to the present* (Edinburgh & London, 1968).

: 'The Electoral System in the Scottish Counties before 1832', in *Stair Society, miscellany* ii, 1984.

Fergusson, A.: *The Honourable Henry Erskine* (Edinburgh & London, 1882).

Fergusson, Sir J.: *Letters of George Dempster to Sir Adam Fergusson 1756–1813* (London, 1934).

: '"Making Interest" in Scottish County Elections', *Scottish Historical Review*, xxvi, 1947.

: *The Sixteen Peers of Scotland* (Oxford, 1960).

Fetter, F. W.: 'The Economic Articles in Blackwood's Edinburgh Magazine', *Scottish Journal of Political Economy*, vii, 1960.

Finlayson, G. B. A. M.: 'A Note on the Employment of the Military in Haddington 1831', *Transactions of the East Lothian Antiquarian Society*, x, 1966.

Finlayson, I.: *The Moth and the Candle, a life of James Boswell* (London, 1984).

Fitzmaurice, Lord E.: *Life of William Earl of Shelburne* (London, 1876).

Fleming, J.: *Robert Adam and his Circle* (London, 1962).

Fletcher, E.: *An Inquiry into the Principles of Ecclesiastical Patronage and Presentation* (Edinburgh, 1783).

Fontana, B.: *Rethinking the politics of commercial society – the Edinburgh Review 1802–1832* (Cambridge, 1986).

Foord, A. S.: *His Majesty's Opposition 1714–1830* (Oxford, 1964).

Forbes, L. L.: *Dundas of Arniston 1570–1880* (n.p., n.d.).

Forbes, Sir W.: *Memoirs of a Banking House* (Edinburgh & London, 1860).

Forbes Leith, W.: *Memoirs of Scottish Catholics during the Seventeenth Century and Eighteenth Century* (London, 1909).

Forman, S.: 'The Dundases of Arniston', *Scottish Field*, ci, 1953.

Forrest, Sir G.: *Selections from the State Papers of the Governors-general of India – Lord Cornwallis* (Oxford, 1926).

Fortescue, Sir J.: *A History of the British Army* (London, 1906).

: *British Statesmen and the Great War 1793–1814* (Oxford, 1911).

(ed.):*A Selection from the Papers of King George III 1781–1783* (Cambridge, 1927).

(ed.): *The Correspondence of King George III 1760–1783* (London, 1928).

Fraser, A. G.: *The Building of Old College – Adam, Playfair and the University of Edinburgh* (Edinburgh, 1989).

Frazer, W.: *Memorials of the Montgomeries* (Edinburgh, 1859).

Fraser, W. H.: 'A Note on the Scottish Weavers' Association 1808–1813', *Scottish Labour History Society Journal*, xx, 1985.

: *Conflict and Class – Scottish Workers 1700–1838* (Edinburgh, 1988).

& Morris, R. J.: *People and Society in Scotland, ii, 1830–1914* (Edinburgh, 1990).

Fritz, P. & Williams, D.: *City and Society in the Eighteenth Century* (Toronto, 1973).

Fry, H. T.: *Alexander Dalrymple (1737–1808) and the Expansion of British Trade* (London, 1970).

Fry, M. R. G.: *Patronage and Principle, a political history of modern Scotland* (Aberdeen, 1987).

: 'Dirty Work in St Andrew Square – Henry and Lawrence Dundas and the control of the Royal Bank of Scotland', *Royal Bank of Scotland Review*, clix, 1988.

Fulford, R. & Strachey, L. (eds.): *The Grenville Memoirs 1814–1860* (London, 1938).

Furber, H.: *Henry Dundas, 1st Viscount Melville 1742–1811* (London, 1931).

(ed.): *An Indian Governor-generalship 1793–1798* (Cambridge, Mass., 1933).

: 'The East India Directors in 1784', *Journal of Modern History*, v, 1933.

: *John Company at Work* (Cambridge, 1948).

Fyfe, J. G. (ed.): *Scottish Diaries and Memoirs 1746–1843* (Stirling, 1942).

Gallin, R. G.: 'Scottish Radicalism 1792–1794' (Columbia University, Ph.D. thesis, 1979).

Gash, N.: *Politics in the Age of Peel* (London, 1953).

: *Mr Secretary Peel* (London, 1961).

Gayer, A., D., Rostow, W. W. & Schwartz, A. J.: *The Growth and Fluctuation of the British Economy* (Hassocks, 1975).

Geggus, D. P.: *Slavery, War and Revolution* (Oxford, 1982).

Gibson, J. S.: *Deacon Brodie* (Edinburgh, 1977).

: *The Thistle and the Crown* (Edinburgh, 1985).

Gifford, D. (ed.): *The History of Scottish Literature, iii, the nineteenth century* (Aberdeen, 1987).

Gifford, J.: *A History of the Political Life of the Rt Hon. William Pitt* (London, 1809).

Gifford, J.: *William Adam 1689–1748* (Edinburgh, 1989).

Ginter, D. E.: *Whig Organisation in the General Election of 1790 – selections from the Blair Adam Papers* (Berkeley & Los Angeles, 1967).

Glover, R.: *Peninsular Preparation* (Cambridge, 1963).

Gordon, J. F. S.: *Journal and Appendix to Scotichronicon and Monasticon* (Glasgow, 1867).

Gordon, W. M.: 'Stair's Use of Roman Law', in Harding (1980).

Gourlay, J. (ed.): *The Provosts of Glasgow* (Glasgow, 1942).

Gourlay, R.: *A Specific Plan for Organising the People* (London, 1809).

The Village System (Bath, 1817).

Graham, G. S.: *The Politics of Naval Supremacy* (Cambridge, 1965).

Graham, I. C. C.: *Colonists from Scotland* (Ithaca, NY, 1956).

Grant, Lady E.: *Memoirs of a Highland Lady* (Edinburgh, 1988).

Grant, I. R. & Withrington, D. J. (eds.): *The Statistical Account of Scotland, ii. The Lothians* (Wakefield, 1975).

Grant, J.: *Random Recollections of the House of Lords* (London, 1836).

Grant, J.: *Old and New Edinburgh* (London, 1883).

Grant, R.: *The Expediency Maintained of Continuing the System by which the Trade and Government of India are now Regulated* (London, 1813).

Granville, Castalia, Countess (ed.): *Lord George Leveson Gower, private correspondence 1781–1821* (London, 1916).

Gray, J. L.: 'The Law of Combination in Scotland', *Economica*, viii, 1928.

Greig, J. Y. T.(ed.): *The Letters of David Hume* (Oxford, 1932).

Grierson, H. J. C.(ed.): *The Letters of Sir Walter Scott* (London, 1932).

: *Sir Walter Scott, Bart.* (London, 1938).

Grimble, I.: *Sea Wolf – the life of Admiral Cochrane* (London, 1978).

Gurwood, Col.: *The Dispatches of the Duke of Wellington* (London, 1844).

Halévy, E.: *Histoire du Peuple Anglais au XIXe Siècle* (Paris, 1912).

Hamilton, H.: 'The Founding of Glasgow Chamber of Commerce 1883', *Scottish Journal of Political Economy*, i, 1954.

: 'The Failure of the Ayr Bank 1772', *Economic History Review*, viii, 1955–6.

: *An Economic History of Scotland in the Eighteenth Century* (Oxford, 1963).

Hamilton, Sir R. V. (ed.): *Letters and Papers of Sir Thomas Byam Martin* (n.p., 1903).

Hamilton, Sir W.: *Collected Works of Dugald Stewart* (Edinburgh, 1854–60).

Hamilton, W. B.: 'Some Letters of George III', *South Atlantic Quarterly*, lxviii, 1969.

Hanham, H.: *The Scottish Political Tradition* (Edinburgh, 1964).

: *Scottish Nationalism* (London, 1969).

Hanna, W.: *Memoirs of Thomas Chalmers* (Edinburgh & London, 1851).

Harcourt, L. V. (ed.): *Diaries and Correspondence of the Rt Hon. George Rose* (London, 1860).

Harding, A. (ed.): *Law-Making and Law-Makers in British History* (London, 1980).

Harlow, V. T.: *The Founding of the Second British Empire* (London, 1952).

& Madden, F.: *British Colonial Developments 1774–1834* (Oxford, 1953).

Harris, P.: *Life in a Scottish Country House* (Whittingehame, 1989).

Harris, W.: *The Radical Party in Parliament* (London, 1885).

Hayton, D. & Szechi, D.: 'John Bull's Other Kingdoms – the English government of Scotland and Ireland', in Jones (1987).

Heron, A.: *The Rise and Progress of the Company of Merchants of the City of Edinburgh* (Edinburgh, 1903).

Hibbert, C.: *George IV, Regent and King* (London, 1973).

Hilton, B.: *Corn, Cash, Commerce – the economic policies of the Tory Governments 1815–1830* (Oxford, 1977).

Historical Manuscripts Commission: iii, *Robert Dundas of Arniston MSS* (London, 1872).

: x, *Drummond Moray MSS* (London, 1885).

: x, *Marquess of Abergavenny MSS* (London, 1887).

: xiii, *J. B. Fortescue MSS* (London, 1892).

: xiv, *Duke of Rutland MSS* (London, 1894).

: xiv, *Graham of Fintry MSS* (London, 1909).

: xv, *Earl of Carlisle MSS* (London, 1897).

: xv, *J. J. Hope Johnstone of Annandale MSS* (London, 1897).

: xli, *Mar and Kellie MSS* (London, 1904).

: xlv, *C. Wykeham-Martin MSS* (London, 1909).

: lxxii, *Laing MSS* (London, 1925).

: lxxviii, *R. R. Harding MSS* (London, 1934).

Hobsbawm, E. J. 'Scottish Reformers and Capitalist Agriculture' in Hobsbawn et al.
    (1980).
    et al. (eds.): Peasants in History (Oxford, 1980).
Holland, Fox, H., Lord: Memoirs of the Whig Party (London, 1852).
    : Further Memoirs of the Whig Party (London, 1905).
Holland Rose, J. (ed.): Select Despatches from the British Foreign Office Archives relating to
    the Formation of the Third Coalition against France (London, 1904).
    : William Pitt and National Revival (London, 1911a).
    : William Pitt and the Great War (London, 1911b).
Holt, P. & Thomis, M. I.: Threats of Revolution in Britain 1789–1848 (London, 1977).
Hope, C.: A Sketch of the Life of George Hope (Edinburgh, 1879).
Horn, B. L. H. (ed.): Letters of John Ramsay of Ochtertyre 1799–1812 (Edinburgh, 1966).
Horn, D. B.: 'George IV and Highland Dress', Scottish Historical Review, xlvii, 1968.
Horner, L. (ed.): Memoirs and Correspondence of Francis Horner, MP (London, 1843).
Hoskins, H. L.: British Routes to India (New York & London, 1928).
Houston, R. A. & Whyte, I. D.: Scottish Society 1500–1800 (Cambridge, 1989).
Hughes, E.: 'The Scottish Reform Movement and Charles Grey 1792–1794; some fresh
    correspondence', Scottish Historical Review, xxxv, 1956.
Hughes, M. & Scott, J.: The Anatomy of Scottish Capital (London, 1980).
Hume Brown, P.: History of Scotland to the Present Time (Cambridge, 1911).
Humes, W. M. & Paterson, H. M. (eds.): Scottish Culture and Scottish Education
    (Edinburgh, 1983).
Hunter, J.: The Making of the Crofting Community (Edinburgh, 1976).
Hutchinson, I. G. C.: A Political History of Scotland 1832–1924 (Edinburgh, 1986).
Hutton, J. (ed.): Selections from the Letters and Correspondence of Sir James Bland Burges
    (London, 1885).
Ilchester, Earl of (ed.): The Journal of Elizabeth, Lady Holland 1791–1811 (London,
    1908).
    : Chronicles of Holland House (London, 1937).
    (ed.): Elizabeth, Lady Holland to her Son (London, 1946).
Ingham, K.: Reformers in India 1793–1833 (Cambridge, 1956).
Ingram, C.: Two Views of British India (Bath, 1970).
Iremonger, L.: Lord Aberdeen (London, 1978).
Jackson, G.: 'Government Bounties and the Establishment of the Scottish Whaling
    Trade', in Butt & Ward (1976).
James, W.: The Naval History of Great Britain (London, 1859).
Jenning, L. J. (ed.): The Correspondence and Diaries of John Wilson Croker (London,
    1885).
Jewell, B. F.: 'The Legislation relating to Scotland after the '45' (University of North
    Carolina, Chapel Hill, Ph.D. thesis, 1975).
Johnson, D.: Developments in the Roman Catholic Church in Scotland 1789–1829
    (Edinburgh, 1983).
    : 'David Downie – a reappraisal', Innes Review, xxxi, 1980.
Johnson, E.: Sir Walter Scott, the Great Unknown (London, 1970).
Jones, C. (ed.): Party and Management in Parliament 1660–1784 (Leicester, 1984).
    (ed): Britain in the First Age of Party (London & Roncevert, 1987).
    : & Jones, D. L. (eds.): Peers, Politics and Power (London, 1986).
Kames, Home, H., Lord: Sketches of the History of Man (Edinburgh, 1774).
Kapstein, E. B.: 'The Improvement of the West Highlands Fisheries 1785–1800',
    Mariner's Mirror, lxvi, 1980.
Kay, J.: Original Portraits (Edinburgh, 1877).
Keith, T.: 'Municipal Elections in the Royal Burghs of Scotland, from the Union to the
    passage of the Scottish Burgh Reform Bill in 1833', Scottish Historical Review, xiii, 1916.

Kelly, P.: 'Constituents' Instructions to Members of Parliament in the Eighteenth Century', in Jones, (1984).

Kennedy, P. M.: *The Rise and Fall of British Naval Mastery* (London, 1976).

Kettler, D.: *The Social and Political Thought of Adam Ferguson* (Ohio State University, 1965).

Kinsley, J. (ed.): *Robert Burns, poems and songs* (Oxford, 1968).

Kitson Clark, G.: *Peel and the Conservative Party* (London, 1964).

Klibansky, R. & Mossner, E. C. (eds.): *New Letters of David Hume* (Oxford, 1964).

Knox, J.: *View of the British Empire, more especially Scotland, with some Proposals for the Improvement of that Country, the extension of its Fisheries and the relief of its people* (Edinburgh 1784).

Kumar, D. (ed.): *Cambridge Economic History of India*, ii, *1757–1790* (Cambridge, 1983).

Large, D.: 'The Decline of "The Party of the Crown" and the Rise of Parties in the House of Lords 1783–1837', *English Historical Review*, lxxviii, 1963.

    : 'The Decline of the Party of the Crown and the Rise of Parties in the House of Lords 1783–1837', in Jones & Jones (1986).

Laughton, Sir J. K. (ed.): *Letters and Papers of Charles, Lord Barham* (London, 1907).

Laurie, J.: 'Reminiscences of a Town Clerk', *Book of the Old Edinburgh Club*, xiv, 1925.

Lawson, J. P.: *History of the Scottish Episcopal Church from the Revolution to the Present Time* (Edinburgh, 1843).

Lee, F. & Stephen, E. (eds): *Dictionary of National Biography* (London, 1908).

Lehmann, W. C.: *Henry Home, Lord Kames and the Scottish Enlightenment* (The Hague, 1971).

Lenman, B.: *An Economic History of Modern Scotland* (London, 1977).

    : *Integration, Enlightenment and Industrialisation – Scotland 1746–1832* (London, 1981).

Levack, B. P.: 'English Law, Scots Law and the Union', in Harding (1980).

Lever, T.: 'Lord Braxfield', *History Today*, xxiii, 1973.

Levitt, I. & Smout, T. C.: *The State of the Scottish Working Class in 1843* (Edinburgh, 1979).

Lewis, M.: *The Navy of Britain* (London, 1948).

Leyland, J. (ed.): *Dispatches and Letters relating to the Blockade of Brest 1803–1805* (Navy Records Society, 1899).

Liebermann, D.: *The Province of Legislation Determined, legal theory in eighteenth-century Britain* (Cambridge, 1989).

Lindsay, J.: *The Canals of Scotland* (Newton Abbot, 1968).

Lloyd, . (ed.): *The Keith Papers* (London, 1950).

Loch, G.: *The Family of Loch* (Edinburgh, 1934).

Lockhart, J. G.: *Peter's Letters to his Kinsfolk* (Edinburgh, 1819).

    :*Memoirs of the Life of Sir Walter Scott* (Edinburgh, 1837).

    : *Life of Sir Walter Scott* (Edinburgh, 1902).

Logue, K. J.: 'The Tranent Militia Riot of 1797', *Transactions of the East Lothian Antiquarian Society*, xiv, 1974.

    : *Popular Disturbances in Scotland 1780–1815* (Edinburgh, 1979).

Londonderry, Charles Vane, Marquis of: *Letters and Despatches of Viscount Castelreagh* (London, 1851).

Lovat-Fraser, J. A.: 'A Famous Lord Advocate', *Juridical Review*, xiv, 1902.

    : *Henry Dundas, Viscount Melville* (Cambridge, 1916).

Lowe, W. C.: 'Bishops and Representative Peers in the House of Lords 1760–1775', *Journal of British Studies*, xviii, 1978.

Lustig, I. S.: 'The Manuscript as Biography – Boswell's Letter to the People of Scotland 1785', *Papers of the Bibliographical Society of America*, lxviii, 1974.

    & Pottle, F. A. (eds.): *Boswell, the applause of the jury* (London, 1981).

    : *Boswell, the English Experiment* (London, 1986).

Macaulay, J.: *The Classical Country House in Scotland 1660–1800* (London, 1987).
McCaffrey, J. F.: 'Thomas Chalmers and Social Change', *Scottish Historical Review*, lx, 1981.
McCahill, M. W.: 'The Scottish Peerage and the House of Lords in the Late Eighteenth
　Century', *Scottish Historical Review*, li, 1972.
　: *Order and Equipoise, the Peerage and the House of Lords 1783–1806* (London, 1978).
　: 'Peerage Creations and the Changing Character of the British Nobility 1750–1830',
　English Historical Review, xcvi, 1981.
MacCallum, N.: *A Small Country, Scotland 1700–1830* (Edinburgh, 1983).
McCleary, J. W.: 'Anglo-French Naval Rivalry' (Johns Hopkins University, Ph.D. thesis,
　1947).
[MacCulloch, J. R]: 'Draft of a proposed Bill for repealing several Acts relating to
　Combinations of Workmen', *Edinburgh Review*, xxxix, 1823–4.
Macdonald, R.: 'The Highland District in 1764', *Innes Review*, xv, 1964.
Macdougall, N.: *Church, Politics and Society – Scotland 1408–1929* (Edinburgh, 1983).
Macgrugar, T.: *Letters of Zeno* (Edinburgh, 1783).
Machin, G. I. T.: 'The Duke of Wellington and Catholic Emancipation', *Journal of
　Ecclesiastical History*, xiv, 1963.
Macinnes, A. I.: 'Scottish Gaeldom – the first phase of clearance', in Devine &
　Mitchison (1988).
Maciver, I. F.: 'The General Assembly of the Church, the State and Society in Scotland
　1815–1843' (University of Edinburgh, M.Litt. thesis, 1977).
　: 'Cockburn and the Church', in Bell (1979).
　: 'The Evangelical Party and the Eldership in General Assemblies 1820–1843', *Records
　of the Scottish Church Historical Society*, xx, 1980a.
　: '"I did not seek … but was sought after" – the election of Thomas Chalmers to the
　chair of divinity at Edinburgh University', October 1827, *Records of the Scottish Church
　History Society*, xx, 1980b.
Mackay, M.: *Memoir of James Ewing* (Glasgow, 1866).
Mackenzie, A. M.: *Scotland in Modern Times* (Edinburgh & London, 1941).
Mackesy, P.: *Statesmen at War – the strategy of overthrow 1798–1799* (London, 1974).
　:*War without Victory – the downfall of Pitt* (Oxford, 1984).
Mackie, J. D. (ed.): 'Thomas Thomson's Memorial on Old Extent', *Stair Society*, x, 1946.
　: *A History of Scotland* (Harmondsworth, 1964).
Mackintosh, R.: *Life of Sir James Mackintosh* (London, 1835).
Maclaurin, J.: *Information for Mungo Campbell* (Edinburgh, 1777).
McWilliam, C.: *The Buildings of Scotland – Lothian except Edinburgh* (Harmondsworth,
　1978).
Mahon, Lord: *Correspondence connected with Mr Pitt's Return to Office in 1804* (London,
　1852).
Malcolm, C. A.: 'The Solicitor General for Scotland', *Juridical Review*, 1942.
　: *The Bank of Scotland 1695–1945* (Edinburgh, 1945).
　: *The History of the British Linen Bank* (Edinburgh, 1950).
Malcomson, A. P. W.: *John Foster, the politics of Anglo-Irish Ascendancy* (Oxford, 1978).
Marcus, G. J.: *A Naval History of England* (London, 1971).
Marshall, P. J.: *Problems of Empire – Britain and India 1757–1813* (London, 1968).
　: *East Indian Fortunes* (Oxford, 1976).
Marshman, J. C.: *History of India* (London, 1867).
Martin, M. (ed.): *The Despatches, Memoirs and Correspondence of the Marquis Wellesley*
　(London, 1837).
Marwick, W. H.: 'Early Trade Unionism in Scotland', *Economic History Review*, v, 1934–5.
　: 'The Beginnings of the Scottish Working Class Movement in the Nineteenth
　Century', *International Review of Social History*, iii, 1938.
　: *Labour in Scotland* (Glasgow, 1948).
　: *Scotland in Modern Times* (London, 1964).

: *A Short History of Labour in Scotland* (Edinburgh & London, 1967).

Mason, R. A. (ed.): *Scotland and England 1280–1815* (Edinburgh, 1987).

Masson, D.: *Edinburgh Sketches and Memories* (Edinburgh, 1892).

Masterson, D. M. (ed.): *Naval History, the sixth symposium of the US Naval Academy* (Wilmington, Del., 1986).

Mather, F. C.: 'Church, Parliament and Penal Laws – some Anglo-Scottish interactions in the eighteenth century', *English Historical Review*, xcii, 1977.

Matheson, D.: *The Life of Henry Dundas, 1st Viscount Melville* (London, 1933).

Mathieson, W. L.: *The Awakening of Scotland* (Glasgow, 1910).
 Church and Reform in Scotland 1797–1843 (Glasgow, 1916).

Maxwell, Sir H.: *The Creevey Papers* (London, 1903).

Meikle, H. W.: 'The King's Birthday Riot in Edinburgh, June 1792', *Scottish Historical Review*, vii, 1910.
 : *Scotland and the French Revolution* (Glasgow, 1912).

Melville, Dundas, H., Viscount: *Disputatio Juridica – de fidejussoribus et mandatoribus et haeredibus tutorum et curatorum* (Edinburgh, 1763).
 : *A Letter from the Rt Hon. Lord Viscount Melville relative to the Management of the Civil Service of the Navy* (London, 1810).
 : *Letters from the Rt Hon. Henry Dundas to the Chairman of the Court of Directors of the East India Company upon an Open Trade in India* (London, 1813).

Melville, L. (ed.): *The Huskisson Papers* (London, 1931).

Mill, J.: *History of British India* (London, 1840).

Miller, K.: *Cockburn's Millennium* (London, 1975).

Mingay, G. E. (ed.): *The Agrarian History of England and Wales, vi, 1750–1850* (Cambridge, 1989).

Minto, Countess of (ed.): *Life and Letters of Sir Gilbert Elliot, First Earl of Minto, from 1751 to 1806* (London, 1874).
 : *Lord Minto in India* (London, 1880).

Mirror, The (Edinburgh, 1781).

Misra, B. B.: *The Central Administration of the East India Company 1773–1834* (London, 1932).

Mitchison, R.: *Agricultural Sir John – the life of Sir John Sinclair of Ulbster* (London, 1962).
 : 'The Making of the Old Scottish Poor Law', *Past and Present*, xliii, 1974.
 : 'The Creation of the Disablement Rule in the Scottish Poor Law', in Smout (1979).
 : (ed.) *The Roots of Nationalism* (Edinburgh, 1980).
 : 'Nineteenth-century Scottish Nationalism, the cultural background', in Mitchison (1980).
 : *History of Scotland* (London, 1982).
 : *Lordship and Patronage, Scotland 1603–1745* (London, 1983).
 : 'The Poor Law', in Devine & Mitchison (1988).
 : 'North and South – the development of the gulf in Poor Law practice', in Houston & Whyte (1989).
 & Phillipson, N. (eds.): *Scotland in the Age of Improvement* (Edinburgh, 1970).

Moffat, C. G.: 'Scotland and the Catholic Emancipation Question' (University of Tennessee, Ph.D. thesis, 1974).

Monboddo, James Burnet, Lord: *Ancient Metaphysics* (Edinburgh, 1797).

Moncreiff Wellwood, Sir H.: *Account of the Life and Writings of John Erskine* (Edinburgh, 1818).

Moorhouse, G.: *India Britannica* (London, 1983).

Morrell, J. B.: 'Professors Robison and Playfair and the Theophobia Gallica – natural philosophy, religion and politics in Edinburgh 1789–1805', *Notes and Records of the Royal Society of London*, xxvi, 1971.
 : 'The Leslie Affair – careers, kirk and politics in Edinburgh in 1805', *Scottish Historical Review*, liv, 1975.

Mossner, E. C.: *Life of David Hume* (Oxford, 1980).
   & Ross, I.: *Correspondence of Adam Smith* (Oxford, 1977).
Mudie, R.: *The Modern Athens* (London, 1825).
Muirhead, I. A.: 'Catholic Emancipation – Scottish Reactions in 1829', *Innes Review*, xxiv, 1973.
Mundell, A.: *Considerations upon the Situation of Elective Franchises as it respects the Counties of Scotland* (London, 1821).
Munro, N.: *The History of the Royal Bank of Scotland 1727–1927* (Edinburgh, 1928).
Munro, R. W.: *Scottish Lighthouses* (Stornoway, 1979).
Murdoch, A.: *The People Above – politics and administration in mid-eighteenth-century Scotland* (Edinburgh, 1980).
   : 'The Advocates, the Law and the Nation in Early Modern Scotland', in Prest (1981).
   : 'The Importance of being Edinburgh – management and opposition in Edinburgh politics 1746–1784', *Scottish Historical Review*, lxii, 1983.
   : 'Lord Bute, James Stuart Mackenzie and the Government of Scotland', in Schweizer (1988).
   & Sher, R. B. 'Patronage and Party in the Church of Scotland 1750–1800', in Macdougall (1983).
   : 'Literary and Learned Culture', in Devine & Mitchison (1988).
   : 'Politics and the People in the Burgh of Dumfries 1758–1760', *Scottish Historical Review*, lxx, 1991.
Mure, W.: *Selections from the Family Papers preserved at Caldwell* (Glasgow, 1854).
Murray, A.: 'Administration and Law', in Rae (1974).
Murray, N.: *The Scottish Hand Loom Weavers 1790–1850, a social history* (Edinburgh, 1978).
Murray, Sir O.: 'The Admiralty', *Mariner's Mirror*, xxiii–xxv, 1937–9.
Nairn, T.: *The Break-up of Britain* (London, 1977).
Napier, M.: *Selections from the Correspondence of the late Macvey Napier* (London, 1877).
Neil, W. (ed.): *The Cleghorn Papers* (London, 1927).
Nenadic, S.: 'The Rise of the Urban Middle Class', in Devine & Mitchison (1988).
New, C.: *Life of Henry Brougham to 1830* (Oxford, 1961).
Nicolson, R. (ed.): *Memoirs of Adam Black* (Edinburgh, 1885).
Nightingale, P.: *Trade and Empire in Western India 1784–1806* (Cambridge, 1970).
Nisbet, J. W.: 'Thomas Chalmers and the Economic Order', *Scottish Journal of Political Economy*, xi, 1964.
Noble, A.: 'John Wilson (Christopher North) and the Tory Hegemony', in Gifford (1987).
Notestein, W.: *The Scot in History* (London, 1946).
Oakley, C. A.: *Our Illustrious Forebears* (Glasgow, 1980).
O'Brien, C. C.: 'Warren Hastings in Burke's Great Melody', in Carnall & Nicholson (1989).
O'Brien, P. K.: 'The Political Economy of British Taxation 1660–1815', *Economic History Review*, xli, 1988.
Old Statistical Account of Scotland (Edinburgh, 1791–9).
Oman, C.: *The Wizard of the North – the life of Sir Walter Scott* (London, 1973).
Omond, G. W. T.: *Arniston Memoirs* (Edinburgh, 1887).
   : *The Lord Advocates of Scotland, from the close of the fifteenth century to the passing of the Reform Bill* (Edinburgh, 1883).
O'Sullivan, N.: *Conservatism* (London, 1976).
Pares, R.: *King George III and the Politicians* (Oxford, 1953).
Parker, C. S.: *Sir Robert Peel, from his private correspondence* (London, 1891).
Parker, J. G. 'Scottish Enterprise in India 1750–1914', in Cage, R. A. (1985).
Parliamentary History of England (to 1804); becoming *Parliamentary Debates* (1804–1827); becoming *Hansard* (from 1827)

Parliamentary Papers: First Report of the Commissioners for Making and Maintaining the Caledonian Canal, (51), 1803–4a.

: *First Report of the Commissioners for Roads and Bridges in the Highlands of Scotland*, (108), 1803–4b.

: *Tenth Report of the Commissioners of Naval Enquiry*, (21), 1805a.

: *King's warrant to Viscount Melville*, (43), 1805b.

: *Trial of Melville*, 1805c.

: *Report of the Number and Value of the Stipends of the Scotch Clergy under £150 per annum*, ii, 1810.

: *Report from the Committee on the Royal Burghs of Scotland*, vi, 1819.

: *Reports from the Select Committee on Petitions from the Royal Burghs of Scotland*, iii, 1820.

: *Report from the Select Committee on Petitions from the Royal Burghs of Scotland*, viii, 1821.

: *Report of the Commissioners on Procedure in the Courts of Law in Scotland*, etc., x, 1824.

: *Third Report of the Select Committee on Emigration*, xiv, 1827.

: *General Report of the Commissioners appointed to visit the Universities and Colleges of Scotland*, October 1830, xii, 1831.

: *Returns relating to the Offices of Privy Seal, etc., Scotland*, xxiii, 1833.

Parry, A.: *Parry of the Arctic* (London, 1963).

Parry, M. L. & Slater, T. R.: *The Making of the Scottish Countryside* (London, 1980).

Paton, C. H.: 'The Eighteenth Century and Later', in *Stair Society* (1958).

Patrick, J.: 'The 1806 Election in Aberdeenshire,'.*Northern Scotland*, i, 1973.

Peel, G. (ed.): *The Private Letters of Sir Robert Peel* (London, 1920).

Pellow, G.: *Life and Correspondence of the Rt Hon. Henry Addington, 1st Viscount Sidmouth* (London, 1847).

Perera, S. G.: *The Douglas Papers* (Colombo, 1933).

Petrie, Sir C.: *Lord Liverpool* (London, 1954).

Philips, C. H.: *The East India Company 1784–1834* (Manchester, 1940).

: 'The New East India Board and the Court of Directors 1784', *English Historical Review*, iv, 1940.

(ed.): *The Correspondence of David Scott 1787–1805* (London, 1951).

Phillipson, N. T.: 'The Scottish Whigs and the Reform of the Court of Session' (University of Cambridge, Ph.D. thesis, 1967).

: 'Nationalism and Ideology', in Wolfe (1969).

: 'Towards a Definition of the Scottish Enlightenment', in Fritz & Williams (1973).

: 'Culture and Society in the Eighteenth-century Province: the case of Edinburgh and the Scottish Enlightenment', in Stone (1975).

: 'Lawyers, Landowners and the Civic Leadership of Post-Union Scotland', *Juridical Review*, 1976.

: 'The Social Structure of the Faculty of Advocates in Scotland 1661–1840', in Harding (1980).

:'The Scottish Enlightenment', in Porter & Teich (1981).

Pool, B.: *Navy Board Contracts 1660–1832* (London, 1966).

Porritt, A. G. & E.: *The Unreformed House of Commons* (Cambridge, 1903).

Pottle, F. A.: *James Boswell, the Earlier Years 1740–1759* (London, 1966).

& Reed, J. W. (eds.): *Boswell, Laird of Auchinleck 1778–1782* (London, 1977).

& Ryskamp, C. (eds.): *Boswell, the ominous years* (London, 1963).

& Weis, C. M. (eds.): *Boswell in Extremis 1776–1778* (London, 1971).

& Wimsatt, W. K. (eds.): *Boswell for the Defence 1769–1774* (London, 1960).

Prebble, J.: *Mutiny* (London, 1975).

: *The King's Jaunt – George IV in Scotland 1822* (Glasgow, 1988).

Prest, W. (ed.): *Lawyers in Early Modern Europe and America* (London, 1981).

Pryde, G. S.: *Central and Local Government in Scotland since 1707*, Historical Association pamphlet, general series, no. 45, 1960.

: *Scotland from 1603 to the Present Day* (London, 1962).
& Rait, Sir R.: *Scotland* (London, 1934).
Rae, T. I, (ed.): *The Union of 1707, its impact on Scotland* (Glasgow & London, 1974).
Raleigh, Sir T.: *Annals of the Church in Scotland* (Oxford, 1921).
Redington, J. (ed.): *Calendar of Home Office Papers of the Reign of George II* (London, 1878).
Rose, G.: *Observations respecting the Public Expenditure and the Influence of the Crown* (London, 1810).
Rose, R. B.: 'The "Red Scare" of the 1790s – the French Revolution and the "agrarian law"', *Past & Present*, ciii, 1984.
Rosebery, Primrose, A., Earl of: *Pitt* (London, 1891).
(ed.): *The Windham Papers* (London, 1913).
(ed.): *The Wellesley Papers* (London, 1914).
Rainy, R.: *Three Lectures on the Church of Scotland* (Edinburgh, 1883).
Rait, R. S.: *The History of the Union Bank of Scotland* (Glasgow, 1930).
Ralston, A. G.: 'The Tron Riot of 1812', *History Today*, xxx, 1980.
Ramsay, A. A. W.: 'The Glasgow Outrages 1820–1825', *Quarterly Review*, ccxlviii, 1927.
Ramsay, J.: *Scotland and Scotsmen in the Eighteenth Century* (Edinburgh & London, 1888).
Renwick, R. (ed.): *Extracts from the Records of the Burgh of Glasgow* (Glasgow, 1912).
Richards, E.: *The Leviathan of Wealth* (London, 1973).
Richardson, Lady M. (ed.): *Autobiography of Mrs Fletcher* (Edinburgh, 1875).
Richmond, A. B.: *Narrative of the Condition of the Manufacturing Population* (London, 1824).
Richmond, Sir H.: *Statesmen and Sea Power* (Oxford, 1946).
Riddy, J.: 'Warren Hastings – Scotland's Benefactor', in Carnall & Nicholson (1989).
Riley, P. W. J.: 'The Structure of Scottish Politics and the Union of 1707', in Rae (1974).
Roach, W. M.: 'Radical Reform Movements in Scotland from 1815 to 1822' (University of Glasgow, Ph.D. thesis, 1970).
: 'Alexander Richmond and the Radical Reform Movements in Glasgow in 1816–1817', *Scottish Historical Review*, li, 1972.
Roberts, P. E.: *India under Wellesley* (London, 1929).
Robertson, J.: *The Scottish Enlightenment and the Militia Issue* (Edinburgh, 1985).
Robertson, M. (ed.): *The Concise Scots Dictionary* (Aberdeen, 1985).
Romilly, S. H.: *Letters to Ivy, from the 1st Earl of Dudley* (London, 1905).
Ross, C.: *Correspondence of Charles, 1st Marquis of Cornwallis* (London, 1859).
Ross, S.: *Lord Kames and the Scotland of his Day* (Oxford, 1972).
Rotwein, E. (ed.): *David Hume – Writings on Economics* (London, 1955).
Roughead, W.: *Twelve Scots Trials* (Edinburgh & London, 1913).
Russell, Lord J.: *Memorials and Correspondence of Charles James Fox* (London, 1853–7).
[St Vincent, Sir John Jervis, Earl of]: *Memoirs of the Administration of the Board of Admiralty* (London, 1805).
Samuel, R. (ed.): *Patriotism, the making and unmaking of British national identity* (London & New York, 1989).
Sanders, C. R. (ed.): *The Collected Letters of Thomas and Jane Carlyle* (Durham, N.C., 1970–).
Saunders, L. J.: *Scottish Democracy 1815–1840* (Edinburgh & London, 1950).
Schom, A.: *Trafalgar* (London, 1990).
Schweizer, K.: *Lord Bute, essays in re-interpretation* (Leicester, 1988).
Scots Magazine, The (1739–1817).
Scotsman, The (1817–).
Scott, R.: 'The Politics and Administration of Scotland 1725–1748' (University of Edinburgh, Ph.D. thesis, 1982).

Scott, Sir W.: 'View of the Changes proposes and adopted in the Administration of
  Justice in Scotland', *Edinburgh Annual Register*, i, 1808.
  : *Letters on the Proposed Change of Currency, by Malachi Malagrowther* (Edinburgh,
  1826).
  : *Familiar Letters* (Edinburgh, 1894).
Scottish Nation, The (n.p., n.d.).
Sedgwick, R. (ed.): *The House of Commons 1715–1754* (London, 1970).
Sefton, H. R.: 'Lord Ilay and Patrick Cuming, a study in eighteenth-century
  ecclesiastical management', *Records of the Scottish Church History Society*, xix, 1977.
Shaw, J. S.: *The Management of Scottish Society 1707–1764* (Edinburgh, 1983).
Sher, R. B.: *Church and University in the Scottish Enlightenment – the Moderate Literati of
  Edinburgh* (Edinburgh, 1985).
  : 'Adam Ferguson, Adam Smith and the Problem of National Defence', *Journal of
  Modern History*, lxi, 1989.
  & Smitten, J.: *Scotland and America in the Age of Enlightenment* (Edinburgh, 1990).
Sibbald, W.: *Facts, Reflections and Queries submitted to the Consideration of the Associated
  Friends of the People* (Edinburgh, 1792).
Sinclair, G. A.: 'Periodical Literature of the Eighteenth Century', *Scottish Historical
  Review*, ii, 1905.
Sinclair, Sir J.: *Correspondence* (London, 1831).
Skinner, A. S. & Wilson, T. (eds.): *Essays on Adam Smith* (Oxford, 1975).
Slater, T. R.: 'The Mansion and the Policy', in Parry & Slater (1980).
Smith, A.: *An Inquiry into the Nature and Causes of the Wealth of Nations* (Oxford, 1976;
  first published, 1776).
Smith, A. M.: 'The Administration of the Forfeited Annexed Estates 1751–1784', in
  Barrow (1974).
  : *Jacobite Estates of the Forty-Five* (Edinburgh, 1982).
Smith, D. C.: *Passive Obedience and Prophetic Protest* (New York, 1987).
Smith, H. S.: *Parliaments of England* (London, 1844).
Smith, J. V.: 'Manners, Morals and Mentalities – reflections on the popular
  enlightenment of early nineteenth-century Scotland' in Humes & Paterson (1983a).
  : 'Reason, Revelation and Reform – Thomas Dick of Methven and the "Improvement
  of Society by the Diffusion of Knowledge"', *History of Education*, xii, 1983b.
Smith, N. C.: *The Letters of Sydney Smith*, (Oxford, 1953).
Smith, T. B.: *British Justice, the Scottish contribution* (London, 1961).
Smith, V.A.: *Oxford History of India* (Oxford, 1958).
Smout, T. C.: 'Scottish Landowners and Economic Growth', *Scottish Journal of Political
  Economy*, xi, 1964.
  : *A History of the Scottish People 1560–1830* (Edinburgh, 1967).
  (ed.): *The Search for Wealth and Stability* (London, 1979).
  : *A Century of the Scottish People 1830–1950* (London, 1986).
Somerville, T.: *My Own Life and Times* (Edinburgh, 1861).
Spilhans, M. W.: *South Africa in the Making 1652–1806* (Cape Town, 1966).
Stair Society: An Introduction to Scottish Legal History (Edinburgh, 1958).
Stanhope, Earl: *Life of the Rt Hon. William Pitt* (London, 1879).
Stanhope, Lady H.: *Memoirs* (London, 1845).
Stanley, A. P.: *Lectures on the History of the Church of Scotland* (London, 1879).
Stein, P.: 'Legal Thought in Eighteenth-century Scotland', *Juridical Review*, 1957.
  : 'The Influence of Roman Law on the Law of Scotland', *Juridical Review*, 1963.
Steuart, A. F.: *The Douglas Cause* (Glasgow & Edinburgh, 1909).
  (ed.): *The Last Journals of Horace Walpole* (London, 1910).
Stewart, D.: *Account of the Life and Writings of William Robertson* (London, 1802).
Stewart, R.:*The Foundation of the Conservative Party* (London, 1978).

: *Henry Brougham, his public career 1778–1868* (London, 1985).

Stone, L. (ed.): *The University in Society* (Princeton, 1975).

Straka, W. W.: 'The Law of Combination in Scotland Reconsidered', *Scottish Historical Review*, lxiv, 1985.

Sunter, R. M.: 'Stirlingshire Politics 1707–1832' (University of Edinburgh, Ph. D. thesis, 1972).

: *Patronage and Politics in Scotland 1707–1832* (Edinburgh, 1986).

Sutherland, L. S.: *The East India Company in Eighteenth-century Politics* (Oxford, 1952).

Swann, E.: *Christopher North* (Edinburgh & London, 1934).

Szechi, D. (ed.): *Letters of George Lockhart of Carnwath 1698–1732* (Edinburgh, 1989).

Tait, A. A.: 'William Adam and Sir John Clerk – Arniston and "The Country Seat"', *Burlington Magazine*, iii, 1969.

Tayler, A. & H. (eds): *Lord Fife and his Factor* (London, 1925).

: *The Domestic Papers of the Rose Family* (Aberdeen 1926).

Teichgraeber, R. F.: 'Politics and Morals in the Scottish Enlightenment' (Brandeis University, Ph.D. thesis, 1978).

: '"Less abused than I had reason to expect" – the reception of the Wealth of Nations in Britain 1776–1790', *Historical Journal*, xxx, 1987.

Temperley, H.: *The Foreign Policy of Canning 1822–1827* (London, 1925).

Terry, C. S. (ed.): *The Albemarle Papers* (Aberdeen, 1902).

Thompson, H. W. (ed.): *Anecdotes and Egotisms of Henry Mackenzie* (Oxford, 1927).

: *A Scottish Man of Feeling – some account of Henry Mackenzie* (Oxford, 1931).

Thorne, R. G. (ed.): *The House of Commons 1790–1820* (London, 1986).

Timperley, L. R.: *A Directory of Landownership in Scotland, c. 1770* (Edinburgh, 1976).

Tinker, C. B.: *Letters of James Boswell* (Oxford, 1924).

Trevelyan, G. M.: *British History in the Nineteenth Century and After* (London, 1937).

Tripathi, A.: *Trade and Finance in the Bengal Presidency 1793–1833* (Bombay, 1956).

Trotter, A.: *The Merit of Statesmen* (London, 1800).

Turberville, A. S.: *The House of Lords in the Age of Reform 1784–1837* (London, 1958).

Twiss, H.: *The Public and Private Life of Lord Chancellor Eldon* (London, 1844).

Twitchett, E. G.: *Life of a Seaman – Thomas Cochrane, 10th Earl of Dundonald* (London, 1931).

Tytler, A. F. J.: *Biographical Account of the Rt Hon. Robert Dundas of Arniston* (Edinburgh, 1789).

Valentine, A.: *The British Establishment 1760–1784* (Norman, Okla., 1970).

Veitch, J.: 'Memoir of Dugald Stewart', in Hamilton (1854–60), vol. x.

Voges, F.: *Das Denken von Thomas Chalmers im Kirchen- und Sozialgeschichtlichen Kontext* (Frankfurt am Main, 1984).

: 'Moderate and Evangelical thinking in the Later Eighteenth Century, differences and shared attitudes', *Records of the Scottish Church History Society*, xxii, 1985.

Walker, D. M.: *The Scottish Jurist* (Edinburgh, 1985).

Walker, E. A. (ed.): *South Africa, etc.*, vol. viii, *Cambridge History of the British Empire* (Cambridge, 1963).

Walker, Sir P.: *To the Subscribers to the Melville Monument* (Edinburgh, 1821).

Wallace, W. (ed.): *Robert Burns and Mrs Dunlop* (London, 1898).

Walpole, H.: *Journal of the Reign of King George III 1771–1783* (London, 1859).

Ward, J. T.: 'A Footnote on the First Reform Act', *Scottish Historical Review*, xlvi, 1967.

: '"The Member" and Parliamentary Reform', in Whatley (1979).

Wilson, R. G.: *Land and Industry* (Newton Abbot, 1971).

Ward, W. R.: 'The Land Tax in Scotland 1797-1798', *Bulletin of the John Rylands Library, Manchester*, xxvii, 1954–5.

Warner, G.: *The Scottish Tory Party – a history* (London, 1988).

Weld, C. R.: *A History of the Royal Society* (London, 1848).

Wellington, 2nd Duke of: *Despatches, Correspondence and Memoranda of Field Marshal Arthur, Duke of Wellington* (London, 1867).
: *Supplementary Despatches and Memoranda of Field Marshal Arthur, Duke of Wellington* (London, 1868).
Western, J. R.: 'The Formation of the Scottish Militia in 1797', *Scottish Historical Review*, xxxiv, 1955.
Whatley, C. A. (ed.): *John Galt 1779–1979* (Edinburgh, 1979).
: *The Scottish Salt Industry 1570–1850* (Aberdeen, 1987a).
: '"The fettering bonds of brotherhood" – combination and labour relations in the Scottish coal-mining industry, c 1690–1775', *Social History*, xii, 1987b.
Wheatley, H. B. (ed.): *The History and Posthumous Memoirs of Sir Nathaniel William Wraxall* (London, 1884).
Wheeler, J. T.: *Short History of India* (London, 1880).
Whetstone, A. E.: *Scottish County Government in the Eighteenth and Nineteenth Centuries* (Edinburgh, 1981).
Wright, A.: *An Inquiry into the Rise and Progress of Parliament, chiefly in Scotland* (Edinburgh, 1784).
Wilberforce, A. M. (ed.): *The Private Papers of William Wilberforce* (London, 1897).
Wilberforce, R. I. & S. (eds.): *The Correspondence of William Wilberforce* (London, 1840).
Wilberforce S.: *Life of William Wilberforce* (London, 1868).
Wilkins, W. H. (ed.): *South Africa a Century Ago – letters written from the Cape of Good Hope (1797–1801) by Lady Anne Barnard* (London, 1901).
Willcock, I. D.: 'The Origins and Development of the Jury in Scotland', *Stair Society*, xxiii, 1966.
Wills, V. (ed.): *Reports on the Annexed Estates* (Edinburgh, 1973).
Winch, D.: *Adam Smith's Politics* (Cambridge, 1978).
Withrington, D. J.: 'What was Distinctive about the Scottish Enlightenment?', in Carter & Pittock (1987).
: 'Schooling, Literacy and Society', in Devine & Mitchison (1988).
Wolfe, J. N. (ed.): *Government and Nationalism in Scotland* (Edinburgh, 1969).
Wood, M.: *The Lord Provosts of Edinburgh* (Edinburgh, 1932).
Woods, C. J.: 'A Plan for a Dutch Invasion of Scotland, 1797', *Scottish Historical Review*, liii, 1974
Yorke, P.: *Life and Correspondence of Philip Yorke, Earl of Hardwicke* (Cambridge, 1913).
Young, J. D.: *The Rousing of the Scottish Working Class* (London, 1979).
Youngson, A. J.: *The Making of Classical Edinburgh* (Edinburgh, 1966).
: *After the '45* (Edinburgh, 1975).

Index

Abbot, Charles, 267, 270
Abercorn, Lord, 47, 150, 151
Abercromby, Alexander, 49
Abercromby, George, elder, 284
Abercromby, George, younger, 378
Abercromby, James, 355, 374, 377
Abercromby, Sir Ralph, 84, 194, 214, 215, 225, 226
Abercromby, Sir Robert, 250, 251
Aberdeen, 68, 146, 149, 159, 167, 285, 287, 341, 346, 369, 379
Aberdeen, university of, 49, 296, 326, 364
Aberdeen, Earl of, 271, 272, 279, 285, 334, 363, 380
Aberdeenshire, 101, 147, 148, 149, 160, 233, 250, 251, 285
Aboukir Bay, Battle of (1798), 214
Act against Wrongous Imprisonment (1701), 172, 338
Adam, Charles, 341
Adam, William (architect), 2
Adam, William (politician), 94, 101, 146, 148, 149, 150, 163, 187, 202, 273, 278, 284, 287, 314, 319, 330, 341
Addington, Henry, see Sidmouth, Viscount
Advocates' Library, 11, 139
Agnew, Sir Andrew, 378
Agnew, John, 203
Airth, 179
Albemarle, Earl of, 10
Albert, Prince, 1
Alexander the Great, 114, 221
Alexander, Boyd, 202
Alexandria, 193, 213, 226, 250
Aliens Act (1793), 189
Alison, Archibald, 184, 332
Alison, William, 326
Alloa, 43
All the Talents, Ministry of, 177, 272, 274, 279-80, 283-6, 289, 295, 298, 301, 342
Amending Act (1786), 118
Amiens, Treaty of (1801), 248, 292
America, 2, 66, 67, 70, 72, 81, 85-9, 104, 113, 126, 137, 181, 210, 218, 247, 248;

see also United States
Angus, *see* Forfarshire
Anne, Queen, 5, 14
Anstruther Burghs, 101, 145, 149, 201, 244, 284, 286, 318, 341, 368
Anti-burgher Church, 183
Antrobus, Edmund, 263-4
Arbroath, 68
Arbuthnott, Viscount of, 342
Arbuthnott, Hugh, 369
Arcot, Nawab of, 115, 119-21
Ardrossan, 43
Argathelians, 7, 9, 10, 11, 18, 25, 26, 27, 33, 37, 55, 56, 78, 136
Argyll (county), 47, 66, 150, 319, 342, 379
Argyll, 2nd Duke of, 7, 8, 9, 25, 33
Argyll, 3rd Duke of, 9, 10, 11, 13, 25, 31, 32, 33, 55, 151
Argyll, 4th Duke of, 31, 32, 37
Argyll, 5th Duke of, 55, 84, 101, 102, 108, 139, 140, 150, 151, 250, 252, 285, 287, 346
Aristotle, 58
Armstrong, William, 133
Arniston House, 2-3, 5, 6, 13, 21, 156, 176-7, 303, 305, 318
Asiatic Society of Bengal, 293
Assaye, Battle of (1803), 221
Atholl, Duchess of, 376
Atholl, 3rd Duke of, 32
Atholl, 4th Duke of, 33, 100, 132, 149, 201, 348
Auchinleck, Alexander Boswell, Lord, 39, 47, 84, 129
Auckland, Lord, 190
Aurangzeb, Emperor, 114
Austerlitz, Battle of (1805), 266, 271
Australia, 199, 323
Austria, 188, 192, 214, 216, 225
Austrian Netherlands, 126, 191
Ayr Bank, 44-5
Ayr Burghs, 55, 150, 234, 287, 319, 342, 345, 362, 378
Ayrshire, 55, 83, 101, 129, 143, 160, 202, 252, 285, 287, 318, 319, 342
Aytoun, W. E., 333